Recent Advances in 3D Imaging, Modeling, and Reconstruction

Athanasios Voulodimos
University of West Attica, Athens, Greece

Anastasios Doulamis
National Technical University of Athens, Athens, Greece

A volume in the Advances in Multimedia and
Interactive Technologies (AMIT) Book Series

Published in the United States of America by
IGI Global
Information Science Reference (an imprint of IGI Global)
701 E. Chocolate Avenue
Hershey PA, USA 17033
Tel: 717-533-8845
Fax: 717-533-8661
E-mail: cust@igi-global.com
Web site: http://www.igi-global.com

Library of Congress Cataloging-in-Publication Data

Names: Voulodimos, Athanasios, editor. | Doulamis, Anastasios, editor.
Title: Recent advances in 3D imaging, modeling, and reconstruction / editors:
    Athanasios Voulodimos and Anastasios Doulamis.
Description: Hershey, PA : Engineering Science Reference, 2019. | Includes
    bibliographical references.
Identifiers: LCCN 2017038324| ISBN 9781522552949 (hardcover) | ISBN
    9781799829966 (softcover) | ISBN 9781522552956 (ebook)
Subjects: LCSH: Three-dimensional imaging. | Image reconstruction.
Classification: LCC TA1560 .E44 2019 | DDC 006.6/93--dc23 LC record available at https://lccn.loc.gov/2017038324

This book is published in the IGI Global book series Advances in Multimedia and Interactive Technologies (AMIT) (ISSN:
2327-929X; eISSN: 2327-9303)

British Cataloguing in Publication Data
A Cataloguing in Publication record for this book is available from the British Library.

For electronic access to this publication, please contact: eresources@igi-global.com.

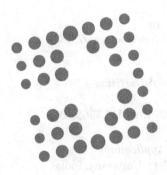

Advances in Multimedia and Interactive Technologies (AMIT) Book Series

Joel J.P.C. Rodrigues

Federal University of Piauí (UFPI), Teresina - Pi, Brazil;
Instituto de Telecomunicações, Portugal

ISSN:2327-929X
EISSN:2327-9303

MISSION

Traditional forms of media communications are continuously being challenged. The emergence of user-friendly web-based applications such as social media and Web 2.0 has expanded into everyday society, providing an interactive structure to media content such as images, audio, video, and text.

The **Advances in Multimedia and Interactive Technologies (AMIT) Book Series** investigates the relationship between multimedia technology and the usability of web applications. This series aims to highlight evolving research on interactive communication systems, tools, applications, and techniques to provide researchers, practitioners, and students of information technology, communication science, media studies, and many more with a comprehensive examination of these multimedia technology trends.

COVERAGE

- Digital Technology
- Social Networking
- Multimedia Streaming
- Multimedia Services
- Digital Games
- Audio Signals
- Internet Technologies
- Digital Communications
- Web Technologies
- Multimedia Technology

IGI Global is currently accepting manuscripts for publication within this series. To submit a proposal for a volume in this series, please contact our Acquisition Editors at Acquisitions@igi-global.com or visit: http://www.igi-global.com/publish/.

Titles in this Series

701 East Chocolate Avenue, Hershey, PA 17033, USA
Tel: 717-533-8845 x100 • Fax: 717-533-8661
E-Mail: cust@igi-global.com • www.igi-global.com

Table of Contents

Section 2
Advances in 3D Reconstruction

Section 3
Advances in 3D Data Handling and Analysis

Detailed Table of Contents

Section 1
Advances in 3D Modelling

Over the last decade or so, laser scanning technology has become an increasingly popular and important tool for forestry inventory, enabling accurate capture of 3D information in a fast and environmentally friendly manner. To this end, the authors propose here a system for tropical tree species classification based on 3D scans of LiDAR sensing technology. In order to exploit the interrelated patterns of trees, skeleton representations of tree point clouds are extracted, and their structures are divided into overlapping equal-sized 3D segments. Subsequently, they represent them as third-order sparse structure tensors setting the value of skeleton coordinates equal to one. Based on the higher-order tensor decomposition of each sparse segment, they 1) estimate the mode-n singular values extracting intra-correlations of tree branches and 2) model tropical trees as linear dynamical systems extracting appearance information and dynamics. The proposed methodology was evaluated in tropical tree species and specifically in a dataset consisting of 26 point clouds of common Caatinga dry-forest trees.

Chapter 2

The implementation of virtual and augmented reality environments on the web requires integration between 3D technologies and web technologies, which are increasingly focused on collaboration, annotation, and semantics. Thus, combining VR and AR with the semantics arises as a significant trend in the development of the web. The use of the Semantic Web may improve creation, representation, indexing, searching, and processing of 3D web content by linking the content with formal and expressive descriptions of its meaning. Although several semantic approaches have been developed for 3D content, they are not explicitly linked to the available well-established 3D technologies, cover a limited set of 3D components and properties, and do not combine domain-specific and 3D-specific semantics. In this chapter, the authors present the background, concepts, and development of the Semantic Web3D approach. It enables ontology-based representation of 3D content and introduces a novel framework to provide 3D structures in an RDF semantic-friendly format.

Millions of people suffering from partial or complete hearing loss use variants of sign language to communicate with each other or hearing people in their everyday life. Thus, it is imperative to develop systems to assist these people by removing the barriers that affect their social inclusion. These systems should aim towards capturing sign language in an accurate way, classifying sign language to natural words and representing sign language by having avatars or synthesized videos execute the exact same moves that convey a meaning in the sign language. This chapter reviews current state-of-the-art approaches that attempt to solve sign language recognition and representation and analyzes the challenges they face. Furthermore, this chapter presents a novel AI-based solution to the problem of robust sign language capturing and representation, as well as a solution to the unavailability of annotated sign language datasets before limitations and directions for future work are discussed.

Chapter 4

Modelling and digitizing performing arts through motion capturing interfaces is an important aspect for the analysis, processing, and documentation of intangible cultural heritage assets. This chapter provides a holistic description regarding the dance preservation topic by describing the capture approaches, efficient preprocessing techniques, and specific approaches for knowledge generation. Presented methodologies take under consideration the existing modelling and interpretation approaches, which may involve huge amounts of information, making them difficult to process, store, and analyze.

Chapter 5

In past decades, for developing a site, engineers used the process of creating a scale model in order to determine their behaviour and to sketch the details collected manually using the drafting process, which behaves as a referring material during the construction of structures. Due to the boom in technology and limitations in drafting, the drawings have been digitized using computer-aided design (CAD) software as a two-dimensional structure (2D). Currently, these drawings are detailed as a three-dimensional structure (3D) that is briefly noted as 3D modelling. Three-dimensional site modelling is an active area that is involved in research and development of models in several fields that has been originated from the scale modelling. In this chapter, the topic 3D site modelling in civil engineering is discussed. First of all, the basic concepts of scale modelling, architectural modelling, and structural modelling are discussed. Then the concept of virtual-based 3D site modelling, its importance, benefits, and steps involved in site modelling are briefed.

Section 2
Advances in 3D Reconstruction

Chapter 6

In recent years, there is a demand for 3D content for computer graphics, communications, and virtual reality. 3D modelling is an emerging topic that is applied in so many real-world applications. The images are taken through camera at multiple angles and medical imaging techniques like CT scan and MRI are also used. From a set of images, intersection of these projection rays is considered to be the position for 3D point. This chapter discusses the construction of 3D images from multiple objects. Various approaches used for construction, triangulation method, challenges in building this model, and the application of 3D models are explained in this chapter.

Cultural heritage (CH) tells us about our roots, and therefore, constitutes a rich value for the society. Its conservation, dissemination, and understanding are of utmost importance. In order to preserve CH for the upcoming generations, it needs to be documented, a process that nowadays is done digitally. Current trends involve a set of technologies (cameras, scanners, etc.) for the shape and radiometric acquisition of assets. Also, intangible CH can be digitally documented in a variety of forms. Having such assets virtualized, a proper dissemination channel is of relevance, and recently, new technologies that make use of interaction paradigms have emerged. Among them, in this chapter, the authors focus their attention in the technologies of virtual reality (VR), augmented reality (AR), and serious games (SGs). They aim to explore these technologies in order to show their benefits in the dissemination and understanding of CH. Though the work involving them is not trivial, and usually a multidisciplinary team is required, the benefits for CH make them worth it.

Chapter 8

Ivan Nikolov, Aalborg University, Denmark
Claus B. Madsen, Aalborg University, Denmark

Capturing details of objects and surfaces using structure from motion (SfM) 3D reconstruction has become an important part of data gathering in geomapping, medicine, cultural heritage, and the energy and production industries. One inherent problem with SfM, due to its reliance on 2D images, is the ambiguity of the reconstruction's scale. Absolute scale can be calculated by using the data from additional sensors. This chapter demonstrates how distance sensors can be used to calculate the scale of a reconstructed object. In addition, the authors demonstrate that the uncertainty of the calculated scale can be computed and how it depends on the precision of the used sensors. The provided methods are straightforward and easy to integrate into the workflow of commercial SfM solutions.

Chapter 9

Athanasios Voulodimos, University of West Attica, Athens, Greece
Eftychios Protopapadakis, National Technical University of Athens, Athens, Greece
Nikolaos Doulamis, National Technical University of Athens, Greece
Anastasios Doulamis, National Technical University of Athens, Greece

Although high quality 3D representations of important cultural landmarks can be obtained via sophisticated photogrammetric techniques, their demands in terms of resources and expertise pose limitations on the scale at which such approaches are used. In parallel, the proliferation of multimedia content posted online creates new possibilities in terms of the ways that such rich content can be leveraged, but only after addressing the significant challenges associated with this content, including its massive volume, unstructured nature, and noise. In this chapter, two strategies are proposed for using multimedia content for 3D reconstruction: an image-based approach that employs clustering techniques to eliminate outliers and a video-based approach that extracts key frames via a summarization technique. In both cases, the reduced and outlier-free image data set is used as input to a structure from motion framework for 3D reconstruction. The presented techniques are evaluated on the basis of the reconstruction of two world-class cultural heritage monuments.

Chapter 10

Claudio Ferrari, University of Florence, Italy
Stefano Berretti, University of Florence, Italy
Alberto Del Bimbo, University of Florence, Italy

3D face reconstruction from a single 2D image is a fundamental computer vision problem of extraordinary difficulty that dates back to the 1980s. Briefly, it is the task of recovering the three-dimensional geometry of a human face from a single RGB image. While the problem of automatically estimating the 3D structure of a generic scene from RGB images can be regarded as a general task, the particular morphology and non-rigid nature of human faces make it a challenging problem for which dedicated approaches are still currently studied. This chapter aims at providing an overview of the problem, its evolutions, the current state of the art, and future trends.

Section 3
Advances in 3D Data Handling and Analysis

Chapter 11

Ioannis Maniadis, Information Technologies Institute, Centre for Research and Technology, Hellas, Greece

Vassilis Solachidis, Information Technologies Institute, Centre for Research and Technology, Hellas, Greece

Nicholas Vretos, Information Technologies Institute, Centre for Research and Technology, Hellas, Greece

Petros Daras, Information Technologies Institute, Centre for Research and Technology, Hellas, Greece

Modern deep learning techniques have proven that they have the capacity to be successful in a wide area of domains and tasks, including applications related to 3D and 2D images. However, their quality depends on the quality and quantity of the data with which models are trained. As the capacity of deep learning models increases, data availability becomes the most significant. To counter this issue, various techniques are utilized, including data augmentation, which refers to the practice of expanding the original dataset with artificially created samples. One approach that has been found is the generative adversarial networks (GANs), which, unlike other domain-agnostic transformation-based methods, can produce diverse samples that belong to a given data distribution. Taking advantage of this property, a multitude of GAN architectures has been leveraged for data augmentation applications. The subject of this chapter is to review and organize implementations of this approach on 3D and 2D imagery, examine the methods that were used, and survey the areas in which they were applied.

Chapter 12

Felix G. Hamza-Lup, Georgia Southern University, USA
Nicholas Polys, Virginia Tech, USA
Athanasios G. Malamos, Hellenic Mediterranean University, Greece
Nigel W. John, University of Chester, UK

As the healthcare enterprise is adopting novel imaging and health-assessment technologies, we are facing unprecedented requirements in information sharing, patient empowerment, and care coordination within the system. Medical experts not only within US, but around the world should be empowered through collaboration capabilities on 3D data to enable solutions for complex medical problems that will save lives. The fast-growing number of 3D medical 'images' and their derivative information must be shared across the healthcare enterprise among stakeholders with vastly different perspectives and different needs. The demand for 3D data visualization is driving the need for increased accessibility and sharing of 3D medical image presentations, including their annotations and their animations. As patients have to make decisions about their health, empowering them with the right tools to understand a medical procedure is essential both in the decision-making process and for knowledge sharing.

Chapter 13

With the recent advancements in supercomputer technologies, large-scale, high-precision, and realistic model 3D simulations have been dominant in the field of solar-terrestrial physics, virtual reality, and health. Since 3D numeric data generated through simulation contain more valuable information than available in the past, innovative techniques for efficiently extracting such useful information are being required. One such technique is visualization—the process of turning phenomena, events, or relations not directly visible to the human eye into a visible form. Visualizing numeric data generated by observation equipment, simulations, and other means is an effective way of gaining intuitive insight into an overall picture of the data of interest. Meanwhile, data mining is known as the art of extracting valuable information from a large amount of data relative to finance, marketing, the internet, and natural sciences, and enhancing that information to knowledge.

Machine learning can be defined as the ability of a computer to learn and solve a problem without being explicitly coded. The efficiency of the program increases with experience through the task specified. In traditional programming, the program and the input are specified to get the output, but in the case of machine learning, the targets and predictors are provided to the algorithm make the process trained. This chapter focuses on various machine learning techniques and their performance with commonly used datasets. A supervised learning algorithm consists of a target variable that is to be predicted from a given set of predictors. Using these established targets is a function that plots targets to a given set of predictors. The training process allows the system to train the unknown data and continues until the model achieves a desired level of accuracy on the training data. The supervised methods can be usually categorized as classification and regression. This chapter discourses some of the popular supervised machine learning algorithms and their performances using quotidian datasets. This chapter also discusses some of the non-linear regression techniques and some insights on deep learning with respect to object recognition.

In general, the diagnosis and treatment planning of pediatric foreign body aspiration is done by medical experts with experience and uncertain clinical data of the patients, which makes the diagnosis a more approximate and time-consuming process. Foreign body diagnostic information requires the evidence such as size, shape, and location classification of the aspired foreign body. This evidence identification process requires the knowledge of human expertise to achieve accuracy in classification. The aim of the proposed work is to improve the performance of automatic anatomic location identification approach (AALIA) and to develop a reasoning-based systematic approach for pediatric foreign body aspiration treatment management. A CBR-based treatment management system is proposed for standardizing the pediatric foreign body aspiration treatment management process. The proposed approach considered a sample set of foreign body-aspired pediatric radiography images for experimental evaluation, and the performance is evaluated with respect to receiver operator characteristics (ROC) measure.

Preface

The world we live in is three-dimensional (3D). 3D geometry and time are probably the two most critical parameters of our lives! We perceive information from this world by several senses but it is doubtful that 3D vision is the most critical one. The 3D geometry plus the time in fact depicts the *whole of our world*, while the conventional 2D representation (using images or videos) is just a subset of the whole (Remondino, F. 2011) . To attribute human-like properties in machines we need to develop new 3D vision algorithms suitable for different types of computer systems, that is, 3D computer vision tools (Cyganek, B., & Siebert, J. P. 2011).

On a different note, time is an essential parameter of our world. We, the humans, the animated beings and the objects of this world are positioning in the 3D space and moving within it to make our world an "active/vivid" environment. Thus, only capturing and digitalizing objects' 3D geometry is not adequate to attain intelligent capabilities to human-made machines and endow them with senses as we, the humans, use to explore, understand and interact with our world. Thus, we need to adopt *a time-varying 3D modelling process* that enables the reconstruction of the spatial and temporal diversity of the objects yielding a 4D (3D geometry plus the time) modelling/analysis (Doulamis, A., Ioannides, M., Doulamis, N., Hadjiprocopis, A., Fritsch, D., Balet, O., Julien, M., Protopapadakis, E., Makantasis, K., Weinlinger, G., Johnsons, P. S., Klein, M., Fellner, D., Stork, A., & Santos, P. 2013).

As dimension increases the complexity exponentially increases as well. Thus, we need to research on new algorithms and tools that can make *3D computer vision applicable to real-life engineering applications* in which *time performance is critical*. To reduce the cost, we exploit spatio-temporal dependencies on the 3D processed data including joint reconstruction, information predictive models and shape repairing algorithms to dramatically reduce the time required for a 3D modelling (Kyriakaki, G., Doulamis, A., Doulamis, N., Ioannides, M., Makantasis, K., Protopapadakis, E., Hadjiprocopis, A., Wenzel, K., Fritsch, D., Klein, M., & Weinlinger, G. 2014). In addition, the models should be enriched with semantics (describing historical, cultural, functional and constructional values of the object) to make them retrievable and searchable. Furthermore, semantics accelerates reconstruction since only the most salient information is taken into account.

Another important aspect is the exploitation of visual information other than of the visible Red Green Blue (RGB) spectrum (Chen, C., Yeh, C., Chang, B. R., & Pan, J. 2015). Currently, almost all the research on 3D analysis is for RGB data while other bands, such as thermal or hyper-spectral sensing, are left behind. These bands can provide useful information on object material type or can indicate material defects and decay phenomena.

THE CHALLENGES

Currently, a plethora of 2D image/video analysis algorithms have been developed, while 3D information is left behind. Representative 2D examples are to: (i) detect objects or track them in video scenes (Redmon, J., Divvala, S., Girshick, R., & Farhadi, A. 2016)., (Doulamis, N., & Doulamis, A. 2012), (ii) understand actions from visual data (Kosmopoulos, D. I., Doulamis, N. D., & Voulodimos, A. S. 2012)., (iii) survey regions for safety and security (Maksymowicz, K., Tunikowski, W., & Kościuk, J. 2014)., (iv) recognize objects of interest (such as pedestrians for accident avoidance) (Cornelis, N., Leibe, B., Cornelis, K., & Van Gool, L. 2007). (Kosmopoulos, D. I., Doulamis, A., Makris, A., Doulamis, N., Chatzis, S., & Middleton, S. E. 2009). or even (v) extract some 2D measurements from the visual data (Knoop, S., Vacek, S., & Dillmann, R. 2009). In the field of 3D processing, some successful paradigms have been derived, especially in photogrammetry research that can achieve 3D models of objects with accuracy that can reach below 1mm (Roncella, R., Forlani, G., & Remondino, F. 2005), (Laggis, A., Doulamis, N., Protopapadakis, E., & Georgopoulos, A. 2017)., (Georgopoulos, A., Ioannidis, C., & Valanis, A. 2010). These models have been applied, for example, for documentation of (mostly) tangible cultural assets (Doulamis, N., Doulamis, A., Ioannidis, C., Klein, M., & Ioannides, M. 2017). or for urban planning (Doulamis, A., 2015) . In addition, within the Information Communication Technology (ICT) society, there exist efforts of 3D data processing that have recently reached some concrete outcomes such as 3D TV (Tam, W. J., Speranza, F., Yano, S., Shimono, K., & Ono, H. 2011)., (Soursos, S., & Doulamis, N. 2012), devices for augmented reality (Georgopoulos, A. 2017) and 3D computer aided engineering mostly applicable for civil applications for monitoring the infrastructures (Jog, G. M., Koch, C., Golparvar-Fard, M., & Brilakis, I. 2012)., (Ma, Z., & Liu, S. 2018)., (Protopapadakis, E., 2016).

However, even these approaches in 3D processing are incomplete in the sense that *the time dimension is lost*. The derived 3D models are created independently in time meaning that the same process is adopted to generate a precise 3D model for an object even if a similar model is already available for a previous time period. That is, we do not exploit 3D information for some object parts (surfaces), being available in previous time periods, so as to accelerate the reconstruction process at the current time. This constitutes a major contribution of this research; to develop algorithms for precise 4D computer vision for various domains under a cost-effective framework.

Nowadays, several methods exist in 3D modelling with applications in various scenarios. Example includes i) image-based photogrammetry methods in creating high fidelity 3D maps (Ioannou, M. T., & Georgopoulos, A. 2013)., ii) photometric stereo that exploits light reflection (Argyriou, V., Zafeiriou, S., & Petrou, M. 2014)., (Georgousis, S., Stentoumis, C., Doulamis, N., & Voulodimos, A. 2016)., iii) real-time depth sensors of low-cost such as Kinect (Izadi, S., Davison, A., Fitzgibbon, A., Kim, D., Hilliges, O., Molyneaux, D., Newcombe, R., Kohli, P., Shotton, J., Hodges, S., & Freeman, D. 2011)., (Protopapadakis, E., Grammatikopoulou, A., Doulamis, A., & Grammalidis, N. 2017)., iv) structured light technologies that capture 3D geometry and the texture (Orghidan, R., Salvi, J., Gordan, M., Florea, C., & Batlle, J. 2013), and v) laser scanning for large-scale automatic 3D reconstruction (Huang, H., Brenner, C., & Sester, M. 2013). Each of these methods present advantages/disadvantages. Photogrammetry creates high fidelity 3D point clouds, but the respective accuracy significantly falls in cases of uniform texture images let alone the manual effort required. Photometric stereo can be applied for reconstructing transparent/ specular surfaces. Real time depth sensors are of very low cost but the derived 3D models are not accurate. Finally, 3D laser scanning, though being automatic, suffers from noise especially in regions where beam reflection fails. In addition, 4D Modelling (Doulamis, A., Doulamis,

N., Protopapadakis, E., Voulodimos, A., & Ioannides, M. 2018)., introduces a novel, computationally efficient framework for 4D modelling based on spatial-temporal change history maps.

In performing arts, such as choreography, dance and theatrical kinesiology, movements of human body signals and gestures are essential elements used to describe a storyline. Although, we, as humans, can inherently perceive such human body signals in a natural way, this process is challenging for a computer system (Rallis, I., Georgoulas, I., Doulamis, N., Voulodimos, A., & Terzopoulos, P. 2017). One important aspect in the analysis of a performing dance is the automatic extraction of the choreographic patterns/elements since these provide an abstract and compact representation of the semantic information encoded in the overall dance storyline ʃ(Rallis, I., Georgoulas, I., Doulamis, N., Voulodimos, A., & Terzopoulos, P. 2017). Regarding 3D dance digitization, the work of ʃ(Hisatomi, K., Katayama, M., Tomiyama, K., & Iwadate, Y. 2011), considered as one of the first approaches, targets Japanese dances. The (Stavrakis, E., Aristidou, A., Savva, M., Himona, S. L., & Chrysanthou, Y. 2012). digitizes Cypriot dances and in (K. Dimitropoulos, S. Manitsaris, F. Tsalakanidou, S. Nikolopoulos, B. Denby, 2014)., the capturing architecture of the i-Treasure EU-funded project is described, focusing on rare folkloric choreographies. Although, Intangible Cultural Heritage (ICH) content, especially traditional performing arts, is commonly deemed worthy of preservation by UNESCO most of the current research efforts are on the focus is on tangible cultural assets, while the ICH content has been overlooked ʃ(Doulamis, Anastasios D., 2017).

3D imaging, modeling and reconstruction have interesting applications in the maintenance and safe operation of the existing civil infrastructure, e.g., pipelines, tunnels, roads and bridges, is a tedious and challenging task (Frangopol, D. M., & Liu, M. 2007). Due to ageing, environmental factors, increased loading, inadequate or poor maintenance and deferred repairs, these structures are progressively deteriorating urgently needing inspection assessment and repair work (Loupos, K., Amditis, A., Stentoumis, C., Chrobocinski, P., Victores, J., Wietek, M., Panetsos, P., Roncaglia, A., Camarinopoulos, S., Kalidromitis, V., Bairaktaris, D., Komodakis, N., & Lopez, R. 2014). In transportation tunnels, there is a widespread evidence of deterioration associated resulting in an increase on inspection and assessment budgets (Montero, R., Victores, J., Martínez, S., Jardón, A., & Balaguer, C. 2015). One should add here that in the next decades the rate of expansion of the transport infrastructure will not keep pace with the increase in transport demand necessitating the maximization of the operational uptime of tunnels (K. Loupos, A. Doulamis, C. Stentoumis, E. Protopapadakis, K. Makantasis, N. Doulamis, (2018).

TARGET AUDIENCE

The target audience of this book will include different engineering disciplines which can exploit 3D information to perform different types of measurements. The book covers all these disciplines and gives a complete view of the new 3D methods, ranging from simple 3D reconstruction techniques to 4D modelling. Computer scientists are also part of the target audience since the computerized structured of the developed models are also examined.

ORGANIZATION OF THE BOOK

The book is organized into 15 chapters, grouped in three Sections. Section 1 (Chapters 1-5) focuses on advances in 3D modelling, Section 2 (Chapters 6-10) addresses developments in 3D reconstruction, and Section 3 (Chapters 11-15) presents advances in 3D data handling and analysis as well as relevant applications. A brief description of each of the chapters follows:

Chapter 1 proposes a system for tropical tree species classification based on 3D scans of LiDAR sensing technology. In order to exploit the interrelated patterns of trees, skeleton representations of tree point clouds are extracted and their structures are divided into overlapping equal-sized 3D segments. Subsequently, the authors represent them as third-order sparse structure tensors setting the value of skeleton coordinates equal to one. Based on the higher-order tensor decomposition of each sparse segment the authors i) estimate the mode-n singular values extracting intra-correlations of tree branches and ii) model tropical trees as linear dynamical systems extracting appearance information and dynamics. The proposed methodology has been evaluated in tropical tree species and specifically, in a dataset consisting of twenty six point clouds of common Caatinga dry-forest trees.

Chapter 2 presents the background, concepts and development of the Semantic Web3D approach. The implementation of virtual and augmented reality environments on the Web requires integration between 3D technologies and web technologies, which are increasingly focused on collaboration, annotation and semantics. Thus combining VR and AR with the Semantics arises as a significant trend in the development of the Web. The use of the Semantic Web may improve creation, representation, indexing, searching and processing of 3D web content by linking the content with formal and expressive descriptions of its meaning. Although several semantic approaches have been developed for 3D content, they are not explicitly linked to the available well-established 3D technologies, cover a limited set of 3D components and properties, and do not combine domain-specific and 3D-specific semantics. In this context, Chapter 2 enables ontology-based representation of 3D content and introduces a novel framework to provide 3D structures in a RDF semantic friendly format.

Chapter 3 reviews current state-of-the-art approaches that attempt to solve sign language recognition and representation and analyzes the challenges they face. Such approaches are important to help people suffering from partial or complete hearing loss use variants of sign language to communicate with each other or hearing people in their everyday life. These systems should aim towards capturing sign language in an accurate way, classifying sign language to natural words and representing sign language by having avatars or synthesized videos execute the exact same moves that convey a meaning in the sign language. Furthermore, this chapter presents a novel AI-based solution to the problem of robust sign language capturing and representation, as well as a solution to the unavailability of annotated sign language datasets before limitations and directions for future work are discussed.

Chapter 4 focuses on modelling and digitizing performing arts, through motion capturing interfaces is an important aspect for the analysis, processing and documentation of intangible cultural heritage assets. This chapter provides a holistic description regarding the dance preservation topic by describing the capture approaches, efficient preprocessing techniques and specific approaches for knowledge generation. Presented methodologies take under consideration the existing modelling and interpretation approaches, which may involve huge amounts of information; making them difficult to process, store and analyze.

Chapter 5 provides an overview of 3D site modelling for civil engineering applications. Three-dimensional site modelling is an active area which is involved in research and development of models in several fields which has been originated from the scale modelling. In this chapter, the topic 3D site modelling in Civil Engineering is discussed. First of all, the basic concept of scale modelling, Architectural modelling and structural modelling would be discussed. After which the concept of virtual-based 3D site modelling, its importance, benefits, and steps involved in site modelling would be briefed.

Chapter 6 discusses 3D reconstruction from multiple objects, including medical images. The chapter describes a variety of approaches used for reconstruction, triangulation, as well as challenges and relevant applications.

Chapter 7 focuses on acquisition, representation and interaction of Cultural Heritage. It focuses on the technologies of Virtual Reality (VR), Augmented Reality (AR) and Serious Games (SGs), exploring these technologies and showcasing their benefits in the dissemination and understanding of Cultural Heritage.

Chapter 8 focuses on Structure from Motion (SfM) 3D reconstruction method for geomapping, medicine, cultural heritage and the energy and production industries. One inherent problem with SfM, due to its reliance on 2D images is the ambiguity of the reconstruction's scale. Absolute scale can be calculated, by using the data from additional sensors. This chapter demonstrates how distance sensors can be used to calculate the scale of a reconstructed object. In addition, the authors demonstrate that the uncertainty of the calculated scale can be computed and how it depends on the precision of the used sensors.

Chapter 9 proposes two approaches for using multimedia content for 3D reconstruction: an image-based approach that employs clustering techniques to eliminate outliers, and a video-based approach that extracts key frames via a summarization technique. In both cases, the reduced and outlier-free image data set is used as input to a Structure from Motion framework for 3D reconstruction. The presented techniques are evaluated on the basis of the reconstruction of two world-class cultural heritage monuments.

Chapter 10 deals with the problem of 3D face reconstruction from a single 2D image, presenting an overview of the problem, its evolutions, the current state-of-the-art, and future trends. Briefly, it is the task of recovering the 3-dimensional geometry of a human face from a single RGB image. While the problem of automatically estimating the 3D structure of a generic scene from RGB images can be regarded as a general task, the particular morphology and non-rigid nature of human faces make it a challenging problem for which dedicated approaches are still currently studied.

Chapter 11 reviews implementations on Generative Adversarial Networks (GANs) for 3D and 2D data augmentation applications. As the capacity of deep learning models increases, data availability becomes the most significant. To counter this issue various techniques are utilized, including data augmentation which refers to the practice of expanding the original dataset with artificially created samples. One approach that has been found is the Generative Adversarial Networks (GANs) which unlike other domain-agnostic transformation-based methods, it can produce diverse samples that belong to a given data distribution. Taking advantage of this property, a multitude of GAN architectures has been leveraged for data augmentation applications. This chapter examines methods that were used for data augmentation in 2D and 3D, and surveys the areas in which they were applied.

Chapter 12 addresses the topic of 3D graphics for medical applications. Medical experts not only within US, but around the world should be empowered through collaboration capabilities on 3D data to enable solutions for complex medical problems that will save lives. The fast growing number of 3D medical 'images' and their derivative information must be shared across the healthcare enterprise among stakeholders with vastly different perspectives and different needs. The demand for 3D data visualization is driving the need for increased accessibility and sharing of 3D medical image presentations, including their annotations and their animations.

Chapter 13 focuses on visualization and analysis of 3D images using data mining approaches. Visualizing numeric data generated by observation equipment, simulations and other means is an effective way of gaining intuitive insight into an overall picture of the data of interest. Meanwhile, data mining is known as the art of extracting valuable information from a large amount of data relative to finance, marketing, the Internet, and natural sciences, and enhancing that information to knowledge. This chapter describes relevant approaches in the above areas.

Chapter 14 reviews various machine learning techniques and their performance with commonly used quotidian datasets.

Finally, Chapter 15 addresses an imaging-based medical application. In particular, the aim of the proposed work is to improve the performance of automatic anatomic location identification approach and to develop reasoning based systematic approach for pediatric foreign body aspiration treatment management. A CBR based treatment management system is proposed for standardizing the pediatric foreign body aspiration treatment management process. The proposed approach considered a sample set of foreign body aspired pediatric radiography images for experimental evaluation and the performance is evaluated with respect to receiver operator characteristics measure.

Athanasios Voulodimos
University of West Attica, Athens, Greece

Anastasios Doulamis
National Technical University of Athens, Athens, Greece

REFERENCES

Argyriou, V., Zafeiriou, S., & Petrou, M. (2014). Optimal illumination directions for faces and rough surfaces for single and multiple light imaging using class-specific prior knowledge. *Computer Vision and Image Understanding*, *125*, 16–36. doi:10.1016/j.cviu.2014.01.012

Chen, C., Yeh, C., Chang, B. R., & Pan, J. (2015). 3D reconstruction from IR thermal images and Re-projective evaluations. *Mathematical Problems in Engineering*, *2015*, 1–8. doi:10.1155/2015/520534

Cornelis, N., Leibe, B., Cornelis, K., & Van Gool, L. (2007). 3D urban scene modeling integrating recognition and Reconstruction. *International Journal of Computer Vision*, *78*(2-3), 121–141. doi:10.100711263-007-0081-9

Cyganek, B., & Siebert, J. P. (2011). *An introduction to 3D computer vision techniques and algorithms*. John Wiley & Sons.

Dimitropoulos, K., Manitsaris, S., Tsalakanidou, F., Nikolopoulos, S., & Denby, B. (2014). Capturing the intangible: An introduction to the I-treasures project. *Proc. the 9th International Conference on66Computer Vision Theory and Applications (VISAPP)*, 773–781. 10.5220/0004871607730781

Doulamis, A. (2015). Selective 4D modelling framework for spatial-temporal land information management system. In *Third International Conference on Remote Sensing and Geoinformation of the Environment (RSCy2015)* (Vol. 9535). International Society for Optics and Photonics.

Doulamis, A., Doulamis, N., Protopapadakis, E., Voulodimos, A., & Ioannides, M. (2018). 4D modelling in cultural heritage. *Lecture Notes in Computer Science, 10754*, 174–196. doi:10.1007/978-3-319-75789-6_13

Doulamis, A., Ioannides, M., Doulamis, N., Hadjiprocopis, A., Fritsch, D., Balet, O., ... Santos, P. (2013). 4D reconstruction of the past. *First International Conference on Remote Sensing and Geoinformation of the Environment (RSCy2013)*. 10.1117/12.2029010

Doulamis, Anastasios D., (2017) Transforming Intangible Folkloric Performing Arts into Tangible Choreographic Digital Objects: The Terpsichore Approach. *VISIGRAPP, 5*.

Doulamis, N., & Doulamis, A. (2012). Fast and adaptive deep fusion learning for detecting visual objects. *Computer Vision – ECCV 2012. Workshops and Demonstrations*, 345-354. doi:10.1007/978-3-642-33885-4_35

Doulamis, N., Doulamis, A., Ioannidis, C., Klein, M., & Ioannides, M. (2017). Modelling of static and moving objects: digitizing tangible and intangible cultural heritage. In *Mixed Reality and Gamification for Cultural Heritage* (pp. 567–589). Cham: Springer. doi:10.1007/978-3-319-49607-8_23

Frangopol, D. M., & Liu, M. (2007). Maintenance and management of civil infrastructure based on condition, safety, optimization, and life-cycle cost. *Structure and Infrastructure Engineering, 3*(1), 29–41. doi:10.1080/15732470500253164

Georgopoulos, A. (2017). Data acquisition for the geometric documentation of cultural heritage. *Mixed Reality and Gamification for Cultural Heritage*, 29-73.

Georgopoulos, A., Ioannidis, C., & Valanis, A. (2010). Assessing the performance of a structured light scanner. *The International Archives of the Photogrammetry, Remote Sensing and Spatial Information Sciences, 38*(Part 5), 251–255.

Georgousis, S., Stentoumis, C., Doulamis, N., & Voulodimos, A. (2016). A hybrid algorithm for dense stereo correspondences in challenging indoor scenes. *2016 IEEE International Conference on Imaging Systems and Techniques (IST)*. 10.1109/IST.2016.7738270

Hisatomi, K., Katayama, M., Tomiyama, K., & Iwadate, Y. (2011). 3D archive system for traditional performing arts. *International Journal of Computer Vision, 94*(1), 78–88. doi:10.100711263-011-0434-2

Huang, H., Brenner, C., & Sester, M. (2013). A generative statistical approach to automatic 3D building roof reconstruction from laser scanning data. *ISPRS Journal of Photogrammetry and Remote Sensing, 79*, 29–43. doi:10.1016/j.isprsjprs.2013.02.004

Ioannou, M. T., & Georgopoulos, A. (2013). Evaluating large scale orthophotos derived from high resolution satellite imagery. *First International Conference on Remote Sensing and Geoinformation of the Environment (RSCy2013)*. 10.1117/12.2028336

Izadi, S., Davison, A., Fitzgibbon, A., Kim, D., Hilliges, O., Molyneaux, D., ... Freeman, D. (2011). KinectFusion. *Proceedings of the 24th annual ACM symposium on User interface software and technology - UIST '11*.

Jog, G. M., Koch, C., Golparvar-Fard, M., & Brilakis, I. (2012). Pothole properties measurement through visual 2D recognition and 3D reconstruction. *Computing in Civil Engineering*, 553-560.

Knoop, S., Vacek, S., & Dillmann, R. (2009). Fusion of 2D and 3D sensor data for articulated body tracking. *Robotics and Autonomous Systems*, *57*(3), 321–329. doi:10.1016/j.robot.2008.10.017

Kosmopoulos, D. I., Doulamis, A., Makris, A., Doulamis, N., Chatzis, S., & Middleton, S. E. (2009). Vision-based production of personalized video. *Signal Processing Image Communication*, *24*(3), 158–176. doi:10.1016/j.image.2008.12.010

Kosmopoulos, D. I., Doulamis, N. D., & Voulodimos, A. S. (2012). Bayesian filter based behavior recognition in workflows allowing for user feedback. *Computer Vision and Image Understanding*, *116*(3), 422–434. doi:10.1016/j.cviu.2011.09.006

Kyriakaki, G., Doulamis, A., Doulamis, N., Ioannides, M., Makantasis, K., Protopapadakis, E., ... Weinlinger, G. (2014). 4D reconstruction of tangible cultural heritage objects from web-retrieved images. *International Journal of Heritage in the Digital Era*, *3*(2), 431–451. doi:10.1260/2047-4970.3.2.431

Laggis, A., Doulamis, N., Protopapadakis, E., & Georgopoulos, A. (2017). A low-cost markerless tracking system for trajectory interpretation. *The International Archives of the Photogrammetry, Remote Sensing and Spatial Information Sciences*, *42*(W3), 413–418. doi:10.5194/isprs-archives-XLII-2-W3-413-2017

Loupos, K., Amditis, A., Stentoumis, C., Chrobocinski, P., Victores, J., Wietek, M., ... Lopez, R. (2014). Robotic intelligent vision and control for tunnel inspection and evaluation - The ROBINSPECT EC project. *2014 IEEE International Symposium on Robotic and Sensors Environments (ROSE) Proceedings* 10.1109/ROSE.2014.6952986

Loupos, K., Doulamis, A., Stentoumis, C., Protopapadakis, E., Makantasis, K., Doulamis, N., ... Singh, P. (2018). Autonomous robotic system for tunnel structural inspection and assessment. *International Journal of Intelligent Robotics and Applications*, *2*(1), 1–24. doi:10.100741315-017-0031-9

Ma, Z., & Liu, S. (2018). A review of 3D reconstruction techniques in civil engineering and their applications. *Advanced Engineering Informatics*, *37*, 163–174. doi:10.1016/j.aei.2018.05.005

Maksymowicz, K., Tunikowski, W., & Kościuk, J. (2014). Crime event 3D reconstruction based on incomplete or fragmentary evidence material – Case report. *Forensic Science International*, *242*, e6–e11. doi:10.1016/j.forsciint.2014.07.004 PMID:25132528

Montero, R., Victores, J., Martínez, S., Jardón, A., & Balaguer, C. (2015). Past, present and future of robotic tunnel inspection. *Automation in Construction*, *59*, 99–112. doi:10.1016/j.autcon.2015.02.003

Orghidan, R., Salvi, J., Gordan, M., Florea, C., & Batlle, J. (2013). Structured light self-calibration with vanishing points. *Machine Vision and Applications*, *25*(2), 489–500. doi:10.100700138-013-0517-x

Protopapadakis, E., (2016). Autonomous robotic inspection in tunnels. *ISPRS Annals of Photogrammetry, Remote Sensing & Spatial Information Sciences*, *3*(5).

Protopapadakis, E., Grammatikopoulou, A., Doulamis, A., & Grammalidis, N. (2017). Folk dance pattern recognition over depth images acquired via kinect sensor. *ISPRS -. The International Archives of the Photogrammetry, Remote Sensing and Spatial Information Sciences, 42*(W3), 587–593. doi:10.5194/isprs-archives-XLII-2-W3-587-2017

Rallis, I., Georgoulas, I., Doulamis, N., Voulodimos, A., & Terzopoulos, P. (2017). Extraction of key postures from 3D human motion data for choreography summarization. *2017 9th International Conference on Virtual Worlds and Games for Serious Applications (VS-Games).*

Redmon, J., Divvala, S., Girshick, R., & Farhadi, A. (2016). You only look once: Unified, real-time object detection. *2016 IEEE Conference on Computer Vision and Pattern Recognition (CVPR).* 10.1109/CVPR.2016.91

Remondino, F. (2011). Heritage recording and 3D modeling with photogrammetry and 3D scanning. *Remote Sensing, 3*(6), 1104–1138. doi:10.3390/rs3061104

Roncella, R., Forlani, G., & Remondino, F. (2005). *Photogrammetry for geological applications: automatic retrieval of discontinuity orientation in rock slopes. In Videometrics VIII* (Vol. 5665). International Society for Optics and Photonics.

Soursos, S., & Doulamis, N. (2012). Connected TV and beyond. *2012 IEEE Consumer Communications and Networking Conference (CCNC).* 10.1109/CCNC.2012.6181009

Stavrakis, E., Aristidou, A., Savva, M., Himona, S. L., & Chrysanthou, Y. (2012). Digitization of Cypriot folk dances. *Progress in Cultural Heritage Preservation*, 404-413.

Tam, W. J., Speranza, F., Yano, S., Shimono, K., & Ono, H. (2011). Stereoscopic 3D-TV: Visual comfort. *IEEE Transactions on Broadcasting, 57*(2), 335–346. doi:10.1109/TBC.2011.2125070

Section 1
Advances in 3D Modelling

Chapter 1
Tropical Tree Species 3D Modelling and Classification Based on LiDAR Technology

Panagiotis Barmpoutis
Imperial College London, UK

Tania Stathaki
Imperial College London, UK

Jonathan Lloyd
Imperial College London, UK

Magna Soelma Bessera de Moura
Brazilian Agricultural Research Corporation, Brazil

ABSTRACT

Over the last decade or so, laser scanning technology has become an increasingly popular and important tool for forestry inventory, enabling accurate capture of 3D information in a fast and environmentally friendly manner. To this end, the authors propose here a system for tropical tree species classification based on 3D scans of LiDAR sensing technology. In order to exploit the interrelated patterns of trees, skeleton representations of tree point clouds are extracted, and their structures are divided into overlapping equal-sized 3D segments. Subsequently, they represent them as third-order sparse structure tensors setting the value of skeleton coordinates equal to one. Based on the higher-order tensor decomposition of each sparse segment, they 1) estimate the mode-n singular values extracting intra-correlations of tree branches and 2) model tropical trees as linear dynamical systems extracting appearance information and dynamics. The proposed methodology was evaluated in tropical tree species and specifically in a dataset consisting of 26 point clouds of common Caatinga dry-forest trees.

DOI: 10.4018/978-1-5225-5294-9.ch001

INTRODUCTION

The many different types of tropical forest are distinguished by differences in the amount and distribution of rainfall throughout the year, as well as by elevation and by soil type. Often categorized on the basis of leaf habit and/or climate (for example "evergreen moist forest" vs. "seasonally dry tropical forest"), although the many different types of tropical forests may have many structural dissimilarities (Torello-Raventos et al., 2013), one common feature is their high diversity and richness of tree species (Banda et al., 2016; Cardoso et al., 2017). However, in sharp contrast to the tropical rain forests and savannas, seasonally dry tropical forests (SDFTs) remain barely studied and under-represented in conservation programs (Banda et al., 2016). As example, the Caatinga SDTF of north-east Brazil not recognized by the scientific community as distinct until a few years ago (Da Silva, et al., 2018).

Caatinga constitutes the largest SDTF region in South America (approximately equal in area to the United Kingdom and Germany combined), also being one of the most diverse and rich species SDTF areas within South America. This area is home for more than 28 million people (Martinelly & Moraes, 2013, Da Silva, et al., 2018) and recent studies have found increased land conversion rates during the past two decades, with over 89.000 km^2.of natural SDTF vegetation lost since 1990 (Santos, et al., 2011, Beuchle, et al., 2015). It is remarkable that more than 250 plant species are currently identified as highly threatened in the Red List of the Brazilian Flora (Martinelly & Moraes, 2013), but only less than 1% of Caatinga is included within the National Protected Area Network (Leal, et al., 2005, Pennington & Ratter, 2006). Although Caatinga has been characterized as a socio-ecological system, mismanagement of SDTFs can lead to biodiversity loss and to reduction in the flows of the ecosystem services required to sustain the livelihoods of millions of low-income people (Da Silva, et al., 2018). For example, a large number of Caatinga species are used by indigenous and rural communities in north-eastern Brazil for medicinal purposes (De Albuquerque, et al., 2007). To this end, the classification of Caatinga tropical tree species is an essential step that plays a crucial role in forestry investigation, forestry planning and environmental protection for maintenance of ecosystem services that underlie human wellbeing.

As described by Szenjner and Emanuelli (2016), there are many requirements for the identification of tree species in tropical forests. This is because structure of tropical tree species is complex with a large diversity of species and with the procedure of species recognition requiring a specimens' collection and taking pictures of each part of the plant (flowers and fruits). The next important step for recognition is the drying of specimens using specific instructions. For the identification process the use of a stereo microscope and the help of literature is suggested. Finally, for the purposes of robust identification, it is often necessary for a local expert to join in the field and/or herbarium. As deduced from the above, in order to have the confidence to identify species at a glance, the identification of tree species in tropical zones requires many years of experience in the field.

Based on the recent advances in the area of three-dimensional analysis, computer vision and pattern recognition, researchers have used 3D laser scanning technology in order to extract accurate information about the structure of large objects as buildings and trees. Light Detection And Ranging (LiDAR) sensors have been proven to be a powerful tool with a variety of capabilities for the analysis of woody vegetation structure and properties (Bournez, et al., 2017). Such LiDAR technologies generally are integrated into three categories: a) airborne laser scanning (ALS) systems, b) terrestrial laser scanning (TLS) systems and c) mobile laser scanning (MLS) systems. ALS systems are able to scan large areas and their use is ideal for modelling of tree crown while the TLS measurements extract more dense point clouds but are restricted by limited areas of surveillance. MLS systems combine components of both

ALS and TLS. In all cases, automatic solutions are required for the effective processing of the data (Favorskaya & Jain, 2017).

Several methods currently exist for the shape and geometric-based analysis of point clouds for object recognition and modelling in urban environments (Golovinskiy, et al., 2009, Bournez, et al., 2017, Wang, et al., 2018). As reviewed by Bournez et al. (2017), some of the characteristics that distinguish tree species, are tree and trunk height, crown shape and volume and branch density and diameter. As examples, Wang et al. (2008) captured point clouds and developed a method for vertical canopy analysis and the estimation of 3D models for trees growing in a temperate mixed (conifer/broadleaf) forest. Taking a different approach, Sirmacek and Lindenbergh (2015), used a probability matrix and calculated the density of point features for classification of urban area point clouds into 'tree' and 'non-tree' categories.

However, the main limitation of the above approaches is the fact that they do not take into account the extreme diversity that appears in the geometric characteristics of trees and particularly of tropical trees. Thus, when the geometry becomes more complex, the modelling, reconstruction and classification of tree species becomes less accurate. Unlike the previous classification methods that rely exclusively on LiDAR data and geometric features, a number of studies have used photogrammetry datasets reaching higher accuracy rates (Becker, et al., 2017). For example, in order to identify forest tree species Puliti et al. (2017) proposed a method that was based on a combination of Dirichlet and linear regression models using photogrammetric data and a pre-existing high-resolution digital terrain model. They classified three dominant tree species of their study area in Norway with 79% accuracy. However, it is considered that laser scanning captures substantially more object details than photogrammetry, a consideration which may be very important for quantifying the sometimes complex structure of tropical tree species (Grussenmeyer, et al., 2008). This later form of data acquisition has served to facilitate many recent studies that have used data-intensive deep learning techniques for any kind of classification (Bobkiv, et al., 2018). A representative method using waveform features in conjunction with a deep learning model for tree species was presented by Guan, et al. (2015) who used many tree samples for training of the model. Another example is by Zou et al. (2017), who proposed a voxel-based deep learning method to classify tree samples using point clouds.

In this chapter, we propose a new point clouds analysis methodology using terrestrial laser scanning and features, that contain unique trees' branches connectivity information in accordance with each tree species' growing pattern. This is then used for a structural analysis of tropical trees and for the subsequent identification of different species. To the best of our knowledge, this is the first study to date focused on modelling and classification of point clouds that are represented by sparse structure tensors. More specifically, in this chapter:

- We propose a methodology for the analysis and classification of point clouds and specifically of tree structures, through the creation of equally sized and overlapping segments and their novel representations as third-order sparse structure tensors.
- We model and describe the third-order tree structure tensors by a) mode-n singular values (MSVs) of core tree skeleton tensors, exploiting unique intra-correlations of tree stems and branches and using b) linear dynamical systems (LDSs) under the assumption that each tree is developed under a growing pattern that exhibit certain stationarity properties in the growing direction of it, extracting appearance information and dynamics.

To evaluate the efficiency of the proposed methodology, we created the dataset "NORDESTE-PC-TREE-SPECIES" that consists of twenty six point clouds of Caatinga tropical tree species. The experimental results show that the proposed methodology outperforms approaches that use geometric characteristics for point clouds tree identification.

The remainder of this chapter is organized as follows: the next section presents the material used for the creation of the tropical tree point cloud dataset, as well as the proposed methodology for automated tree species recognition. Subsequently, experimental results are discussed, while finally conclusions are drawn in the last section.

MATERIAL AND METHODS

Dataset Description

This research was conducted at the center of Caatinga Biome in the experimental field of the Brazilian Agricultural Research Corporation - Embrapa Tropical Semi-arid (9°05' S; 40°19' W; 350 m a.s.l.), municipality of Petrolina, Pernambuco state, Brazil. The study area covers, approximately 600 *ha* of natural mixed species of drought-deciduous trees and shrubs and with the study area having been free from and significant human interference for at least the last 35 years. The climate, according to Koppen, is classified as BSwh', i.e. semiarid with rainy season between the months of January and April, average annual rainfall of 510 *mm*. average annual temperatures of 26.2°C and Acrisol soil type.

This research focused on the following four tree species: Manihot pseudoglaziovii Pax & K.Hoffm., Commiphora leptophloeos (Mart.) J.B.Gillett, Sapium glandulosum (L.) Morong, and Cnidoscolus quercifolius Pohl. (Figure 1). M. pseudoglaziovii is a wild relative of cassava and can be found as a shrub or small tree up to 6 *m* high, occasionally taller. It is sometimes grown for forage under semi-arid conditions (Nassar et al., 2008). C. leptophloeos a spiny, deciduous tree with a spreading, roundish crown; which can grow 6 - 9 metres tall. The tree is sometimes harvested from the wild for local use as a medicine and source of wood and a gum (Lorenzi, 2002). S. glandulosum is a tree that can grow as tall as 35 *m* in moist forest areas, but which typically reaches only 3 to 8 *m* in height in the Caatinga region. It is used in traditional medicine and its use has also been recommended for the recovery of degraded areas in the semi-arid zone (Ferreira et al., 2009). C. quercifolius is a deciduous shrub or tree with a sparse, longish or roundish crown which can grow up to 8 metres tall and which often branches from the base. The tree is harvested from the wild for local use as a source of oil and wood and it can be used as a pioneer when restoring native woodland (Lorenzi, 2002).

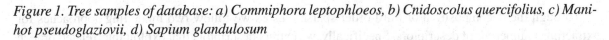

Figure 1. Tree samples of database: a) Commiphora leptophloeos, b) Cnidoscolus quercifolius, c) Manihot pseudoglaziovii, d) Sapium glandulosum

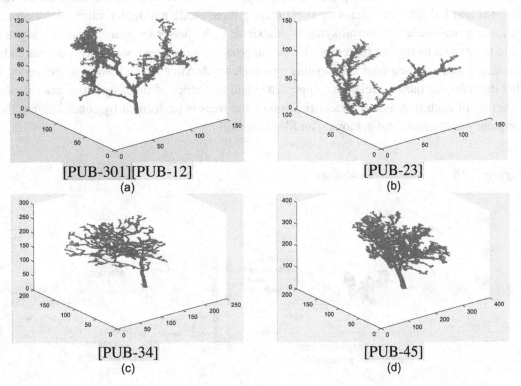

A FARO Focus 3D scanner was used for the scanning of trees with the settings of resolution 1/2 and of quality 4x. Furthermore, four scans per tree were performed either indoors or outdoors from different directions, viewing angles and heights. To process and register the multiple raw scans, the scene software version 6.2.4 was used. Finally, the point cloud of each tree was exported in XYZ format in order to be used. The experiments were performed in a PC that has an E5 2.4 GHz processor and 32 GB memory ram.

Methodology

The framework of the proposed methodology is shown in Figure 2. In the proposed methodology, a 3D laser scanner was used to capture the point clouds of isolated trees. Even though it is clear that the increase of the point clouds density improves the classification results, more data points require further computation time and memory for the point clouds processing. To this end, the initial pre-processing step relates to the denoising of the captured point clouds. Then, in order to further reduce the complexity of data and to reconstruct the architecture and geometry of trees accurately, skeletons of trees and resampling of them into local voxel spaces are estimated through the Fast Marching Method (FMM). Subsequently, in order to exploit the interrelated branch patterns, we divide these skeletons into overlapping equal-sized segments and we represent them as third-order sparse structure tensors.

Through the decomposition of third-order sparse tensors we follow two modelling approaches for extracting a numerous of descriptors. Specifically, we extract descriptors that exploit interrelated branch patterns and hidden correlations by i) estimating three mode-n singular values descriptors and by ii) extracting one linear dynamical systems descriptor of higher-order sparse structure segments. As we need to create a histogram representation per approach for each tree, we apply k-means and k-medoids clustering and each segment is described by a codeword. After which, two term frequency histograms that describe the intra-correlations, appearance and dynamics of trees skeletons are calculated for the structure of each tree. Finally, identification of the trees is performed by concatenating the two term frequency histograms and deploying an SVM classifier.

Figure 2. The proposed methodology

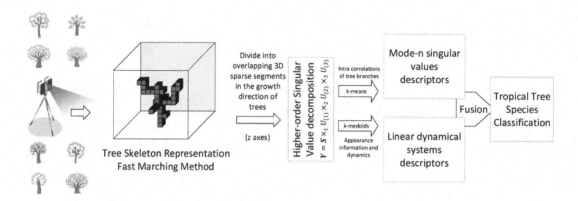

3D Modelling

After obtaining the point clouds it is necessary to perform noise and extraneous scan point removal as well as resampling of the retained points into local voxel spaces. The subsequent voxel representation is used for the estimation of tree skeletons. This is a significant step for the modeling of connectivity and topology of branches, structure analysis and classification of a trees' data. In most studies, estimating of skeletons or skeletonization of point clouds is achieved in four different ways: a) removing the boundary of a point cloud layer by layer, known as morphological thinning (Zhou & Toga, 1999), b) computing Voronoi diagrams of discrete polylines like boundaries known as geometric and topological structure methods (Ying, et al., 2015), c) computing distance transform (DT) of the object's boundary (Hassouna & Farag, 2007, Van Uitert & Bitter, 2007) and d) generating quantitative structure models (QSMs) (Raumonen, et al., 2013, Raumonen, et al., 2015). In our methodology, we used the Fast Marching Method (FMM) that has shown to be superior to other methods with regards to fast execution and accurate skeletonization results.

Fast Marching Method (FMM) is one of the most representative distance transform methods and it has been applied so far to binary images or to voxel representations with skeletonization usages mainly for medical purposes (Van Uitert & Bitter, 2007). In this chapter, for tree structure skeletonization, we applied the FMM approach that was proposed by Van Uitert & Bitter (2007). This approach takes into account level sets with a positive evolution speed, which is based on distance values, and represents the isosurface by solving the Eikonal equation:

$$|\nabla T| F = 1, T = 0 \text{ on } \Gamma \tag{1}$$

where T is the arrival time function, F is the speed of evolution function and Γ is the initial isosurface at time zero. According to the skeletonization procedure, the processing of voxels is performed in a sorted order based on increasing values of T. Furthermore, the Euclidean distance was used to compute the point with the largest distance from the object's boundary, i.e., the global maximum distance point, and to determine a speed image in order to use it as input for the fast marching propagation with a constant step size of unity. The discretization of Eq. (1) is given by:

$$max\left(D_{i,j,k}^{-x},0\right)^2 + min\left(D_{i,j,k}^{+x},0\right)^2 + max\left(D_{i,j,k}^{-y},0\right)^2 + min\left(D_{i,j,k}^{+y},0\right)^2 + max\left(D_{i,j,k}^{-z},0\right)^2 + min\left(D_{i,j,k}^{+z},0\right)^2 = F_{i,j,k}^{-2} \tag{2}$$

where $D_{i,j,k}^{-x}$ and $D_{i,j,k}^{+x}$ .are values resulting from standard backward and forward difference calculations at location (i,j,k). The start point for a fast marching propagation was defined the point at the global maximum distance from the object's boundary.

Skeletons Representation Through Higher-Order Tensors

The extracted tree skeletons contain spatially-evolving characteristics that reflect the connectivity and topology of branches with both inter-correlated and intra-correlated patterns that are unique for each one of species. In order to exploit this information, we divide the skeleton of trees into equal-sized segments and a numerous of tensors are created for each segment, following a patching approach which divides each tree skeleton into overlapping segments in the growing direction of trees. Thus, we consider each skeleton segment as a sparse binary tensor for which tree skeleton coordinates are equal to one. The corresponding dimensions for each segment are l_1, l_2 and h respectively for tree length, width and height respectively.

To this end, we represent each segment as a sparse third order tensor $Y \in \mathcal{R}^{l_1 \times l_2 \times h}$ .and we apply higher order singular value decomposition (Higher-Order SVD) using sequential truncation and a randomized SVD algorithm based on randomized subspace iteration (Halko, et al., 2011): this allowing the computation of singular values and vectors of large sparse matrices with high accuracy. In summary, for each mode-n unfolding $Y_{(n)}$ of the sparse third order tensor Y we estimate a Gaussian random matrix Ω and we compute the $I_{(n)} = Y_{(n)} \Omega$ and its QR factorization so that it is $I_{(n)} = QR$. Then we form the matrix $B_{(n)} = Q^T I_{(n)}$ and compute the corresponding singular value decomposition: $B_{(n)} = \tilde{U} \Sigma V^T$. Thus, the orthonormal matrices of the higher-order singular value decomposition are described by the equation $U_{(n)} = Q\tilde{U}$. Therefore, the tensor Y is written as the multilinear tensor-matrix product of S and $U_{(n)}$.

$$Y = S \times_1 U_{(1)} \times_2 U_{(2)} \times_3 U_{(3)}. \tag{3}$$

where, $S \in \mathcal{R}^{l_1 \times l_2 \times h}$ is the core tensor, while $U_{(1)} \in \mathcal{R}^{l_1 \times l_1}$, $U_{(2)} \in \mathcal{R}^{l_2 \times l_2}$ and $U_{(3)} \in \mathcal{R}^{h \times h}$ are orthogonal matrices containing the orthonormal vectors spanning the column space of the matrix and with the operator $\times_j$ denoting the j mode product between a tensor and a matrix. After obtaining the core tensor and the set of U matrices, we evaluated two modelling approaches for the extraction of a features set.

Modelling of Tree Branches' Through Mode-N Singular Values

The singular values of mode-n tensor unfoldings extract topological properties of tensors for which they can also be considered as artificial characteristics providing crucial measures (Hackbusch and Uschmajew, 2017). Generally, the singular values are different for mode-n unfoldings but not completely independent. Here, in order to model inter-correlations and intra-correlations of tree branches and by the assumption that topological changes and branches patterns reflected by the sums of squared SVs, mode-n singular values (MSVs) are computed using the core tensor S of each segment. The MSVs descriptors, denoted as $\sigma^{(n)}$ are given by:

$$\sigma_t^{(1)} = \sqrt{\sum_{i=1}^{l_1}\sum_{j=1}^{l_2} s_{ijt}^2} \in \mathcal{R}^h, \; t=1,2,\dots,h \tag{4}$$

$$\sigma_j^{(2)} = \sqrt{\sum_{i=1}^{l_1}\sum_{t=1}^{h} s_{ijt}^2} \in \mathcal{R}^{l_2}, \; j=1,2,\dots,l_2$$

$$\sigma_i^{(3)} = \sqrt{\sum_{j=1}^{l_2}\sum_{t=1}^{h} s_{ijt}^2} \in \mathcal{R}^{l_1}, \; i=1,2,\dots,l_1$$

where l_1, l_2 and h are the sizes of mode-n dimensions and s_{ijt} are the elements of the core tensor. As a mode-n SV descriptor corresponds to each segment, a total number of $H-h$ descriptors are produced for each tree structure. Comparing the results of Figure 3 which shows the variations of the first three SVs of each mode for the different tree species, it is clear that the SVs can be used as discriminating features for species differentiation. Furthermore, we observe that singular values for mode-n unfoldings are not completely independent, and there are slight variations between consecutive singular values.

Figure 3. Distributions of mode-n SVs of core tensors for different tree samples: a-b-c) First, second and third SV of Commiphora leptophloeos, d-e-f) First, second and third SV Cnidoscolus quercifolius, g-h-i) First, second and third SV Manihot pseudoglaziovii, j-k-l) First, second and third SV Sapium glandulo-sum. Red line corresponds in mode-1 SV, the blue line in mode-2 SV and the black line in mode-3 SV.

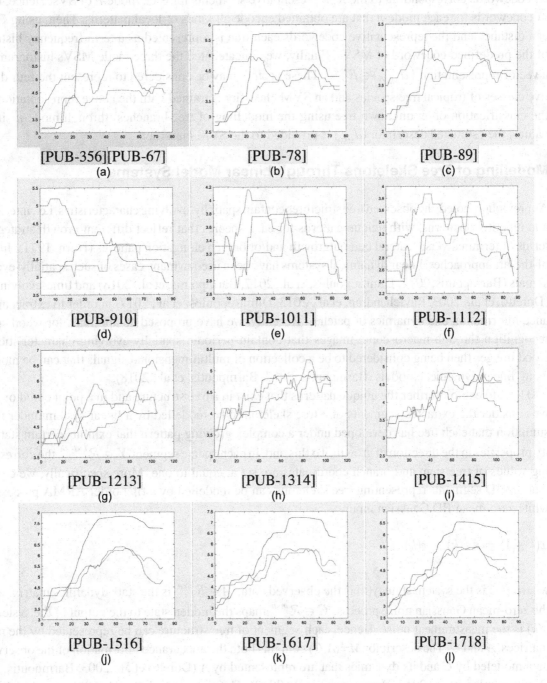

[PUB-356][PUB-67] (a)
[PUB-78] (b)
[PUB-89] (c)

[PUB-910] (d)
[PUB-1011] (e)
[PUB-1112] (f)

[PUB-1213] (g)
[PUB-1314] (h)
[PUB-1415] (i)

[PUB-1516] (j)
[PUB-1617] (k)
[PUB-1718] (l)

After obtaining mode-n SV descriptors, to estimate a histogram representation for each tree structure we apply the bag of systems approach by using k-means clustering method for the collection of H–h descriptors for the three modes and by defining three different codebooks. Each codebook consists of K_1 codewords corresponding to the K_1 representative segments for each mode-n of SVs. Hence, the set of codewords for each mode-n that are obtained encode all kinds of local patterns. Then, using Euclidean distance and the representative codewords each tree is represented as a term frequency histogram of the predefined codeword of MSVs. Finally, we concatenated the three mode MSVs histograms into a vector representation $\left(d_{MSV}\right) \in R^{3 \times K_1}$. These vectors may be considered to represent the four distinctive classes of tropical tree species and an SVM classifier is trained with the above representations. For the classification of an unknown tree using the modelling of tree branches' through mode-n singular values, the estimated descriptor (d_{MSV}) is provided to the SVM classifier.

Modelling of Tree Skeletons Through Linear Model Systems

As previously noted, the observed tree structures contain spatially-evolving characteristics, i.e., interrelated and repetitive patterns, with unique patterns for each species that reflect different growth strategies in terms of terminal versus lateral bud outgrowth and/or branch elongation patterns (Horn, 1971). In state-of-the-art approaches, linear dynamical systems have been used in many cases of such spatially-evolving signals (Barmpoutis, 2017, Dimitropoulos, et al., 2017, Barmpoutis, et al., 2018) and time-evolving data (Doretto, et al., 2003, Ravichandran, et al., 2013, Dimitropoulos, et al., 2017) in order to extract appearance information and dynamics of patches. Recently, we have proposed an approach for wood species recognition through macroscopic images that contain periodic spatially-evolving characteristics: the wood images then being considered to be a collection of multidimensional signals that can be modelled using linear dynamical models (Barmpoutis, 2017, Barmpoutis, et al., 2018).

Here, to exploit further the unique patterns that exist in a tree structure and in a point cloud of a tree, we consider the extracted segments of a tree skeleton to be modelled by a linear system under the assumption that each tree has developed under a complex growing pattern that exhibits certain stationarity properties in the direction of growth. To this end, in each sparse segment $Y \in \mathcal{R}^{l_1 \times l_2 \times h}$ the corresponding values of tree stem and branch coordinates are set at equal to one. More specifically, we consider that the 3D segments representing tree skeletons can be modelled by a first order ARMA process with white zero mean IID Gaussian input:

$$x(k+1) = Ax(k) + w(k) \tag{5}$$

where $x(k)$ is the system state, $y(k)$ is the observed data, $A \in \mathcal{R}^{n \times n}$ is the state dynamics matrix, $w(k)$ is the zero-mean Gaussian noise process, $C \in \mathcal{R}^{m \times n}$ maps the hidden state to the output of the system and $q(k)$ is the measurement noise. Hence, each segment of tree structure can be represented by the pair of matrices, A and C. The descriptor $M=(A,C)$ contains both the appearance information of the observation data modeled by C and its dynamics that are represented by A (Doretto et al., 2003, Barmpoutis, 2017, Dimitropoulos, et al., 2017, Barmpoutis, et al., 2018). The sizes of both A and C are related to the total number of the observed data.

Considering that the decomposition of Y is obtained from equation (3) and that the choice of matrices A and C in equations (5) is not unique, we can consider $C=U_{(3)}$ and

$$\boldsymbol{X} = S \times_1 U_{(1)} \times_2 U_{(2)} \qquad (6)$$

Hence, equation (3) can be reformulated as follows:

$$\boldsymbol{Y} = X \times_3 C \Leftrightarrow Y_{(3)} = CX_{(3)} \qquad (7)$$

where $Y_{(3)}$ and $X_{(3)}$ indicate the unfolding along the third dimension of tensors $\boldsymbol{Y}$ and $\boldsymbol{X}$ respectively and $X_{(3)} = [x(1),x(2),....,x(n)]$ are the estimated states of the system. Here, to further reduce the computational cost of the method we reduce the dimensions of A and C through reducing the dimension of the hidden space which is represented by tensor $\boldsymbol{X}$. Hence, we select the first n orthonormal columns of the core tensor S as well as of the orthogonal matrices $U_{(1)}$, $U_{(2)}$ and $U_{(3)}$. Thus, if we define $X_1 = [x(2),x(3),...$ $..,x(n)]$ and $X_2 = [x(1),x(2),.....,x(n-1)]$ the transition matrix A that contains the dynamics of the signal, can be easily computed by using least squares as:

$$A = X_2 X_1^T (X_1 X_1^T)^{-1} \qquad (8)$$

After the estimation of the system parameters, we define a codebook, and similarly to MSVs approach as already described, we apply a bag of systems approach to create a Term Frequency (TF) histogram representation $(d_{LDS}) \in R^{K_2}$ .of tree structures for each one of species. The codebook consists of K_2 codewords corresponding to the K_2 representative segments defined through a k-medoid clustering approach (Ravichandran, 2013, Barmpoutis, 2017, Dimitropoulos, et al., 2017).

Specifically, for the creation of codebook and for the classification of the descriptors we adopt the Martin distance as similarity metric. Thus, in order to determine the similarity degree between two descriptors $M_1 = (A_1, C_1)$ and $M_2 = (A_2, C_2)$ subspace angles between the two descriptors are initially calculated and a Martin distance then used as a comparison metric (Cock and Moor, 2002) similarly to previous works (Ravichandran, 2013, Barmpoutis, 2017, Dimitropoulos, et al., 2017, Barmpoutis, et al., 2018). For the classification of an unknown tree using the modelling of tree skeletons through linear model systems approach, the estimated descriptor (d_{LDS}) is provided to an SVM classifier.

Classification of Caatinga Tree Species

In order to improve the classification accuracy, because the branching structure of tropical trees is necessarily complex, the proposed method uses the combination of *MSVs* and *LDS* descriptors. The formula for the concatenation of features that are derived from skeleton segments is described as follows:

$$d = [d_{MSV}, d_{LDS}] \qquad (9)$$

Finally, for the classification of $d \in R^{3 \times K_1 + K_2}$ .descriptors into tree species classes, a multi-class Support Vector Machines (SVM) classifier is used. The accuracy of the proposed methodology represents the proportion of true results, and is calculated as:

$$Accuracy = \frac{TP + TN}{TP + FP + FN + TN} \qquad (10)$$

Where TP, FP, TN and FN are true positives, false positives, true negatives and false negatives.

RESULTS AND DISCUSSION

In this section, we present a detailed experimental evaluation of our methodology using "NORDESTE-PC-TREE-SPECIES" dataset. The goal of this experimental evaluation is three-fold: a) initially, we want to define the optimum set of parameters for our algorithm; b) subsequently, we aim to show that the late fusion of proposed descriptors improves significantly the classification accuracy and c) finally, we intend to demonstrate the superiority of the proposed algorithm in tree species recognition against a number of current state of the art approaches. In all experimental results we split the tree species dataset into *ds* (in our experiments, *ds*=5 training and testing subsets. For each subset the 80% of samples is used as training dataset and the remaining subset is used for testing the developed methodology. Then, we repeat the above procedure five times. The overall classification accuracy is estimated by averaging the accuracy of all iterations.

Figure 4. Results for the tree species recognition using mode-1 singular values

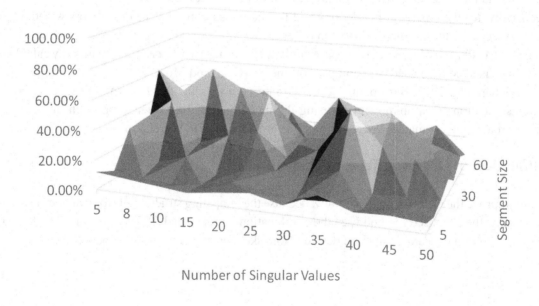

MSVs Evaluation

In order to have a clear view of the performance of the MSVs descriptors, we present a complete evaluation analysis: with this taking into account all the factors that can directly affect the result of the MSVs analysis. More precisely, we focus on the size h of the 3D segment, on the number of singular values that are considered in each mode and on the sizes of codebooks that are defined using k-means clustering. More specifically, we run experiments with seven different segment sizes (5, 10, 20, 30, 40, 50, and 60) and eleven numbers of singular values sizes that are considered (viz. 5, 8, 10, 15, 20, 25, 30, 35, 40, 45 and 50 SVs), i.e., 77 experiments in total. Figure 4, illustrates recognition results of the mode-*1* singular values analysis using segments of eleven different height sizes $l_1 \times l_2 \times k$ where l_1 is the length of each tree, l_2 is the width of each tree and k is the size of the segment height. As can be seen, the best recognition rate of 64%, is achieved by setting the segment height equal to 40 and by selecting the first ten mode-*1* singular values.

Figure 5 illustrates recognition results of the mode-*2* singular values analysis using the same evaluation scheme. Here, the best recognition rate of 76% is achieved by setting the segment height equal to 50 and selecting the first forty mode-*2* singular values.

Figure 5. Results for the tree species recognition using mode-2 singular values

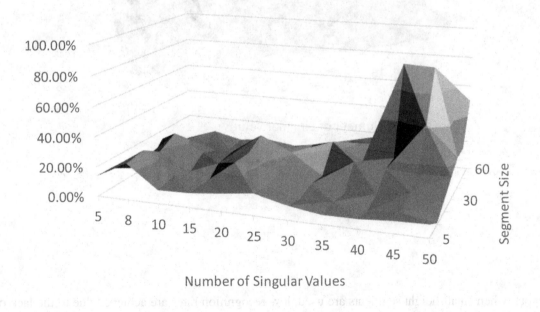

Similarly, the recognition rates of the mode-*3* singular values analysis are presented in Figure 6. Here, the best recognition rate of 64% is achieved by setting the segment height *h* equal to 60 and selecting the first forty-five mode-*3* singular values. Experimental results of mode-*2* and mode-*3* show that the recognition rates follow a similar trend due to the randomness of scanning direction and similarities in the structure of trees in the two tree dimensions (width and length as defined in the chapter).

Figure 6. Results for the tree species recognition using mode-3 singular values

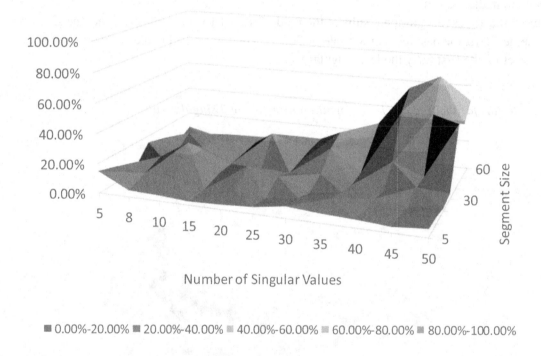

■ 0.00%-20.00% ■ 20.00%-40.00% ■ 40.00%-60.00% ■ 60.00%-80.00% ■ 80.00%-100.00%

Of note, when small-height segments are used, low recognition rates are achieved due to the lack of structure information of trees. Thus, growing patterns and variations of branches are not adequately reflected in the MSV descriptors. Similarly, when the height of segments increases significantly, the performance of descriptors falls due to the high complexity of patterns identified in these tropical tree species. After the selection of optimum parameters for the size *h* of the 3D segment and for the number of consecutive singular values to be used, it is further necessary to define the size of codebooks. Taking into account the experimental results and with computational costs increasing with codebooks size, we selected 32 codewords to extract the three components of the d_{MSV} descriptor in respect to each mode-*n* unfolding.

Linear Dynamical Systems Evaluation

In this subsection, we present a detailed analysis aimed to define the optimum set of parameters for the linear dynamical systems modelling approach. More specifically, we run experiments using seven different codebook sizes (16, 32, 48, 64, 80, 96 and 128 codewords) and seven different segment sizes (5, 10, 20, 30, 40, 50, and 60), i.e., 49 experiments in total. As can easily be seen from Figure 7 the proposed method produces the best results for segment size equal to 40 and codebook size of 32 codewords, yielding a detection rate of 76%.

Figure 7. Results for the tree species recognition using modelling through linear dynamical systems

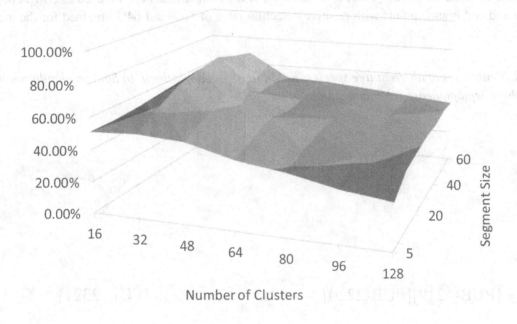

Subsequently, to further exploit the performance of the proposed methodology and sparse formation of tree data in a tensor, we formed patches which consisted of the coordinates of tree stem and branches and classified them using Histograms of Grassmannian Points similarly to state-of-the-art methodologies (Dimitropoulos, et al., 2016, Ding, et al., 2018). The true positive accuracy was estimated at 4%, much less than the proposed approach at 72%.

Having defined the best parameters of the algorithm, i.e., segment size, number of singular values and codebook size, in the next experiment we aim to show that the fusion of these features can improve the recognition rates. The performance of the proposed fusion method, and the explanation of how the different descriptors contribute to classification rates, from which it can be seen that the proposed methodology achieves a 92% classification rate using both MSVs descriptor and LDS descriptor and an SVM classifier.

Comparison Performance

Finally, we evaluated the performance of the proposed methodology against other state-of-the-art techniques. First, the geometric approach of Bournez, et al., (2017) which incorporates tree structure characteristics viz. tree and trunk height, crown shape, volume and surface and branch density, order, position and diameter and is which able to characterize the geometric complexity of trees and to perform segmentation and reconstruction of trees results in a recognition rate using the above measurements and an SVM classifier of 64%. Second, we considered an alternative approach which employs a set of features that are based on perimeters and surface areas of Voronoi Diagrams and Delaunay Triangulations of the given sets of critical points of trees. 3D Voronoi diagrams (VD) and Delaunay Triangulations (DT) are able and have been used to describe and quantify 3D objects defining spatial pattern and relationships between the selected 3D points (Ying, et al., 2015). For the comparison here we used as critical points the node and end branch points with positive detection rates of 56% and 64% obtained for the use of

Figure 8. Similarities of different tree species: a) Manihot pseudoglaziovii, b) Sapium glandulosum, c) Commiphora leptophloeos, d) Sapium glandulosum

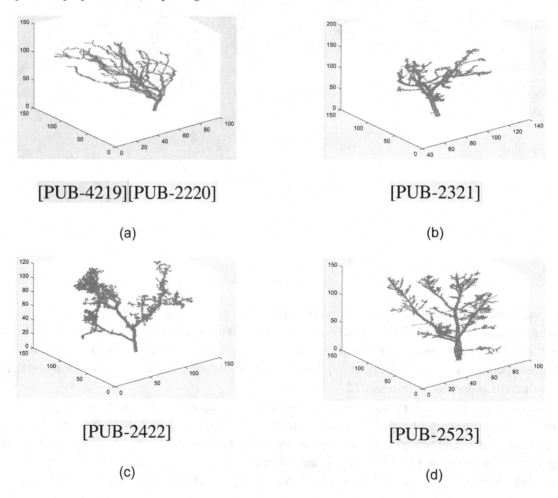

[PUB-4219][PUB-2220]

(a)

[PUB-2321]

(b)

[PUB-2422]

(c)

[PUB-2523]

(d)

VD and DT respectively. Third, using an SVM classifier and the late fusion combination of VD and DT extracted features, we found a successful classification rate estimated at 72%. Obviously then, for the current dataset at least, our proposed new method outperforms previously presented tree recognition approaches that rely solely on geometric characteristics as described in the previous sections.

Figure 8 provides examples of obtained skeletons for the different tree species, for which both similarities and differences in size and structure are readily evident. For example, M. pseudoglaziovii (Fig. 8a) and S. glandulosum (Fig. 8b) are both of a similar height and with broadly similar branching patterns giving rise to a reasonably high probability of misclassification. Similarly, some misclassifications of C. leptophloeos (Fig. 8c) as S. glandulosum (Fig. 8d) and vice versa are explained by the fact that both of them have short main stem length and relatively long second-level branches.

Figure 9. Dissimilarities of same tree species: a-b) Sapium glandulosum, c-d) Manihot pseudoglaziovii

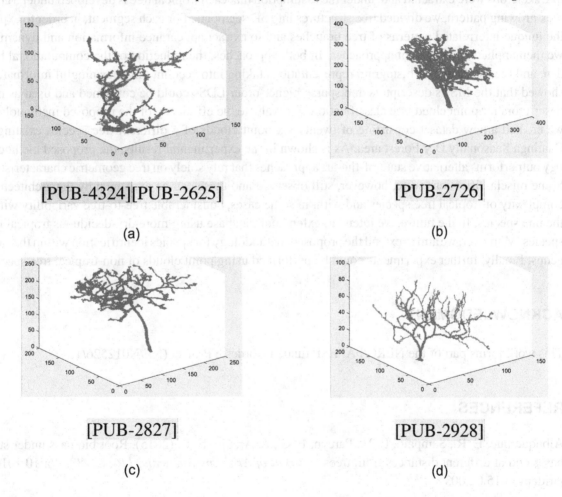

[PUB-4324][PUB-2625]

(a)

[PUB-2726]

(b)

[PUB-2827]

(c)

[PUB-2928]

(d)

On the other hand, Figure 9 provides two examples where intraspecific differences in structure are obviously clear, these being for S. glandulosum (Figure 9a&b) and M. pseudoglaziovii (Figure 9c&d). For S. glandulosum there are differences in the size of trees as well as in the structure and inter-correlations. But nevertheless, our new proposed methodology successfully recognizes them. For M. pseudoglaziovii there are obvious differences in stem length, branches topology and height, but again with these also differences similarly not confounding our new species recognition algorithm.

CONCLUSION AND FUTURE RESEARCH DIRECTIONS

In this chapter we have presented a novel approach for automated tropical tree species recognition using point clouds through skeleton extraction and analysis using higher order tensor representations. Initially, tree skeletons were extracted and, under the assumption that each tropical tree is developed under a complex growing pattern, we divided tree structures into 3D segments. For each segment, in order to exploit the unique interrelated patterns of tree branches and to extract appearance information and dynamics, we then applied two different approaches. In both approaches, the reduction of the computational burden, and the estimation of histogram representations taking into account only meaningful information, showed that the MSVs descriptors and sparse higher-order LDSs could be combined and used as new descriptors for point cloud tree classification. To evaluate the efficiency of the proposed methodology, we created a new dataset consisting of twenty six point clouds of 4 different tree species existing in Caatinga Seasonally Dry Forest area. As is shown in the experimental results, the proposed methodology outperforms alternative state-of-the-art approaches that rely solely on tree geometric characteristics. Some misclassifications were, however, still observed and these can be explained by the architectural complexity of tropical tree species and with, in some cases, considerable tree-to-tree variability within the one species. In the future, we intend to extend our database using more dry-deciduous tropical tree species. Moreover, we aim to extend the proposed methodology for species identification within the same genus. Finally, further experiments could be performed using point clouds of non-tropical tree species.

ACKNOWLEDGMENT

This work forms part of the NERC/FAPESP funded Nordeste Project (NE/N012526/1).

REFERENCES

Albuquerque, E. R., Sampaio, E. V., Pareyn, F. G., & Araújo, E. L. (2015). Root biomass under stem bases and at different distances from trees. *Journal of Arid Environments*, *116*, 82–88. doi:10.1016/j.jaridenv.2015.02.003

Banda-R, K., Delgado-Salinas, A., Dexter, K. G., Linares-Palomino, R., Oliveira-Filho, A., Prado, D., ... Rodríguez, M. (2016). Plant diversity patterns in neotropical dry forests and their conservation implications. *Science*, *353*(6306), 1383–1387. doi:10.1126cience.aaf5080 PMID:27708031

Barmpoutis, P. (2017). *Design and Development of a System for the Processing of Wood Images of Greek Forest Species* (Doctoral dissertation). Aristotle University of Thessaloniki, Greece.

Barmpoutis, P., Dimitropoulos, K., Barboutis, I., Grammalidis, N., & Lefakis, P. (2018). Wood species recognition through multidimensional texture analysis. *Computers and Electronics in Agriculture, 144,* 241–248. doi:10.1016/j.compag.2017.12.011

Becker, C., Häni, N., Rosinskaya, E., d'Angelo, E., & Strecha, C. (2017). Classification of Aerial Photogrammetric 3d Point Clouds. *ISPRS Annals of Photogrammetry, Remote Sensing and Spatial Information Sciences,* 3-10.

Beuchle, R., Grecchi, R. C., Shimabukuro, Y. E., Seliger, R., Eva, H. D., Sano, E., & Achard, F. (2015). Land cover changes in the Brazilian Cerrado and Caatinga biomes from 1990 to 2010 based on a systematic remote sensing sampling approach. *Applied Geography (Sevenoaks, England), 58,* 116–127. doi:10.1016/j.apgeog.2015.01.017

Bobkov, D., Chen, S., Jian, R., Iqbal, Z., & Steinbach, E. (2018). Noise-resistant Deep Learning for Object Classification in 3D Point Clouds Using a Point Pair Descriptor. *IEEE Robotics and Automation Letters.*

Bournez, E., Landes, T., Saudreau, M., Kastendeuch, P., & Najjar, G. (2017). From TLS point clouds to 3D models of trees: A comparison of existing algorithms for 3D tree reconstruction. ISPRS-International Archives of the Photogrammetry. *Remote Sensing and Spatial Information Sciences, 42,* 2.

Cardoso, D., Särkinen, T., Alexander, S., Amorim, A. M., Bittrich, V., Celis, M., ... Giacomin, L. L. (2017). Amazon plant diversity revealed by a taxonomically verified species list. *Proceedings of the National Academy of Sciences of the United States of America, 114*(40), 10695–10700. doi:10.1073/pnas.1706756114 PMID:28923966

Cock, D. K., & Moor, D. B. (2002). Subspace angles between ARMA models. *Systems & Control Letters, 46*(4), 265–270. doi:10.1016/S0167-6911(02)00135-4

Da Silva, J. M. C., Leal, I. R., & Tabarelli, M. (Eds.). (2018). *Caatinga: The Largest Tropical Dry Forest Region in South America.* Springer.

De Albuquerque, U. P., De Medeiros, P. M., De Almeida, A. L. S., Monteiro, J. M., Neto, E. M. D. F. L., de Melo, J. G., & Dos Santos, J. P. (2007). Medicinal plants of the caatinga (semi-arid) vegetation of NE Brazil: A quantitative approach. *Journal of Ethnopharmacology, 114*(3), 325–354. doi:10.1016/j.jep.2007.08.017 PMID:17900836

Dimitropoulos, K., Barmpoutis, P., & Grammalidis, N. (2017). Higher order linear dynamical systems for smoke detection in video surveillance applications. *IEEE Transactions on Circuits and Systems for Video Technology, 27*(5), 1143–1154. doi:10.1109/TCSVT.2016.2527340

Dimitropoulos, K., Barmpoutis, P., Kitsikidis, A., & Grammalidis, N. (2016). Classification of multidimensional time-evolving data using histograms of Grassmannian points. *IEEE Transactions on Circuits and Systems for Video Technology.*

Dimitropoulos, K., Barmpoutis, P., Zioga, C., Kamas, A., Patsiaoura, K., & Grammalidis, N. (2017). Grading of invasive breast carcinoma through Grassmannian VLAD encoding. *PLoS One*, *12*(9), e0185110. doi:10.1371/journal.pone.0185110 PMID:28934283

Ding, W., Liu, K., Belyaev, E., & Cheng, F. (2018). Tensor-based linear dynamical systems for action recognition from 3D skeletons. *Pattern Recognition*, *77*, 75–86. doi:10.1016/j.patcog.2017.12.004

Doretto, G., Chiuso, A., Wu, Y. N., & Soatto, S. (2003). Dynamic textures. *International Journal of Computer Vision*, *51*(2), 91–109. doi:10.1023/A:1021669406132

Favorskaya, M. N., & Jain, L. C. (2017). Overview of LiDAR Technologies and Equipment for Land Cover Scanning. In *Handbook on Advances in Remote Sensing and Geographic Information Systems* (pp. 19–68). Cham: Springer. doi:10.1007/978-3-319-52308-8_2

Golovinskiy, A., Kim, V. G., & Funkhouser, T. (2009). Shape-based recognition of 3D point clouds in urban environments. In *Computer Vision, 2009 IEEE 12th International Conference on* (pp. 2154-2161). IEEE.

Grussenmeyer, P., Landes, T., Voegtle, T., & Ringle, K. (2008). Comparison methods of terrestrial laser scanning, photogrammetry and tacheometry data for recording of cultural heritage buildings. *The International Archives of the Photogrammetry, Remote Sensing and Spatial Information Sciences*, *37*(B5), 213–218.

Guan, H., Yu, Y., Ji, Z., Li, J., & Zhang, Q. (2015). Deep learning-based tree classification using mobile LiDAR data. *Remote Sensing Letters*, *6*(11), 864–873. doi:10.1080/2150704X.2015.1088668

Hackbusch, W., & Uschmajew, A. (2017). On the interconnection between the higher-order singular values of real tensors. *Numerische Mathematik*, *135*(3), 875–894. doi:10.100700211-016-0819-9 PMID:28615745

Halko, N., Martinsson, P. G., & Tropp, J. A. (2011). Finding structure with randomness: Probabilistic algorithms for constructing approximate matrix decompositions. *SIAM Review*, *53*(2), 217–288. doi:10.1137/090771806

Hassouna, M. S., & Farag, A. A. (2007). Multistencils fast marching methods: A highly accurate solution to the eikonal equation on cartesian domains. *IEEE Transactions on Pattern Analysis and Machine Intelligence*, *29*(9), 1563–1574. doi:10.1109/TPAMI.2007.1154 PMID:17627044

Horn, H. S. (1971). *The adaptive geometry of trees*. Princeton, NJ: Princeton University Press.

Kankare, V., Holopainen, M., Vastaranta, M., Puttonen, E., Yu, X., Hyyppä, J., ... Alho, P. (2013). Individual tree biomass estimation using terrestrial laser scanning. *ISPRS Journal of Photogrammetry and Remote Sensing*, *75*, 64–75. doi:10.1016/j.isprsjprs.2012.10.003

Larsen, R. M. (1998). Lanczos bidiagonalization with partial reorthogonalization. *DAIMI Report Series*, *27*(537).

Leal, I. R., da Silva, J. O. S. E., Cardoso, M., Tabarelli, M., & Lacher, T. E. (2005). Changing the course of biodiversity conservation in the Caatinga of northeastern Brazil. *Conservation Biology*, *19*(3), 701–706. doi:10.1111/j.1523-1739.2005.00703.x

Lorenzi, H. (2002). Brazilian Trees. A Guide to the Identification and Cultivation of Brazilian Native Trees, Vol. 2 (2nd ed.). Instituto Plantarum de Estados da Flora LTDA, Nova.

Martinelli, G., & Moraes, M. A. (2013). *Livro vermelho da flora do Brasil*. Academic Press.

Nassar, N. M., Hashimoto, D., & Fernandes, S. (2008). Wild Manihot species: Botanical aspects, geographic distribution and economic value. *Genetics and Molecular Research*, 7(1), 16–28. doi:10.4238/vol7-1gmr389 PMID:18273815

Pennington, R. T., & Ratter, J. A. (Eds.). (2006). *Neotropical savannas and seasonally dry forests: plant diversity, biogeography, and conservation*. CRC Press. doi:10.1201/9781420004496

Prado, D. E. (2000). Seasonally dry forests of tropical South America: From forgotten ecosystems to a new phytogeographic unit. *Edinburgh Journal of Botany*, 57(3), 437–461. doi:10.1017/S096042860000041X

Puliti, S., Gobakken, T., Ørka, H. O., & Næsset, E. (2017). Assessing 3D point clouds from aerial photographs for species-specific forest inventories. *Scandinavian Journal of Forest Research*, 32(1), 68–79. doi:10.1080/02827581.2016.1186727

Raumonen, P., Casella, E., Calders, K., Murphy, S., Åkerblom, M., & Kaasalainen, M. (2015). Massive-scale tree modelling from TLS data. ISPRS Annals of the Photogrammetry. *Remote Sensing and Spatial Information Sciences*, 2(3), 189.

Raumonen, P., Kaasalainen, M., Åkerblom, M., Kaasalainen, S., Kaartinen, H., Vastaranta, M., ... Lewis, P. (2013). Fast automatic precision tree models from terrestrial laser scanner data. *Remote Sensing*, 5(2), 491–520. doi:10.3390/rs5020491

Ravichandran, A., Chaudhry, R., & Vidal, R. (2013). Categorizing dynamic textures using a bag of dynamical systems. *IEEE Transactions on Pattern Analysis and Machine Intelligence*, 35(2), 342–353. doi:10.1109/TPAMI.2012.83 PMID:23257470

Santos, J. C., Leal, I. R., Almeida-Cortez, J. S., Fernandes, G. W., & Tabarelli, M. (2011). Caatinga: The scientific negligence experienced by a dry tropical forest. *Tropical Conservation Science*, 4(3), 276–286. doi:10.1177/194008291100400306

Särkinen, T., Iganci, J. R., Linares-Palomino, R., Simon, M. F., & Prado, D. E. (2011). Forgotten forests-issues and prospects in biome mapping using Seasonally Dry Tropical Forests as a case study. *BMC Ecology*, 11(1), 27. doi:10.1186/1472-6785-11-27 PMID:22115315

Sirmacek, B., & Lindenbergh, R. (2015). Automatic classification of trees from laser scanning point clouds. ISPRS Annals of Photogrammetry, Remote Sensing & Spatial. *Information Sciences*, 2.

Szejner, M., & Emanuelli, P. (2016). Tree Species Identification in the Tropics. *Tropical Forestry Handbook*, 451-470.

Thomas, S., & Baltzer, J. (2002). Tropical forests. Encyclopedia of life sciences.

Torello-Raventos, M., Feldpausch, T. R., Veenendaal, E., Schrodt, F., Saiz, G., Domingues, T. F., ... Lloyd, J. (2013). On the delineation of tropical vegetation types with an emphasis on forest/savanna transitions. *Plant Ecology & Diversity*, 6, 101–137. doi:10.1080/17550874.2012.762812

Van Uitert, R., & Bitter, I. (2007). Subvoxel precise skeletons of volumetric data based on fast marching methods. *Medical Physics*, *34*(2), 627–638. doi:10.1118/1.2409238 PMID:17388180

Wang, H., Zhihong, D., Bo, F., Hongbin, M., & Yuanqing, X. (2017). An adaptive Kalman filter estimating process noise covariance. *Neurocomputing*, *223*, 12–17. doi:10.1016/j.neucom.2016.10.026

Wang, R., Peethambaran, J., & Chen, D. (2018). LiDAR Point Clouds to 3-D Urban Models: A Review. *IEEE Journal of Selected Topics in Applied Earth Observations and Remote Sensing*, *11*(2), 606–627. doi:10.1109/JSTARS.2017.2781132

Wang, Y., Weinacker, H., & Koch, B. (2008). A lidar point cloud based procedure for vertical canopy structure analysis and 3D single tree modelling in forest. *Sensors (Basel)*, *8*(6), 3938–3951. doi:10.33908063938 PMID:27879916

Ying, S., Xu, G., Li, C., & Mao, Z. (2015). Point Cluster Analysis Using a 3D Voronoi Diagram with Applications in Point Cloud Segmentation. *ISPRS International Journal of Geo-Information*, *4*(3), 1480–1499. doi:10.3390/ijgi4031480

Zhou, Y., & Toga, A. W. (1999). Efficient skeletonization of volumetric objects. *IEEE Transactions on Visualization and Computer Graphics*, *5*(3), 196–209. doi:10.1109/2945.795212 PMID:20835302

Zou, X., Cheng, M., Wang, C., Xia, Y., & Li, J. (2017). Tree Classification in Complex Forest Point Clouds Based on Deep Learning. *IEEE Geoscience and Remote Sensing Letters*, *14*(12), 2360–2364. doi:10.1109/LGRS.2017.2764938

Chapter 2
Recent Advances in Web3D Semantic Modeling

Jakub Flotyński
Poznań University of Economics and Business, Poland

Felix G. Hamza-Lup
(iD) https://orcid.org/0000-0002-8532-4228
Georgia Southern University, USA

Athanasios G. Malamos
Hellenic Mediterranean University, Greece

Nicholas Polys
Virginia Tech, USA

Don Brutzman
Naval Postgraduate School, Monterey, USA

Leslie F. Sikos
Edith Cowan University, Australia

Krzysztof Walczak
(iD) https://orcid.org/0000-0001-8170-7910
Poznań University of Economics and Business, Poland

ABSTRACT

The implementation of virtual and augmented reality environments on the web requires integration between 3D technologies and web technologies, which are increasingly focused on collaboration, annotation, and semantics. Thus, combining VR and AR with the semantics arises as a significant trend in the development of the web. The use of the Semantic Web may improve creation, representation, indexing, searching, and processing of 3D web content by linking the content with formal and expressive descriptions of its meaning. Although several semantic approaches have been developed for 3D content, they are not explicitly linked to the available well-established 3D technologies, cover a limited set of 3D components and properties, and do not combine domain-specific and 3D-specific semantics. In this chapter, the authors present the background, concepts, and development of the Semantic Web3D approach. It enables ontology-based representation of 3D content and introduces a novel framework to provide 3D structures in an RDF semantic-friendly format.

DOI: 10.4018/978-1-5225-5294-9.ch002

INTRODUCTION

Immersive virtual reality (VR) and augmented reality (AR) environments are becoming more and more popular in various application domains due to the increasing network bandwidth as well as the availability of affordable advanced presentation and interaction devices, such as headsets and motion tracking systems. One of the most powerful and promising platforms for immersive VR/AR environments is the Web. It offers suitable conditions for collaborative development and use of VR/AR environments, including indexing, searching and processing of interactive 3D content of the environments. Development of web-based VR and AR has been enabled by various 3D formats (e.g., VRML (Web3D Consortium, 1995) and X3D (Web3D Consortium, 2013)), programming libraries (e.g., WebGL (WebGL, 2020) and WebXR (W3C Consortium, 2019)) and game engines (e.g., Unreal (Unreal engine, 2019) and Unity (Unity Technologies, 2019)).

A potential searching procedure may refer to matching using geometrical and structural characteristics of the scenes (Tangelder, J. W. H. et al., 2008)(Attene, M. et al., 2007)(Papaleo, L. at al., 2009). However, files containing complex 3D scenes are difficult to handle due to their enormous size. Thus, shape and structure matching may be inefficient in terms of computational effort and response time (Grana, C. et al., 2006). Alternatively, the use of textual information in order to retrieve semantic references will fail in most cases. The annotation performed by authors depends on subjective factors, such as language, culture, etc. Therefore, results based on textual matching are even more degraded than the structural matching (Min, P., 2004) The need for a reliable searching mechanism led to the advent of the Semantic Web (W3C Consortium, 2014), which is currently a prominent trend in the evolution of the Web. It transforms the Web into a network that links structured content with formal and expressive semantic descriptions. Semantic descriptions are enabled by structured data representation standards (in particular, the Resource Description Framework, RDF (W3C Consortium, 2014), and by ontologies, which are explicit specifications of a conceptualization (Tom Gruber, 2009), i.e. knowledge organization systems that provide a formal conceptualization of the intended semantics of a knowledge domain or common sense human knowledge. Ontologies consist of statements that describe terminology (conceptualization)—particular classes and properties of objects. Ontologies are intended to be understandable to humans and processable by computers (Berners-Lee, T., 2001).

In the 3D/VR/AR domain, ontologies can be used to specify data formats and schemes with comprehensive properties and relationships between data elements. In turn, collections of individuals of a knowledge domain, including their properties and relationships between them are referred to as knowledge bases. Knowledge bases consist of statements about particular objects using classes and properties that have been defined in ontologies. Hence, in the 3D/VR/AR domain, knowledge bases can be used to represent individual 3D scenes and objects.

The Resource Description Framework Schema (RDFS) and the Web Ontology Language (OWL) (W3C Consortium, 2012) are languages for building statements in RDF-based ontologies and knowledge bases. In turn, SPARQL (W3C Consortium, 2013) is the most widely used query language to RDF-based ontologies and knowledge bases. In contrast to other techniques of content representation, ontologies and knowledge bases enable reasoning over the content. Reasoning leads to inferred tacit (implicit) statements on the basis of statements explicitly specified by the authors. These, in turn, represent implicit content properties.

The overall knowledge obtained from reasoning can be subject to semantic queries. For instance, connections between 3D objects that form hierarchies in scenes can be subject to reasoning and querying about the scenes' complexity. Similarly, position and orientation interpolators in a 3D scene can be subject to reasoning and querying about the motion categories of objects (linear, curved, rotary, etc.). A semantically represented 3D piston engine can be subject to reasoning to infer and query about its type on the basis of the cylinder arrangement (in-line, multi-row, star or reciprocating).

A number of approaches use semantic web technologies to improve creation, representation and processing of various types of media, including text, images, audio and video. However, comprehensive standardized solutions for semantic creation, representation and processing of 3D content are yet to be developed. This gap is the major obstacle for integration and wide dissemination of VR and AR on the Web.

In this chapter we present a novel 3D description approach that is based on X3D structure with RDF syntax. This Semantic Web3D approach developed by the X3D Semantic Web Working Group (Web3D Consortium, 2018), which is a part of the Web3D Consortium. The approach enables ontology-based representation of 3D content on top of the available 3D technologies, including 3D formats. The representation includes different levels of specificity: 3D-specific and domain-specific knowledge. At every level, different classes, objects and properties may be used. The 3D-specific level is constituted by the X3D Ontology, which is a semantic counterpart to the Extensible 3D (X3D) (Web3D Consortium, 2004). X3D is a widely used standardized 3D format (ISO/IEC 197751) for web-based applications. It has been developed by the Web3D Consortium as the successor to the Virtual Reality Modeling Language (VRML) (Web3D Consortium, 1995). The domain-specific level can be described using arbitrary domain ontologies, e.g., pertaining to cultural heritage, medicine, design, engineering or e-commerce. Ontologies at both levels are linked by mappings. The Semantic Web3D has the following advantages over the previous approaches to semantic 3D representation:

1. It is strictly integrated with leading standardized 3D web technologies by an automatic transformation of the X3D format to the X3D Ontology, which is the foundation of our approach.
2. It covers a comprehensive and up-to-date set of 3D components and properties, including geometry, structure, presentation and animation, since it is generated from X3D.
3. It combines 3D-specific semantics with domain-specific semantics, thereby being applicable to arbitrary areas. Semantic querying, reasoning and processing of 3D content can be performed for both: inherent 3D components and properties (understandable to technical users) as well as domain components and properties (related to a particular usage of the approach and understandable to domain experts).

The remainder of this chapter is structured as follows. Section 2 provides an overview of the current state of the art in semantic representation of 3D content. In Section 3, we overview the Semantic Web3D approach. The X3D Ontology, which is a key element of the approach, is presented in Section 4. Examples of queries utilizing the ontology are discussed in Section 5. Finally, Section 6 concludes the chapter and indicates possible future research.

BACKGROUND AND RELATED WORKS

MPEG-7 - Based Annotations

Multimedia applications require the concurrent presence of raw as well as synthetic media content. The co-existence of different content types in the same application imposes the requirement of a uniform annotation among all multimedia content schemes. Thus, first attempts on semantical annotation were engaging MPEG-7 description standard for the annotation of multimedia content. MPEG-7 is a multimedia content description standard (defined as ISO/IEC 15938) aimed to provide additional functionality to the previous MPEG standards by describing the content of multimedia files in a unified format (Dasiopoulou, S. et al., 2010).

Previous related research literature on the semantic annotation of X3D content with MPEG-7 focuses mainly on defining methods on extending MPEG-7 Description Schemes to provide multiple 3D model locators for indexing and retrieval purposes (Bilasco, M., et al., 2005)(Bilasco, M., et al., 2007)(Bilasco, M., et al., 2006) or on presenting generalized methods to describe specific characteristics of a 3D model, such as object interactivity (Chmielewski, J., 2008a) (Chmielewski, J., 2008b).

Bilasco et al. (Bilasco, M., et al., 2005)(Bilasco, M., et al., 2007)(Bilasco, M., et al., 2006) use MPEG-7 to index 3D content within X3D files with the use of localization descriptors. As stated in their research, due to the fact that an X3D object can be stored over numerous file entries, or even a larger X3D scene may be split over several smaller files, multiple MPEG-7 MediaLocator descriptors are necessary to describe one entity by referencing all according locations. For this reason, Bilasco et al. propose new description tools, namely Structural Locator and 3D Region Locator. StructuralLocatorType aims to support the localization of objects situated over various file entries by allowing multiple URIs in the descriptor. While the work described above facilitates in the indexing and retrieval of X3D objects allowing the reuse of the models which are indexed in the content repository, it lacks in generating a complete semantic description profile of X3D models, as issues such as animation, textures and interactivity are not addressed.

Chmielewski presents the Multimedia Interaction Model designed to provide a solution in describing object interactions (Chmielewski, J., 2008a)(Chmielewski, J., 2008b). It utilizes an Interaction Interface concept based on the fact that 3D objects have some common properties that can be grouped together through the interface. Again, even though this work is considered important, it provides a generalized method on describing 3D object interactions, whereas the X3D XML format already provides direct estimation of object interactivity through the XML definition itself, making the semantic annotation process faster and more efficient when generated directly from an X3D document.

The association of X3D documents to an external domain-specific ontology approach provides an interesting case on describing real and virtual semantic objects in X3D worlds. The authors propose the solution of inserting metadata nodes into the existing X3D XML representation. With this method, sets of MetadataSet nodes are associated with the WorldInfo node, with every MetadataSet containing the semantic information on a specific object from the corresponding scene. The semantic annotations are then associated with an external RDF Schema based ontology to provide a scene-independent semantic description. Again, while the solution provides an external ontology for the semantics, at the same time it requires modifications to be made on the existing X3D files by inserting additional metadata information.

Papaleo et al. introduce a framework for the segmentation of X3D complex scenes to primitives that may be annotated manually by using a semantic graph (Papaleo, L., 2009). In, Spala et al. and Zampoglou et al. introduce an extended MPEG7 set of descriptors that takes advantage of the fully annotated XML representation of X3D and produce semantical information (Spala, P., et al. 2012)(Zampoglou, P., et al., 2013). In Table 1 the is a presentation of the recommended descriptors.

Table 1. MPEG 7 extended descriptors (Spala, P., et al. 2012)(Zampoglou, P., et al., 2013)

	Name	Usage
MPEG-7 Part 3 - Visual	BoundingBox3D	Specifies the position and size of a complex 3D object in a scene, by providing the volumetric coordinates of the group of shape nodes that composite the complex model.
	Geometry3D	Describes the types of primitive or complex geometries contained in the X3D scene along with curvature details.
	Metadata3D	Specifies any additional metadata information provided with an X3D node (such as MatadataFloat, MetadataInteger, MetadataSet).
	Interactivity3D	Describes how an X3D object interacts with other objects in the scene or with the end user, by extracting interaction details from the corresponding X3D ROUTE elements.
	MotionTrajectory	Describes the animation characteristics of a 3D moving object within an X3D Scene by determining the type of animation it contains through the X3D Interpolator or Follower nodes bound to that object, along with the motion path keypoint values.
	Viewpoint3D	Describes each viewpoint nodes' position, orientation, animation and coordinate properties contained in an X3D file.
	Lighting3D	Specifies the type of X3D Light nodes used within an X3D Scene in addition to their distinct characteristics, illumination specifications and whether they are used globally in the scene or scoped to a targeted area of objects in the X3D world.
MPEG-7 Part 5 – MDS	Profile3D	Describes the X3D profile in use for the file described in order to gain all additional functionality and specify browser and rendering requirements.
	Script3D	If the X3D file described contains scripting nodes controlling interactions and animations, this datatype specifies the script class location (internally in the content file or in an external file location) and the scripting language used, in order to define all necessary rendering and control requirements.

RDF/OWL Ontologies

In recent literature there are many ontology implementations related to 3D content annotation. A comparison of such solutions is presented in Table 2. The 3D and domain specificity levels are almost equally addressed by the ontologies. The ontologies also enable representation of different features of 3D content, such as geometry, structure, appearance and animation. In most cases, only some content features are represented by a single ontology. All the ontologies enable representation of 3D structure, in particular spatial relations and hierarchies between 3D objects. Only one third of the ontologies support representation of animation, making it the least covered feature. Five ontologies enable representation of all content features. An extensive comparison of 3D content representations has been presented in (Flotyński, J., 2017).

Table 2. Comparison of 3D ontology description solutions

Ontology	Specificity level 3D	Domain	Geom.	Struct.	Appear.	Anim.
(Bille, W., et al., 2004)	✓	✓	✓	✓	✓	
(AIM@SHAPE), (Spagnuolo, et al., M., 2008)	✓		✓	✓	✓	✓
(Gutierrez, et al., M., 2007)	✓		✓	✓	✓	✓
(Kalogerakis, E., et al., 2006)	✓		✓	✓	✓	✓
(Pittarello, F., et al., 2006)		✓		✓		
(Attene, M., et al., 2007)		✓		✓		
(Floriani, L., et al., 2007)	✓		✓	✓		
(Chu, Y., et al., 2012)	✓		✓	✓		✓
(Kapahnke, P., et al., 2010)		✓		✓		
(Vasilakis, G., et al., 2010)	✓		✓	✓	✓	
(Albrecht, S., et al., 2011)		✓		✓		
(Wiebusch, D., et al., 2012)		✓		✓	✓	
(Flotyński, J., et al., 2013)	✓		✓	✓	✓	✓
(Flotyński, J., et al., 2014, 2016)		✓		✓	✓	
(Sikos, L.F., 2017)	✓		✓	✓	✓	✓
(Perez-Gallardo, Y., et al., 2017)	✓			✓		
(Drap, P., et al. 2017)		✓	✓	✓		
(Trellet, M., et al., 2018)		✓		✓	✓	
(Kontakis, K., et al., 2017)		✓		✓	✓	
(Radics, P.J., et al., 2015)		✓		✓	✓	
(Flotyński, J., et al., 2017)		✓		✓		✓

The available solutions have the following limitations:

1. They are not integrated with 3D formats. It hinders transformation between knowledge bases, which can be used for reasoning and querying, and 3D scenes, which can be rendered using available browsers.
2. They do not combine 3D and domain specificity levels. This hinders the use of content by average users and domain experts who are not IT specialists.
3. They do not cover important areas adhering to 3D representation such as humanoid animation, geospatial data, CAD, printing and scanning, do they integrate with separate formats designed for such areas.

Semantic Information Extraction

The adoption of Web3D technologies goes hand in hand with the native support of real-time rendering offered by most modern browsers, allowing an on-the-fly conversion of countless images and video that ship with X3DOM, OBJ and other textual formats of 3D graphics. So, the question that quickly arises is whether is feasible the searching and retrieval of the information enclosed inside such files. At first sight, it's obvious that several parts of these files comply with a technical standard, specification sheet or API, allowing web users to search for specific features like shapes, colors, URLs, animations, etc. Yet, the majority of users are interested in the non-technical aspects of them, where there is available a vast semantic content about the 3D scene (e.g. what this scene represents, where is an object located in relation to its surroundings). Thus, a research branch in 3D graphics deals with the problem of object identification, which is mainly based on techniques that take advantage of objects' shape and volume data. Meanwhile, designers and producers provide some primitive annotation in their scenes, which is usually limited to a textual description or object definition of a 3D model. On the other hand, most advanced solutions may apply several identification rules that can be perceived as semantic attributes based on human ranking data, but such methodologies have proven to be time-consuming and error-prone. A first attempt to extensively annotate such scenes and move from a CAD-oriented to a human-oriented spatial environment took place with an artificial intelligence framework which did not support a spontaneous mechanism for spatial relations. Kontakis et al. introduce a novel computational model for the automated implication of spatial relations (Kontakis, K., 2018)(Kontakis, K., 2017). This model makes use of successive topological and directional predicates between each pair of indexed objects, eliminating pairwise entries for improved performance. Such objects are associated with the Cartesian coordinate system, a three-dimensional distance metric which specifies their position with a signed triplet of numerical coordinates.

Customization of 3D Content with Semantic Queries to Generic Meta-Scenes

In the work Flotyński et al. (2016a) extends the semantic 3D content creation pipeline proposed in (Flotyński, J., 2015) with query-based content customization proposed in (Walczak, K., et al. 2014) (Walczak, K., et al. 2016)(Flotyński, J., et al. 2016b). The input data of the method are generalized domain-specific semantic 3D meta-scenes created using an ontology mapping proposed in (Flotyński, J., 2014a). Further, customized semantic 3D scenes created using the method are transformed into final scenes encoded in different formats using the approach proposed in (Flotyński, J., 2014b).

Previous approaches to adaptation of 3D content have been designed mostly to permit content presentation on diverse hardware and software platforms. In (Almer, A., et al., 2006), an approach to visualization of 2D and 3D tourism information on multiple platforms (in particular Google Earth and Google Maps) has been proposed. In (Tack, K., et al. 2006), an approach to adaptation of 3D content complexity with respect to the available hardware resources has been proposed. In (Dachselt, R., et al., 2006), an approach to 3D content adaptation to different devices and contexts of use has been proposed. In (Bilasco, I. M., et al., 2007), a rule-based framework has been proposed to enable adaptation of content for different access devices. Adaptation may include such operations as geometry and texture degradation as well as filtering of objects. In (Maglo, A., et al, 2010), a solution for streaming X3D content for remote visualizations with the adaptation of the level of detail based on several parameters (e.g., network bandwidth, device capabilities and user preferences) has been proposed.

In (Tzompanaki, K., et al., 2012), a framework for semantic querying for 3D models has been proposed. The framework is intended to combine the responsiveness of keyword-based search systems with the precision of semantic systems by using semantic networks of fundamental categories and relationships extracted from more specialized semantic networks.

The presented languages and frameworks have been designed for content exploration, and they do not enable content customization. In (Kalogerakis, E., et al., 2006), an ontology providing elements and properties that are equivalent to elements and properties specified in X3D has been proposed. Moreover, a set of semantic properties have been proposed to enable description of 3D scenes with domain knowledge. In (Bille, W., et al., 2004)(De Troyer, O., et al., 2007) an approach to generating virtual environments upon mappings of domain ontologies has been proposed. The following three content generation stages are distinguished: specification of a domain ontology, mapping the domain ontology to a 3D content representation language, and generation of a final presentation. In (Flotyński, J., et al., 2013a) (Flotyński, J., et al., 2013b) an approach to building semantic descriptions embedded in 3D web content and a semantic representation of 3D content have been proposed. In (Rabattu, P. Y., et al., 2015), a semantic representation of evolving human embryo has been proposed. The approach leverages RDF, OWL and SPARQL as well as an ontology describing stages, periods and processes.

The aforementioned approaches address semantic content description and creation using different ontologies and knowledge bases. However, in the approaches, 3D content is created by specifying instances of ontologies (knowledge bases) that determine the final form of the created content. The available solutions do not permit on-demand customization of 3D content according to specific consumers' requirements to enable the generation of various forms of final 3D content.

Several works provide an overview of the use of semantic descriptions of 3D content in artificial intelligence systems. The idea of semantic description of 3D environments has been summarized in (Latoschik, M. E., et al., 2008). In (Spagnuolo, M., et al., 2009), a review of the main aspects related to the use of 3D content in connection with the semantic web technologies has been provided. An overview of approaches to semantic representation and creation of 3D content has been presented in (Flotyński, J., et al., 2017).

Recent trends in the development of VR, AR and the web provide new requirements for efficient and flexible content creation, which go beyond the current state of the art in 3D modeling.

1. Content creation should be declarative, stressing the specification of the results to be presented rather than the way in which the results are to be achieved.
2. Content creation should be supported by the discovery of hidden knowledge covering content properties, dependencies and constraints, which are not explicitly specified, but which may be extracted from the explicit data, and which have an impact on the modeled content.
3. Content objects and properties should be conceptually created at arbitrarily chosen levels of abstraction, including both aspects that are directly related to 3D content and aspects that are specific to a particular application or domain.
4. Modeling activities related to different parts of content representation should be decoupled, enabling separation of concerns between different modeling users with different expertise, who are equipped with different modeling tools, e.g., to facilitate content creation by domain experts who are not IT-specialists.
5. 3D content should be independent of particular hardware and software platforms to enable creation of multi-platform 3D content presentations.

The *Semantic Modeling of Interactive 3D Content* (SEMIC) covers various aspects of 3D content such as geometry, structure, space, appearance, scene, animation and behavior (Flotyński, J., et al., 2015). In the approach, semantic web techniques are applied to satisfy the aforementioned requirements.

THE SEMANTIC WEB3D APPROACH

The Semantic Web3D approach, which is an extension of the approach proposed in (Flotyński, J., 2016b). The Semantic Web3D encompasses a queryable ontology-based 3D content representation, which enables creation, modification and analysis of 3D content (Fig. 1). The representation is described in Section 3. Semantic queries possible with the proposed representation are discussed in Section 3.2. In Section 3.3, we analyze the possible use contexts of the Semantic Web3D, which determine new research and application areas, and provide the main motivations for the further development of the approach.

Ontology-Based 3D Content Representation

The ontology-based 3D content representation, which is the main element of the Semantic Web3D, is a stack of ontologies and knowledge bases. Ontologies specify 3D content schemes at different levels of specificity, whereas knowledge bases specify 3D models and scenes in line with the ontologies. The representation includes two levels of specificity: the 3D-specific level and the domain-specific level.

The 3D-specific level uses classes, objects and properties that are related to 3D content, including geometry (e.g., vertices, edges and faces), structure (e.g., hierarchy of objects), appearance (e.g., textures and materials) and animation (e.g., event generators and interpolators). 3D-specific classes and properties are defined in a *3D ontology*, which has been generated from a 3D format schema. So far, we have automatically generated the *X3D Ontology* from the *X3D Unified Object Model* (X3DUOM) using an XSL transformation (cf. Section 4). The ontology is a counterpart to the X3D format, and consists of classes and properties that are equivalents of X3D elements and attributes. Hence, the X3D Ontology can be suited to a wide range of practical 3D applications, including humanoid animation, geospatial visualization, CAD, printing and scanning. Also other 3D ontologies for different formats can be used at this specificity level. 3D ontologies are intended to be an augmentation of available 3D formats (implemented by 3D browsers) with reasoning and queries. However, in some cases, it may be useful to treat ontologies as independent (semantic) 3D formats directly processable by (semantic) 3D browsers (cf. Section 3.3/9). 3D ontologies can be subject to 3D-specific *meta-queries* (cf. Section 3.2) for *information retrieval* (cf. Section 3.3/6).

Figure 1. The Semantic Web3D approach

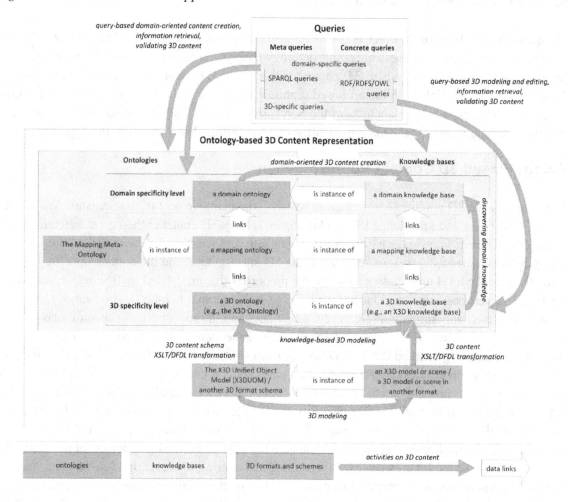

Collections of information about particular 3D models and scenes specified using classes and properties defined in a 3D ontology are referred to as *3D knowledge bases*. 3D knowledge bases may be created by content authors within *knowledge-based 3D modeling* (cf. Section 3.3/1), or automatically generated from 3D models and scenes encoded in a textual or binary 3D format, using the Data Format Description Language (DFDL) (Apache, 2014) (cf. Section 3.3/8). 3D knowledge bases can be subject to 3D-specific *concrete queries* (cf. Section 3.2) for *query-based 3D modeling, editing* and *information retrieval* (cf. Section 3.3/3 and 6).

The domain-specific level uses classes, objects and properties that are related to an arbitrary domain, which is determined by a particular use case of the approach. For instance, in cultural heritage, classes may correspond to different artifacts (weapons, armors, decorations, etc.), while properties can describe features of the artifacts (types of swords, materials used to make jewelry, etc.). Domain classes and properties are defined in a *domain ontology*, which is determined by a particular Semantic Web3D application. Domain ontologies can be subject to domain specific *meta-queries* (cf. Section 3.2) for *information retrieval* (cf. Section 3.3/6).

Collections of information about particular domain objects and properties that build 3D models and scenes using classes and properties defined in a domain ontology are referred to as *domain knowledge bases*. Domain knowledge bases may be created by content authors within *domain-oriented 3D content creation* (cf. Section 3.3/2) or automatically generated from 3D knowledge bases via *discovering domain knowledge* (cf. Section 3.3/5). Domain knowledge bases can be subject to domain-specific *concrete queries* (cf. Section 3.2) for *query-based 3D modeling, editing* and *information retrieval* (cf. Section 3.3/3 and 6).

Ontologies at both levels of specificity are aligned using *mapping ontologies*. A mapping ontology is a specification of how domain-specific classes and properties are represented by 3D-specific classes and properties. Hence, it enables visualization of domain-specific concepts. A mapping ontology is created by a content author or automatically generated by machine learning techniques within *generating mappings* (cf. Section 3.3/4). A mapping ontology is a specialization of the *Mapping Meta-Ontology*, which defines basic, general concepts for mapping. Classes and properties of a mapping ontology are inherited from classes and properties of the Mapping Meta-Ontology. They are specific to a particular Semantic Web3D application. An individual mapping ontology is used for a distinct pair of a 3D ontology and a domain ontology. Hence, it can be reused for different 3D models and scenes built with these ontologies.

Knowledge bases at both levels of specificity are linked by a *mapping knowledge base*, which is a collection of information about how particular domain-specific objects and properties are represented by particular 3D-specific objects and properties. For such a specification, classed and properties defined in the corresponding mapping ontology are used. Hence, a mapping knowledge base specifies visual representations of particular domain objects in a 3D scene, e.g., cars, exhibits and appliances. It is automatically generated during a *domain-oriented 3D content creation* (cf. Section 3.3/2).

Queries to the Representation

Possible queries to the ontology-based representation of 3D content may be distinguished in terms of the target dataset type, specificity level, encoding standards used, and initiated activity. These four classifications are orthogonal, i.e. every query fits all of them.

Classification of queries in terms of the **target dataset type**:

1. **Meta-queries** are about schemes of 3D models and scenes, e.g., data types of properties of particular 3D components, classes of components for which particular properties are used, specializations and hierarchies of components.
2. **Concrete queries** are about particular 3D models and scenes, e.g. the distance between two objects in a scene, the number of objects of a particular class in a scene, the value of an object property.

Classification of queries in terms of the **specificity level**:

1. **3D-specific queries** are related to 3D components and properties, e.g., the number of vertices and faces of a model, the period of an animation, the color of a material.
2. **Domain-specific queries** are related to a particular domain for which the target model or scene has been created, e.g., the age of a virtual museum exhibition, the species of plants in a virtual garden, the functionality of virtual home appliances.

Classification of queries in terms of the **encoding standards** used:

1. **SPARQL queries** are encoded in SPARQL (W3C Consortium, 2013), which is the primary query language for ontologies and knowledge bases on the Semantic Web.
2. **RDF/RDFS/OWL queries** are knowledge bases combined with the target dataset (ontology or knowledge base) and next, used to accomplish reasoning. RDF, RDFS and OWL-based queries have the same encoding as the target datasets. On the one hand, it makes the solution syntactically more uniform then using SPARQL, and liberates content consumers from applying additional software for query processing. Moreover, it enables to determine the computational properties of the overall dataset, in particular decidability. On the other hand, since RDF, RDFS and OWL are knowledge representation formats but not query languages, they lack some query-specific constructs that are available in SPARQL, e.g., order by, limiting the number of results and selecting only distinct results. In addition, they do not permit numerical operations.

Classification of queries in terms of the **initiated action**:

1. **Information retrieval** provides information about 3D models or scenes, e.g., get the coordinates of a shape, get the trajectory of a moving object.
2. **Modeling and editing 3D content** creates or modifies 3D models or scenes, e.g., add a shape to a scene, change the trajectory of a moving object.

Contexts of Use

The queryable ontology-based representation of 3D content enables the following activities related to content creation and analysis (marked by blue arrows in Fig. 1).

1. **Knowledge-based 3D modeling**, which a 3D is modeling process supported by knowledge contained in a 3D ontology. The result of this activity is a 3D knowledge base, which represents models or scenes at the 3D-specific level. The use of a 3D ontology can facilitate modeling of 3D content, e.g., by suggesting components and properties, with data types and ranges, that can be set for a particular object. In contrast to available 3D modeling tools, which provide proprietary implementations of such functions, ontologies can describe such features in a standardized way, while reasoning engines can process such descriptions using standard, well-known algorithms.
2. **Domain-oriented 3D content creation**, within which 3D content is created using a domain ontology with domain-specific classes, objects and properties, without appealing to 3D-specific classes, objects and properties (like in typical 3D modeling). For instance, a marketing expert designs an exhibition of home appliances including stoves, dishwashers and washing machines. In this activity, first, a domain knowledge base, which represents models or scenes at the domain-specific level, is created. Next, due to a mapping ontology, which determines 3D representations of domain concepts, final 3D scenes are generated upon the domain knowledge base.
3. **Query-based 3D modeling and editing**, in which concrete queries are issued by content consumers to create or edit content at different specificity levels—using 3D or domain knowledge bases. Such queries can specify new or modify existing objects and properties, e.g., move an artifact to a museum room with a collection dated to the appropriate historical period.

4. **Generating mappings** may be useful for domain ontologies that have no mapping ontologies linking them to 3D ontologies. Therefore, they cannot be used for domain oriented content creation, query-based modeling and editing, or information retrieval. However, there are some examples of mapping knowledge bases linking domain knowledge bases to 3D knowledge bases. In such a case, machine learning software can generalize the available examples to produce a mapping ontology. For instance, the availability of multiple examples of 5 regularly arranged shapes may be a prerequisite how a table can be constructed (a countertop and 4 legs).

5. **Discovering domain knowledge** can be useful for 3D knowledge bases that have no associated domain knowledge bases, because have been modeled by content authors (*knowledge based 3D modeling*—p. 1) or automatically generated from models and scenes encoded in 3D formats (*transforming 3D content*—p. 8). Since this activity requires a mapping ontology, it can follow *generating mappings*.

6. **Information retrieval** is possible from ontologies (about schemes of content) and knowledge bases (about individual models and scenes) at different specificity levels. For example, select positions of emergency vehicles in a virtual city.

7. **Validating 3D content** allows content authors and consumers to automatically verify the correctness of 3D models and scenes at different specificity levels against corresponding 3D and domain ontologies, in particular: the use of appropriate classes as well as data types and cardinality of properties. Content validation can by performed by standard reasoning algorithms for RDF, RDFS and OWL implemented by semantic environments, e.g., plugins to Protege [2]. For instance, a virtual car must have 4 wheels; the vertices of a mesh must form polygons.

8. **Transforming available 3D content to semantic 3D content**, which is enabled by automatic transformation of 3D format schemes to 3D ontologies, and automatic transformation of 3D content encoded in the formats to 3D knowledge bases compliant with these ontologies. XSLT can be used to transform XML-based 3D formats and content, e.g., in case of X3D, whereas the Data Format Description Language (DFDL) (Apache, 2014) can be used for any (textual or binary) format and content. This opens new opportunities to convert the available repositories and libraries of 3D content to their semantic equivalents, thus enabling the range of new operations on content described in this section.

9. Rendering ontology-based 3D scenes can be done in two ways.

    (a) Maintaining the conformance of 3D ontologies to their underlying 3D formats will enable transformation of 3D knowledge bases (compliant with the ontologies) to 3D scenes encoded in the formats. This will integrate our approach with the currently available technologies and enable 3D visualization with a number of well established, efficient content browsers. However, final 3D content encoded in a 3D format can no longer be subject to reasoning and queries.

    (b) The development of semantic 3D browsers is possible to permit direct visualization of 3D knowledge bases. In such a case, transformation of the content could be implicitly accomplished within a browser, while maintaining the possibility of semantic reasoning and queries over dynamically changing content properties with their temporal values, e.g., the volatile position of an object moving in a 3D scene.

THE X3D ONTOLOGY

The X3D Ontology, which is an RDF/RDFS/OWL document, is a 3D ontology we have developed for the Semantic Web3D approach (Web3D Consortium, 2019a). It is the successor to the 3D Modeling Ontology (3DMO) (Sikos, L.F., 2020). 3DMO has been developed manually based on the X3D format. Therefore, modifications of the ontology necessary to keep its consistency with new versions of the X3D format were problematic. The goal of the Semantic Web3D is to provide flexible integration of available 3D technologies with semantic web technologies. Hence, the X3D Ontology, as the evolution of 3DMO, is automatically generated from the X3D schema, which is described by the X3D Unified Object Model (X3DUOM).

The X3DUOM is a description of the X3D schema, which is a set of object-oriented interfaces for X3D nodes and fields (Web3D Consortium, 2019b). The X3DUOM is encoded as an XML document that contains a list of the names of the X3D nodes, interfaces and fields, information about inheritance of the nodes and fields, and the field's data types. This is useful to implement various encodings of X3D as well as bindings to programming languages.

The X3D Ontology is generated using an XSL transformation (Web3D Consortium, 2019c). A fragment of the XSLT document in the Turtle format is presented in Table 3. The code transforms X3D XML elements to declarations of individual classes in the ontology. It processes every XML element (line 1) by extracting its name attribute (2) and printing it as the subject of a new RDF statement in the ontology. The subject is a new *class* within the local namespace in the ontology (3–4). The predicate in the statement is a (5), which is a shorthand notation for rdf:type. The object in the statement is owl:Class (6). In addition, if the processed XML element has sub-elements with the path InterfaceDefinition/ Inheritance, including the baseType attribute (7), it is used to specify the superclass of the *class* (8–11).

Table 3. A fragment of the XSLT document describing transformation of the X3DUOM to the X3D Ontology in Turtle

<xsl:template match="*"> <!-process each element --> 1
<xsl:variable name="elementName" select="@name"/> 2
<xsl:text>:</xsl:text><!-local namespace --> 3
<xsl:value-of select="$elementName"/> 4
<xsl:text> a </xsl:text> 5
<xsl:text>owl:Class</xsl:text> 6
<xsl:if test="(string-length(InterfaceDefinition/ Inheritance/@baseType) > 0)"> 7
<xsl:text> ;
 </xsl:text><!-new line --> 8
<xsl:text>rdfs:subClassOf </xsl:text> 9
<xsl:text>:</xsl:text><!-local namespace --> 10
<xsl:value-of select="InterfaceDefinition/Inheritance/@baseType"/> 11
</xsl:if> 12
... 13
</xsl:template> 14

An example of an X3DUOM fragment transformed using the XSLT document is presented in Table 4. Like every element, Shape (line 1) is transformed to a class, while information about the inheritance of the Shape node (its baseType, line 3) is transformed to the superclass specification. The resulting statements are:

:Shape a owl:Class ; rdfs:subClassOf:X3DShapeNode .

Table 4. A fragment of the X3DUOM document describing the X3D Shape node

<ConcreteNode name="Shape"> 1
<InterfaceDefinition specificationUrl="https://www.web3d 2.org/documents/specifications/19775-1/V3.3/Part01/ components/shape. html#Shape"> 2
<Inheritance baseType="X3DShapeNode"/> 3
... 4
</InterfaceDefinition> 5
</ConcreteNode> 6

Fragments of the generated hierarchies of classes as well as object and datatype properties of the X3D Ontology visualized in the Protege ontology editor are depicted in Figure 2.

Figure 2. Hierarchies of classes as well as object and datatype properties of the X3D Ontology presented in Protege

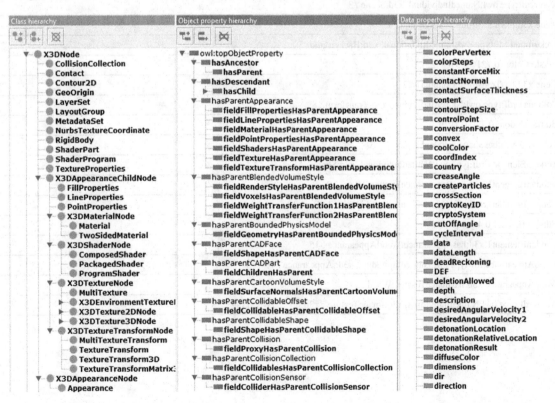

Another XSLT document has been developed to enable transformation of X3D scenes to X3D knowledge bases compliant with the X3D Ontology.

EXAMPLE

In this section, we present an example of transforming an X3D scene to an X3D knowledge base compliant with the X3D Ontology. The scene presents the San Carlos Cathedral in Monterey, CA, USA[2] (Figure 3).

Table 5 includes a fragment of the generated X3D knowledge base, covering some scene properties as well as the altar. The scene has a background with a sky color represented by an RDF list of values (lines 3–6). In addition, there is a transform node applied to a shape that is a wooden element of the altar (7–11). The shape of the element is determined by a box with a given size (12–14). Like sky color, translation and size are also represented by RDF lists. In addition, the element has appearance with an image texture (15–18).

Every X3D knowledge base can be subject to semantic queries. The following SPARQL query provides the number of shapes composing the altar. The result of the query is: 14.

Table 5. A fragment of an X3D knowledge base describing the altar in the San Carlos Cathedral1

Prefixes: 'x3d', ':', 'rdf' and 'owl' indicate: the X3D
Ontology and knowledge base as well as RDF and OWL. 2
:scene rdf:type owl:NamedIndividual, x3d:Scene . 3
:scene x3d:hasBackground:background . 4
:background rdf:type owl:NamedIndividual, x3d:Background; 5
x3d:skyColor (0.7216 0.8 0.9922). 6
:scene x3d:hasTransform:Colonna1 . 7
:Colonna1 rdf:type owl:NamedIndividual, x3d:Transform ; 8
x3d:translation (0.7 0 -0.7) . 9
:Colonna1 x3d:hasShape:woodenElement1 . 10
:woodenElement1 rdf:type owl:NamedIndividual, x3d:Shape . 11
:woodenElement1 x3d:hasBox:woodenElement1Box . 12
:woodenElement1Box rdf:type owl:NamedIndividual, x3d:Box; 13
x3d:size (0.4 1.2 0.4) . 14
:woodenElement1 x3d:hasAppearance:WoodAppearance . 15
:WoodAppearance rdf:type owl:NamedIndividual, x3d: Appearance . 16
:WoodAppearance x3d:hasImageTexture:Wood . 17
:Wood rdf:type owl:NamedIndividual, x3d:ImageTexture ; x3d:url ".../Wood.jpg". 18

Figure 3. An X3D model of the San Carlos Cathedral2 (Monterey, CA, USA): a view from outside and the altar

```
SELECT (count(distinct ?shape) as ? numberShapes) WHERE {
?shape rdf:type x3d:Shape. }
```

The following query provides the paths of all textures used within the scene. The result is the wood texture: .../Wood.jpg (cf. Listing 3, line 18).

```
SELECT ?textureUrl WHERE {
?appearance x3do:hasTexture ?texture .
?texture x3do:url ?textureUrl .
BIND (strafter(xsd:string(?appearance),"#") AS ?appearanceNode) }
```

The following query retrieves the color of the sky used in the scene. The result is the following list of RGB values: (0.7216 0.8 0.9922) (cf. Table 5 line 6).

```
SELECT ?color WHERE {
        ?background rdf: x3do:Background ;
        x3do:skyColor/rdf:rest*/rdf:first ?skyColorListValues .
BIND (strafter(xsd:string(?background),"#") AS ?backgroundNode) }
```

CONCLUSION AND FUTURE WORKS

In this chapter, we have presented the concept of the Semantic Web3D approach, which has been developed by the X3D Semantic Web Working Group. The approach enables comprehensive ontology-based representation of 3D content at different specificity levels, which integrates with available 3D technologies. The primary implementation of the Semantic Web3D encompasses the XSL transformation of the X3DUOM to the X3D Ontology as well as the XSL transformation of X3D scenes to X3D knowledge bases. This sets directions to a variety of new 3D/VR/AR applications in different domains, which determine new opportunities for future research.

The use of the OWL-based X3D Ontology permits inference of knowledge about objects as well as their classes and properties, which can facilitate modeling by providing suggestions to content authors and by validating the modeling results. With a mapping to domain ontologies, the approach can be used in domain-oriented 3D content creation by domain experts who are not IT-specialists, thereby improving dissemination of 3D content on the web. Discovering such mappings from examples is a new field on the border between 3D/VR/AR and AI. Moreover, since ontologies and knowledge bases are queryable data sources, the X3D Ontology and knowledge bases can be subject to queries intended to modify and edit content. This opens new possibilities of content creation in collaborative web-based VR/AR environments. The comprehensive 3D representation – at 3D and domain levels of specificity – enables retrieval of information about different content components and properties that may be interesting to different content authors and users, and for very different purposes. In particular, we plan to continue the development of DFDL-based transformations of different textual and binary 3D formats to make the solutions available to a wider range of tools. Other topics related to implementation of the approach are tools for semantic 3D scene validation as well as semantic 3D browsers to directly render 3D knowledge bases.

REFERENCES

AIM@SHAPE. (n.d.). http://visionair.ge.imati.cnr.it/ontologies/ shapes/

Albrecht, S., Wiemann, T., Gunther, M., & Hertzberg, J. (2011). Matching CAD object models in semantic mapping. In *Proceedings ICRA 2011 Workshop: Semantic Perception, Mapping and Exploration*. SPME.

Almer, A., Schnabel, T., Stelzl, H., Stieg, J., & Luley, P. (2006). A tourism information system for rural areas based on a multi platform concept. In *International Symposium on Web and Wireless Geographical Information Systems* (pp. 31-41). Springer. 10.1007/11935148_4

Apache. (2014). *Data Format Description Language (DFDL) v1.0 Specification*. https://daffodil.incubator.apache.org/ docs/dfdl/

Attene, M., Robbiano, F., Spagnuolo, M., & Falcidieno, B. (2007). Semantic Annotation of 3D Surface Meshes Based on Feature Characterization, Semantic Multimedia. Springer Berlin/Heidelberg.

Attene, M., Robbiano, F., Spagnuolo, M., & Falcidieno, B. (2007). Semantic Annotation of 3D Surface Meshes Based on Feature Characterization. In Semantic Multimedia, (pp. 126–139). Springer Berlin Heidelberg.

Behr, J., Eschler, P., Jung, Y., & Zöllner, M. (2009). X3DOM: a DOM-based HTML5/X3D integration model. In *Proceedings of the 14th international conference on 3D web technology* (pp. 127-135). ACM.

Berners-Lee, T., Handler, J., & Lassila, O. (2001). *The Semantic Web. A new form of Web content that is meaningful to computers will unleash a revolution of new possibilities* (Vol. 284). Scientific American.

Berners-Lee, T., Hendler, J., & Lassila, O. (2001). The semantic web. *Scientific American*, *284*(5), 34–43. doi:10.1038cientificamerican0501-34 PMID:11681174

Bilasco, I. M., Gensel, J., Villanova-Oliver, M., & Martin, H. (2005). 3DSEAM: a model for annotating 3D scenes using MPEG-7. *Seventh IEEE International Symposium on Multimedia (ISM'05)*. DOI 10.1109/ISM.2005.2

Bilasco, M., Genzel, J., Villanova, M. O., & Martin, H. (2005). On Indexing of 3D Scenes Using MPEG-7. *Proceedings of ACM Multimedia '05*, 471-474. 10.1145/1101149.1101254

Bilasco, M., Genzel, J., Villanova, M. O., & Martin, H. (2006). An MPEG-7 framework enhancing the reuse of 3D models. *Proceedings of Web3D Symposium '06*, 65-73.

Bilasco, M., Genzel, J., Villanova, M. O., & Martin, H. (2007). Semantic-based Rules for 3D Scene Adaptation. *Proceedings of IEEE International Symposium on Multimedia '07*, 97-100.

Bille, W., Pellens, B., Kleinermann, F., & De Troyer, O. (2004). Intelligent Modelling of Virtual Worlds Using Domain Ontologies. *IVEVA, 97*.

Bille, W., Pellens, B., Kleinermann, F., & De Troyer, O. (2004). Intelligent modelling of virtual worlds using domain ontologies. *Proceedings of the Workshop of Intelligent Computing (WIC), held in conjunction with the MICAI 2004 conference*, 272–279.

BlenderA. P. I. (n.d.). https://www.blender.org/api/.JSON

Broekstra, J., & Kampman, A. (2004). *SeRQL: An RDF query and transformation language. Semantic Web and Peer-to-Peer.* https://gate.ac.uk/sale/dd/related-work/SeRQL.pdf

Celakovski, S., & Davcev, D. (2009). Multiplatform real-time rendering of mpeg-4 3D scenes with Microsoft XNA. In *International Conference on ICT Innovations*. Springer.

Chittaro, L., & Ranon, R. (2007). Web3D technologies in learning, education and training: Motivations, issues, opportunities. *Computers & Education, 49*(1), 3–18. doi:10.1016/j.compedu.2005.06.002

Chmielewski, J. (2008a). Interaction Descriptor for 3D Objects. *Proceedings of the International Conference on Human System Interaction*, 18-23.

Chmielewski, J. (2008b). Interaction Interfaces for Unrestricted Multimedia Interaction Descriptions. *Proceedings of the Mobile Computing and Multimedia Conference*, 397-400. 10.1145/1497185.1497270

Chu, Y., & Li, T. (2012). Realizing semantic virtual environments with ontology and pluggable procedures. *Applications of Virtual Reality*.

COLLADA Homepage. (n.d.). https://www.khronos.org/collada/

Dachselt, R., Hinz, M., & Pietschmann, S. (2006). Using the AMACONT architecture for flexible adaptation of 3D web applications. In *Proceedings of the eleventh international conference on 3D web technology*. ACM.

Dasiopoulou, S., Tzouvaras, V., Kompatsiaris, I., & Strintzis, M. G. (2010). Enquiring MPEG-7 based multimedia ontologies. *Multimedia Tools and Applications, 46*(2-3), 331–370. doi:10.100711042-009-0387-4

Daum, S., & Borrmann, A. (2013). Definition and implementation of temporal operators for a 4D query language. *Computing in Civil Engineering, 2013*(2013), 468–475. doi:10.1061/9780784413029.059

De Floriani, L., Hui, A., Papaleo, L., Huang, M., & Hendler, J. (2007). A semantic web environment for digital shapes understanding. In *Semantic Multimedia* (pp. 226–239). Springer. doi:10.1007/978-3-540-77051-0_25

De Troyer, O., Kleinermann, F., Pellens, B., & Bille, W. (2007). Conceptual modeling for virtual reality. In *Tutorials, posters, panels and industrial contributions at the 26th international conference on Conceptual modeling-Volume 83* (pp. 3-18). Australian Computer Society, Inc.

Doller, M., & Kosch, H. (2008). The MPEG-7 Multimedia Database System (MPEG-7 MMDB). *Journal of Systems and Software, 81*(9), 1559–1580. doi:10.1016/j.jss.2006.03.051

Döller, M., Tous, R., Gruhne, M., Yoon, K., Sano, M., & Burnett, I. S. (2008). The MPEG Query Format: Unifying access to multimedia retrieval systems. *IEEE MultiMedia*, (4): 82–95.

Doulamis, N., Ceacero, C., Collantes, L., & Tektonidis, D. (2006). DESYME: Development System for Mobile Services. 15th IST Mobile & Wireless Communications Summit, Mykonos, Greece.

Drap, P., Papini, O., Sourisseau, J. C., & Gambin, T. (2017). Ontology-based photogrammetric survey in underwater archaeology. In *European Semantic Web Conference*, (pp. 3–6). Springer.

EncoderA. P. I. (n.d.). https://docs.python.org/2/library/json.html.urllib, https://docs.python.org/2/library/urllib.html.Restlet

EngineU. (2019). https://www.unrealengine.com/what-is-unreal-engine-4

Evans, A., Romeo, M., Bahrehmand, A., Agenjo, J., & Blat, J. (2014). 3D graphics on the web: A survey. *Computers & Graphics*, *41*, 43–61. doi:10.1016/j.cag.2014.02.002

Flotyński, J. (2014). Semantic modelling of interactive 3D content with domain-specific ontologies. *Procedia Computer Science*, *35*, 531–540. doi:10.1016/j.procs.2014.08.134

Flotynski, J., Krzyszkowski, M., & Walczak, K. (2017). Semantic Composition of 3D Content Behavior for Explorable Virtual Reality Applications. In *Proceedings of EuroVR 2017* (pp. 3–23). Springer. doi:10.1007/978-3-319-72323-5_1

Flotyński, J., & Walczak, K. (2013). Semantic Multi-layered Design of Interactive 3D Presentations. In *Proceedings of the Federated Conference on Computer Science and Information Systems*, (pp. 541–548). Krakow, Poland: IEEE.

Flotyński, J., & Walczak, K. (2013a). Microformat and microdata schemas for interactive 3d web content. In *2013 Federated Conference on Computer Science and Information Systems*. IEEE.

Flotyński, J., & Walczak, K. (2013b). Semantic multi-layered design of interactive 3d presentations. In *2013 Federated Conference on Computer Science and Information Systems*. IEEE.

Flotyński, J., & Walczak, K. (2014). Semantic representation of multi-platform 3D content. *Computer Science and Information Systems*, *11*(4), 1555–1580. doi:10.2298/CSIS131218073F

Flotyński, J., & Walczak, K. (2015). Conceptual knowledge-based modeling of interactive 3D content. *The Visual Computer*, *31*(10), 1287–1306. doi:10.100700371-014-1011-9

Flotyński, J., & Walczak, K. (2015). Ontology-based creation of 3D content in a service-oriented environment. In *International Conference on Business Information Systems*. Springer. 10.1007/978-3-319-19027-3_7

Flotyński, J., & Walczak, K. (2016). Customization of 3D content with semantic meta-scenes. *Graphical Models*, *88*, 23–39. doi:10.1016/j.gmod.2016.07.001

Flotyński, J., & Walczak, K. (2016). Customization of 3D Content with Semantic Meta-Scenes, July 2016. *Graphical Models*, *88*, 23–39. doi:10.1016/j.gmod.2016.07.001

Flotyński, J., & Walczak, K. (2017). Ontology-Based Representation and Modelling of Synthetic 3D Content: A State-of-the-Art Review. *Computer Graphics Forum*, *36*(8), 2017. doi:10.1111/cgf.13083

Flotyński, J., & Walczak, K. (2017). Knowledge-based Representation of 3D Content Behavior in a Service-oriented Virtual Environment. In *Proceedings of the 22Nd International Conference on 3D Web Technology, Web3D '17*, (pp. 14:1–14:10). New York, NY: ACM.

FOCUS K3D Homepage. (n.d.). http://www.focusk3d.eu/

Funkhouser, T., Min, P., Kazhdan, M., Chen, J., Halderman, A., Dobkin, D., & Jacobs, D. (2003). A search engine for 3D models. *ACM Transactions on Graphics, 22*(1), 83–105. doi:10.1145/588272.588279

Glantz, A., Krutz, A., Sikora, T., Nunes, P., & Pereira, F. (2010). Automatic MPEG-4 sprite coding Comparison of integrated object segmentation algorithms. *Journal of Multimedia Tools and Applications, 49*(3), 483–512. doi:10.100711042-010-0469-3

Grana, C., & Cucchiara, R. (2006). Performance of the MPEG-7 Shape Spectrum Descriptor for 3D objects retrieval. In *Second Italian Research Conference on Digital Library Management Systems*. IRCDL.

Gruber, T. (2009). *Encyclopedia of database systems*. http://tomgruber.org/writing/ontology-definition-2007.htm

Gutierrez, M., Garcıa-Rojas, A., Thalmann, D., Vexo, F., Moccozet, L., Magnenat-Thalmann, N., ... Spagnuolo, M. (2007). An ontology of virtual humans: Incorporating semantics into human shapes. *The Visual Computer, 23*(3), 207–218.

Gutierrez, M., Vexo, F., & Thalmann, D. (2005). Semantics-based representation of virtual environments. *International Journal of Computer Applications in Technology, 23*(2-4), 229-238.

Halabala, P. (2003). Semantic metadata creation. *Proceedings of CESCG 2003: 7th Central European Seminar on Computer Graphics*.

Halkos, D., Doulamis, N., & Doulamis, A. (2009). A Secure Framework Exploiting Content Guided and Automated Algorithms for Real Time Video Searching. *Multimedia Tools and Applications, 42*(3), 343–375. doi:10.100711042-008-0234-z

Hejazi, M. R., & Ho, Y.-S. (2007). An efficient approach to texture-based image retrieval. *International Journal of Imaging Systems and Technology, 17*(5), 295–302. doi:10.1002/ima.20120

Hejazi, M. R., & Ho, Y.-S. (2007). Efficient approach to extraction of texture browsing descriptor in MPEG-7. *Electronics Letters, 43*(13), 709–711. doi:10.1049/el:20070208

Hughes, S., Brusilovsky, P., & Lewis, M. (2002). Adaptive navigation support in 3D e-commerce activities. *Proc. of Workshop on Recommendation and Personalization in eCommerce at AH*, 132-139.

ISO 15938:3. (2002). Multimedia Content Description Interface – Part 3: Visual.

ISO 15938:5. (2003). Multimedia Content Description Interface – Part 5: Multimedia Description Schemes. May.

JenaA. (n.d.). http://jena.apache.org/

Kalogerakis, E., Christodoulakis, S., & Moumoutzis, N. (2006). Coupling ontologies with graphics content for knowledge driven visualization. In *IEEE Virtual Reality Conference (VR 2006)*. IEEE. 10.1109/VR.2006.41

Kalogerakis, E., Christodoulakis, S., & Moumoutzis, N. (2006). Coupling ontologies with graphics content for knowledge driven visualization. In *VR '06 Proceedings of the IEEE conference on Virtual Reality*, (pp. 43–50). 10.1109/VR.2006.41

Kapahnke, P., Liedtke, P., Nesbigall, S., Warwas, S., & Klusch, M. (2010). ISReal: An Open Platform for Semantic-Based 3D Simulations in the 3D Internet. *International Semantic Web Conference*, 2, 161–176. 10.1007/978-3-642-17749-1_11

Karpathy, A., Miller, S., & Fei-Fei, L. (2013). Object discovery in 3d scenes via shape analysis. In *Robotics and Automation (ICRA), 2013 IEEE International Conference on* (pp. 2088-2095). IEEE.

Koller, D., Frischer, B., & Humphreys, G. (2009). Research challenges for digital archives of 3D cultural heritage models. *ACM J. Comput. Cult. Herit., 2*(3).

Kontakis, K., Malamos, A. G., Steiakaki, M., & Panagiotakis, S. (2017). Spatial Indexing of Complex Virtual Reality Scenes in the Web. *International Journal of Image and Graphics, 17*(2), 00523. doi:10.1142/S0219467817500097

Kontakis, K., Malamos, A. G., Steiakaki, M., Panagiotakis, S., & Ware, J. A. (2018). Object Identification Based on the Automated Extraction of Spatial Semantics from Web3D Scenes. *Annals of Emerging Technologies in Computing, 2*(4), 1–10. doi:10.33166/AETiC.2018.04.001

Kontakis, K., Steiakaki, M., Kalochristianakis, M., & Malamos, A. G. (2015). Applying Aesthetic Rules in Virtual Environments by means of Semantic Web Technologies. In *Augmented and Virtual Reality* (Vol. 9254, pp. 344–354). Springer International Publishing; doi:10.1007/978-3-319-22888-4_25

Kontakis, K., Steiakaki, M., Kapetanakis, K., & Malamos, A. G. (2014). DEC-O: an ontology framework and interactive 3D interface for interior. In *Proceedings of the 19th International ACM Conference on 3D Web Technologies* (pp. 63-70). Vancouver, British Columbia, Canada: ACM.

Kontakis, K., Steiakaki, M., Kapetanakis, K., & Malamos, A. G. (2014). DEC-O: An Ontology Framework and Interactive 3D Interface for Interior Decoration Applications in the Web. In *Proceedings of the 19th International ACM Conference on 3D Web Technologies, Web3D '14*, (pp. 63–70). New York, NY: ACM.

Latoschik, M. E., Blach, R., & Iao, F. (2008). *Semantic modelling for virtual worlds a novel paradigm for realtime interactive systems?* VRST. doi:10.1145/1450579.1450583

Lee, K.-L., & Chen, L.-H. (2005). An efficient computation method for the texture browsing descriptor of MPEG-7. *Image and Vision Computing, 23*(5), 479–489. doi:10.1016/j.imavis.2004.12.002

Loewenstein, Y., Raimondo, D., Redfern, O. C., Watson, J., Frishman, D., Linial, M., ... Tramontano, A. (2009). Protein function annotation by homology-based inference. *Genome Biology, 10*(2), 207. doi:10.1186/gb-2009-10-2-207 PMID:19226439

Maglo, A., Lee, H., Lavoué, G., Mouton, C., Hudelot, C., & Dupont, F. (2010). Remote scientific visualization of progressive 3D meshes with X3D. In *Proceedings of the 15th International Conference on Web 3D Technology* (pp. 109-116). ACM.

Malamos, A. G., & Mamakis, G. (2006). VCLASS-3D: A Multimedia Educational Collaboration Platform With 3D Virtual Workspace Support. WBE '06, Puerto Vallarta.

Malamos, A. G., & Mamakis, G. (2009). Extending X3D-based Educational Platform for Mathematics with Multicast Networking Capabilities. WBE ' 09, 644-038, Phuket, Thailand.

Mikolajczyk, K., Zisserman, A., & Schmid, C. (2003). Shape recognition with edge-based features. *BMVC'03*, 779–788.

Min, P., Kazhdan, M., & Funkhouser, T. (2004). A comparison of text and shape matching for retrieval of online 3D models. *Proc. European conference on digital libraries*, 209. 10.1007/978-3-540-30230-8_20

MPEG-4 Homepage. (n.d.). https://mpeg.chiariglione.org/standards/mpeg-4/mpeg-4.htm

MPEG-7 Homepage. (n.d.). https://mpeg.chiariglione.org/standards/mpeg-7/mpeg-7.htm

O'Connor, M. J., & Das, A. (2009). *SQWRL: A Query Language for OWL* (Vol. 529). OWLED.

Panagiotakis, C., Doulamis, A., & Tziritas, G. (2009). Equivalent Key Frames Selection Based on Iso-Content Principle. *IEEE Transactions on Circuits and Systems for Video Technology*, *19*(3), 447–451. doi:10.1109/TCSVT.2009.2013517

Papaleo, L., & De Floriani, L. (2009). Semantic-Based Segmentation and Annotation of 3D Models. In Image Analysis and Processing – ICIAP 2009, (pp. 103-112). Springer Berlin/Heidelberg.

Pavlopoulos, G. A., Wegener, A.-L., & Schneider, R. (2008). A survey of visualization tools for biological network analysis. *BioData Mining*, *1*(1), 12. doi:10.1186/1756-0381-1-12 PMID:19040716

Pein, R. P., Amador, M., Lu, J., & Renz, W. (2008). Using CBIR and semantics in 3D-model retrieval. In *8th IEEE International Conference on Computer and Information Technology*. IEEE. 10.1109/CIT.2008.4594669

Perez-Gallardo, L. C., Crespo, G., & de Jesus, G. (2017). GEODIM: A Semantic Model-Based System for 3D Recognition of Industrial Scenes. In Current Trends on Knowledge-Based Systems (pp. 137–159). Springer.

Pitarello, F., & Faveri, A. (2006). Semantic Description of 3D Environments: a Proposal Based on Web Standards. *Proceedings of Web3D Symposium '06*, 85-95.

Pittarello, F., & Faveri, A. (2006). Semantic Description of 3D Environments: A Proposal Based on Web Standards. In *Proceedings of the Eleventh International Conference on 3D Web Technology, Web3D '06*, (pp. 85–95). New York, NY: ACM.

PlatformA. P. I. (n.d.). http://restlet.com/.Apache

Protégé. (2019). https://protege.stanford.edu/

Rabattu, P. Y., Massé, B., Ulliana, F., Rousset, M. C., Rohmer, D., Léon, J. C., & Palombi, O. (2015). My Corporis Fabrica Embryo: An ontology-based 3D spatio-temporal modeling of human embryo development. *Journal of Biomedical Semantics*, *6*(1), 36. doi:10.118613326-015-0034-0 PMID:26413258

Radics, P. J., Polys, N. F., Neuman, S. P., & Lund, W. H. (2015). OSNAP! Introducing the open semantic network analysis platform. In Visualization and Data Analysis 2015 (vol. 9397, pp. 38–52). International Society for Optics and Photonics, SPIE.

Ro, Y. M., Kim, M., Kang, H. K., Manjunath, B. S., & Kim, J. (2001). MPEG-7 Homogeneous Texture Descriptor. *ETRI Journal*, *23*(2), 41–51. doi:10.4218/etrij.01.0101.0201

Shen, Y., Ong, S. K., & Nee, A. Y. C. (2008). Product information visualization and augmentation in collaborative design. *Computer Aided Design, 40*(9), 963–974. doi:10.1016/j.cad.2008.07.003

Sikora, T. (2001). The MPEG-7 Visual standard for content description an overview. *IEEE Trans. on Circuits and Systems for Video Technology, 11*(6), 696–702.

Sikos, L. F. (2017a). A novel ontology for 3D semantics: Ontology-based 3D model indexing and content-based video retrieval applied to the medical domain. *International Journal of Metadata, Semantics and Ontologies, 12*(1), 59–70. doi:10.1504/IJMSO.2017.087702

Sikos, L. F. (2017b). *Description Logics in Multimedia Reasoning* (1st ed.). Springer Publishing Company, Incorporated. doi:10.1007/978-3-319-54066-5

Sikos, L. F. (2020). 3D Modeling Ontology (3DMO). http://purl.org/ontology/x3d/

Spagnuolo, M., & Falcidieno, B. (2008). *The Role of Ontologies for 3D Media Applications* (pp. 185–205). Springer London. doi:10.1007/978-1-84800-076-6_7

Spagnuolo, M., & Falcidieno, B. (2009). 3D media and the semantic web. *IEEE Intelligent Systems, 24*(2), 90–96. doi:10.1109/MIS.2009.20

Spala, P., Malamos, A. G., Doulamis, A. D., & Mamakis, G. (2012). Extending MPEG-7 for efficient annotation of complex web 3D scenes. *Multimedia Tools and Applications, 59*(2), 463–504. doi:10.100711042-011-0790-5

Sylaiou, Liarokapis, Kotsakis, & Patias. (2009). Virtual museums, a survey and some issues for consideration. *Journal of Cultural Heritage, 10*(4), 520–528.

Tack, K., Lafruit, G., Catthoor, F., & Lauwereins, R. (2006). Platform independent optimisation of multi-resolution 3D content to enable universal media access. *The Visual Computer, 22*(8), 577–590. doi:10.100700371-006-0036-0

Tangelder, J. W. H., & Veltkamp, R. C. (2008). A survey of content based 3D shape retrieval methods. *Multimedia Tools and Applications, 39*(3), 441–471. doi:10.100711042-007-0181-0

TechnologiesU. (2019). *Unity*. http://unity3d.com

Tejada, S., Knoblock, C. A., & Minton, S. (2001). Learning object identification rules for information integration. *Information Systems, 26*(8), 607–633. doi:10.1016/S0306-4379(01)00042-4

Trellet, N., Férey, N., Flotyński, J., Baaden, M., & Bourdot, P. (2018). Semantics for an integrative and immersive pipeline combining visualization and analysis of molecular data. *Journal of Integrative Bioinformatics, 15*(2), 1–19. doi:10.1515/jib-2018-0004 PMID:29982236

Tzompanaki, K., & Doerr, M. (2012). A new framework for querying semantic networks. *Proceedings of Museums and the Web 2012: the international conference for culture and heritage on-line.*

Vasilakis, G., García-Rojas, A., Papaleo, L., Catalano, C. E., Robbiano, F., Spagnuolo, M., ... Pitikakis, M. (2010). Knowledge-Based Representation of 3D Media. *International Journal of Software Engineering and Knowledge Engineering, 20*(5), 739–760.

W3C. (2004). *RDQL a query language for RDF (member submission)*. http://www.w3.org/Submission/2004/SUBM-RDQL-20040109/

W3C. (2008). *SPARQL query language for RDF*. http://www.w3.org/TR/2008/REC-rdf-sparql-query-20080115/

W3C. (2013). *SPARQL 1.1 update*. http://www.w3.org/tr/sparql11-update/

W3C Consortium. (2012). *OWL*. https://www.w3.org/TR/owl2- syntax/

W3C Consortium. (2013). *SPARQL*. https://www.w3.org/TR/ sparql11-query/

W3C Consortium. (2014a). *RDF*. https://www.w3.org/TR/rdf11- concepts/

W3C Consortium. (2014b). *RDFS*. https://www.w3.org/TR/rdfschema/

W3C Consortium. (2019). *WebXR*. https://www.w3.org/TR/ webxr/

Walczak, K. (2008). Flex-VR: Configurable 3D Web Applications. *Proceedings of the International Conference on Human System Interaction, HSI'08*, 135-140.

Walczak, K., & Flotyński, J. (2014). On-demand generation of 3D content based on semantic meta-scenes. In *International Conference on Augmented and Virtual Reality*. Springer. 10.1007/978-3-319-13969-2_24

Walczak, K., & Flotyński, J. (2016). Semantic query-based generation of customized 3D scenes. In *Proceedings of the 20th International Conference on 3D Web Technology*. ACM.

Walczak, K., & Flotynski, J. (2019). Inference-based creation of synthetic 3D content with ontologies. *Multimedia Tools and Applications*, 78(9), 12607–12638. doi:10.100711042-018-6788-5

Web3D Consortium. (1995). *VRML*. https://www.w3.org/ MarkUp/VRML/.Web3D

Web3D Consortium. (2004). *Extensible 3D (X3D) ISO/IEC 19775:2004*. http://www.web3d.org/x3d/specifications/ISOIEC-19775-X3DAbstractSpecification/2004S

Web3D Consortium. (2013). *X3D*. https://www.web3d.org/ documents/specifications/19775-1/V3.3/Part01/ X3D.html

Web3D Consortium. (2018). *X3D Semantic Web Working Group*. https://www.web3d.org/working-groups/x3d- semantic-web/.Web3D

Web3D Consortium. (2019a). *X3D Ontology for Semantic Web*. https://www.web3d.org/x3d/content/semantics/ semantics.html

Web3D Consortium. (2019b). *X3D Unified Object Model (X3DUOM)*. https://www.web3d.org/specifications/ X3DUOM.html

Web3D Consortium. (2019c). *Export stylesheet to convert X3D XML models into Turtle RDF/OWL triples*. https://www.web3d.org/x3d/stylesheets/X3dToTurtle.xslt

WebG. L. (2020). https://get.webgl.org/

Wiebusch, D., & Latoschik, M. E. (2012). Enhanced Decoupling of Components in Intelligent Realtime Interactive Systems using Ontologies. In *Software Engineering and Architectures for Realtime Interactive Systems (SEARIS), Proceedings of the IEEE Virtual Reality 2012 Workshop*. IEEE.

Wu, Z., Xu, G., Zhang, Y., Cao, Z., Li, G., & Hu, Z. (2012). GMQL: A graphical multimedia query language. *Knowledge-Based Systems*, *26*, 135–143. doi:10.1016/j.knosys.2011.07.013

Zaharia, T., & Preteux, F. (2001). 3D Shape-based retrieval within the MPEG-7 framework. *Proceedings of the SPIE/EI Conference on Nonlinear Image Processing, SPIE/EI 2001*.

Zampoglou, P., Spala, K., Kontakis, A. G., Malamos, & Ware, J. A. (2013). Direct mapping of x3d scenes to mpeg-7 descriptions. *Proceeding of the 18th International Conference on 3D Web Technology*.

Zhang, J. M., Xu, X., & Yuan, B. (2007). Rotation Invariant Image Classification Based on MPEG-7 Homogeneous Texture Descriptor. *Eighth ACIS International Conference on Software Engineering, Artificial Intelligence, Networking, and Parallel/Distributed Computing (SNPD 2007)*, 3, 798-803.

Zhou1, N., & Deng, Y. (2009). Virtual reality: A state-of-the-art survey. *International Journal of Automation and Computing, 6*(4), 319-325.

ENDNOTE

[1] https://x3dgraphics.com/examples/X3dForAdvancedModeling/SanCarlosCathedral/SanCarlosCathedralIndex.html

Chapter 3
3D Technologies and Applications in Sign Language

Kiriakos Stefanidis
https://orcid.org/0000-0002-9922-1916
The Visual Computer Lab, Information Technologies Institute, Centre for Research and Technology, Hellas, Greece

Athanasios Kalvourtzis
The Visual Computing Lab, Information Technologies Institute, Centre for Research and Technology, Hellas, Greece

Dimitrios Konstantinidis
https://orcid.org/0000-0002-7391-6875
The Visual Computing Lab, Information Technologies Institute, Centre for Research and Technology, Hellas, Greece

Kosmas Dimitropoulos
The Visual Computing Lab, Information Technologies Institute, Centre for Research and Technology, Hellas, Greece

Petros Daras
https://orcid.org/0000-0003-3814-6710
The Visual Computing Lab, Information Technologies Institute, Centre for Research and Technology, Hellas, Greece

ABSTRACT

Millions of people suffering from partial or complete hearing loss use variants of sign language to communicate with each other or hearing people in their everyday life. Thus, it is imperative to develop systems to assist these people by removing the barriers that affect their social inclusion. These systems should aim towards capturing sign language in an accurate way, classifying sign language to natural words and representing sign language by having avatars or synthesized videos execute the exact same moves that convey a meaning in the sign language. This chapter reviews current state-of-the-art approaches that attempt to solve sign language recognition and representation and analyzes the challenges they face. Furthermore, this chapter presents a novel AI-based solution to the problem of robust sign language capturing and representation, as well as a solution to the unavailability of annotated sign language datasets before limitations and directions for future work are discussed.

DOI: 10.4018/978-1-5225-5294-9.ch003

INTRODUCTION

Sign language is the only way of communication among deaf or hearing-impaired people around the world. The importance of sign language can be illustrated by the fact that it is used not only for the communication among hearing-impaired people, but also for the interaction of hearing-impaired people with their environment and speaking people. Sign language enables people with hearing loss to remove the barriers to the use of mainstream products and services, such as TV and other media and improves their social inclusion by giving them equal opportunities with people having no hearing loss problems. Sign language is a visual-spatial language based on positional and visual components, such as the shape of fingers and hands, the location and orientation of the hands, arm and body movements and facial expressions. These components are combined together to form utterances that convey the meaning of words or sentences (Kendon, 2004).

Being able to capture and understand the relation between utterances and words is crucial for the deaf community in order to guide us to an era where the translation between utterances and words can be achieved automatically. To enable such translation, automatic systems should be developed that include methodologies for precise capturing of the hand and facial movements, robust recognition and classification of utterances to words and accurate representation of the utterances in a 2D environment using synthesized signed videos or in a 3D environment, using 3D avatars that represent humans performing utterances.

Unfortunately, current sign language capturing techniques either depend on too costly or complicated sensor setups or suffer from significant hand and finger occlusions. Moreover, sign language recognition methodologies face significant challenges as: a) each country has its own sign language, b) there is a lack of large publicly available annotated sign language recognition datasets, c) there are variations in the way people sign based on their individual signing style and d) each sign language consists of thousands of signs that can differ by subtle changes in hand, finger and facial movements. Finally, the 3D representation of utterances using avatars is challenging due to the mediocre accuracy of computed human skeletal joints, the lack of avatar realism and the problems in translation from skeletal points in the 3D space to quaternions. On the other hand, the synthesis of signed videos is still at its infancy due to lack of large datasets, although current deep learning approaches has shown promising results.

The need of deaf community for accurate and robust sign language recognition and representation makes the development of such systems imperative. However, the great many challenges these systems face put significant limitations and obstacles to current sign language recognition and representation systems. Although the sign language recognition and representation field has captured the attention of the research community and a lot of progress has been made in this field, there is still a lot of work that should be performed towards improving the accuracy and robustness of sign language recognition and representation systems.

In the next sections, we initially present a literature review of the state-of-the-art sign language capturing, recognition and representation approaches before we move on and present our proposed Artificial Intelligence (AI) – based approach to solve the sign language 3D animation task based on capturing and 3D representation. Finally, we also present our approach towards collecting annotated signed videos to form a large sign language repository based on the notion of crowdsourcing.

BACKGROUND

In this section, we present and categorize existing sign language capturing technologies and then we perform a literature review on sign language recognition and representation.

Sign Language Capturing

Sign language capturing is concerned with the collection of every significant piece of information regarding hand, body and face motions that can describe a sign and can be used for both sign language recognition and sign language representation purposes. Sign language capturing is highly dependent on the sensor technology used for the data collection. As a result, sign language capturing technologies can be split in three major categories: marker-based, markerless and other, as shown in Figure 1.

Figure 1. Categorization of sign language capturing technologies

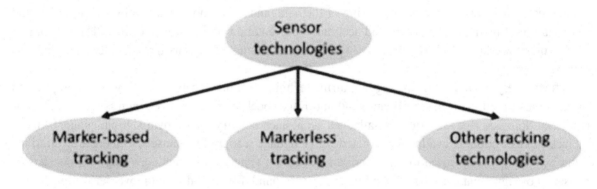

Marker-based Tracking Technologies

Marker-based technologies include inertia and optical motion capture (mocap) systems, which involve sensors attached to the body of a signer while signing. Inertial motion capture systems include smart gloves, such as CyberGlove (CyberGlove Systems, n.d.), Manus VR (Manus VR, n.d.) and VR gluv (VRgluv, n.d.), that have the ability to capture finger motions, rotations and orientations in 3D space by employing tiny IMU based sensors on each finger segment. Because the inertial sensors are capturing movements in all 3 directions, flexion, extensions and abduction can be captured for all fingers and then interpreted into useful information that can be used for sign language recognition and representation. Smart gloves offer many advantages, such as accuracy and robustness during capturing of movements, real-time performance and finger and hand occlusion handling. However, they also have significant disadvantages as they are available at a high cost, they are obtrusive to the signers and they face problems with capturing the absolute position of hands in 3D space, as well as problems with magnetic interference among the inertial sensors that can affect overall accuracy.

Figure 2. From left to right: Images of CyberGlove (CyberGlove Systems, n.d.), Manus VR (Manus VR, n.d.) and VR gluv (VRgluv, n.d.) taken from the corresponding websites

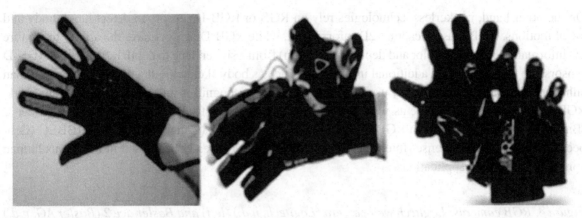

Optical motion capture systems rely on the use of retroreflective, color and light-emitting markers attached to a human body that provide information about location, orientation and velocity of each marker, and thus human body joint to which the marker is attached. Optical systems, like Vicon (VICON, n.d.) or ART (ART, n.d.), provide real-time information on human motion using multiple high-resolution cameras. Such optical systems provide robust results even though some markers may not be visible due to bad illumination, motion blur or occlusions. Because the spatial relationships of all the markers are known, the positions of the markers that are not visible can be computed by using the markers that are detected. Although accurate and robust, such motion capture systems are considered obtrusive and depend on costly setups that limit their use to specialized laboratories.

Figure 3. Optical motion capture setups using Vicon (VICON, n.d.) (left) and ART (ART, n.d.) (right) technologies

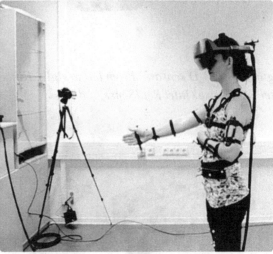

Markerless Tracking Technologies

On the other hand, markerless technologies rely on RGB or RGB-D sensors to detect hand, body and facial motions. RGB sensors capture 2D information, while RGB-D sensors have the ability to capture 3D information (i.e., both color and depth information) from a signer. Due to depth information, RGB-D sensors can usually provide additional information, such as body skeletal joints, face points and human silhouette that can be proved really useful in a sign language recognition and representation framework. RGB sensors can be as simple as web-cameras or elaborate industrial cameras, such as Basler ace 2 (Basler AG, n.d.). Well-known RGB-D sensors are the Kinect v2 (Callaham, 2015), ORBBEC (Orbbec, n.d.) and Intel RealSense (Intel RealSense, n.d.) that have already been used in numerous human computer interaction applications.

Figure 4. RGB cameras: Logitech web-camera (Logitech, n.d.) (left) and Basler ace 2 (Basler AG, n.d.) industrial camera (right)

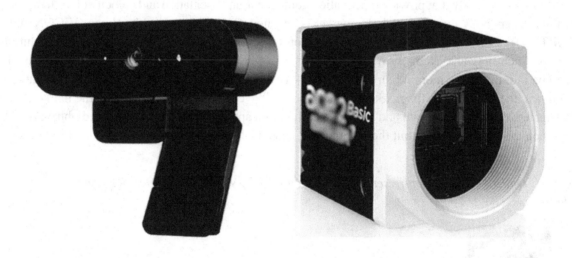

Figure 5. RGB-D sensors: From left to right, Kinect v2 (Callaham, 2015), ORBBEC (Orbbec, n.d.) and Intel RealSense (Intel RealSense, n.d.)

Other Tracking Technologies

Other technologies can also be used to capture hand and finger movements, such as Virtual and Augmented Reality (VR/AR), smartbands, smartwatches, etc. Below, we present a few representative examples of such technologies that can be employed for sign language recognition and representation. HTC Vive (Vive, n.d.) is a virtual reality headset, which comes with two wireless controllers that act as the virtual "arms" to track hand and arm movements in space in real time. Leap Motion (Leap Motion, n.d.) is a hands-free solution specifically designed for virtual reality. Leap Motion is a depth sensor that provides a wide field of view of 135 degrees, almost-zero latency, pinpoint accuracy, and high robustness and can be used to track hand movements and turn the user's hands as the sole controller of anything on screen. A limitation of Leap Motion for sign language recognition lies in the fact that the user should stand exactly above the sensor and in a really close distance to the sensor. Finally, Fitbit (Fitbit, n.d.) develop several different types of smartbands that are equipped with various sensors, such as accelerometer, gyroscope, etc. that can be used for the detection of arm movements. The aforementioned technologies can be really useful for sign language recognition, especially if combined with other marker-based or markerless approaches.

Figure 6. Other technologies for sign language capturing: From left to right, HTC Vive (Vive, n.d.), Leap Motion (Leap Motion, n.d.) and Fitbit Charge 3 smartband (Fitbit, n.d.)

Sign Language Recognition

Sign language recognition is often considered as a sub-category of the more general gesture recognition and is concerned with the identification of hand, body and facial motions and the classification of these motions to specific signs in a sign language vocabulary. Gesture recognition has been widely studied and several state-of-the-art methods have been proposed to successfully recognize human motion (Kosmopoulos, Doulamis & Doulamis, 2005, September; Dimitropoulos, Barmpoutis, Kitsikidis & Grammalidis, 2016; Konstantinidis, Dimitropoulos & Daras, 2018, September), in various interactive environments, e.g., in dancing and pottery learning (Kitsikidis et al., 2015, August; Dimitropoulos et al., 2018), educational video games (Psaltis et al., 2016, October; Psaltis, Apostolakis, Dimitropoulos & Daras, 2017) etc. In the literature, sign language recognition systems are often categorized based on the data acquisition method used to capture the various sign language positional and visual components to sensor-based and vision-based approaches (Cheok, Omar & Jaward, 2019). Sensor-based approaches rely on data gloves, inertial measurement unit (IMU) sensors, Electromyography (EMG) sensors and other types of technologies that are physically attached to users, such as flex sensors, ultrasound, mechanical and electromagnetics technologies. On the other hand, vision-based approaches are based on the collection of visual information from one or more cameras or depth sensors. Another categorization can be made based on the sign language recognition task, where isolated sign language recognition approaches are concerned with the classification of signs to isolated words, while continuous sign language recognition approaches involve the classification of signs to phrases or sequences of words.

Most continuous sign language recognition approaches are vision-based as they process videos to identify sequences of words. Such approaches employ deep learning concepts, such as Convolutional Neural Networks (CNNs) and Long Short-Term Memory (LSTM) units, as well as concepts from natural language and audio processing, such as connectionist temporal classification (CTC) and language modelling to solve the continuous sign language recognition task. Below, we present an overview of the most significant research work performed in the task of continuous sign language recognition. Koller, Forster & Ney (2015) were one of the first that tracked and extracted hand features in videos and combined them with language models to train a Hidden Markov Model (HMM) to recognize signs. Later on, other works were introduced to combine the discriminative power of CNNs with HMMs for sign language recognition (Koller, Zargaran, Ney & Bowden, 2016; Koller, Zargaran, & Ney, 2017). Cui, Liu & Zhang (2017) employed the concept of CTC and developed a CNN-LSTM deep network that achieved good performance in continuous sign language recognition datasets. Similarly, Camgoz, Hadfield, Koller & Bowden (2017, October) employed CTC and CNN-LSTM with a special type of temporal network, called subunet, that consisted of forward and backward LSTM units. Finally, Cui, Liu & Zhang (2019) employed RGB and optical flow images in a two-stream deep network, as well as proposed a novel video-to-word alignment that managed to achieve state-of-the-art performance in the continuous sign language recognition task.

Next, we present representative work on isolated sign language recognition for both sensor-based and vision-based approaches. Most sensor-based sign language recognition approaches utilize data gloves that have IMU sensors, such as gyroscope and accelerometer attached to them. Kim, Jang & Bien (1996) used raw data generated from a flex-sensor glove that capture finger bending information to categorize the motion of both hands into ten basic motions, which are then used as input to a Fuzzy Min-max Neural Network (FMNN). On the other hand, Liang & Ouhyoung (1998, April) used a data glove to capture position, angles and motion trajectory data from fingers and fed them as input to a HMM in order to classify Taiwanese sign language words. Fang, Gao & Zhao (2004) used 2 data gloves and trackers placed on the wrists of signers to feed HMM and decision tree models for Chinese sign language classification. In a similar fashion, Kong & Ranganath (2008) used a data glove and magnetic trackers, as well as a linear decision tree with Fisher's linear discriminant to classify English signs. Zhang, Chen, Li, Lantz, Wang & Yang (2011) combined 3-axis input from accelerometer and 5-channel of EMG signals attached on the hand of the user and employed Fuzzy K-means clustering to recognize Chinese sign language with a high level of accuracy. Similarly, Kosmidou & Hadjileontiadis (2009) employed the intrinsic-mode sample entropy on EMG signals and accelerometer data for Greek sign language recognition. Sensor-based approaches have the advantage of providing really accurate and robust shape, orientation and motion data as they overcome the problem of occlusions of fingers and hands from which the vision-based approaches suffer. Unfortunately, sensor-based approaches depend on costly and complicated setups that can only exist in a laboratory environment, Furthermore, data gloves and other human body attached sensors are obtrusive, as they severely restrict the movements of a signer.

As already mentioned, vision-based sign language recognition approaches rely on cameras and depth sensors to collect data from a signer and then process them to achieve accurate and robust classification of signs. In the case depth sensors are utilized, the extraction of skeleton joints can be very handy, along with hand regions for the task of sign language classification (Almeida, Guimarães & Ramírez, 2014; Sun, Zhang & Xu, 2015). Otherwise, most vision-based sign language approaches attempt to detect and extract hand regions by performing skin color detection and segmentation (Rautaray & Agrawal, 2011; Zhang & Huang, 2013, December). However, other body parts, such as face and arms has similar skin color information, which can lead to their erroneous recognition as hands. To overcome this problem, recent methodologies rely also on face detection and background subtraction in order to identify and extract only the moving parts of a scene (Lim, Tan & Tan, 2016a; Lim, Tan & Tan, 2016b). Another common practice in vision-based sign language approaches is to employ tracking techniques, such as Kalman and particle filters in order to handle occlusion problems and achieve accurate and robust hand detection and extraction (Lim et al., 2016b; Gaus & Wong, 2012, February). As far as classification is concerned, several methods take advantage of the detected hand regions to compute distances between histograms of optical flow (Lim et al., 2016a), feature covariance matrices (Lim et al., 2016b) or Grassmann covariance matrices from pixel values (Wang, Chai, Hong, Zhao & Chen, 2016). HMMs are widely employed in vision-based sign language approaches as well, in order to take as input hand shapes and locations and classify them to signs (Tanibata, Shimada & Shirai, 2002, May; Ni et al., 2013, August; Ronchetti, Quiroga, Estrebou, Lanzarini & Rosete, 2016). Additionally, HMMs have been successfully used for sign language recognition based on multi-camera systems (Starner, Weaver & Pentland, 1998; Kumar, Gauba, Roy & Dogra, 2017).

The superb performance of deep learning on several computer vision tasks has led to its use on vision-based isolated sign language recognition well. Huang, Zhou, Li & Li (2015, June) proposed the use of 3D CNNs to automatically capture both temporal and spatial information from the raw video sequences without the need for handcrafting features. On the other hand, Liu, Zhou & Li (2016, September) employed an LSTM unit with fully connected layers for accurate Chinese sign language recognition. Similarly, Masood, Srivastava, Thuwal & Ahmad (2018) combined a CNN with a LSTM unit for accurate Argentinian sign language recognition.

Although the aforementioned approaches allow a signer to perform gestures with no restrictions, the data gathered can be noisy and inaccurate due to overlaps and occlusions between fingers and other body parts, especially when a single sensor (i.e., camera or depth) is used. To overcome this problem and improve the robustness in vision-based sign language recognition, new approaches have been proposed that process body, hand and facial features extracted from videos in order to classify signs. Such approaches have been based on state-of-the-art deep learning algorithms, such as OpenPose (Simon, Joo, Matthews & Sheikh, 2017; Cao, Hidalgo, Simon, Wei & Sheikh, 2018) and AlphaPose (Fang, Xie, Tai & Lu, 2017; Xiu, Li, Wang, Fang & Lu, 2018), that are capable of extracting 2D skeletal and facial features from images or videos. Skeletal features have been shown to be more robust to illumination changes and color information than raw pixel values. Konstantinidis, Dimitropoulos & Daras (2018, June) proposed a skeleton-based sign language recognition approach that employed body and hand features extracted from videos and processed such features with LSTM units and linear dynamical systems (Dimitropoulos, Barmpoutis, Kitsikidis & Grammalidis, 2016) so as to accurately classify signs. In a later work, the same authors expanded their previous work by including facial features, along with body and hand features, as well as colour and optical flow information extracted using convolutional and recurrent neural networks (Konstantinidis, Dimitropoulos & Daras, 2018, October). Moreover, Konstantinidis et al. (2018, October) experimented with different data fusion techniques to merge the multimodal information and improve the accuracy and robustness of their proposed algorithm in sign language recognition. In a similar fashion, De Amorim, Macêdo & Zanchettin (2019) employed hand and body skeletal joints and processed them with graph convolutional networks in order to classify signs from the American sign language.

Sign Language Representation

One of the first successful implementations of avatar technologies for sign language is the signing avatar PAULA by Davidson (2006). This avatar served as an educational tutor focused on the development and practice of sign language recognition skills. The latter was accomplished by providing demonstrations of signs to users and tracking user performance in quizzes. PAULA also allowed the sign language learner to control the practice of sign language and guide the feedback process. The benefits of presenting educational content using avatar technologies instead of videos are properly addressed in Yorganci, Kindiroglu & Kose (2016). In particular, the authors of this work argue that the creation of educational support material specifically designed to aid and assess learning, such as books and worksheets, is hard to create, edit, store and transfer with videos. For that reason, avatar-based tutoring has proven to be more effective than regular video content in assessing a child's knowledge of certain sign language words.

The gradual adoption of virtual signing by the Deaf and Hearing Impaired communities over the years created the need for standardization. Thus, many research projects shed their focus on defining declarative, XML-like specifications of sign language that, in most cases, map individual words to avatar-specific gesture information. The majority of the efforts are grounded upon the famous HamNoSys notation, which is an alphabetic system describing signs on a mostly phonetic level (Hanke, 2004). Towards that end, the EU-funded project ViSiCAST defined SiGML (Signing Gesture Markup Language), a specification that is known as the first XML-equivalent of HamNoSys (Elliott, Glauert, Kennaway & Marshall, 2000). Moreover, ViSiCAST and its successor project eSign, showcased the benefits of using synthetic signing from HamNoSys/SiGML notation instead of implicating with sophisticated and costly motion capture technology (Elliott et al., 2000). In that context, Elliott, Glauert, Kennaway, Marshall & Safar (2008) used synthetic signing and high-level linguistic analysis for translating English into British Sign Language (BSL), and then generated the HamNoSys/SiGML notation for animation playback on the eSign avatar. Similarly, synthetic signing with the eSign avatar was part of the 'Research Toolkit Project' (Nelson, 2009), which aimed at developing tools in the areas of fingerspelling, facial expression, syntax, and semantics. A review on synthetic signing approaches for HCI that use HamNoSys/SiGML is given in Smith, Morrissey & Somers (2010). In a more recent work, Kaur & Kumar (2016) created an automated conversion system able to generate HamNoSys from Indian Sign Language (ISL) and also produce SiGML in order to use the 'virtual human' player in the JA SiGML URL APP for animating a signing avatar.

Another popular transcription system for sign language is SignWriting. In one of the earliest works, Papadogiorgaki, Grammalidis, Tzovaras & Strintzis (2005) presented an approach for the generation of VRML (Virtual Reality Modeling Language) animation sequences from SignWriting Markup Language (SWML), which is the XML version of SignWriting. Their system was based on MPEG-4 face and body animation, receiving text sentences as input and generating 3D animated VRML sequences that could be visualized on any VRML-compliant browser. More recently, Ferreira (2017) created the 3DSL system that uses speech-to-text technology and SignWriting representation in order to translate Portuguese into Portuguese Sign Language for playback by a 3D humanoid avatar. On the contrary, other research works on synthetic signing avoid the use of HamNoSys and SignWriting transcriptions and develop novel scripting schemes for sign language animation (Bouzid & Jemni, 2014). Moreover, in a recent PhD Thesis, Murtagh (2019) created a lexicon definition for 3D animation of Irish Sign Language (ISL) that is based on Role and Reference Grammar (RRG), which is a structural functionalist theory of grammar.

Another important area of research in signing avatars is animation synthesis. Animation synthesis refers to the blending of individual words into a single animation clip. A review on methods for animation synthesis for American Sign Language (ASL) based on sparse input specifications is provided in Huenerfauth (2014). More specifically, the author of this work created a lexicon of ASL signs that can be used to rapidly synthesize sentences or longer passages. Furthermore, Maarif, Akmeliawati & Gunawan (2018) review SL synthesis technologies and describe a framework for synthesizing SL from speech input (NLP). The speed and timing in SL animation is discussed in Al-khazraji, Berke, Kafle, Yeung & Huenerfauth (2018) and a new method based on machine learning is presented for the automatic calculation of three key values: selection of locations to insert pauses, setting the differential speed of individual words, and adjusting the time duration of the pauses. Establishing smooth transitions in synthesized animation is discussed in Punchimudiyanse (2015) and Punchimudiyanse & Meegama (2015). More recently, Uchida et al. (2019) used animation synthesis for Japanese Sign Language (JSL) applied on live sports data. Their method included a 'collocation synthesis' phase for representing two concepts with a single sign. Moreover, the ongoing EU-funded project Content4All is developing a sign interpreter in a remote studio, process it and render it via broadcast by making use of a state-of-the-art photorealistic 3D human avatar ("Content4All Project" (Content4All Project website, n.d.)). Finally, one of the most comprehensive animation synthesis systems for sign language up-to-date, SiMAX, combines several highly sophisticated ICT technologies: a real-time 3D-engine, an animation/clip exporter, an animation builder, a "learning" database, a clip database, a sign database, a translation engine based on statistical methods, a translator interface, an emotion editor, and a video converter.

Many problems may arise in the creation process of animation for sign language. One of the major issues concerns the high degree of freedom (DoF) of finger movements, which is hard to capture even with today's motion capture technology. Alexanderson & Beskow (2015) try to solve this problem by defining an accurate underlying hand model within a dual-sensor approach, which combines optical motion capture with bend sensors. Another important issue is robotic motion. In the context of virtual signing, despite reducing realism in animations, robotic motion may also reduce the understandability of sign language. McDonald et al. (2016) argue that animations procedurally created from a library of signs based on linguistic parameters, naturally produce a sparse distribution of keys which may make it easy to modify the animations based on linguistic context, yet the same sparseness of keys can easily lead to robotic motion. An example of such case is the Signed Language Phonetic Annotation (SLPA) model of ASL.

Establishing a two-way communication with deaf people using realistic avatar technologies is the ultimate goal, a problem that still remains open and drives research in Sign Language. An initial effort to accomplish that is the Deaf Talk system described in Ahmed, Idrees, ul Abideen, Mumtaz & Khalique (2016). Deaf Talk used Microsoft's Kinect v2.0 sensor and predefined stored animations to implement modules for both speech-to-sign and sign-to-speech procedures. Similarly, the Greek project "Επικοινωνώ" (Epikoinwnw Project, n.d.) aims to implement a mobile/tablet application which will provide easy and efficient communication for the deaf and hearing impaired individuals, in real time. The main objective of the project is the recognition of hand gestures using innovative deep learning methods executed on Greek Sign Language (GSL).

Several research works have shed their focus on the understandability of sign language animation. In particular, Kipp, Heloir & Nguyen (2011) present methods and discuss challenges for the creation and evaluation of signing avatars while introducing delta testing as a novel comprehensibility method for comparing avatars with human signers. In order to produce signing animation, the authors of this work used the EMBR character animation engine that executes HamNoSys-like scripts. In another work, the same authors conducted online studies for assessing whether deaf people like signing avatars (Kipp, Nguyen, Heloir & Matthes, 2011). While results showed a positive baseline response on the idea of signing avatars, they also revealed that there is a statistically significant increase in positive opinions caused by participating in the studies. For that reason, the authors argue that the inclusion of Deaf people in avatar evaluation phases has the potential to foster acceptance, as well as provide important feedback regarding key aspects of avatar technologies that need to be improved. In a more recent study, Malala, Prigent, Braffort & Berret (2018) highlighted the crucial role of movement in SL understandability and created an online test consisting of four types of avatars: a baseline version with a real human signer, a more complete version of a virtual signer, and two degraded versions of a virtual signer (one with non-visible hands and one without movements of head/trunk). Each video showed the description of a picture in French Sign Language (LSF). The novelty of this work was the inclusion of two types of confusable pictures for users: one was supposed to induce errors by confounding the lexical signs while the other disturbed the spatial structure of the picture. Even more recently, Bigand, Prigent & Braffort (2019) studied anonymity on signing 3D avatars and conducted an experiment where users tried to identify if a signer/actor could be recognized solely by looking at the 3D avatar. The experiment, however, was conducted without any facial expressions. In fact, facial expressions are of central importance for enhancing the understandability of signing avatars. Smith & Nolan (2016) made the hypothesis that augmenting an avatar with Ekman's 7 emotions (happiness, sadness, anger, disgust, contempt, fear and surprise) can make it more human-like and improve the understandability of ISL users. The 7 Ekman emotions were created as facial morphs using the ARPtoolkit. The authors' evaluation results revealed no significant differences with baseline avatars.

Researchers also made efforts for creating a corpus of sign language recordings intended for avatar playback. In a multi-year project, Braffort, Benchiheub & Berret (2015) tried to create a 3D corpus of French Sign Language that includes motion capture, video and eye-tracker data, as well as user annotations. In the recording sessions, signers were engaged into four distinct tasks under a setup consisting of 10 OptiTrack cameras and 40 markers placed on their body. However, the MoCap system used did not include accurate tracking of fingers. In another work, Heloir & Nunnari (2013) introduce the concept of crowdsourcing for creating a corpus of sign language through an online platform. Their setup included a Microsoft Kinect and a Leap Motion device in a system supporting two editing modes for creating animation interchangeably: performance capture and pose-to-pose animation. The first mode involved the core recording process while the later served as a refinement phase by regarding the recordings as key poses and offering further adjustment to the user. A shortcoming of this method was the long calibration process required for performance capture. Finally, in an ongoing effort, the EasyTV project (EasyTV Project website, n.d.) aims to offer a multi-language approach for delivering sign language content through a crowdsourcing platform supporting the translations among different sign languages using a multilingual ontology. The result of this process will be a corpus of sign language animation data ready for playback by a realistic 3D avatar on TV or companion screens.

AI-BASED 3D ANIMATION

In this section, we present our own work on AI-based 3D animation for sign language purposes. More specifically, we present our approach based on machine learning techniques for accurate extraction of skeletal features from a motion capturing system that relies on a single depth sensor and the proposed post-processing steps that follow in order to remove noisy data and transform them in a way that they are better manageable from a 3D avatar. Moreover, we present our attempt to perform accurate avatar playback for sign language and the challenges we face. Finally, we present a crowdsourcing platform we developed in the framework of the EasyTV project in order to collect signed videos and annotations from users around the world and thus create a large sign language repository for recognition and representation purposes.

Motion Capturing

Capturing human motion is generally a complex and challenging task. The process becomes even more cumbersome in the context of Sign Language, considering the demands for capturing accurate finger motion of the signer. In fact, Sign Language requires a full body motion capture setup that includes body gestures, as well as, finger movements and facial expressions. Towards that end, the EasyTV project provides an innovative and easy-to-use solution for full body motion capture via a simple desktop application. The main objective is to combine a motion capture technology with a crowdsourcing system and, in that way, create the potential for developing a multilingual corpus for Sign Language across Europe. Towards that end, the capturing module of EasyTV offers a simple yet complete graphical user interface (GUI) for recording Sign Language. The application GUI has been designed especially for the Deaf and Hearing Impaired communities according to feedback gathered from end-users.

As illustrated in Figure 7, the main window of the application includes the following:

- **Signer viewer:** A display screen for visualizing the signer while recording. This is important so that the admin can see if the signer is in the right position and his moves do not exceed the sensor's viewing area. Also, the effects that the lighting conditions of the room may have on the sensor can be observed.
- **Path for file storage:** A textbox for defining the folder where data will be written into. This data concerns both the acquired images and the final output of the application.
- **Start/stop recording button:** The admin starts and stops the image acquisition phase. When the acquisition stops, files are stored in the specified folder.
- **Detection button:** The keypoint detection phase starts for the body, fingers and face of the signer.
- **Visualization button:** 3D keypoints are shown in an OpenGL viewer window.
- **Store annotation button:** Annotations written in the textbox are stored in a text file.

Figure 7. The EasyTV motion capture application GUI

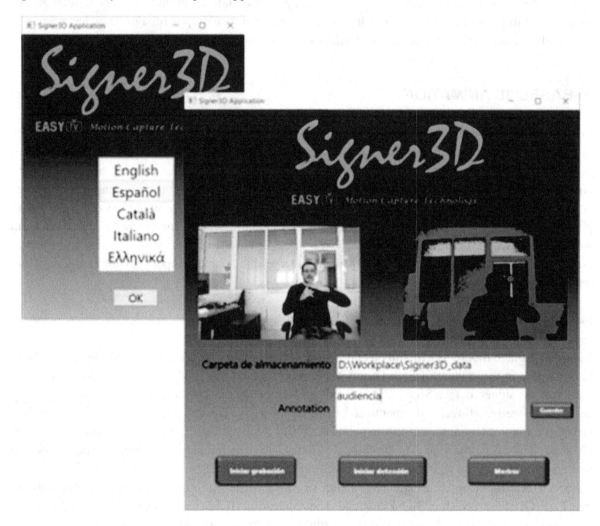

For the acquisition of images, the capturing application uses Intel's RealSense RGB-D sensor. Two types of images are acquired from the sensor: RGB and depth images. Both types of images are necessary for the generation of 3D motion data. The native resolution of RealSense for color frames is fixed at Full HD quality, i.e., 1920 x 1080 pixels, captured at a frame rate of 30 FPS. On the other hand, the maximum resolution for the depth images is 1280 x 720 at a rate up to 30 FPS. However, the sensor's SDK does not include detectors for skeletal keypoints on either the body, fingers or face. For this reason, third-party detectors were included so that the requirements of the EasyTV project are met and accurate hand tracking is provided.

In order to synthese 3D data, the depth frames should not only be aligned in time with RGB frames, but also be spatially aligned. This means that each color frame and its corresponding depth frame, should also have the same resolution. In fact, RGB-D devices like Intel's RealSense or Microsoft's Kinect sensor offer the choice of either mapping depth frames to color space or color frames to depth space.

When the acquisition process completes with all RGB and depth frames been collected, frames are also merged into videos. The purpose of generating videos of the recorded content is for the admin of the capturing process to review the recordings in the annotation phase, as well as for the moderator of the crowdsourcing platform can review the recordings in the validation phase.

An RGB video of the recording is also exported in MP4 format. For the generation of videos, the popular ffmpeg software is used. ffmpeg is a free command-line application for processing video or audio files, and is widely used for format transcoding, basic editing (trimming and concatenation), and video scaling. The video is uploaded along with the exported motion data to the crowdsourcing platform.

For extracting the skeleton keypoints, specific algorithms process each color image and detect keypoints on the body of the signer. Keypoints are points of interest on the captured frames that identify the important visual content on the image. In the present case, the important parts of images are landmarks on the hands, face and body of the signer. Keypoints can be either 2D or 3D keypoints. Currently, a detection process for 2D keypoints is used. The number of keypoints and their position depends on the training of the detection algorithms. In the current state-of-the-art, such detection algorithms are usually deep neural networks trained on annotated images.

Keypoint detectors find application in a wide area of computer vision tasks, such as, image processing and analysis, object recognition and classification, and also, motion capturing. Some desirable properties of a keypoint detector are: i) accurate localization, ii) invariance against shift, rotation, scale, brightness change, iii) robustness against noise, high repeatability. The keypoint detector of choice is OpenPose (Simon et al., 2017; Cao et al., 2018) which offers full body keypoint detection in 2D, including keypoints for the face, body and fingers. OpenPose offers parameters to control the quality/speed ratio such as the resolution of the detection networks.

Sign Language detection is a very demanding process requiring the motion capture of fingers, as well as, body movements and facial expressions. For that reason, keypoints need to be detected for not only the hands of the signer, but also for the body and the face. In order to accomplish that, three distinct keypoint detectors are integrated with the capturing module. Except for hand detection, OpenPose also includes robust keypoint detectors for the face and body, making it a complete keypoint detection solution that doesn't require any extra third-party software to integrate with. In fact, OpenPose is able to detect a total of 137 keypoints on the acquired RGB images, which are sufficient for accurately capturing the motion of the signer.

Each keypoint detector in OpenPose is a deep neural network and, more specifically, a special type of CNN called Convolutional Pose Machine (CPN). CPNs have the ability to learn long-range dependencies among images and multi-part cues, and also, inherit a modular sequential design. These features combine with the advantages afforded by convolutional architectures, thus making the networks capable of learning feature representations for both image and spatial context directly from data. In the first stage, the convolutional pose machine predicts part beliefs from only local image evidence, while the convolutional layers in the subsequent stage allow the classifier to freely combine contextual information by picking the most predictive features. More comprehensive information about the architecture of a CPN can be found in Wei, Ramakrishna, Kanade & Sheikh (2016).

In order to avoid the problem of annotating databases for hand detection, the training process of a CPN is done using a technique called Multiview Bootstrapping. While a thorough analysis of this method is provided in Simon et al. (2017), we will also mention some important aspects of it for the completeness of presentation. Multiview bootstrapping is an approach that allows the generation of large annotated datasets using a weak initial detector. More specifically, the weak detector is trained on a small annotated dataset in order to detect subsets of keypoints in the so called "good views" which are the views for a certain frame achieving the highest scores as evaluated by a heuristic scoring policy. A robust 3D trian-

Figure 8. Full body 3D keypoints for Sign Language drawn in OpenGL, formed by merging 2D keypoints detected on RGB images with values from spatially aligned depth frames

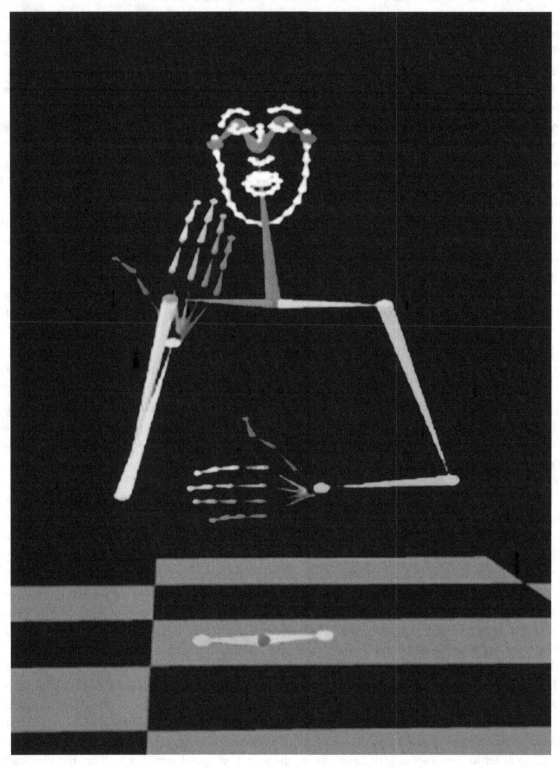

gulation procedure is then used to filter out incorrect detections. Images where severe occlusions exists are then labeled by reprojecting the triangulated 3D hand joints. The inclusion of the newly generated annotations in the training set, iteratively improves the detector, and thus, in each iteration we obtain more and more accurate detections. With this approach we generate geometrically consistent hand keypoint annotations using constraints from the multiple views as an external source of supervision. In this way, one can label images that are difficult or impossible to annotate due to occlusion.

In order to provide avatar playback, the keypoints extracted from the captured images have to be mapped to specific control points on the avatar. Using a 2D detection algorithm, we only get the values corresponding to the width and height of an image which is not appropriate for controlling a 3D avatar. Therefore, a technique to infer the depth dimension is required in order to construct 3D keypoints. It is more practical and reliable to use the aligned depth frames given by an RGB-D sensor over a multi-view 3D reconstruction solution. The process involves simply extracting the values from depth frames for each X and Y coordinate, and then merge all three values and store them in a single file.

Figure 8 shows how the 3D keypoints look if we draw them using OpenGL. The result shows that in the given frame, all keypoints were accurately detected without being affected by occlusions or noise. However, in most cases data from the detection process contain errors. This means that either some key-points are not detected by the algorithms, i.e., missing keypoints, or the algorithms produce erroneous values for some keypoints, i.e., mis-detections. The first case can occur due to occlusions by other body parts while the signer makes the gestures. For example, the gestures made for a certain sign might involve hiding some fingers behind the hand. When the acquired images are given to the detection algorithms, the keypoints of the hidden parts would not be detected. The second case can be encountered in the presence of noise. Such noise can be generated due to sensor specifications, room lighting conditions, or even colors of the clothes that the signer wears.

Noisy data can have negative effects when propagated in formated motion data. Most motion file formats follow a hierarchical structure under which the position of each body part is defined as an offset from the previous one. Thus, errors in joint detection will affect other joints in the hierarchy as well. It should be apparent that under such a scheme, even a single error occuring on a keypoint value might disturb the skeletal structure and motion greatly, and produce unwanted results when the motion file is imported for avatar playback.

A common form of side effects encountered in motion data is spikes. A spike is an extreme value in the signal, usually of short duration. In our case, its presence is mainly due to sensor accuracy in captur-ing certain movements/gestures (i.e., the depth/RGB alignment), and occurs especially in the outer-most skeletal joints. Spikes should be removed from the signal because they produce unnatural animation. For effective spike removal, we utilized a median filter. Moreover, motion capture data can be affected by jitter. Jitter refers to the shaking of skeletal data and is inherent to any motion detection system. Jitter can be effectively removed by using a smoothing filter. Our choice for effective smoothing is the moving average filter. Furthermore, speaking Sign Language heavily involves occlusions of different body parts, i.e., one hand hiding some joints. In these situations, missing values are recorded for the coordinates of the occluded joints. Currently, we have implemented a simple rule-based strategy using previous posi-tions and joint confidence levels for eliminating occlusions on upper body joints.

The EasyTV capturing module will finally output a number of different file types. These files are es-sential to other EasyTV services and modules. Examples are the realistic 3D avatar and the multilingual ontology. The files are initially uploaded to the crowdsourcing platform and then stored into repositories in order to be accessible by these services and modules. Below are some types of files that are exported by the capturing module.

- **Motion files:** These files contain the motion data generated in the detection phase of the capturing module. The selection of the right file format affects the simplicity in calculations when creating the file and the availability of solutions when importing it for avatar playback. For that reason, data is exported in C3D format which is the industry standard for motion capture applications. A C3D file contains only positional data, i.e., X, Y, Z values, and is composed of two sections: a header section and a data section. The former contains flags that describe the data, as well as, the labels for each marker, while the latter contains the actual 3D data that was recorded and also the residual values for the quality of the data. The benefit for choosing C3D is that it can be imported into applications such as Autodesk's MotionBuilder and used in the process of solving in order to provide realistic motion playback to the avatar. These procedures are described in the next session.
- **Image lists:** These are the RGB and depth images acquired by the RGB-D sensor. They are both written in PNG format and are aligned both in time and spatially.
- **Video files:** These are video files containing frames acquired by the RGB-D sensor. Only RGB videos are exported by the capturing module. The file format of choice is MP4. The videos are used in the validation phase of the crowdsourcing process by the moderator of the crowdsourcing platform, as well as in search options for database content retrieval.
- **Annotation file:** This is a text file containing annotations corresponding to a sign language recording session.
- **Visualisation files:** These are simple text files containing 3D positional data information and are used only for visualisation purposes.

3D Animation

The EasyTV project encompasses a novel architecture for providing signing avatar animation through a series of processing steps applied on motion capture data, eventually leading to crowdsourcing ready-to-play motion files (Figure 9). The first steps include the acquisition of RGB and depth images, the construction of 3D data from 2D keypoint detection algorithms, as well as, data filtering for motion refinement and exporting to an industry standard motion file format. These topics have already been discussed in detail in Section 3.1. After these steps complete, motion is retargeted to the EasyTV avatar to produce 3D animation. Although animation for the body and face is generated on the same 3D avatar, the two retargeting procedures are different. At the final step, animation data is exported in another industry standard file format, the FBX format, and uploaded to the crowdsourcing platform for later use by the EasyTV services and modules. Whenever necessary, the EasyTV avatar service can issue a request to the platform's repository and receive the required motion files in order to synthesize animation for translating TV content to Sign Language.

Animation requires motion to be encoded as translation, rotation, and scale values of a given object. As mentioned earlier in this work, a C3D file contains only positional data, i.e. translation values of markers (in our case, skeletal joints). Autodesk's MotionBuilder (MB) software offers the 'Flexible Mocap' pipeline with which a kinematic skeleton can be fitted to positional data within a C3D file. The first step is importing the C3D data to the current scene. Then, the animator has to place a generic 3D human model (MB's Actor) properly close to the corresponding keypoints in the scene (Figure 10). A

Figure 9. Architectural scheme for generating crowdsourced 3D animation for Sign Language in EasyTV

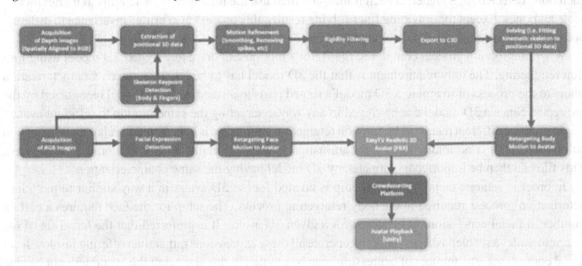

Figure 10. Solving using the Actor asset in Autodesk's MotionBuilder

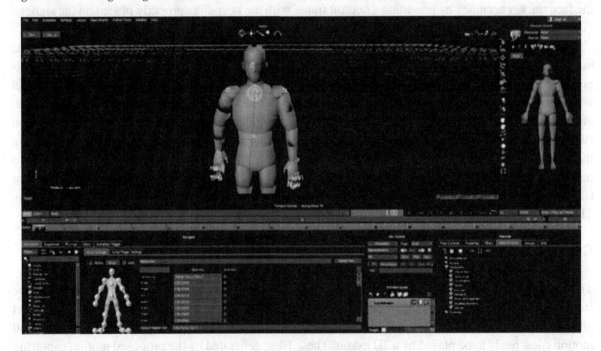

'markerset' is then created to map the Actor's body parts and fingers to the corresponding 3D keypoints. Finally, the solving process is executed to fit the constrained skeleton model to the 3D point cloud. The above process is executed just once. Solving to any other motion data of the same structure and scale is executed automatically (i.e., without the animator's intervention), using the same Actor model.

An extra step included in the EasyTV pipeline and necessary for achieving finer results in the solving process is rigidity filtering. In this step, a skeleton of fixed bone lengths is defined and serves as a reference for scaling the bone lengths captured for each signer. This is done by calculating the unit vectors for each bone detected for a signer, at each frame, and then use the reference bone lengths to hierarchically scale all bones. Except for providing finer solving results, this process also brings invariance to different body sizes of signers, as well as, camera distances.

When the solving process completes, the Actor's motion can drive any rigged 3D model using motion retargeting. The only requirement is that the 3D model has to be 'characterized'. Characterization refers to the process of mapping a 3D model's rigged parts to a standard body model recognized by the retargeter. Since a 3D model can be rigged in any way, retargeting the same motion to different avatars might produce different results. After motion retargeting, animation is baked onto the character's skeleton so that the Actor is no longer needed for animation playback. Finally, a FBX motion file is exported. This file can then be imported to animate any 3D model having the same characterization.

In order to retarget facial motion, a setup is created for the 3D avatar in a way similar to the 'characterization' process required in the body retargeting process. The setup for the face requires a certain number of facial expressions to be stored for a given 3D avatar. It is preferred that the facial rig of the avatar includes a set blendshapes that can generate all these expressions rather than offering just low level facial controllers. Any number of expressions can be omitted in this setup, but the avatar will not be able to reproduce them in the retargeting phase. For every signing session, facial tracking is applied on the RGB images and the motion of the eyes, brows, nose and mouth is extracted. It is important to enhance the face tracker accuracy by providing a neutral frame with the keypoints properly placed on the signer's face. Finally, the extracted motion can be retargeted to any avatar having the aforementioned setup.

Although the retargeted body motion can be exported in a FBX motion file without including the avatar, the same does not hold for face motion. This is due to an inability of MotionBuilder's FBX exporter to separately store blendshape/morph information without including the corresponding 3D model within the file. For that reason, the final output of the EasyTV animation pipeline are FBX files that also include the animated avatar (i.e., animation files) instead of just motion information (i.e., motion files). This raises a problem on space requirements for storing animation files, since each file containing the avatar model reaches approximately 80MB in size and is impractical for uploading and storing to a remote crowdsourcing repository. In order to resolve the issue, a low-spec version of the EasyTV avatar (i.e., without any assets) has been created especially for storing body and face animation information. This way, space requirements are reduced to ~10MB per file.

Crowdsourcing

The crowdsourcing platform that is described in this section is based on the work performed in the framework of the EasyTV project. The aim of this platform is the development of a web service that allows users around the world to upload signed videos, along with their corresponding annotations and motion files, ready to be played by a 3D avatar. These files, generated by the proposed motion capturing system, described in Section 3.1 are stored in a repository, linked with the crowdsourcing platform. The purpose of this repository is the creation of a sign language database that can constantly expand with new material, ultimately reaching sizes much bigger than any existing dataset. Additionally, the use of a multi-lingual ontology inside the crowdsourcing platform enables the translation of sign language across different languages. Finally, another aim of the crowdsourcing platform is to connect with a 3D avatar, feeding it with a multi-lingual vocabulary of sign language utterances.

Drawing upon the crowdsourcing paradigm (Crowdsourcing definition, n.d.), the development of the EasyTV Crowdsourcing Platform is based upon a generic micro-tasking framework that has been designed for providing infrastructure for crowdsourcing applications. The proposed crowdsourcing platform supports the secure login of two types of users, namely crowd-workers and moderators. The crowd-workers can interact with the platform from their web browsers by completing sign language tasks (i.e., upload of annotated signed videos and corresponding motion files), issued by the moderators. The moderators are allowed to launch and manage projects through a web Graphical User Interface (GUI) or from connected clients through an Application Programming Interface (API). The moderators can also evaluate the work performed by crowd-workers, leading to the approval of a sign language task and the storage of sign language files to the repository or the disapproval of a sign language task and a request towards the crowd-worker responsible for the task to make necessary changes.

The EasyTV Crowdsourcing Platform is designed in a way that aims to provide an intuitive User Interface (UI) for the creation, distribution and assessment of crowdsourcing tasks. More specifically the platform provides a number of functionalities targeting to facilitate the creation of an online sign language repository with the collaboration of crowd workers. For this purpose, the platform provides user interfaces that allow the creation and management of user profiles and web-based annotation tools for their participation in the sign language production procedures through their browser. The full realization of the pipeline is based on the integration of various EasyTV components, which take part in the sign language production communicating as presented in Figure 11. The outcome of the generated crowdsourcing content is intended to be made available back to the users in two main ways, by the multilingual sign language translations and retrievable 3D motion-data playable by animation engines.

Figure 11. The pipeline of the proposed crowdsourcing platform

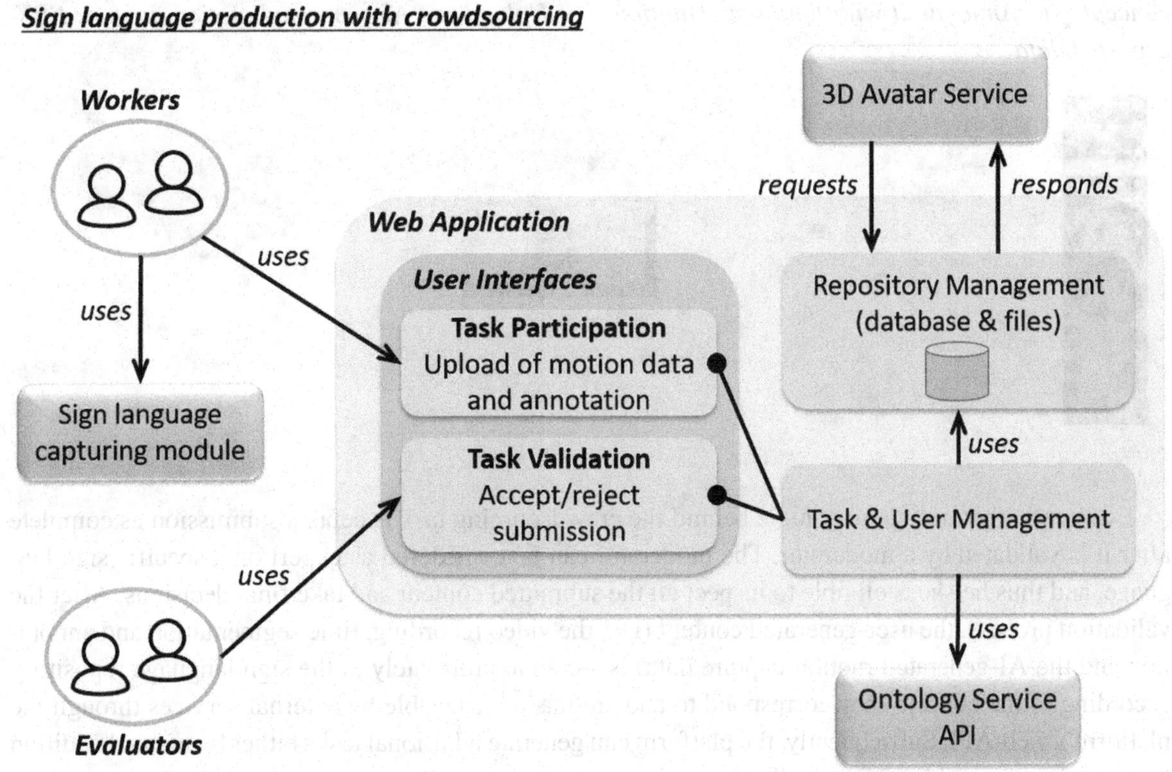

A typical scenario towards the completion of a crowdsourcing task is described below. At the end of a capturing session using the EasyTV sign language capturing module described earlier, a crowd-worker of sign language can sign in the crowdsourcing application and contribute with the produced content by participating in tasks or by introducing new sign languages concepts at will, thus expanding the sign language repository. The crowd-workers are prompted to complete a series of steps in order for their submission to be considered complete, otherwise the platform automatically tags the submission as a pending task and will present it to other registered users. Following the steps presented in the screenshots of Figure 12, the user is prompted to upload the appropriate video recording corresponding to a concept written in a certain natural language. In the second step, the platform redirects the user to a browser-based video-annotation tool and prompts her/him to annotate by selecting specific time segments in two different sentence orders: one corresponding to sign language order and the second to natural language order. These annotations are necessary since in the context of EasyTV project the crowdsourcing tasks are generating input for the enrichment of the EasyTV Sign Language Multilingual Ontology that creates connections between similar words in different languages, thus enabling the translation of sign language content from one language to another. The platform performs API requests to the Multilingual Ontology web-service with which properly formatted data (i.e., video-url and time-segmented annotations) are submitted in order to create a new record, or a new translation according to the type of the sign language task that is performed. In the third step, the user is prompted to upload the generated motion-capture data that correspond to the previous video recording in an appropriate format (i.e., MP4 for video and FBX for motion data) to make the data playable by popular animation engines.

Figure 12. Steps during completion of a crowdsourcing task – a) Upload a video for the sign language concept – b) Annotate it with time-segmentation – c) Upload the AI-generated motion-capture FBX-exported data

Eventually the management logic behind the crowdsourcing task accepts a submission as complete after it is validated by a moderator. The moderator can be considered as expert on a specific sign language, and thus he/she is eligible to inspect all the submitted content and take final decisions. After the validation process, the user-generated content (i.e., the video recording, time segmentation and annotation and the AI-generated motion-capture data) is stored appropriately in the sign language repository according to the concept they correspond to and are made retrievable by external services through the platform's web-API. Subsequently, the platform can generate additional tasks either by manual addition from moderators or by automatically registering tasks upon unmet concept search requests.

CONCLUSION

Overall, there is a critical need in deaf community for systems that can automatically, accurately and robustly capture, recognize and represent sign language that current systems does not fulfill. The lack of large publicly available datasets of sign language can be attributed to the need of manual annotation that can be very time consuming, as well as the variations in sign language from country to country. This problem has led researchers to the development of crowdsourcing platforms that can be used by millions of users around the globe to upload signed videos, along with their corresponding annotations. On the other hand, there is a trade-off in current sign language capturing systems between accuracy and affordability. RGB or depth sensors are affordable, but their accuracy is affected by finger and hand occlusions, while smart gloves can be costly but they can overcome the problem of occlusions.

As far as sign language recognition methodologies is concerned, deep learning-based approaches seem to produce really accurate results in the isolated sign language recognition task and promising results in the continuous sign language recognition task. The extraction of skeletal features from videos that are invariant to color and illumination changes and their use on deep learning networks currently seems to be the way towards more accurate and robust sign language recognition approaches, however there is still much work that can be done in this direction. Finally, current avatars face serious realism problems as a lot of work is required both towards improving the visualization part of the avatar (i.e., skin, clothes, textures, etc.) and towards the execution of the sign part of the avatar. The execution of the sign language from 3D avatars currently suffer from two limitations: a) the extracted skeletal finger joints are not really accurate especially when single RGB or depth sensors are employed and b) the transformation of the absolute positions of the skeletal joints in the 3D space to the motion file required by the avatar is very challenging. Novel AI-based approaches, like the ones presented in this chapter, have recently been developed to mitigate this problem with some success, but there is still room for improvements. To overcome the aforementioned avatar playback problems, there is also nowadays a tendency to design deep learning networks that can automatically produce synthesized signed videos based on given utterances, however this technology is not yet mature enough to produce accurate and robust results.

ACKNOWLEDGMENT

This work has been supported from the European Commission through the European project H2020-ICT-19-2016-2 "EasyTV: Easing the access of Europeans with disabilities to converging media and content" [grant number 761999].

REFERENCES

Advanced Realtime Tracking, A. R. T. (n.d.). Retrieved November 22, 2019, from https://ar-tracking.com/

Ahmed, M., Idrees, M., ul Abideen, Z., Mumtaz, R., & Khalique, S. (2016). Deaf talk using 3D animated sign language: A sign language interpreter using Microsoft's kinect v2. *2016 SAI Computing Conference (SAI)*, 330–335. 10.1109/SAI.2016.7556002

Al-khazraji, S., Berke, L., Kafle, S., Yeung, P., & Huenerfauth, M. (2018). Modeling the Speed and Timing of American Sign Language to Generate Realistic Animations. *Proceedings of the 20th International ACM SIGACCESS Conference on Computers and Accessibility*, 259–270. 10.1145/3234695.3236356

Alexanderson, S., & Beskow, J. (2015). Towards Fully Automated Motion Capture of Signs--Development and Evaluation of a Key Word Signing Avatar. *ACM Transactions on Accessible Computing*, 7(2), 7. doi:10.1145/2764918

Almeida, S. G. M., Guimarães, F. G., & Ramírez, J. A. (2014). Feature extraction in Brazilian Sign Language Recognition based on phonological structure and using RGB-D sensors. *Expert Systems with Applications*, 41(16), 7259–7271. doi:10.1016/j.eswa.2014.05.024

Basler AG – Industrial Camera Manufacturer. (n.d.). Retrieved November 22, 2019, from https://www.baslerweb.com/en/

Bigand, F., Prigent, E., & Braffort, A. (2019). Animating Virtual Signers: The Issue of Gestural Anonymization. *Proceedings of the 19th ACM International Conference on Intelligent Virtual Agents*, 252–255. 10.1145/3308532.3329410

Bouzid, Y., & Jemni, M. (2014). A Virtual Signer to Interpret SignWriting. In K. Miesenberger, D. Fels, D. Archambault, P. Pevnáz, & W. Zagler (Eds.), *Computers Helping People with Special Needs* (pp. 458–465). Cham: Springer International Publishing. doi:10.1007/978-3-319-08599-9_69

Braffort, A., Benchiheub, M.-F., & Berret, B. (2015). APLUS: a 3D Corpus of French Sign Language. *International ACM SIGACCESS Conference on Computers and Accessibility*. 10.1145/2700648.2811380

Callaham, J. (2015). *Kinect for Windows v2 sensor sales end, developers can use Xbox One version instead.* Retrieved November 22, 2019, from https://www.windowscentral.com/kinect-windows-v2-sensor-sales-end-developers-can-use-xbox-one-version

Camgoz, N. C., Hadfield, S., Koller, O., & Bowden, R. (2017, October). Subunets: End-to-end hand shape and continuous sign language recognition. In *2017 IEEE International Conference on Computer Vision (ICCV)* (pp. 3075-3084). IEEE. 10.1109/ICCV.2017.332

Cao, Z., Hidalgo, G., Simon, T., Wei, S. E., & Sheikh, Y. (2018). *OpenPose: realtime multi-person 2D pose estimation using Part Affinity Fields.* arXiv preprint arXiv:1812.08008

Cheok, M. J., Omar, Z., & Jaward, M. H. (2019). A review of hand gesture and sign language recognition techniques. *International Journal of Machine Learning and Cybernetics*, 10(1), 131–153. doi:10.100713042-017-0705-5

Content4All Project website. (n.d.). Retrieved November 22, 2019, from http://content4all-project.eu/

Crowdsourcing definition. (n.d.). Retrieved November 22, 2019, from https://searchcio.techtarget.com/definition/crowdsourcing

Cui, R., Liu, H., & Zhang, C. (2017). Recurrent convolutional neural networks for continuous sign language recognition by staged optimization. In *Proceedings of the IEEE Conference on Computer Vision and Pattern Recognition* (pp. 7361-7369). 10.1109/CVPR.2017.175

Cui, R., Liu, H., & Zhang, C. (2019). A Deep Neural Framework for Continuous Sign Language Recognition by Iterative Training. *IEEE Transactions on Multimedia, 21*(7), 1880–1891. doi:10.1109/TMM.2018.2889563

CyberGlove Systems LLC. (n.d.). Retrieved November 22, 2019, from http://www.cyberglovesystems.com/

Davidson, M. J. (2006). PAULA: A computer-based sign language tutor for hearing adults. *Intelligent Tutoring Systems 2006 Workshop on Teaching with Robots, Agents, and Natural Language Processing.*

De Amorim, C. C., Macêdo, D., & Zanchettin, C. (2019). *Spatial-Temporal Graph Convolutional Networks for Sign Language Recognition.* arXiv preprint arXiv:1901.11164

Dimitropoulos, K., Barmpoutis, P., Kitsikidis, A., & Grammalidis, N. (2016). Classification of multidimensional time-evolving data using histograms of grassmannian points. *IEEE Transactions on Circuits and Systems for Video Technology, 28*(4), 892–905. doi:10.1109/TCSVT.2016.2631719

Dimitropoulos, K., Tsalakanidou, F., Nikolopoulos, S., Kompatsiaris, I., Grammalidis, N., Manitsaris, S., ... Hadjileontiadis, L. (2018). A multimodal approach for the safeguarding and transmission of intangible cultural heritage: The case of i-Treasures. *IEEE Intelligent Systems, 33*(6), 3–16. doi:10.1109/MIS.2018.111144858

EasyTV Project website. (n.d.). Retrieved November 22, 2019, from https://easytvproject.eu/

Elliott, R., Glauert, J. R. W., Kennaway, J. R., & Marshall, I. (2000). The development of language processing support for the ViSiCAST project. *Annual ACM Conference on Assistive Technologies, Proceedings*, 101–108. 10.1145/354324.354349

Elliott, R., Glauert, J. R. W., Kennaway, J. R., Marshall, I., & Safar, E. (2008). Linguistic modelling and language-processing technologies for Avatar-based sign language presentation. *Universal Access in the Information Society, 6*(4), 375–391. doi:10.100710209-007-0102-z

Epikoinwnw Project. (n.d.). Retrieved November 22, 2019, from http://iti.gr/iti/projects/Επικοινωνώ.html

Fang, G., Gao, W., & Zhao, D. (2004). Large vocabulary sign language recognition based on fuzzy decision trees. *IEEE Transactions on Systems, Man, and Cybernetics. Part A, Systems and Humans, 34*(3), 305–314. doi:10.1109/TSMCA.2004.824852

Fang, H. S., Xie, S., Tai, Y. W., & Lu, C. (2017). Rmpe: Regional multi-person pose estimation. In *Proceedings of the IEEE International Conference on Computer Vision* (pp. 2334-2343). IEEE.

Ferreira, A. (2017). *Character Animation Using Sign Language Character Animation Using Sign Language*. Academic Press.

Fitbit Official Site for Activity Trackers and More. (n.d.). Retrieved November 22, 2019, from https://www.fitbit.com/eu/home

Gaus, Y. F. A., & Wong, F. (2012, February). Hidden Markov Model-based gesture recognition with overlapping hand-head/hand-hand estimated using kalman filter. In *2012 Third International Conference on Intelligent Systems Modelling and Simulation* (pp. 262-267). IEEE. 10.1109/ISMS.2012.67

Hanke, T. (2004). HamNoSys-representing sign language data in language resources and language processing contexts. *LREC, 4*, 1–6.

Heloir, A., & Nunnari, F. (2013). Towards an intuitive sign language animation authoring environment for the deaf. *Proceedings of the 2nd Workshop in Sign Language Translation and Avatar Technology.*

Huang, J., Zhou, W., Li, H., & Li, W. (2015, June). Sign language recognition using 3d convolutional neural networks. In 2015 IEEE international conference on multimedia and expo (ICME) (pp. 1-6). IEEE.

Huenerfauth, M. (2014). Learning to generate understandable animations of American Sign Language. *Proceedings of the 2nd Annual Effective Access Technologies Conference.*

Intel RealSense Depth and Tracking Cameras. (n.d.). Retrieved November 22, 2019, from https://realsense.intel.com/stereo/

Kaur, K., & Kumar, P. (2016). HamNoSys to SiGML conversion system for sign language automation. *Procedia Computer Science, 89*, 794–803. doi:10.1016/j.procs.2016.06.063

Kendon, A. (2004). *Gesture: Visible action as utterance.* Cambridge University Press. doi:10.1017/CBO9780511807572

Kim, J. S., Jang, W., & Bien, Z. (1996). A dynamic gesture recognition system for the Korean sign language (KSL). *IEEE Transactions on Systems, Man, and Cybernetics. Part B, Cybernetics, 26*(2), 354–359. doi:10.1109/3477.485888 PMID:18263039

Kipp, M., Heloir, A., & Nguyen, Q. (2011). Sign Language Avatars: Animation and Comprehensibility. In H. H. Vilhjálmsson, S. Kopp, S. Marsella, & K. R. Thórisson (Eds.), *Intelligent Virtual Agents* (pp. 113–126). Berlin: Springer Berlin Heidelberg. doi:10.1007/978-3-642-23974-8_13

Kipp, M., Nguyen, Q., Heloir, A., & Matthes, S. (2011). Assessing the Deaf User Perspective on Sign Language Avatars. *The Proceedings of the 13th International ACM SIGACCESS Conference on Computers and Accessibility*, 107–114. 10.1145/2049536.2049557

Kitsikidis, A., Dimitropoulos, K., Uğurca, D., Bayçay, C., Yilmaz, E., Tsalakanidou, F., ... Grammalidis, N. (2015, August). A game-like application for dance learning using a natural human computer interface. In *International Conference on Universal Access in Human-Computer Interaction* (pp. 472-482). Springer. 10.1007/978-3-319-20684-4_46

Koller, O., Forster, J., & Ney, H. (2015). Continuous sign language recognition: Towards large vocabulary statistical recognition systems handling multiple signers. *Computer Vision and Image Understanding, 141*, 108–125. doi:10.1016/j.cviu.2015.09.013

Koller, O., Zargaran, O., Ney, H., & Bowden, R. (2016). Deep sign: Hybrid CNN-HMM for continuous sign language recognition. *Proceedings of the British Machine Vision Conference 2016*. 10.5244/C.30.136

Koller, O., Zargaran, S., & Ney, H. (2017). Re-sign: Re-aligned end-to-end sequence modelling with deep recurrent CNN-HMMs. In *Proceedings of the IEEE Conference on Computer Vision and Pattern Recognition* (pp. 4297-4305). 10.1109/CVPR.2017.364

Kong, W. W., & Ranganath, S. (2008). Signing exact english (SEE): Modeling and recognition. *Pattern Recognition*, *41*(5), 1638–1652. doi:10.1016/j.patcog.2007.10.016

Konstantinidis, D., Dimitropoulos, K., & Daras, P. (2018, June). Sign language recognition based on hand and body skeletal data. In *2018-3DTV-Conference: The True Vision-Capture, Transmission and Display of 3D Video (3DTV-CON)* (pp. 1-4). IEEE. 10.1109/3DTV.2018.8478467

Konstantinidis, D., Dimitropoulos, K., & Daras, P. (2018, September). Skeleton-based action recognition based on deep learning and Grassmannian pyramids. In *2018 26th European Signal Processing Conference (EUSIPCO)* (pp. 2045-2049). IEEE. 10.23919/EUSIPCO.2018.8553163

Konstantinidis, D., Dimitropoulos, K., & Daras, P. (2018, October). A deep learning approach for analyzing video and skeletal features in sign language recognition. In *2018 IEEE International Conference on Imaging Systems and Techniques (IST)* (pp. 1-6). IEEE. 10.1109/IST.2018.8577085

Kosmidou, V. E., & Hadjileontiadis, L. J. (2009). Sign language recognition using intrinsic-mode sample entropy on sEMG and accelerometer data. *IEEE Transactions on Biomedical Engineering*, *56*(12), 2879–2890. doi:10.1109/TBME.2009.2013200 PMID:19174329

Kosmopoulos, D. I., Doulamis, A., & Doulamis, N. (2005, September). Gesture-based video summarization. In *IEEE International Conference on Image Processing 2005* (Vol. 3, pp. III-1220). IEEE. 10.1109/ICIP.2005.1530618

Kumar, P., Gauba, H., Roy, P. P., & Dogra, D. P. (2017). Coupled HMM-based multi-sensor data fusion for sign language recognition. *Pattern Recognition Letters*, *86*, 1–8. doi:10.1016/j.patrec.2016.12.004

Leap Motion. (n.d.). Retrieved November 22, 2019, from https://www.leapmotion.com/

Liang, R. H., & Ouhyoung, M. (1998, April). A real-time continuous gesture recognition system for sign language. In *Proceedings third IEEE international conference on automatic face and gesture recognition* (pp. 558-567). IEEE. 10.1109/AFGR.1998.671007

Lim, K. M., Tan, A. W., & Tan, S. C. (2016a). Block-based histogram of optical flow for isolated sign language recognition. *Journal of Visual Communication and Image Representation*, *40*, 538–545. doi:10.1016/j.jvcir.2016.07.020

Lim, K. M., Tan, A. W., & Tan, S. C. (2016b). A feature covariance matrix with serial particle filter for isolated sign language recognition. *Expert Systems with Applications*, *54*, 208–218. doi:10.1016/j.eswa.2016.01.047

Liu, T., Zhou, W., & Li, H. (2016, September). Sign language recognition with long short-term memory. In *2016 IEEE International Conference on Image Processing (ICIP)* (pp. 2871-2875). IEEE. 10.1109/ICIP.2016.7532884

Logitech - Webcams for Video Conferencing and Video Calling. (n.d.). Retrieved November 22, 2019, from https://www.logitech.com/en-us/video/webcams?filters=consumer

Maarif, H., Akmeliawati, R., & Gunawan, T. S. (2018). Survey on Language Processing Algorithm for Sign Language Synthesizer. *International Journal of Robotics and Mechatronics*, *4*(2), 39–48. doi:10.21535/ijrm.v4i2.1001

Malala, V. D., Prigent, E., Braffort, A., & Berret, B. (2018). Which Picture? A Methodology for the Evaluation of Sign Language Animation Understandability. In Multimodal Signals: Cognitive and Algorithmic Issues (pp. 83–93). Berlin: Springer Berlin Heidelberg.

Manus, V. R. | World's leading VR gloves for training. (n.d.). Retrieved November 22, 2019, from https://manus-vr.com/

Masood, S., Srivastava, A., Thuwal, H. C., & Ahmad, M. (2018). Real-time sign language gesture (word) recognition from video sequences using CNN and RNN. In *Intelligent Engineering Informatics* (pp. 623–632). Singapore: Springer. doi:10.1007/978-981-10-7566-7_63

McDonald, J., Wolfe, R., Schnepp, J., Hochgesang, J., Jamrozik, D. G., Stumbo, M., ... Thomas, F. (2016). An automated technique for real-time production of lifelike animations of American Sign Language. *Universal Access in the Information Society*, *15*(4), 551–566. doi:10.100710209-015-0407-2

Murtagh, I. E. (2019). *A Linguistically Motivated Computational Framework for Irish Sign Language*. Trinity College.

Nelson, D. (2009). Using a Signing Avatar as a Sign Language Research Tool. Academic Press.

Ni, X., Ding, G., Ni, X., Ni, X., Jing, Q., Ma, J., ... Huang, T. (2013, August). Signer-independent sign language recognition based on manifold and discriminative training. In *International Conference on Information Computing and Applications* (pp. 263-272). Springer. 10.1007/978-3-642-53932-9_26

Orbbec – Intelligent computing for everyone everywhere. (n.d.). Retrieved November 22, 2019, from https://orbbec3d.com

Papadogiorgaki, M., Grammalidis, N., Tzovaras, D., & Strintzis, M. G. (2005). Text-to-sign language synthesis tool. *2005 13th European Signal Processing Conference*, 1–4.

Psaltis, A., Apostolakis, K. C., Dimitropoulos, K., & Daras, P. (2017). Multimodal student engagement recognition in prosocial games. *IEEE Transactions on Games*, *10*(3), 292–303. doi:10.1109/TCIAIG.2017.2743341

Psaltis, A., Kaza, K., Stefanidis, K., Thermos, S., Apostolakis, K. C., Dimitropoulos, K., & Daras, P. (2016, October). Multimodal affective state recognition in serious games applications. In *2016 IEEE International Conference on Imaging Systems and Techniques (IST)* (pp. 435-439). IEEE. 10.1109/IST.2016.7738265

Punchimudiyanse, M. (2015). *3D Animation framework for sign language.* Academic Press.

Punchimudiyanse, M., & Meegama, R. G. N. (2015). 3D signing avatar for Sinhala Sign language. *2015 IEEE 10th International Conference on Industrial and Information Systems (ICIIS),* 290–295.

Rautaray, S. S., & Agrawal, A. (2011). A real time hand tracking system for interactive applications. *International Journal of Computers and Applications, 18*(6), 28–33. doi:10.5120/2287-2969

Ronchetti, F., Quiroga, F., Estrebou, C., Lanzarini, L., & Rosete, A. (2016). LSA64: A dataset of Argentinian sign language. *XX II Congreso Argentino de Ciencias de la Computación (CACIC).*

Simon, T., Joo, H., Matthews, I., & Sheikh, Y. (2017). Hand keypoint detection in single images using multiview bootstrapping. In *Proceedings of the IEEE conference on Computer Vision and Pattern Recognition* (pp. 1145-1153). IEEE. 10.1109/CVPR.2017.494

Smith, R., Morrissey, S., & Somers, H. (2010). *HCI for the Deaf community: Developing human-like avatars for sign language synthesis.* Academic Press.

Smith, R. G., & Nolan, B. (2016). Emotional facial expressions in synthesised sign language avatars: A manual evaluation. *Universal Access in the Information Society, 15*(4), 567–576. doi:10.100710209-015-0410-7

Starner, T., Weaver, J., & Pentland, A. (1998). Real-time american sign language recognition using desk and wearable computer based video. *IEEE Transactions on Pattern Analysis and Machine Intelligence, 20*(12), 1371–1375. doi:10.1109/34.735811

Sun, C., Zhang, T., & Xu, C. (2015). Latent support vector machine modeling for sign language recognition with Kinect. *ACM Transactions on Intelligent Systems and Technology, 6*(2), 20. doi:10.1145/2629481

Tanibata, N., Shimada, N., & Shirai, Y. (2002, May). Extraction of hand features for recognition of sign language words. In *International conference on vision interface* (pp. 391-398). Academic Press.

Uchida, T., Sumiyoshi, H., Miyazaki, T., Azuma, M., Umeda, S., Kato, N., ... Yamanouchi, Y. (2019). Systems for Supporting Deaf People in Viewing Sports Programs by Using Sign Language Animation Synthesis. *ITE Transactions on Media Technology and Applications, 7*(3), 126–133. doi:10.3169/mta.7.126

VICON | Award Winning Motion Capture Systems. (n.d.). Retrieved November 22, 2019, from https://www.vicon.com/

Vive | Discover Virtual Reality Beyond Imagination. (n.d.). Retrieved November 22, 2019, from https://www.vive.com/eu/

VRgluv | Force Feedback Haptic Gloves for VR Training. (n.d.). Retrieved November 22, 2019, from https://vrgluv.com/

Wang, H., Chai, X., Hong, X., Zhao, G., & Chen, X. (2016). Isolated sign language recognition with grassmann covariance matrices. *ACM Transactions on Accessible Computing, 8*(4), 14. doi:10.1145/2897735

Wei, S.-E., Ramakrishna, V., Kanade, T., & Sheikh, Y. (2016). Convolutional Pose Machines. *The IEEE Conference on Computer Vision and Pattern Recognition (CVPR).*

Xiu, Y., Li, J., Wang, H., Fang, Y., & Lu, C. (2018). *Pose flow: Efficient online pose tracking.* arXiv preprint arXiv:1802.00977

Yorganci, R., Kindiroglu, A. A., & Kose, H. (2016). Avatar-based Sign Language Training Interface for Primary School Education. *Workshop: Graphical and Robotic Embodied Agents for Therapeutic Systems.*

Zhang, X., Chen, X., Li, Y., Lantz, V., Wang, K., & Yang, J. (2011). A framework for hand gesture recognition based on accelerometer and EMG sensors. *IEEE Transactions on Systems, Man, and Cybernetics. Part A, Systems and Humans, 41*(6), 1064–1076. doi:10.1109/TSMCA.2011.2116004

Zhang, Z., & Huang, F. (2013, December). Hand tracking algorithm based on superpixels feature. In *2013 International Conference on Information Science and Cloud Computing Companion* (pp. 629-634). IEEE. 10.1109/ISCC-C.2013.77

Chapter 4
Digitizing the Intangible:
Machine Learning Applications Over Complex 3D Trajectories

Eftychios Protopapadakis
National Technical University of Athens, Greece

Ioannis Rallis
National Technical University of Athens, Athens, Greece

Nikolaos Bakalos
National Technical University of Athens, Athens, Greece

Maria Kaselimi
National Technical University of Athens, Athens, Greece

ABSTRACT

Modelling and digitizing performing arts through motion capturing interfaces is an important aspect for the analysis, processing, and documentation of intangible cultural heritage assets. This chapter provides a holistic description regarding the dance preservation topic by describing the capture approaches, efficient preprocessing techniques, and specific approaches for knowledge generation. Presented methodologies take under consideration the existing modelling and interpretation approaches, which may involve huge amounts of information, making them difficult to process, store, and analyze.

INTRODUCTION

In performing arts, such as dance, classical or contemporary, body signals, i.e. movements and gestures, are intentionally used to punctuate a storyline, in an aesthetically pleasing and thorough way. The observed kinesiology is a form of Intangible Cultural Heritage (ICH), directly connected to local culture and identity (Marolt et al., 2009). ICH preservation is of great interest to both the scientific and cultural communities, as well as, the general public. The most prominent challenges involved are associated with

DOI: 10.4018/978-1-5225-5294-9.ch004

the complex structure of ICH; i.e. its dynamic nature, the interactions among objects and environment, and emotional elements, e.g. dancers' expressions and style (Aristidou et al., 2015).

The preservation of folk dances is, nowadays, a basic requirement (A. D. Doulamis et al., 2017). The history and style of dance should become available to the public, through a system that includes descriptive information, videos, movement, and 3D modelled data relevant to it. Digital documentation of tangible and intangible heritage, data formats and standards, metadata and semantics, linked data, crowdsourcing and cloud, the use and reuse of data and copyright issues are some of the rising challenges in the field (Nikolaos Doulamis et al., 2017). However, prior to any of the above challenges the digitization of the information itself, i.e. moving patterns and tempo remains the main task.

Recent technological advancements, including ubiquitous mobile devices, pervasive video capturing sensors and software, increased camera and display resolutions, cloud storage solutions, and motion capture technologies, have unleashed tremendous possibilities in capturing, documenting and storing ICH content. However, utilizing the full potential of the massive, high-quality multimodal (text, image, video, 3D, mocap) ICH data is not an easy feat. Researchers need to appropriately adopt state-of-the-art techniques or invent new ones; multiple fields are involved as artificial intelligence (AI), computer vision, and image processing. Existing knowledge is essential for the ICH—in our case, dance—content's efficient and effective organization and management, fast indexing, browsing, and retrieval, but also semantic analysis, such as automatic recognition (Kosmopoulos et al., 2013; A. S. Voulodimos et al., 2012) and classification (N. D. Doulamis et al., 2010; A. Voulodimos et al., 2011).

Ever since the introduction of the first Kinect sensor, depth cameras were widely used as low-cost peripherals for several applications. Furthermore, the advent of motion sensing devices and depth cameras has boosted the fields of motion analysis and monitoring, including human tracking (N. Doulamis & Voulodimos, 2016; Lalos et al., 2014), action recognition (Kosmopoulos et al., 2010; A. S. Voulodimos et al., 2014), and pose estimation(Bakalos et al., 2019). The main advantage of a depth camera is that produces dense and reliable depth measurements, albeit over a limited range and offers balance in usability and cost.

These, relatively recent, advances in depth sensors lead to the development of low-cost 3D capturing systems, such as Microsoft Kinect (Zhang, 2012) or Intel RealSense (Keselman et al., 2017), and allowed for easy capturing of human skeleton joints in 3D space, which are then properly analyzed to extract dance kinematics (A. Voulodimos, Rallis, et al., 2018). Nevertheless, digitization does not guarantee preservation in the case of folklore performing arts. The documentation and the development of interactive frameworks, that enhances the learning procedure, or generate additional knowledge, is required; e.g. the creation serious game platforms, allowing the users to achieve a rich learning experience (Kitsikidis et al., 2015).

Machine learning (ML) algorithms provide multiple tools, capable to support multiple preservation tasks, e.g. evaluating and comparing users' movement, identifying the dances, or extracting the main steps. The purpose of an ML tool is to spatiotemporally analyze the captured 3D human joints (and the respective kinematic features of them) in order to identify the main choreographic patterns which are then compared against targeted dance motives. These ML tools support the creation of robust systems capable to identify primitive choreographic postures and be coupled with serious games platforms, as monitoring mechanisms that ensure the achievement of the serious games' learning goals.

The remainder of this book chapter is structured as follows: Section 2 briefly reviews the state of the art in the field; Section 3 describes the methodology employed for motion capturing, data preprocessing and feature extraction, while Section 4 presents the classifiers whose applicability for dance pose identification are explored; the related experimental evaluation is given in Section 5; and, finally, Section 6 concludes the chapter with a brief summary of presented work.

Related Work

The use of computer technology for folklore performing arts modeling and digitization has been recently studied in scientific literature. The works can be distinguished into multiple categories, including, but not limited to 3D digitization, labanotation, posture identification, dance recognition, serious games development, or any type of choreographic analysis.

One of the first approaches regarding 3D digitization of performing arts introduces a 3D archive system for Japanese traditional dances (Hisatomi et al., 2011). A digitization approach for Cypriot dances using the Phasespace Impulse X2 motion capture system is proposed in (Stavrakis et al., 2012). The architectures utilize eight cameras that are able to capture 3D motion on modulated LEDs. In (Kosmas Dimitropoulos et al., 2014), the capturing architecture schema of the i-Treasure European Union-funded project is analyzed targeting on 3D digitization and analysis of rare European folkloric dances.

The main limitation of the aforementioned approaches is that they require a marker capturing framework, while the capturing process fails to include choreographic metadata. The first limitation is addressed in (Zhang, 2012), where 3D wireframe skeleton structures are extracted based on a markerless interface, reducing however, the overall digitization accuracy. The second limitation is addressed in (Aristidou et al., 2015), where the captured motion trajectories are transformed into meaningful and semantically enriched LMA features.

As far as choreographic analysis is concerned, classification algorithms have been proposed in order to analyze the captured digitized 3D data and then to identify the human body kinesiology entities. More specifically, the work of (Masurelle et al., 2013) combines principal component analysis (PCA) and two classification schemes (specifically a Gaussian mixture and a hidden Markov model) for dance movement classification. Additionally, a combination of PCA and Fischer's linear discriminant analysis for classifying Korean pop dances is introduced in (Kim et al., 2017).

In this framework, style analysis algorithms have been proposed in (Aristidou et al., 2018), exploiting principles drawn from Labanotation. The method leverages knowledge from anatomy, kinesiology and psychology as that is incorporated in the Laban Movement Analysis. The work of (Laggis et al., 2017) introduces a markerless tracking system for motion trajectory identification. Another folklore dance pattern interpretation theme involving keyframe extraction and matching is presented by (Protopapadakis, Grammatikopoulou, et al., 2017a), while the work of (Raptis et al., 2011) proposes a real-time classification system in detecting choreographed gesture classes.

Recently, summarization methods have been introduced for a more precise and representative choreographic analysis. These methods are capable of abstractly modeling a folklore dance, and they are distinguished into two main categories. The first group spatially analyzes motion-captured features, while the second group relies on temporal fluctuations of the descriptors in order to extract the key choreographic postures.

As far as the first group is concerned, the work of (I. Rallis et al., 2017) introduces a key posture extraction framework, exploiting spatial classification algorithms, such as the k-means. Instead, the work of (A. Voulodimos, Doulamis, et al., 2018) performs selection of the main dancer's postures using temporal segmentation algorithms. In particular, the work of (Vögele et al., 2015) relies on a neighborhood graph to partition a dance sequence into distinct activities and motion primitives according to self-similar structures, while the work of (A. Voulodimos, Doulamis, et al., 2018) detects variations in the kinematic-based motion characteristics. The main limitation of a spatially based summarization algorithm is that temporal interrelationships of a dance are lost. On the contrary, temporal analysis algorithms are highly sensitive to noise and dancer's micro-movement variations.

The aforementioned drawbacks are addressed in (Ioannis Rallis, Doulamis, et al., 2018) where a spatiotemporally enriched summarization algorithm is considered. Spatiotemporal decomposition improves precision of extracting the main dance choreographic primitives. In particular, spatial clustering identifies major choreographic postures and temporal analysis identifies microchoreographic dancer's movements. Spatiotemporal hierarchical algorithms are also considered in (Zhou et al., 2013).

As regards Labanotation, several methods have been proposed in the literature for transforming the captured 3D motion into Laban scores. The work of (Hachimura & Nakamura, 2001) can be considered as one of the first approaches for automatic Labanotation. Recently, serious game platforms (Ballas et al., 2017; Ioannis Rallis, Langis, et al., 2018) have been proposed for providing a friendly interface for educational purposes. These interactive platforms have two forms of operations: to make the user familiar to the Laban scores and to provide an educational framework of folklore dances.

CAPTURING THE INTAGIBLE

Human motion capturing is a rapidly growing research area due to the large number of potential applications and its inherent complexity. Motion capture (MoCap) is the process of recording a live movement event to obtain a single 3D representation of the performance by translating it into usable mathematical terms and using a number of tracking key points in space over time (Wan Idris et al., 2019). In other words, MoCap refers to the technology of translating a live performance into a digital performance. In this section we describe the folk dances, used for the experiments, and the adopted capturing methodologies.

Folk Dances

Cultural expression, among many, includes fragile intangible live expressions, which involve knowledge and skills such as music, dance, singing, theatre, human skills and craftsmanship. These manifestations of human intelligence and creativeness constitute our Intangible Cultural Heritage (ICH), a basic factor of local cultural identity and a guaranty for sustainable development (K. Dimitropoulos et al., 2014). Folk dances are important to ICH; they are directly connected to local culture and identity (Shay & Sellers-Young, 2016).

Greek traditional dances were for centuries one of the most valuable and expressive cultural assets of Greek society. Through the ages, the side of traditional culture contributed decisively to maintaining of the national identity of the Greek nation, especially the difficult moments, as was the main means of expression of social and, to a certain extent, of religious events Greek population. In this chapter utilized data consider five dances and variations:

1. **Syrtos at three beats** is a Greek folklore dance in a slow three-beat rhythm. Syrtos (3-Beat) danced with small variants in Epirus, D. Macedonia, Thessaly, Central Greece, Peloponnese and elsewhere. In these regions, it constitutes one of the main dances of local repertoires. It is danced by men and women in an open cycle in all situations. The hand grip is with hands tied by palms, in W position,

sometimes common to the above position is hands only between the first and second, while the rest have their hands tied by palms with stretched elbows relaxed down. The musical tempo is at 3/ 4 beat. The motor pattern has 6 movements. (Gait in three)

2. **Syrtos at two beat (Pogonisios)** is a Greek folklore dance in a slow two-beat rhythm. It is danced by men and women in an open circle. It is danced in Pogoni region and in other regions of Epirus. The hand grip is palms with elbows stretched down or bent in position W. However, it is common the handle with arms in the arm position. In the past, the dance was performed separately by men and women, in one, two or more circles, but today this is not observed. The musical tempo is at 4/4 beat. The motor pattern has 6 movements. (Gait in both)

3. **Makedonikos** is a Greek folkloric dance, one of the most famous folklore dances in the whole Greece and one of the most basic dances of local repertories. It is danced by men and women in an open circle. The basic pattern of dance performed in twelve movements. The hand grip is with hands tied by palms, in W position, and sometimes is customary above the hand positions exist only between the first and second, while the rest have their hands tied by palms down. All over Greece, there are a lot of different songs accompanied the dance. The musical tempo is at 7/8 beat. The motor pattern has 12 movements. (Crosswise)

Figure 1.

Initial Posture (IP)	Left Leg Back (LLB)	Cross Legs (CL)	Cross Legs (CL)
Cross Legs (CL)	Initial Posture (IP)	Right Leg Back (RLB)	

4. **Trehatos** (Running) is a Greek folkloric circle dance performed by both men and women which is danced in the village Neochorouda of Thessaloniki. The kinetic tempo of the dance is composed of three different dance patterns. The first, which looks like the Syrtos in three, the second, which is once performed, and it is essentially the connecting mode of the first to the second pattern, and the third, which is characterized by strong kinetic activity. The grip of the hands in the first pattern is from the palms with the elbows in position W, while on the other two alternated up – down. The music tempo is at 7/8 beat. The motor pattern has 20 (10+10) movements. (Hops/Simple-complex steps) .

Figure 2.

5.   **Enteka** is a Greek folkloric dance performed by women and men by at a line. Enteka is a Greek folklore dance performed by both men and women. It is a very popular folklore dance in the large urban centres of Western Macedonia. It is danced freely in the streets as outbound carnival dance, but also around the carnival fires. The hands during the dance move freely or come in the middle. It consists of five main choreographic steps. The musical tempo is at 9/8 beat. The motor pattern has 8 (4+4) movements. (Hops).

Figure 3.

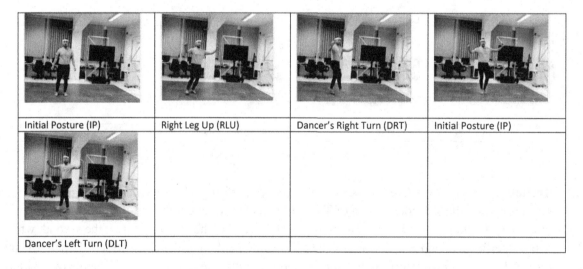

Initial Posture (IP)	Right Leg Up (RLU)	Dancer's Right Turn (DRT)	Initial Posture (IP)
Dancer's Left Turn (DLT)			

Capturing Tools

MoCap techniques can be marker-based or marker-less. The markers usually are small spheres or blobs. The purpose of these markers is to identify the parts of the human skeleton during performance of suitable motion sequences (Rallis et al. 2018). The images are normally recorded in infra-red light. Meanwhile the marker-less MoCap technique may track and recognize precisely the human motion and activities (Bakalos et al., 2019). The technique can provide a detailed representation of human shape and posture. MoCap tools as Vicon, Kinect, PhaseSpace and Xsens, have been used (Pfister et al., 2014) in applications such as gait analysis, rehabilitation, 3D animation and special effects in cinema.

The recent progress in digitization technology as regards tangible cultural assets and especially in the area of 3D virtual reconstruction, the e-documentation of intangible cultural assets is not yet evident, especially of folklore performing arts. This is mainly due to the complex multi-disciplinarily of the folklore performances which presents a series of challenges ranging from the choreography and the traditional/folk music to the digitization and computer vision to spatio-temporal (4D) dynamic modeling and virtual scene generation.

The Computer vision (CV) research field is a multi-disciplinary area with a variety of applications, both in science and industry. The common objectives of CV are the recognition and the pose estimation of the research object. In parallel, human motion capture is a discipline which nowadays gains popularity through the quick growth of the technology and the film industry. Due to, the necessity to animate the human body as consecutive sequences, the human body capturing systems are targeting to digitalizing the human movements. For this purpose, is adopted capture system that allows for mapping of the observed movements and kinematics variations.

Kinect sensors Vicon and Optitrack motion capture systems are the most recognizable trademarks and are adopted to our project as the tools for capture, analyze and reach out our project goals. Subsequently, many approaches to the digitalization of the Intangible Cultural Heritage are discussed. It is important to mention that this is an innovative project, which aims to act as a pioneering unified mechanism for ICH, but also patents, which has an added value to the deployable EU economy. The motion capture system is characterized by the sensor type, the scientific framework and the capturing space that is used. Figure 1 indicates the Kinect sensor used for extracting in real time constraints the 3D coordinators of the human skeleton of the dancers.

Kinect Sensor

Microsoft Kinect II was one of the most advanced motion sensing input devices that is available to the public. It is a physical device with depth sensing technology, built-in color camera, infrared (IR) emitter, and microphone array, which projects and captures an infrared pattern to estimate depth information. Based on the depth map data, the human skeleton joints are located and tracked via the Microsoft Kinect II for Windows SDK (*Kinect—Windows app development*, 2017). Figure 1 shows a snapshot of our experiment conducted.

More specifically, the Microsoft Kinect II sensor can achieve real-time 3D skeleton tracking, while at the same time it is relatively cheap and easy to setup and use. The tracked skeleton consists of twenty five joints with each one to include the 3D position coordinates, its rotation and a tracking state property: "Tracked", "Inferred", and "UnTracked" (Webb & Ashley, 2012). Moreover, the sensor can work in dark and bright environments and the capture frame rate is 30fps. On the other hand, there are some limitations that should be considered: it is designed to track the front side of the user and as a result the front and back side of the user cannot be distinguished, and that the movement area is limited (approximately 0.7–6 m).

Figure 4. The dance capturing process. Image on the left demonstrates the sensor position. On the right, we can see the dancer while acting.

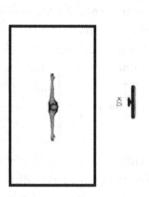 

VICON

VICON is a high-cost, motion-capturing system, which exploits markers attached on dancers' joints to extract motion variations and the trajectory of a choreography. The VICON motion-capturing system requires i) a properly equipped room of cameras and trackers, ii) experienced staff to manage the VICON devices, iii) a pre-capturing procedure, which is obligatory to calibrate the whole system.

The effectiveness of motion capturing systems depending on their system setup and is sensitive against variations, marker properties, optical projections, video-digital conversion, camera configuration, lens distortion, and calibration procedures. Typically, a set of spherical reflective markers are attached to the research object(s), i.e. the dancer(s). The reflective markers are tracked by several grayscale cameras, which are placed around the research area and via the Vicon software is calculating and calibrating the 3D position for each reflective marker. Figure 2 depicts the Vicon camera used in the experimentation framework of the third capturing process.

Data Sequences

Two type of sensors were used for the feature extraction: Kinect and VICON. Despite their differences (Table 1) both sensors provide similar information in many body joints.

Table 1. Key aspects of the employed motion captured techniques

Motion capture system	cost	Accuracy	Calibration	Camera resolution
Kinect	Low	Low	Simple	Low
Vicon	High	High	Difficult	High

In VICON implementation, ten Bonita B3 cameras were used, running the Nexus 1.8.5.61009h software. The movement area is 6.75 square meters. The origin of the Vicon coordinate system is the centre of the square surface. A wand with markers is used to calibrate the ten cameras. User body is measured by attaching 35 markers on it at fixed positions. After sticking all the markers, the height, weight and other specific anthropometric characteristics of the user are measured. The capture frame rate is around 100Hz.

A total of 10 cameras were used in our Vicon-based acquisition system to capture the dancer moving trajectory. In (Rallis et al., 2019) we present the topology of the markers used for capturing the motion properties of the dancer. The markers are exploited by the Vicon component for modelling the 3D dancer attributes so as to extract the joints. The recorded data from Vicon system is used to estimate a transformation matrix by a closed-form solution using unit quaternions. Based on this transformation matrix, a skeleton from the Vicon system is created.

In the following, let us denote as $\vec{J}_k^G = \left(x_i^G, y_i^G, z_i^G \right)$ the kth joint out of the N=35 extracted by the Vicon architecture. Variables x_i^G, y_i^G .and z_i^G .indicates the coordinates of the respective joint with respect to a reference coordination system of the Vicon. We assume that these joints have been obtained after a density-based filtering of the detected joints to remove possible noise from the acquisition process. Then, the center of mass of the dancer with respect to the Vicon coordination system can be obtained as:

$$\vec{C}_{cm} = \sum_{k=1}^{N} \frac{\vec{J}_k^G}{N}$$

The main problem of processing directly the joints $\vec{J}_k^G$, k=1,2,..,N is that the spatial positioning of the dancer affecting the joints properties and therefore the processing performance. To address the limitations of using the global Vicon coordination system, the joint attributes are transformed to a local coordinate system the center of which coincide with the center of mass of the dancer.

Figure 2 presents the approach adopted in this chapter to transform the global Vicon coordinates of the joints $\vec{J}_k^G$ into a local coordinate system. The adopted local coordinate system coincides with the center of mass of the dancer. Therefore, the captured skeleton coordinates is transformed with respect to the dancer movement, making them independent from the spatial location of the dancer. It should be mentioned that the local coordinate system is dynamically updated as the dancer is moving in the space throughout the capturing experiment.

It is clear that after the transformation to the local coordinate system, the properties of each of the N detected skeleton joints will be expressed as:

$$\vec{J}_k^L = \vec{J}_k^G - \vec{C}_{CM}$$

Regarding the Kinect capturing, the approach was less complicated. used a motion capture system using one Kinect II depth sensor and the ITGD module, developed within the i-Treasures project (K. Dimitropoulos et al., 2014) by UMONS. The ITGD module enables the user to record and annotate motion capture data received from a Kinect sensor.

Figure 5. Transformation of the Vicon global coordination system to a local one, the center of which coincides with the center of mass of the dancer. This is an important aspect of analysing the captured moving trajectory of the dance, since dancer spatial positioning is compensated.

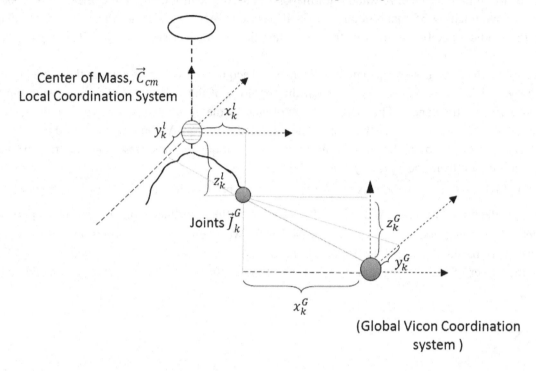

Figure 6. An example depicting 10 image frames of the "syrtos" dance by a dancer. In this figure, we have also depicted the skeleton as well as the joints extracted by the Vicon motion acquisition component.

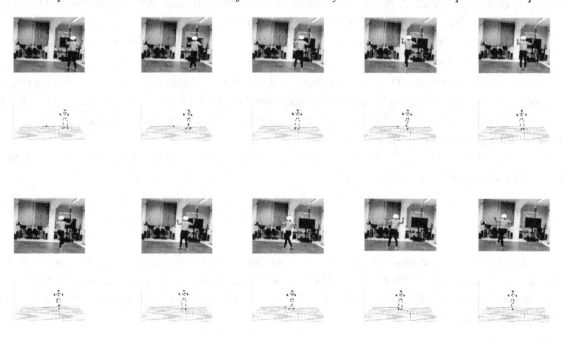

The recording process took place at the School of Physical Education and Sport Science of the Aristotle University of Thessaloniki. Six Greek traditional dances with a different degree of complexity were recorded. Each dance was performed by three dancers twice: The first time in a straight line and the second in a semi-circular curving line. Table 2 provides additional details on the captured dances.

Table 2. Captured dances duration, when Kinect sensor is used

Dance	Variation	Short name	Duration (frames)		
			D1	D2	D3
Enteka	Straight	Syrt_11_Str8	749	807	858
Kalamatianos	Circular	Kal_Circ	655	593	561
	Straight	Kal_Str8	304	378	455
Makedonitikos	Circular	Mak_Circ	424	582	409
	Straight	Mak_Str8	283	367	418
Syrtos 2	Circular	Syrt_2_Circ	608	543	352
	Straight	Syrt_2_Str8	623	639	334
Syrtos 3	Circular	Syrt_3_Circ	608	964	947
	Straight	Syrt_3_Str8	1366	678	511
Trehatos	Circular	Treh_Circ	991	723	443
	Straight	Treh_Str8	315	295	355

KNOWLEDGE EXTRACTION

Up to this point, we focused on capturing processes, dances description and generic preprocessing steps. Dance data, multimedia by nature, consists primarily of visual (image and video) ques. Analysis, classification and indexing of dance data depend significantly on our ability to recognize the relevant information in each of the data streams, and fuse it, so that the collective semantics of all parts will be consistent with the perception of the real world (Golshani et al., 2004). In this section we focus on how to utilize provided information, in a meaningful way, to be beneficial, any way possible. Some of the investigated scenarios involve: a) frame sequence summarization, b) dance identification and c) trajectories similarities.

Dance Summarization

An important aspect, during any dance analysis task, is the automatic extraction of the choreographic patterns. These elements provide an abstract representation of the semantics of the dance and encode the overall dance storytelling (Ioannis Rallis, Doulamis, et al., 2018). However, application of conventional video summarization algorithms on dance sequences cannot appropriately retrieve their choreographic patterns, since a dance is composed of an ordered set of sequential elements which are often repeated in time. Additionally, 3D geometry is lost using color information.

The duration, tempo and variation related to the performer are few, among many, factors, that should be dealt with, prior to do anything related to interpretation or preservation. Towards that direction, video summarization through identification and extraction of main key image frames is an important process in multimedia and computer graphics research. It allows fast content-based browsing, efficient indexing, storing in multimedia repositories and content-based retrieval (Nikolaos Doulamis & Doulamis, 2005). It is a content-based sampling procedure, where a set of image key frames are extracted for providing a meaningful abstraction of the video sequence, that is the choreography in our application scenario.

Figure 4 demonstrates how the summarization technique is applied. The concept lies in the consecutive utilization of SMRS algorithm (Vidal et al., 2012), until a converging criteria are met. The initial sequence is separated in smaller ones, then for each sub sequence the same approach is applied. Process terminates when no more sampling is feasible, given some threshold provided values or other, user defined, criteria are met. Figure 6 illustrates the keyframe extraction form a video sub-segment.

Figure 7. An example of the proposed hierarchical decomposition scheme

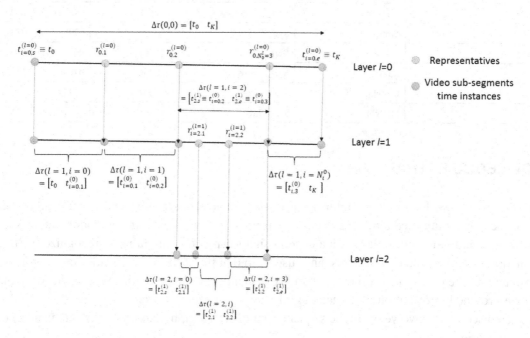

Dance Identification Using Body Postures

This section focuses on the evaluation of classification algorithms on Kinect-captured skeleton data from folkloric dance sequences for dance pose identification. We explore the applicability of raw skeleton data from a single low-cost sensor for determining dance genres through well-known classifiers by incorporating multiple pose identification schemes, temporal constraints, spatial information, and feature space distributions (Protopapadakis, Voulodimos, Doulamis, et al., 2018).

A three-step approach is adopted for the evaluation of dance pattern over traditional folk dances: the motion capturing, data preprocessing and feature extraction, and comparative evaluation among well-known classification techniques. In this case, dance trajectories were captured using a single Kinect sensor. Sensor's output were the position and the rotation of specific body joints, at a constant frame rate. The available information is processed to form low-level features which will support the dance recognition mechanism. The problem at hand, i.e. dance recognition, entails to a traditional multi-class classification problem. Given a frame, or sequence of frames, during the performance of a dancer, we would like to identify correctly the dance type.

Figure 8. Keyframe extraction from a video subsegment

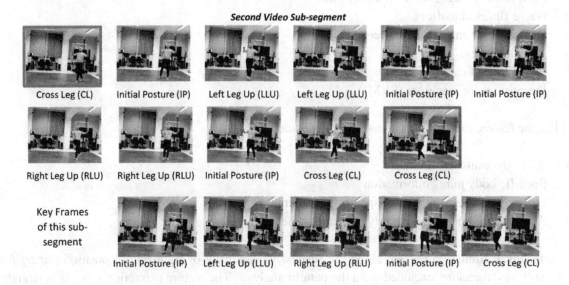

Identifying Key Postures

There are multiple sources of variation when investigating dance patterns: a) temporal variations or movement speed, related to the music tempo, b) dancer's body build variations and c) personalized interpretation of the steps. When building analytical predictive models for dance analysis, all possible sources of variation must be included. Crucial factors influencing the predictive performance of classification models, involve outliers, low quality features, and differences in the size of the classes. In our case three sampling approaches for the creation of an adequate train data set are employed: Temporal constrained, cluster based, and uniform feature space selection.

Temporal constrained selection breaks a dance sequence in consecutive clusters exploiting information as the fps rate of the motion tracking device. In each of the initially created clusters, a density-based approach, i.e. OPTICS algorithm output analysis, identifies possible outliers and representative samples. Since similar instances are likely to be clustered together, the few random samples from each cluster are expected to provide adequate information, over the entire data set. Exploitation of density based approaches for data selection has been used in many cases (Protopapadakis & Doulamis, 2014).

The classic KenStone algorithm is a uniform mapping algorithm; it yields a flat distribution of the data. It is a sequential method that uniformly covers the experimental region. The procedure consists of selecting, as the next sample (candidate object), the one that is most distant from those already selected (calibration objects). For initialization, one can select either the two observations that are most distant from each other, or preferably, the one closest to the mean.

Employed Classifiers and Feature Extraction

A set of well-known classifiers were applied to evaluate the detection rates:

a)   the k nearest neighbors (k.n) algorithm.
b)   Naive Bayes classifiers.
c)   Discriminant analysis classifiers.
d)   Decision trees.
e)   Ensembles of classifiers.
f)   Support vector machines (SVMs).

For the feature extraction four cases were considered:

a)   All body joints information
b)   Specific body joints information
c)   Difference in values between specified moments
d)   Application of a dimensionality reduction scheme

A technical limitation did not allow the successful capturing of right thumb position during few dances; it was, therefore, excluded from the pattern analysis. The feature extraction process is straight-forward. For any dance D_i, we have $24 \times 9 \times n$ values, or, in a 2D form, a $216 \times n$ matrix. Thus, each captured frame describes the entire body posture via 216 values. We decide to maintain the 99.1% of the initial feature space variance since the projection space was less than 1/9 of the original. However, the dance is not a static act; the time dimension should be also considered. Therefore, we utilized the information of consecutive frames, I_i and I_{i+1} by subtracting them. In the end, each dance, D_i, was of size $b \times (2m) \times n-1$. Prior to the dimensionality reduction via PCA step, data were normalized using min-max normalization. In the former case, i.e. single frame analysis, PCA resulted in 21 dimensions. For the latter case, i.e. 2 successive frames, we had 41 dimensions in the reduced space.

Experimental results provide various insights on a set of questions. If we investigate the results as a hole, i.e. the combined approach of all four factors (feature type, projection space, sampling, and clas-sifier), the Single-Frame, PCA projected, kmeans-random sampler, kNN classifier provides the best possible results (0.52) with a marginal mean significantly different from 167 different groups. However, if we investigate separately each factor, results vary greatly.

At first, using difference in values from consecutive frames does not provide enough information and, thus, cannot contribute to higher dance identification performance as shown in Figure 9. It is advised to either use difference in values between longer time intervals, e.g. 1 second or more.

Figure 9. F1 scores for different input feature setups

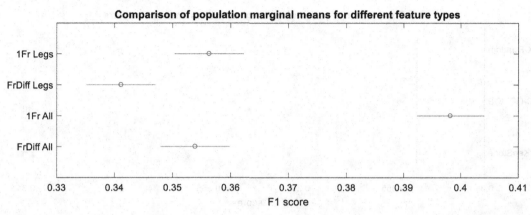

Secondly, using linear dimensionality reduction approaches does not benefits the classifiers outcomes. Even if dimensionality related problems are handled (Protopapadakis, Voulodimos, et al., 2017a), provided information does not suffice. Figure 9 demonstrates described case.

Figure 10. F1 scores for raw and projected data

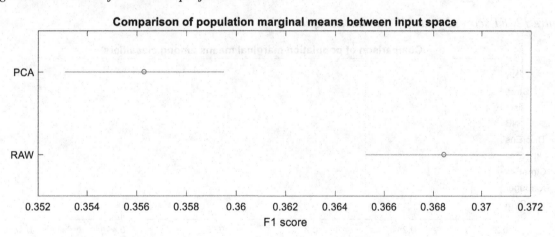

Thirdly, it appears that random selection over data clusters, provides the most appropriate training data samples. Figure 10 demonstrates the case. One should also mention that depending on the application scenario, the same sampling approaches can result in significantly different results (Protopapadakis, Voulodimos, & Doulamis, 2018a; Protopapadakis et al., 2019).

Figure 11. F1 scores for the employed samplers

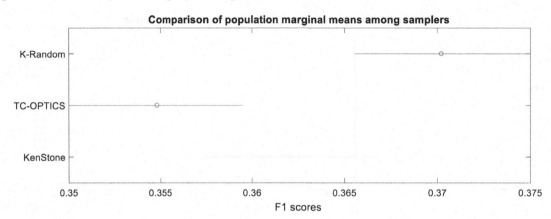

Lastly, regarding the selected classifiers, Random Forests (TreeBager) and the traditional *k*.N classifier performed better that the rest. Figure 10 demonstrates the outcomes. At this point, we should emphasize that the dance identification is hard to achieve by using single frames, or limited sequences of frames; most dances share the same basic postures (choreography).

Figure 12. F1 scores by classification technique

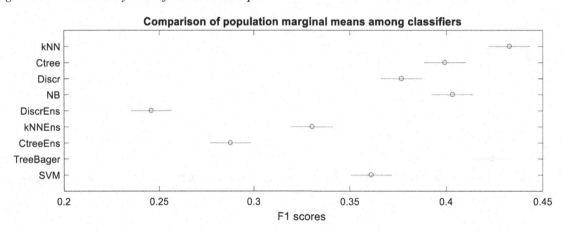

Posture Identification Using RGB Sequences

This section presents briefly a deep learning scheme for classification of dance postures using Kinect II RGB data and Convolutional Neural Networks (Bakalos et al., 2019). This is achieved through the analysis of a dataset that includes three traditional Greek dances, where each dance was performed by 3 different dancers. The obtained data were processed and analyzed using a deep convolutional neural network, in order to identify the primitive postures that comprise the choreography. To enhance the classification performance, a background subtraction framework was utilized, while the CNN architecture was adapted to simulate a moving average behavior. The overall system can be used as an AI module for assessing the performance of users in a serious game for learning traditional dance choreographies

The proposed framework consists of three main components. The first is responsible for the data acquisition. In this case Kinect-II sensor RGB data, not the skeletal data, are used. The second component is related with the background subtraction for noise reduction. The first two components are adopted as pre-processing stage (Data Input Layer) and function as input data to the CNN component. The third component is the CNN structure, modified to operate on a memory window. Additionally, the last component comprises the classification layer and the adjusted CNN. The final layer encompasses the evaluation procedure, taking as ground truth, the sequence of the professional dancer.

Step 1: Background Subtraction.

A Gaussian Mixture Model (GMM) creates the dancers' mask. This algorithm provides an accurate disunion of foreground and background information. Moreover, we do not use the BS simply to eliminate background noise, rather we use the foreground information, i.e. pixels assigned to the foreground class, as input data for the CNN. This step helps eliminating information not relevant with the choreography (e.g. dancer's attire, and background items).

The output of the background subtraction module can be seen in Figure 13, where the initial capture data (in RGB format) are transformed in two a black-and-white image of the same size keeping only the choreographic information of the dataset, i.e. foreground class of a dancer's captured data.

Figure 13. Background Subtraction Module

Step 2: Moving average behaviour.

The dynamic behaviour of a choreographic performance means that the classification of a primitive posture should be based on a cumulative behaviour over a time period, instead of relying only on the current measurable observations, in order to avoid having outliers in the input data, which in turn could trigger misclassifications. Moving average is often used with input data to smooth out short-term fluctuations and highlight mid and long-term trends.

Thus, to enhance the performance of the proposed system, the input to the proposed CNN should not be limited to a single frame, but rather to a set of q frames. This assumption is adopted and tested during the experimental validation of this chapter. The classification in the proposed CNN is performed in each frame individually.

Step 3: Defining the CNN architecture.

A set of parameterizable filters is convolved with the input data, selecting appropriate features and estimating kernel parameters. This process results in L feature maps, denoted as $f_1, f_2, \ldots, f_L$ that are in turn used as inputs in the classification layer. The convolutional layer employed in this chapter consists of two convolutional/pooling layers with a convolutional, ReLU and Max Pooling component. The first convolutional layer consists of 32 filters with a 5x5x3 filter size, while the second convolutional layer consists of 64 filters of 5x5x32 size. The stride of the convolutional layers is 1x1 while the max pooling stride is 2x2.

Finally, the classification layer uses the $f_1, f_2, \ldots, f_L$ feature maps and trigger the final (supervised) posture classification. The classification layer consists of on fully connected hidden layer with 64 neurons and one output layer of 8 output neurons. An overview of the CNN architecture can be seen in Figure 10.

Figure 14. The CNN Structure

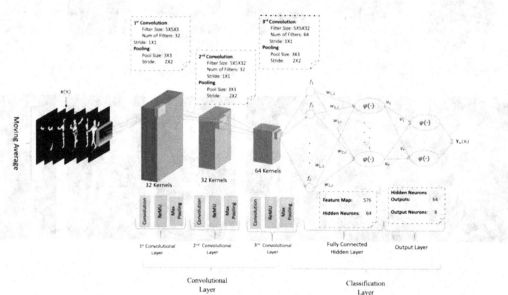

For the investigated dances, you may find bellow the choreography steps (key postures):

1. Syrtos in 3 beats: Initial Posture (IP), Cross Legs (CL), Initial Posture (IP), Left Leg Up (LLU), Initial Posture (IP), Right Leg Up (RLU)
2. Kalamatianos: Initial Posture (IP), Cross Legs (CL), Initial Posture (IP), Cross Legs (CL), Initial Posture (IP), Cross Legs (CL), Initial Posture (IP), Cross Legs (CL), Initial Posture (IP), Cross Legs, Backwards (CLB)
3. Makedonikos: Initial Posture (IP), Left Leg Back (LLB), Cross Legs (CL), Initial Posture (IP), Cross Legs (CL), Initial Posture (IP), Cross Legs (CL), Initial Posture (IP), Right Leg Back (RLB), Initial Posture (IP)

Figure 11 provides a further insight of the classifiers capability in distinguish among the postures, over all dances. These are average scores; they do not depict the detection capabilities per investigated case. Actually, a CNN which uses 30 past frames as input and background subtraction as a preprocessing step achieves more than 75% F1 score values.

Figure 15. Comparative Analysis of the performance of the tested classifiers

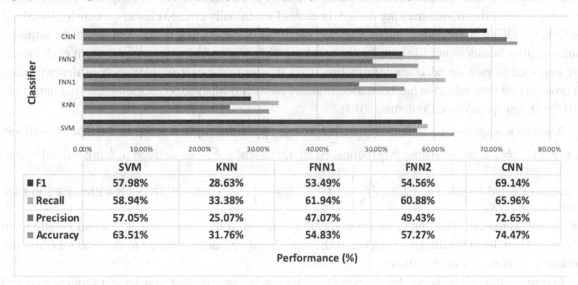

	SVM	KNN	FNN1	FNN2	CNN
■ F1	57.98%	28.63%	53.49%	54.56%	69.14%
■ Recall	58.94%	33.38%	61.94%	60.88%	65.96%
■ Precision	57.05%	25.07%	47.07%	49.43%	72.65%
■ Accuracy	63.51%	31.76%	54.83%	57.27%	74.47%

Performance (%)

Trajectories Interpretation

Dance sequences can be interpreted as multi-channel signals, containing information over dancer's joints' position and rotation (Ioannis Rallis et al., 2019). Therefore, any signal similarity technique, e.g. employing correlation measurements, can be used to match different signals. In this section, we consider two different approaches: representative keyframe matching using correlation scores and entire sequence matching using dynamic time wrapping.

Dance Similarities via Spatial and Temporal Embedding and Signal Analysis

The proposed approach consists of three steps: a) feature extraction, b) descriptive frames selection and c) similarity assessment. At first, a second-generation Kinect sensor is utilized to record dancers' performance. Secondly, the idea of spatial-temporal information management (A. Doulamis, Doulamis, et al., 2015; A. Doulamis, Soile, et al., 2015) is applied, so that recorded dance sequences are summarized to create keyframe sequences.

An iterative clustering scheme, imposing time constraints, is applied. Then, for each of the created data sets, keyframes are selected using density-based clustering. At the end, any dance sequence is reduced to a set of few steps. It is important to note that noise or tempo variations do not affect the proposed approach. Thirdly, the keyframe sequences, for different dances, are compared to each other. The sequences are signals containing information over dancer's joints' position and rotation. Signal similarity, employing the correlation measure is performed. Consequently, variations of the same dance can be easily identified, due to high similarity scores.

Extracting the Keyframes

Temporal constrained selection breaks a dance sequence in consecutive clusters exploiting information as the fps rate of the motion tracking device. In each of the initially created clusters, a density-based approach, i.e. OPTICS algorithm output analysis, identifies possible outliers and representative samples. Since similar instances are likely to be clustered together, the few random samples from each cluster are expected to provide adequate information, over the entire data set. Exploitation of density based approaches for data selection has been used in many cases (Protopapadakis, Grammatikopoulou, et al., 2017b; Protopapadakis & Doulamis, 2014).

Assume a sequence of frames $F_{d,t_d} = \left[f_1, \ldots, f_{t_d} \right]$. describing a dance, among the d available dances, i.e. $d=1,\ldots,d$ consisting o t_d frames. At first, sequence F_{d,t_d} .is divided in h predefined subsequences of equal length, i.e. $\left\{ f_1, \ldots, f_{\frac{t_d}{h}} \right\}, \left\{ f_{\frac{t_d}{h}+1}, \ldots, f_{2 \cdot \frac{t_d}{h}} \right\}, \ldots$ Then, OPTICS algorithm runs in each of the subsequences. The output of the algorithm is assessed by identifying peaks and creating sub clusters. Then, local maxima are selected as the representative frames, similar to the work of (Protopapadakis, Voulodimos, et al., 2017b).

Figure 12 illustrates the keyframe extraction approach. Assume that you have a sequence of 120 frames, which correspond to a duration of 4 seconds. Successive frames will have similar feature values and, thus, small distance scores among them. However, when dancer proceed to the next step, according to the choreography, feature values change significantly. That change is depicted as a peak. The representative samples are located somewhere between consecutive peaks.

Figure 16. Illustration of OPTICS outputs while assessing posture frames

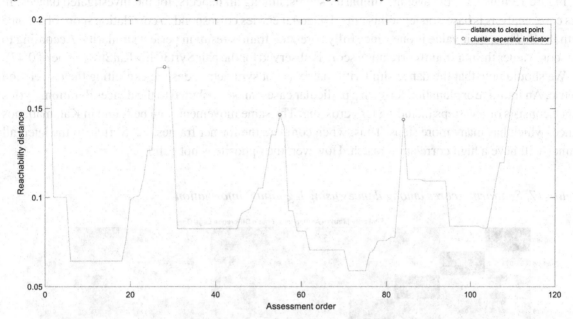

Signal Comparison

The outcome of keyframe extraction, as described above, summarizes a dance sequence F_{d,t_i} to a new sequence $F_{d,m}^{(R)} = \left[f_1^{(R)}, \ldots, f_m^{(R)} \right]$, $m \ll t_i$. Two sequences, e.g. $F_{d_1,m_1}^{(R)}$ and $F_{d_2,m_2}^{(R)}$ similarity can be assessed using the typical correlation score. Assume two random frames originated from two different dances, d_l and d_m denoted as $x = \left\{ f_i^{(R)} \right\}_{d_l}$ and $y = \left\{ f_j^{(R)} \right\}_{d_m}$ respectively. Both feature frames are of same length n. The correlation among these two is defined as:

$$r_{xy} = \frac{n \cdot \sum_{i=1}^{n} x_i \cdot y_i - \sum_{i=1}^{n} x_i \cdot \sum_{i=1}^{n} y_i}{\sqrt{n \cdot \sum_{i=1}^{n} x_i^2 - \left(\sum_{i=1}^{n} x_i \right)^2} \cdot \sqrt{n \cdot \sum_{i=1}^{n} y_i^2 - \left(\sum_{i=1}^{n} y_i \right)^2}}$$

Scores close to one indicate high similarity between observed vectors.

However, dances' duration varies significantly. As such, the overall correlation between two dances d_l and d_m is defined as:

$$C \left(d_l, d_m \right) = \frac{1}{m_1} \cdot \sum_{i=1}^{m_1} c_i$$

where c_i is the maximum correlation of frame $\left\{ f_i^{(R)} \right\}_{d_l}$ for all frames $\left\{ f_j^{(R)} \right\}_{d_m}$.

Figure 13 illustrates the average similarity scores, among all dancers, for the investigated dances. In this case, analysis is based on leg joints only. Diagonal entries correspond to correlation score of a dance with itself. Thus, their value is one, since fully corelated frames result in perfect similarity. According to the score values the minimum correlation score is observed for the pair Syrt3Circ-KalStr8 (value of 0.47).

We should note that the dance similarity matrix is not symmetric, despite exploiting the correlation metric. An intuitive explanation for such a pellicular case can be attributed to the dances duration. Syrtos dance consists of few steps including legs crossing. The same movements can be found in Kalamatianos dance, which has many more steps. Thus, when compare the former frames, i.e. Syrtos, to the later, all frames will have a high correlation match. However, the opposite is not valid.

Figure 17. Similarity scores among dances using leg joints' information

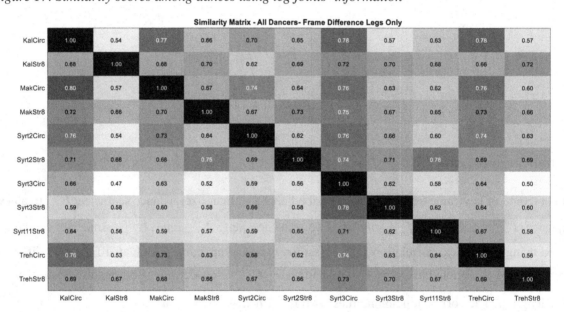

Matching Based on Dynamic Time Warping

DTW (Berndt & Clifford, 1994) calculates an optimal match between two temporal sequences, which may vary in speed. DTW generated matching path is based on linear matching but has specific conditions that need to be satisfied: the continuity condition, the boundary condition, and the monotonicity condition.

In the following a brief description on matching between curve points is provided. If N_1 and N_2 are the number of points in the two curves, the ith point of curve 1 and the jth point of curve 2 match if:

$$\frac{i-1}{N_1} \cdot N_2 \le j \le \frac{i}{N_1} \cdot N_2 \tag{1}$$

Figure 18. Moving trajectory of left foot joint, indicating the rhythm of the dance

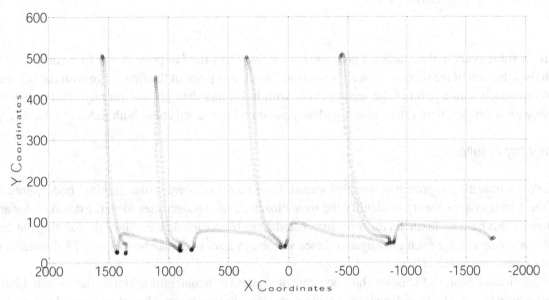

Figure 19. Performance illustration for the matching process

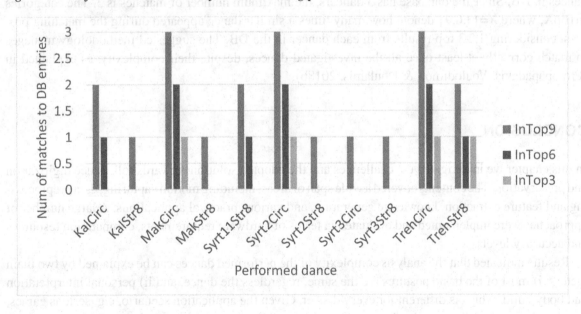

Please note that each point can match with no more than one point of the other curve. The boundary condition forces a match between the first points of the curves and a match between the last points of the curves.

The continuity condition decides how much the matching can differ from linear matching. This condition is the core of the Dynamic Time Warping. It was formulated as (Vuori et al., 2000):

$$\frac{N_2}{N_1} \cdot i - c \cdot N_2 \le j \le \frac{N_2}{N_1} \cdot i + c \cdot N_2 \qquad (2)$$

If, at some point in the matching process, it is decided that the i.th point of the first curve matches with the j.th point of the second curve, it is not possible for any point of the first curve with index greater than i to match with a point of the second curve with index less than j.th and for any point on the first curve with index less than i.th to match with any point on the second curve with index greater than j.

Similarity Analysis

The dance matching approach is straightforward. Given a set of points from multiple body joints, using the Vicon system, we try to identify the most closely related trajectories form the database for each dancer. In this case we maintain the top 3 matched dances from each dancer. Since the existing database contains 3 dancers, for each investigated dance we obtain a set of 9 matches. Figure 14 illustrates the joint movement over the floor.

Performance analysis focuses on how accurate the system is in matching correctly the recorded dance. In other words, we asked the dancer to execute a specific choreography. Then the recorded trajectory is subsampled in a ratio 1 to 4; that way the framerate matches the Kinect. Finally, we run the similarity tests with existing entries in the database.

Figure 15 illustrates the number of matches for each of the recorded dances using Vicon to the existing dances in DB. Since the database has 3 dancers, the maximum number of matches is 3. The categories InTopX, where $X=\{3.6.9\}$ denote how many times a similar dance appeared during the matching process, considering 1,2,3 top results from each dancer in the DB. The suggested methodology manages to match correctly at least once all the investigated dances, despite their complexity, as explained in (Protopapadakis, Voulodimos, & Doulamis, 2018b).

CONCLUSION

In this chapter we investigated the challenges and the adopted solutions towards folk dance digitization and preservation. The contents covered a wide span of areas, including motion capturing, data preprocessing and feature extraction, knowledge generation, and various practical applications. A large number of approaches were implemented and evaluated in terms of hardware requirements, computation resources and accuracy levels.

Results indicated that the analysis complexity of the performed dances can be explained by two main factors: i) most of the basic postures are the same, regardless the dance, and ii) personal interpretation and body build, which is different for every dancer. Given the application scenario, e.g. serious games, preservation, etc., researchers should consider too many different aspects during the development process.

ACKNOWLEDGMENT

This work is supported by the EU funded project TERPSICHORE "Transforming Intangible Folkloric Performing Arts into Tangible Choreographic Digital Objects", Grant agreement ID: 691218.

REFERENCES

Aristidou, A., Stavrakis, E., Charalambous, P., Chrysanthou, Y., & Himona, S. L. (2015). Folk Dance Evaluation Using Laban Movement Analysis. *Journal on Computing and Cultural Heritage, 8*(4), 20:1–20:19. doi:10.1145/2755566

Aristidou, A., Stavrakis, E., Papaefthimiou, M., Papagiannakis, G., & Chrysanthou, Y. (2018). Style-based motion analysis for dance composition. *The Visual Computer, 34*(12), 1725–1737. doi:10.100700371-017-1452-z

Bakalos, N., Rallis, I., Doulamis, N., Doulamis, A., Protopapadakis, E., & Voulodimos, A. (2019). Choreographic Pose Identification using Convolutional Neural Networks. *2019 11th International Conference on Virtual Worlds and Games for Serious Applications (VS-Games)*, 1–7. 10.1109/VS-Games.2019.8864522

Ballas, A., Santad, T., Sookhanaphibarn, K., & Choensawat, W. (2017). Game-based system for learning labanotation using Microsoft Kinect. *2017 IEEE 6th Global Conference on Consumer Electronics (GCCE)*, 1–3. 10.1109/GCCE.2017.8229481

Berndt, D. J., & Clifford, J. (1994). Using dynamic time warping to find patterns in time series. *KDD Workshop, 10*, 359–370.

Dimitropoulos, K., Manitsaris, S., Tsalakanidou, F., Nikolopoulos, S., Denby, B., Kork, S. A., … Grammalidis, N. (2014). Capturing the intangible an introduction to the i-Treasures project. *2014 International Conference on Computer Vision Theory and Applications (VISAPP), 2*, 773–781.

Dimitropoulos, K., Manitsaris, S., Tsalakanidou, F., Nikolopoulos, S., Denby, B., Kork, S. A., … Grammalidis, N. (2014). Capturing the intangible an introduction to the i-Treasures project. *2014 International Conference on Computer Vision Theory and Applications (VISAPP), 2*, 773–781.

Doulamis, A., Doulamis, N., Ioannidis, C., Chrysouli, C., Grammalidis, N., Dimitropoulos, K., … Ioannides, M. (2015). 5D modelling: An efficient approach for creating spatiotemporal predictive 3D maps of large-scale cultural resources. *ISPRS Annals of the Photogrammetry. Remote Sensing and Spatial Information Sciences, 2*(5), 61.

Doulamis, A., Soile, S., Doulamis, N., Chrisouli, C., Grammalidis, N., Dimitropoulos, K., . . . Ioannidis, C. (2015). Selective 4D modelling framework for spatial-temporal land information management system. *Third International Conference on Remote Sensing and Geoinformation of the Environment (RSCy2015), 9535*, 953506.

Doulamis, A. D., Voulodimos, A., Doulamis, N. D., Soile, S., & Lampropoulos, A. (2017). Transforming Intangible Folkloric Performing Arts into Tangible Choreographic Digital Objects: The Terpsichore Approach. *VISIGRAPP, 5*, 451–460.

Doulamis, N., Doulamis, A., Ioannidis, C., Klein, M., & Ioannides, M. (2017). Modelling of Static and Moving Objects: Digitizing Tangible and Intangible Cultural Heritage. In Mixed Reality and Gamification for Cultural Heritage (pp. 567–589). Springer. doi:10.1007/978-3-319-49607-8_23

Doulamis, N., & Doulamis, A. (2005). Non-sequential multiscale content-based video decomposition. *Signal Processing*, *85*(2), 325–356. doi:10.1016/j.sigpro.2004.10.004

Doulamis, N., & Voulodimos, A. (2016). FAST-MDL: Fast Adaptive Supervised Training of multi-layered deep learning models for consistent object tracking and classification. *2016 IEEE International Conference on Imaging Systems and Techniques (IST)*, 318–323. 10.1109/IST.2016.7738244

Doulamis, N. D., Voulodimos, A. S., Kosmopoulos, D. I., & Varvarigou, T. A. (2010). Enhanced Human Behavior Recognition Using HMM and Evaluative Rectification. *Proceedings of the First ACM International Workshop on Analysis and Retrieval of Tracked Events and Motion in Imagery Streams*, 39–44. 10.1145/1877868.1877880

Golshani, F., Vissicaro, P., & Park, Y. (2004). A Multimedia Information Repository for Cross Cultural Dance Studies. *Multimedia Tools and Applications*, *24*(2), 89–103. doi:10.1023/B:MTAP.0000036838.87602.71

Hachimura, K., & Nakamura, M. (2001). Method of generating coded description of human body motion from motion-captured data. *Proceedings 10th IEEE International Workshop on Robot and Human Interactive Communication. ROMAN 2001 (Cat. No.01TH8591)*, 122–127. 10.1109/ROMAN.2001.981889

Hisatomi, K., Katayama, M., Tomiyama, K., & Iwadate, Y. (2011). 3D Archive System for Traditional Performing Arts. *International Journal of Computer Vision*, *94*(1), 78–88. doi:10.100711263-011-0434-2

Keselman, L., Woodfill, J. I., Grunnet-Jepsen, A., & Bhowmik, A. (2017). Intel(R) RealSense(TM) Stereoscopic Depth Cameras. *2017 IEEE Conference on Computer Vision and Pattern Recognition Workshops (CVPRW)*, 1267–1276. 10.1109/CVPRW.2017.167

Kim, D., Kim, D.-H., & Kwak, K.-C. (2017). Classification of K-Pop Dance Movements Based on Skeleton Information Obtained by a Kinect Sensor. *Sensors (Basel)*, *17*(6), 1261. doi:10.339017061261 PMID:28587177

Kinect—Windows app development. (2017). https://developer.microsoft.com/en-us/windows/kinect

Kitsikidis, A., Dimitropoulos, K., Uğurca, D., Bayçay, C., Yilmaz, E., Tsalakanidou, F., ... Grammalidis, N. (2015). A Game-like Application for Dance Learning Using a Natural Human Computer Interface. In M. Antona & C. Stephanidis (Eds.), *Universal Access in Human-Computer Interaction. Access to Learning, Health and Well-Being* (pp. 472–482). Springer International Publishing. doi:10.1007/978-3-319-20684-4_46

Kosmopoulos, D. I., Voulodimos, A. S., & Doulamis, A. D. (2013). A System for Multicamera Task Recognition and Summarization for Structured Environments. *IEEE Transactions on Industrial Informatics*, *9*(1), 161–171. doi:10.1109/TII.2012.2212712

Kosmopoulos, D. I., Voulodimos, A. S., & Varvarigou, T. A. (2010). Robust Human Behavior Modeling from Multiple Cameras. *2010 20th International Conference on Pattern Recognition*, 3575–3578. 10.1109/ICPR.2010.872

Laggis, A., Doulamis, N., Protopapadakis, E., & Georgopoulos, A. (2017). A low-cost markerless tracking system for trajectory interpretation. *ISPRS International Workshop of 3D Virtual Reconstruction and Visualization of Complex Arhitectures, Nafplio,* 1–3. 10.5194/isprs-archives-XLII-2-W3-413-2017

Lalos, C., Voulodimos, A., Doulamis, A., & Varvarigou, T. (2014). Efficient tracking using a robust motion estimation technique. *Multimedia Tools and Applications, 69*(2), 277–292. doi:10.100711042-012-0994-3

Marolt, M., Vratanar, J. F., & Strle, G. (2009). Ethnomuse: Archiving folk music and dance culture. *IEEE EUROCON, 322–326,* 322–326. doi:10.1109/EURCON.2009.5167650

Masurelle, A., Essid, S., & Richard, G. (2013). Multimodal classification of dance movements using body joint trajectories and step sounds. *2013 14th International Workshop on Image Analysis for Multimedia Interactive Services (WIAMIS),* 1–4. 10.1109/WIAMIS.2013.6616151

Pfister, A., West, A. M., Bronner, S., & Noah, J. A. (2014). Comparative abilities of Microsoft Kinect and Vicon 3D motion capture for gait analysis. *Journal of Medical Engineering & Technology, 38*(5), 274–280. doi:10.3109/03091902.2014.909540 PMID:24878252

Protopapadakis, E., & Doulamis, A. (2014). Semi-Supervised Image Meta-Filtering Using Relevance Feedback in Cultural Heritage Applications. *International Journal of Heritage in the Digital Era, 3*(4), 613–627. doi:10.1260/2047-4970.3.4.613

Protopapadakis, E., Grammatikopoulou, A., Doulamis, A., & Grammalidis, N. (2017). Folk Dance Pattern Recognition Over Depth Images Acquired via Kinect Sensor. *3D ARCH-3D Virtual Reconstruction and Visualization of Complex Architectures.*

Protopapadakis, E., Niklis, D., Doumpos, M., Doulamis, A., & Zopounidis, C. (2019). Sample selection algorithms for credit risk modelling through data mining techniques. *Int. J. Data Mining, Modelling and Management, 11*(2), 103–128. doi:10.1504/IJDMMM.2019.10019369

Protopapadakis, E., Voulodimos, A., & Doulamis, A. (2018a). On the Impact of Labeled Sample Selection in Semisupervised Learning for Complex Visual Recognition Tasks. *Complexity, 2018,* 1–11. doi:10.1155/2018/6531203

Protopapadakis, E., Voulodimos, A., Doulamis, A., Camarinopoulos, S., Doulamis, N., & Miaoulis, G. (2018). Dance Pose Identification from Motion Capture Data: A Comparison of Classifiers. *Technologies, 6*(1), 31. doi:10.3390/technologies6010031

Protopapadakis, E., Voulodimos, A., Doulamis, A., Doulamis, N., Dres, D., & Bimpas, M. (2017a). Stacked autoencoders for outlier detection in over-the-horizon radar signals. *Computational Intelligence and Neuroscience, 2017,* 2017. doi:10.1155/2017/5891417 PMID:29312449

Protopapadakis, E., Voulodimos, A., Doulamis, A., Doulamis, N., Dres, D., & Bimpas, M. (2017b). *Stacked Autoencoders for Outlier Detection in Over-The-Horizon Radar Signals.* Academic Press.

Protopapadakis, E., Voulodimos, A., & Doulamis, N. (2018b). Multidimensional Trajectory Similarity Estimation via Spatial-Temporal Keyframe Selection and Signal Correlation Analysis. *Proceedings of the 11th PErvasive Technologies Related to Assistive Environments Conference,* 91–97. 10.1145/3197768.3201533

Rallis, I., Langis, A., Georgoulas, I., Vouldimos, A., Doulamis, N., & Doulamis, A. (2018). An Embodied Learning Game Using Kinect and Labanotation for Analysis and Visualization of Dance Kinesiology. *2018 10th International Conference on Virtual Worlds and Games for Serious Applications (VS-Games)*, 1–8. 10.1109/VS-Games.2018.8493410

Rallis, I., Doulamis, N., Doulamis, A., Vouldimos, A., & Vescoukis, V. (2018). Spatio-temporal summarization of dance choreographies. *Computers & Graphics, 73*, 88–101. doi:10.1016/j.cag.2018.04.003

Rallis, I., Georgoulas, I., Doulamis, N., Vouldimos, A., & Terzopoulos, P. (2017). Extraction of key postures from 3D human motion data for choreography summarization. *2017 9th International Conference on Virtual Worlds and Games for Serious Applications*, 94–101. 10.1109/VS-GAMES.2017.8056576

Rallis, I., Protopapadakis, E., Vouldimos, A., Doulamis, N., Doulamis, A., & Bardis, G. (2019). Choreographic Pattern Analysis from Heterogeneous Motion Capture Systems Using Dynamic Time Warping. *Technologies, 7*(3), 56. doi:10.3390/technologies7030056

Raptis, M., Kirovski, D., & Hoppe, H. (2011). Real-time classification of dance gestures from skeleton animation. *Proceedings of the 2011 ACM SIGGRAPH/Eurographics Symposium on Computer Animation*, 147–156. 10.1145/2019406.2019426

Shay, A., & Sellers-Young, B. (2016). *Dance and Ethnicity*. doi:10.1093/oxfordhb/9780199754281.013.38

Stavrakis, E., Aristidou, A., Savva, M., Himona, S. L., & Chrysanthou, Y. (2012). Digitization of Cypriot Folk Dances. In M. Ioannides, D. Fritsch, J. Leissner, R. Davies, F. Remondino, & R. Caffo (Eds.), *Progress in Cultural Heritage Preservation* (pp. 404–413). Springer. doi:10.1007/978-3-642-34234-9_41

Vidal, R., Sapiro, G., & Elhamifar, E. (2012). See all by looking at a few: Sparse modeling for finding representative objects. *2012 IEEE Conference on Computer Vision and Pattern Recognition*, 1600–1607.

Vögele, A., Krüger, B., & Klein, R. (2015). Efficient unsupervised temporal segmentation of human motion. *Proceedings of the ACM SIGGRAPH/Eurographics Symposium on Computer Animation*, 167–176.

Vouldimos, A., Doulamis, N., Doulamis, A., & Rallis, I. (2018). Kinematics-based Extraction of Salient 3D Human Motion Data for Summarization of Choreographic Sequences. *2018 24th International Conference on Pattern Recognition (ICPR)*, 3013–3018. 10.1109/ICPR.2018.8545078

Vouldimos, A., Kosmopoulos, D., Veres, G., Grabner, H., Van Gool, L., & Varvarigou, T. (2011). Online classification of visual tasks for industrial workflow monitoring. *Neural Networks, 24*(8), 852–860. doi:10.1016/j.neunet.2011.06.001 PMID:21757322

Vouldimos, A., Rallis, I., & Doulamis, N. (2018). Physics-based keyframe selection for human motion summarization. *Multimedia Tools and Applications*. doi:10.100711042-018-6935-z

Vouldimos, A. S., Doulamis, N. D., Kosmopoulos, D. I., & Varvarigou, T. A. (2012). Improving Multi-Camera Activity Recognition by Employing Neural Network Based Readjustment. *Applied Artificial Intelligence, 26*(1–2), 97–118. doi:10.1080/08839514.2012.629540

Vouldimos, A. S., Kosmopoulos, D. I., Doulamis, N. D., & Varvarigou, T. A. (2014). A top-down event-driven approach for concurrent activity recognition. *Multimedia Tools and Applications, 69*(2), 293–311. doi:10.100711042-012-0993-4

Vuori, V., Aksela, M., Laaksonen, J., Oja, E., & Kangas, J. (2000). Adaptive character recognizer for a hand-held device: Implementation and evaluation setup. *Proc. of the 7th IWFHR*, 13–22.

Wan Idris, W. M. R., Rafi, A., Bidin, A., Jamal, A. A., & Fadzli, S. A. (2019). A systematic survey of martial art using motion capture technologies: The importance of extrinsic feedback. *Multimedia Tools and Applications*, 78(8), 10113–10140. doi:10.100711042-018-6624-y

Webb, J., & Ashley, J. (2012). *Beginning Kinect Programming with the Microsoft Kinect SDK*. Apress. doi:10.1007/978-1-4302-4105-8

Zhang, Z. (2012). Microsoft Kinect Sensor and Its Effect. *IEEE MultiMedia*, 19(2), 4–10. doi:10.1109/MMUL.2012.24

Zhou, F., la Torre, F. D., & Hodgins, J. K. (2013). Hierarchical Aligned Cluster Analysis for Temporal Clustering of Human Motion. *IEEE Transactions on Pattern Analysis and Machine Intelligence*, 35(3), 582–596. doi:10.1109/TPAMI.2012.137 PMID:22732658

Chapter 5
An Overview on 3D Site Modelling in Civil Engineering

Muthuminal R.
Info Institute of Engineering, India

ABSTRACT

In past decades, for developing a site, engineers used the process of creating a scale model in order to determine their behaviour and to sketch the details collected manually using the drafting process, which behaves as a referring material during the construction of structures. Due to the boom in technology and limitations in drafting, the drawings have been digitized using computer-aided design (CAD) software as a two-dimensional structure (2D). Currently, these drawings are detailed as a three-dimensional structure (3D) that is briefly noted as 3D modelling. Three-dimensional site modelling is an active area that is involved in research and development of models in several fields that has been originated from the scale modelling. In this chapter, the topic 3D site modelling in civil engineering is discussed. First of all, the basic concepts of scale modelling, architectural modelling, and structural modelling are discussed. Then the concept of virtual-based 3D site modelling, its importance, benefits, and steps involved in site modelling are briefed.

INTRODUCTION

As all knows that Shelter is one among the basic needs of people to survive in this world, it leads to the development of shelter in the form of structures that is buildings. The development of buildings deals with the design, construction and maintenance of them which were carried out by the developers or engineers. The engineers usually communicate their ideas through their personalized language named Engineering Graphics. In the ancient history the structures were build by the creation of a scale model as a reference. Scale model is the one which was used to identify the behaviour of the structure initially. After which engineers spend numerous time to draft manual drawing using pencils, drafters, compass, protractors, triangular scales and other drawing devices. Since the hand drawings were time consuming and larger efforts were needed by the engineers to draft, computer program was evolved. In the late twentieth century the evolution of drawing occurred through the usage of computerized software. The

DOI: 10.4018/978-1-5225-5294-9.ch005

first and foremost computer program was Computer Aided Drafting and Design software (CADD) which was implemented by the usage of engineering graphics.

CAD system was easier and faster than manual drawing process and also it had capability to reduce the time period for the development of design. It also helped to reduce time consumption and the workload levied by the engineers. Drafting with the software had an advantage in storing the drawing electronically so that viewing; editing could be done directly at any time when it is necessary. Initially the drafting was done two dimensionally (2D) which also had a drawback in communicating. In order to build from the drafted drawing, an engineer must visualise the referral document for the purpose of constructing it which was an error prone area as it was very difficult to interpret the data. Two dimensional models had also drawback in designing. Hence due to these drawbacks the two dimensional models were evolved into a three dimensional model recently (Songer, Dickmann., & Al.Rasheed, 1998) (Zbigniew & Tomasz, 2014). In order to understand the concept of three dimensional models it is necessary to comprehend the basic concepts of models which are going to be discussed in the fore coming topics.

SCALE MODEL

The concept of three dimensional model was progressed from the basics of scale model. To express in simple words, Scale model is nothing but a miniature of an object which maintains exact relationship between all aspects of a model. This scale model usually helps in testing the behaviour or property of original object without directly demonstrating test over the original model. Toy cars, Madurai Meenakshi Amman Temple model, a scale replica model of demolished capitol theatre in Causeway Bay are some of the examples of a scale model. The Toy model in Figure 1 represents an example of a scale model.

Scale models are opted at many fields such as engineering, architecture, film industry, military field etc. Though each field used scale model for different purposes, the physical property and the principle was similar in all such types but the detail functional requirements may vary. To be a perfect scale model, the materials to be used must be the same as that of the original object in accordance to verify its behaviour in the outside world. From this concept several types has been emerged, among which the most important ones in civil engineering field are as follows.

- Architectural Scale Model
- Structural Scale Model

ARCHITECTURAL SCALE MODEL

Architectural model is one of the types of Scale model which was opted by the engineers. It was defined as the physical representation of a structure which was used to communicate design ideas, the aspects of the exterior view and the interior view of a structure. In other words, it is simply known as the miniature of a structure to be built. Models could be created by considering variety of scales depending over the purpose and the needs of the modeller. In the past the architectural scale model was developed using several materials whereas some of the models were produced as a readymade pieces or components such as people figurines, vehicle, furniture, and vegetation etc., Due to the emerging techniques and trends in the current scenario the architectural model could be provided as a rapid prototyping model that incorporates rapid prototyping techniques such as CNC routing, 3D printing which automatically build the models directly from the CAD design plans (Gibson, Kvan, & Ming, 2002). A township replica in Figure 2 represents an example of an architectural model.

Figure 1. Toy model that represents an example of a Scale model

Purpose of Architectural Model

Engineers and architects use architectural model for wide range of varieties which are as follows

- In accordance to learn about the relationship between the volumes, concepts during design process the sketch models or Adhoc models are used. In other simple words it is used in the discussion of design ideas between designers and consultants about the complicated design and unusual design to the builders.
- In order to showcase, visualize a final design the presentation models are used. For Example, Scale replicas of historical buildings in the museum are presentation models.

Figure 2. A township replica that represents an example of an Architectural Model

Scales Used in Architectural Model

Architectural models are designed at several smaller scale ratios which are as follows.

- 1:1 scale for Full size details
- 1:2 scale for details
- 1:5 scale for details
- 1:10 scale for interior design details
- 1:20 scale for interior design details
- 1:50 scale for interior spaces, detailed floor plan, different floor level
- 1:100 scale for building plan or layout details
- 1:500 scale for building site layout details
- 1:1000 scale for urban models
- 1:1250 scale for site plan details
- 1:2500 scale for site plans or city map details

Types of Architectural Model

There are several types of architectural models that are as follows

- **Exterior Models**
  It is one of the types of architectural models which shows the model of a building along with the exterior landscaping or the civic space around the building.

- **Interior Models**
  Interior models are the one that shows several details over the interior works done in the building (i.e.) the ceiling decorations, wall decorations, interior space filling using furniture, finishing works that include painting and beautification done through the usage of lightings.

- **Landscaping Design Models**
  These models are the one that represents the design and development of the surrounding using several feature such as vegetation patterns, beautification, small bridges, pergolas, walkways etc., In other words, landscaping design models usually represents public spaces and sometimes it may include buildings in it.

- **Urban Models**
  These are the one in which the models are built at a smaller scale typically starting from 1:500 and less, 1:700, 1:1000, 1:1200, 1:2000, 1:20000 that represents city blocks, large resort, campus, industrial facility and so on. This kind of model plays a vital role in the planning and development.

- **Engineering and Construction Models**
  Engineering and construction models are the one that represents isolated buildings / structural elements and components. In simple words, this is a model that represents details minutely in a single building.

STRUCTURAL SCALE MODEL

Structural scale model is the one which is widely used in the field of structural engineering. In this field many analytical and numerical techniques are used in appropriate to solve several field related problems. Certain problems are too complicated to be solved by these techniques; hence structural scale model is opted. In order to solve the problem, a scale model is constructed and tested for its behaviour. Figure 3 represents an example of a structural scale model.

From these kinds of techniques that are used over the past to represent the design ideas has now paved a new way in creation of a computerised 3D model from the evolution of 2D drafted or handmade drawings that helps the engineers to communicate their idea of design.

Figure 3. An Example of a structural scale model

Types of Structural Scale Model

The structural scale models are broadly classified into four major groups which are briefed as follows ("Autodesk Inc," 2014)

- **Components structural Model**
  This type of structural model involves the components of the building which are located above the ground level surface such as columns, beam, joints, etc., which are commonly known as super structure components

- **Sub assemblages Structural Model**
  Sub assemblages structural models are the one which indicates group of components at certain axis in accordance to calculate their behaviour under the action of loads. For example – Beam to Column to Slab.

- **Substructure Model**

  This is one of the types of structural scale model which includes the components that are situated below the ground level of the surface. Some of the sub structure components are foundation, frames etc.

- **Structural Model**

  This type of model deals with the whole structure that is the models which showcases buildings, bridges, space structures etc.

Scales Used in Structural Scale model

In the structural engineering scale models it is necessary to use specific quantities according to the theory of similitude in order to develop a structural model. These specific quantities are broadly classified into three major groups such as loading, geometry and material properties. The typically used geometry scales for the development of structural scale models under the loading condition is indicated in Table 1. (Harris, Sagnis, & Gajanan, 1999)

Table 1. Scales in Structural Scale Model

Components	Elastic models	Strength models
Buildings	1:25	1:10 – 1:3
Shells, Roofs	1:200 – 1:50	1:30 – 1:10
Bridges	1:25	1:20 – 1:4
Reactor vessels	1:100 – 1:50	1:20 – 1:4
Slabs	1:25	1:10 – 1:4
Dams	1:400	1:75
Wind effects	1:300 – 1:50	-

3D SITE MODELLING

From the outlook of scale model, the advancement of 2D drawing into 3D model occurred. Initially, the engineers used two dimensional drafting methods to communicate their view of design ideas. Since, it was time consuming and it required larger effort from the engineers, a change in the way of approach through the creation of 3D models came into existence. Three dimensional models have a capability to reduce the efforts made by an engineer and it also reduces the time consumption.

Now a day, 3D site modelling is an emerging trend to create a smart city (Jobst.& Dollner, 2008). In order to build a structure physically it is initially necessary to make the site suitable for it .3D site modelling is defined as virtually modelling the topographical surface into a perfect site which would be suitable for erecting a structure over it. Through the usage of 3D modelling technique it is easy to devoid the errors in design that overlaps over the other and helps to provide the design data as accurate as possible. Three dimensional models could be created using the software that opt the concept of building information modelling. Figure 4 represents the site which is virtually modelled.

Figure 4. Site which is virtually modelled

BUILDING INFORMATION MODELLING (BIM)

Three dimensional site modelling is carried out through the most intelligent 3D model based processor named building information modelling.BIM is defined as the process that involves management of digital representation of physical and functional characteristics of locations (Autodesk Inc. (2014a), (Autodesk Inc. (2014b). It is used by the professionals to efficiently plan, design, construct, maintain buildings and infrastructure such as water, refuse, electricity, gas, communication, utilities, roads, bridges, ports, tunnels, etc., Now a days, building information modelling is not only used for planning and designing phase of project alone but also for the processes such as cost management, construction management, project management and facility management.

Origin of BIM

In 1970, the concept of building information model came into existence (Eastman, Fisher, Lafue, Lividini, Stocker, & Yessios, 1974) (Eastman, Tiecholz, Sacks, & Liston, 2008). (Eastman, Tiecholz, Sacks, & Liston, 2011) but it was not so popular until the year of 2002. In 2002, Autodesk company released a white paper named Building Information Model and since then other software vendors started to show their involvement in this field. In the year 2003, Building information model was popularized as the common name for digital representation of a building process through the help of contributions from Autodesk, Bentley systems, Graphisoft and Jerry Laiserin (Laiserin, 2003)(Laiserin, in his foreword to Eastman, et al 2008). Among the developing applications, ArchiCAD by Laiserin is regarded as the most mature BIM solution on the market by 1987, as it was the first product on the personal computer able to create two dimensional and three dimensional geometry.

BIM in Construction Management

At present in the building process engineers are challenged to deliver successful projects inspite of tight budgets, limited manpower, accelerated schedules and limited or conflicting information. It is necessary for the designs such as architectural, structural, MEP to be well coordinated in order to avoid design errors (Smith, 2007). Hence, building information modelling helps in identifying the discrepancies in exact location at initial stage itself.

The concept of BIM helps in the virtual construction of facility prior to its original physical construction, in appropriate to reduce uncertainty, improve safety, workout problems, simulate and analyze potential impacts. Through the assembling of some systems offsite it will help to reduce the wastes onsite and the products could be delivered on just in time. By virtue of this concept, the quantity of material required, scope of work can be identified easily. It also has a capability of identifying clash detection in certain location which helps in the prevention of errors.

BIM in Facility Operation

Building information modelling helps in analysing information loss associated with handling a project from design team, construction team and building owner / operator. BIM allows each group to add certain details and to refer back the information that acquired from the building information model which benefits the owner or the operator. As a result of this any error occurrence could be identified at exact location before the physical development of the project and it could be redesigned without causing any major consequences.

BIM in Land Administration and Cadastre

Building information modelling potentially provides benefit in maintaining cadastral spaces in urban built environment. Its first benefit is that BIM offers visual communication of cadastral spaces. The rich amount of semantic information about the spaces in BIM could be used for identifying ownership, rights, responsibilities and restrictions. Also using BIM the data gathered in the land administration system could be converted into three dimensional digital, dynamic, interactive one (Atazadeh, Kalantari, Rajabifard, Ho, & N, 2016). This would help to unlock the value by creation of bridge between information and the interactive lifecycle and the management of buildings.

Future Potential of BIM

Building information modelling is a relatively new technology which faces a very slow change in the industrial field. But its followers believe that it will play a vital role in the revolution of development of environment.

Adopters claim that building information modelling offers

- Improved visualization
- Due to easy retrieval of information, it leads to improved productivity
- Increased coordination of building documents
- Information such as specific materials, quantities required, tendering, location details are linked for vendors.
- Minimise cost

The data needed for the analysis of building energy performance are available in building information modelling. Through the usage of BIM the input file could be automatically created through the usage of building properties. This will save greater amount of time and effort done by the engineers. The error occurrence in the design could also be reduced through the automation process and also the differences in the building energy simulation process. It also has a facility named walkthrough that enables the user to tour the model virtually along with the rendering effects.

LIST OF SOFTWARE THAT OPT BIM

In the field of construction there is several software that incorporates the Building information modelling process (Broquetas, 2010).

In the field of architectural works the software used are as follows.

- Autodesk Revit Architecture
- Graphisoft ArchiCAD
- Nemestschek Allplan Architecture
- Gehry Technologies – Digital project designer
- Nemetchel vectorworks Architect
- Bentley Architecture
- 4MSA IDEA Architectural Design (IntelliCAD)
- CADsoft Envisioneer
- Softtech Spirit
- RhinoBIM (BETA)

In the field of structural engineering works the software used are as follows

- Autodesk Revit Structure
- Bentley Structural Modeler
- Bentley RAM, STAAD and ProSteel

- Tekla Structures
- Cype CAD
- Graytec Advance Design
- Structuresoft Metal wood framer
- Nemetschek Scia
- 4MSA Strad and steel
- Autodesk Robot Structural analysis

In the field of Mechanical, Electrical and Plumbing (MEP) works the software used are as follows

- Autodesk Revit MEP
- Bentley Hevacomp Mechanical Designer
- 4MSA FineHVAC + FineLIFT + FineELEC + FineSANI
- Gehry Technologies – Digital Project MEP systems Routing
- CADMEP (CADduct / CADmech)

In the field of sustainability works the software used are as follows

- Autodesk Ecotect Analysis
- Autodesk Green building Studio
- Grphisoft EcoDesigner
- IES Solutions Virtual Environment VE-Pro
- Bentley Tas Simulator
- Bentley Hevacomp
- DesignBuilder

In the construction works the software used are as follows

- Autodesk Navisworks
- Solibri Model Checker
- Vico Office Suite
- Vela Field BIM
- Bentley ConstrucSim
- Tekla BIMSight
- Glue (by horizontal systems)
- Synchro Professional
- Innovaya

In the facility management work the software used are as follows

- Bentley Facilities
- FM: Systems FM: Interact
- Vintocon ArchiFM (For ArchiCAD)

- Onuma System
- EcoDomus

BENEFITS OF 3D MODELLING

There are several benefits in using 3D modelling in the construction field (Haymaker & Fischer, 2001). They are as follows

- Sensible, simple and speedy
- An illustration speaks thousand words
- Better for promoting and project approval
- Trouble-free remodelling and correction
- Impact on project implementation
- Boon for interior designers
- Measurements
- Precision and control
- Reduced time consumption
- Fewer instruction and no language barrier

Sensible, Simple and Speedy

It reduces the larger effort provided by the engineers to draft a design through the automated building material properties. This makes it a way faster way to complete a job and also it makes it a easier way to complete the job for the designers. Through the creation of virtual building it makes it easier for the consumers to understand the design in a realistic manner by the facility of virtual tour throughout the model of the building.

An Illustration Speaks Thousand Words

In accordance to understand the architectural two dimensional models, it takes a greater time period to interpret, visualize and communicate it to the contractors by the engineers. But through the three dimensional model, the imaginary design of the building could be simply visualized without any kind of barrier.

Better for Promoting and Project Approval

While comparing with two dimensional drawings, three dimensional models has larger advantage in showcasing the design. Through the three dimensional design it is easy to communicate the design without any problem in understanding the theme. Three dimensional images have a capability to remain in the consumer's mind for a longer period of time and hence the engineers stand a better chance of winning the customer. Similarly the project approval rate is also higher when compared to the two dimensional referral documents in the field of construction business.

Trouble-free Remodelling and Correction

In a three dimensional model, if the design is not upto the expectation it is easy to make minor and major changes in the model and view its appearance. Rather than making changes in the design of two dimensional model drawing it is easier to remodel the three dimensional model with lesser effort made by the engineers. Through this it also easier to determine the design errors made and to correct them.

Impact on Project Implementation

Construction engineers could complete the construction process at low cost and minimal time duration with a proper design plan. It has several impacts which are as follows.

- It helps in to get rid of field interferences
- Reduces rework
- Enhances prolifically
- Lesser demand for details
- Fewer change orders
- Lesser cost growth
- Minimise time period

Boon for Interior Designers

Through three dimensional modelling engineers could create a commercial flat or a residential building as a life like model with all the facilities such as furnitures, wall paints and designs, show cases, designer ceiling etc., so that the client could outlook the virtual view of the building.

Measurements

In a three dimensional designs, the exact dimensions of a building could be shown in a scale ratio. Thus the arrangements of the facilities inside the room could also be placed at certain required distance which helps in showing the room's space available and also its appearance. By this we could also avoid costly mistakes in the design since all types of designs are included in the three dimensional model such as exterior view, interior view, MEP etc., It also paves the way for the non engineers to see and adjust the arrangements based on their sizes to achieve varied objectives like space, movement problems, room size correction and so on.

Precision and Control

There is a recent trend called laser scanning which has a capability to collect accurate data on sites and also engineers can use such data to create models of real space. It is not necessary for architects and engineers to spend time in surveying the site to develop a precise model. This reduces occurrences of costly mistake by making engineers to notice the design issues or weakness of the structure in site as a virtual model before the physical construction of the building.

Reduced Time Consumption

In accordance to construct a building, engineers need to interpret the design drawing as a referral document. Engineers need to spend longer time and effort to visualize the details provided in the two dimensional drawing while comparing with the three dimensional virtual model. Three dimensional models could be easily understood even by the non engineers. Hence the time spend over the interpretation of drawing is reduced. Since the fault in the design could be avoided before the construction of the building, the time spend over the physical construction of them is also reduced.

Fewer Instructions and No Language Barrier

In a two dimensional design, it is necessary for the engineers to detail the drawing and to brief it to the contractors with a clear instruction to build it physically. 2D design has a greater disadvantage in communicating the design at the site. But, in a three dimensional design the clear instruction about the design is not necessary as it is easier for anyone to understand the three dimensional model through the virtual tour of the building model. In other words, the three dimensional model doesn't have any language barrier.

STEPS INVOLVED IN CREATION OF A 3D SITE MODEL

The three dimensional site model is developed through the following steps.

Step 1: Collection of source map of the site
Step 2: Creation of two dimensional drawing
Step 3: Importing the two dimensional site drawing into the BIM software
Step 4: Modification of two dimensional site drawing into a three dimensional site model
Step 5: Output is obtained in the form of three dimensional site model

Step 1

Usually the source map of the site is obtained from the Google earth application if only the source data is necessary and not an accurate source map along with the perfect contour coordinates is needed. In order to obtain accurate data of the site located in India along with the contour lines, it could be obtained from the database which is maintained by the survey of India. Initially the map could be obtained by the organizations only by paying for it. Recently, the datasheets over the topography of the site could be obtained freely from the website named soinakshe.uk.gov.in which is maintained by the department of survey of India. In this website the datasheets with standard data on shape, extent and geographical features of the country for the defence and civilian purpose is available.

Step 2

The datasheet which is collected from the website with the accurate survey data along with the contour coordinates of the site could be opened as a two dimensional drawing in the civil engineering software. For instance, the software used in this chapter is AutoCAD software which was developed by Autodesk

Company. In this software the two dimensional site map is opened as a DWG file format where the map could be edited into the required form along with the required data.

Step 3

The two dimensional site drawing obtained from the CAD software could be converted into a three dimensional site model by importing the DWG file into the BIM software such as Revit Architecture, Sketchup etc., The software which is opted for example is Revit Architecture and the process of importing the site map could be carried out through the option LinkCAD but while linking the site map it is necessary to keep the screen page at site floor plan in the project browser. The process involved in importing the drawing is shown in the following flow process.

The screenshot in figure 5 shows the process of importing site plan.

Figure 5. Process of Importing Site Plan

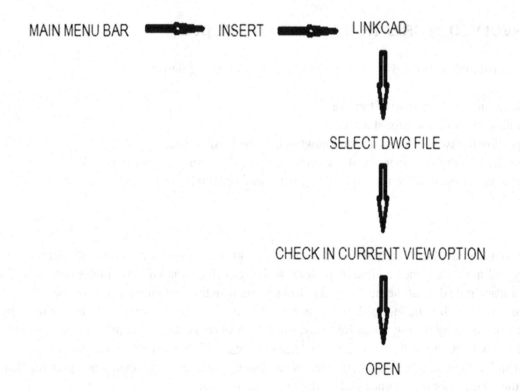

Step 4

After importing the site plan into Revit Architecture software the three dimensional site plan could be created using several ways. Initially in accordance to develop a site plan it is necessary to create an accurate topographical surface. This could be created through the following work process.

- If the contour coordinates of the site is given properly then the toposurface could be created from the massing and site option. At first, select massing and site option from the main menu bar and then click over the toposurface option. In that select modify / edit surface tab opens, at which use place points option and change the elevation accordingly, then place the contour lines to create the topography of the site as shown in the following work flow process
Massing and site toposurface Modify / edit surface
Place points option
Change Elevation
Place points at screen
Click OK

The screenshot in figure 6 represents the creation of toposurface.

Figure 6.

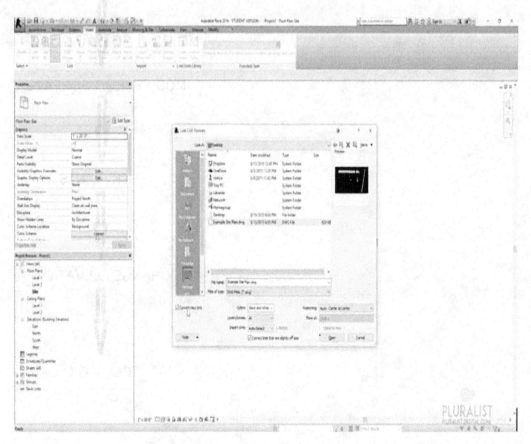

- After the creation of toposurface of the site, the three dimensional site model could be created as per the designer's idea / imagination. The site could be modelled as such it is suitable for creation of building over it through several options such as subregion, property line, site components, parking components and building pad. Once the site is modelled the building could be designed over it. Massing and site Subregion, Property line,
Site components,
Parking components,
Building pad.
Modify / edit surface
Select pick points
Click OK

The screenshot in figure 7 represents the creation of site.

Figure 7. Creation of Site

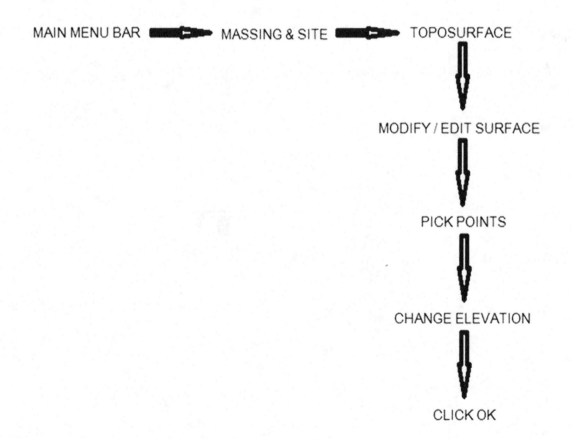

Step 5

The final output three dimensional site model could be viewed through the 3D view option and the step involved is shown in the following flow process.

Main Menu Bar View 3D view
Default 3D view
Camera
Walkthrough

In the Revit architecture, it has a facility to view the model through the virtual tour by the walkthrough option and also we can take the snapshot of the model through the camera option. The screenshot in figure 8 represents the three dimensional site model.

Figure 8. Three Dimensional Site model

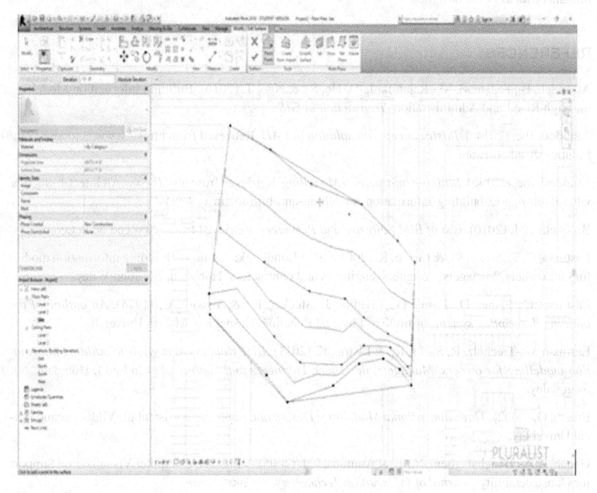

CONCLUSION

Software plays a vital role in all aspects of the daily life since it has a capability to perform a specific type of data processing for the completion of the task within the limited time period. In this chapter, it is clearly briefed about the development of the environment or the surroundings by the architects or engineers through the usage of computer programs. Through the usage of building information modelling process incorporating software the design ideas could be created sensibly in a realistic manner with the lesser effort provided by the designers. While considering the construction phase of the building in the site can be completed within the scheduled time duration, since the fault occurrence in the construction site could be avoided at the design phase itself and also the time required to produce the paperwork is shorter while comparing to the traditional workflow. Building information modelling allows for realization of the each and every project by the non engineers undoubtedly. But in working with the building information modelling it is necessary to choose the software carefully since it also has certain drawbacks such as it has several options to make the model realistic but it is important to choose only one option which would be suitable for the model by the designer. Hence the outcome of the model relays over the imaginary ideas of the designer.

REFERENCES

Atazadeh, B., Kalantari, M., Rajabifard, A., Ho, S., & Ngo, T. (2016). Building Information Modelling for High Rise Land Administration. *Transaction in GIS*.

Autodesk Inc. (2014a). *Basic concepts on solution in CAD*. Retrieved from https://www.autodesk.com/Solutions/Cad-software

Autodesk Inc. (2014b). *Building Information Modelling*. Retrieved from http://www.Architect-bim.com/what-is-bim-part2-building-information-modelling-and-bim-maturity-levels/

Broquetas, M. (2010). *List of BIM Software and Providers*. Retrieved from www.cad-addict.com

Eastman, C. T., Sacks, R., & Liston, K. (2008). BIM Handbook: A guide to building information modelling for owners, Managers, designers, engineers and contractors. Hoboken, NJ: John Wiley.

Eastman, C., Fisher, D., Lafue, G., Lividini, J., Stocker, D., & Yessios, C. (1974). *An outline of the building description system*. Institute of Physical Planning, Carnegie – Mellon University.

Eastman, C., Tiecholz, P., Sacks, R., & Liston, K. (2011). *BIM Handbook: A guide to building information modelling for owners, Managers, designers, engineers and contractors* (2nd ed.). Hoboken, NJ: John wiley.

Emem, O. (2002). *Three dimensional Modelling: Design and applications*. Istanbul: Yildiz Technological University.

Ganah, A.A., Bouchalaghem, N.M., & Anumba, C.J. (2005). VISCON: Computer Visualization Support for Constructability. *Journal of Information Technology in Construction*.

Gibson, I., Kvan, T., & Ming, L.W. (2002). *Rapid prototyping for Architectural Models.* doi:10.1108 / 13552540210420961

Harris, H., & Sagnis, G. (1999). *Structural Modelling and Experimental Techniques.* CRC Press LLC. doi:10.1201/9781420049589

Haymaker, J., & Fischer, M. (2001). *Challenges and Benefits of 4D Modelling on the Walt Disney Concert Hall Project.* Working paper No.64. Stanford University.

Jobst, M., & Dollner, J. (2008). 3D City Model Visualization with cartography-oriented design. REAL CORP 2008 Proceedings.

Laiserin, J. (2003). *The BIM Page.* Laiserin Letter.

Lewis, R. (1996). Generating 3D Building Models from 2D Architectural Plans (Master's Project). University of California, Berkeley, CA.

Shreyl, S., & Atub, K. (2007). 3D and 4D Modelling for Design and Construction Coordination: Issues and lessons learned. Academic Press.

Smith, D. (2007). An Introduction to Building Information Modelling. *Journal of Building Information Modelling.*

Songer, A. D., Dickmann, J., & Al Rasheed, K. (1998). The Impact of 3D Visualization on construction planning. In *Proceedings of the international congress on computing in civil engineering.* ASCE.

Zbigniew, K., & Tomasz, K. (2014). Building Information Modelling- 4D Modelling Technology on the example of the reconstruction of stairwell. Academic Press.

Section 2
Advances in 3D Reconstruction

Chapter 6
Emerging Trends in 3D Image Reconstruction and Modeling:
3D Construction From Multiple Images

Parimala Boobalan

Vellore Institute of Technology, India

ABSTRACT

In recent years, there is a demand for 3D content for computer graphics, communications, and virtual reality. 3D modelling is an emerging topic that is applied in so many real-world applications. The images are taken through camera at multiple angles and medical imaging techniques like CT scan and MRI are also used. From a set of images, intersection of these projection rays is considered to be the position for 3D point. This chapter discusses the construction of 3D images from multiple objects. Various approaches used for construction, triangulation method, challenges in building this model, and the application of 3D models are explained in this chapter.

INTRODUCTION

There is an essential need for generating 3D models from multiple images in movie industry, gaming and in mapping. Creating a three dimensional model from group of images is called 3D construction from multiple images. When an image is projected from a 3D scene onto a 2D view, the depth of the image is lost. To perform this reverse process of obtaining 2D from 3D images, image point for a specific images ie., line of sight has to be found. But it is impossible to determine which point is the line of sight for a specific image. If two images are present then the intersection of two projections is found to be the position of 3D point. The process used to find this intersection of projection is called as triangulation. The important task for this process is to find the relation between multiple views which delivers the information that corresponds to set of points that contain the structure related to poses and calibration of the camera.

The significance of 3D images is highly visible in computer graphics, virtual reality and communications. The traditional system that is used for constructing 3D images results in high cost and cannot

DOI: 10.4018/978-1-5225-5294-9.ch006

satisfy the need of new application. This gap is filled with the use of digital mapping facilities. Recently, various approaches are developed to extract three dimensional images from sequence of images.

The sequence of processing steps involved in converting multiple 2D images into 3D model is as follows.

(i)   Depth determination: This step involves in finding the missing depth component from any 3D image. The matching position of two images can then be triangulated in 3D space. Finding this matching position is the biggest challenge in depth determination.

(ii)   Registration: Multiple depth maps are combined and final mesh is created by calculating the depth and projection out of camera.

(iii) Material Application: This step involves in applying the colour from original photographs to the mesh.

In late decades, there is an important urge for 3D content for personal digital assistant graphics, virtual reality and communication, triggering a need in elaboration for the requirements. Many current systems for constructing 3D models are built over specialized hardware (e.g. audio sound system) bring about a steep cost, which cannot answer the specification of new applications. This defoliated area stimulates the act mutually regard to digital imaging facilities (like a camera). Moore's law furthermore tells us that more fields can be done in software. Affine factorization approach is used to recognize 3D from image sequences. However, the chief ingredient of orthographic outlook is an important limitation about system.

The difficulty of converting multiple 2D images into 3D model consists of a chain of processing steps. Autocalibration or self-calibration is an traditional approach, in which camera proposition and parameters are recovered sooner, for rigidity, then structure is well calculated. Two methods implementing this subject are presented as follows, Kruppa equations and Mendonca and cipolla. Another way of doing Startification consists of Projective reconstruction, Afffine reconstruction and Euclidean reconstruction. The concept of 3D models has been a popular research topic earlier for a long time now, and important advance has literally been made as a result of the early days. Nonetheless, the research society is well observant of the specific that still for all practical purposes remains subsequent done.

There is a wide variety of techniques for creating 3D models, but limited to the geometry and material characteristics of the object or scene, a well-known technique may be much better qualified than another. For concrete illustration, untextured objects are illusion for traditional stereo, but too much texture may interfere by the whole patterns of structured-light techniques. Hence, a well-known method can be developed to deal with the variability of objects — e.g., in a museum — to be modeled. As a case of picture, having to model the realized collections of different museums is a useful investigation aspect to visualize about, as it poses large amount of the unanswered challenges, constantly all at once. Another trend is 3D city modeling, which has all of a sudden grown in importance everywhere the last years. It is another extreme in terms of demand under which report have to be captured, in that cities describe an absolutely uncontrolled and considerable environment. Also in that application aspect, multiple problems remain to be resolved.

Given the above considerations, the 3D reconstruction of shapes from infinite, uncalibrated images are one of the practically promising 3D acquisition techniques. In terms of taxonomy of techniques, self-calibrating structure-from-motion is a passive, multi-vantage point strategy. It offers valuable degrees of power in that one can easily move a camera around an object or scene. Most people have a camera and recognize how to handle it. Objects or scenes can be small or large, assuming that the optics and the approach of camera motion are appropriate. These methods further give clear access to both shape and surface reflectance information, where both can be aligned without special alignment techniques. Efficient implementations of several subparts have been proposed earlier, in case the online application of well-known methods is gradually becoming a reality. Also, the required hardware is minimal, and in large amount cases consumer type cameras will suffice. This keeps prices for data capture relatively low.

Reverse engineering has emerged as an important concept in modern manufacturing. There is a growing interest in transforming images to models, i.e., to construct geometric and descriptive models of 3D objects from sensed data for applications ranging from component inspection, manufacturing, surgical planning to entertainment industries, Automatic object model construction is useful in duplicating or modifying parts and in verifying the tolerance of manufactured parts for which CAD models may not be available. Accurate models of already existing complex shaped objects are required for synthesizing arbitrary views and also for recognizing them in many applications such as robot navigation, part inspection, animation and visualization in virtual museums and vision augmented environments.

Automatic construction of geometric models of 3D objects (Figure 1) involves three major steps: (i) data acquisition, (ii) registration of different views, and (iii) integration. Data acquisition involves obtaining either intensity or depth data of an object from multiple viewpoints. In this paper the term data refers to surface depth data that can be obtained using a laser range scanner or an interferometric sensor. Note that the accurate 3D spatial relations between different views may not be easily and directly obtained in many cases. Therefore, integration of data from multiple views is not only dependent on the representation chosen for the model description, but also requires knowledge of the transformations relating the data obtained from multiple views. The goal of registration, also known as the correspondence problem, is to find the transformations that relate multiple views, thus bringing the object regions that are shared between them into alignment. Integration merges data from multiple views using the computed view transformations, to create a single surface representation in a unique coordinate frame. Various approaches, taxonomy and challenges of 3D construction are discussed in this chapter.

TAXONOMY OF 3D IMAGES

Taxonomy of 3D Images is shown in Figure 2. The Extraction of 3D images is broadly classified as active and passive methods. Controlling the light sources is considered as one of the effective strategy for extracting 3D information. Active lighting includes some system of temporal or spatial variation of the illumination. On the other hand in passive method, light is not controlled or with respect to image quality. From a practical point of view, active techniques tend to be less demanding, as the special light source is used to simplify some of the steps involved in 3D capturing process. Their usage is limited to environments where the special illumination methods can be applied.

A second difference is between the numbers of vantage points from where the scene is illuminated. Two methods are involved in vantage points such as single-vantage and multi-vantage methods. When a system works from a single point of location it is called as single-vantage method. In case if there are multiple view point, these points are positioned close to each other and obviously they would coincide. This can also be handled by using semi-transparent mirrors. In multi-vantage systems, various viewpoints and positions are involved. The position of viewpoint should be far enough from each other so that the baseline between the components should be wide. The main advantage of single-vantage methods is that

Figure 1. Steps involved in 3D Modelling

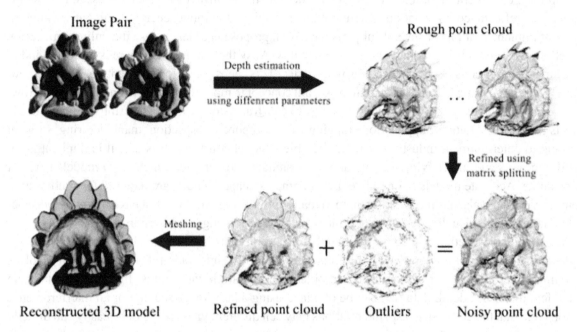

they are compact and they do not suffer from occlusion problems that occur in multi-vantage systems when views of the scene are not visible from all vantage points.

TRIANGULATION

3D surface is measured using the projection of laser on the surface. Of all traditional methods triangulation provides the practical way for locating a high speed accuracy product. Triangulation is the process of finding a point in 3D space from the projection of multiple images. Figure 3 depicts the triangulation method. Given the two view points from two images, position of point in space is found as intersection of two viewpoints. The parameters required for projection function from 3D to 2D is represented in the form of camera matrices. Triangulation is also known as reconstruction method. Triangulation is a trivial problem where each point in a 2D space corresponds to a line in 3D image. The set of lines generated by the image points must intersect at a common 3D point. However, the coordinates may contain geometric noise from lens distortion. Due to this noise present in the coordinates, the generated image points do not intersect in 3D space. In the literature, there are various methods to find the optimal image coordinates for achieving 3D intersection point. Some of the triangulation methods studied in the literature is mid-point method, direct linear transformation method, optimal triangulation technique and so on. Triangulation method can be categorized into two group namely passive and active techniques.

Figure 2. Taxonomy of 3D Images

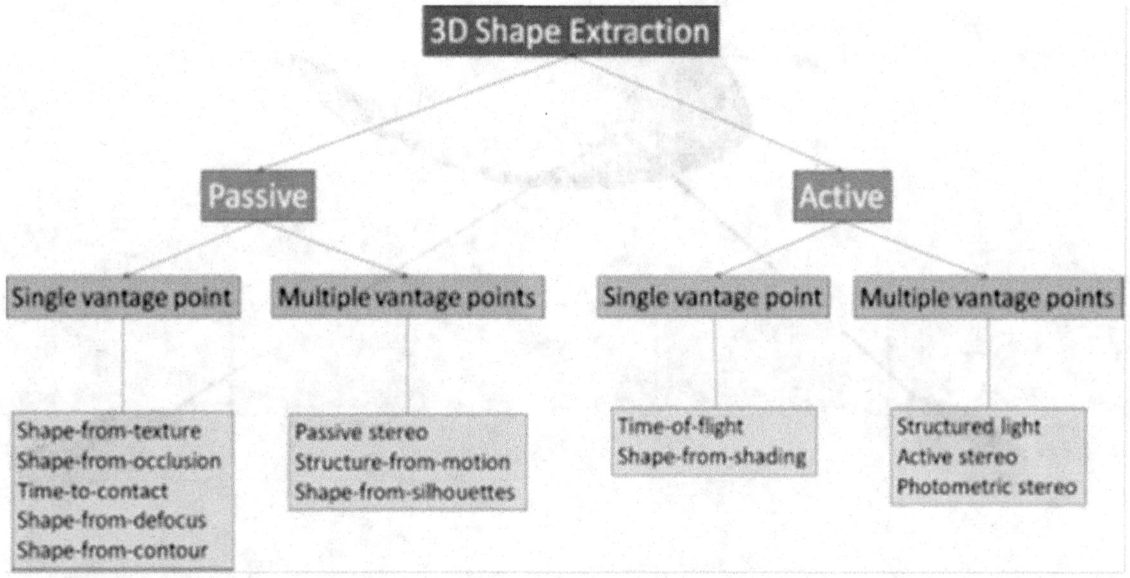

Passive Triangulation

Triangulation approach is used to extract depth information in multi-vantage method. This is the key concept exploited by self-calibrating structure-from-motion (SfM) methods. This method does not require any specific light source to calculate any range calculation.

Active Triangulation

Active triangulation uses controlled source of light or energy emission from camera, scanning laser source, detector or projected pattern of light. Finding the corresponding points can be derived by replacing the camera by projection setup. So, one illumination source is combined with one camera. For example, if an object surface is spotted with laser, particular spot can be easily detected by camera. 3D surface point is the intersection of position and angle of both laser and camera ray. This structure is clearly shown in the Figure 4. The laser light L project light on the object O. The intersection point P is formed on the object and is viewed by the camera. Point P' is formed as spot in the camera on the image plane I.

Even though triangulation methods have many advantages, it does not efficiently handle the problem of occlusion or shadowing. There are two types of occlusion such as laser and camera occlusion. If the laser light (Figure 5) does not cover the area covered by the camera it is known as laser occlusion. This problem can be solved by using multibeam (Figure 7) to cover more space. If the camera does not cover the area reached by laser light is called camera occlusion (Figure 6). This can be rectified using multiple cameras placed to cover the source.

Figure 3. Triangulation Process

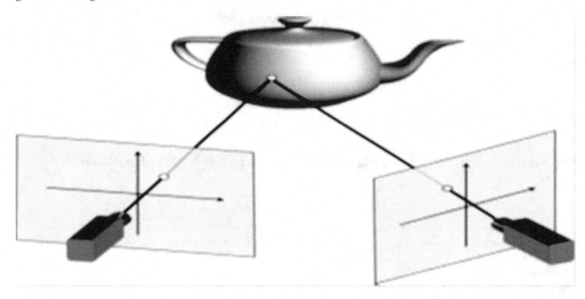

Figure 4. Active Triangulation

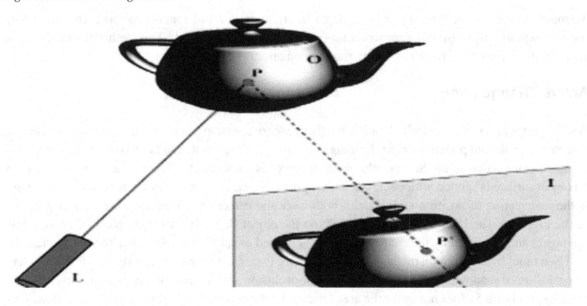

Figure 5. Laser occlusion

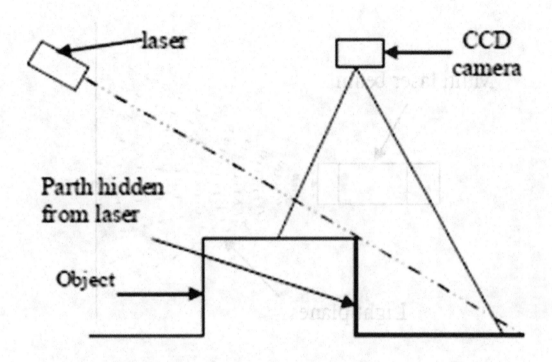

Figure 6. Camera occlusion

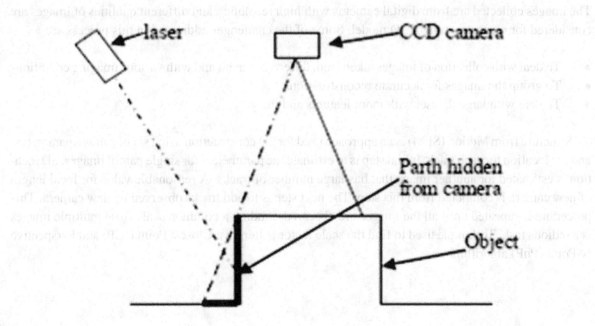

Figure 7. Multibeam Laser

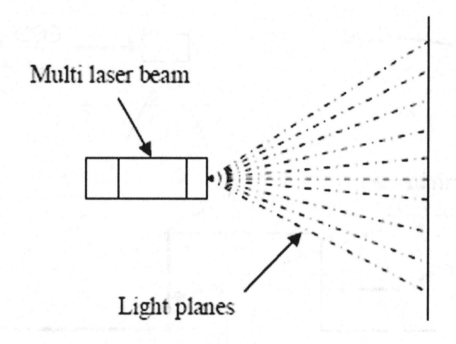

APPROACHES FOR 3D RECONSTRUCTION

Structure From Motion

The images collected are from digital cameras with high resolution and different qualities of images are considered for reconstruction of 3D model. Some of the challenges addressed in this process are

- To deal with collection of images taken from different camera and with various imaging conditions
- To group the images for accurate reconstruction.
- To deal with large dataset with more features and images.

Structure from Motion (SFM) is an approach used for 3D construction using set of camera parameters and 3D location for each track. Initial step is to estimate the parameters for single pair of images. 3D location is estimated for another image that has large number of tracks. A reasonable value for focal length of new camera is computed from this step. The next step is to add tracks observed by new camera. This procedure is repeated until all the images are observed. Finding a common scale from multiple images is a tedious task. Technique used to find the scale factor is Iterative Closest Point (ICP) and Perspective N-Point (PnP) algorithm.

Figure 8. Set of images from Foundation dataset

Figure 9. Sparse and Dense 3D models in Foundation dataset

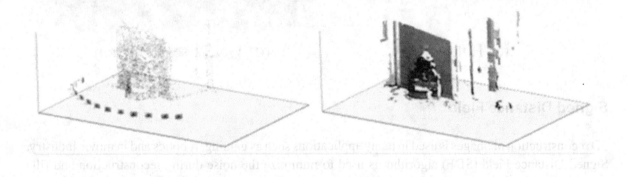

SfM algorithm is tested with Fountain dataset (Figure 8) that has set of 24 images at approximately 5 degree increments from Dense Multi View Stereo datasets collected from EPFL Computer Vision Lab. The images that do not have the estimated key points are removed from the model. The points that are not found in the below Figure 9 is due to the fact that there is not sufficient key point match. This problem is dealt by adjusting SfM parameters. Additional dataset used to test the algorithm are Topoi Lowen images and oxford dataset. The key issues in this algorithm is, these models are CPU and memory intensive specifically when the dataset size is large for reconstruction of 3D model.

Figure 10. Signed Distance Field

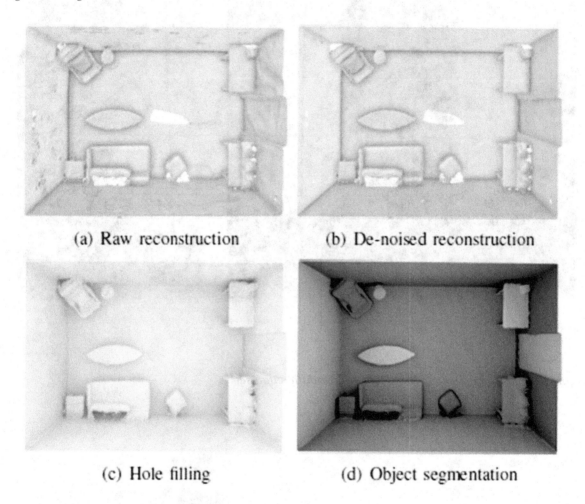

(a) Raw reconstruction   (b) De-noised reconstruction

(c) Hole filling   (d) Object segmentation

Signed Distance Field

3D reconstruction of images is used in many applications such as gaming, robotics and in movie industry. Signed Distance Field (SDF) algorithm is used to minimize the noise during reconstruction and fills the unobserved and occluded regions. Traditional 3D algorithms target on offline images, whereas this SDF algorithm is well suitable to tackle online use. The various interesting issues that are faced during reconstruction of 3D images are discussed below. First, the change in 3D model that happens in every observation leads to wobbling. Secondly, when the 3D image is reconstructed it contains holes and incomplete, Third factor the final image is noisy after reconstruction. Figure 10 given below illustrates concept of significantly reducing noise in planar surfaces that results in appealing 3D construction.

Figure 11. Object Segmentation. Checkboard patterns are planes and different colors are given to each object

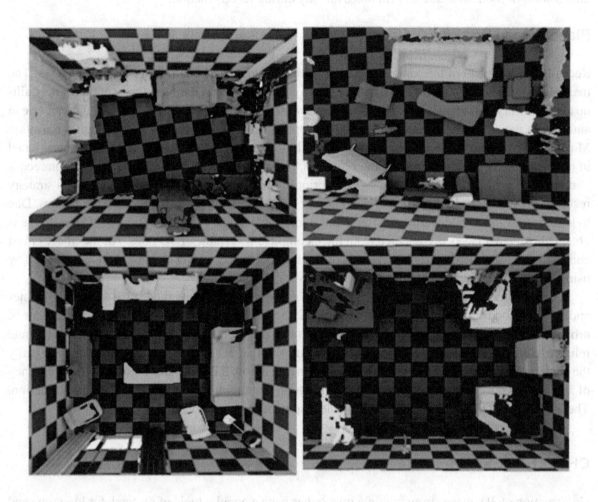

This technique uses least square method which is faster than the other traditional methods. The local plane that are detected are merged to find the globally consistent planes. By applying this approach the noise is reduced, holes are filled, object-level and segmentation using plane surface. As a post processing step, object segmentation is carried out. Segmentation is performed correctly, as long as there is no connectivity between objects and walls. In Figure 11, the top row exhibits how topologically connected objects are wrongly segmented as one object. So this method works well for indoor environments where all objects are related to planar surface.

Various new approaches are uses planar surfaces during online 3D reconstruction of indoor environments. Plane detection algorithm consists of local plane fitting and global plane merging. Local candidate generation can be efficiently tackled by least squares plane estimation directly on the SDF grid. Global clustering can be effectively done by 1-point RANSAC on all candidates. By using this approach we can significantly reduce noise in online and offline 3D reconstructions and make them more visually appealing. Omitting re-meshing of planar regions resolves the vertex jitter problem of flat surfaces. By extending planar regions into unobserved and occluded parts of the scene we are able to recover missing information of room structure and fill holes already during reconstruction.

Plane Sweep Strategy

Recently, huge growth of telecommunication network has increased the need for urban databases. The main challenge in reconstruction of 3D images from urban database is the complexity of the scene, built-up areas are very dense and boundaries of image have poor contrast. All these factors play a major role in automating reconstruction of images. One of the approaches to handle these issues is Digital Elevation Model (DEM) which is used for matching objects based on cross-correlation. DEM is the partitioned in order to provide 3D boundaries of the buildings. However these approaches always focus on reconstruction of specific 3D models having strong prior knowledge about the image. Plane sweep strategy reconstructs the image by grouping of neighboring coplanar 3D lines generated from the images. Due to low contrast image boundaries and fragment or missing boundary lines, incomplete 3D wireframe is obtained. A planar facets is computed from the incomplete wireframe of 3D lines. All the images must contribute both geometric and photometric constraints. Therefore, the 3D plain model is determined by using both 3D lines and neighborhood of images over multiple views.

In general, reconstruction of 3D images using plane sweep strategy method is based on the 3D lines and neighborhood of multiple images. The Figure 12 shown below represents the image of aerial view of urban buildings. This approach involves three steps to reconstruct the 3D image. First step is to compute reliable half-planes, second step is line grouping completion of 3D lines based on half planes and finally the plane delineation and verification. The results generated from this method demonstrates the efficiency of automated construction of piecewise planar models from multiple image with minimal information. The quality of the 3D model is quite reasonable inspite of the complex input images.

CHALLENGES

Construction of 3D images from multiple images has been a popular topic of research for long time and lot of progress has been made in recent days. Some of the challenges are listed below

i. Selecting the best 3D modelling technique is a challenging job. Even though there are various techniques available, methods are selected based on their location of object, geometry and texture of objects. For instance, for structured objects stereo types systems are well suited.

ii. Most of the objects have complex shape which needs high precision camera to capture cavities that deals with self-occlusion.

iii. Apart from the shape of the objects to be captured, the properties and characteristics of the material also must be handled. There is no single technology to handle the objects like ceramics, jewellery and wooden sculptures.

iv. The 3D techniques developed must handle the objects of all sizes, from tiny like needle to large scale like city.

v. Data collection should be done on-site under any conditions or implying equipment to remote environments.

vi.   Portable scanner can be used for the objects that are too fragile or valuable. Scanner will move around the objects without touching it.

vii. Volume of data captured must be high. For example like museum and city there are masses of data to be captured.

viii. The cost invested on 3D modelling techniques must be relatively cheaper. In many applications investment is very limited.

ix.   Achieving higher precision is the moving target in the present applications. For example to study the paintings of 3D surface must be accurate.

Figure 12. Six overlapping aerial views of urban area

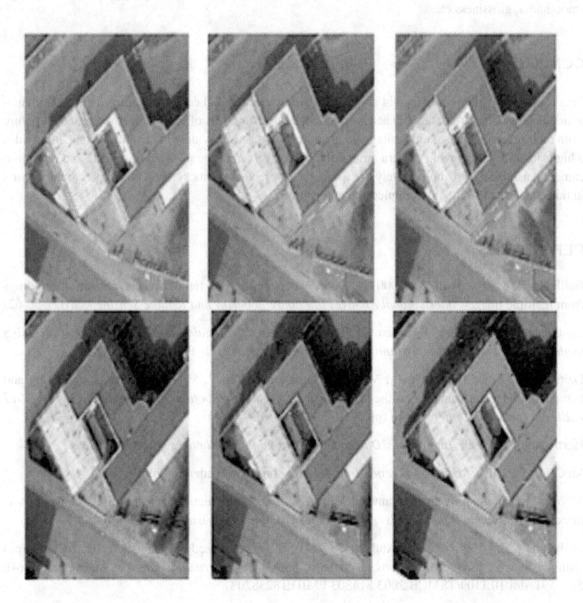

Based on these challenges, so many models have been developed and led to technological developments of 3D data acquisition. 3D scanning technology is used to extract the surface reflection properties. The device not only extracts the shape, it also scans the surface properties. In order to achieve high quality precision it can be combined with BRDF (Bidirectional Reflectance Distribution Function) or BTF (Bidirectional Texture Function). Surface reflection method works with all types of materials such as metals, glass, etc. On-line scanning of 3D objects is done in two steps. First, the objects are scanned followed by processing of scanned data. During this process, there is a chance of incompleteness and low quality of result. This can be solved be extracting the 3D information on fly which would help in locating the position for next scan. The other refinement process can be performed in off-line. Opportunistic scanning is based on the volume and mass of the application, type of scanner and techniques has to be decided on-the-fly. Scanners with multiple cameras must be used to capture the texture, surface smoothness, glossiness etc.

CONCLUSION

This chapter provides a deep insight about the basic concepts of 3D construction from multiple images which is one of the promising 3D acquisition techniques. In terms of various methods used, structure from motion technique is multi-vantage point strategy that is used widely in all applications. It provides a high flexibility by moving camera around the object or scene. The position of objects and motion of camera must be aligned appropriately to capture the image viewpoints. Several techniques are discussed in this chapter with suitable examples and applications.

REFERENCES

Baillard, C., & Zisserman, A. (2000). A plane-sweep strategy for the 3D reconstruction of buildings from multiple images. *International Archives of Photogrammetry and Remote Sensing, 33*(B2), 56-62.

Costineanu, D., Fosalau, C., Damian, C., & Plopa, O. (n.d.). *Triangulation-based 3D image processing method and system with compensating shadowing errors*. Academic Press.

Dzitsiuk, M., Sturm, J., Maier, R., Ma, L., & Cremers, D. (2017, May). De-noising, stabilizing and completing 3d reconstructions on-the-go using plane priors. In *Robotics and Automation (ICRA), 2017 IEEE International Conference on* (pp. 3976-3983). IEEE.

Hertzmann, A. (1999). *Interactive 3D Scene Reconstruction from Images*. Academic Press.

McCann, S. (2015). *3D Reconstruction from Multiple Images*. Academic Press.

Moons, T., Van Gool, L., & Vergauwen, M. (2010). 3D reconstruction from multiple images part 1: principles. *Foundations and Trends® in Computer Graphics and Vision, 4*(4), 287-404.

Mulayim, A. Y., Yilmaz, U., & Atalay, V. (2003). Silhouette-based 3-D model reconstruction from multiple images. *IEEE Transactions on Systems, Man, and Cybernetics. Part B, Cybernetics, 33*(4), 582–591. doi:10.1109/TSMCB.2003.814303 PMID:18238208

Chapter 7
Current Trends on the Acquisition, Virtual Representation, and Interaction of Cultural Heritage:
Exploring Virtual and Augmented Reality and Serious Games

Cristina Portalés
ⓘ https://orcid.org/0000-0002-4520-2250
Universitat de València, Spain

Lucía Vera
ⓘ https://orcid.org/0000-0003-0749-7243
Universitat de València, Spain

Sergio Casas
ⓘ https://orcid.org/0000-0002-0396-4628
Universitat de València, Spain

Javier Sevilla
Universitat de València, Spain

ABSTRACT

Cultural heritage (CH) tells us about our roots, and therefore, constitutes a rich value for the society. Its conservation, dissemination, and understanding are of utmost importance. In order to preserve CH for the upcoming generations, it needs to be documented, a process that nowadays is done digitally. Current trends involve a set of technologies (cameras, scanners, etc.) for the shape and radiometric acquisition of assets. Also, intangible CH can be digitally documented in a variety of forms. Having such assets virtualized, a proper dissemination channel is of relevance, and recently, new technologies that make use of interaction paradigms have emerged. Among them, in this chapter, the authors focus their attention in the technologies of virtual reality (VR), augmented reality (AR), and serious games (SGs). They aim to explore these technologies in order to show their benefits in the dissemination and understanding of CH. Though the work involving them is not trivial, and usually a multidisciplinary team is required, the benefits for CH make them worth it.

DOI: 10.4018/978-1-5225-5294-9.ch007

INTRODUCTION

Cultural Heritage (CH) is an essential expression of the richness and the diversity of our culture and therefore, its analysis, documentation, interpretation, conservation, recreation and dissemination are considered crucial tasks. The traditional way of dealing with CH is being left aside as it has become evident that past events cannot be studied only by means of static books since those events were lived by their actors in a similar way as we experience current events and CH should be studied, presented and disseminated in an interactive, appealing way.

The application of Information and Communication Technologies (ICT) to achieve digital acquisition, storage, conservation, recreation, reconstruction and representation of CH assets, both tangible and intangible, is of high interest for many different reasons, namely the accurate documentation of our cultural legacy, the increase of awareness about CH, the determination of possible mechanical alterations suffered by tangible assets, or the mere shape acquisition prior to restoration and/or reconstruction works, etc. The application of these technologies to CH is often coined as Virtual Heritage (VH), Virtual Cultural Heritage (VCH) or Virtual Archaeology when it deals with archaeological sites. The virtual representation of objects involves the process of 3D modelling and visualization. Additionally, for these Virtual Heritage objects to be successfully disseminated and accessed, the interaction paradigms are essential, i.e., how users can have access to those objects. They enhance the value of CH by means of virtually reconstructed objects/stories that can be used in computer graphic applications with several potential benefits.

However, both the way objects are virtually represented and interacted/accessed and the type of application should be correctly chosen to achieve the desired goals for the system. In this regard, VCH applications could have many different goals, and thus the application of ICT to the CH field constitutes a very broad field and different levels of immersion and realism can be provided. Luckily, these technologies have evolved very rapidly in recent years and now offer the possibility of portraying very realistic graphics, scanning objects with high detail, simulating events, and providing effective ways to perform pervasive meetings. However, realism is not the only important thing in VCH. The significance of CH is not always directly correlated with its mere visual appearance. It is also necessary to create meaningful content to engage people. The challenge, thus, is to create VCH applications that are at the same time realistic, educational and engaging. For this reason, in most of these applications, the end-user should be the focus of the process, and technology should be a mean but not an end. In this sense, it is very important also to be historically accurate, performing a comprehensive documentation and choosing proper sources before releasing a CH-related computer application, since VCH applications that fail to properly account for representing the cultural legacy could be harmful instead of beneficial.

Although there are many different approaches and technologies to deal with the digital acquisition, virtual representation and interaction of CH assets (acquisition devices, methods and techniques), many of them involve the intervention of expert technicians in different areas of knowledge. The synergies among humanities and computer science engineering is not trivial, since these fields belong to very distant areas, sometimes with different views and biases about life, history, culture and technology. Technicians are more aware of representation, implementation and technical issues, whereas historians are very much concerned about accuracy and authenticity. In addition, these interdisciplinary and highly technical requirements sometimes lead to elevated costs that not all the conservationists and professionals are able to cover. This is one of the biggest criticisms of VCH and one of the reasons why technology may be underused in this field. However, the benefits of these kinds of approaches, when they are correctly performed, are not always acknowledged and must be emphasized. This is one of the main objectives of this chapter, given that recent computer-based virtual representation technologies and interactive methods have improved vastly over a few years. In this sense, it would be of great importance if cultural institutions are engaged in this task and are able to get rid of some mistaken preconceptions about VCH. The synergies that the joint work of humanistic and technologic institutions could provide are enormous, and should mark the decisive step in making VCH the default way of presenting and accessing our digitalized cultural legacy.

In a previous work (Portalés, Casas, Alonso-Monasterio, & Viñals, 2017) we performed a study on a similar topic, where the focus was given on tangible assets and considering multi-dimensional data. In this chapter, however, we will focus on the acquisition, virtual representation and interaction of both tangible and intangible assets without restricting to multi-dimensional information. Tangible and intangible assets are not completely separable, as objects, buildings and monuments are the consequence of ideas, beliefs and battles. Therefore, it is more than convenient to deal with them in a joint way.

The aim of this chapter is to enhance the existing works related to VCH, being most of them the outcomes of a successful work involving multidisciplinary teams. To that end, we will provide a review on the current trends in the digital acquisition, virtual representation and interaction of tangible and intangible CH assets, which involve different disciplines. We will provide some insights in the technologies of Virtual Reality (VR) and Augmented Reality (AR) as paradigms for interacting with the virtually represented CH objects, and in the technology of Serious Games (SGs) as a way to further get an added value of VCH for the society. These technologies have greatly evolved in the last years, as a variety of new computational capabilities, methods and low-cost devices have emerged, and also a variety of them are now integrated in e.g. smartphones or tablets. This can lead to several kinds of applications, such as 3D immersive simulators, 2D interactive applications, virtual museums, virtual flights, etc. We will address to the reader about the benefits of using these technologies regarding e.g. the dissemination capabilities of our past legacy or their appealing for the engagement of new audiences. The following principle should always be kept in mind: "through interpretation, understanding; through understanding, appreciation; through appreciation, protection" (Tilden, 1957). If we want to preserve our legacy for future generations it is mandatory to emphasize its importance and educate the general public in its appreciation. New technologies are very appealing for almost everybody, including children. This constitutes another reason to bet on these technologies in CH.

The chapter is organized as follows. First, digital acquisition devices and techniques are described and reviewed. These methods are particularly useful for tangible assets, which constitute a sizable amount of the work done in VCH. Next, the virtual representation and interaction paradigms (and their corresponding display hardware) are discussed, emphasizing the advantages each of them provides in CH applications. In this section, we discuss the application of VR and AR technologies. Then, a section on SGs is given, which provides some successful case studies in this field and constitute one of the leading trends in CH as they allow a sensible combination of tangible and intangible assets providing engaging and entertaining environments. Finally, conclusions are drawn.

DIGITAL ACQUISITION OF CULTURAL HERITAGE

Devices

From ancient manuscripts to artworks or architectural buildings, the digital acquisition of cultural heritage is of great importance. To that end, different devices can be used depending on the characteristics to be acquired and the nature of the object itself. To name some, in the following lines a set of technologies are introduced, focusing only on those from which 3D representations are commonly derived.

- *Conventional cameras*: Conventional cameras, working in the visible range of the spectrum, can be used to record the visual (surface) appearance of objects. They are useful to document a huge variety of tangible assets, both planar and non-planar, such as manuscripts, artworks, textiles, sculptures, buildings, etc. They can also be used to acquire the 3D shape of objects by means of stereo-photogrammetry or structured-light-based techniques, for what a pair of images of at least two cameras or two camera positions are used, or a combination of a camera and a projector. Additionally, cameras can be mounted on drones in order to access assets that are at a certain height, such as the roof of buildings.
- *Mobile phones and tablets*: Nowadays mobile technologies are provided with integrated cameras, which are used in many cases to quick-document objects, events, testimonies, etc., both in image and in video forms. These technologies are spread over the great public, making them recursive devices that can be used if expert/expensive devices are not available at a certain moment.
- *Cameras in different spectral ranges*: This category includes cameras working in the ultra-violet, infrared or thermal spectral ranges, which can be monospectral (the acquisition is done in a single band), multispectral (usually, 3 to 10 bands) or even hyperspectral (from 10 to hundreds of bands). These cameras are usually more expensive and less portable than the ones working in the visible range, and so their use is not so much widely extended. They have been used in CH to add texture to the 3D models of objects.
- *Low-cost scanners*: In the last few years, new technologies have evolved that allow a quick acquisition of object's shape. Examples are the Microsoft Kinect or the Occipital Structure Sensor. With these technologies both the shape and the visual appearance of objects can be acquired at a low cost, but with the loss of high accuracies.
- *Laser scanners*: With the laser scanning technique usually a dense cloud of points is acquired, which might include RGB information combined with cameras. Laser scanning provides many advantages that makes it quite suitable to document the shape of objects (Vidal & Muñoz, 2015). Nevertheless, safety and cost issues may be an important restriction of this technology.
- *Microphones*: Microphones are used to record sound, and thus they are the natural way to record musical pieces and spoken testimonies. Some works can be found that try to visualize musical pieces by means of 3D graphics (Portalés & Perales, 2009), and thus these devices are here mentioned.
- *Others*: This category includes other means that can be used in order to derive a virtual representation of objects. When dealing with intangible assets, or even tangible assets that are nowadays not present (totally or partially destroyed), it is not possible to directly document them with an acquisition device. In these cases, usually interpretation is necessary departing from other sources, such as old written documents, drawings, testimonials, etc.

All of the aforementioned technologies allow the digital acquisition of one or several characteristics of the CH assets. Therefore, it seems logic that the combined use of these technologies can lead to a richer documentation of the assets. However, in this case a mapping between the different kinds of data is required. For instance, one can scan the shape of an object with a scanner, and then collect images with a thermal camera. In order to fuse this information into a single object which can be inspected and analysed, it is required to map the images to the 3D model. To that end, photogrammetric techniques are used. This and other examples are given in the next section.

Techniques

In order to document CH tangible assets that have some volumetric (non-planar) shape, usually their surface is reconstructed from images or by means of laser scanning. The first ones include several techniques, such as stereo-photogrammetry, structure from motion (SFM), simultaneous localization and mapping (SLAM) or a variety of different structured light techniques. Additionally to the 3D reconstructed shape, textures (RGB values) are usually added to the object's' shape. With the laser scanning technique, the acquired cloud of points might include also RGB information provided by cameras (Blais & Beraldin, 2006; Chow & Chan, 2009; Guarnieri, Remondino, & Vettore, 2006; Lerones, Fernández, Gil, Gómez-García-Bermejo, & Casanova, 2010; Navarro et al., 2009; Trinchão Andrade, Mazetto Mendes, de Oliveira Santos Jr, Pereira Bellon, & Silva, 2012; Yastikli, 2007). Although laser scanning technology is reliable and provides high accuracy (Vidal & Muñoz, 2015), it is not always the preferred solution because cost and safety issues impose important restrictions on this technology. On the other hand, the many different approaches provided by structured light techniques (Salvi, Fernandez, Pribanic, & Llado, 2010) bring also high acquisition rates, with the advantage that high resolution images are directly available from the acquisition camera(s). Nevertheless, these techniques are usually dependent on the environment conditions and may be highly demanding in terms of computational cost (depending on the technique). Stereo-photogrammetry and other image-based approaches, though computationally demanding, have been researched by the research community during decades, and robust and accurate algorithms exist nowadays (Cabrelles et al., 2010). Nevertheless, its accuracy is restricted to well-defined targets (1). Other techniques such as shape from motion or texture gradients, do present some weaknesses (e.g. low accuracy) that make them not suitable for the high fidelity 3D reconstruction of CH assets (Sansoni et al. 2009).

On the other hand, the visual appearance or photometric properties of CH objects is of great importance to correctly digitally preserve objects, and these properties are used to provide a texture to the 3D models. As pointed before, they can be acquired from the use of conventional cameras, mobile phones, or cameras working in the visible range or even in other spectral ranges, such as thermal or infrared cameras (Bodnar et al., 2012; Imposa, 2010; Lerma, Cabrelles, & Portalés, 2011). In these works, the 3D shape of the objects is complemented with radiometric information at different levels and thus providing a more accurate documentation of the CH assets. Other works use multispectral or hyperspectral cameras in order to retrieve both the shape and spectral properties of the assets. For instance, in (Granero-Montagud et al., 2013; Groves, Portalés, & Ribes-Gómez, 2014) a pre-industrial prototype was built for diagnosing the deterioration on movable assets, such as paintings, by the acquisition of 3D-hyperspectral imaging, thus acquiring much more information than just the 3D shape of objects, which is important, but it is not the only relevant aspect.

Figure 1. Cloud of points of a building façade obtained with the VisualSFM (Wu, 2017). Gathered images are also represented from where they were taken.

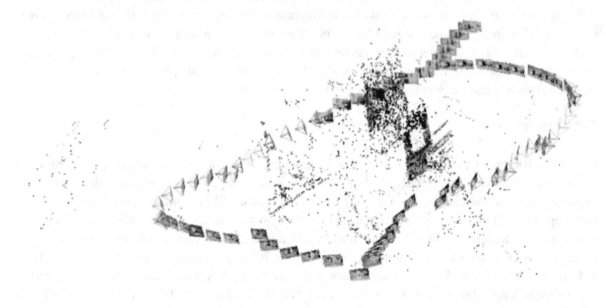

With respect to intangible assets, such as battles, speeches, historical events, celebrations, dances, funerals, rituals, skills, ancient habits, artistic techniques or social recreation, the 3D reconstruction process is very different, since no direct physical elements could be analysed, but usually documentation mainly in textual or graphic (images, drawings, pictures) forms needs to be studied. In this case, historians, archaeologists, musicologists, linguistics, etc. play an important role, since a professional research and interpretation of the existing documentation is not just necessary, but indispensable. For instance, in (Christopoulos, Mavridis, Andreadis, & Karigiannis, 2011) the famous battle of the Termopylae is recreated by means of an interactive virtual game. In a similar way, archaeological sites need interpretation in order to be reconstructed/modeled, as the ancient buildings are partially destroyed nowadays. An example of such an interpretation is explained in (Portalés, Alonso-Monasterio, & Viñals, 2017) that involved different kinds of data (written texts, aerial images, documentation on similar sites better conserved, etc.) and a multidisciplinary team of archaeologists, engineers and graphic designers (Figure 2).

Figure 2. Virtual reconstruction of the Castellet de Bernabé, where: (a) initial proposal of the graphic designer for the textures; (b) result after the first round of review with the archaeologist advice; (c) final design approved by the archaeologist

VIRTUAL REPRESENTATION AND INTERACTION

In this section we provide an introduction of the displays commonly used for presenting VCH, then we provide an insight of the VR and AR interaction paradigms, and finally we review their use in the field of CH. Both technologies are useful to recreate tangible and intangible CH assets, although VR is more suited for the recreation of intangible or destroyed tangible assets and AR is very useful to enhance existing tangible assets that have been deteriorated, such as archaeological sites or damaged monuments.

Visual Displays

Currently there are a variety of devices that allow the visualization of digital information. Here, we focus on those commonly used in VR and AR applications.

- *Head mounted display (HMD)*: Some HMD use live video stream to render the real scene and others use a half-silvered or semi-transparent mirror onto where the digital information is projected. The first design is known as video-based HMD, and the second is referred as optical-based HMD (Azuma, 1997; Bimber & Raskar, 2005, pp. 71-92; Rolland, Holloway, & Fuchs, 1994). Since the first HMD, these devices have evolved considerably in the last years, and currently there are different solutions on the market, including affordable solutions. To cite some examples described in (Nguyen, Tran, & Le, 2017): portable pocket stereoscopes, low-cost Google Cardboard, Oculus Rift, Samsung Gear VR, premium Google Day Dream.
- *Mobile phones and tablets*: These technologies have significantly been improved in the last years. Issues such as the increased computational capabilities, the touch screen interaction or the integration of small sensors (e.g. inclinometers) and cameras make them suitable for interactive applications demanding rich 3D graphics. Many AR and VR applications can be found that make use of these technologies (Andreetto, Brusco N Fau - Cortelazzo, & Cortelazzo, 2004; Chang et al., 2014; Jesus Gimeno, Portalés, Coma, Fernández, & Martínez, 2017; Michele, Michele, & Fabio, 2013).

- *Projectors*: Multimedia projectors are another alternative to show visual content. They are becoming more and more affordable and small, especially those with integrated LED technology. They are still the preferred solution for being used in static applications and indoors. The projected images can be rendered on top of planar (Figure 3) or curved surfaces, on 3D objects, on building façades, on the body, etc. (Jesus Gimeno, Olanda, Martinez, & Sanchez, 2011). Also, a set of projectors can be used together in order to increase the projection size and avoid shadows, as long as they are properly calibrated (Portalés, Casas, Coma, & Fernández, 2017).
- *Screens*: This category includes other kind of screens not mentioned before (remind that e.g. smartphones also have a screen), such as the screens of computers, laptops, televisions, etc. (overall referred as regular screens). Also, surfaces can act as screens if visual content is depicted on them based on projections (overall referred as projection screens). Following the same concept as in HMD, video-based or optical-based solutions can be found. A good example of both kind of construction is usually found in AR-mirrors (Portalés, Gimeno, Casas, Olanda, & Giner, 2016).
- *Cave Automatic Virtual Environment* (*CAVE*): the CAVE was first introduced in (Cruz-Neira, Sandin, DeFanti, Kenyon, & Hart, 1992) and it basically consists on a series of projection screens arranged in a cubic form, such as a user is placed inside, one projector per screen, an HMD and interactive globes. Then, instead of a single device, this technology is composed of a set of technologies that are synchronized in order to properly show and interact with the virtual contents. Because of its nature, this technology is used for VR applications, and many examples can be found such as in (Gaitatzes, Christopoulos, & Roussou, 2001b; Gutierrez, Seron, Magallon, Sobreviela, & Latorre, 2004).

Figure 3. Examples of projection screens with added interaction, where: (a) table-like interactive screen with rear projection; (b) wall-like screen with frontal projection

As given above, a variety of displays can be used for virtual representation and interaction in VR and AR applications. The kind of display used mainly depends on the characteristics of the project, but also economic aspects might be of great importance. For instance, a CAVE system can be integrated as part of an indoor exhibition to represent rich virtual content. As it involves a variety of heavy technologies that need to be placed on site, it is obviously a solution not appropriate for mobile applications. The same would be the case for projectors and big screens. On the contrary, small devices such as smartphones or tablets can be used for mobile applications, both indoors and outdoors. Regarding to HMDs, recently a variety of low-cost solutions have emerged, opening the door for its greater use in VR and AR.

Virtual Reality and Augmented Reality Interaction Paradigms

VR is a technology that allows replacing the real world by a synthetic one, making the user believe that she/he is in another realm. VR is a convenient technological solution in many cases, as it provides, among others: safety and risk reduction; costs reduction; greater trial availability; no damage; possibility of recreating a variety of situations; possibility of repeating the same situations under the same conditions; etc. (Casas, Portalés, García-Pereira, & Fernández, 2017). In a different way, the AR technology allows displaying virtual information/stimuli attached or related to the real world. The term 'AR' was first coined by Caudell and Mizell (1992) to describe a digital display used by aircraft electricians that blended virtual graphics onto a physical reality. At that time, the definition of the AR technology was linked to head-mounted displays (HMDs), as being the unique displays using this technology (Portalés Ricart, 2009). Azuma (1997) defines AR as the technology that allows to build systems that simultaneously: 1) combine real and virtual objects; 2) are interactive in real time and 3) are registered in 3D. The restriction to include 3D registration is key, so that the virtual (augmented) information presented to the user is spatially and temporally synchronized with the real information. Interaction is also important, because the user can experience the real world from different points, and the AR system should be able to generate the appropriate virtual content from any location. In Figure 4, these interaction paradigms are schematized.

Figure 4. VR and AR interaction paradigms, adapted from (Rekimoto & Nagao, 1995)

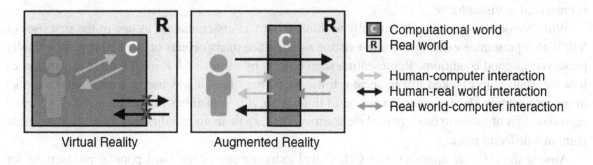

As VR allows simulating elements that are not present or do not exist in the real world, they can be depicted to users in a way that they can focus their attention on them. Moreover, it also allows recreating specific situations at certain moments or during a certain interval of time, as many times is required. Thus, this kind of interaction paradigm results more interesting when it is required that users are more aware of the virtual content, to centre there their attention. Additionally, the interaction with this virtual environment is done at the display level, and thus it does not imply a change in the real world. Interaction is also considered a key element of VR, since the deceived user needs to interact with the VR world as naturally as possible, and do it in (ideally) the same way as he/she would do it the real world. This is often the most difficult part of the system and it is usually simplified or limited. Thus, many VR applications are not fully immersive, do not use natural interfaces and, thus, do not provide a full alternative reality. However, it is common to still consider them as VR systems.

Regarding AR, although users interact by means of a device, it allows that virtual and real worlds are seamlessly blended (Azuma, 1997), in a way that it simulates that the interaction is done directly on the real world and thus, it improves the interaction feeling. In this case, the attention of the user is centred in the real world, onto where the virtual information is depicted, and thus AR is commonly used for those situations where it is of relevance that the user is present in a certain place.

Therefore, while VR substitutes the real world by a synthetic one, AR enriches the real world by means of virtual stimuli, without (completely) replacing the real world. Both technologies have (different) advantages for the visualization and interaction of CH assets. On the one hand, VR allows the general public to appreciate remote (in space and time) cultural assets; users can access the virtual content from anywhere, which can be very advantageous since users with mobility difficulties or inaccessible sites (private ownership assets, physical difficulties, etc.) can easily reach them. On the other hand, through the use of AR technology, users have to physically visit/access the assets to trigger the related virtual contents, so that in, some way, users are encouraged to visit such assets, promoting the tourism of the zone and creating a strong link between the CH site and the augmented content. In any case, both technologies provide unarguable advantages: VR recalls memories or trigger new sensations, encouraging visiting a place and appreciating a historical site/event, while AR adds value to existing CH sites and attractions.

Virtual Reality Approaches and Applications in Cultural Heritage

VR uses simulation techniques to deceive the human senses so that the perceptual cues that reach the brain are consistent with the belonging of an alternative/simulated reality. Although these perceptual cues can be of different nature (e.g. acoustic, visual, haptic, etc.), the most common is that information is presented in visual forms.

With this definition, it comes naturally to think about CH dissemination as one of the first uses of VR, both representing existing and non-existing assets, since many objects of our heritage are not fully preserved in good conditions. Representing such objects by means of VR allows users to experience how a certain object looked like in ancient times, or perhaps how it was used, or even what was like to live in a certain place at a certain period of time. Also, it is sometimes interesting to build a virtual representation of assets in order to analyse them in detail, show them in a different fashion or integrate them in a different place.

Among the different approaches in CH, virtual tours are one of the most popular productions for dissemination purposes (Bastanlar et al., 2008; Wessels, Ruther, Bhurtha, & Schröeder, 2014). For instance, in (Maicas & Viñals, 2016), a virtual tour of the Lliria heritage town (Valencia, Spain) named Edeta 360° is presented. The virtual enhancement of the cultural heritage is based on panorama photos following a straightforward procedure with off-the-self equipment and using the freely available software Hugin-2014.0.0 and Easypano Tourweaver 7.90®, while keeping the high quality of the final product. Virtual tours or virtual flights can be integrated as part of museum exhibitions, as it is the case of the virtual flight of Castellet the Bernabé described in (Portalés, Alonso-Monasterio, et al., 2017) (Figure 5).

Many VR-based CH applications are designed to reconstruct ancient assets that have been altered, partially destroyed or even are nowadays inexistent. This is the case of archaeological sites by reconstructing damaged structures or remains allowing users to know a whole and realistic vision of some

Figure 5. Some image sequences of the Virtual flight of the Castellet de Bernabé

ancient buildings (Ercek, Viviers, & Warzée, 2010; Guidi, Russo, & Angheleddu, 2014; Portalés, Alonso-Monasterio, et al., 2017; Rodrigues, Magalhaes, Moura, & Chalmers, 2008).

VR techniques can also be used to recreate architectural museums or CH items that are nowadays in good conservation state, but that need to be digitally preserved or be widely disseminated. In the first case, it is important to digitally preserve a good representation of current assets in order to avoid their loss in case of any damage, such as the result of a vandalism act. In the second case, digitally disseminating art collections or even architectural buildings is a good way of attracting new audiences. There are many virtual museum applications (Miguélez Fernández, 2013; Reffat & Nofal, 2013; Styliania, Fotisb, Kostasa, & Petrosa, 2009), which offer the opportunity of exploring a remote site by manipulating (rotate, enlarge, etc.) fragile and precious objects with no risk of damage. Examples of virtual museums are very common, although not all the applications tagged as virtual museums are really VR applications since most of them lack a sense of immersion and natural interaction (like (Wojciechowski, Walczak, White, & Cellary, 2004)).

Intangible assets have also been virtually represented and interacted by means of the VR technology. For instance, in (Sevilla et al., 2000) an VR application was built to recreate the daily life of famous neurologist Santiago Ramón y Cajal (Figure 6). Users could access the rooms and navigate through them by means of a HMD and gloves. They could make use of some objects existing in the rooms.

Figure 6. VR space that recreated the life of the famous neurologist Santiago Ramón y Cajal

Regardless of the objective of the system and the data acquisition technique used to gather information to build the CH application, the display and simulation of the represented assets in VR-based CH applications follows basically the same rules as other VR systems. In this regard, older VR-applications used generic graphics libraries (Christou, Angus, Loscos, Dettori, & Roussou, 2006; Gaitatzes, Christopoulos, & Roussou, 2001a) such as OpenGL, OpenGL Performer, or Open Scene Graph or specific VR libraries such as CAVElib, but their use has diminished with the maturity of new game development engines. Newer VR-based CH applications are now benefiting from the existence of increasingly complex game development platforms, such as Unreal or Unity (Jiménez Fernández-Palacios, Morabito, & Remondino, 2016), allowing the development of realistic VR applications for CH in shorter time periods, even for non-experts in VR technology. Web deployment (Kiourt, Koutsoudis, & Pavlidis, 2016) can also be considered for some applications where immersion is less important than universal access.

Nevertheless, there are certain requirements that CH applications need to emphasize in terms of visualization and interaction. The first one is the ability to optimize 3D models that are sometimes obtained with high-resolution devices (such as laser scanners). As the number of polygons increases, so does the complexity of the graphics pipeline calculations. The second one is to choose the appropriate devices for the generation of the perceptual cues. This also influences the interaction paradigm and the role of the user in the CH application. Some applications use VR glasses/helmets such as Oculus Rift (Jiménez Fernández-Palacios et al., 2016), allowing users to walk around a reconstructed CH site. Other applications use more natural interfaces using depth-sensing devices like Kinect or tracking systems like Leap Motion (Webel, Olbrich, Franke, & Keil, 2013).

Regarding to the visual display technology used in VR, many applications use the CAVE system (Christou et al., 2006; Gaitatzes et al., 2001a) in order to provide fully immersive experiences. Other approaches use other kind of big screens, as in (Bruno et al., 2010). More modest approaches include the traditional display with tactile or even standard input devices (keyboard/mouse) (Wojciechowski et al., 2004). Depth cues are also applied using stereoscopic screens, as in (Bruno et al., 2010), although recent approaches prefer the use of HMD that already include stereoscopy and motion tracking. Regarding to HMD, the natural choice for VR applications are the ones that are video-based, as no information of the real world is depicted to the users. The problem with this highly immersive HMD is that they have been traditionally expensive and somehow uncomfortable. This is the reason of its little use in CH. However, recent advances have allowed this technology to be relatively affordable and comfortable (such as Oculus Rift). Therefore, their use in VCH applications is expected to grow.

Augmented Reality Approaches and Applications in Cultural Heritage

AR has a distinctive and special capability in CH. While VR "extracts" people from the current reality trying to teleport them to a different place and time, AR-based CH applications allow people to perform a mental time travel, while making a strong spatial connection with the actual CH location, which can be very relevant.

Sometimes, the displayed CH assets are partially destroyed or have suffered modifications through history. In those cases where there are some remains, it is not necessary to show a complete virtual model of the assets but only some parts, enhancing/augmenting them, so that the missing CH assets can be displayed together with the existing ones. An example of this is the past and present book of the Castellet de Bernabé (Portalés, Alonso-Monasterio, et al., 2017), where the virtual reconstruction of the site is merged with the existing parts. However, the generated images are static, so they cannot be strictly referred as AR, but as augmented/enhanced images. Also, in other cases it might be relevant to visually show the existing assets with added data, that gives extra information of them, or just show them in a different way, such as how they look liked some centuries ago.

Moreover, it has to be pointed out that AR outstands as a very valuable tool when historical events have to be interpreted for visitors. For instance, in Gandía Marsh (Valencia, Spain), under the framework of a Visitor Center, it was implemented an AR application (referred as AR-Cinema) to interpret historical events for school-aged audiences (Portalés, Viñals, Alonso-Monasterio, & Morant, 2010). In this application the visitor, who carried some AR markers that transformed him/her in an augmented user (Giner Martínez & Portalés Ricart, 2005), was visually integrated with the actors of a sketch, and an augmented scene was presented with a video-based AR mirror (Figure 7). This emerged as a useful application to raise awareness about the intangible heritage to locals.

Figure 7. User interacting with the actors of the AR-Cinema, where: (a) the user is not yet augmented, so the marker she carries in one of her hands is appreciated; (b) the user is already augmented, so she is virtually wearing an ancient dress

Figure 8. Images of the AR-Jazz application where the virtual objects represented sound are depicted together with the musicians, in a video-based AR mirror

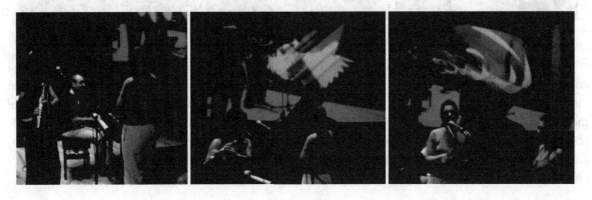

AR mirrors have also been used to depict other kind of intangible assets, such as in (Portalés & Perales, 2009), where virtual representations of traditional Jazz pieces were shown. The AR scene included both the virtual objects and the interpreters (Figure 8).

AR visualization and content-generation shares many aspects with VR systems, and some of the visualization devices can be shared, too. However, AR-based applications often use mobile phones, tablets, cameras, projectors or even mirrors to mix real and virtual information, such as in (Chang et al., 2014; Chen, Chang, & Huang, 2014; Portalés Ricart, Giner Martínez, & Sanmartín Piquer, 2005). All these technologies can be applied to CH. AR-based CH applications use the same techniques as other AR applications, with some particular considerations and restrictions: many CH sites can be visited both outdoors and indoors, so AR needs to be applicable for both scenarios. In addition, CH sites cannot usually be altered or modified so the placement of AR-markers or the use of invasive technologies is often forbidden Therefore, markerless or feature-based AR technology should be the preferred choice, such as in (Portalés, Lerma, & Pérez, 2009), where a Baroque vault was recreated on top of a Gothic vault and a present-day reredos. The existing assets served as a feature-based image for the positioning in real time (Figure 9). Another example can be found in (Jesus Gimeno et al., 2017), where the user positioning was achieved with a combination of Bluetooth and the sensors integrated in the mobile phone, to show, by means of indirect AR, the ancient furniture at the Casa Batlló museum.

Outdoor AR-based CH applications are harder to build since the 3D registration process, which is in many cases based on computer vision, is more complex due to the less controllable environmental conditions (mainly natural light). Some examples can be found in (Haugstvedt & Krogstie, 2012) and (Vlahakis et al., 2002). In the later, three different interaction systems and interaction paradigms are presented to enjoy a time travel to ancient Olympia, Greece.

Figure 9. Images of the Valencia Cathedral with augmentations, where: (a) selected area for the positioning in real time; (b) key points for the image correspondences; (c) augmented environment. From (Portalés Ricart, 2009)

Mobile AR-based CH applications (using HMD, glasses or mobile devices) represents the most common set-up such as in (Haugstvedt & Krogstie, 2012; Portalés et al., 2009), as it is very common that interaction is triggered through navigation, and thus users need to carry a device that is portable/ movable. In this sense, mobile phones and tablets are the preferred choice since it is the most affordable and portable configuration, especially for outdoor use. For instance, in (Jesús Gimeno & Morillo) a mobile-based outdoor AR application was developed to see the Sagrada Familia monument (under construction) as it will look like when it is finished. However, other paradigms, like spatial AR have also been used to project information over real CH items (Ridel et al., 2014). Regarding to HMD, one could think that the natural choice for AR applications are the ones that are optical-based, as the virtual information needs to be merged with the real world. However this is not always the case for different reasons, mainly because optical-based HMD is a less mature technology that video-based HMD; for instance, occlusions are more difficult to handle. On the other hand, the merging of real and virtual worlds can also be achieved with a video-based HMD provided with an integrated camera.

SERIOUS GAMES IN CULTURAL HERITAGE

An emergent trend in CH is the use of Serious Games (SGs). The term Serious Game is usually confused with other related terms such as "Simulator" or "Virtual Reality". Although the differences are sometimes subtle, it is important to clarify these terms.

A simulator is an application that replicates some experience, process, natural phenomenon or real situation. Although a simulator may not need a computer, computer-based simulation represent the majority of the simulation applications. In addition, a simulator does not need to visualize the result. Nevertheless, most of them do visualize the final result and the simulation process. Visualization is very important in CH.

VR, as defined earlier, deals with generating an alternative world so that users believe they are actually living this alternative (virtual) reality. In this regard, the virtual world needs to be simulated, and thus VR could be considered as a particular case of computer-based simulation in which the center of the process is a human being, since the goal is to simulate the perceptual cues a person would perceive in a real situation so as to make them believe they are experiencing the artificial world instead of the real one. VR has been widely used in CH.

Although many VR-applications and simulators are designed as games, they do not have to be games. For instance, an electrical simulator is an application that simulates the behavior of an electrical circuit but it is not a game and the result may not be visualized. SGs, on the contrary are usually defined as computer-based games with a particular learning purpose. It is widely accepted that SG are videogames designed for educational objectives. In this regard, they do not need to simulate a particular phenomenon (and if they do, simulation accuracy may not need to be high) and can use several interaction paradigms such as VR and AR. The important part is to get people learning by playing a game.

SGs have been successfully used to provide awareness about different aspects of life (Cetto et al., 2014; Madeira et al., 2011; Rebolledo-Mendez, Avramides, de Freitas, & Memarzia, 2009). Research suggests that these applications are hugely successful in generating public interest and an increase of awareness (Rebolledo-Mendez et al., 2009) since they can be both appealing for young people due to its ludic nature, and to adults as they provide rigorous information about diverse issues. In addition, they can benefit from the latest technological advances (stereo systems, VR headsets, AR displays, etc.), producing multimodal SGs (Liarokapis, Petridis, Andrews, & de Freitas, 2017) which increase productivity in different ways. CH is of course no exception and CH awareness-raising is one of the most important uses of SGs. In fact, SGs are probably the best envelope to promote CH and increase awareness since SGs are very effective at the affective domain; SGs do foster empathy as players can experience how was to live in a different culture probably at a different time. The advantages of computer-based applications is that the history clock can be traced back to almost any moment at any place. Although this kind of application was not common in CH a few years ago (Anderson et al., 2010), the number of CH-applications that are shaped as SGs is rapidly increasing (Mortara et al., 2014).

CH content is of course quite diverse. Therefore, the different CH-related SGs are very diverse as well. One the one hand, there are CH tangible assets. The SGs that deal with these assets focus on buildings, monuments, machines, landscapes, documents or works of art. These topics are usually covered with non-game VR applications, but they can also be designed as SG to engage people. Examples of SGs focused on tangible assets are: (Antoniou, Lepouras, Bampatzia, & Almpanoudi, 2013) where a systematic approach for the description and development of CH SGs is studied and applied to the case study of the Sanctuary of Vravrona (Greece), (Coenen, Mostmans, & Naessens, 2013) a pervasive serious game for use in museums, (Lercari, Mortara, & Forte, 2013) where Unity 3D is utilized to create a Virtual Reality SG about a fort in northern California, (Djaouti, Alvarez, Rampnoux, Charvillat, & Jessel, 2009) where two SGs about the prehistoric Gargas caves in France are presented and analyzed. In Figure 10, some examples of the application "Hablando con el Arte" are depicted. These applications were built to transmit artistic knowledge and values, and foster creativity to a very special public: persons with ASD (Autism Spectrum Disorder) and people with other mental disabilities (Orange, 2017).

Figure 10. Apps from "Hablando con el Arte", where: (a) "el sueño"; (b) "la ventana abierta"; (c) "la gallina ciega"

One the other hand, there are also intangible assets, such as traditions, dances, language, funerals, folklore, battles, stories, etc. There are fewer SGs about intangible assets because of the difficulty of knowing the details of intangible cultural aspects distant in time. Tangible assets are sometimes preserved (although, more often than not, they need reconstruction), whereas intangible assets are transmitted from generation to generation in chronicles, books or even orally. For this reason, it is fairly easy that they get distorted as generations pass. Therefore, in this case studio, historians play a key role, since interpretation of history is very important and draws a line between a fictional game and a CH-related SG. However, when enough information is available, these intangible assets are well reproduced by means of SG. Example of SGs dealing with intangible assets are: (Francis, 2006), where a role play game is used for players to experience the daily life of ordinary citizens in a virtual reconstruction of the 18th century colony of Williamsburg; (Gaitatzes, Christopoulos, & Papaioannou, 2004) a SGs about the ancient Olympic games in Olympia, Greece; (Mortara, Catalano, Fiucci, & Derntl, 2013) where a SG about Japanese culture, Icura, is described and assessed; (Huang & Huang, 2013), a SG about Taiwanese indigenous culture, focusing on the Atayal tribe. These SGs are crucial to engage people into active learning instead of being passive spectators. The fact that new technologies provide a way to interact and play with intangible assets that no longer exist, produce a better understanding of CH and it is a simple but effective way to increase awareness about CH. SGs have also a crucial advantage: they can be the perfect place where both tangible and intangible assets meet. The acquisition, recreation and 3D representation of tangible assets is of the utmost importance, but it is sometimes equally important to explain the relationship between these objects and their culture. This is sometimes overlooked and SGs offer the possibility of showing this relationship in a clear and fun way, linking for instance a battle with its weapons, a monument with their designers and architects, or an artwork with their creators.

CH-related SGs come in various formats: puzzles, action and adventure games, simulation games, role-playing and trivia games. Some are designed to be played for one person, but others are multiplayer games. The specific format depends on the CH asset and on the specific targets of the application. Therefore, few general guidelines can be offered.

Awareness is one of the objectives of CH-related SGs. However, they can also be used for economic reasons. One of these other reasons is tourism (Georgopoulos, Kontogianni, Koutsaftis, & Skamantzari, 2017) (Bujari, Ciman, Gaggi, & Palazzi, 2017; Xu, Buhalis, & Weber, 2017). Virtual tourism and virtual museums are two of the most exploited case scenarios for CH SGs.

In any case, the use of SGs provides indubitable benefits and represent an emerging trend in CH dissemination and understanding. However, on the down side, the design of a SG is complex as it involves the collaboration of multidisciplinary teams: engineers, artists, software developers (for the IT part), historians (to recreate or interpret history) and also (possibly differently from other VCH applications), psychologists and educators (for the learning part), etc. In addition it is difficult to provide a methodology to create and assess CH-related SG (Mortara et al., 2013), due to the diversity of topics and cultural aspects and the intrinsic difficulty of evaluating these applications. In this regard, CH-related applications should direct their effort in improving the assessment of their tools (Bellotti, Kapralos, Lee, Moreno-Ger, & Berta, 2013), although the potential benefits of these applications are so extensive that the task is worth doing.

CONCLUSIONS

In this chapter we have given an insight on different technologies and approaches that are nowadays relevant to proper document, disseminate and transmit added value of CH. The focus has been given to the virtual representation of both tangible and intangible assets, to what a previous step of acquisition or digitalization is required. Once 3D models of objects are achieved, it is crucial to select the appropriated means to depict them to the end-users, also providing the capabilities to inspect them or interact with them. In this sense, we have given an insight on the AR and VR technologies, also pointing to existing works in the CH sector. These technologies, though sharing many issues – especially those related to 3D graphics – have their own characteristics and benefits for disseminating and having access to the digitized CH. In essence, VR allows having access to virtual objects almost from everywhere, while users are immersed in a completely virtual environment. On the other hand, AR allows having an enhanced access to real objects by seamlessly blending them with virtual information. Thus, end-users need to visit the real environment, what can give an extra dimension in the CH interpretation and understanding. Another extra dimension to transfer our CH legacy to further generations is brought by the SGs technology, where the knowledge and skill transfer to end-users is possible by means of appealing games. SGs involve a gaming motor, where both the VR and AR interaction paradigms are possible, alone or in combination.

The described approaches and techniques arise as highly efficient tools to support documentation, dissemination and interpretation of CH, including also those cases where the objects do not exist nowadays (they are partially or totally destroyed) or in cases of intangible assets (battles, historical events, artistic techniques, etc.), where it is necessary to describe and create mental images of the objects to boost the deep understanding of the heritage and of the civilizations that created them. They provide a synoptic image upon which the interpretation discourse can be constructed.

Finally we would like to highlight that, in many occasions, the required work to design and implement interactive applications with rich virtual objects is not trivial, and usually a multidisciplinary team is required to handle the different steps, from documentation to reconstruction, modeling, interpretation, etc. This might involve different experts such as engineers, graphic artists, historians, archaeologists, etc. Despite of this, we believe that the benefits that these technologies bring for CH make them worth, as we have shown by the many different applications that are currently being used and that are focused on end-users, mainly the great public.

REFERENCES

Anderson, E. F., McLoughlin, L., Liarokapis, F., Peters, C., Petridis, P., & De Freitas, S. (2010). Developing serious games for cultural heritage: A state-of-the-art review. *Virtual Reality (Waltham Cross)*, *14*(4), 255–275. doi:10.100710055-010-0177-3

Andreetto, M., Brusco, N., & Cortelazzo, G. M. (2004). Automatic 3-d modeling of textured cultural heritage objects. *IEEE Transactions on Image Processing*, *13*(3), 354–369. doi:10.1109/TIP.2003.821351 PMID:15376927

Antoniou, A., Lepouras, G., Bampatzia, S., & Almpanoudi, H. (2013). An approach for serious game development for cultural heritage: Case study for an archaeological site and museum. *Journal on Computing and Cultural Heritage*, *6*(4), 17. doi:10.1145/2532630.2532633

Azuma, R. T. (1997). A survey of augmented reality. *Presence: Teleoper. Virtual Environ.*, *6*(4), 355–385. doi:10.1162/pres.1997.6.4.355

Bastanlar, Y., Grammalidis, N., Zabulis, X., Yilmaz, E., Yardimci, Y., & Triantafyllidis, G. (2008). 3D Reconstruction for a Cultural Heritage virtual tour system. *Paper presented at the The International Archives of the Photogrammetry, Remote Sensing and Spatial Information Sciences, 37*(b5).

Bellotti, F., Kapralos, B., Lee, K., Moreno-Ger, P., & Berta, R. (2013). Assessment in and of serious games: An overview. *Advances in Human-Computer Interaction*, *2013*, 1. doi:10.1155/2013/120791

Bimber, O., & Raskar, R. (2005). *Spatial Augmented Reality: Merging Real and Virtual Worlds*. A. K. Peters, Ltd. doi:10.1201/b10624

Blais, F., & Beraldin, J. A. (2006). Recent Developments in 3D Multi-modal Laser Imaging Applied to Cultural Heritage. *Machine Vision and Applications*, *17*(6), 395–409. doi:10.100700138-006-0025-3

Bodnar, J. L., Candoré, J. C., Nicolas, J. L., Szatanik, G., Detalle, V., & Vallet, J. M. (2012). Stimulated infrared thermography applied to help restoring mural paintings. *NDT & E International, 49*(0), 40–46. doi:10.1016/j.ndteint.2012.03.007

Bruno, F., Bruno, S., De Sensi, G., Luchi, M.-L., Mancuso, S., & Muzzupappa, M. (2010). From 3D reconstruction to virtual reality: A complete methodology for digital archaeological exhibition. *Journal of Cultural Heritage, 11*(1), 42–49. doi:10.1016/j.culher.2009.02.006

Bujari, A., Ciman, M., Gaggi, O., & Palazzi, C. E. (2017). Using gamification to discover cultural heritage locations from geo-tagged photos. *Personal and Ubiquitous Computing, 21*(2), 235–252. doi:10.100700779-016-0989-6

Cabrelles, M., Seguí, A. E., Navarro, S., Galcerá, S., Portalés, C., & Lerma, J. L. (2010). *3D Photorealistic modelling of stone monuments by dense image matching.* Paper presented at the International Archives of Photogrammetry, Remote Sensing and Spatial Information Sciences. Commission V Symposium, Newcastle upon Tyne, UK.

Casas, S., Portalés, C., García-Pereira, I., & Fernández, M. (2017). On a First Evaluation of ROMOT – a RObotic 3D MOvie Theatre – for Driving Safety. *Multimodal Technologies and Interaction.*

Caudell, T. P., & Mizell, D. W. (1992). Augmented reality: an application of heads-up display technology to manual manufacturing processes. *Proceedings of the Twenty-Fifth Hawaii International Conference on System Sciences.*

Cetto, A., Netter, M., Pernul, G., Richthammer, C., Riesner, M., Roth, C., & Sänger, J. (2014). *Friend inspector: a serious game to enhance privacy awareness in social networks.* arXiv preprint arXiv:1402.5878

Chang, K.-E., Chang, C.-T., Hou, H.-T., Sung, Y.-T., Chao, H.-L., & Lee, C.-M. (2014). Development and behavioral pattern analysis of a mobile guide system with augmented reality for painting appreciation instruction in an art museum. *Computers & Education, 71*(0), 185–197. doi:10.1016/j.compedu.2013.09.022

Chen, C.-Y., Chang, B., & Huang, P.-S. (2014). Multimedia augmented reality information system for museum guidance. *Personal and Ubiquitous Computing, 18*(2), 315–322. doi:10.100700779-013-0647-1

Chow, S.-K., & Chan, K.-L. (2009). Reconstruction of photorealistic 3D model of ceramic artefacts for interactive virtual exhibition. *Journal of Cultural Heritage, 10*(2), 161–173. doi:10.1016/j.culher.2008.08.011

Christopoulos, D., Mavridis, P., Andreadis, A., & Karigiannis, J. N. (2011). *Using Virtual Environments to Tell the Story:" The Battle of Thermopylae".* Paper presented at the Games and Virtual Worlds for Serious Applications (VS-GAMES), 2011 Third International Conference on.

Christou, C., Angus, C., Loscos, C., Dettori, A., & Roussou, M. (2006). A versatile large-scale multimodal VR system for cultural heritage visualization. *Proceedings of the ACM symposium on Virtual reality software and technology.* 10.1145/1180495.1180523

Coenen, T., Mostmans, L., & Naessens, K. (2013). MuseUs: Case study of a pervasive cultural heritage serious game. *Journal on Computing and Cultural Heritage, 6*(2), 8. doi:10.1145/2460376.2460379

Cruz-Neira, C., Sandin, D. J., DeFanti, T. A., Kenyon, R. V., & Hart, J. C. (1992). The CAVE: Audio visual experience automatic virtual environment. *Communications of the ACM, 35*(6), 64–73. doi:10.1145/129888.129892

Djaouti, D., Alvarez, J., Rampnoux, O., Charvillat, V., & Jessel, J.-P. (2009). *Serious games & cultural heritage: a case study of prehistoric caves.* Paper presented at the Virtual Systems and Multimedia, 2009. VSMM'09. 15th International Conference on. 10.1109/VSMM.2009.40

Ercek, R., Viviers, D., & Warzée, N. (2010). 3D reconstruction and digitalization of an archeological site, Itanos, Crete. *Virtual Archaeology Review, 1*(1). doi:10.4995/var.2010.4794

Francis, R. (2006). Revolution: Learning about history through situated role play in a virtual environment. *Proceedings of the American educational research association conference.*

Gaitatzes, A., Christopoulos, D., & Papaioannou, G. (2004). The ancient olympic games: being part of the experience. *Proceedings of the 5th International conference on Virtual Reality, Archaeology and Intelligent Cultural Heritage.*

Gaitatzes, A., Christopoulos, D., & Roussou, M. (2001a). Reviving the past: cultural heritage meets virtual reality. *Proceedings of the 2001 conference on Virtual reality, archeology, and cultural heritage.* 10.1145/584993.585011

Gaitatzes, A., Christopoulos, D., & Roussou, M. (2001b). Reviving the past: cultural heritage meets virtual reality. *Proceedings of the 2001 conference on Virtual reality, archeology, and cultural heritage.* 10.1145/584993.585011

Georgopoulos, A., Kontogianni, G., Koutsaftis, C., & Skamantzari, M. (2017). *Serious Games at the Service of Cultural Heritage and Tourism. In Tourism, Culture and Heritage in a Smart Economy* (pp. 3–17). Springer. doi:10.1007/978-3-319-47732-9_1

Gimeno, J., & Morillo, P. (n.d.). *A Mobile Augmented Reality System to Enjoy the Sagrada Familia.* Academic Press.

Gimeno, J., Olanda, R., Martinez, B., & Sanchez, F. M. (2011). Multiuser augmented reality system for indoor exhibitions. *Proceedings of the 13th IFIP TC 13 international conference on Human-computer interaction.* 10.1007/978-3-642-23768-3_86

Gimeno, J., Portalés, C., Coma, I., Fernández, M., & Martínez, B. (2017). Combining Traditional and Indirect Augmented Reality for Indoor Crowded Environments. A Case Study on the Casa Batlló Museum. *Computers & Graphics, 69*, 92–103. doi:10.1016/j.cag.2017.09.001

Giner Martínez, F., & Portalés Ricart, C. (2005). *The Augmented User: A Wearable Augmented Reality Interface.* Paper presented at the International Conference on Virtual Systems and Multimedia (VSMM'05), Ghent, Belgium.

Granero-Montagud, L., Portalés, C., Pastor-Carbonell, B., Ribes-Gómez, E., Gutiérrez-Lucas, A., Tornari, V., . . . Dietz, C. (2013). *Deterioration estimation of paintings by means of combined 3D and hyperspectral data analysis.* Paper presented at the SPIE - Optics for Arts, Architecture, and Archaeology IV. 10.1117/12.2020336

Groves, R. M., Portalés, C., & Ribes-Gómez, E. (2014). *Assessment of Mechanical and Chemical Deterioration of Artworks.* Paper presented at the International Conference on Ageing of Materials & Structures (AMS), Delft, The Netherlands.

Guarnieri, A., Remondino, F., & Vettore, A. (2006). Digital photogrammetry and TLS data fusion applied to Cultural Heritage 3D modeling. *International Archives of Photogrammetry, Remote Sensing and Spatial Information Sciences. ISPRS Commission V Symposium, Dresden, Germany, 36*(part 5).

Guidi, G., Russo, M., & Angheleddu, D. (2014). 3D Survey and virtual reconstruction of archeological sites. *Digital Applications in Archaeology and Cultural Heritage, 1*(2), 55–69. doi:10.1016/j.daach.2014.01.001

Gutierrez, D., Seron, F. J., Magallon, J. A., Sobreviela, E. J., & Latorre, P. (2004). Archaeological and cultural heritage: Bringing life to an unearthed Muslim suburb in an immersive environment. *Journal of Cultural Heritage, 5*(1), 63–74. doi:10.1016/j.culher.2003.10.001

Haugstvedt, A.-C., & Krogstie, J. (2012). *Mobile augmented reality for cultural heritage: A technology acceptance study.* Paper presented at the Mixed and Augmented Reality (ISMAR), 2012 IEEE International Symposium on. 10.1109/ISMAR.2012.6402563

Huang, C.-H., & Huang, Y.-T. (2013). An annales school-based serious game creation framework for taiwanese indigenous cultural heritage. *Journal on Computing and Cultural Heritage, 6*(2), 9. doi:10.1145/2460376.2460380

Imposa, S. (2010). Infrared thermography and Georadar techniques applied to the "Sala delle Nicchie" (Niches Hall) of Palazzo Pitti, Florence (Italy). *Journal of Cultural Heritage, 11*(3), 259–264. doi:10.1016/j.culher.2009.04.005

Jiménez Fernández-Palacios, B., Morabito, D., & Remondino, F. (2016). Access to complex reality-based 3D models using virtual reality solutions. *Journal of Cultural Heritage.*

Kiourt, C., Koutsoudis, A., & Pavlidis, G. (2016). DynaMus: A fully dynamic 3D virtual Museum framework. *Journal of Cultural Heritage, 22,* 984–991. doi:10.1016/j.culher.2016.06.007

Lercari, N., Mortara, M., & Forte, M. (2013). *Unveiling California history through serious games: Fort Ross virtual warehouse.* Paper presented at the International Conference on Games and Learning Alliance.

Lerma, J. L., Cabrelles, M., & Portalés, C. (2011). Multitemporal thermal analysis to detect moisture on a building façade. *Construction & Building Materials, 25*(5), 2190–2197. doi:10.1016/j.conbuildmat.2010.10.007

Lerones, P. M., Fernández, J. L., Gil, Á. M., Gómez-García-Bermejo, J., & Casanova, E. Z. (2010). A practical approach to making accurate 3D layouts of interesting cultural heritage sites through digital models. *Journal of Cultural Heritage, 11*(1), 1–9. doi:10.1016/j.culher.2009.02.007

Liarokapis, F., Petridis, P., Andrews, D., & de Freitas, S. (2017). *Multimodal Serious Games Technologies for Cultural Heritage. In Mixed Reality and Gamification for Cultural Heritage* (pp. 371–392). Springer. doi:10.1007/978-3-319-49607-8_15

Madeira, R. N., Silva, A., Santos, C., Teixeira, B., Romão, T., Dias, E., & Correia, N. (2011). LEY! Persuasive pervasive gaming on domestic energy consumption-awareness. *Proceedings of the 8th International Conference on Advances in Computer Entertainment Technology.* 10.1145/2071423.2071512

Maicas, J. M., & Viñals, M. J. (2016). Edeta 360° Virtual Tour for visiting the heritage of Lliria (Spain). *Proceedings of the Archaeologica 2.0. 8th International Congres on Archaeology, Computer Graphics, Cultural Heritage and Innovation.*

Michele, G., Michele, D. D., & Fabio, S. (2013). *VisitAR: a mobile application for tourism using AR.* Paper presented at the SIGGRAPH Asia 2013 Symposium on Mobile Graphics and Interactive Applications, Hong Kong, Hong Kong. 10.1145/2543651.2543665

Miguélez Fernández, L. (2013). *Tour virtual por la red de museos de Gijón* (Master). Univeridad de Oviedo.

Mortara, M., Catalano, C. E., Bellotti, F., Fiucci, G., Houry-Panchetti, M., & Petridis, P. (2014). Learning cultural heritage by serious games. *Journal of Cultural Heritage, 15*(3), 318–325. doi:10.1016/j.culher.2013.04.004

Mortara, M., Catalano, C. E., Fiucci, G., & Derntl, M. (2013). *Evaluating the effectiveness of serious games for cultural awareness: the Icura user study.* Paper presented at the International Conference on Games and Learning Alliance.

Navarro, S., Seguí, A. E., Portalés, C., Lerma, J. L., Akasheh, T., & Haddad, N. (2009). *Integration of tls data and non-metric imagery to improve photo models and recording-a case study on djin block no. 9, petra (jordan).* Paper presented at the Virtual Systems and Multimedia.

Nguyen, M., Tran, H., & Le, H. (2017). Exploration of the 3D World on the Internet Using Commodity Virtual Reality Devices. *Multimodal Technologies and Interaction, 1*(3), 15. doi:10.3390/mti1030015

Orange. (2017). *Fundación Orange. Hablando con el arte.* Retrieved from http://www.fundacionorange.es/aplicaciones/hablando-con-el-arte-apps/

Portalés, C., Alonso-Monasterio, P., & Viñals, M. J. (2017). 3D virtual reconstruction and visualisation of the archaeological site Castellet de Bernabé (Llíria, Spain). *Virtual Archaeology Review, 8*(16), 75–82. doi:10.4995/var.2017.5890

Portalés, C., Casas, S., Alonso-Monasterio, P., & Viñals, M. J. (2017). Multi-Dimensional Acquisition, Representation and Interaction of Cultural Heritage Tangible Assets. An Insight on Tourism Applications. In J. M. F. Rodrigues, C. M. Q. Ramos, P. J. S. Cardoso, & C. Henriques (Eds.), *Handbook of Research on Technological Developments for Cultural Heritage and eTourism Applications.* IGI-Global.

Portalés, C., Casas, S., Coma, I., & Fernández, M. (2017). A Multi-Projector Calibration Method for Virtual Reality Simulators with Analytically Defined Screens. *Journal of Imaging, 3*(2), 19. doi:10.3390/jimaging3020019

Portalés, C., Gimeno, J., Casas, S., Olanda, R., & Giner, F. (2016). Interacting with augmented reality mirrors. In J. Rodrigues, P. Cardoso, J. Monteiro, & M. Figueiredo (Eds.), *Handbook of Research on Human-Computer Interfaces, Developments, and Applications* (pp. 216–244). IGI-Global. doi:10.4018/978-1-5225-0435-1.ch009

Portalés, C., Lerma, J. L., & Pérez, C. (2009). Photogrammetry and augmented reality for cultural heritage applications. *The Photogrammetric Record, 24*(128), 316–331. doi:10.1111/j.1477-9730.2009.00549.x

Portalés, C., & Perales, C. D. (2009). *Sound and Movement Visualization in the AR-Jazz Scenario.* Paper presented at the International Conference on Entertainment Computing (ICEC). 10.1007/978-3-642-04052-8_15

Portalés, C., Viñals, M. J., Alonso-Monasterio, P., & Morant, M. (2010). AR-Immersive Cinema at the Aula Natura Visitors Center. *IEEE MultiMedia, 17*(4), 8–15. doi:10.1109/MMUL.2010.72

Portalés Ricart, C. (2009). *Entornos multimedia de realidad aumentada en el campo del arte* (Doctoral Thesis). Universidad Politécnica de Valencia, Valencia.

Portalés Ricart, C., Giner Martínez, F., & Sanmartín Piquer, F. (2005). Back to the 70's. *Proceedings of the ACM SIGCHI International Conference on Advances in Computer Entertainment Technology.*

Rebolledo-Mendez, G., Avramides, K., de Freitas, S., & Memarzia, K. (2009). Societal impact of a serious game on raising public awareness: the case of FloodSim. *Proceedings of the 2009 ACM SIGGRAPH Symposium on Video Games.* 10.1145/1581073.1581076

Reffat, R. M., & Nofal, E. M. (2013). Effective Communication with Cultural heritage using Virtual Technologies. *The International Archives of the Photogrammetry, Remote Sensing and Spatial Information Sciences, XL-5*(W2), 519–524. doi:10.5194/isprsarchives-XL-5-W2-519-2013

Rekimoto, J., & Nagao, K. (1995). The world through the computer: computer augmented interaction with real world environments. *Proceedings of the 8th annual ACM symposium on User interface and software technology.* 10.1145/215585.215639

Ridel, B., Reuter, P., Laviole, J., Mellado, N., Couture, N., & Granier, X. (2014). The Revealing Flashlight: Interactive spatial augmented reality for detail exploration of cultural heritage artifacts. *Journal on Computing and Cultural Heritage, 7*(2), 6. doi:10.1145/2611376

Rodrigues, N., Magalhaes, L. G., Moura, J. P., & Chalmers, A. (2008). Automatic Reconstruction of Virtual Heritage Sites. *Proceedings International Symposium on Virtual Reality, Archaeology and Intelligent Cultural Heritage.*

Rolland, J. P., Holloway, R. L., & Fuchs, H. (1994). *A comparison of optical and video see-through head-mounted displays.* Paper presented at the SPIE - Telemanipulator and Telepresence Technologies.

Salvi, J., Fernandez, S., Pribanic, T., & Llado, X. (2010). A state of the art in structured light patterns for surface profilometry. *Pattern Recognition, 43*(8), 2666–2680. doi:10.1016/j.patcog.2010.03.004

Sevilla, J., Martin, G., Casillas, J., Martinez, B., Blasco, J., & Pérez, M. (2000). *Utilización de entornos de visualización inmersiva en la transmisión del conocimiento. Un museo virtual de Santiago Ramón y Cajal.* Paper presented at the CEIG 2000:X Congreso Español de Informática Gráfica.

Styliania, S., Fotisb, L., Kostasa, K., & Petrosa, P. (2009). Virtual museums, a survey and some issues for consideration. *Journal of Cultural Heritage*, *10*(4), 520–528. doi:10.1016/j.culher.2009.03.003

Tilden, F. (1957). Interpreting our heritage (R. B. Graig, Ed.; 4th ed.). The University of North Carolina Press.

Trinchão Andrade, B., Mazetto Mendes, C., de Oliveira Santos Jr, J., Pereira Bellon, O. R., & Silva, L. (2012). 3D preserving xviii century barroque masterpiece: Challenges and results on the digital preservation of Aleijadinho's sculpture of the Prophet Joel. *Journal of Cultural Heritage*, *13*(2), 210–214. doi:10.1016/j.culher.2011.05.003

Vidal, C., & Muñoz, G. (2015). Métodos avanzados para el análisis y documentación de la arqueología y la arquitectura maya: los "mascarones" de Chiloé y La Blanca. In C. Vidal & G. Muñoz (Eds.), *Artistic Expressions in Maya Architecture: Analysis and Documentation Techniques* (pp. 75–90). Oxford, UK: Archaeopress.

Vlahakis, V., Ioannidis, N., Karigiannis, J., Tsotros, M., Gounaris, M., Stricker, D., ... Almeida, L. (2002). Archeoguide: An Augmented Reality Guide for Archaeological Sites. *IEEE Computer Graphics and Applications*, *22*(5), 52–60. doi:10.1109/MCG.2002.1028726

Webel, S., Olbrich, M., Franke, T., & Keil, J. (2013). *Immersive experience of current and ancient reconstructed cultural attractions*. Paper presented at the Digital Heritage International Congress (DigitalHeritage). 10.1109/DigitalHeritage.2013.6743766

Wessels, S., Ruther, H., Bhurtha, R., & Schröeder, R. (2014). *Design and creation of a 3D Virtual Tour of the world heritage site of Petra, Jordan*. Paper presented at the AfricaGeo.

Wojciechowski, R., Walczak, K., White, M., & Cellary, W. (2004). Building virtual and augmented reality museum exhibitions. *Proceedings of the ninth international conference on 3D Web technology*. 10.1145/985040.985060

Wu, C. (2017). *VisualSFM: A Visual Structure from Motion System*. Retrieved from http://ccwu.me/vsfm/

Xu, F., Buhalis, D., & Weber, J. (2017). Serious games and the gamification of tourism. *Tourism Management*, *60*, 244–256. doi:10.1016/j.tourman.2016.11.020

Yastikli, N. (2007). Documentation of cultural heritage using digital photogrammetry and laser scanning. *Journal of Cultural Heritage*, *8*(4), 423–427. doi:10.1016/j.culher.2007.06.003

KEY TERMS AND DEFINITIONS

Augmented Reality: A technology that allows seamlessly displaying virtual information blended with the real world.

Digital Representation of Data: Reproduction of data by means of digital forms, as enabled by computers.

Intangible Assets: Assets that do not have a physical form, including stories, beliefs, ideas, traditions, folklore, etc.

Interaction: A kind of action that occurs as two or more objects have an effect upon one another.

Serious Game: A game designed for a primary purpose different than entertainment, usually a computer-based game designed for learning and awareness-raising.

Tangible Assets: Assets that have a physical form, including buildings, places, monuments, tools, artefacts, etc.

Three-Dimensional (3D) Data: Data that is realized in a three-dimensional space, a geometric setting in which three values are required to determine the position of an element.

Virtual Reality: A technology that allows replacing the real world by a synthetic one, making the user believe that she/he is in another realm.

Virtual Reconstruction: Modelling of structures by means of computational tools.

Chapter 8
Calculating Absolute Scale and Scale Uncertainty for SfM Using Distance Sensor Measurements:
A Lightweight and Flexible Approach

Ivan Nikolov
https://orcid.org/0000-0002-4952-8848
Aalborg University, Denmark

Claus B. Madsen
https://orcid.org/0000-0003-0762-3713
Aalborg University, Denmark

ABSTRACT

Capturing details of objects and surfaces using structure from motion (SfM) 3D reconstruction has become an important part of data gathering in geomapping, medicine, cultural heritage, and the energy and production industries. One inherent problem with SfM, due to its reliance on 2D images, is the ambiguity of the reconstruction's scale. Absolute scale can be calculated by using the data from additional sensors. This chapter demonstrates how distance sensors can be used to calculate the scale of a reconstructed object. In addition, the authors demonstrate that the uncertainty of the calculated scale can be computed and how it depends on the precision of the used sensors. The provided methods are straightforward and easy to integrate into the workflow of commercial SfM solutions.

INTRODUCTION

Structure from Motion (SfM) techniques have matured throughout the years to become viable commercial solutions for 3D reconstruction. This is due to the techniques' scalability, relative ease of use and the fact that they do not rely on specialized equipment. This positions SfM as a useful substitute for other reconstruction approaches that require both specialized hardware and software, like structured

DOI: 10.4018/978-1-5225-5294-9.ch008

light (Sarbolandi, 2015), stereo (Sarker, 2017) or time-of-flight cameras (Corti, 2016), when real-time performance is not necessary.

The algorithm pipeline for SfM is extensively documented by (Özyeşil, 2017) and the accuracy of different solutions for varying use cases are discussed by (Nikolov I. A., 2016), (Knapitsch, 2017) . There are several approaches to performing SfM reconstruction, but a typical algorithm takes 2D images looking at the reconstructed object or surface, from different positions and directions. Another important feature of SfM is the possibility to use it both with images from precisely calibrated capturing setups (Martell, 2018), as well as with in the wild image datasets (Makantasis, 2016), requiring more post-processing in filtering the image data and clustering it, but saving on long capturing times.

In the SfM processing pipeline, a number of feature points are extracted from each image and matched with features from the input images. These feature matches are filtered and together with the intrinsic parameters of the cameras are used in a bundle adjustment algorithm to triangulate the camera positions in 3D space, as well as a sparse point cloud. A depth map and dense point cloud are then computed. Finally, if needed, the dense point cloud is meshed and a texture is calculated from the images. One drawback of using only uncalibrated 2D images as input is that the scale of the reconstruction is ambiguous. To calculate the absolute scale, additional information is needed. This information can be captured manually, by using objects of known sizes in the images or by using additional sensors.

This chapter focuses on using additional sensors for calculating the absolute scale of the 3D reconstruction. It demonstrates a step-by-step solution which uses external distance sensors to provide the necessary information. In addition, the authors take into consideration that real-world sensors' readings contain level of uncertainty, which in turn is transferred to the calculated scale. The discussed solutions take this into consideration and demonstrate that these uncertainties can be quantified.

The chapter's contributions to the field of SfM can be summarized as:

- A lightweight and easy to implement method for finding the absolute scale of a SfM reconstruction using distance sensors;
- The method is easy to integrate into existing commercial SfM solutions, as it requires only simple outputs, such as a 3D mesh and camera positions and orientations;
- The method is flexible and can be used both with expensive LiDAR solutions, as well as cheap distance measurement sensors, as it does not require capturing the object surface;
- The uncertainty of the computed absolute scale can be calculated, when high precision is required.

STATE OF THE ART

All state of the art SfM solutions, both open-source (Wu, 2011), (Sweeney, 2015), (Schonberger, 2016) and commercial (Agisoft, 2010), (Bentley, 2016), (CapturingReality, 2016), contain some kind of built-in way to manually scale the final 3D reconstruction using information captured from the environment. Normally, users can manually measure parts of the real and reconstructed objects and compute the resultant scaling factor. Another widely used method is relying on markers with predefined shapes and sizes. These markers are put on the reconstructed object or surface and are captured in the images. Later the scale of the object can be calculated from the ratio between the real-world size of the marker and the captured size. Both methods rely on the fact that the real object is easily accessible and are time consuming, which makes them not ideal for all use cases. In addition, there is no easy way to predict any introduced uncertainty to the calculated absolute scale.

Other approaches for estimating the scale, base assumptions on known factors of the capturing environment, like the height (Giubilato, 2018), (Zhou, 2016) or the kinematic model of the motion (Li, 2019). Finally, some approaches rely on data from external sensors. Positioning data is widely used for geo-referencing and scaling the reconstruction, as seen in the work by (Rabah, 2018), (Turner, 2012), (Clapuyt, 2016), (Nikolov & Madsen, 2019). Other multimodal approaches (Kim, 2015), (Schöps, 2015) take advantage of inertial measuring units (IMU) for calculating the positioning, rotation and movement of the cameras. Combining SfM and LiDAR scans has the added benefit of determining the scale of the reconstruction, as shown by (Ding, 2017), (Lu, 2020) .

Building on the findings of the state of the art, a lightweight scaling solution can be achieved by introducing additional sensor data. This way data for the scaling can be captured together with the image data without the need for additional manual measurements. Position sensors are widely used for outdoor SfM reconstruction, but their reliance on GPS and other external position sensors makes them impractical for indoor use. Another problem with these systems can arise if the captured object or surface moves, while images are taken, as the captured positions are normally of the camera. To mitigate this problem, the position of the captured object needs to be tracked as well, making the setup even more complicated. Movement tracking sensors like IMUs are another possibility, but they require filtering and constant calibration to offset the possible drifting. Finally, distance sensors like LiDAR solutions give high precision measurements, but most present systems try to create a full 3D scan of the environment, which can introduce considerable computation load.

The solution described in the chapter takes the idea of using distance measurements from the camera to the captured object or surface, to calculate the scale of the reconstruction, but minimizes the necessary readings. It does not need to create a full 3D scan and can be used with both single direction distance measurement sensors, as well as high-quality multi-directional LiDAR solutions. This can streamline the often long and complicated process of capturing additional data for SfM reconstructions and provide a simple scaling way to already existing 3D reconstruction pipelines (Voulodimos, 2016).

Additionally, because all sensors possess a certain amount of noise in their readings, the solution takes that into account and computes the scale together with the amount of uncertainty. This way highly precise measurements can be taken from the reconstructions.

METHODOLOGY

The methodology is divided into parts, containing the different steps that go into building the proposed solution. As an initial step, a basic SfM pipeline will be described and the production of a 3D reconstruction, with an unknown absolute scale, together with the other outputs needed for the proposed solution. Using this as a basis, the proposed solution of using distance sensors is introduced. For producing a 3D reconstruction with an absolute scale, two main parts are needed – a calibrated fixed rig containing the distance sensor and the camera used for SfM and an algorithm for comparing the real distance measurements, to the ones captured from the reconstructed objects or surfaces. Finally, when needing high degree of accuracy in the calculated scaling factors, the uncertainty introduced by the used distance sensors needs to be taken into account. To do this, two additional parts are introduced in the proposed solution – an initial sensor uncertainty modeling and an algorithm for propagating this uncertainty to the calculated scaling factor.

SfM RECONSTRUCTION OVERVIEW

For reconstructing objects or surfaces using SfM, only a normal color camera sensor is required. More importantly, images need to be taken of the scanned object, from varying positions and angles, so the overall shape, size and surface detail can easily be described. Images need to be taken with a certain degree of overlap, normally at least 70% to 80% overlap, as specified in the work by (Özyeşil, 2017) and (Nikolov I. A., 2016). From each image a number of feature points are extracted and matched between images. Feature extractors and descriptors like SURF (Bay, 2006), SIFT (Lowe, 2004), FAST (Rosten, 2006) or ORB (Rublee, 2011) are used with a lot of commercial SfM, having proprietary solutions. From these matched features, together with the calculated intrinsic camera calibrations, a 3D triangulation is done between the unordered images, using any of the many bundle adjustment implementations (Triggs, 1999). This results in the creation of a sparse 3D point cloud, plus the calculation of the back-projected camera positions. The sparse point cloud can then be densified, by interpolating the information from the calculated 3D points. The resultant dense point cloud can be meshed if needed, with additional steps like texture calculation from projecting the camera images onto the 3D model, removing noise, closing holes, etc. If no additional information is provided to the application, the final output is scaled to an unknown scale, with the SfM applications trying to guess a correct one depending on the calculated camera positions, intrinsic parameters, size of the captured object, etc. This calculated scale can vary from one object to another and can be different even between multiple computations on the same datasets, as seen in Figure 1.

Figure 1. Example of a SfM reconstruction, resulting in a 3D object with unknown absolute scale. Several images of the object are taken from different positions and angles

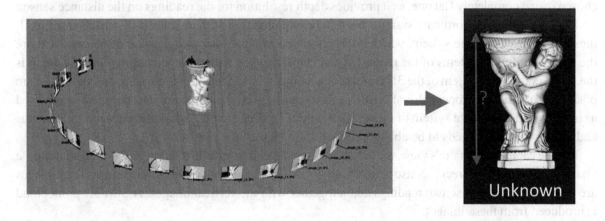

SCALED SfM RECONSTRUCTION USING DISTANCE SENSORS

To introduce an absolute scale to the SfM pipeline additional real-world data is needed. In the method proposed by the authors this data comes from distance sensors. In the next chapter the basis for the proposed algorithm will be explained. For this chapter the sensor used as an example is the mid-range LiDAR solution by Hokuyo - the UTM-30LX (Hokuyo, 2010). As it will be shown in the later chapters and the Results section, this sensor can easily be interchanged with other cheaper alternatives and the proposed methods will retain their validity. Initially the chosen sensor needs to be attached to a fixed rig together with the camera, used for capturing images for SfM. The transformation between the two needs to be calibrated as well. This initial calibration needs to be done only once and after that the rig can be used together with the proposed algorithms for calculating the absolute scale of the captured objects.

Extrinsic Calibration Between Camera and Sensor

An initial extrinsic calibration between the real-world camera and each used distance sensor needs to be calculated. This calibration provides the position and orientation of the sensor compared to the camera, which eliminates problems that can arise from the lever-arm effect (Daakir, 2016), which is normally present when using GPS sensors for georeferencing. It also gives an initial guess for the scale of the reconstructed object. It is important to note that in a perfect world this calibration would be enough to give a correct absolute scaling factor, but because of possible errors in the calibration and initial positions of the camera and sensor, here the authors use it only as an initial guess, which is used as a basis for the second part of the proposed method. Also, this part needs to be done just once as long as the transformation between the sensor and the camera is not changed. The proposed calibration steps are the same for any used distance sensor.

To prevent any unintended movements, the sensor is mounted on a bracket together with the camera with the forward direction of the two pointing at the same direction, as seen in Figure 2a). The position and orientation between the two in unknown and the proposed calibration is done using a 3D checkerboard, consisting of a flat plane with a set of 24 four sided pyramids, as shown in Figure 2b). This design is chosen over a completely flat one, as it provides depth resolution for the readings on the distance sensor.

Here the required coordinate systems need to be explained. First there are the distance sensor readings' 2D local coordinate system, which are represented as polar, using angles and distances. Next are the local coordinate systems of the reconstructed cameras, each with their orientation. Finally, there is the world coordinate system of the 3D reconstructed object, in which both the cameras and the object are position. To achieve a proper calibration, the sensor readings' 2D local coordinates, need to be expressed as in the world coordinate system of the reconstruction. To perform the calibration between the cameras and the sensors, each needs to be able to produce a 3D view of the checkerboard.

For the capturing camera's view, the 3D model is produced from a SfM reconstruction from multiple images. To ensure a correct reconstruction both horizontal images in a semi-circle and vertical images are taken, with distance sensor readings taken together with the vertical images. A SfM 3D point cloud is produced from these images.

Figure 2. The 3D checkerboard calibration artifact, used for finding the transformation between the sensors and the camera

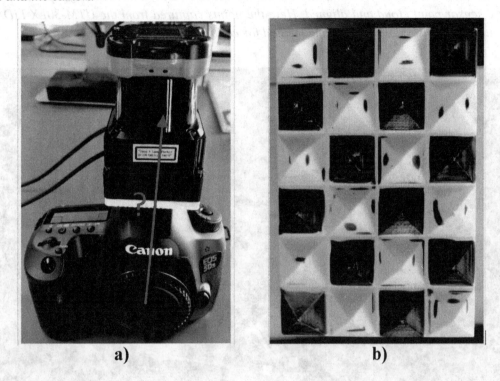

a)   b)

Next the same needs to be done from the distance sensor's readings. Because the sensor's readings are in its local coordinate system, they need to be transformed into the unified coordinate system of the SfM reconstructed point cloud. SfM solutions calculate the camera positions together with the reconstructed objects. For simplicity, the authors will show the calculation for one camera, from the full set $k=[1,2,...,C]$ same calculations are valid for all other cameras.

The camera position is used as an origin point to transform the distance sensor's readings to the proper coordinate system. To do this first, the sensor readings are transformed from polar to Cartesian coordinates, with the camera position as origin, using Equation 1, where in the case of the HC-SR04, the direction angle of the only distance measurement is set at 0 degrees. In the equation, x_{origin}, y_{origin}, z_{origin} are the coordinates of the camera position origin, l_i is the sensor distance at angle φ_i for each of the readings, where the number of readings can vary and for simplicity it is expressed as $i=[1,2,...,n_k]$.

$$x_i = x_{origin} - l_i \cos(\varphi_i), \ y_i = y_{origin} - l_i \cos(\varphi_i), \ z_i = z_{origin} \tag{1}$$

The transformed sensor point set is then rotated in 3D space from the camera's local coordinate system to the global coordinate system of the reconstruction, using the camera's calculated rotation matrix, denoted in Equation 2 as R. The SfM dense point cloud and transformed Cartesian readings from the UTM-30LX LiDAR can be seen in Figure 3.

Figure 3. The two-point clouds used for the initial calibration process for detecting the transformation between the camera and sensor. Point pairs are manually selected from the dense SfM point cloud and the sparse sensor point cloud and aligned. Here the points captured from the UTM-30LX LiDAR are shown, with other sensors, using the same method for calibration.

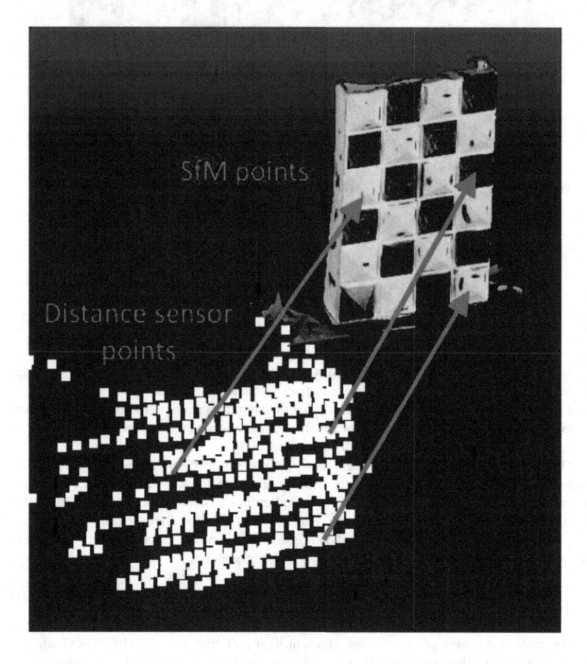

$$\begin{bmatrix} x_{i_w} \\ y_{i_w} \\ z_{i_w} \end{bmatrix} = R\left(\begin{bmatrix} x_i \\ y_i \\ z_i \end{bmatrix} \right) \tag{2}$$

Once the 3D point cloud, created from combining all the distance readings, is in the same coordinate system, as the one created from the SfM reconstruction, the final transformation between them can be done. This transformation finds the position of the distance sensor's origin compared to the capturing camera, at each position. There are a number of manual and automatic ways to achieve this, but because there is no direct correspondence between the points of the two point clouds, the authors use the manual cloud alignment tool, which comes with CloudCompare (Girardeau-Montaut, 2003).To calculate the transformation matrix, a number of equivalent points are selected from the two point clouds and the distance error between them is minimized. As a result, a transformation matrix is calculated, which is used in the next part of the method.

Absolute Scale Calculation Using Distance Measurements

Once the initial calibration is done once, the next steps can be done for each measured object or surface. For each camera position, a sensor reading of the distance to the object is taken. These distance readings are used as input for the proposed solution, together with the reconstructed SfM object and the camera positions and orientations. The process is shown in Figure 4 and explained in the next paragraphs.

Figure 4. Second part of the solution for finding the absolute scale of a SfM reconstruction using the ratio between real-world and calculated distance measurements

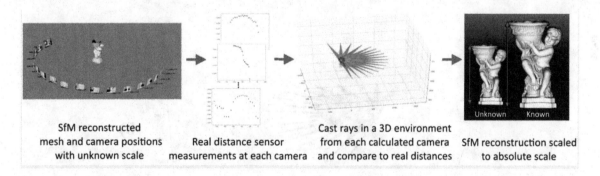

SfM reconstructed mesh and camera positions with unknown scale

Real distance sensor measurements at each camera

Cast rays in a 3D environment from each calculated camera and compare to real distances

SfM reconstruction scaled to absolute scale

To calculate the absolute scale of the SfM reconstruction, the real-life sensor measurements from each camera position need to be compared to the distances calculated from reconstructed camera position to the reconstructed object or surface. Naturally, in a best-case scenario these two distances can be the same, but because of the way SfM calculates the reconstructed object, as well as imperfections in the calibration, etc., the two distances can be far off. Initially each camera position is taken and the inverse transformation matrix, calculated in the initial calibration part, is used to find the position of the distance sensor for that camera. A ray is cast from the distance sensor's position toward the reconstructed object and if they hit it, the distance between the two is calculated and saved. The number of rays cast from the position of the sensor for each camera depends on the angular resolution of that sensor. To demonstrate the idea, in Figure 5a the rays that hit the reconstruction from one sensor position are shown, while in Figure 5b, the same is shown for a number of sensor position. The two figures show calculated distance rays created using the characteristics of the UTM-30LX LiDAR.

Figure 5. Visualization of the rays from a single camera and the points hit on the object (a), together with the ray hits from each camera on the reconstructed mesh (b). UTM-30LX LiDAR readings. For easier visualization only a subset of the vertices of the mesh is visualized.

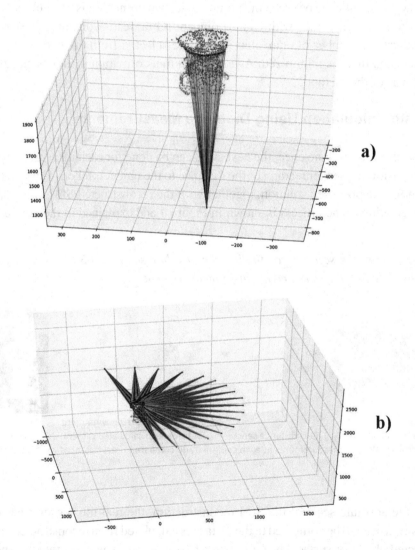

To simplify the calculations, an average distance $\bar{r}$. is computed from all the calculated distance rays r_j for each camera position. The number of distance rays $j=[1,2,\ldots,m_k]$ can vary from camera to camera, depending on the shape of the reconstructed mesh and is denoted with m_k.

To calculate the scale factor between the real-life object and the reconstruction, real sensor readings are needed from each camera position. Here it is important to note that a hypothesis is made that for each camera position that the real sensors have readings on the object, the same camera position also has calculated ray distances from the reconstructed object mesh. With this the number of cameras is denoted by $k=[1,2,…,C]$ where C is the number of camera positions with readings both from the real and reconstructed object. The real-life sensor measurements are denoted in the same way, as the one used for the extrinsic calibration – l_i where $i=[1,2,..,n_k]$. Here again the readings can vary from camera to camera and for simplicity they are marked with one variable. From all the sensor readings of each camera an average distance measurement is calculated $\bar{l}$. From the two average distance readings – the real life one and the reconstructed one the scaling factor s_k can be calculated as a ratio for each camera position. An average scaling factor is calculated from the factors calculated for each camera position. This calculation is presented in Equation 3. Here is important to note that if a single direction distance sensor is used, like the HC-SR04, then $n_k=m_k=1$ for each camera and the average values of both the real and the calculated distances, can be substituted for the single reading.

$$ s = \frac{1}{c} \sum_{k=1}^{c} \left(\frac{\frac{1}{n_k} \sum_{i=1}^{n_k} l_i}{\frac{1}{m_k} \sum_{j=1}^{m_k} r_j} \right) = \frac{1}{c} \sum_{k=1}^{c} \left(\frac{\bar{l}_k}{\bar{r}_k} \right) \tag{3} $$

Normally one pass should be sufficient to calculate a proper scale factor, but there are a number of complicating factors, which can make this calculation incorrect:

- Imperfections in the initial extrinsic calibration – because the initial calibration requires manual input and uses a distance minimization algorithm, there is always a possibility of falling into a local minimum, not representative of the best possible solution of the transformation;
- Captured objects or surfaces can have complex shapes with both micro- and macro-roughness, which can present problems for both the real distance sensor's readings, as well as for the distance readings from the reconstructed object. Small changes in the direction of the cast ray can give large changes in the returned distances. This can be mitigated with the use of distance sensors with higher angular resolutions in both 2D and 3D, but it is still a large factor for less complex sensors;
- Because of the way SfM works, by matching features from multiple 2D images, it is prone to creating surface noise and reconstruction inaccuracies, when the capturing conditions are sub-optimal. These problems can be mitigated somewhat with the use of surface smoothing and denoising algorithms, but can still interfere with the calculated distances from the reconstructions, throwing off the initial computed scaling factors.

A way to deal with these possible problems is to do multiple iterative passes on calculating the scaling factor. Before each pass the previously calculated factor is used to scale the reconstruction. Rays are then cast again and a new factor is calculated. The algorithm stops either after a predetermined number of times or when the calculated Root Mean Square Error (RMSE) between the real sensor distances and the calculated ones from the reconstruction drops below a certain threshold. Once the end criteria are reached, the final scaling factor s_{final} is calculated, by multiplying all the temporary factors s as seen in Equation 4, where g is the number of iterations needed to reach the end criteria. Here it is important to note that the average sensor distance l_{avg} is measured in [mm]. In the first iteration of the algorithm the ray distances are unitless [.] while in the consecutive iterations the they are again in [mm]. This means that the final unit of the scaling factor is also [mm].

$$s_{final} = \prod_1^g s \qquad (4)$$

For most SfM reconstruction this can be a final result, which would be useful for detecting the absolute scale in a simple and straightforward way, with minimal additional captured data. But when a high degree of precision is required from the reconstruction, for example for surface inspection, where millimeter or even sub-millimeter accuracy is the norm, additional steps are required. Each used sensor has inherent noise and uncertainty in its readings and this uncertainty can propagate to the calculated scale, making data measurements from the reconstruction more unreliable. This problem has been expressed in the paper by (Nikolov & Madsen, 2019), using the notion that uncertainties from one type of variables, in this case scale, can propagate to another type of measurements, for example surface measurements. In Equation 5 taken from the paper, the uncertainty of a calculated scale factor is denoted as its variance σ_s^2. The measurement D_{SfM} in unknown scale is taken from the surface of a 3D object and subsequently scaled to absolute scale using that scale factor. Then it will display a measurement uncertainty σ_{metric}^2, proportional to the scale factor's uncertainty. If the scaling uncertainty is known, then this can be predicted and better-quality measurements can be achieved.

$$\sigma_{metric}^2 = D_{SfM} \bullet \sigma_s^2 \qquad (5)$$

The next chapters look into modeling the distance measurement sensors' uncertainties and propagating this uncertainty through the algorithms used for calculating the absolute scale factors.

UNCERTAINTY MODELING AND PROPAGATION

To demonstrate the uncertainty modeling of a distance sensor, a number of hardware solutions are chosen. These solutions range in price, the type of distance data they capture and their performance. The three sensors are a low-cost ultrasonic distance sensor HC-SR04, a low-cost LiDAR solution - the rpLidar-A1 (Slamtec, 2013) and the already mentioned Hokuyo UTM-30LX. Figure 6. shows the sensors, as well as examples of the captured uncertainties from each one. A more in-depth explanation is given below. Initially their distance capture uncertainty is calculated, which will later be used as an input in the propagation algorithm.

Figure 6. The distance sensors used for testing the proposed solution – a) ultrasonic distance sensor HC-SR04, b) LiDAR rpLiDAR-A1 and c) LiDAR Hokuyo UTM-30LX

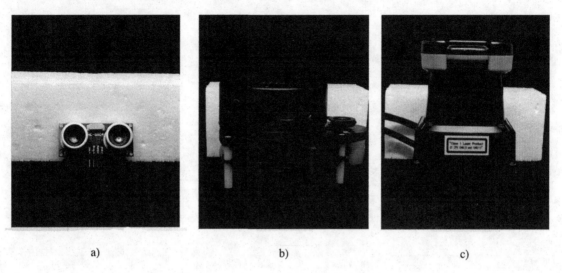

a)   b)   c)

Distance Sensor Modeling

The three used sensors provide different measurement resolutions and uncertainties, as well as maximum measured distances. The HC-SR04 provides a single measurement and can measure between 0.1-4m, the rpLidar-A1, can measure between 0.5-12m and has an angular resolution of around 1 degree, the UTM-30LX can measure between 0.5-30m and has an angular resolution of 0.25 degrees. The distance measurement uncertainty of the sensors at multiple distances needs to be captured for use in the scale uncertainty calculation. To do this, readings of each sensor are taken in intervals of 0.2m, from 0.5m to 3.1m. The bottom interval is chosen, because of the limitations of the tested sensors. The top interval is chosen, because of the size of the laboratory where the tests were conducted. A ground truth is taken for all the readings using a Leica DISTO laser distance meter, with a known accuracy of less than 0.03m. A matte, flat and smooth surface is used for taking the readings to minimize errors from laser beam reflections. For the two LiDAR units, only the central beam is taken into consideration, for simplification of the measurements. At each distance 500 readings are taken. Both the distance error between the ground truth and the measurement and the standard deviation between the 500 measurements are calculated. These are shown in Figure 7 and Figure 8. To verify that the method for capturing the readings is correct, the standard deviation of the measurements captured by (Cooper, 2018) for the similar Hokuyo UST-20LX are plotted as a comparison. It can be seen that the authors' results exhibit similar standard deviation to those. To create the uncertainty values used in the second part of the proposed solution, the standard deviation measurements for each of the devices are interpolated and smoothed using a spline fitting. The created values are used as a look-up table depending on the capturing distance. The distance errors are also used to correct the captured measurements when using the sensors.

Figure 7. Captured distance standard deviations from the tested sensors - UTM-30LX, rpLidar-A1 and HC-SR04, together with the results taken from (Cooper, 2018) for comparison

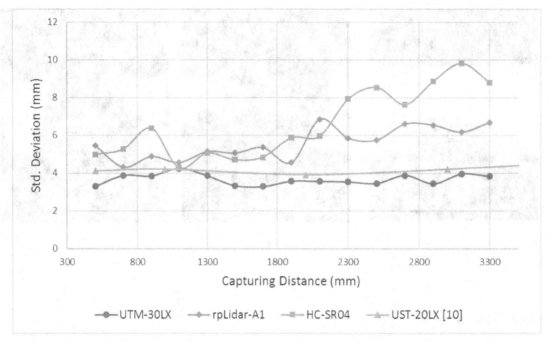

Figure 8. Captured distance errors from the tested sensors - UTM-30LX, rpLidar-A1 and HC-SR04. The distance errors are calculated from as a difference between the captured measurement and ground truth measurements.

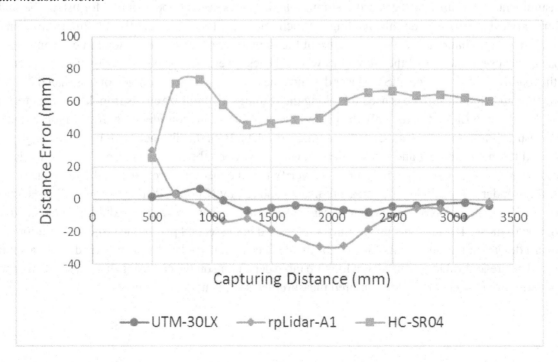

Propagation of Distance Uncertainty to Scale

As the final scaling factor is calculated, the next important thing to take into account is the possible noise and uncertainty, that the used sensor might have introduced to it. The authors' proposed solution is based on the described approach for covariance propagation of noise for computer vision as described by (Haralick, 2000). This method is chosen as it has been demonstrated to give good results in the work by (Madsen, 1997) and (Nikolov & Madsen, 2019), as long as the input parameters used are independent from one another and are used in a function to calculate the output parameters, whose uncertainty needs to be found. The method works for both analytically and iteratively computed functions. In the work by (Nikolov & Madsen, 2019) the method is used for calculating the uncertainty of the calculated scale, when using position measurements from a GPS. In that case the position in each dimension is used as a separate input parameter. To use the same numerical approach with distance measurements, the proposed equations needs to be simplified, so it can be used with only one input parameter. Equation 6 described in the paper, can be used with the data produced by the authors' proposed solution, but the differentiation needs to be calculated only for the average measured distance from each camera position.

$$\sigma_s^2 = \frac{\partial s}{\partial l} \Delta \frac{\partial s^T}{\partial l} \tag{6}$$

To do this the modelled sensor variance is subtracted and added to the average sensor measurements for each camera in turn and the scale is calculated for each, as seen in Equation 7. The other part of Equation 6 that needs to be changed is the calculation of the covariance matrix, again as there is only one input parameter. The new matrix is shown in Equation 8. where the average sensor uncertainty is the calculated one from Equation 9.

$$\frac{\partial s}{\partial l} = \left[\frac{\partial s}{\partial \overline{l_1}}, \cdots \frac{\partial s}{\partial \overline{l_c}} \right] \tag{7}$$

$$\Delta = \begin{bmatrix} \overline{\sigma_{l_1}^2} & \cdots & 0 \\ \vdots & \ddots & \vdots \\ 0 & \cdots & \overline{\sigma_{l_c}^2} \end{bmatrix}_{CxC} \tag{8}$$

$$\overline{\sigma_{l_k}^2} = \frac{1}{n_k} \sigma_l^2 \tag{9}$$

If the captured sensor readings for each camera positions are used as random variables, then they will contain the already extracted uncertainty, in the form of variance, which is denoted as σ_l^2 for each reading. In Equation 9, the average variance $\overline{\sigma_{l_k}^2}$ for the average sensor distance for each camera $k=[1,2,\ldots,C]$ is taken from Equation 3, where only the real sensor's data contains uncertainty. From the average of the real distance sensor's readings the variance can be represented using Equation 10, based on the theorem 2 from (DeGroot, 2012), describing representing the variance of a linear function and a variable, in the current case that variable is the number of measurements per camera, n_k. From there the average variance can be represented using theorem 4 (DeGroot, 2012) as a sum of all the variances of all measurements per camera.

$$\overline{\sigma_{l_k}^2} = \frac{1}{n_k^2} \sigma_{\sum_{i=1}^{n_k} l_i}^2 \tag{10}$$

$$\sigma_{\sum_{i=1}^{n_k} l_i}^2 = n_k \sigma_l^2 \tag{11}$$

By using Equation 6 and taking two simplifications into account, the scale uncertainty can be computed in a more straightforward manner:

- The measured distances from the cameras to the object should be roughly the same for all images;
- The number of distance readings per camera from the real world and the cast rays to the reconstructed object needs to be the same.

The first simplification can be restrictive, but in the work by (Nikolov I. A., 2016) and (Marčiš, 2013), it is demonstrated that for achieving the best results in SfM reconstruction, a circular or hemispherical capturing path is needed. For this type of capturing the distances can be relatively uniform. The second simplification can also be followed if a set number of measurements are selected depending on the distance sensor and the same number is set for the calculated measurements from the reconstructed object. Taking this into account and expressing that $n_k=m_k$ and $f = \overline{r_k}$, is the average distance measurement for all cameras $k=[1,2,\ldots,C]$ then a new simplified expression can be made, as shown in Equation 12.

$$\overline{A_s^2} = \frac{1}{n_k cf^2} \sigma_l^2 \tag{12}$$

This expression gives a number of relations between the used variables. From the above, it can be seen that the scale uncertainty drops with both the number of camera positions with sensor measurements and the number of measurements per positions. This can be explained by the fact that the more positions there are, the more information for the distances between the cameras and the object's surface there is. Also, the more measurements there are per camera position, the less likely it is that the sensor's uncertainty will affect. In addition, the distance from the camera to the object can affect the uncertainty in a number of ways. If measuring large distances, a small millimetre sensor uncertainty will not give a

Figure 9. Pipeline of the proposed solution. The bulk of the calculations are done using Python, with the needed inputs coming either from the distance sensor or as output from the chosen SfM software.

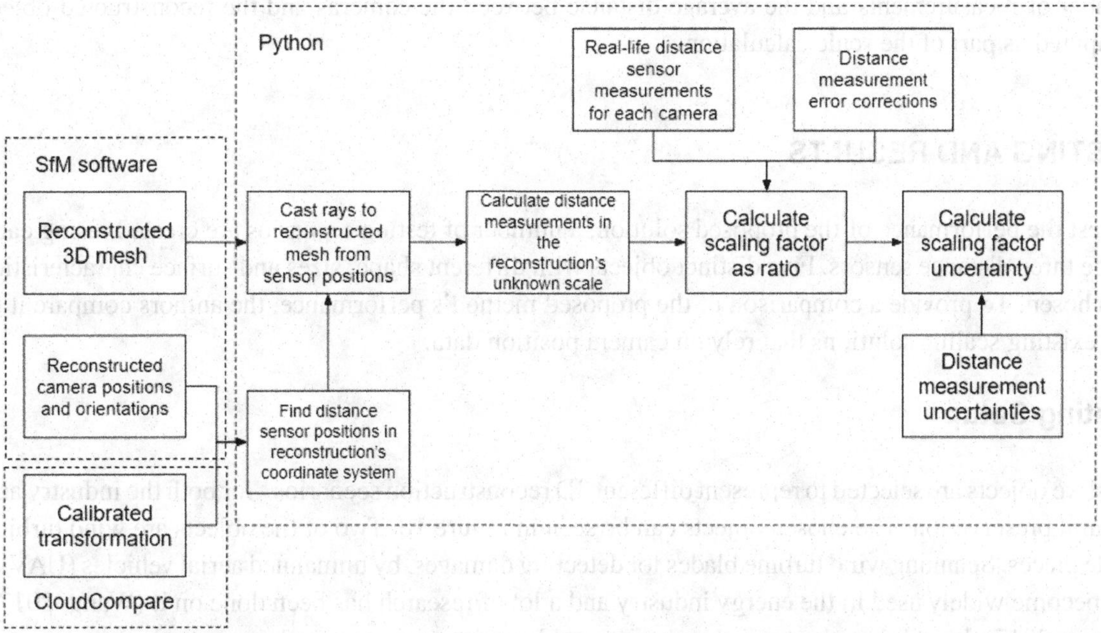

lot of weight to the scale calculation, but if the reconstruction is done using images and measurements close to the object the distance uncertainty will be more pronounced. The proposed uncertainty solution is tested in the Results section and compared to two additional uncertainty calculation solutions.

IMPLEMENTATION

An overview of the implementation of the proposed solution is given in Figure 9. The initial data comes as an output from the chosen SfM solutions. Because the reconstructed object or surface is going to be used for casting rays and measuring distances, a mesh is suggested. The calculated camera positions and orientations are also used as input for the proposed solution. These inputs are used in the main implementation together with the calibrated transformation between the camera and the sensor in the rig. The used algorithms are built in Python, together with the library trimesh (Dawson-Haggerty, 2019), used for the implementation of casting rays and calculating the distance between their origin and the hit point. The position of the distance sensor is calculated for each camera location using the calibration transformation matrix and the position and orientation of the camera. Once the location and orientation of the sensor is known, a number of rays are cast from it. The number and density of the rays depends on the chosen sensor and set input parameters – single or multi distance measurement sensor, angle resolution and maximum working distance. The distances of all rays hitting the reconstructed object are captured. The real-life sensor measurement for each camera, corrected using the distance error expectation is used together with the ray distance to calculate a scaling factor. The average scale factor for all camera positions is calculated. This scaling factor is used to scale the reconstruction and camera positions and the process is repeated until the difference between the real measurement and the ray one is minimized. The sensor measurement uncertainty is calculated using Equation 12, with the average number of measurements and the average distance between the cameras and the reconstructed object computed as part of the scale calculation.

TESTING AND RESULTS

To test the performance of the proposed solution, a number of testing scenarios are created, using each of the three distance sensors. Five distinct objects with different shape, sizes and surface characteristics are chosen. To provide a comparison of the proposed method's performance, the authors compare it to two existing scaling solutions that rely on camera position data.

Testing Setup

The five objects are selected to represent different 3D reconstruction scenarios - for both the industry and cultural preservation. The chosen objects can be seen in Figure 10. Two of the objects are wind turbine blade pieces. Scanning wind turbine blades for detecting damages, by unmanned aerial vehicles (UAVs), has become widely used in the energy industry and a lot of research has been done on it (Wang, 2017), (Zhang, 2017). In addition, this type of scenario would require a sensor-based way to scale the computed SfM reconstructions, as it is normally hard to manually measure the real-life blade surfaces or to place markers on them. The other three objects represent examples of digital cultural heritage preservation. Scanning fragile or hard to reach objects is another common use of SfM reconstruction, where access can be restricted and neither manual or marker-based scaling can easily be used. In addition, the five

Figure 10. The five objects were selected to represent two types of application scenarios, which may require the use of SfM reconstruction with absolute scale. The first group represents is artifacts for digital cultural preservation - an angel statue (a), a duck statue (b) and a vase (c). The second group represents surface inspection for the industry, with examples of two types of wind turbine blade, denoted as the small one (d) and large one (e).

objects were chosen based on widely varying surface profiles and shapes, which can be used to judge the robustness of the proposed method.

Initially, a number of images are taken from each of the five objects, in a 180-degree semi-circular pattern. This method of capturing the image is used, as it has been shown by (Schöning, 2016) and (Nikolov I. A., 2016) that it produces good reconstruction results with the minimum needed image positions. For each image a sensor measurement is also taken. A Canon 5Ds DSLR camera is used with a 30-105 mm zoom lens and the taken images are with a resolution of 8688x5792. This way the possibility of inaccuracies on the reconstruction can be minimized and the only possible error can come from the scaling methods. Once the images are taken, a reconstruction is made of each object using Agisoft Metashape.

Scale Test Results

The method presented in this chapter is compared to the built-in solution present in Metashape and the positioning-based solution used by (Nikolov & Madsen, 2019), from here on referred to as NM. The built-in solution from Metashape, takes the positioning data as input and as it reconstructs the object, it tries to use the data as initial guess where the cameras are. This has the effect that it also scales the model, but the used algorithm itself is proprietary and undisclosed by the company. No possible scaling uncertainties are calculated as well. The NM method uses positioning data for each camera. The data is captured from a GPS, with a real-time kinematic (RTK) add-on, which makes the positioning information much more accurate, compared to the normal GPS. A least-squares estimation is then used to calculate the transformation between these positions and the ones calculated by the SfM algorithm. The method makes the assumption that for each measured position there is a corresponding calculated one, without outliers. For testing purposes, the GPS-RTK sensor uncertainties in each direction are taken as they are and used in the present chapter. Because both the built-in solution and the NM one requires camera positions and the testing scenarios for these chapters are conducted indoor, the positioning data is captured manually, using the same laser range finder used for capturing the distance sensor uncertainty. In each direction the readings of the range finder are calculated and put in a global coordinate system, contained in the room where the experiments are conducted. As an added benefit this means that the captured positioning data is much more accurate than possible with a real positioning sensor like a GPS. In turn this will ensure that the two methods produce the best possible results for comparison to the proposed solution.

The reconstruction is first created in Metashape, without an absolute scale. It is then scaled with all three tested solutions. To compare the accuracy of each of the calculated scale factors, a number of ground truth measurements need to be done. A number of parts of each of the real objects are manually measured with a digital calliper with an accuracy of 0.02mm. The same parts are measured on the reconstructed objects after they have been scaled with the scaling factor from each of the methods. To minimize the possible effect of human error from the manual measurements, each part is measured multiple times and an average measurement is calculated. To measure how close, the scaling from each method is to the real-life scale of the objects the absolute percentage difference between the real and the scaled measurements is calculated. The absolute percentage differences for each part of the object are then averaged for the whole object and a final scaling accuracy metric is calculated. The results from that can be seen in Table 1, with graphical representation in Figure 11.

Table 1. Absolute percentage difference between the averaged real-world and scaled 3D object measurements. For the proposed method three different sensors are used and for comparison the position-based built-in solution in Metashape and the solution by NM are tested. The two LiDAR sensors provide better or similar scaling performance than the position-based solution, while the low-cost single distance sensor still produces usable scaling factors.

Object	Metashape [%]	NM Solution [%]	UTM-30LX [%]	rpLidar-A1 [%]	HC-SR04 [%]
Angel	4.12	3.20	2.07	3.89	5.53
Duck	1.99	1.44	0.90	2.33	2.82
Vase	0.55	0.36	0.22	0.50	0.69
Small Blade	7.60	7.09	5.49	7.06	10.12
Big Blade	13.92	13.64	12.52	13.79	18.63

Figure 11. The absolute percentage difference between the average real-world and 3D object measurements for each of the reconstructed objects. The proposed solution is tested with each of the distance sensors, together with the Metashape build-in solution and the method proposed by NM.

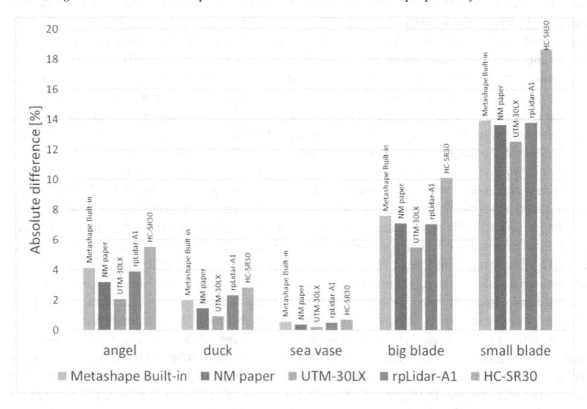

Scale Uncertainty Test Results

The calculated scale uncertainty is also tested for each of the tested distance sensors from the proposed solution. For inputs each of the distance sensors, uses the calculated distance uncertainty lookup table. The results from the final scale factor uncertainty are given in Table 2.

Table 2. Calculated scale uncertainties for each of the five tested objects, with each of the distance sensors

Object	UTM-30LX [mm^2]	rpLidar-A1 [mm^2]	HC-SR04 [mm^2]
Angel	2.86e-10	1.01e-08	3.52e-08
Duck	5.79e-10	5.02e-08	2.90e-08
Vase	1.84e-10	4.34e-09	3.03e-08
Small Blade	1.04e-10	6.21e-09	1.25e-08
Big Blade	1.42e-10	2.65e-09	5.51e-08

To test if the proposed simplified scale uncertainty solution gives proper results, it needs to be compared to other methods for calculating uncertainty. The work from (Nikolov & Madsen, 2019), describes two different ways for introducing and computing scale uncertainty – a repeated approach and the numerical differentiation approach, already explained in the Methodology chapter. Each of the two methods is implemented with distance measurements as the input parameter and their results are compare to the ones produced by the simplified calculation. The angel statue has been chosen as a test object.

Repeated Approach

The most straightforward way to compute the scale uncertainty from the distance sensor uncertainty is through repeated calculations. A zero mean Gaussian distribution is created from the standard deviations, obtained from the sensor uncertainty modelling. This distribution is then randomly sampled and values from it are added to the real sensor measurements for the 3D reconstruction. The scale is then calculated as normal and saved. This process is done repeatedly 1000 times, by randomly sampling the measurement fluctuations. Once all the final scale factors are calculated, their variance is calculated. This approach is easy to implement, but requires a lot of computation time to achieve good results, as well as a large pool of sensor measurements.

Results

The scale uncertainty for each of the three sensors is calculated for the angel statue. The results from each of the three used methods are given in Table 3. As it can be seen from the table, the simplified model demonstrates discrepancy in the produced results for the sensors, which have higher uncertainty, combined with a smaller number of measured distances. The other two uncertainty computation approaches give comparable results.

Table 3. Comparison between three methods for calculating the scaling uncertainty – simplified model demonstrated by the authors and two methods described by (Nikolov & Madsen, 2019) – a numerical model using covariance propagation and a repeated calculation model

Sensor	Simplified $[mm^2]$	Numerical $[mm^2]$	Repeated $[mm^2]$
UTM-30LX	2.86e-10	3.14e-10	2.95e-10
rpLidar-A1	1.01e-08	1.15e-08	1.05e-08
HC-SR04	3.52e-08	3.53e-08	3.65e-08

DISCUSSION

Analysing the results from the testing, it can be seen that the authors' proposed solution using the UTM-30LX LiDAR gives the best scaling results, together with the lowest scale uncertainty. This is an expected result, as the sensor has the highest angular resolution, together with the lowest distance measurement uncertainty. The other distance sensors also give progressively worse results depending on their distance measurement accuracy and the angular resolution. More interesting are the results from the HC-SR30 distance sensor. Even though the sensor has a comparatively small measurement distance and low distance accuracy, it manages to provide satisfactory results in all cases, expect the second wind turbine blade. All tested algorithms show difficulties in scaling the wind turbine blades. It is theorized that this can be a problem from the reconstruction itself, as both objects are relatively harder to reconstruct and have noise in the reconstructed 3D models, as well as in the positioning of the cameras. This can result from glossiness of the surfaces and the lack of features. Additionally, the two blades have elongated shapes, which could additionally present problems, especially for the single distance measuring sensors, while with the help of more measuring points the two LiDAR solutions give a better average representation.

Looking at the scale uncertainty calculation, the same trend can be seen. The images with distance reading from the three sensors are taken from roughly the same positions and the same number of camera positions are used. From Equation 12, that leaves only the number of distance measurements per camera position and measurement uncertainty as changing variables. It can be seen that, because the sonic sensor relies only on one reading and has the highest uncertainty, the produced scale from it also exhibits the highest uncertainty. On the other hand, the UTM-30LX sensor produces a lot of distance readings and together with the relatively smaller uncertainty, it achieves lower scale uncertainty values. That said, the cheap sensor still manages to produce good results and is viable for use.

When comparing the proposed simplified method to the other two computationally more expensive methods, comparable results are achieved. This shows that simplified method can be a useful approximation, when the longer computational times of the other method are prohibitive. More tests need to be conducted to get a predictive trend how the simplified method's results will behave with different distances, number of measurements and sensors.

Overall the proposed method gives better or comparable results to the two solutions using positioning sensors. Combined with the robustness of a distance sensor, which can be used both indoor and outdoor and in varying conditions, the fact that the method does not require additional external hardware, and the flexibility that switching to a cheaper, but lower resolution sensor still gives usable results, shows the validity of the proposed solution.

CONCLUSION

One of the problems connected to SfM is the inability to compute the absolute scale of a reconstructed object, without additional information. This chapter proposed a method for finding the absolute scale and scale uncertainty, by using the readings of distance sensors. The method can be made to work with a wide array of sensors and can easily be integrated into a SfM working pipeline, as it requires minimal additional information. Furthermore, the solution is robust enough to provide usable results with as little as one distance measurement per image.

The proposed method requires a one-time extrinsic calibration for getting the transformation between the camera used for SfM reconstruction and the distance sensor. After that, the scale calculation can be done with only the captured distance measurements and an iterative method used to improve the accuracy of the computed scale, as well as the uncertainty brought about by the used distance sensor.

To test the flexibility of the proposed method, three different distance sensors are used - from a low-cost single direction sensor to two 2D LiDAR solutions. The authors compare the proposed solution to two position-based scaling methods, using five different objects from different application scenarios. It is shown that the proposed method gives better performance to built-in scaling solutions and position based solutions, when used with comparably high-grade sensors and that the performance is still usable, when dropping to a low-cost single direction sensor.

Finally, it is shown that the scaling uncertainty is proportional to the input sensor's measurement uncertainty, and the proposed simplified method achieves comparable results to the more computationally intensive methods. This gives the possibility that both the scaling calculation approach and the uncertainty computation can be simply computed with only base sensor readings and modelling.

REFERENCES

Agisoft. (2010). *Metashape*. Retrieved from http://www.agisoft.com

Bay, H. T. (2006). Surf: Speeded up robust features. *European conference on computer vision*, 404-417.

Bentley. (2016). *ContextCapture*. Retrieved from https://www.bentley.com

CapturingReality. (2016). *Reality Capture*. Retrieved from https://www.capturingreality.com

Clapuyt, F. V., Vanacker, V., & Van Oost, K. (2016). Reproducibility of UAV-based earth topography reconstructions based on Structure-from-Motion algorithms. *Geomorphology*, *260*, 4–15. doi:10.1016/j.geomorph.2015.05.011

Cooper, M. R., Raquet, J., & Patton, R. (2018). Range Information Characterization of the Hokuyo UST-20LX LIDAR Sensor. *Photonics*, *5*(2), 12. doi:10.3390/photonics5020012

Corti, A. G., Giancola, S., Mainetti, G., & Sala, R. (2016). A metrological characterization of the Kinect V2 time-of-flight camera. *Robotics and Autonomous Systems*, *75*, 584–594. doi:10.1016/j.robot.2015.09.024

Daakir, M. P.-D. (2016). Study of Lever-arm Effect Usign Embedded Photogrammetry and On-board GPS Receiver on UAV for Metrological Mapping Purpose and Proposal of a Free Ground Measurements Calibration Procedure. *ISPRS Annals of Photogrammetry, Remote Sensing & Spatial. Information Sciences, §§§,* 6.

Dawson-Haggerty. (2019). *trimesh.* Retrieved from https://trimsh.org

DeGroot, M. H. (2012). *Probability and statistics.* Pearson Education.

Ding, L. &. (2017). Fusing structure from motion and lidar for dense accurate depth map estimation. *IEEE International Conference on Acoustics, Speech and Signal Processing (ICASSP),* 1283-1287. 10.1109/ICASSP.2017.7952363

Girardeau-MontautD. (2003). *CloudCompare.* Retrieved from http://www.cloudcompare.org

Giubilato, R. C. (2018). Scale correct monocular visual odometry using a lidar altimeter. *IEEE/RSJ International Conference on Intelligent Robots and Systems (IROS),* 3694-3700. 10.1109/IROS.2018.8594096

Haralick, R. M. (2000). *Propagating covariance in computer vision.* Performance Characterization in Computer Vision.

Hokuyo. (2010). *UTM-30LX.* Retrieved from https://www.hokuyo-aut.jp

Kim, O. &. (2015). A sensor fusion method to solve the scale ambiguity of single image by combining IMU. *15th International Conference on Control, Automation and Systems (ICCAS),* 923-925. 10.1109/ICCAS.2015.7364754

Knapitsch, A. P., Park, J., Zhou, Q.-Y., & Koltun, V. (2017). Tanks and temples: Benchmarking large-scale scene reconstruction. *ACM Transactions on Graphics, 36*(4), 78. doi:10.1145/3072959.3073599

Li, L., & Lan, H. (2019). Recovering absolute scale for Structure from Motion using the law of free fall. *Optics & Laser Technology, 112,* 514–523. doi:10.1016/j.optlastec.2018.11.045

Lowe, D. G. (2004). Distinctive image features from scale-invariant keypoints. *International Journal of Computer Vision, 60*(2), 91–110. doi:10.1023/B:VISI.0000029664.99615.94

Lu, Y. L. (2020). *Sharing heterogeneous spatial knowledge: Map fusion between asynchronous monocular vision and lidar or other prior inputs.* Robotics Research.

Madsen, C. B. (1997). A comparative study of the robustness of two pose estimation techniques. *Machine Vision and Applications, 9*(5-6), 291–303. doi:10.1007001380050049

Makantasis, K. D., Doulamis, A., Doulamis, N., & Ioannides, M. (2016). In the wild image retrieval and clustering for 3D cultural heritage landmarks reconstruction. *Multimedia Tools and Applications, 75*(7), 3593–3629. doi:10.100711042-014-2191-z

Marčiš, M. (2013). Quality of 3D models generated by SFM technology. *Slovak Journal of Civil Engineering,* 13-24.

Martell, A. L. (2018). Benchmarking structure from motion algorithms of urban environments with applications to reconnaissance in search and rescue scenarios. *IEEE International Symposium on Safety, Security, and Rescue Robotics*, 1-7. 10.1109/SSRR.2018.8468612

Nikolov, I., & Madsen, C. (2019). Performance Characterization of Absolute Scale Computation for 3D Structure from Motion Reconstruction. *International Conference on Computer Vision Theory and Applications*. 10.5220/0007444208840891

Nikolov, I. A. (2016). Benchmarking close-range structure from motion 3D reconstruction software under varying capturing conditions. *Euro-Mediterranean Conference*, 15-26. 10.1007/978-3-319-48496-9_2

Özyeşil, O. V., Voroninski, V., Basri, R., & Singer, A. (2017). A survey of structure from motion*. *Acta Numerica*, *26*, 305–364. doi:10.1017/S096249291700006X

Rabah, M. B. (2018). *Using RTK and VRS in direct geo-referencing of the UAV imagery*. *NRIAG Journal of Astronomy and Geophysics*.

Rosten, E. &. (2006). Machine learning for high-speed corner detection. *European conference on computer vision*, 430-443.

Rublee, E. R. (2011). ORB: An efficient alternative to SIFT or SURF. *International Conference for Computer Vision*, 2. 10.1109/ICCV.2011.6126544

Sarbolandi, H. L., Lefloch, D., & Kolb, A. (2015). Kinect range sensing: Structured-light versus Time-of-Flight Kinect. *Computer Vision and Image Understanding*, *139*, 1–20. doi:10.1016/j.cviu.2015.05.006

Sarker, M. M., Ali, T. A., Abdelfatah, A., Yehia, S., & Elaksher, A. (2017). A cost-effective method for crack detection and measurement on concrete surface. *The International Archives of the Photogrammetry, Remote Sensing and Spatial Information Sciences*, *42*(W8), 237–241. doi:10.5194/isprs-archives-XLII-2-W8-237-2017

Schonberger, J. L. (2016). Structure-from-motion revisited. *Proceedings of the IEEE Conference on Computer Vision and Pattern Recognition*, 4104-4113.

Schöning, J. (2016). Taxonomy of 3D sensors. *Argos*, 9–10.

Schöps, T. S. (2015). 3D modeling on the go: Interactive 3D reconstruction of large-scale scenes on mobile devices. *International Conference on 3D Vision*, 291-299. 10.1109/3DV.2015.40

Slamtec. (2013). *rpLidar A1*. Retrieved from http://www.slamtec.com/en/lidar/a1

Sweeney, C. H. (2015). Theia: A fast and scalable structure-from-motion library. *Proceedings of the 23rd ACM international conference on Multimedia*, 693-696. 10.1145/2733373.2807405

Triggs, B. M. (1999). Bundle adjustment—a modern synthesis. *International workshop on vision algorithms*, 298-372.

Turner, D. L., Lucieer, A., & Watson, C. (2012). An automated technique for generating georectified mosaics from ultra-high resolution unmanned aerial vehicle (UAV) imagery, based on structure from motion (SfM). *Remote Sensing*, *4*(5), 1392–1410. doi:10.3390/rs4051392

Voulodimos, A. D., Doulamis, N., Fritsch, D., Makantasis, K., Doulamis, A., & Klein, M. (2016). Four-dimensional reconstruction of cultural heritage sites based on photogrammetry and clustering. *Journal of Electronic Imaging*, 26(1), 011013. doi:10.1117/1.JEI.26.1.011013

Wang, L., & Zhang, Z. (2017). Automatic detection of wind turbine blade surface cracks based on UAV-taken images. *IEEE Transactions on Industrial Electronics*, 64(9), 7293–7303. doi:10.1109/TIE.2017.2682037

Wu, C. (2011). *VisualSFM: A visual structure from motion system.* Retrieved from http://ccwu.me/vsfm/doc.html

Zhang, D. B. (2017). Remote inspection of wind turbine blades using UAV with photogrammetry payload. *56th Annual British Conference of Non-Destructive Testing-NDT.*

Zhou, D. D. (2016). Reliable scale estimation and correction for monocular visual odometry. *IEEE Intelligent Vehicles Symposium*, 490-495.

KEY TERMS AND DEFINITIONS

3D Reconstruction: The process of capturing the 3D shape of an object or parts of an object, in contract to images, which capture a 2D representation of an object from a certain direction.

Absolute Scale: Scale which is equal to real life measurements in a known measurement system like mm, cm, m, inches, etc.

Color Images: Images containing three color channels, represented in a certain way, for example RGB—red, green, blue—or HSI—hue, saturation, intensity.

Distance Measurement Sensor: Sensors used to measure real-life distances. They can use different hardware to do it – lasers, ultrasound, etc. The number of distance measurements can also vary from one to many.

LiDAR: Light detection and sensing. A type of distance sensor, which uses laser light pulses to measure distances in one or many directions.

Structure From Motion: A computer vision based 3D reconstruction technique, using a number of unordered color images, to capture both the 3D shape, as well as the color of an object or surface.

Value Uncertainty: The variance in the measured or calculated values, which can be cause by noise or random fluctuations.

Chapter 9
Image Clustering and Video Summarization for Efficient 3D Modelling and Reconstruction

Athanasios Voulodimos
University of West Attica, Athens, Greece

Eftychios Protopapadakis
National Technical University of Athens, Athens, Greece

Nikolaos Doulamis
National Technical University of Athens, Greece

Anastasios Doulamis
National Technical University of Athens, Greece

ABSTRACT

Although high quality 3D representations of important cultural landmarks can be obtained via sophisticated photogrammetric techniques, their demands in terms of resources and expertise pose limitations on the scale at which such approaches are used. In parallel, the proliferation of multimedia content posted online creates new possibilities in terms of the ways that such rich content can be leveraged, but only after addressing the significant challenges associated with this content, including its massive volume, unstructured nature, and noise. In this chapter, two strategies are proposed for using multimedia content for 3D reconstruction: an image-based approach that employs clustering techniques to eliminate outliers and a video-based approach that extracts key frames via a summarization technique. In both cases, the reduced and outlier-free image data set is used as input to a structure from motion framework for 3D reconstruction. The presented techniques are evaluated on the basis of the reconstruction of two world-class cultural heritage monuments.

DOI: 10.4018/978-1-5225-5294-9.ch009

INTRODUCTION

The free and online availability of large collections of images and videos located on distributed and heterogeneous platforms over the Web is one of the prominent characteristics of today's digital era, reigned by the Internet, social media and powerful mobile devices. The abundance of shared photographs spurred the emergence of new image retrieval techniques based not only on images' visual information, but also on geo-location tags and camera exif data. These massive visual collections provide a unique opportunity for urban areas and cultural heritage documentation and 3D reconstruction. The main challenge, nevertheless, is that Internet image datasets are unstructured containing many outliers. Therefore, content-based image filtering is necessary to discard image outliers that either confuse or significantly delay the employed 3D reconstruction frameworks, such as, for example, Structure from Motion (e.g. VisualSFM).

In contrast with sophisticated airborne and close range photogrammetric approaches, where 3D data acquisition is accomplished in a constrained environment using specialized equipment and sophisticated techniques, Web-based collections can be exploited for a much easier and more "user-friendly" cultural heritage e-documentation. However, the main difficulty in implementing a precise 3D reconstruction of an object from unstructured internet image collections (being captured for personal use instead of reconstruction purposes), is that there are usually several outliers in the set of retrieved data deteriorating both performance and computational cost. Consider, for example, a query containing the keywords "Acropolis, Parthenon." As a response to that query, a large set of images are retrieved, which depict not only the Parthenon monument itself, but also the view of the city of Athens from the Acropolis hill or of people being photographed in the environment of the monument. These image outliers confuse any e-documentation algorithm. Although auto-generated geo-location tags can improve visual content characterization and therefore the retrieval performance, they suffer from low precision since geo-information does not correctly describe what is actually depicted. While there exist 3D reconstruction algorithms, such as Structure from Motion (SfM), which demonstrate robustness against noisy data, their computational complexity significantly increases with respect to the number of input data. This makes direct implementation of such methods for large image volumes practically impossible. Therefore, in the cases where retrieved images are used as input, content-based filtering algorithms are necessary for an effective and computationally efficient 3D reconstruction exploiting distributed Web based image collections. Content-based filtering algorithms, apart from discarding image outliers, also organize the retrieved unstructured content into well-structured forms to optimize both 3D reconstruction performance and computational cost.

In more detail, the accuracy of 3D reconstruction over a given image dataset is inherently dependent on the number of images that will be fed as input to the Structure from Motion (SfM) scheme. Given an image dataset the best 3D reconstruction accuracy is achieved when all visually similar images are fed into a SfM method. One way to exploit all visually similar images is to give as input to the SfM method the entire image dataset. However, the time complexity for a typical incremental SfM method is of order where N stands for the number of images. This complexity makes SfM not scalable to large image collections. In order to decrease computational cost associated with 3D reconstruction, the initial image dataset can be pruned by removing outliers. When outliers' removal process is very precise, dataset reduction does not affect reconstruction accuracy, since the relevant (reduced) dataset will contain only all visually similar images. Therefore, the metric that can be associated with reconstruction accuracy is the metric of recall. On the other hand, the reduction of SfM computational time is dependent on the percentage of reduction of the initial image dataset, which implicitly can be computed by using the metric of precision. When the precision metric is close to one, the cluster of visually similar images contains no outliers, achieving this way the most accurate dataset reduction.

It is therefore clear that the goal is to obtain a dataset of images devoid of outliers and with little redundancies, in other words decrease the number of input images without loss of information. As mentioned above, the described approach exploits User Generated Content in terms of image and video collections, stored on distributed multimedia platforms, such as Flickr and Picasa to derive 3D reconstructed models of monuments or urban landmarks. We will therefore explore two main different alternatives: an image-based approach, where outlier removal and representative images selection is performed employing clustering techniques, and a video-based approach, where representative image selection and outlier elimination is based on a video summarization technique.

BACKGROUND

Several methods have been proposed in the literature for 3D modeling: image based methods that exploit photogrammetric aspects in creating high fidelity 3D maps (Haala & Rothermel, 2012; Hullo, Grussenmeyer, & Fares, 2009), photometric stereo that exploits light reflection properties for 3D modeling (Argyriou, Zafeiriou, & Petrou, 2014), real-time depth sensors, such as Kinect, to create cost-effective but of low fidelity RGBD images (Izadi et al., 2011), structured light technologies with the capability of simultaneously capture 3D geometry and texture (Orghidan, Salvi, Gordan, Florea, & Batlle, 2014; Soile, Adam, Ioannidis, & Georgopoulos, 2013) and laser scanning for large scale automated 3D reconstruction (Barone, Paoli, & Razionale, 2012; Huang, Brenner, & Sester, 2013; Sitnik & Karaszewski, 2010; Valanis, Tapinaki, Georgopoulos, & Ioannidis, 2009, p. 3). Each of the suggested methods presents advantages and drawbacks. Automatic photogrammetric matching techniques present the advantage of creating high fidelity 3D point clouds, but the respective accuracy falls in cases of uniform texture images.

Photometric stereo can be applied either for improving the results of image based matching or for reconstructing transparent/specular surfaces, where conventional methods fail. Real time depth sensors, such as Kinect, present the advantage of providing a cost-effective 3D modeling, but the respective 3D meshes are of low resolution and therefore not suitable for many CH application scenarios (e.g., reconstruction, monitoring). Structured light 3D methods are suitable for high accuracy modeling, but present difficulties in scanning large scale archaeological sites. Finally, 3D laser scanning alone presents the advantage of automation, but it fails in capturing textured point clouds and the cost of 3D modeling is high due to use of expensive terrestrial laser scanners.

The construction of high fidelity 3D models using the most precise among the above methods certainly contributes to the preservation of detailed, precise digital models of important cultural heritage objects, landmarks or sites; at the same time however, it is a complex, arduous process - let alone when repeated at different time instances to capture changes - which requires a great amount of different resources, such as specialized equipment, manual labor, professionals' expertise, time; it is therefore both computationally and financially expensive.

In contrast with the previous approaches, where input image data acquisition is a complex, often sophisticated, and certainly non-trivial process, web multimedia repositories (such as Flickr, Picasa, Photosynth) contain millions of photos uploaded by users, among which a significant number cover cultural heritage objects, monuments and sites, and constitute a valuable source of image data that could be leveraged for cultural heritage e-documentation. However, there have been limited technological tools and research methods for retrieving, mining and ultimately exploiting such vast cultural heritage collections for 3D reconstruction applications, although important works (Agarwal et al., 2011; Goesele, Snavely, Curless, Hoppe, & Seitz, 2007; Kamberov et al., 2006) have shown that geometry can be recovered for uncontrolled Internet collected data. In general, one significant drawback of exploiting "in the wild" web image collections is the fact that irrelevant images, namely outliers, are bound to "infiltrate" an input data set that was created as a result of an online query. Such outliers severely deteriorate the performance and computational cost of 3D reconstruction algorithms, such as Structure from Motion (SfM) (Snavely, Seitz, & Szeliski, 2006; Wu, Agarwal, Curless, & Seitz, 2011), in which the computational cost also significantly increases with respect to the amount of input data. These facts make the direct application of such reconstruction methods difficult for large volumes of image data and usually dictate the need for content-based filtering, outlier removal and clustering methods.

Previous works in these areas include Content Based Image Retrieval (CBIR) tools that mine relevant images from large repositories based on a visual matching process, since they use image filtering and clustering algorithms to appropriately organize image data into groups of similar visual properties. Therefore, CBIR methods can be considered as suitable tools towards efficient content-based image filtering (Anastasios D. Doulamis, Doulamis, & Kollias, 2000). The work of (Min & Cheng, 2009) proposes the dominant color descriptor to encode visual information, while clustering is performed using fuzzy Support Vectors Machines (fSVMs); however, its performance depends on illumination conditions since color descriptors are used to encode visual information.

In some works, textual or geo-location information are exploited to filter out the retrieved results. Authors of (Papadopoulos, Zigkolis, Kompatsiaris, & Vakali, 2010) describe an image analysis algorithm that automates the detection of landmarks and events from large multimedia databases in order to improve content-consumption experience. The idea of geo-clustering is also exploited in (Zheng et al., 2009) for retrieving landmark images. However, the retrieved set contains a lot of image outliers that are photos of several adjacent landmarks. Although such approaches are useful for content-based image retrieval applications, where the aim is to extract similar images upon a query, they present many shortcomings when applied in the context of 3D reconstruction scenarios. The proposed approach of (Toldo, Gherardi, Farenzena, & Fusiello, 2015) employs agglomerative clustering to build a hierarchical framework for structure-and-motion (Samantha), which proved more efficient than the sequential approach when applied in datasets of approximately 300 images.

Video summarization has not been used as a driver for 3D reconstruction, to the authors' knowledge, although there is significant related work in the literature. The first approaches for automatic video summarization had the goal of extracting key frames at regular time instances or within a shot (Verykokou, Doulamis, Athanasiou, Ioannidis, & Amditis, 2016), but such a selection cannot really be considered very representative. Related research has also often focused on specific types of video content like sports (Chen & Vleeschouwer, 2011) and instructional videos (Choudary & Liu, 2007). Algorithms were proposed maximizing entropy and exploiting information-theoretic measures (Li, Schuster, & Katsaggelos, 2005; Panagiotakis, Doulamis, & Tziritas, 2009), cross correlation (A. D. Doulamis & Doulamis, 2004), and/or perceptual users' centric video summaries (Liu, Hua, & Chen, 2010). In this chapter, an efficient algorithm for video content representation is described, which is not threshold dependent and thus the number of extracted keyframes varies according to the shot complexity (A. D. Doulamis, Doulamis, & Kollas, 2000). This is of great importance in the application scenario at hand, where the output of the summarization module will be used as input for a 3D reconstruction framework such as VisualSFM.

IMAGE-BASED CLUSTERING AND OUTLIER REMOVAL FOR 3D RECONSTRUCTION

Effective and efficient generation of local features, from an image is a well-studied problem in the literature and forms the basis of various cultural heritage applications, including image selection (Protopapadakis & Doulamis, 2014), outlier removal (Makantasis, Doulamis, Doulamis, & Ioannides, 2014) and 3D reconstruction (Kyriakaki et al., 2014). The term local feature refers to any keypoints together with its descriptor. Thus, prior to any advancement to manifold projection and outlier's detection, we should discuss about key-point detectors, descriptors and how are these two connected.

A local feature is an image pattern which differs from its immediate neighborhood. It is usually associated with a change of an image property or several properties simultaneously, although it is not necessarily localized exactly on this change (Tuytelaars, Mikolajczyk, & others, 2008). The image properties commonly considered are intensity, color, and texture. Local features can be points, but also edges or small image patches. Typically, some measurements are taken from a region centered on a local feature and converted into descriptors. The descriptors can then be used for various applications.

Keypoint Detectors

An interest point (key point, salient point) detector is an algorithm that chooses points from an image based on some criterion. The ideal keypoint detector finds salient image regions such that they are repeatably detected despite change of viewpoint; more generally it is robust to all possible image transformations.

In other words, the surface around the keypoint must contain sufficient descriptive information, which uniquely characterizes that point; ideally, the local feature extracted at the keypoint will be unique facilitating accurate recognition among different images. Typically, an interest point is a local maximum of some function, such as a "cornerness" metric. Harris, Min Eigen, and FAST are interest point detectors, or more specifically, corner detectors.

The Harris corner detector (Harris & Stephens, 1988) is a popular interest point detector due to its strong invariance to: rotation, scale, illumination variation and image noise. The Harris corner detector is based on the local auto-correlation function of a signal (i.e. second moment matrix); it measures the local changes of the signal with patches shifted by a small amount in different directions.

The Shi-Tomasi corner detector (Shi & Tomasi, 1994), also known as minimum eigenvalue algorithm, is based on the Harris corner detector, having a slight variation in a "selection criteria"; only the eigenvalues are used to check if the pixel was a corner or not

The FAST detector (Rosten & Drummond, 2005) adopts a segment-test approach, which investigates whether a continuous arc of pixels around a point on the image are either much brighter or much darker compared to the image point. A comparison of the point detectors is shown in Figure 1.

Keypoint Descriptors

A descriptor is a vector of values, which somehow describes the image patch around an interest point. It could be as simple as the raw pixel values, or it could be more complicated, such as distribution based descriptors, spatial-frequency techniques, differential descriptors, or other type of techniques. Many of the descriptors include keypoint detectors.

Scale Invariant Feature Transform (SIFT), as described in (Lowe, 2004), consists of four major stages: scale-space peak selection, keypoint localization, orientation assignment, and keypoint descriptor. Therefore, SIFT includes both a detector and a descriptor. The detector is based on the difference-of-Gaussians (DoG), which approximates the Laplacian. The DoG detector detects centers of blob-like structures. The descriptor is a based on a histogram of gradient orientations.

Speeded-Up Robust Features (SURF) is meant to be a fast approximation of SIFT, as described in (Bay, Tuytelaars, & Gool, 2006). SIFT, approximates Laplacian of Gaussian with DoG for finding scale-space. SURF approximates LoG with Box Filter. The main advantage of this approximation is that, convolution with box filter can be easily calculated with the help of integral images, and it can be done in parallel for different scales. Also, SURF rely on determinant of Hessian matrix for both scale and location.

BRISK, like SIFT and SURF, includes a detector and a descriptor. The detector is a corner detector. The descriptor is a binary string representing the signs of the difference between certain pairs of pixels around the interest point.

Projecting Data to Manifold

The main idea, as proposed in the work of (Makantasis et al., 2014), is to relate the visual similarities between images, as Euclidean distances between points onto a multi-dimensional manifold over which these images are projected. Such an approach allows for further analysis on the set, including clustering and outliers selection. In the following lines, we explain briefly the adopted methodology.

Estimation of Similarity Metric in a Set of Images

The similarity between two images can be estimated by the number of correspondent points. The idea is straightforward, calculate n local features in each of the images and, then, perform a nearest-neighbor matching algorithm on the available keypoints. The local features can be calculated using any form the previous section's algorithms.

Let's denote as k_i^A the i-th keypoint, $i=1,\ldots,n$, of the image A extracted via some computer vision algorithm. We also have k_j^B the j-th keypoint, j=1,\ldots,n, of the image B. It is possible that $p \neq q$, since different images result in different keypoints. Then, its corresponding keypoint $ck_j^B(i)$, belonging to image B can be estimated by performing a k-nn search keypoints matching algorithm. A corresponding pair of points (PoP) between image A and B is described as $PoP_l = \left(k_l^A, ck_j^B(l)\right)$, $l=1,\ldots,m$. The expected number of corresponding PoPs, m, is expected to be many times lesser than the number of local features n, i.e. $m \ll n$.

Having detected all corresponding points between two images A and B a set $C(A,B)$ that contains pairs of all keypoints from the first image along with the correspondent points from the second image can be formed as:

$$C(A,B) = \{PoP_l\}_{l=1}^m \tag{1}$$

Figure 1. Illustration of the point detector output over the same image. Image above will be used for the 3D reconstruction. Image bellow is considered an outlier due to the partial occlusions (i.e. car).

The similar approach can be used to form the set $C(B,A)$. The set of final matches, $M(A,B)$, between images A and B can be defined as the intersection of the sets $C(A,B)$ and $C(B,A)$.

$$M(A,B) = C(A,B) \cup C(B,A) \tag{2}$$

Please note that the corresponding point identification is a threshold based approach; two feature vectors match when the distance between them is less than a pre-defined threshold. In case of binary feature vectors (e.g. FREAK or BRISK descriptors) a larger value, for the match threshold, is required. In case of "large" feature sets, an approximate nearest neighbor search can be applied (Muja & Lowe, 2009).

As the number of extracted keypoints for each image is at most n, a visual similarity metric between two images i,j, e.g. images A and B, can be defined as:

$$s(i,j) = \frac{1}{n} \cdot |M(A,B)| \tag{3}$$

where $|M(A,B)|$ stands for the cardinality of the set $M(A,B)$. The output of the process, assuming a set of N images, is a $N{\times}N$ symmetric matrix S defined as:

$$S = \begin{bmatrix} s(1,1) & \ldots & s(1,N) \\ \vdots & \ddots & \vdots \\ s(N,1) & \ldots & s(N,N) \end{bmatrix} \tag{4}$$

Variable $s(i,j)$ takes value of zero if the visual content of image i has no relation with the content of image j; i.e. no corresponding points found. Instead, for two similar images variable $s(i,j)$ takes value $\in(0,1)$; higher the value, more corresponding points. The negative logarithmic version of matrix S, denoted as D, serve as the dissimilarity matrix between images:

$$D = -\log(S) \tag{5}$$

D is a square $N{\times}N$ symmetric matrix with non-negative elements and zeros on the main diagonal.

IMAGES AS POINTS ON MANIFOLDS

The next step of the analysis is establishing a meaningful relation between the dissimilarity metric and the Euclidean distances between points that lie on a manifold. Let's define as $p_i \in \mathbb{R}^{\mu}$ the coordinates of i-th image in the μ-dimensional space. The μ-dimensional space is defined so that the norm between two points p_i and p_j should be equal to their respective image distance $d{ij}=-log(s{ij})$. The coordinates of all N images in the dataset can be compactly represented by a matrix P, which has the following form:

$$P = [p_1, \ldots, p_N]^T \in \mathbb{R}^{N \times \mu}.$$

Figure 2. An illustration of the calculating corresponding points over the same image pair from Parthenon, using different combinations of point detectors and descriptors. In this case, the Shi-Tomasi corner detector combined with SURF descriptor resulted in many more point connections compared to Harris detector and FREAK descriptor. Also note that many of the corresponding points are not accurate.

Density Based Clustering

Clustering refers to the task of identifying groups or clusters in a data set. In density-based clustering, a cluster is a set of data objects spread in the data space over a contiguous region of high density of objects. Density-based clusters are separated from each other by contiguous regions of low density of objects. Data objects located in low-density regions are typically considered noise or outliers (Kriegel, Kröger, Sander, & Zimek, 2011).

OPTICS algorithm (Ankerst, Breunig, Kriegel, & Sander, 1999), as one among various approaches for hierarchical density based clustering, includes ordering points to identify the clustering structure. OPTICS is based on DBSCAN (Ester, Kriegel, Sander, Xu, & others, 1996) and the work in (Stuetzle, 2003).

OPTICS computes a Minimum Spanning Tree of the data, where edge weights represent pairwise distances. These distances are smoothed by a density estimator, called core distance. The core distance of a point x_i is the smallest threshold r such that x_i is still considered a core object by the DBSCAN algorithm, i.e., x_i has still at least k objects in its neighborhood with radius r. The resulting distance, which is used to construct the Minimum Spanning Tree, is called reachability distance (RD). Taking k as input parameter for smoothing the density estimation, the reachability distance of point x_i is defined relative to a reference object y as the minimum of the core distance of y and the actual distance between x_i and y. The outcome of the algorithm can provide us information about the clustering of the objects.

Figure 3. An illustration of OPTICS outputs, for different minimum cluster sizes for Heidentor case. Note that regardless the selected minimum cluster size we have a relatively smooth increase in the reachability distance score. Image ranked 35 to 40 is expected to be outliers.

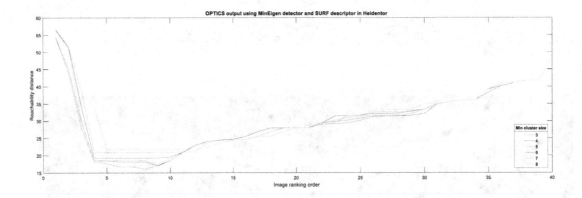

Outlier Identification

Outlier detection is a combinatory threshold-based approach build on the interquartile range rule, as in (Xiao & Fan, 2014), OPTICS output, and images matched data (i.e. see sec. IMAGES AS POINTS ON MANIFOLDS). OPTICS outputs (i.e. reachability distances of the investigated images) is treated as a continuous signal, over which we identify the peaks. Peaks correspond in significand changes between the closest compared vehicles. As such, anything that varies from the norm, has a peak, allowing us the easy identification of a possible outlier. Then, we calculate a threshold value *ths* defined as

$$ths = \frac{1}{m} \sum_{i}^{m} RD_o(i), \quad m=0.1 \cdot N,$$ where N denotes the number of available images and RD_o is the reach-

ability distances vector, in a descending order.

If we have a set of N images describing all sides of a building and some outliers there are two possible outcomes regarding the **RD**. We have a relatively smooth **RD** related signal (i.e. no peaks) or not. The former case is expected. Typically, there should be a smooth connection between adjacent images on each of the building's sides. Even when we move from one side to the other, there should be some corresponding points. Thus, the reachability distances should have minor variations as we progress around the monument. Regarding the outliers, they depict a small part of the monument. Thus, the reachability distances will increase at a significant pace; i.e. they likely belong to 10% of the higher values. Outliers are then provided as:

$$Outliers = argmax(\mathbf{RD} \geq ths) \tag{6}$$

Structure-From-Motion

After the elimination of outliers, the representative images are fed into a Structure from Motion module. In the present case, VisualSFM ("VisualSFM : A Visual Structure from Motion System - Documentation," n.d.) software was used to derive a sparse feature point cloud and orientation parameters. Figure 4 shows an example of VisualSFM's results on determining the cameras' focal length and positions at the time of image acquisition. Other software tools could be used such as Agisoft PhotoScan ("Agisoft PhotoScan," n.d.), MicMac ("Micmac - LOGICIELS," n.d.) and MeshLab (Cignoni et al., 2008). A quantitative comparative study regarding reconstruction accuracy and computational cost among these commercial, free and/or open-source software tools is shown in (Verykokou et al., 2016). The results show that the minimum computational time required for the acquisition of a coarse 3D model is lower in PhotoScan (commercial software), but the generated model has significantly lower density than the one created by the other toolkits due to the smoothing effect. On the contrary, PhotoScan models may contain some holes, which are not present in other software tools such as VisualSFM and MicMac. The comparisons were performed using different parametric settings. VisualSFM was selected because it is open (free) software and yields good precision results (although being slower in terms of execution time).

VIDEO SUMMARIZATION FOR 3D RECONSTRUCTION

Video summarization pertains to the extraction of keyframes from a video sequence. In the case of cultural heritage monuments, brief video shots of monuments are often acquired by visitors and tourists who make them available online. Extracting the keyframes of such videos can provide for an effective alternative approach in creating the input dataset for 3D reconstruction frameworks such as Structure from Motion. In the context of a video summarization technique, since a feature vector is assigned for each frame of a shot, the vectors of all frames form a trajectory in a high dimensional feature space, which expresses their temporal variation. Thus, selection of the most representative frames within a shot is equivalent to selection of appropriate curve points, able to represent the corresponding trajectory. The selected curve points should provide sufficient information about the trajectory, so that it can be reproduced using some kind of interpolation. This can be achieved by extracting the time instances, i.e., the frame numbers, which reside in extreme locations of this trajectory.

The magnitude of the second derivative of feature vectors for all frames within a shot with respect to time is used as a curvature measure. The second derivative expresses the degree of acceleration or deceleration of an object that traces out the feature trajectory. Local maxima correspond to time instances of peak variation of an object velocity, i.e., large acceleration or deceleration. On the other hand, local minima indicate low variation of the object velocity. Thus, these time instances are selected as the most representative points of the feature trajectory.

Figure 4. Example of determining camera positioning and focal length in Visual SFM

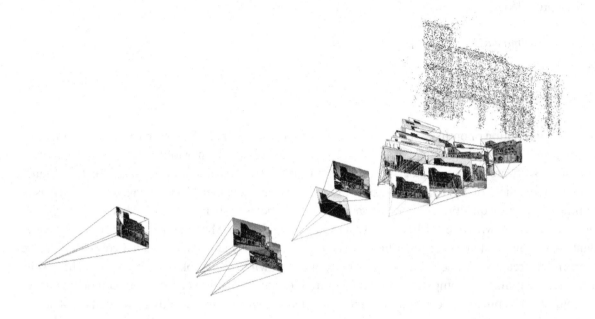

Let us denote as $\mathbf{f}(k)$ the feature vector corresponding to the kth frame of an examined video shot. Vectors $\mathbf{f}(k)$, $k = 1, \ldots, M$ correspond to the descriptors presented in the previous sections also having the additional index k, which indicates the time instance of the respective frame within the examined shot. Variable M indicates the number of frames of the shot. Initially, the first derivative of vector $\mathbf{f}(k)$, say d'(k), is evaluated with respect to time index k. Since, however, variable k takes values in discrete time, the first derivative is approximated as the difference of feature vectors between two successive frames,

$$\mathbf{d}'(k) = \mathbf{f}(k+1) - \mathbf{f}(k), k = 0,1,\ldots,M-2 \tag{7}$$

However, the previous operator is rather sensitive to noise since differentiation of a signal stresses the high pass components. For this reason, a weighted average of the first derivative, say $\mathbf{d}'_w$ over a window, is used to eliminate the noise influence. Particularly, the weighted first derivative is given as

$$\mathbf{d}'_w(k) = \sum_{l=a_1(k)}^{\beta_1(k)} w_{l-k} \mathbf{d}'(l) = \sum_{l=a_1(k)}^{\beta_1(k)} w_{l-k} \left(\mathbf{f}(l+1) - \mathbf{f}(l) \right), k = 0,1,\ldots,M-2 \tag{8}$$

where

$$a_1(k) = \max\left(0, k - N_w\right), \beta_1(k) = \max\left(\mathrm{M} - 2, k + N_w\right)$$

and $2N_w+1$ is the length of the window, centered at frame k. It can be seen from (16) that the window length linearly reduces at shot limits. The weights w_l are defined for $l \in \{-N_w, N_w\}$; in the simple case, all weights w_l are considered equal to each other, meaning that the derivatives of all frame feature vectors within the window interval present the same importance. Then,

$$w_l = \frac{1}{2N_w+1}, l = -N_w, \ldots, N_w \tag{9}$$

Similarly, the second weighted derivative, $\mathbf{d}''_w(k)$ for the k-th frame is defined as:

$$\mathbf{d}''_w(k) = \sum_{l=a_2(k)}^{\beta_2(k)} w_{l-k} \mathbf{d}''(l) = \sum_{l=a_1(k)}^{\beta_1(k)} w_{l-k} \left(\mathbf{d}'(l+1) - \mathbf{d}'(l) \right), k = 0,1,\ldots,M-3 \tag{10}$$

where $a_2(k) = \max(0, k - N_w), \beta_2(k) = \max(\mathrm{M}-3, k+N_w)$.

The second weighted derivative, as defined in (18), is a vector, the elements which express the variation of the elements of $\mathbf{f}(k)$ with respect to time. In order to take into consideration the effect of all elements of $\mathbf{f}(k)$, the magnitude of $\mathbf{d}''_w(k)$ is computed as:

$$D(k) = |\mathbf{d}''_w(k)| \tag{11}$$

As explained previously, the local maxima and minima of $D(k)$ are considered as appropriate curve points, i.e., as time instances for the selected key-frames. Given that $D(k)$ is a discrete time sequence here, the local maxima and minima can be estimated in this case as follows. Let us denote as X the set containing the indices of the most representative frames within a given shot. Then, X can be considered as the union:

$$X = X_M \cup X_m \tag{12}$$

of two sets; X_M contains the time instances of frames corresponding to the local maxima of $D(k)$, while X_m the time instances of local minima of $D(k)$. Thus, sets X_M and X_m are estimated as:

$$X_M = \left\{ k : D(k-1) < D(k) < D(k+1) \right\} \text{ and } X_m = \left\{ k : D(k-1) > D(k) > D(k+1) \right\} \tag{13}$$

EXPERIMENTAL EVALUATION

Experimental Setting

Two cultural heritage related monuments were selected, for evaluation purposes of the described approaches: Parthenon and Heidentor. The Parthenon is a former temple on the Athenian Acropolis, Greece, dedicated to the goddess Athena. Construction began in 447 BC. It is the most important surviving building of Classical Greece, generally considered the zenith of the Doric order. Heidentor is a triumphal monument erected between 354 AD and 361 AD, located in Petronell-Carnuntum, Austria. Contemporary reports suggest that Emperor Constantius II had it built to commemorate his victories. When the remains of Carnuntum disappeared after the Migration Period the monument remained as an isolated building in a natural landscape and led Medieval people to believe it was the tomb of a pagan giant. Hence, they called it "Heidentor" (pagan gate).

The proposed approach assumes that a CBIR method is already applied; most of the images should relevant to the search query, e.g. images of Parthenon for 3D reconstruction. Both sets described by forty images in total. Images were selected so that all sides of the monuments are available and around 20% of them be outliers. Two types of outliers exist within the set: a) images with occlusions, i.e. the monument is not the main object in the foreground) and b) irrelevant pictures, e.g. a PC rendered model, book cover, animals, etc.

The code has been implemented using MatLab software. The OPTICS algorithm was provided by (Daszykowski, Walczak, & Massart, 2002). In order to maintain a relatively shoirt point matching time, we set an upper limit in the detected points; at most 2000 points can be detected per image. In case that more points occur, we select the most confident ones.

Experimental Results

The first step of the analysis involves the number of detected keypoints over an image. On one hand, more keypoints could lead to more corresponding points' matches between image pairs; i.e. improve images correlation scores. On the other hand, the more point we use, higher the matching times. Figure 6 illustrates the number of detected points. The Shi-Tomasi corner detector (MinEigen) provides with more points regardless the investigated monument.

Secondly, we are interested in the similarity between the images; i.e. the applied point descriptors should be correctly correlated among different images, allowing for the identification of similar images. We need high similarity among monuments images and low similarity scores in the case of outliers. Figure 7 illustrates the average corresponding points when using various descriptors. Both FREAK and SURF descriptors provide more point matches for the non-outliers. However, depending on the monument a different descriptor should be applied.

Having established the similarities among images and projected the onto a new manifold, OPTICS clustering should provide additional information regarding the structure of the data. As described in previous sections, images should be clustered in one set. In case of limited matched points among images (e.g. using BRISK descriptor), it is possible to observe a dense chance in reachability distances (i.e. a peak) which indicates the existence of another cluster.

Figure 5. Examples of outlier images in the dataset. Top row refers to Heidentor, bottom row to Parthenon.

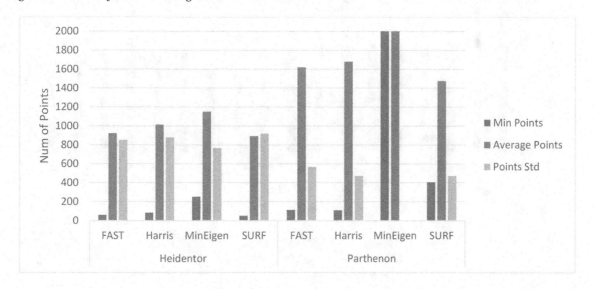

UB-311][PUB-72] UB-83] UB-94]

UB-105] UB-116] UB-127]

Figure 6. Points of interest using various detectors

Figure 7. Average number of corresponding points between two images

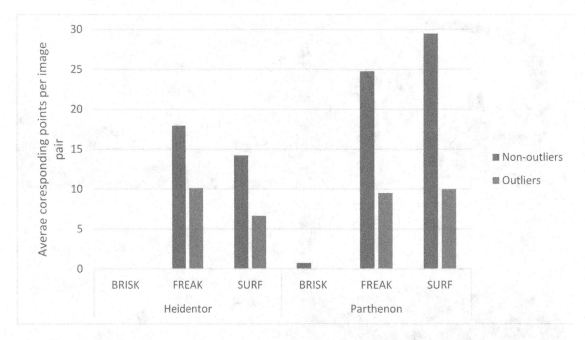

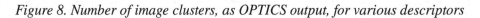

Figure 8. Number of image clusters, as OPTICS output, for various descriptors

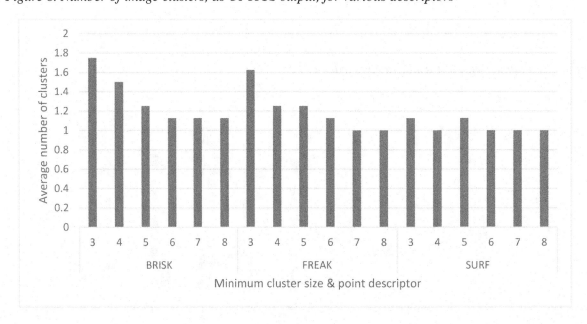

Figure 9. Outlier detection performance metrics

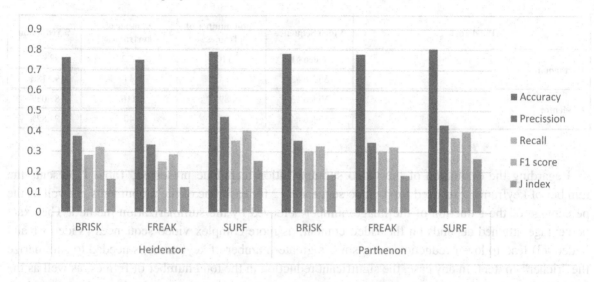

The outlier detection problem actually pertains to a traditional binary classification problem: an image should be considered as an outlier or not? The results are analyzed through standard measures of predictive performance for binary classification tasks. First, the confusion matrices (i.e. 2 × 2 matrices) are formed for each of the suggested combinations of the classifier algorithms with the sampling approaches. The elements of the confusion matrices in our case involve: (1) the number of non-outlier images correctly classified as non- outlier (true negatives, TN), (2) the number of actual outliers misclassified as non- outliers (false negatives, FN), (3) the number of non- outlier images misclassified as outliers (false positives, FP), and (4) the number of outliers correctly classified as outliers (true positives, TP). Using these elements, four well-known classification performance indices are calculated:

1. Accuracy: ACC = (TP + TN) / (P + N), representing the percentage of correct classification for *all* classes.
2. Recall: Rec=TP / P, indicating the fraction of the defaulted cases identified by a model.
3. Specificity: SPC = TN / N, representing the probability of a correct identification of non-defaulted cases.
4. Precision: PPV = TP / (TP + FP), indicating the correct positive predictions, i.e. how many defaulted companies exist among the cases classified (by a model) in the default class.
5. F1 score: is the harmonic mean of precision and sensitivity.
6. Youden's index: J = Rec + SPC − 1, is a single statistic that captures the performance of a dichotomous diagnostic test.

Figure 9 illustrates the performance of the point descriptor on the outliers' detection. Both monuments achieved higher detection rates when SURF descriptor is used.

Table 1. Number of keyframes extracted by the video summarization technique

Landmark	Video Sequence	Total number of frames	Number of keyframes	% reduction
Parthenon	Video #1	1102	122	88.93%
	Video #2	645	44	93.18%
Heidentor	Video #3	898	116	87.08%
	Video #4	772	40	94.82%

Regarding the evaluation of the video summarization technique presented, Table 1 presents the number of keyframes extracted for 4 video sequences, 2 for each one of the monuments, as well as the percentage of the reduction of the image number achieved by the summarization method. The exact percentage attained depends on the video content, as more complex video sequences (Video #1 and Video #3) lead to lower reduction rates, since a greater number of keyframes is needed to summarize the "richer" content. In any case, the significant reduction in the total number of frames, as well as the outlier removal process described above, lead to an important improvement in the computational efficiency of the Structure from Motion module that uses these images as input for reconstructing a 3D model of the depicted cultural landmark.

CONCLUSION

The proliferation of image and video content posted online on multimedia repositories and social media creates new possibilities in terms of the ways that this content can be used for 3D modelling and reconstruction of cultural monuments. Nevertheless, significant challenges have to be tackled which are associated the massive volume, unstructured nature, and outliers residing within these input data. We have presented two an image-based and a video-based approach. In the former, we explore different keypoint detectors and descriptors, similarity based metrics and employ density-based clustering algorithms to identify and eliminate outliers, the existence of which are detrimental to the computational efficiency of Structure from Motion approaches for 3D reconstruction. In the latter, we employ a video summarization technique to extract a set of the most informative frames from a video shot, that will be used as input in a 3D reconstruction framework. The presented approaches are showcased and evaluated in two application scenarios: Parthenon and Heidentor. As further work, we will scrutinize the effectiveness and efficiency of additional visual descriptors, clustering algorithms and video summarization approaches in terms of their applicability, accuracy and computational complexity as drivers of 3D modelling and reconstruction.

ACKNOWLEDGMENT

This research was implemented through scholarships by the Greek State Scholarship Foundation (IKY), co-financed by the European Union (European Social Fund - ESF) and Greek national funds through the action titled "Reinforcement of Postdoctoral Researchers", in the framework of the Operational Programme "Human Resources Development Program, Education and Lifelong Learning" of the National Strategic Reference Framework (NSRF) 2014 – 2020.

REFERENCES

Agarwal, S., Furukawa, Y., Snavely, N., Simon, I., Curless, B., Seitz, S. M., & Szeliski, R. (2011). Building Rome in a Day. *Communications of the ACM, 54*(10), 105–112. doi:10.1145/2001269.2001293

Agisoft PhotoScan. (n.d.). Retrieved July 26, 2017, from https://www.agisoft.com/

Ankerst, M., Breunig, M. M., Kriegel, H.-P., & Sander, J. (1999). OPTICS: Ordering Points to Identify the Clustering Structure. In *Proceedings of the 1999 ACM SIGMOD International Conference on Management of Data* (pp. 49–60). New York, NY: ACM. 10.1145/304182.304187

Argyriou, V., Zafeiriou, S., & Petrou, M. (2014). Optimal illumination directions for faces and rough surfaces for single and multiple light imaging using class-specific prior knowledge. *Computer Vision and Image Understanding, 125*, 16–36. doi:10.1016/j.cviu.2014.01.012

Barone, S., Paoli, A., & Razionale, A. V. (2012). 3D virtual reconstructions of artworks by a multiview scanning process. In *2012 18th International Conference on Virtual Systems and Multimedia* (pp. 259–265). 10.1109/VSMM.2012.6365933

Bay, H., Tuytelaars, T., & Gool, L. V. (2006). SURF: Speeded Up Robust Features. In *Computer Vision – ECCV 2006* (pp. 404–417). Berlin: Springer. doi:10.1007/11744023_32

Chen, F., & Vleeschouwer, C. D. (2011). Formulating Team-Sport Video Summarization as a Resource Allocation Problem. *IEEE Transactions on Circuits and Systems for Video Technology, 21*(2), 193–205. doi:10.1109/TCSVT.2011.2106271

Choudary, C., & Liu, T. (2007). Summarization of Visual Content in Instructional Videos. *IEEE Transactions on Multimedia, 9*(7), 1443–1455. doi:10.1109/TMM.2007.906602

Cignoni, P., Callieri, M., Corsini, M., Dellepiane, M., Ganovelli, F., & Ranzuglia, G. (2008). *MeshLab: an Open-Source Mesh Processing Tool*. The Eurographics Association.

Daszykowski, M., Walczak, B., & Massart, D. L. (2002). Looking for Natural Patterns in Analytical Data. 2. Tracing Local Density with OPTICS. *Journal of Chemical Information and Computer Sciences, 42*(3), 500–507. doi:10.1021/ci010384s PMID:12086507

Doulamis, A. D., Doulamis, N., & Kollas, S. (2000). Non-sequential video content representation using temporal variation of feature vectors. *IEEE Transactions on Consumer Electronics, 46*(3), 758–768. doi:10.1109/30.883444

Doulamis, A. D., & Doulamis, N. D. (2004). Optimal content-based video decomposition for interactive video navigation. *IEEE Transactions on Circuits and Systems for Video Technology, 14*(6), 757–775. doi:10.1109/TCSVT.2004.828348

Doulamis, A. D., Doulamis, N. D., & Kollias, S. D. (2000). A fuzzy video content representation for video summarization and content-based retrieval. *Signal Processing*, *80*(6), 1049–1067. doi:10.1016/S0165-1684(00)00019-0

Ester, M., Kriegel, H.-P., Sander, J., Xu, X., & Associates. (1996). A density-based algorithm for discovering clusters in large spatial databases with noise. In *Kdd* (Vol. 96, pp. 226–231). Retrieved from https://www.aaai.org/Papers/KDD/1996/KDD96-037

Goesele, M., Snavely, N., Curless, B., Hoppe, H., & Seitz, S. M. (2007). Multi-View Stereo for Community Photo Collections. In *2007 IEEE 11th International Conference on Computer Vision* (pp. 1–8). 10.1109/ICCV.2007.4408933

Haala, N., & Rothermel, M. (2012). Dense multiple stereo matching of highly overlapping UAV imagery. *ISPRS-International Archives of the Photogrammetry. Remote Sensing and Spatial Information Sciences*, *39*(B1), 387–392.

Harris, C., & Stephens, M. (1988). A combined corner and edge detector. In *Alvey vision conference* (Vol. 15, pp. 10–5244). Retrieved from http://courses.daiict.ac.in/pluginfile.php/13002/mod_resource/content/0/References/harris1988.pdf

Huang, H., Brenner, C., & Sester, M. (2013). A generative statistical approach to automatic 3D building roof reconstruction from laser scanning data. *ISPRS Journal of Photogrammetry and Remote Sensing*, *79*, 29–43. doi:10.1016/j.isprsjprs.2013.02.004

Hullo, J. F., Grussenmeyer, P., & Fares, S. (2009). Photogrammetry and dense stereo matching approach applied to the documentation of the cultural heritage site of Kilwa (Saudi Arabia). *Proceedings of CIPA*.

Izadi, S., Kim, D., Hilliges, O., Molyneaux, D., Newcombe, R., Kohli, P., ... Fitzgibbon, A. (2011). KinectFusion: Real-time 3D Reconstruction and Interaction Using a Moving Depth Camera. In *Proceedings of the 24th Annual ACM Symposium on User Interface Software and Technology* (pp. 559–568). New York, NY: ACM. 10.1145/2047196.2047270

Kamberov, G., Kamberova, G., Chum, O., Obdržálek, Š., Martinec, D., & Kostková, J. ... Šára, R. (2006). 3D Geometry from Uncalibrated Images. In Advances in Visual Computing (pp. 802–813). Springer. doi:10.1007/11919629_80

Kriegel, H.-P., Kröger, P., Sander, J., & Zimek, A. (2011). Density-based clustering. *Wiley Interdisciplinary Reviews. Data Mining and Knowledge Discovery*, *1*(3), 231–240. doi:10.1002/widm.30

Kyriakaki, G., Doulamis, A., Doulamis, N., Ioannides, M., Makantasis, K., Protopapadakis, E., ... Weinlinger, G. (2014). 4D Reconstruction of Tangible Cultural Heritage Objects from Web-Retrieved Images. *International Journal of Heritage in the Digital Era*, *3*(2), 431–452. doi:10.1260/2047-4970.3.2.431

Li, Z., Schuster, G. M., & Katsaggelos, A. K. (2005). MINMAX optimal video summarization. *IEEE Transactions on Circuits and Systems for Video Technology*, *15*(10), 1245–1256. doi:10.1109/TC-SVT.2005.854230

Liu, D., Hua, G., & Chen, T. (2010). A Hierarchical Visual Model for Video Object Summarization. *IEEE Transactions on Pattern Analysis and Machine Intelligence*, *32*(12), 2178–2190. doi:10.1109/TPAMI.2010.31 PMID:20975116

Lowe, D. G. (2004). Distinctive Image Features from Scale-Invariant Keypoints. *International Journal of Computer Vision*, *60*(2), 91–110. doi:10.1023/B:VISI.0000029664.99615.94

Makantasis, K., Doulamis, A., Doulamis, N., & Ioannides, M. (2014). In the wild image retrieval and clustering for 3D cultural heritage landmarks reconstruction. *Multimedia Tools and Applications*, *§§§*, 1–37. doi:10.100711042-014-2191-z

Micmac - LOGICIELS. (n.d.). Retrieved July 26, 2017, from http://logiciels.ign.fr/?Micmac

Min, R., & Cheng, H. D. (2009). Effective image retrieval using dominant color descriptor and fuzzy support vector machine. *Pattern Recognition*, *42*(1), 147–157. doi:10.1016/j.patcog.2008.07.001

Muja, M., & Lowe, D. G. (2009). Fast approximate nearest neighbors with automatic algorithm configuration. *VISAPP*, *1*(2)331–340.

Orghidan, R., Salvi, J., Gordan, M., Florea, C., & Batlle, J. (2014). Structured light self-calibration with vanishing points. *Machine Vision and Applications*, *25*(2), 489–500. doi:10.100700138-013-0517-x

Panagiotakis, C., Doulamis, A., & Tziritas, G. (2009). Equivalent Key Frames Selection Based on Iso-Content Principles. *IEEE Transactions on Circuits and Systems for Video Technology*, *19*(3), 447–451. doi:10.1109/TCSVT.2009.2013517

Papadopoulos, S., Zigkolis, C., Kompatsiaris, Y., & Vakali, A. (2010). Cluster-based Landmark and Event Detection on Tagged Photo Collections. *IEEE MultiMedia*. doi:10.1109/mmul.2010.68

Protopapadakis, E., & Doulamis, A. (2014). Semi-Supervised Image Meta-Filtering Using Relevance Feedback in Cultural Heritage Applications. *International Journal of Heritage in the Digital Era*, *3*(4), 613–627. doi:10.1260/2047-4970.3.4.613

Rosten, E., & Drummond, T. (2005). Fusing points and lines for high performance tracking. In *Tenth IEEE International Conference on Computer Vision (ICCV'05)* (Vol. 2, pp. 1508–1515). 10.1109/ICCV.2005.104

Shi, J., & Tomasi, C. (1994). Good features to track. In *1994 Proceedings of IEEE Conference on Computer Vision and Pattern Recognition* (pp. 593–600). 10.1109/CVPR.1994.323794

Sitnik, R., & Karaszewski, M. (2010). Automated Processing of Data from 3D Scanning of Cultural Heritage Objects. In *Digital Heritage* (pp. 28–41). Berlin: Springer. doi:10.1007/978-3-642-16873-4_3

Snavely, N., Seitz, S. M., & Szeliski, R. (2006). Photo Tourism: Exploring Photo Collections in 3D. In *ACM SIGGRAPH 2006 Papers* (pp. 835–846). New York, NY: ACM; doi:10.1145/1179352.1141964

Soile, S., Adam, K., Ioannidis, C., & Georgopoulos, A. (2013). Accurate 3D textured models of vessels for the improvement of the educational tools of a museum. *Proceedings of 3D-ARCH*, 219–226.

Stuetzle, W. (2003). Estimating the Cluster Tree of a Density by Analyzing the Minimal Spanning Tree of a Sample. *Journal of Classification*, *20*(1), 25–47. doi:10.100700357-003-0004-6

Toldo, R., Gherardi, R., Farenzena, M., & Fusiello, A. (2015). Hierarchical structure-and-motion recovery from uncalibrated images. *Computer Vision and Image Understanding, 140*, 127–143. doi:10.1016/j.cviu.2015.05.011

Tuytelaars, T., Mikolajczyk, K., & others. (2008). Local invariant feature detectors: a survey. *Foundations and Trends® in Computer Graphics and Vision, 3*(3), 177–280.

Valanis, A., Tapinaki, S., Georgopoulos, A., & Ioannidis, C. (2009). *High resolution textured models for engineering applications*. Retrieved from https://dspace.lib.ntua.gr/handle/123456789/28564

Verykokou, S., Doulamis, A., Athanasiou, G., Ioannidis, C., & Amditis, A. (2016). UAV-based 3D modelling of disaster scenes for Urban Search and Rescue. In *2016 IEEE International Conference on Imaging Systems and Techniques (IST)* (pp. 106–111). 10.1109/IST.2016.7738206

Visual, S. F. M. (n.d.). *A Visual Structure from Motion System - Documentation*. Retrieved July 26, 2017, from http://ccwu.me/vsfm/doc.html

Wu, C., Agarwal, S., Curless, B., & Seitz, S. M. (2011). Multicore bundle adjustment. In CVPR 2011 (pp. 3057–3064). doi:10.1109/CVPR.2011.5995552

Xiao, F., & Fan, C. (2014). Data mining in building automation system for improving building operational performance. *Energy and Building, 75*, 109–118. doi:10.1016/j.enbuild.2014.02.005

Zheng, Y.-T., Zhao, M., Song, Y., Adam, H., Buddemeier, U., & Bissacco, A., … Neven, H. (2009). Tour the world: Building a web-scale landmark recognition engine. In *IEEE Conference on Computer Vision and Pattern Recognition, 2009. CVPR 2009* (pp. 1085–1092). 10.1109/CVPR.2009.5206749

KEY TERMS AND DEFINITIONS

3D Reconstruction: The process of capturing the shape and appearance of real objects.

Density-Based Clustering: A category of clustering in which clusters are defined as areas of higher density than the remainder of the data set. Data points belonging in sparse areas are usually considered to be noise and border points.

Descriptor: A description of the visual features of the contents in images or videos, or the algorithm that generates this description.

Keypoint Detector: An algorithm that chooses points from an image based on some criterion.

Outlier Removal: Process of identifying and eliminating observations that are distant or unrelated from/to other observations. In the context of the chapter, outliers pertain to images whose content is not closely related to the content of the remaining group of images.

Structure From Motion (SfM): A photogrammetric range imaging technique for estimating 3D structures from 2D image sequences that may be coupled with local motion signals.

Video Summarization: The process of creating a brief synopsis of the content of a longer video by selecting and presenting the most informative or representative image frames of the video.

Chapter 10
Single View 3D Face Reconstruction

Claudio Ferrari
 https://orcid.org/0000-0001-9465-6753
University of Florence, Italy

Stefano Berretti
 https://orcid.org/0000-0003-1219-4386
University of Florence, Italy

Alberto Del Bimbo
University of Florence, Italy

ABSTRACT

3D face reconstruction from a single 2D image is a fundamental computer vision problem of extraordinary difficulty that dates back to the 1980s. Briefly, it is the task of recovering the three-dimensional geometry of a human face from a single RGB image. While the problem of automatically estimating the 3D structure of a generic scene from RGB images can be regarded as a general task, the particular morphology and non-rigid nature of human faces make it a challenging problem for which dedicated approaches are still currently studied. This chapter aims at providing an overview of the problem, its evolutions, the current state of the art, and future trends.

INTRODUCTION

Estimating the 3D information of a scene from 2D images using computer vision techniques is a research topic with a quite long tradition that dates back to '80. Now, remaining the 3D acquisition limited to a certain constrained domain, the deployment of powerful deep learning tools has pushed forward this research field, with innovative solutions that appeared recently.

DOI: 10.4018/978-1-5225-5294-9.ch010

Estimating the 3D geometry from single or multiple images under the most general conditions, where no *a priori* knowledge is available about the imaged scene and the capturing conditions is a very challenging task. Hence, to make the problem solvable to some extent, priors are usually assumed. In the case a 3D model of the face, the prior knowledge can be in the form of camera parameters and reflectance properties of the face considering either a single image, as in the shape from shading (SfS) solution (Horn and Brooks, 1989) or multiple images with different illuminations in the photometric stereo approach (Woodham, 1980). Though quite accurate reconstructions can be obtained with these solutions, the given assumptions are rarely verified in real contexts. However, recent technical advancements in scanning technologies are making it possible to acquire 3D data of sufficient quality at an affordable cost, so that reconstruction algorithms can leverage additional data. Not only 3D data but also the increased availability of 2D imagery can be exploited to this aim; in (Ioannides et al, 2013), authors employ online image repositories to collect multi-view imagery of cultural heritage sites to reconstruct the 3D structure. Multi-view reconstruction is usually achieved using multiple photographs of the same object taken at subsequent time steps from different view-points, which are not easily available. However, multiple images collected from the internet can still be used with some additional effort; clearly this reasonably implies less accurate reconstructions. In a similar way, researchers are putting effort in collecting 4D databases containing temporal sequences of 3D scans as in (Cheng et al, 2018). The temporal consistency is indeed an importan source of information that can be exploited in place of other constraints.

Nevertheless, to overcome such limitations, in 1999 the 3D Morphable face Model (3DMM) was first proposed (Blanz and Vetter, 1999) to be used as a statistical human face shape prior. Despite being originally developed as a generative model, it has been subsequently used in many applications as a means to limit the shape deformations to statistically plausible motions. The main idea behind the 3DMM is that of exploiting the statistics of 3D face shapes to generate new faces by controlling a set of parameters learned from a training set of real 3D face scans. This statistical model limits the shape of the reconstructed face to the combination, according to a set of parameters, of an average face model and some deformation components. Thanks to its intuitiveness and simplicity, it is still exploited as a means for relieving constraints on the general problem. Different solutions have been proposed in the literature for solving for these parameters. In the original 3DMM, as firstly proposed in (Blanz and Vetter, 1999), this was formulated as the problem of iteratively minimizing the difference between the 2D target image and the face image rendered from the 3D reconstruction. This line of research was extended by many others, as it allows a pretty accurate shape reconstruction, though computationally onerous. Later works proposed many alternatives to learn the parameters, for example via linear regression from the position of a set of corresponding 2D and 3D landmarks or exploiting geometrical constraints. These latter solutions, though efficient, often result in coarse reconstructions that can be sensitive to inaccurate landmarks detection in the 2D images.

Despite these drawbacks, the 3DMM has been the founding idea of several recent solutions that use deep neural networks to learn complex non-linear regression functions or as a tool for generating synthetic training data. Nonetheless, the main limitation of the 3DMM is that the results of such reconstructions appear still approximated, lacking fine-grained details of the face. The current trend is moving towards solutions that start from an initial smooth estimation of the face shape, then add local, fine-grained details.

Since the vast majority of works addressing the problem of single-view 3D face reconstruction are based on the morphable model, in the following the latter is detailed and relevant works are presented.

3D MORPHABLE MODEL

Blanz and Vetter were the first proposing to create a 3D morphable model from a set of exemplar 3D faces and showed the potential and versatility of this solution. 3DMM and its variants have been used with success in many recognition applications, such as pose robust face recognition and 3D face recognition. In their work, they first presented a complete solution to derive a 3DMM by transforming the shape and texture from a training set of 3D face scans into a vector space representation based on PCA. The 3DMM was further extended into the Basel Face Model (Paysan et al., 2009). This allowed better shape and texture accuracy thanks to an improved scanning device, and a lower number of artifacts using an improved registration algorithm based on the non-rigid iterative closest point (ICP) (Amberg and Romdhani and Vetter, 2007).

The work by (Booth et al., 2016) also defined a pipeline for building a 3DMM. Initially, a dense correspondence is estimated applying the non-rigid ICP to a template. Then, the so-called LSFM-3DMM was built applying PCA to derive the basis on a dataset of approximately 10.000 scans including a wide variety of age, gender, and ethnicity. Though the LSFM-3DMM was built from the largest dataset compared to the current state-of-the-art, the face shapes did not include any expressive variation, thus limiting the modeling ability of the 3DMM. Following a different approach, (Patel and Smith, 2009) showed that Thin-Plate Splines (TPS) and Procrustes analysis can be employed to construct a 3DMM. Procrustes analysis was used to establish a dense correspondence between a set of 104 landmarks labeled on the facial scans, and the mean coordinates of these landmarks were used as anchor points. A complete deformable model was then constructed by warping the landmarks of each sample to the anchor points and interpolating the regions between landmarks using TPS. Finally, consistent resampling was performed across all faces, but using the estimated surface between landmarks rather than the real one. In (Cosker et al.), the authors depicted a framework for building a dynamic 3DMM, which extended static 3DMM construction by incorporating temporal data. This was obtained by proposing an approach based on the Active Appearance Model and TPS for non-rigid mesh registration. Results showed this method overcomes optical flow-based solutions that are prone to temporal drift and effectively used such to build a 3DMM from the densely registered scans.

Brunton et al. (Brunton et al., 2014), instead, proposed a statistical model for 3D human faces in varying expression. The approach decomposed the face using a wavelet transform in place of PCA and learned many localized, decorrelated multilinear models on the resulting coefficients. In (Luthi et al., 2016), it is presented a Gaussian Process Morphable Model (GPMM), which generalizes PCA-based Statistical Shape Models (SSM). GPMM was defined by a Gaussian process, which makes it inherently continuous. Further, it can be specified using arbitrary positive definite kernels, which makes it possible to build shape priors, even in the case where many examples to learn an SSM are not available.

All the above methods, however, only rely on training scans in a neutral expression as expressive scans represent a challenge in this scenario. This is mainly due to the difficulty to realize a dense correspondence (registration) between the scans, which is an essential step in order to compute the average model. In fact, intuitively, the average model is computed on a predefined number N of 3D points of the face, and each point pi should be located in the same position of the face across all the scans. If this condition can be obtained quite easily for a reduced set of face landmarks with a clear semantic meaning (this are often between 16 to 68, and include, for example, the nose tip, the eye corners, the mouth corners, the eyebrows, etc.), the problem becomes ill posed when the correspondence should be extended to points that densely cover the face of scans of different subjects or scans of the same subject, but with

Figure 1. Example of 3D shape deformation by means of the 3DMM. A generic face model is deformed by linearly combining a set of deformation components. Each components is learned from a training set of registered 3D scans.

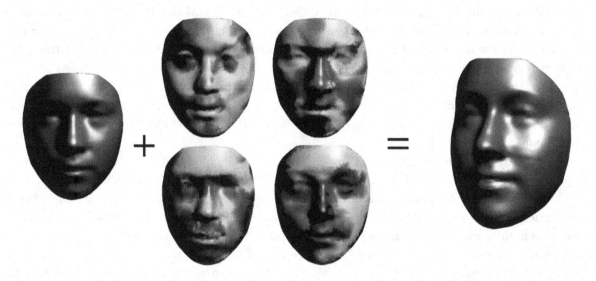

different expressions. This obviously limits the modeling ability of the resulting model. An illustrative example of the 3DMM is shown in Figure 1.

From the discussion of existing solutions for generating a 3DMM, it is quite evident the presence of some aspects that play a major relevance in characterizing the different solutions: (1) the human face variability captured by the model, which directly depends on the number and heterogeneity of training examples; (2) the capability of the model to account for facial expressions; also this feature of the model directly derives from the presence of expressive scans in the training.

The first problem to be solved in the construction of a 3DMM is the selection of an appropriate set of training data. This should include sufficient variability in terms of ethnicity, gender, age, so as to enable the model to include a large variance in the data. Apart for this, as mentioned above, the most difficult aspect in preparing the training data is the need to provide dense, i.e., vertex-by-vertex, alignment between the 3D scans. In the original work of Blanz and Vetter this was solved with the optical-flow method that provided reasonable results just in the case of neutral scans of the face. Several subsequent works used non-rigid variants of the Iterative Closest Point (ICP) algorithm (Amberg et al., 2007), thus solving some problem related to the optical-flow, but without the explicit capability of addressing large facial expressions in the training data. One of the few 3DMM that included expressive scans in the training set is the one proposed by (Ferrari et al., 2017). Expressive scans are put in dense correspondence by means of a resampling strategy applied on a set of geodesic paths connecting a set of sparse landmarks. Then, the deformation components are learned by exploiting a Dictionary Learning (DL) technique, which demonstrated to be effective in modeling both identity and expression variations in a single model.

Definition

Once a dense correspondence is established across the training data, these are used to estimate a set of deformation components that will be used to generate novel shapes. In the classic 3DMM framework, new 3D shapes **S** and textures **T** are generated by deforming an average 3D model **m** and an average texture map **t** with a linear combination of a set of M principal components **Cs**, **Ct** usually derived by PCA as follows:

$$S = m + \sum_{i=1}^{M} Cs_i \alpha_i \quad T = t + \sum_{i=1}^{M} Ct_i \beta_i$$

From the equations above, the deformation coefficients α, β are used to deform the average shape and texture, constrained by the variabilities included in the training data. This is done both for generating arbitrary novel shapes and textures or reconstructing a target face. In the former case, arbitrary linear combinations are applied and new 3D textured models are generated. With little additional effort, the identity (and, optionally, expression) labels from the training dataset can be used to learn characteristic-specific components, so that peculiar traits can be controlled in a human-understandable way, e.g., large/thin, short/long. In the second case, the parameters need to be estimated in order to match the target face.

Several approaches have been proposed to regress the optimal parameters; in the following, it is provided an overview of the possible strategies that can be employed.

Face Reconstruction Using a 3DMM

To reconstruct the 3D shape from a single RGB image using a 3DMM, many approaches have been developed. Such methods can be mainly divided into two categories: Analysis-by-Synthesis and Geometric based. The former methods attempt to estimate the correct shape by minimizing the difference between the original RGB image and a rendering of the 3DMM. The shape and texture parameters of the 3DMM are optimized such that it matches as accurately as possible the appearance of the RGB image. This should ensure to some extent a correct matching of the geometry. However, the image appearance resulting from a projection of a 3D model to a 2D plane can be generated from very different shapes in different poses. Other than that, those are usually approaches that take a considerable time for converging and can work mostly under constrained conditions. Only a few methods attempted to generalize the approach to unconstrained scenarios. On the opposite, the obtained reconstructions usually result rather accurate in the former case. The second category of techniques shares the common concept of deforming the shape by matching some geometrical elements, such as sparse landmark points. Other subsequent extensions included soft constraints on edges or local image features such as SIFT keypoints. The latter methods have the advantage of being much faster and less computationally onerous. On the opposite, the accuracy of such reconstruction is limited, as the whole shape is estimated by just controlling a set of sparse control points. In any case, geometric methods are still being widely employed for their versatility and a sufficient level of approximation. An example is shown in Figure 2.

Figure 2. Example of textured rendering of a face reconstructed using the method in (Ferrari et al., 2017)

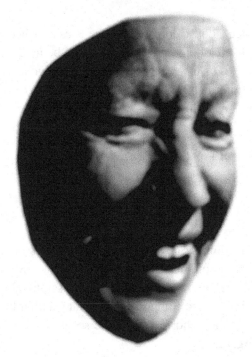

Some of the earliest methods like the one in (Hassner and Basni, 2006) and also more recent methods (Hassner, 2013) used 3D reference models to modify the shape estimated from an input face image.

For example, in (Hassner, 2013) a data-driven method was presented for estimating the 3D shape of faces viewed in single "in-the-wild" photos, where an optimization process was used to jointly maximize the similarity of appearances and depths to those of a reference model.

These methods favor robustness to challenging viewing conditions over detailed reconstructions, thus they were only used to synthesize new views from unseen poses for face recognition. Also, these methods emphasized more the appeal of rendered face images, rather than the quantitative evaluation of the accuracy of the reconstructed face shape. In (Booth et al., 2017) an in-the-wild 3DMM was proposed by combining a statistical model of facial shape, which describes both identity and expression, with an in-the-wild texture model. The latter represented one of the first attempts to extend the reconstruction to faces captured in unconstrained conditions, that is with unpredictable changes in the imaging conditions such as illumination, outdoor/indoor, spontaneous poses and expressions and so on. This represents still now the main challenge in the field of single view reconstruction. As said previously, the total absence of constraints make the problem much more challenging.

Some other reconstruction techniques fit the 3DMM surface to detected facial landmarks rather than to face intensities directly. These methods include solutions designed for videos, like in (Saito et al., 2016), and the CNN based approaches of (Jourabloo and Liu, 2016).

For example, in (Jourabloo and Liu, 2016) a face alignment method for large-pose face images was proposed that combines the powerful cascaded CNN regressor method and the 3DMM. In particular, the face alignment is formulated as a 3DMM fitting problem, where the camera projection matrix and the

3D shape parameters are estimated by a cascade of CNN-based regressors. The dense 3D shape allows designing pose-invariant appearance features for effective CNN learning.

The face recognition method also used 3D modeling of the face based on fiducial points to warp a detected facial crop to a 3D frontal mode.

These latter methods, however, focus more on landmark detection and alignment than 3D shape estimation, and so do not attempt to produce detailed and discriminative facial geometries.

Applications

Reconstructing the geometry and texture of a face given an image opens the way to a broad range of applications, ranging from entertainment, security, biometrics, to healthcare. It can be employed for analyzing subtle changes in the facial structure for detecting alterations for healthcare applications; other applications can span from the generation of user-specific avatars to be used in entertainment and gaming; facial expression recognition can be performed to aid human-computer interaction systems or simply to detect the emotional state of a person. In any case, face recognition and facial expression recognition are central in most of these applications as the specific user of emotion must be recognized. In a broad sense, face recognition performs coarse-grained face analysis, where face variations that separate different identities are accounted for. Convincing results have been obtained for 2D still images and videos, where 2D large and heterogeneous corpora can be easily collected, with the ultimate effect of making machine learning tools work effectively. Conversely, in applications that recognize facial expressions or Action Units (AU), fine-grained face analysis is required, where subtle and local variations of the face occur under the action of groups or individual facial muscles. In this case, 2D data manifest more evident limitations, and performing face analysis in 3D can be convenient. However, the acquisition of 3D data is surely more complex than collecting 2D imagery; as a result, the idea that developed in the research community was to design techniques aimed at recovering the 3D structure directly from the images. This is employed for a variety of applications. Among them, the most widespread consists in normalizing the face image by compensating the out-of-plane rotation of the head. This is possible since the 3D structure allows performing movements out of the 2D image plane and rebuild the image.

Nevertheless, the main important limitation of all the above is that the accuracy of the reconstructions provided by a morphable model or similar statistical priors is limited to a smooth and approximated estimation lacking fine-grained details and usually distant from the real underlying geometry of the subject. In addition, the 3DMM formulation is inherently linear, and so not capable to model non-linear deformations as can happen in the reality. To surpass such obstacles, recently the power of deep learning solutions is being employed to a great extent.

DEEP LEARNING FOR 3D FACE RECONSTRUCTION

The recent success of deep learning and Convolutional Neural Networks (CNNs) began with the work of Krizhevsky (Krizhevsky et al. 2012), which won the LSVRC image classification competition on the ImageNet dataset. Nowadays, the use of such technology extended also to the field of 3D vision, with hybrid methodologies that allowed the extension of CNNs also to 3D data. The main bottleneck for using such technology is the lack of training data. Indeed, deep learning methods require huge computational resources and data to effectively train. While collecting RGB images can leverage an almost infinite source such as the Internet, this does not apply for 3D data. For some time, high resolution scans were required, thus further limiting the applicability of deep learning to 3D data. One idea is that of generating such face shapes synthetically using a 3DMM. Following this approach, in (Richardson et al., 2016) a rather shallow network is trained on synthetic shapes with an iterative process, and facial details are also added by training an end-to-end system to additionally estimate SfS. However, many workarounds have been then studied to address the problem. The first straightforward solution consisted in rendering multi-views of a 3D object to simultaneously increase the size of the data and providing richer information, but still represented as RGB images, so that classic architectures could be used (Su et al. 2015).

In any case, two principal pathways can be identified to address the representation problem; one is developing dedicated architectures and methodologies to deal with 3D data. The chapter will not discuss such architectures as it is not the primary scope. It is important to remark, however, that 3D data can be represented in many different forms, e.g., point-clouds, triangular meshes, adjacency matrices, or range images, to mention some. The problem is that most of them are unordered data structures, which are not suitable for direct use with deep networks. As an example, one trivial obstacle is represented by the number of vertices in the point-clouds; neural networks are made such that the input necessarily needs to have a fixed size. On the contrary, each 3D model (face or any other object), is likely to be made up of a variable number of 3D points. Other way around, one can try to represent the 3D data in a way such that it becomes suitable for standard architectures. The most widely employed representation is the depth image, in which each pixel encodes the distance between the camera and a 3D point. In this way, a regular grayscale image is built encoding the 3D structure of the data. A nice property of such kind of solutions is that, similarly to the z-coordinate, many other geometrical properties can be encoded into an image. For example, one can compute the normal vectors at each vertex and encode the polar angles, which give information on the local direction of the surface. Another property that can be used is the surface curvature. This is particularly informative when dealing with human faces as some regions, e.g., cheeks, forehead, are highly smooth, while some others like the nose or mouth, tend to have a more irregular structure. All such informations can be encoded into an image and exploited to enrich the information. However, such information is usually not easy to retrieve from RGB face images.

Other methods in this category, used deep networks by emphasizing more the aspect of estimating 3D shapes from unconstrained photos, like in (Tran et al., 2017). These methods estimate shapes that are highly invariant to viewing conditions, but provide only coarse 3D details. In (Tran et al., 2017), authors proposed to use a very deep CNN to regress 3DMM parameters and facial details directly from image intensities, rather than by using the analysis by synthesis approach of earlier methods. In (Jackson, 2017), regression of a volumetric representation of the 3D facial geometry from a single 2D image is directly performed using a simple CNN architecture denoted as Volumetric Regression Network that was based on the "hourglass network". In other works, like in (Sengupta et al., 2017), the SfSNet designs an end-to-end learning framework, which reflects a physical Lambertian rendering model for producing decomposition of an unconstrained image of a human face into shape, reflectance and illuminance. To allow for detailed reconstructions the face shape is directly estimated using a depth map. An image-to-image translation network is proposed that jointly maps the input image to a depth image and a facial correspondence map. This explicit pixel-based mapping can then be utilized to provide high-quality reconstructions of diverse faces under extreme expressions, using a purely geometric refinement process. Other approaches reconstructed a 3D face from a single in-the-wild color image by combining a convolutional encoder network with an expert-designed generative model that serves as decoder. All the reported solutions exploit the 3DMM in some way, demonstrating the usefulness and the modernity of such tool.

Current State-of-the-Art

Still, all the latter approaches tend to recover smooth and approximated face shapes, without accounting for realistic details of the surface. To account for this issue, in (Richardson et al., 2017) an end-to-end CNN framework is introduced, which derives the shape in a coarse-to-fine fashion. This architecture is composed of a network that recovers the coarse facial geometry (CoarseNet), followed by a CNN that refines the facial features of that geometry (FineNet). Also in this case, the solution space is modeled by a 3DMM. Different from other works that reconstruct and refine the 3D face in an iterative manner using both an RGB image and an initial 3D facial shape rendering, in (Dou et al., 2017) an end-to-end DNN model was proposed that avoids the complicated 3D rendering process. In doing so, two components are integrated in the DNN architecture: a multi-task loss function, and a fusion-CNN to improve facial expression reconstruction. With the multi-task loss function, 3D face reconstruction is divided into neutral 3D facial shape reconstruction and expressive 3D facial shape reconstruction. With the fusion-CNN, features from different intermediate layers are fused and transformed for predicting the 3D expressive facial shape.

However, the recent trend is moving towards solutions able to both recover an accurate geometry of the face image, but also to generate fine-grained details, such as wrinkles. Most of the recent techniques developed to this aim make use of the Generative Adversarial Network (GAN) learning mechanism. Briefly, the GAN mechanism involves two (or more) network components that are trained concurrently; the founding idea is that of learning to generate, while learning to discriminate between true or generated in a min-max adversarial game. Despite simple, this idea led to a noticeable improvement in the realism of the generated output. GANs were first proposed in (Goodfellow et al., 2014), and subsequently modified in a series of works, for improved training, or extended to unsupervised learning as with the Deep Convolutional GANs (DCGANs).

Since their introduction, GANs have rapidly established as state-of-the-art solutions to improve the quality of generated 2D images in a variety of image synthesis tasks. Generative parametric models were further introduced capable of producing high-quality samples of natural images.

To allow for detailed reconstructions, in (Sela et al., 2017) the face shape is directly estimated using a depth map. An image-to-image translation network is proposed that jointly maps the input image to a depth image and a facial correspondence map. This explicit pixel-based mapping can then be utilized to provide high-quality reconstructions of diverse faces under extreme expressions, using a purely geometric refinement process. The method designed in (Tran et al., 2018) provides detailed 3D reconstructions of faces viewed under out of plane rotations, and occlusions. Motivated by the concept of bump mapping, a layered approach is proposed, which decouples estimation of a global shape from its mid-level details. A coarse 3D face shape is first estimated, which acts as a foundation, and then details represented by a bump map are layered on this foundation. A deep convolutional encoder-decoder was used to estimate such bump maps.

An approach based on a Conditional Generative Adversarial Network (CGAN) was proposed in (Galteri et al., 2019) for refining the coarse face reconstruction provided by a 3DMM. The latter is represented as a three channels image, where the pixel intensities represent the depth, curvature and elevation values of the 3D vertices. The architecture is an encoder–decoder trained progressively, starting from the lower-resolution layers. This resulted in a more stable training, and ultimately in the generation of high quality outputs even when high-resolution images are fed during the training.

In light of the success and accurate results obtained with GANs, researchers are trying to adapt the adversarial learning protocol also to more complex architectures specifically designed for dealing with 3D data. In (Cheng et al., 2019), a mesh-GAN architecture is proposed based on spectral mesh convolutions to build a non-linear 3DMM. With respect to other linear formulations, 3DMM directly learned with a deep network allows for more complex deformations, with a noticeable improvement in the representation power. In (Bouritsas et al., 2019), another variant is proposed, which makes use of spiral convolutions to capture latent information in the 3D structure of an unordered point-cloud.

Issues and Future Trends

Thanks to the development of deep learning, the quality and precision of methods addressing the 3D face reconstruction from single image is increased dramatically, reaching a level of accuracy that is satisfactory for a broad range of applications. However, there is still room for improvements; indeed, all the methods reported in the literature are able to get very good results also in unconstrained environments only if the resolution of the input image is rather high. One pathway that still poses challenges is the case of lower-resolution images. In such scenario, the level of visual information is not sufficient to make deep learning based methods work properly, and researchers are working towards solutions that can effectively derive accurate reconstructions also in case the input image is of lower quality. Another line of research that is currently being studied is that of generalizing the face model to the entire head. In (Ploumpis et al., 2019), authors built a complete morphable model of the whole head, including ears, neck, and the cranium. The complete model includes scans of huge diversity, including different ethnicities, ages, gender etc.

One main difficulty in developing accurate approaches is represented by the evaluation protocols that are used. In the vast majority of works, the evaluation is carried out in a qualitative way; this is forced by the fact ground-truth 3D models of the reconstructed faces are rarely available. This poses another challenge as the realism and apparent accuracy of the reconstruction obtained by performing textured renderings often impairs a correct understanding of the real accuracy of the reconstructed geometry.

CONCLUSION

This chapter provided an overview and solutions to the problem of 3D face reconstruction from single RGB images. The difficulty of the problem is demonstrated by its longevity and by the fact that it still represents an active research field with a wide range of practical applications. The 3D Morphable Model has been presented and discussed as it represents the most widespread statistical tool used in this field, as also demonstrated by the huge number of works including the 3DMM in the pipeline. Finally, the chapter presented the recent state-of-the-art solutions and discussed the current and future research trends and limitations, so as to provide the reader an overview of what was done, what is being done and what can be done in the future.

REFERENCES

Amberg, B., Romdhani, S., & Vetter, T. (2007, June). Optimal step nonrigid ICP algorithms for surface registration. In *2007 IEEE Conference on Computer Vision and Pattern Recognition* (pp. 1-8). IEEE. doi:10.1109/AVSS.2009.58

Blanz, V., & Vetter, T. (1999, July). A morphable model for the synthesis of 3D faces. In Siggraph (Vol. 99, No. 1999, pp. 187-194). ACM.

Booth, J., Antonakos, E., Ploumpis, S., Trigeorgis, G., Panagakis, Y., & Zafeiriou, S. (2017, July). 3D face morphable models "In-The-Wild". In *2017 IEEE Conference on Computer Vision and Pattern Recognition (CVPR)* (pp. 5464-5473). IEEE. 10.1109/CVPR.2017.580

Booth, J., Roussos, A., Zafeiriou, S., Ponniah, A., & Dunaway, D. (2016). A 3d morphable model learned from 10,000 faces. In *Proceedings of the IEEE Conference on Computer Vision and Pattern Recognition* (pp. 5543-5552). IEEE.

Bouritsas, G., Bokhnyak, S., Ploumpis, S., Bronstein, M., & Zafeiriou, S. (2019). Neural 3d morphable models: Spiral convolutional networks for 3d shape representation learning and generation. In *Proceedings of the IEEE International Conference on Computer Vision* (pp. 7213-7222). 10.1109/ICCV.2019.00731

Brunton, A., Bolkart, T., & Wuhrer, S. (2014, September). Multilinear wavelets: A statistical shape space for human faces. In *European Conference on Computer Vision* (pp. 297-312). Springer. 10.1007/978-3-319-10590-1_20

Cheng, S., Bronstein, M., Zhou, Y., Kotsia, I., Pantic, M., & Zafeiriou, S. (2019). *MeshGAN: Non-linear 3D Morphable Models of Faces.* arXiv preprint arXiv:1903.10384

Cheng, S., Kotsia, I., Pantic, M., & Zafeiriou, S. (2018). 4dfab: A large scale 4d database for facial expression analysis and biometric applications. In *Proceedings of the IEEE conference on computer vision and pattern recognition* (pp. 5117-5126). 10.1109/CVPR.2018.00537

Cosker, D., Krumhuber, E., & Hilton, A. (2011, November). A FACS valid 3D dynamic action unit database with applications to 3D dynamic morphable facial modeling. In *2011 International Conference on Computer Vision* (pp. 2296-2303). IEEE. 10.1109/ICCV.2011.6126510

Dou, P., Shah, S. K., & Kakadiaris, I. A. (2017). End-to-end 3D face reconstruction with deep neural networks. In *Proceedings of the IEEE Conference on Computer Vision and Pattern Recognition* (pp. 5908-5917). 10.1109/CVPR.2017.164

Ferrari, C., Lisanti, G., Berretti, S., & Del Bimbo, A. (2017). A dictionary learning-based 3D morphable shape model. *IEEE Transactions on Multimedia*, *19*(12), 2666–2679. doi:10.1109/TMM.2017.2707341

Galteri, L., Ferrari, C., Lisanti, G., Berretti, S., & Del Bimbo, A. (2019, August). Deep 3D Morphable Model Refinement via Progressive Growing of Conditional Generative Adversarial Networks. *Computer Vision and Image Understanding*, *185*, 31–42. doi:10.1016/j.cviu.2019.05.002

Goodfellow, I., Pouget-Abadie, J., Mirza, M., Xu, B., Warde-Farley, D., Ozair, S., . . . Bengio, Y. (2014). Generative adversarial nets. In Advances in neural information processing systems (pp. 2672-2680). Academic Press.

Hassner, T. (2013). Viewing real-world faces in 3D. In *Proceedings of the IEEE International Conference on Computer Vision* (pp. 3607-3614). IEEE.

Hassner, T., & Basri, R. (2006, June). Example based 3D reconstruction from single 2D images. In *2006 Conference on Computer Vision and Pattern Recognition Workshop (CVPRW'06)* (pp. 15-15). IEEE. 10.1109/CVPRW.2006.76

Horn, B. K., & Brooks, M. J. (1989). *Shape from shading*. MIT Press.

Ioannides, M., Hadjiprocopi, A., Doulamis, N., Doulamis, A., Protopapadakis, E., Makantasis, K., ... Julien, M. (2013). Online 4D reconstruction using multi-images available under Open Access. *ISPRS Photogr. Rem. Sens. Spat. Inf. Sc.*, *2*(W1), 169–174. doi:10.5194/isprsannals-II-5-W1-169-2013

Jackson, A. S., Bulat, A., Argyriou, V., & Tzimiropoulos, G. (2017). Large pose 3D face reconstruction from a single image via direct volumetric CNN regression. In *Proceedings of the IEEE International Conference on Computer Vision* (pp. 1031-1039). 10.1109/ICCV.2017.117

Jourabloo, A., & Liu, X. (2016). Large-pose face alignment via CNN-based dense 3D model fitting. In *Proceedings of the IEEE conference on computer vision and pattern recognition* (pp. 4188-4196). 10.1109/CVPR.2016.454

Krizhevsky, A., Sutskever, I., & Hinton, G. E. (2012). Imagenet classification with deep convolutional neural networks. In Advances in neural information processing systems (pp. 1097-1105). Academic Press.

Lüthi, M., Jud, C., Gerig, T., & Vetter, T. (2016). *Gaussian Process Morphable Models*. Academic Press.

Patel, A., & Smith, W. A. (2009). Shape-from-shading Driven 3D Morphable Models for Illumination Insensitive Face Recognition. In BMVC (pp. 1-10). Academic Press.

Paysan, P., Knothe, R., Amberg, B., Romdhani, S., & Vetter, T. (2009, September). A 3D face model for pose and illumination invariant face recognition. In *2009 Sixth IEEE International Conference on Advanced Video and Signal Based Surveillance* (pp. 296-301). IEEE.

Ploumpis, S., Ververas, E., Sullivan, E. O., Moschoglou, S., Wang, H., Pears, N., . . . Zafeiriou, S. (2019). *Towards a complete 3D morphable model of the human head.* arXiv preprint arXiv:1911.08008

Richardson, E., Sela, M., & Kimmel, R. (2016, October). 3D face reconstruction by learning from synthetic data. In *2016 Fourth International Conference on 3D Vision (3DV)* (pp. 460-469). IEEE. 10.1109/3DV.2016.56

Richardson, E., Sela, M., Or-El, R., & Kimmel, R. (2017). Learning detailed face reconstruction from a single image. In *Proceedings of the IEEE Conference on Computer Vision and Pattern Recognition* (pp. 1259-1268). 10.1109/CVPR.2017.589

Saito, S., Li, T., & Li, H. (2016, October). Real-time facial segmentation and performance capture from rgb input. In *European Conference on Computer Vision* (pp. 244-261). Springer. 10.1007/978-3-319-46484-8_15

Sela, M., Richardson, E., & Kimmel, R. (2017). Unrestricted facial geometry reconstruction using image-to-image translation. In *Proceedings of the IEEE International Conference on Computer Vision* (pp. 1576-1585). 10.1109/ICCV.2017.175

Sengupta, S., Kanazawa, A., Castillo, C. D., & Jacobs, D. W. (2018). SfSNet: Learning Shape, Reflectance and Illuminance of Facesin the Wild'. In *Proceedings of the IEEE Conference on Computer Vision and Pattern Recognition* (pp. 6296-6305). 10.1109/CVPR.2018.00659

Su, H., Maji, S., Kalogerakis, E., & Learned-Miller, E. (2015). Multi-view convolutional neural networks for 3d shape recognition. In *Proceedings of the IEEE international conference on computer vision* (pp. 945-953). 10.1109/ICCV.2015.114

Tran, A. T., Hassner, T., Masi, I., Paz, E., Nirkin, Y., & Medioni, G. G. (2018, June). Extreme 3D Face Reconstruction: Seeing Through Occlusions. In CVPR (pp. 3935-3944). Academic Press.

Tuan Tran, A., Hassner, T., Masi, I., & Medioni, G. (2017). Regressing robust and discriminative 3D morphable models with a very deep neural network. In *Proceedings of the IEEE Conference on Computer Vision and Pattern Recognition* (pp. 5163-5172). 10.1109/CVPR.2017.163

Woodham, R. J. (1980). Photometric method for determining surface orientation from multiple images. *Optical Engineering (Redondo Beach, Calif.)*, *19*(1), 191139. doi:10.1117/12.7972479

Section 3
Advances in 3D Data Handling and Analysis

Chapter 11
Data Augmentation Using GANs for 3D Applications

Ioannis Maniadis

Information Technologies Institute, Centre for Research and Technology, Hellas, Greece

Vassilis Solachidis

Information Technologies Institute, Centre for Research and Technology, Hellas, Greece

Nicholas Vretos

(iD) https://orcid.org/0000-0003-3604-9685

Information Technologies Institute, Centre for Research and Technology, Hellas, Greece

Petros Daras

(iD) https://orcid.org/0000-0003-3814-6710

Information Technologies Institute, Centre for Research and Technology, Hellas, Greece

ABSTRACT

Modern deep learning techniques have proven that they have the capacity to be successful in a wide area of domains and tasks, including applications related to 3D and 2D images. However, their quality depends on the quality and quantity of the data with which models are trained. As the capacity of deep learning models increases, data availability becomes the most significant. To counter this issue, various techniques are utilized, including data augmentation, which refers to the practice of expanding the original dataset with artificially created samples. One approach that has been found is the generative adversarial networks (GANs), which, unlike other domain-agnostic transformation-based methods, can produce diverse samples that belong to a given data distribution. Taking advantage of this property, a multitude of GAN architectures has been leveraged for data augmentation applications. The subject of this chapter is to review and organize implementations of this approach on 3D and 2D imagery, examine the methods that were used, and survey the areas in which they were applied.

DOI: 10.4018/978-1-5225-5294-9.ch011

INTRODUCTION

The advances that have been made in the field of deep learning have provided us with ever more potent tools, which can be applied in an increasing number of tasks, computer vision being foremost among them. Concurrently, the potential value of data has become apparent, and so data gathering and mining are now employed in several domains in order to make it possible for deep learning techniques to be applied in those domains. Deep learning models require data for their training which constitute a representative sampling of a given task. When the available data only relate to a subset of cases, a model will only learn to address those cases only and fail in the task overall. For this reason, deep learning models generally require significant amounts of data for their training. Nonetheless, in many cases the available data is not sufficient for training models that generalise adequately. That may occur either because data gathering might be difficult in a given setting (due to scarcity of subject cases or due to difficulties in collecting them) or because the available data are not annotated. In all the above cases, other methods must be employed to make deep learning feasible.

Several techniques have been developed in order to tackle the above-mentioned problems, particularly when dealing with 2D and 3D image data. One point of focus is to develop architectural modifications that make models generalize better in a given task, such as dropout and weight regularization (Sutskever, Hinton, Krizhevsky, & Salakhutdinov, 2014). Another approach suggests expanding the initial dataset by manipulating the existing data and creating new synthetic samples. This approach is usually refered to as data augmentation. The most frequent implementations of data augmentation are the addition of random noise to the data and the application of geometric and/or other transformations (Taylor & Nitschke, 2019). The latter is particularly effective in image data, whose features have spatial properties. Those data augmentation methods however, while suitable for image data, are domain-agnostic, since they apply transformations without taking into account the nature, characteristics and features of the original data, and produce synthetic samples that could deviate from the original distribution.

In order to achieve these two objectives, that is to augment a dataset with meaningfully and significantly diverse samples, a method would be required that augments a dataset in ways specific to its properties, so that the generated samples would cover the largest area of the sample space possible, without deviating from it. GANs (Goodfellow et al., 2014), (Zoumpourlis, Doumanoglou, Vretos, & Daras, 2017), (Shijie, Ping, Peiyi, & Siping, 2017) as is demonstrated in (Shijie, Ping, Peiyi, & Siping, 2017), can be used to augment data in this exact way, and so they are an attractive alternative to the above domain agnostic methods. Ideally, GANs produce samples that belong to the original data distribution, while at the same time they differ from any given sample of that distribution. In this way they fulfill the essential objective of data augmentation, which is to provide to the model a diverse sample pool with which to train, which is representative of a given task. Additionally, the fundamental formulation of GANs has proven to be remarkably flexible, in that GANs can be modified to generate samples in many different ways, and can be combined with a variety of architectures to tackle different data augmentation tasks. However, GANs are also remarkably hard to train (Goodfellow I., 2016), and so have been the subject of intense study in an effort to develop mode efficient architectures (Arjovsky & Bottou, 2017), (Salimans et al., 2016). It is important to note at this point that unlike other GAN review papers, such as (Z. Wang, She, & Ward, 2019) and (Pan et al., 2019), this work does not provide a broad review of GAN models. Rather, it limits its purview to cases where GANs have been used in the context of 2D and 3D image data augmentation for the purpose of improved performance in classification, segmentation, object detection/identification and motion tracking tasks. This work studies these cases with regard to the GAN architecture that was used, the domain in which it was used, and the specific way it was leveraged to augment the available data.

Considering the volume of our findings and their diversity, the authors decided that the first step of our survey should be to provide the reader with a detailed description of the significant terms and symbols that will be used in this work (Section *Background*). Following that, the authors will outline the tasks for which GAN-based data augmentation was utilized, the types of GANs encountered, and the ways in which data augmentation could be done depending on the dataset and the problem in question (Section *Tasks & Augmentation Techniques*). Then, the studied specific GAN models are described with regard to their function and architecture (Section *GAN models*), Finally, the domains and applications in which GAN-based data augmentation was used are presented, organised according to their domain (Section Applications). Table 1 summarises our findings by providing an extensive listing of the works encountered, including their domain of application, the task in question, as well as the GAN and dataset(s) used. With regard to the distinction between 2D and 3D data, while applications that deal with 3D data are noted as such, it must be stressed that, as will be made apparent in section *GAN models* and subsection *3D Generative Adversarial Network (3D-GAN)* in particular, the transition from 2D to 3D data generation usually requires no significant architectural modifications and the working principles of each model are maintained.

BACKGROUND

Notation and Definitions

Labeled Sample

In the context of this work, it is considered that a sample is labeled when it is paired with the information we are interested in and that we expect a trained model to be able to infer, depending on the task in question. That might be the sample's class(es), a segmentation mask, the location of objects etc.

Conditioning Input

In the earliest GAN formulations, the input, based on which samples are generated, is a random vector. However, later models introduced conditionality. In those models, the input includes user defined information which aims to restrict generated samples to specific subspaces. This is referred to as conditioning input. For example, if a sample is generated with conditioning information that corresponds to a specific class c, we expect that sample to belong to that class. The term *conditioning input* will then refer to use-defined information fed to a GAN, which restricts a synthetic sample to a specific subset of the datasets' broader distribution.

True (Real) and Fake (Synthetic) Samples

True (or real) samples are those that belong to the original dataset in each given task. Fake (or synthetic) samples are those that were generated by a GAN or other augmentation approach.

Noise Vector z

Most GAN variants make use of a noise vector z as a latent input variable from which to draw to generate diverse samples. This vector is frequently drawn from a uniform distribution $N(0,1)$ and its length depends on the architecture in question. It is also referred to as noise prior, symbolised with $p(z)$.

Domain

A domain can be thought of as a specific subset of existing data. Each domain's properties may be defined by annotations (e.g. classes) or other less discernible properties determined by the samples themselves. Broadly speaking, a domain is defined by the common attributes of the group of samples it consists of. This definition becomes particularly relevant in domain transfer applications (see section *Domain Transfer (DT)*), where models are used to transform samples from one domain to another, without user defined knowledge of the properties of each domain.

Data Augmentation

Data augmentation been established as an effective method to improve a model's performance in various tasks with regard to generalization. The term data augmentation relates to a number of techniques used to expand a dataset with artificially created samples, so that a model trained with that dataset will generalize better. Data augmentation has been found to be particularly effective in image-related tasks, where label-preserving transformations such as rotation, flipping, noise, cropping etc. have been studied and applied to great success (Simard, Steinkraus, & Platt, 2003). These methods are used to artificially expand datasets to assist the model in learning more robust interpretations of the available data. Building on these augmentation approaches, more complex techniques have been proposed over time, such as Colour Jittering, Edge Enhancement and Fancy PCA (Taylor & Nitschke, 2019), which, except for the latter, are again mostly applicable to image-related tasks. Finally, there are also algorithms such as SMOTE (Chawla, Bowyer, Hall, & Kegelmeyer, 2002) and its variants (Bunkhumpornpat, Sinapiromsaran, & Lursinsap, 2012), which artificially expand a dataset by synthesizing new samples based on the original dataset's feature space. This technique has the advantage of being domain-agnostic, in that it can be used on non-image datasets. Finally, generative models such as GANs and Variational Autoencoders (VAEs) (Kingma & Welling, 2013) can also be used to create synthetic samples for data augmentation purposes. It is important to note that the above approaches are not necessarily mutually exclusive, and can be used in various combinations at a given task.

Generative Adversarial Networks

Generative Adversarial Networks (GANs) were first proposed in 2014 by (Goodfellow et al., 2014). They are a class of generative networks whose fundamental operating principle is that of a competition between two distinct models, the generator and the discriminator, that are trained jointly. The original GAN's architecture is demonstrated in Figure 1, and their training process is as follows. In each iteration, the generator produces a batch of synthetic (fake) samples. The discriminator is then fed these samples, along with true samples from the original dataset. The objective of the discriminator is to accurately distinguish true from fake samples, while the generator's objective is to generate fake samples that fool the discriminator. That is, samples that the discriminator falsely assigns *True* labels to. This function, which amounts to a minimax game between the two components, ideally results in a discriminator having learned to perfectly discern true from fake samples, and a generator that still manages to fool it, which would mean that it has learned to create perfectly realistic samples. At this point we consider the GAN to have converged. This process is illustrated in Algorithm 1 below. It should be noted that the above description corresponds to the GAN as described in (Goodfellow et al., 2014). Subsequent works have modified this approach is significant ways, however the principle of the adversarial game between the generator and the discriminator remains the central idea in which all GAN variants are rooted.

Figure 1. GAN Architecture: The discriminator receives true samples X and fake samples X', which, through its training, it learns to distinguish and assign appropriate True and Fake labels to. The generator is provided with a noise vector z, and is trained to generate sample X', such that the discriminator would label as True. Through their iterative training, as described in Algorithm 1, the generator learns to create samples X' that are realistic enough to be indistinguishable from true samples X by the discriminator.

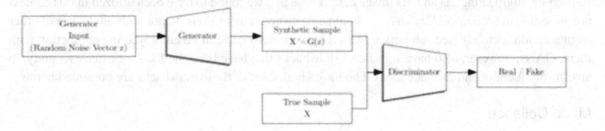

Algorithm 1

Minibatch stochastic gradient descent training of generative adversarial nets. The number of steps to apply to the discriminator, *k*, is a hyperparameter whose value is set to *k=1* based on experimentation.

for number of training iterations **do**

for k steps **do**

- Sample minibatch of *m* noise samples $\{z^{(1)},..., z^{(m)}\}$ from noise prior $p_g(z)$.
- Sample minibatch of *m* examples $\{x^{(1)},..., x^{(m)}\}$ from data generating distribution $p_{data}(x)$.
- Update the discriminator by ascending its stochastic gradient:

$$\nabla_{\theta_g} \frac{1}{m} \sum_{i=1}^{m} [\log D(x^{(i)}) + \log(1 - D(G(z^{(i)})))]$$

end for

- Sample minibatch of *m* noise samples $\{z^{(1)},..., z^{(m)}\}$ from noise prior $p_g(z)$.
- Update the discriminator by ascending its stochastic gradient:

$$\nabla_{\theta_g} \frac{1}{m} \sum_{i=1}^{m} \log(1 - D(z^{(i)}))$$

end for

This algorithm amounts to a minimax game of:

$$\min_G \max_D V(D,G) = \mathbb{E}_{x \sim p_{data(x)}}[\log D(x)] + \mathbb{E}_{z \sim p_{data(z)}}[\log(1 - D(G(z)))] \qquad (1)$$

GANs present a simple yet powerful concept which, particularly after it was expanded on in ways that are examined in section *GAN models*, can be leveraged to create high quality, realistic and diverse data. Specifically from a data augmentation perspective, GANs can be used to generate synthetic samples that share the specific properties of the original dataset, while at the same time being more diverse. Also, while GANs have been used to generate various types of data, including text and sound, most GAN models focus on image data generation, which means that there is a wide array of approaches that can be used for augmenting 2D and 3D image data. Those that we found to have been utilized in this context are presented in section *GAN models*. It should also be noted that GANs do not prohibit the use of other augmentation methods (see subsection *Data Augmentation*) and can be employed in conjunction with them. GANs, however, also have significant drawbacks that have been the focus of extensive study, in an effort to identify and mitigate them. The most significant of those drawbacks are presented below.

Mode Collapse

A frequent problem in GAN training, mode collapse refers to the cases where the generator only produces a very small number of distinct samples. Those samples might fulfill the objectives defined by the GANs architecture, that is to be realistic enough to fool the discriminator, which means that the GAN shows signs of convergence. However, the fact that the synthetic samples are not diverse means that the model overall has failed. Mode collapse is then an issue that relates with the quantity of diverse samples that the GAN synthesizes.

Overfitting

Overfitting occurs when the discriminator learns to only assign true labels to samples that are almost identical to those in the original dataset. This, in turn, forces the generator to produce samples that are, in fact, near exact copies of the original dataset. Although overfitting is a problem that seems similar to mode collapse, it is not, in fact these drawbacks are mutually exclusive. Their difference is that given N real samples, in the case of mode collapse the GAN produces $M << N$ distinct samples, each of which may or may not be identical to some sample in N. When a GAN overfits, it produces as many as $M \approx N$ distinct samples, where for each synthetic sample $m \in M$, there exists an almost identical sample $n \in N$. In that sense, overfitting relates to the diversity of synthetic samples compared to the original dataset.

Non-Convergence

The adversarial nature of a GAN's training process means that both the generator and discriminator have no fixed objective. Rather, they receive feedback from each other. It is then possible they reach a point where neither provides the other with useful information and both diverge from the point of convergence. This development is referred to as non-convergence, a point at which both discriminator and generator no longer provide each other with beneficial feedback and the synthetic samples deteriorate. It is common for GANs to deteriorate in this way if they keep being trained after having converged.

Diminished and Exploding Gradients

The nature of GANs means that the generator and discriminator depend on each other for guidance. However, it is possible possible for either one to significantly outpace the other (Arjovsky & Bottou, 2017). In this case, the component that has fallen behind may not be able to perceive a viable path through which to progress. A generator might produce samples more realistic than the discriminator can identify, which usually leads to its gradients increasing rapidly and it being unable to make meaningful updates. Conversely, the discriminator might discern true from synthetic samples so well that the generator is unable to identify ways to fool it, which leads to its gradients converging to zero and it not being trained at all. In both cases, training fails.

Sensitivity to Hyper-Parameters and Computational Load

In addition to the above issues, GANs are particularly difficult to be designed with regard to their hyperparameters. Due to their unsupervised training, significant experimentation is required to identify the optimal design for a given task. Also, given the minimax nature of GANs' function, even when a successful tuning has been identified, a small change in hyperparameters might disturb the balance at some stage of the training process, and lead to any of the problems outlined above. This is an ongoing challenge, though significant progress is being made, such as in the case of (Gong, Chang, Jiang, & Wang, 2019), which applied Neural Architecture Search (NAS) (Elsken, Metzen, & Hutter, 2019) in the context of GANs.

Lack of Evaluation Metrics

Evaluating the output of a GAN is a major problem in evaluating their quality. The discriminator only provides a relative evaluation of how realistic a sample is. It is then a statement related to the state of the generator at each time, rather than relevant to the actual quality of the synthetic samples. The diversity of synthetic samples is also hard to bequantified. Considerable work has been done in this area (Lucic, Kurach, Michalski, Gelly, & Bousquet, 2017), (Shmelkov, Schmid, & Alahari, 2018) and several metrics have been proposed, most prominently the Inception Score (IS) (Heusel, Ramsauer, Unterthiner, Nessler, & Hochreiter, 2017), the Frechet Inception Distance (FID) (Salimans et al., 2016) and the Classification Accuracy Score (CAS) (Ravuri & Vinyals, 2019). Regardless, evaluating GANs remains a significant open problem. In the specific context of data augmentation however, the criterion that is used is simply how much the performance is improved in a given task when a given data augmentation method is applied, compared with using only the original data or other augmentation techniques.

Various proposals have been made proposed to address the above-mentioned issues and some of them are presented on Section *GAN models*, along with the respective models. It should be noted that, while some approaches have been proven to be more effective than others, there has yet to emerge a clear consensus regarding optimal GAN training parameters, and finding such a consensus remains the subject of a number of works (Arjovsky & Bottou, 2017), (Lucic et al., 2017), (Salimans et al., 2016), (Kurach, Lucic, Zhai, Michalski, & Gelly, 2018), (Odena et al., 2018).

TASKS AND AUGMENTATION TECHNIQUES

In this section definitions will be provided with regard to the tasks in which data augmentation was found to have been applied and the approaches that were used. Given the quantity and diversity of the works examined in this survey, this section is important in understanding *GAN models*, as well as Table 1, where these works are enumerated for the reader to examine collectively.

Tasks

Classification (CL)

The model is trained to assign the correct class label(s) to the samples it examines. While there are many ways to augment a dataset in the context of a classification task (see *Samples Generation Method* subsection), the most frequent way is to use GANs that generate labeled synthetic samples through some conditional input.

Object Detection (OD)

The model is expected to locate user-specified objects in an image. To do this, the model is most often expected to define a space with a bounding box, in which space the object has been found to exist. This task may or may not include an object recognition aspect, wherein objects are not only located, but also classified.

Segmentation (SG)

The model is expected to detect the exact shape of an object in a given image. This can be seen as an expansion of object detection, where not only the position but also the shape of an object are requested. In most cases, this amounts to creating a segmentation mask, by assigning a label to each pixel in an image, where pixels that belong to the same object have the same label. Data augmentation in this case is done by generating samples paired with their corresponding desired segmentation masks.

Object Tracking (OT)

An extension of object detection, the task of object tracking requires for the model in question to not only be able to locate an object in a given image, but also to track that object's movements in the various frames that make up a video sequence (Doumanoglou, Vretos, & Daras, 2019).

Person Re-Identification (PID)

Given an image of a specific person and a set of other images, the model is expected to identify that person in those images (if indeed they appear in them). It differs from classification in that models that do classification learn to assign a finite number of identities to the samples they examine. Rather than assign identities, PID models learn to use people's images to detect if those people appear in other samples.

Samples Generation Method

A significant distinguishing factor among GAN variants relates to their inputs and, more specifically, if and how those inputs apply restrictions to the generated samples. Three broad categories are presented: a) GANs generating samples unconditionally, b) GANs generating samples conditionally via some conditioning input and c) and Domain Transfer GANs, which do not generate entirely new synthetic samples, but rather a transition of an input sample to another domain. Finally, considering the increasing importance of 3D applications, as well as the fact that the handling of 3D imagery differs in some cases to that of 2D, cases where 3D imaging is either the input or output of the examined GAN will be noted with (*3D*).

Unconditional Samples Generation (USG)

Unconditional Samples Generation refers to the approach by which samples are generated independent to any label or other condition, only under the constraint that they belong to the sample space which is defined by the dataset used to train the GAN. GANs adhering to this approach generally use a noise vector as input. It should be noted that "Unconditional" does not require synthetic samples to be unlabeled. It only means that the user cannot influence the kind of sample (e.g. with regard to its class) the GAN will generate. While this approach seems impractical in the context of data augmentation, several methods were found to have been used to apply it. 1) A separate unconditional model is trained to generate samples for each label (USGa). While this approach could be effective in producing labeled samples, it becomes computationally impractical as the number of distinct labels increase. 2) Samples are generated unconditionally, drawing from the entire dataset in question, and are labeled by a model trained on that original dataset. The model is then re-trained or fine-tuned with some combination of original and synthetic data (USGb). 3) The labels are themselves included in the samples (USGc). This method is, for example, applicable when each sample is an N dimensional vector, in which case m class labels can be included via concatenation. It can also be applied in segmentation tasks, where the segmentation mask may be generated along with the original image via depth-wise concatenation. In adding the labels to the samples, the assumption can be made that a realistic synthetic sample is one whose content and label are a) realistic and b) match each other. 4) For a dataset with *n* classes, all generated samples are assigned class memberships of *1/n* for each class and are then used along the original dataset (USGd). This methods is limited to classification tasks.

Conditional Samples Generation (CSG)

Per this approach, in order to produce synthetic samples the GAN receives (alongside other possible inputs, most often a noise vector) some conditioning input, which restricts the sample space to which the synthetic sample is expected to belong. Depending on the task in question, the conditioning input might be related to a particular class, the location and/or ID of an object, information regarding segmentation etc. This method is also the simplest one conceptually in the context of data augmentation, in that it produces labeled synthetic samples. It should be noted that, while the conditioning input is usually expressed as a vector, it can also be represented in other ways. An example is DAGAN where the generator receives a sample image as input, and is expected to generate a sample of the same class as that image. In this case, we consider the conditioning input to be the image itself, as a representation of its class.

Domain Transfer (DT)

Also referred to as image translation when applied to images, this approach to generate samples is distinct in that the generator's inputs include the same kind of data as those that it is expected to produce (e.g. *Image → Image*). Its function is to receive input sample X that belongs to a domain A, and generate sample Y that belongs to a different domain B. An example would be to have generic images of *angry faces* (domain A), and expect them to be changed to *happy faces* (domain B). Some GANs in this category also enforce that transferred samples Y differ from their origin samples X *only* in the properties required to make the transition $A → B$. In the prior example, that would mean that for each *angry face*, we expect its transition to *happy face* not to alter that face's distinguishing features and for the person to remain identifiable. We will refer to this property as *identity-preservation*. Regarding cases where the GAN in question allows for Domain Transfer to any one of multiple domains, which are chosen in accordance with some conditioning input, we will refer to their function as Conditional Domain Transfer (DTc).

A significant subcategory of domain transfer applications relates to transitioning visual data from 2D to 3D or the inverse. These applications (Alexiadis et al., 2016) are rapidly becoming more relevant in terms of their academic and industrial impact, due to the increasing number of 3D applications being developed and deployed, which increases the availability of 3D datasets, as well as the requirement for additional annotated data. We will refer to this function as Domain Transfer 2D to 3D (DT2t3) when the GAN in question transitions samples from 2D to 3D, Domain Transfer 3D to 2D (DT3t2) when the transition is from 3D to 2D, and Domain Transfer 2D and 3D (DT2a3) when the transition can happen in either direction.

Augmentation Approach

A final distinction that should be made in this section relates to the specific ways in which a dataset may be augmented. Augmentation is not necessarily done in a uniform way. Depending on the dataset, a model may benefit from augmenting only specific sample subsets, or by augmenting various subsets to uneven degrees. As such, two distinct approaches can be discerned.

Uniform Data Augmentation (UA)

In this approach, samples are generated uniformly, without distinctions being made among existing subsets (i.e. labels). An open question within the context of this approach regards to the ratio of real to synthetic samples. A fixed figure does not exist and is determined in a case-to-case basis via experimentation, with values ranging from *0.2* to *10* synthetic samples for each real one. This is the most frequent approach and, as such, in *Applications* section it will be assumed to be the one implemented, unless stated otherwise.

Dataset Balancing (DB)

In cases where, in a dataset, some labels have considerably fewer samples than others, this imbalance may significantly degrade a model's performance in a given task. In those cases, data augmentation can be used to generate samples that belong to those specific labels' distributions, in order to mitigate this imbalance, a practice with is referred to as dataset balancing. GANs have been used in this way, and can perform this function via all three sample generation methods described later in *Samples Generation Method* subsection. In terms of the quantity of synthetic data, the most frequent approach is to generate enough so that the minority class(es) have approximately the same number of samples as the other(s).

GAN MODELS

In this section various GAN architectures are examined. Those architectures have been selected either because they have been applied in Data Augmentation tasks with 3D or 2D imagery, and so are of direct interest to this paper, or because their presentation is considered to be fundamental in understanding subsequent GAN models. It should be understood that each model will not be discussed in depth and small variations of each that might have been applied will be presented, but will not be separately analyzed. The objective of this section is to provide sufficient technical information for each GAN model for the reader to be able to understand their functions and how they were used in each application. Subsequently, not all GANs that are presented in this work will be analyzed in equal length. We will expand only on the models that we consider to be the most significant in terms of their impact on the field, their novelty, or the frequency with which they were found to have been used. Also, in order to maintain cohesion, GANs will be organised in accordance with the way they generate samples, a distinction made in *Samples Generation Method* subsection. While this distinction is not absolute and in the case of some GANs it is unclear whether their function is closer to CSG or DT (e.g. the TAGAN and GANs used for content infilling), we believe it is a strong taxonomy criterion for the purposes of this survey.

Unconditional GANs

For the original GAN, proposed in (Goodfellow et al., 2014), see *Generative Adversarial Networks* in the *Background* section.

Deep Convolutional GAN (DCGAN)

At the time they were first formulated, GANs had significant difficulties in incorporating deep convolutional architectures. This issue was tackled by the Deep Convolutional GAN (DCGAN), proposed in (Radford, Metz, & Chintala, 2015). The authors studied the use of CNNs in GANs, proposed guidelines for stable training, and suggested an architecture template. The DCGAN was notable for using no fully connected layers in its generator (seen in Figure 2), instead relying entirely on convolutions. The guidelines that were suggested in this work are as follows:

- Rather than pooling layers, use strided convolutions in the discriminator and fractional-strided convolutions in the generator.

- Use Batch Normalization in both the generator and the discriminator.
- Use no fully connected hidden layers for deeper architectures.
- Use ReLU activation in the generator for all layers except for the output, which uses Tanh.
- Use LeakyReLU activation in the discriminator for all layers.

Figure 2. DCGAN generator used for LSUN scene modeling. The discriminator's architecture follows the same architectural principles as a standard deep convolutional classifier, subject to the guidelines outlined for DCGANs
Figure from (Radford, Metz, & Chintala, 2015)

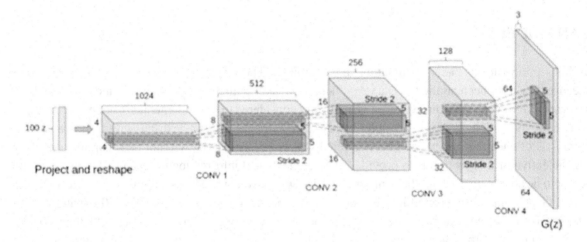

3D Generative Adversarial Network (3D-GAN)

Based on the DCGAN, (J. Wu, Zhang, Xue, Freeman, & Tenenbaum, 2016) proposed 3D-GAN, the first instance of a GAN being used to create synthetic 3D images. Its architecture is similar to the DCGAN, the most significant alteration being that 3D-GAN used volumetric convolutional layers to produce 3D samples (Figure 3). Its impact is significant in that it proved that GANs can also be applied in the field of 3D imagery. A conditional variant called 3D-CGAN was later suggested by (Jin, Xu, Tang, Harrison, & Mollura, 2018), which, rather than creating samples by drawing from a random vector, uses as its input a distorted real sample. In the context of the original work, the 3D-CGAN is used for content infilling, where the distortion takes the form of cropping specific areas of the original samples.

Figure 3. 3D-GAN generator. The discriminator mostly mirrors that architecture
Figure from (J. Wu, Zhang, Xue, Freeman, & Tenenbaum, 2016)

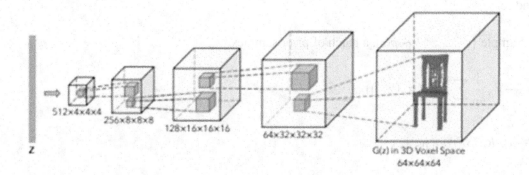

Wasserstein GAN (WGAN) and WGAN-Gradient Penalty (WGAN-GP)

In (Arjovsky, Chintala, & Bottou, 2017), the authors observed that, up until that point, the objective functions used by GANs were limited to variations of the Jensen Shannon and Kullback-Leibler divergences. However, the paper proves that the Earth Mover (EM) distance provides superior convergence properties, and is thus more sensible to use for GANs. To enforce the K-Lipschitz discriminator requirement of the EM distance, the paper proposes that 1-Lipschitz continuity be enforced via weight clipping. Thus, the paper concludes to a novel GAN formulation, the Wasserstein-GAN (WGAN), which is trained per Algorithm 2, and displayed far superior results with regard to its stability and the quality and diversity of its generated samples compared to other contemporary models.

Algorithm 2

WGAN algorithm. Suggested default values by (Arjovsky & Bottou, 2017) are $\alpha = 0.00005$, $c = 0.01$, $m = 64$, ncritic = 5

Require: α, the learning rate. c, the clipping parameter. m, the batch size. n_{critic}, the number of iterations of the critic per generator iteration. w_0, initial critic parameters. θ_0, initial generator's parameters.

while θ has not converged **do**

for $t = 0,...,n_{critic}$ **do**

- Sample $\{x^{(1)},...,x^{(m)}\} \sim Pr$, a batch from the real data.
- Sample $\{z^{(1)},...,z^{(m)}\} \sim p(z)$, a batch of prior samples.

$$g_w \leftarrow \nabla_w \left[\frac{1}{m} \sum_{i=1}^{m} f_w \left(x^{(i)} - \frac{1}{m} \sum_{i=1}^{m} f_w (g_\vartheta(z^{(i)})) \right) \right]$$

$$w \leftarrow w + a \cdot RMSProp(w, g_w)$$

$$w \leftarrow clip(w, -c, c)$$

end for

- Sample $\{z^{(1)}, ..., z^{(m)}\} \sim p(z)$, a batch of prior samples.

$$g_w \leftarrow -\nabla_\theta \frac{1}{m} \sum_{i=1}^{m} f_w(g_\vartheta(z^{(i)}))$$

$$\theta \leftarrow -a \cdot RMSProp(w, g_\theta)$$

end while

Algorithm 3

WGAN with gradient penalty (WGAN-GP). Suggested default values by (Gulrajani, Ahmed, Arjovsky, Dumoulin, & Courville, 2017) are $\lambda = 10$, $\alpha = 0.0001$, $\beta1 = 0$, $\beta2 = 0.9$, ncritic = 5

Require: The gradient penalty coefficient λ. The number of critic iterations per generator iteration n_{critic}. The batch size m. Adam hyperparameters $\alpha, \beta_1, \beta_2.\alpha$. Initial critic parameters w_0. Initial generator's parameters θ_0.

while θ has not converged **do**
for $t = 1, ..., n_{critic}$ **do**
for $i = 1, ..., m$ **do**

- Sample real data $x \sim \mathbb{P}_r$, latent variable $z \sim p(z)$, a random number $\varepsilon \sim U[0,1]$

$$\tilde{x} \leftarrow G_\theta(z)$$

$$\tilde{x} \leftarrow \varepsilon x + (1 - \varepsilon)\tilde{x}$$

$$L^{(i)} \leftarrow D_w(\tilde{x}) - D_w(x) + \lambda(\| \nabla_{\hat{x}} D_w(\hat{x}) \|_2 - 1)^2$$

end for

$$w \leftarrow Adam(\nabla_w \frac{1}{m} \sum_{i=1}^{m} L^{(i)}, w, a, \beta_1, \beta_2)$$

end for

- Sample a batch of latent variables $\{z^{(1)}, ..., z^{(m)}\} \sim p(z)$.

$$w \leftarrow Adam(\nabla_w \frac{1}{m} \sum_{i=1}^{m} -D_w(G_\vartheta(z)), \theta, a, \beta_1, \beta_2)$$

end while

The weight clipping approach is problematic in the blunt way in which it manipulates the model's weights, which (Arjovsky & Bottou, 2017) acknowledges. (Gulrajani et al., 2017) sought to solve this issue and proposed a modification of the WGAN which used Gradient Penalty (WGAN-GP). In their work, they proposed imposing the Lipschitz constraint through an additional objective in the GAN's discriminator loss function, as can be seen in the WGAN-GP's training Algorithm 3 above. This modification was proven to fulfil the Lipschitz constraint requirement, as well as to provide significantly improved performance compared to the original WGAN.

It should be noted that the WGAN and WGAN-GP essentially propose methodologies that enforce constraints which improve GAN training, more so than they constitute distinct GAN models in themselves. As such, these approaches can be combined with other conditional and unconditional GAN architectures, which will in fact be the case for many of the applications that will be examined in Section *Applications*. Until spectral normalization was proposed by (Miyato, Kataoka, Koyama, & Yoshida, 2018), the WGAN-GP's formulation served as the basis for most subsequent GAN variants.

Other Unconditional GANs

Laplacian GAN (LAPGAN). As mentioned earlier, training GANs with deep CNNs was particularly difficult before the DCGAN proposed a concrete methodology for doing so. Prior to that, LAPGAN (Denton, Chintala, Szlam, & Fergus, 2015) proposed overcoming that difficulty by leveraging the methodology of the Laplacian Pyramid (Burt & Adelson, 1983) to combine multiple shallow, and thus easier to train, CNNs in a single GAN architecture. Per this approach, LAPGAN consists of a cascade of small GANs using CNNs. A smaller sized sample is generated by the first GAN and is progressively enlarged as it passes through the pyramid until it reaches the desired level. Each GAN contributes via the application of a mask to the sample, so that images of higher resolution and quality are produced progressively.

Progressive Growing GGAN (PGGAN). The Progressively Growing GAN (Karras, Aila, Laine, & Lehtinen, 2017) expands on previous works that attempted to use GANs in a cascade structure. However, rather than training multiple GANs, PGGAN consists of a single generator-discriminator pair. Both models are initially shallow. As training progresses, however, more layers gradually are added to both, so that they *are both mirror images of each other and grow in synchrony*. This continues until the generated samples has the desirable properties in terms of dimensions, diversity and realism. A conditional variant of the PGGAN is proposed in (Han, Murao, et al., 2019).

Consistency Term GAN (CT-GAN) Proposed in (Wei, Gong, Liu, Lu, & Wang, 2018), it builds on the WGAN-GP by modifying its loss function. Specifically, it introduces a component named consistency regularization which, introduced to the GP loss, is claimed by the authors to enforce Lipschitz continuity in a way that improves the model's performance, particularly with regard to avoiding overfitting.

WaveGAN Introduced in (Donahue, McAuley, & Puckette, 2018), WaveGAN is the result of an effort to make advances with regard to using GANs for the generation of sound. The authors did so by building on DCGAN and WGAN-GP to propose an architecture more appropriate to this task, by modifying the components proposed by the DCGAN, using WGAN-GP's training objectives, and suggesting that the discriminator use the proposed *Phase Shuffle* method for evaluating samples.

Conditional GANs

Conditional GAN (cGAN)

Following the publication of the first GAN, (Mirza & Osindero, 2014) proposed the Conditional GAN, which could produce samples dependent on user defined information, as seen in Figure 4. The cGAN approach modifies the original minimax game from equation 1 to:

$$min_G max_D V(D,G) = Ex_{\sim pdata}(_x)[logD(x|y)] + Ez_{\sim pdata}(_z)[log(1 - D((G(z|y)))] \qquad (2)$$

Per the cGAN formulation, synthetic samples are not generated randomly, rather they are generated based on conditioning input vector y. Realistic samples are then required be the discriminator to be such that they belong to the specific distribution defined by the conditioning input y.

Auxiliary Classifier GAN (AC-GAN)

Seeking to improve on the cGAN in the task of generating synthetic samples using a conditional input, (Odena, Olah, & Shlens, 2016) introduced the Auxiliary Classifier GAN. Similar to the cGAN, this model suggests that the generator use a random noise vector z and a conditioning input vector y in order to produce synthetic samples $X_{fake}=G(y,z)$. Where the AC-GAN deviates from the cGAN is that, given a sample X, the AC-GAN's discriminator produces both an assessment $S=\{True,False\}$ regarding how realistic X is, and an estimate C, representing the sample's class. The two outputs $D(X) = P(S|X), P(C|X)$ of the discriminator are used to estimate the log-likelihood of the correct source L_S and that of the correct class L_C, as displayed below in the equations below:

$$L_S = E[logP(S = real|X_{real}] + E[logP(S = fake|X_{fake}] \qquad (3)$$

$$L_C = E[logP(C = y|X_{real}] + E[logP(C = y|X_{fake}] \qquad (4)$$

Working with these equations, the discriminator D is trained to maximise L_C+L_S, and the generator G is trained to maximize L_C-L_S. In that way, the discriminator's objective is changed to assign a *True* or *Fake* label to each sample, but also to assign a correct class label. Concurrently, the generator's objective is now to not only produce realistic synthetic samples, but also to provide samples appropriate to its conditioning input y. This modification, combined with deeper convolutional architectures such as those suggested in (Radford et al., 2015), yielded significantly improved results compared to previous approaches.

Figure 4. cGAN Architecture: The generator is provided with a noise vector z, drawn from a uniform distribution, and a vector y, which includes the information to which samples must be conditioned, which it uses to generate sample x. x is then passed on to the discriminator, along with information y, which determines whether x is real or synthetic.
Figure from (Mirza & Osindero, 2014)

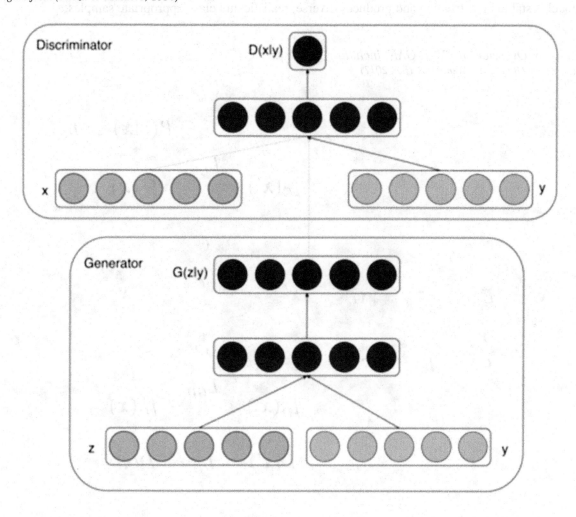

Conditional Variational Auto-Encoder GAN (CVAE-GAN)

CVAE-GAN (Bao, Chen, Wen, Li, & Hua, 2017) is an architecture that draws from both Conditional GANs and autoencoders. Specifically, it combines a GAN and a Variational Autoencoder (VAE) into a single architecture, as seen in Figure 5. The model consists of an encoder (E), a generator (G), a discriminator (D), and a classifier (C), which are trained jointly (contrary to most GAN architectures where the discriminator and generator are trained separately). Following the notation of Figure 5, the encoder is given data sample x and it's corresponding class c. It then maps x to an encoding z, through a learned distribution $P(z|x,c)$, which is then used by G, along with c, to generate a synthetic sample x'. Subsequently, G and D functions as they would in a GAN. D learns to identify synthetic samples and

G tries to create samples that can fool D. Finally, the Classifier C tries to accurately assess the class c that samples x and x' correspond to.

Other than its architecture, the model is notable in that it is trained with a combination of six loss functions. They each apply to specific components of the model and combined aim to ensure that the model is stable in its training and produces diverse, realistic and class-appropriate samples.

Figure 5. Overview of CVAE-GAN, including its losses
Figure from (Bao, Chen, Wen, Li, & Hua, 2017)

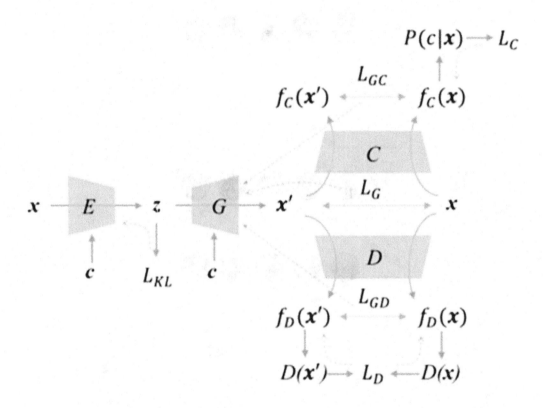

Data Augmentation GAN (DAGAN)

Data Augmentation GAN (DAGAN) was proposed by (Antoniou, Storkey, & Edwards, 2017) as a GAN aimed specifically towards Data Augmentation, and was tested on Few-Shot and One-Shot Learning classification tasks. It's architecture and function can be seen in Figure 6. It is an example of a GAN where the generator's conditional input is not a vector, but rather a sample. DAGAN receives samples as inputs and generates synthetic samples that match each input sample's class, through the process described in Figure 6. The fact that the DAGAN uses a real sample as input to produce class preserving synthetic samples, means that it can also augment classes it has not been trained on, and thus can tackle one-shot learning problems as well.

Figure 6. Overview of DAGAN. For each class c for which a synthetic sample is to be generated, a pair of random samples $(x_i, x_j) \in c$ are chosen. The generator then produces a synthetic sample $x_g = G(x_i, z)$, where z is a random noise vector. The samples are evaluated as real or fake by the discriminator, which receives either Fake pair (x_i, x_g) or Real pair (x_i, x_j). In this way the DAGAN's architecture promotes the generation of realistic, conditional samples that avoid mode collapse, all while using only the standard adversarial loss (the paper uses the WGAN-GP loss proposed by (Gulrajani et al., 2017)
Figure from (Antoniou, Storkey, & Edwards, 2017)

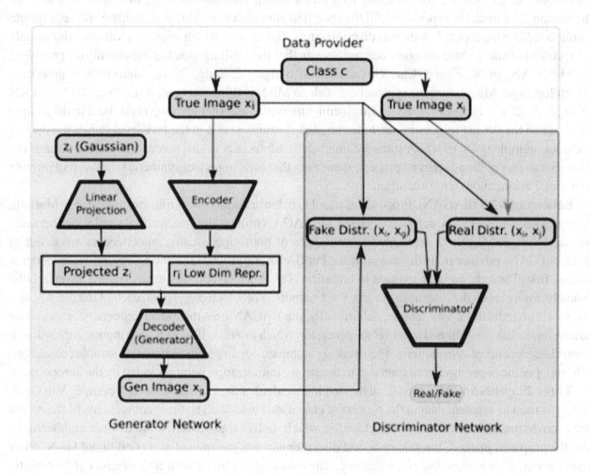

Other Conditional GANs

Deep Adversarial Data Augmentation (DADA). Expanding approaches proposed in (Salimans et al., 2016) and (Odena et al., 2016), (X. Zhang, Wang, Liu, & Ling, 2018) proposed a novel GAN based data augmentation framework. DADA recommends that the GAN's discriminator not assign $k + 1$ probabilities to each sample (where k probabilities correspond to each of k classes and the $(k + 1)$th probability corresponds to a *True/Fake* label). Rather, it was proposed that the model and its loss function be modified so that the discriminator would assign $2k$ probabilities, where to each class c_k corresponds 2 possible outcomes c_{kTrue} and c_{kFake}.

Multiple Distribution GAN (MD-GAN). Proposed by (Yirui Wu, Yue, Tan, Wang, & Lu, 2018), the MD-GAN enforces conditionality by drawing its input from multiple distinct distributions per label via a Gaussian Mixture Model, rather than a noise vector z drawn drom a single distribution. This modification, the paper claims, also results to more diverse samples.

3D Multi-Conditional GAN (3D MCGAN). The 3D MCGAN (Han, Kitamura, et al., 2019) is proposed for 3D conditional infilling. It's generator receives 3D images, areas of which are replaced with noise, and which are concatenated with conditioning information along the input samples' 4th dimension. The model is expected to fill the specified area with content that is realistic and appropriate to the conditioning input. It uses two discriminators, the first of which evaluates whether the sample as a whole is realistic, and the other determines whether the infilling matches the conditions provided.

MetaGAN. In (R. Zhang, Che, Grahahramani, Bengio, & Song, 2018), MetaGAN is proposed, which leverages Meta-Learning approaches, such as MAML (Finn, Abbeel, & Levine, 2017) and RN (Sung et al., 2017), to tackle supervised and semi-supervised few-shot learning tasks, both in the sample level (when the dataset in question includes unlabeled samples) and in the task level (when the dataset includes multiple tasks, of which some are unlabeled). MetaGAN is also noteworthy in that it trains the classifier as part of the adversarial process, theorizing that even imperfect synthetic samples will provide beneficial information to the classifier.

Balancing GAN (BAGAN). Proposed as a tool to balance datasets with minority classes by (Mariani, Scheidegger, Istrate, Bekas, & Malossi, 2018), the BAGAN utilizes the architectural similarities between autoencoders and GANs to leverage the advantages of both. Specifically, autoencoders are easier to train, but GANs produce more diverse samples. Per BAGAN's proposed methodology, an autoencoder is trained first. Then, the weights are used to initialize a GAN, which is subsequently trained adversarially. Notably, for n classes the discriminator has $n + 1$ outputs, n of which correspond each of the classes, and the $(n + 1)th$ indicates a *fake* sample. Additionally, the BAGAN uses the trained autoencoder's encoder to develop a class-conditioned input vector generator, which provides the GAN with input samples drawn from class-dependent distributions. The resulting architecture can generate synthetic samples conditionally and, per the paper, is easy to train due to the strong initialization point provided by the autoencoder.

Three-Player GAN. This model, suggested in (Vandenhende, De Brabandere, Neven, & Van Gool, 2019), is used to augment data in the context of classification tasks. The three components of the model are a generator, a discriminator and a classifier which, unlike the AC-GAN, are distinct architectures. Per the proposed method, the generator and discriminator are pre-trained as a conditional GAN. After that, the classifier is included in the training. The classifier is trained with both original and synthetic samples, while the generator is concurrently trained to produce samples that are harder for the classifier to classify. It is important to note that in each step both models are trained.

Conditional Infilling GAN (ciGAN). CiGAN (Yirui Wu et al., 2018) tackles the task of conditional image infilling. That is, to fill specific areas of a given image with content that is a) realistic and b) appropriate to conditions that ciGAN received as input. To achieve this, ciGAN's inputs consist of a sample from the original dataset, with the content of the area to be filled replaced by random noise, a class-related conditioning input, and a mask which identifies the area to be filled. This input information is fed to various stages of the generator as the sample is gradually upscaled to match the desired dimensions. CiGAN also uses a slightly modified loss function compared to regular GANs, more suitable to the task in question.

Adversarial in-painting based framework (AIPBF). This model, suggested in (Jie Yang et al., 2018), was unnamed by the writers of the paper. Used for conditional infilling of 3D images, it's inputs are a class label and a 3D image with a mask which determines the area to be filled. The model has two generators that function sequentially in a coarse-to-fine scheme and two discriminators that both promote realistic and class adhering sample generation, though one of the two enforces those qualities locally and the other globally.

Domain Transfer GANs

pix2pix

The pix2pix architecture was first presented in (Isola, Zhu, Zhou, & Efros, 2017) and was one of the first GAN models to tackle the image-to-image translation task. Its objective is to establish a way for images to transition from one domain to another (e.g. grayscale to colored, Google Maps to aerial photo etc.).

For the pix2pix framework to function, pairs of the same sample in both examined domains are needed. The generator G receives a sample x from source domain X and generates sample $ŷ = G(x)$, which we expect to be a realistic interpretation of x in target domain Y. The discriminator D then attempts to distinguish *true* pairs (x,y) from *fake* pairs $(x, ŷ)$ of samples using the loss function in equation 5 below. To improve the quality of generated images, another component is added to the model's objective, which tasks the generator with producing samples $ŷ$ that not only succeed in fooling the discriminator, but that are close to the ground truth image y in terms of their L_1 distance (equation 6). These two components combine to form the model's final objective, as seen in equation 7, where in the paper $\lambda = 100$. It is also notable that pix2pix uses a Markovian discriminator (C. Li & Wand, 2016) and U-NET generator (Ronneberger, Fischer, & Brox, 2015).

$$LcGAN(G,D) = Ex,y \sim pdata(x,y)[logD(x,y] + Ex \sim pdata(x),z \sim pz(z)[log(1 - D(x,G(x,z)))] \tag{5}$$

$$L_1(G) = E_{x,y \sim p_{data}}(x,y),z \sim p_z(z)[k \, y - G(x,z) \, k_1] \tag{6}$$

$$G^* = arg \, min_G \, max_D \, L_{cGAN}(G,D) + \lambda L_{L1}(G) \tag{7}$$

Cycle-GAN

Pix2pix is limited by the fact that it requires pairs of the same content in both the source and target domains. Expanding on pix2pix, Cycle-GAN (J. Y. Zhu, Park, Isola, & Efros, 2017) suggested an approach that allows for domain transition without using paired samples. Furthermore, it allows for transition from each domain to the other, rather than from the source to the target domain only.

Given two domains X and Y, with samples x and y respectively, the model consists of two mapping functions (generators) $G: X \to Y$ and $F: Y \to X$, and their corresponding discriminators D_y and D_x, which encourage G and F to generate samples indistinguishable from those in domains Y and X respectively. Each pair (G,D_y) and (F,D_x) have their own adversarial loss objective, per equation below.

$$L_{GAN}(G,D_Y, X,Y) = E_y \sim_{pdata}(_y)[logD_Y(y)] + E_x \sim_{pdata}(_x)[log(1 - D_Y(G(x))] \tag{8}$$

The paper also introduces the Cycle Consistency Loss, an objective that tasks the generators with not only producing samples that belong in their respective target domain, but that also correspond to their input sample from the source domain. This is achieved by forcing them to satisfy *backward cycle consistency:* $y \rightarrow F(y) \rightarrow G(F(y)) \approx y$ and $x \rightarrow G(x) \rightarrow F(G(x)) \approx x$. The loss function for this objective can be seen in equation 9.

$$L_{cyc}(G,F) = E_x \sim_{pdata}(_x)[\mathrm{k}\ F(G(x)) - x\ \mathrm{k}_1] + E_y \sim_{pdata}(_y)[\mathrm{k}\ G(F(y)) - y\ \mathrm{k}_1] \qquad (9)$$

The above combine for the Cycle-GAN's full objective function (in experiments $\lambda = 10$) and its corresponding minimax formulation in equations below. The model's function can also be seen in Figure 7 below.

$$L(G,F,D_X,D_Y) = L_{GAN}(G,D_Y,X,Y) + LGAN(F,D_X,Y,X) + \lambda Lcyc(G,F) \qquad (10)$$

$$G*,F* = arg\ minG,F\ maxDX,DY\ L(G,F,DX,DY) \qquad (11)$$

Figure 7. The Cycle-GAN's function. (a) An overview of the model with regard to its two mapping functions G: X → Y and F: Y → X, and their corresponding discriminators DX and DY . (b) The forward cycle-consistency loss x → G(x) → F(G(x)) ≈ x. (c) The backward cycle-consistency loss y → F(y) → G(F(y)) ≈ y
Figure from (J. Y. Zhu, Park, Isola, & Efros, 2017)

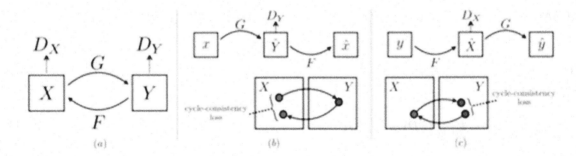

The Cycle-GAN served as the basis for a number of variants such as the covariance-preserving conditional cycle-GAN (cCov-GAN) (Gao, Shou, Zareian, Zhang, & Chang, 2018), which expanded on the Cycle-GAN's objective to allow for conditional domain transfer and preserving intra-class covariance information, as well as other variants that will be examined in the next subsection.

Other Domain Transfer GANs

StarGAN Proposed by (Choi et al., 2018), StarGAN expands on the Cycle-GAN. Each Cycle-GAN is limited to domain transfer between two specific domains X and Y. However, StarGAN allows for conditional transition to multiple domains. Trained with data from N domains, it can transfer any sample x from domain $X \in N$ to any of domain $Y \in N$. To achieve that, during training it receives a sample as input, but it also receives a label indicative of the domain the sample is expected to transition to. A classification error is also incorporated in the training process to facilitate this function, that is to restrict each generated sample to a domain determined by a conditioning input. StarGANs allow for N to N domain transition with only one model, whereas the use of Cycle-GANs would have required the training of a distinct model for each domain pair.

A StarGAN variant named CTGAN was also encountered in (Zhou, Ke, & Luo, 2019), where an *ID consistent* loss is added to the objective in the form of an L_1 distance between the synthetic image and its original.

DavinciGAN. In (K. Lee, Choi, & Jung, 2019) the DavinciGAN is proposed as an alternative to Cycle-GAN for unpaired image-to-image translation. Its contribution lies in the use of loss functions that promote the generation of samples that are realistic with regard, belong to the desired domain, and whose background (i.e. the parts of the image that are irrelevant to the source and target domains) has not been altered. The later objective is achieved via a combination of unsupervised segmentation and attention. The DavinciGAN is then particularly suitable for applications which require that only very specific sections and/or objects of each image should be altered as the image transitions between domains, with the rest of it remaining relatively intact.

Tonality-Alignment GAN (TAGAN). Proposed in (L. Chen et al., 2018), TAGAN is a domain transfer GAN designed to augment 2D and 3D hand gesture datasets for the purpose of hand pose estimation. It consists of a generator and discriminator. The generator receives as input the shape drawing of a palm in a given gesture and a color map, to generate a 2D or 3D rendering a realistic palm with the corresponding gesture and color properties. The TAGAN uses multiple objectives to encourage the generation of samples that are realistic and maintain the required shape and color consistency. It should be noted that, while we group TAGAN as a domain transfer GAN, in the sense that it transitions samples in the domain of shape drawings to that of images of hand gestures, it could also be thought of as a conditional GAN, generating samples based on the conditioning input of the shape drawing and the color map.

AugGAN. AugGAN is a variant of the Cycle-GAN suggested in (S. W. Huang et al., 2018) meant for use in the context of object detection and segmentation tasks. In AugGAN's architecture, the generator produces a segmentation mask along with the synthetic image, which is guided by a loss function to correspond to a specific object. Via this modification, AugGAN learns to transition samples between domains without distorting the shape and placement of the object that is under examination.

Differential GAN (D-GAN). Proposed in (Gu, Kim, Kim, Baddar, & Ro, 2017) and focused on facial expression alteration, D-GAN transfers an image x from domain X to image y at domain Y, as defined by a conditional input, using pairs of the same image in both domains as ground truth for training. The mask is created by projecting a class conditioning vector to the shape of the image in a learned way, so that it can be depth-wise concatenated with the image to be modified. The resulting tensor includes both the original image and the conditioning mask. It is then fed to the generator, with produces a synthetic image. The model then uses two discriminators, the *standard* one, tasked with determining how realistic the synthetic image is, and the *differential* one, which determines if the differential image $x - y$ is acceptable. In that way, the generator is forced to create realistic synthetic samples that alter the original image only in areas and ways that are required by the domain transition task.

Expression GAN (ExprGAN). Combining elements of autoencoders and conditional GANs, the ExprGAN proposed by (Ding, Sricharan, & Chellappa, 2017) performs identity preserving domain transfer. ExprGAN is novel in that its conditioning input relates to information not only about the synthetic sample's the desired class, but its intensity as well. In the context it was used in the original paper, this formulation related to the intensity with which certain emotions were expected to appear in synthetic images of faces. Another notable element of the ExprGAN is that, due to the fact it uses multiple loss functions, each relating to specific components of its architecture, the authors suggest training those components independently in distinct stages. The ExprGAN was designed for the purposes of face expression alteration, but is not by design restricted to this application.

Identity Preserved Conditional GAN (IPCGAN). (X. Tang, Wang, Luo, & Gao, 2018) is designed to perform conditional domain transfer in the context of age on images of faces. In addition to the discriminator, the model makes use of a classifier and a pre-trained AlexNet model. The classifier determines the age group a given image belongs to and is used to force the generator to produce synthetic samples that correspond to the age group determined by the conditioning input. The AlexNet is used to extract features of the original and the synthetic image, whose distance the generator is motivated to minimize, so that the identity of the subject is preserved. Those three components ensure that the synthetic images are realistic, belong to the expected age group, and are of the same person as that of their input. Similar to the ExprGAN, it is designed and tested in the context of a specific task, that of face aging, but is not restricted to it with regard to its applicability.

Deep Attention GAN (DA-GAN). DA-GAN (Not to be confused with DAGAN (Antoniou et al., 2017)) was introduced by (Ma, Fu, Chen, & Mei, 2018). It uses a deep attention encoder to produce latent space representations based on the localized properties of each sample. The generator uses those representation to produce synthetic samples, which both locally and collectively have features that correspond to those of the target domain (as defined by samples of that domain). The paper proposes a combination of four loss function components to facilitate the use of DAEs and to enforce desirable properties on the model. Additionally, due to the fact that the synthetic samples are generated based on a localized interpretation of their properties projected to a latent space (which in the case of image-to-image translation is extracted via the DAE), DA-GAN is flexible regarding its applications which include, for instance, text-to-image generation.

Pedestrian Synthesis GAN (PS-GAN). This model, proposed in (Ouyang, Cheng, Jiang, Li, & Zhou, 2018), focuses on content infilling. Its input is two versions of the same image, the second of which has had a specific part of it corrupted by noise. The PS-GAN is expected to fill that area with realistic content. This application is used specifically in the context of a pedestrian detection task (though it can be used in other domains), wherein the PS-GAN is tasked with inserting pedestrians in sections of images defined by the corrupting noise. To achieve this, PS-GAN uses two discriminators rather than one. The first determines if the area in question is filled with realistic content in itself. The second discriminator determines if the synthetic image as a whole is realistic, when considered along with its noisy original.

Stacked GAN (SGAN) The SGAN, proposed in (Y. Tang et al., 2018), uses two GANs, whose architectures draw heavily from the SRGAN (Ledig et al., 2016), to perform two consecutive domain transfers on their input images in order to achieve desirable properties in the end result. In the case of (Y. Tang et al., 2018), the SGAN is used to improve an image's quality and resolution, and the two functions of the SGAN are to first denoise, and then to increase the resolution of its input image samples.

Domain Invariance & Feature Augmentation (DIFA) A framework designed for data augmentation for unsupervised domain adaptation tasks proposed in (Volpi, Morerio, Savarese, & Murino, 2018). It expands on the cGAN so that it performs data augmentation in the feature space, rather than by synthesizing new samples. The architecture is trained in 3 steps. Initially, a classifier is trained on the source domain. Then, the trained model is used as a feature extractor and a GAN is trained to produce realistic class-conditioned synthetic feature vectors. Finally, the encoder is trained again in the context of a GAN on both the source and target domains. Its objective is for the encoder to create common feature vector representations for samples in both domains. Ultimately, the framework results in an encoder trained for domain-invariant feature extraction, which can be used for augmentation, as well as for class inference in the cases of unlabeled datasets.

3DMM Cycle-GAN. (Gecer, Bhattarai, Kittler, & Kim, 2018) propose an adversarial approach for generating 2D images conditioned by a 3D Morphable Model. Being a method with similar objectives to the Cycle-GAN, its objective is to transfer samples generated by a 3DMM to a photorealistic domain. To do that, the model requires unpaired samples of both domains, and a proportionally small number of paired samples. Similar to the Cycle-GAN, the model uses a pair of generators $G: X \rightarrow Y$ and $F: Y \rightarrow X$ and their respective generators, but on the other hand it uses a Classifier along with the discriminator, as well as different loss functions to guide its training, in order to enforce identity preservation and pair matching, with limited paired samples from each domain.

Background Augmentation Generative Adversarial Network (BAGAN). BAGAN (M. Yan et al., 2018) is designed to function as part of a framework that generates 2D samples by drawing from renderings of 3D models of objects and augmenting them with diverse synthetic backgrounds while maintaining the objects' identities. It should be noted that the full pipeline of the framework involves multiple techniques and components that inform and utilize the actual GAN component, but the framework's purpose overall is to generate diverse and realistic annotated 2D samples from a limited 3D dataset. The Background Augmentation Generative Adversarial Network is distinct from the Balancing GAN (Mariani et al., 2018), though their acronyms are identical.

APPLICATIONS

Having surmised in section *GAN models* the technical features of each GAN that will be mentioned, and having defined the tasks they were used for in section *Tasks*, this section presents the specific Data Augmentation applications that GANs were identified to have been used in by our research on the topic. We organize this section in three distinct groups based on the fields in which each application belongs to. The first groups relates to medicine, the second to people and faces, and the third includes all remaining applications that could not be grouped into a broader category. It is this section's objective to list the ways in which GANs have been used to augment datasets in each domain and application. We will refer to sample generation techniques using the notation described in subsection *Samples Generation Method*. The specific datasets used in each work described in this section is listed in Table 1.

Medicine

GAN-based data augmentation was found to have been used extensively in applications related to medicine, where scarcity of data and difficulty in annotating them coincides with enormous potential benefits if machine learning could be applied to facilitate various tasks, especially diagnostic ones. The motivating promise of significant returns for healthcare systems can explain the fact that most applications we found were related to this domain. 2D and 3D imagery analysis is particularly important in extracting information from CT, MRI and other diagnostic tools.

*Table 1. Data augmentation with GANs - Applications. Datasets marked with * were gathered for the purposes of each work and have not necessarily been made public*

Dataset	GAN Model	Reference	Sample Gen.
Domain: Medicine			
DDSM (Heath, Bowyer, Kopans, Moore, & Kegelmeyer, 2001)	ciGAN	(Yirui Wu et al., 2018)	CSG
CBIS-DDSM (R. S. Lee et al., 2017)	DADA	(X. Zhang et al., 2018)	CSG
LIDC (McNitt-Gray et al., 2008)	3D-CGAN	(Jin et al., 2018)	CSG(3D)
LIDC	3D MCGAN	(Han, Kitamura, et al., 2019)	CSG(3D)
LIDC	AIPBF	(Jie Yang et al., 2018)	CSG(3D)
Cardiac CT & MRI scans *	3D Cycle-GAN Var.	(Z. Zhang, Yang, & Zheng, 2018)	DT(3D)
Combination of fMRI datasets	Cond. WGAN-GP (3D) Var.	(Zhuang, Schwing, & Koyejo, 2019)	CSG
Liver Lesions *	DCGAN, AC-GAN	(Frid-Adar et al., 2018)	CSG, USGa
Chest X-Rays dataset *	DCGAN	(Salehinejad, Valaee, Dowdell, Colak, & Barfett, 2017)	USGa
Chromosome Karyotyping Cell Dataset *	MD-GAN	(Yirui Wu et al., 2018)	USGb
Pulmonary nodule CT dataset *	WGAN	(Onishi et al., 2019)	USGa
Breast Cancer Wisc. (Diagnostic) Data Set (UCI, 2011)			
BRATS (Menze et al., 2015)	PGGAN	(Han, Murao, et al., 2019)	USGa
Surgery Images *	DavinciGAN	(K. Lee et al., 2019)	DT
BCDR (Guevara Lopez et al., 2012), INbreast (Moreira et al., 2011), CBIS-DDSM (R. S. Lee et al., 2017)	Cycle-GAN	(Jendele, Skopek, Becker, & Konukoglu, 2019)	DT
MITOS-ATYPIA-14 Challenge[1]	Cycle-GAN	(R. S. Lee et al., 2017; Shaban, Baur, Navab, & Albarqouni, 2018)	DT
TCGA (Kandoth et al., 2013), CINJ Histopathology Dataset *	GAN var.	(Ren, Hacihaliloglu, Singer, Foran, & Qi, 2018)	DT
MITOS-ATYPIA-14 Challenge, MICCAI'16(Sirinukunwattana et al., 2016),	AC-GAN var.	(Bentaieb & Hamarneh, 2017)	DTc
Ovarian Carcinoma whole slide images *			
DeepLesion (K. Yan et al., 2018)	SGAN	(Y. Tang et al., 2018)	DT
Blood smears images *	pix2pix	(Bailo, Ham, & Shin, 2019)	DT
BRATS, ADNI[2]	pix2pix	(Shin et al., 2018)	DT(3D)
CT & FLAIR datasets *	PGGAN	(Bowles, Gunn, Hammers, & Rueckert, 2018)	USGc
Brain MRI dataset *	Cond. PGGAN	(Han, Murao, et al., 2019)	CSG
Domain: People & Faces			
VGG Face (Parkhi, Vedaldi, & Zisserman, 2015)	DAGAN	(Antoniou et al., 2017)	CSG
CASIAWebFace (D. Yi, Lei, Liao, & Li, 2014)	CVAE-GAN	(Bao et al., 2017)	CSG
VGG Face, LFW (G. B. Huang, Ramesh, Berg, & Learned-Miller, 2007), IJB-A (Klare et al., 2015)	3DMM Cycle-GAN	(Gecer et al., 2018)	DT3t2(3D)
CASIA Palmprint Dataset [3]	DCGAN	(G. Wang, Kang, Wu, Wang, & Gao, 2019)	USGa
IIT Delhi Palmprint database[4]			
CACD (B.-C. Chen, Chen, & Hsu, 2014)	IPCGAN	(X. Tang et al., 2018)	DTc
Oulu-CASIA (Zhao, Huang, Taini, Li, & Pietikäinen, 2011)	ExprGAN	(Ding et al., 2017)	DTc
FER2013 (Dhall, Goecke, Lucey, & Gedeon, 2011), SFEW (Goodfellow et al., 2015), JAFFE (Kamachi, Lyons, & Gyoba, 1997)	Cycle-GAN	(Y. Zhu, Aoun, Science, Krijn, & Vanschoren, 2018)	DT
MMI (Valstar & Pantic, 2010), LFW	D-GAN	(Gu et al., 2017)	DT
Tsinghua-Daimler Cyclist Benchmark (X. Li et al., 2016),	PS-GAN	(Ouyang et al., 2018)	DT
CASIA gait dataset (Shiqi Yu, Daoliang Tan, & Tieniu Tan, 2006), VOT2013, VOT2014,	StarGAN	(K. Chen, Zhou, Zhou, & Xu, 2019)	DTc
VOT2015 (Kristan et al., 2015), OTB100 (Y Wu, Lim, & Yang, 2013)			
Market-1501 (L. Zheng et al., 2015), DukeMTMC-ReID (Ristani, Solera, Zou, Cucchiara, & Tomasi, 2016)	CTGAN	(Zhou et al., 2019)	DTc
Market-1501, DukeMTMC-ReID	Cycle-GAN	(Zhong, Zheng, Zheng, Li, & Yang, 2017)	DT
Market-1501, DukeMTMC-ReID, CUHK03 (W. Li, Zhao, Xiao, & Wang, 2014)	DCGAN	(Z. Zheng, Zheng, & Yang, 2017)	USGd
Domain: Other			
ImageNet	cCov-GAN	(Gao et al., 2018)	DTc
X-Rays of various items*	DCGAN, CT-GAN,	(J Yang, Zhao, Zhang, & Shi, 2019)	USGb

continues on following page

Table 1. Continued

Dataset	GAN Model	Reference	Sample Gen.
Domain: Medicine			
ObjectNet3D (Xiang et al., 2016), ShapeNet (Chang et al., 2015)	BAGAN	(M. Yan et al., 2018)	DT3t2(3D)
Omniglot (M Lake, Salakhutdinov, & B Tenenbaum, 2015), EMNIST (Cohen, Afshar, Tapson, & van Schaik, 2017)	DAGAN	(Antoniou et al., 2017)	CSG
RHP (Zimmermann & Brox, 2017), STB (J. Zhang et al., 2016), CMU-PS (Simon, Joo, & Sheikh, 2017)	TAGAN	(L. Chen et al., 2018)	DT, DT2t3(3D)
HMDB51, UCF101	WGAN	(Y. Zhang, Jia, Chen, Zhang, & Yong, 2019)	USGa
Omniglot, Mini-Imagenet (Vinyals, Blundell, Lillicrap, Kavukcuoglu, & Wierstra, 2016)	MetaGAN	(R. Zhang et al., 2018)	CSG
CURE-TSR (Temel, Kwon, Prabhushankar, & AlRegib, 2017)	Three-Player GAN	(Vandenhende et al., 2019)	CSG
MNIST (Lecun, Bottou, Bengio, & Haffner, 1998), CIFAR-10 (Krizhevsky, 2012), Flowers[5]	BAGAN	(Mariani et al., 2018)	CSG
CUB-200-2011 (Wah, Branson, Welinder, Perona, & Belongie, 2011)	DA-GAN	(Ma et al., 2018)	DT
MNIST, USPS (Denker et al., 1989), SVHN (Netzer et al., 2011), SYN DIGITS (Ganin & Lempitsky, 2015), NYUD (Silberman, Hoiem, Kohli, & Fergus, 2012)	DIFA	(Volpi et al., 2018)	DT
SYNTHIA (Ros, Sellart, Materzynska, Vazquez, & Lopez, 2016), GTA (Richter, Vineet, Roth, & Koltun, 2016), KITTI (Geiger, Lenz, & Urtasun, 2012), ITRI*[6]	AugGAN	(S. W. Huang et al., 2018)	DT
Cityscapes (Cordts et al., 2016)	PS-GAN	(Ouyang et al., 2018)	DT
CVPPP 2017 LSC Plant Dataset ("Jonathan Bell and Hannah M Dee. Aberystwyth leaf evaluation dataset. 2016.," n.d.)	cGAN	(J. Y. Zhu et al., 2017)	CSG

In this fields, GAN-based data augmentation has been used most frequently in augmenting datasets consisting of MRIs, X-Rays and other medical images to improve on classification or segmentation related diagnostic tasks. With regard to classification, (Han, Rundo, et al., 2019) used USGa with the PGGAN on brain MRIs for cancer diagnoses, and subsequently (Han, Murao, et al., 2019) used a conditional PG-GAN in a similar application with a tumor detection objective (OD). PGGAN was also used by (Bowles et al., 2018) in a transfer learning framework to augment brain CTs and MRIs for improved segmentation via USGc. Another application of USGa was found in (Frid-Adar et al., 2018) and (Salehinejad et al., 2017), where the DCGAN was used to augment datasets consisting of liver lesions CT scans and chest X-rays respectively. With regard to Conditional Samples Generation (CSG), (Frid-Adar et al., 2018) also used the AC-GAN to generate samples conditionally to augment a dataset of CT scans. An interesting application of data augmentation via USGa is found in (Onishi et al., 2019), where a WGAN is used on a pulmonary CT dataset, but the classifier is trained only on synthetic samples, and then fine-tuned with the originals. (X. Zhang et al., 2018) used the DADA framework to augment a dataset of scanned film mammography studies after experimenting with CIFAR-10, while (E. Wu, Wu, Cox, & Lotter, 2018) used the ciGAN in a similar dataset, to augment mammograms via content infilling (filling specific sections of each sample conditionally to facilitate classification) for dataset balancing. Moving on to GANs performing domain transfer, (Bentaieb & Hamarneh, 2017) proposed a combination of an AC-GAN and an autoencoder in order to perform conditional domain transfer (DTc) on various histopathology image datasets, in order to solve the problem of stain color inconsistencies for both classification and segmentation purposes. On the same subject, (Shaban et al., 2018) used the Cycle-GAN on a histopathology dataset to improve on tumor classification, and (Ren et al., 2018) used an architecture combining a GAN with a Siamese network to augment two prostate histopathology image datasets in an unsupervised way, also to improve classification results. (Y. Tang et al., 2018) used the SGAN to augment CT images for lesion segmentation purposes and (Jendele et al., 2019) used the Cycle-GAN for breast cancer diagnosis (classification). Regarding 3D imagery, (Jin et al., 2018) used for content infilling to create synthetic lung nodules which are then used to fine tune a nodule segmentation model. Using the same dataset of lung nodules, (Han, Kitamura, et al., 2019) proposes the 3D MCGAN for 3D conditional infilling in the context of object detection, and (Jie Yang et al., 2018) proposed the AIPBF GAN based framework for augmented classification. (Shin et al., 2018) utilized the pix2pix methodology, adjusted for 3D data, to augment brain MRIs and improve on a tumor segmentation task. (Z. Zhang et al., 2018) proposed a modification on the Cycle-GAN, such that allowed for domain transition between two 3D domains, which was utilized to improve segmentation performance using CT and MRI cardiac scans by transitioning samples to either domain. In (Zhuang et al., 2019), a conditional WGAN-GP variant was used to augment 3D fMRI datasets for a classification task.

Diagnostics aside, GANs have also been used in other applications. (Yirui Wu et al., 2018) used MD-GAN to improve on chromosome classification (Karyotyping). (Bailo et al., 2019) augmented a dataset of blood smear slides with pix2pix and improved on segmentation performance. In (K. Lee et al., 2019), the DavinciGAN is used to augment a dataset consisting of frames of surgeries which include the tools used be the surgeon, to improve on instrument classification.

For a broader overview of GANs used in medical applications, we suggest reading (Kazeminia et al., 2018) and (X. Yi, Walia, & Babyn, 2018).

People and Faces

This section lists works that tackled the datasets whose subjects were people, whether in terms of faces, body shapes or other characteristics. Regarding face data augmentation techniques more broadly, we also suggest (X. Wang, Wang, & Lian, 2019), which reviews approaches that are not limited to GANs.

In this domain, the only cases were samples were generated unconditionally were (G. Wang et al., 2019) and (Z. Zheng et al., 2017), in both of which the DCGAN was used. The former applied USGa on a palmprint dataset, applying classification in terms of identifying the owner of each print. The later used USGd in a person identification (PID) task using datasets consisting of images of pedestrians captured by cameras. (Gecer et al., 2018) used the 3DMM Cycle-GAN to augment 2D face datasets with samples originating from using 3D models. (Antoniou et al., 2017) used the DAGAN in a CSG application to augment a dataset of faces to improve person classification, which was also done by (Bao et al., 2017) with the CVAE-GAN. The rest of the works in this domain used Domain Transfer. In the area of classification, (X. Tang et al., 2018) used the IPCGAN to augment dace datasets age-wise in an identity preserving way (DTc) and (Y. Zhu et al., 2018) used the Cycle-GAN to augment face datasets emotion-wise, which was done both uniformly (UA) and for specific classes (DB) to improve on emotion classification. Finally, (Gu et al., 2017) used the ExprGAN for DTc and (Ding et al., 2017) used the D-GAN both for UA and DB, to augment face datasets with regard to their expresions. It should be noted that works performing domain transfer on faces provide for identity-preservation, as defined in section *Domain Transfer (DT)*. Regarding person identification (PID), (Zhou et al., 2019) uses the CTGAN on images of pedestrians and (Zhong et al., 2017) uses the Cycle-GAN to improve on a multi-camera person re-identification task. Finally, object detection (OD) is tackled in (Ouyang et al., 2018) on a dataset of cyclist images using the PS-GAN, and (K. Chen et al., 2019) does object tracking (OT) with the StarGAN on various videos of people.

Other Data

This subsection relates to works whose area of focus does not fall into a concrete application domain, and includes publications that tackled popular machine learning datasets, as well as data specific to particular applications.

Regarding classification tasks, USGb was used in (J Yang et al., 2019), which compared the DCGAN, WGAN-GP and CT-GAN's performances in augmenting a dataset consisting of X-rays of various items which were to be classified. Conditional approaches included (Antoniou et al., 2017), which used the DAGAN on two datasets with written characters and (R. Zhang et al., 2018) which used the MetaGAN on datasets of characters and various images. CSG was also used in (Vandenhende et al., 2019), which used the Three-Player GAN to augment a dataset of traffic signs to improve classification accuracy. Finally, (Mariani et al., 2018) use the BAGAN on various machine learning datasets performing CSG and DB. Domain Transfer for classification purposes is used by (Ma et al., 2018) with the DA-GAN on a dataset of birds that are augmented pose-wise, by (Volpi et al., 2018), where DIFA is used to augment data using other similar datasets or domains, and by (Gao et al., 2018), where a variation of the Cycle-GAN, the cCov-GAN, was used to augment a downsampled ImageNet dataset in a low-shot learning classification task. Lastly, (J. Y. Zhu et al., 2017) utilized a cGAN conditioned on plant masks to conditionally generate diverse plant images to facilitate accurate leaf segmentation and counting, (S. W. Huang et al., 2018) used the AugGAN to perform day/night DT on various datasets of images of cars in streets in order to improve object detection efficiency, and (Ouyang et al., 2018) performed DT on a dataset of city street images with the PS-GAN, also to improve OD. Data augmentation in video was applied in (Y. Zhang et al., 2019), where WGAN was used as part of a pipeline to augment video classification datasets. In the area of 3D to 2D transitions, BAGAN (M. Yan et al., 2018) was used with the ObjectNet3D and ShapeNet databases to augment a 2D classification task with samples generated from 3D models, arguing that 3D models are easier to generate than it is to gather annotated 2D data, and so using them to synthesize diverse 2D samples is more efficient. TAGAN, which is proposed in (L. Chen et al., 2018) to augment datasets used for hand pose estimation is also used to generate both 2D and 3D samples.

CONCLUSION

In summarizing our findings, we first have to observe that the number and diversity of the GAN models that were found to have been used for Data Augmentation on 2D and 3D imagery, as well as the various techniques that were employed, make it difficult to suggest a strict methodology for choosing the optimal approach for any given problem. We would, however, make note of the following conclusions that can be drawn from the works that were studied. The first conclusion is that using Unconditional Samples Generation is rarely the best option for Data Augmentation. While there are ways that it might be applied, those approaches have significant drawbacks and were found to be largely outdated. Considering the need for annotated samples in the context of data augmentation, Conditional Samples Generation is the most straightforward tool, particularly when augmenting data for a classification problem. Among conditional GANs, the AC-GAN presents itself as a simple, efficient and versatile model. Finally, with regard to Domain Transfer, the Cycle-GAN proved to be a very potent and adaptive architecture, which can also be attested to by the number of variants it has inspired (e.g. the StarGAN and the cCov-GAN).

The above are in no way guaranteed to augment all datasets in an satisfactory way. They constitute, however, potent and versatile architectures that can easily be modified to match the specific requirements of various problems, which was the case in most of the cases that were examined in this survey.

It is also important to point out that many of the papers we studied used approaches that were largely outdated by the time those papers were written. Expanding on this observation, it must be made clear that this work does not include more recent and advanced GANs that have not, to the best of our knowledge, been used in the context of image data augmentation. For the study of state of the art models and the techniques they employ we recommend (H. Zhang, Goodfellow, Metaxas, & Odena, 2018), (Brock, Donahue, & Simonyan, 2018) and (Lucic et al., 2019) with regard to CSG and (Park, Liu, Wang, & Zhu, 2019) with regard to Domain Transfer. We attribute the relative delay in applying state of the art GAN models to data augmentation tasks to the fact that GANs are considerably complex architectures, and their level of complexity increases steeply as more advanced models are examined. Consequently, it is not easy to adapt such models to new applications. It should also be pointed out that the increased capacity of state of the art GANs may not be required in cases where data are limited, as well as that more powerful GANs are more difficult to train successfully, particularly with limited data and computational resources. Consequently, GANs that perform better in large benchmark datasets are not necessarily appropriate for data augmentation purposes.

Finally, it is important to examine the applications listed in this survey with regard to the 2D/3D distinction. 3D data augmentation applications were considerably more scarce than 2D. This mirrors the general trend in machine learning research overall, where 3D data and tasks have only recently attracted interest. This can be attributed to the fact that 3D applications are only now becoming prominent enough to motivate extensive study and the creation of annotated datasets. GAN-based data augmentation however is proven in the works we surveyed to be a potent tool in overcoming the relative scarcity of annotated 3D data. Most 2D architectures can easily be adapted to generate 3D data (e.g. the 3D-GAN in section *3D Generative Adversarial Network (3D-GAN)*), while domain transfer GANs can be used to transfer images from 2D to 3D and the inverse. This is an interesting application related to the generation of diverse samples from 3D models, which can also serve as a source of annotated data.

Overall, research in data augmentation can be shown by the surveyed works to be largely driven by real-life data shortages in specific applications rather than academic interest. However, there is consensus in the works we surveyed that GANs can be an invaluable tool in overcoming data scarcity, which is itself a major impediment in the use of machine learning in many domains. It is then our expectation that, considering the potential for applying machine learning solutions in many of the subject areas we examined, considerable effort will be invested in the future toward making advanced GAN models more accessible and easier to use

ACKNOWLEDGMENT

This work was supported by the EU funded project NADINE H2020 under the grant agreement 822601

REFERENCES

Alexiadis, D. S., Chatzitofis, A., Zioulis, N., Zoidi, O., Louizis, G., Zarpalas, D., & Daras, P. (2016). An integrated platform for live 3D human reconstruction and motion capturing. *IEEE Transactions on Circuits and Systems for Video Technology, 27*(4), 798–813. doi:10.1109/TCSVT.2016.2576922

Antoniou, A., Storkey, A., & Edwards, H. (2017). *Data Augmentation Generative Adversarial Networks.* Retrieved from https://arxiv.org/abs/1711.04340

Arjovsky, M., & Bottou, L. (2017). *Towards Principled Methods for Training Generative Adversarial Networks.* Retrieved from https://arxiv.org/abs/1701.04862

Arjovsky, M., Chintala, S., & Bottou, L. (2017). *Wasserstein GAN.* Retrieved from https://arxiv.org/abs/1701.07875

Bailo, O., Ham, D., & Shin, Y. M. (2019). *Red blood cell image generation for data augmentation using Conditional Generative Adversarial Networks.* Retrieved from https://arxiv.org/abs/1901.06219

Bao, J., Chen, D., Wen, F., Li, H., & Hua, G. (2017). *CVAE-GAN: Fine-Grained Image Generation through Asymmetric Training.* Retrieved from https://arxiv.org/abs/1703.10155

Bell & Dee. (2016). *Aberystwyth leaf evaluation dataset.* Academic Press.

Bentaieb, A., & Hamarneh, G. (2017). Adversarial Stain Transfer for Histopathology Image Analysis. *IEEE Transactions on Medical Imaging, PP, 1.* doi:10.1109/TMI.2017.2781228 PMID:29533895

Bowles, C., Gunn, R., Hammers, A., & Rueckert, D. (2018). *GANsfer Learning: Combining labelled and unlabelled data for GAN based data augmentation.* Retrieved from https://arxiv.org/abs/1811.10669

Brock, A., Donahue, J., & Simonyan, K. (2018). *Large Scale GAN Training for High Fidelity Natural Image Synthesis.* Retrieved from https://arxiv.org/abs/1809.11096

Bunkhumpornpat, C., Sinapiromsaran, K., & Lursinsap, C. (2012). DBSMOTE: Density-based synthetic minority over-sampling technique. *Applied Intelligence, 36*(3), 664–684. doi:10.100710489-011-0287-y

Burt, P. J., & Adelson, E. H. (1983). The Laplacian Pyramid as a Compact Image Code. *IEEE Transactions on Communications, 31*(4), 532–540. doi:10.1109/TCOM.1983.1095851

Chang, A. X., Funkhouser, T. A., Guibas, L. J., Hanrahan, P., Huang, Q.-X., Li, Z., … Yu, F. (2015). *ShapeNet: An Information-Rich 3D Model Repository.* Retrieved from https://arxiv.org/abs/1512.03012

Chawla, N. V., Bowyer, K. W., Hall, L. O., & Kegelmeyer, W. P. (2002). SMOTE: Synthetic minority over-sampling technique. *Journal of Artificial Intelligence Research, 16*, 321–357. doi:10.1613/jair.953

Chen, B.-C., Chen, C.-S., & Hsu, W. H. (2014). Cross-Age Reference Coding for Age-Invariant Face Recognition and Retrieval. *Proceedings of the European Conference on Computer Vision ({ECCV}).* 10.1007/978-3-319-10599-4_49

Chen, K., Zhou, X., Zhou, Q., & Xu, H. (2019). Adversarial Learning-based Data Augmentation for Rotation-robust Human Tracking. In *ICASSP 2019 - 2019 IEEE International Conference on Acoustics, Speech and Signal Processing (ICASSP)* (pp. 1942–1946). IEEE. 10.1109/ICASSP.2019.8683451

Chen, L., Lin, S.-Y., Xie, Y., Tang, H., Xue, Y., Xie, X., … Fan, W. (2018). *Generating Realistic Training Images Based on Tonality-Alignment Generative Adversarial Networks for Hand Pose Estimation.* Retrieved from https://arxiv.org/abs/1811.09916

Choi, Y., Choi, M., Kim, M., Ha, J. W., Kim, S., & Choo, J. (2018). StarGAN: Unified Generative Adversarial Networks for Multi-domain Image-to-Image Translation. *Proceedings of the IEEE Computer Society Conference on Computer Vision and Pattern Recognition*, 8789–8797. 10.1109/CVPR.2018.00916

Cohen, G., Afshar, S., Tapson, J., & van Schaik, A. (2017). *{EMNIST:} an extension of {MNIST} to handwritten letters.* Retrieved from https://arxiv.org/abs/1702.05373

Cordts, M., Omran, M., Ramos, S., Rehfeld, T., Enzweiler, M., & Benenson, R., … Schiele, B. (2016). The Cityscapes Dataset for Semantic Urban Scene Understanding. *Proceedings of the IEEE Computer Society Conference on Computer Vision and Pattern Recognition,* 3213–3223. 10.1109/CVPR.2016.350

Denker, J. S., Gardner, W. R., Graf, H. P., Henderson, D., Howard, R. E., & Hubbard, W. … Guyon, I. (1989). Neural Network Recognizer for Hand-Written Zip Code Digits. In D. S. Touretzky (Ed.), *Advances in Neural Information Processing Systems 1* (pp. 323–331). Morgan-Kaufmann. Retrieved from http://papers.nips.cc/paper/107-neural-network-recognizer-for-hand-written-zip-code-digits.pdf

Denton, E., Chintala, S., Szlam, A., & Fergus, R. (2015). *Deep Generative Image Models using a Laplacian Pyramid of Adversarial Networks.* Retrieved from https://arxiv.org/abs/1506.05751

Dhall, A., Goecke, R., Lucey, S., & Gedeon, T. (2011). Static facial expression analysis in tough conditions: Data, evaluation protocol and benchmark. In *2011 IEEE International Conference on Computer Vision Workshops (ICCV Workshops)* (pp. 2106–2112). 10.1109/ICCVW.2011.6130508

Ding, H., Sricharan, K., & Chellappa, R. (2017). *ExprGAN: Facial Expression Editing with Controllable Expression Intensity.* Retrieved from https://arxiv.org/abs/1709.03842

Donahue, C., McAuley, J., & Puckette, M. (2018). *Adversarial audio synthesis.* ArXiv Preprint ArXiv:1802.04208

Doumanoglou, A., Vretos, N., & Daras, P. (2019). Frequency--based slow feature analysis. *Neurocomputing, 368*, 34–50. doi:10.1016/j.neucom.2019.08.067

Elsken, T., Metzen, J. H., & Hutter, F. (2019). Neural Architecture Search: A Survey. *Journal of Machine Learning Research, 20*(55), 1–21. Retrieved from http://jmlr.org/papers/v20/18-598.html

Finn, C., Abbeel, P., & Levine, S. (2017). *Model-Agnostic Meta-Learning for Fast Adaptation of Deep Networks.* Retrieved from https://arxiv.org/abs/1703.03400

Frid-Adar, M., Diamant, I., Klang, E., Amitai, M., Goldberger, J., & Greenspan, H. (2018). GAN-based synthetic medical image augmentation for increased CNN performance in liver lesion classification. *Neurocomputing, 321*, 321–331. doi:10.1016/j.neucom.2018.09.013

Ganin, Y., & Lempitsky, V. (2015). Unsupervised Domain Adaptation by Backpropagation. In *Proceedings of the 32Nd International Conference on International Conference on Machine Learning - Volume 37* (pp. 1180–1189). JMLR.org. Retrieved from https://dl.acm.org/citation.cfm?id=3045118.3045244

Gao, H., Shou, Z., Zareian, A., Zhang, H., & Chang, S.-F. (2018). *Low-shot Learning via Covariance-Preserving Adversarial Augmentation Networks*. Retrieved from https://arxiv.org/abs/1810.11730

Gecer, B., Bhattarai, B., Kittler, J., & Kim, T.-K. (2018). *Semi-supervised Adversarial Learning to Generate Photorealistic Face Images of New Identities from 3D Morphable Model*. doi:10.1007/978-3-030-01252-6_14

Geiger, A., Lenz, P., & Urtasun, R. (2012). Are we ready for autonomous driving? The KITTI vision benchmark suite. In *2012 IEEE Conference on Computer Vision and Pattern Recognition* (pp. 3354–3361). 10.1109/CVPR.2012.6248074

Gong, X., Chang, S., Jiang, Y., & Wang, Z. (2019). *AutoGAN: Neural Architecture Search for Generative Adversarial Networks*. Retrieved from https://arxiv.org/abs/1908.03835

Goodfellow, I. J., Erhan, D., Carrier, P. L., Courville, A., Mirza, M., Hamner, B., … Bengio, Y. (2015). Challenges in representation learning: A report on three machine learning contests. *Neural Networks, 64*, 59–63.

Goodfellow, I. J., Pouget-Abadie, J., Mirza, M., Xu, B., Warde-Farley, D., Ozair, S., … Bengio, Y. (2014). *Generative Adversarial Networks*. Retrieved from https://arxiv.org/abs/1406.2661

Gu, G., Kim, S. T., Kim, K., Baddar, W. J., & Ro, Y. M. (2017). *Differential Generative Adversarial Networks: Synthesizing Non-linear Facial Variations with Limited Number of Training Data*. Retrieved from https://arxiv.org/abs/1711.10267

Guevara Lopez, M. A., González Posada, N., Moura, D., Pollán, R., Franco-Valiente, J., Ortega, C., … Ferreira M Araújo, B. (2012). BCDR: A breast cancer digital repository. Academic Press.

Gulrajani, I., Ahmed, F., Arjovsky, M., Dumoulin, V., & Courville, A. (2017). *Improved Training of Wasserstein GANs*. Retrieved from https://arxiv.org/abs/1704.00028

Han, C., Kitamura, Y., Kudo, A., Ichinose, A., Rundo, L., Furukawa, Y., … Li, Y. (2019). *Synthesizing Diverse Lung Nodules Wherever Massively: 3D Multi-Conditional GAN-based {CT} Image Augmentation for Object Detection*. Retrieved from https://arxiv.org/abs/1906.04962

Han, C., Murao, K., Noguchi, T., Kawata, Y., Uchiyama, F., Rundo, L., … Satoh, S. (2019). *Learning More with Less: Conditional PGGAN-based Data Augmentation for Brain Metastases Detection Using Highly-Rough Annotation on MR Images*. Retrieved from https://arxiv.org/abs/1902.09856

Han, C., Rundo, L., Araki, R., Furukawa, Y., Mauri, G., Nakayama, H., & Hayashi, H. (2019). *Infinite Brain MR Images: PGGAN-based Data Augmentation for Tumor Detection*. Retrieved from https://arxiv.org/abs/1903.12564

Heath, M., Bowyer, K., Kopans, D., Moore, R., & Kegelmeyer, P. (2001). The digital database for screening mammography. *Proceedings of the Fifth International Workshop on Digital Mammography*. 10.1007/978-94-011-5318-8_75

Heusel, M., Ramsauer, H., Unterthiner, T., Nessler, B., & Hochreiter, S. (2017). *GANs Trained by a Two Time-Scale Update Rule Converge to a Local Nash Equilibrium*. Retrieved from https://arxiv.org/abs/1706.08500

Huang, G. B., Ramesh, M., Berg, T., & Learned-Miller, E. (2007). *Labeled Faces in the Wild: A Database for Studying Face Recognition in Unconstrained Environments*. Academic Press.

Huang, S. W., Lin, C. T., Chen, S. P., Wu, Y. Y., Hsu, P. H., & Lai, S. H. (2018). AugGAN: Cross domain adaptation with GAN-based data augmentation. Lecture Notes in Computer Science, 11213, 731–744. doi:10.1007/978-3-030-01240-3_44

Isola, P., Zhu, J. Y., Zhou, T., & Efros, A. A. (2017). Image-to-image translation with conditional adversarial networks. In *Proceedings - 30th IEEE Conference on Computer Vision and Pattern Recognition, CVPR 2017* (pp. 5967–5976). Institute of Electrical and Electronics Engineers Inc. 10.1109/CVPR.2017.632

Jendele, L., Skopek, O., Becker, A. S., & Konukoglu, E. (2019). *Adversarial Augmentation for Enhancing Classification of Mammography Images*. Retrieved from https://arxiv.org/abs/1902.07762

Jin, D., Xu, Z., Tang, Y., Harrison, A. P., & Mollura, D. J. (2018). *CT-Realistic Lung Nodule Simulation from 3D Conditional Generative Adversarial Networks for Robust Lung Segmentation*. Retrieved from https://arxiv.org/abs/1806.04051

Kamachi, M., Lyons, M., & Gyoba, J. (1997). *The Japanese female facial expression (jaffe) database*. Http://Www. Kasrl. Org/Jaffe. Html

Kandoth, C., McLellan, M. D., Vandin, F., Ye, K., Niu, B., & Lu, C. … Ding, L. (2013). Mutational landscape and significance across 12 major cancer types. *Nature*. doi:10.1038/nature12634 PMID:24132290

Karras, T., Aila, T., Laine, S., & Lehtinen, J. (2017). *Progressive Growing of GANs for Improved Quality, Stability, and Variation*. Retrieved from https://arxiv.org/abs/1710.10196

Kazeminia, S., Baur, C., Kuijper, A., van Ginneken, B., Navab, N., Albarqouni, S., & Mukhopadhyay, A. (2018). *GANs for Medical Image Analysis*. Retrieved from https://arxiv.org/abs/1809.06222

Kingma, D. P., & Welling, M. (2013). *Auto-Encoding Variational Bayes*. Retrieved from https://arxiv.org/abs/1312.6114

Klare, B. F., Klein, B., Taborsky, E., Blanton, A., Cheney, J., & Allen, K., … Jain, A. K. (2015). Pushing the frontiers of unconstrained face detection and recognition: IARPA Janus Benchmark A. In *2015 IEEE Conference on Computer Vision and Pattern Recognition (CVPR)* (pp. 1931–1939). 10.1109/CVPR.2015.7298803

Kristan, M., Matas, J., Leonardis, A., Felsberg, M., Cehovin, L., Fernandez, G., … Solis Montero, A. (2015). The Visual Object Tracking VOT2015 Challenge Results. In *2015 IEEE International Conference on Computer Vision Workshop (ICCVW)* (pp. 564–586). 10.1109/ICCVW.2015.79

Krizhevsky, A. (2012). *Learning Multiple Layers of Features from Tiny Images*. University of Toronto.

Kurach, K., Lucic, M., Zhai, X., Michalski, M., & Gelly, S. (2018). *A Large-Scale Study on Regularization and Normalization in GANs*. Retrieved from https://arxiv.org/abs/1807.04720

Lake, M., Salakhutdinov, R., & Tenenbaum, J. B. (2015). Human-level concept learning through probabilistic program induction. *Science*, *350*(6266), 1332–1338. doi:10.1126cience.aab3050 PMID:26659050

Lecun, Y., Bottou, L., Bengio, Y., & Haffner, P. (1998). Gradient-based learning applied to document recognition. *Proceedings of the IEEE, 86*(11), 2278–2324. doi:10.1109/5.726791

Ledig, C., Theis, L., Huszar, F., Caballero, J., Aitken, A. P., Tejani, A., … Shi, W. (2016). *Photo-Realistic Single Image Super-Resolution Using a Generative Adversarial Network*. Retrieved from https://arxiv.org/abs/1609.04802

Lee, K., Choi, M.-K., & Jung, H. (2019). DavinciGAN: Unpaired Surgical Instrument Translation for Data Augmentation. In M. J. Cardoso, A. Feragen, B. Glocker, E. Konukoglu, I. Oguz, G. Unal, & T. Vercauteren (Eds.), *Proceedings of The 2nd International Conference on Medical Imaging with Deep Learning* (Vol. 102, pp. 326–336). London, UK: PMLR. Retrieved from http://proceedings.mlr.press/v102/lee19a.html

Lee, R. S., Gimenez, F., Hoogi, A., Miyake, K. K., Gorovoy, M., & Rubin, D. L. (2017). Data Descriptor: A curated mammography data set for use in computer-aided detection and diagnosis research. *Scientific Data, 4*(1), 170177. doi:10.1038data.2017.177 PMID:29257132

Li, C., & Wand, M. (2016). *Precomputed Real-Time Texture Synthesis with Markovian Generative Adversarial Networks*. Retrieved from https://arxiv.org/abs/1604.04382

Li, W., Zhao, R., Xiao, T., & Wang, X. (2014). DeepReID: Deep Filter Pairing Neural Network for Person Re-identification. In *2014 IEEE Conference on Computer Vision and Pattern Recognition* (pp. 152–159). 10.1109/CVPR.2014.27

Li, X., Flohr, F., Yang, Y., Xiong, H., Braun, M., Pan, S., … Gavrila, D. (2016). *A new benchmark for vision-based cyclist detection*. doi:10.1109/IVS.2016.7535515

Lucic, M., Kurach, K., Michalski, M., Gelly, S., & Bousquet, O. (2017). *Are GANs Created Equal? A Large-Scale Study*. Retrieved from https://arxiv.org/abs/1711.10337

Lucic, M., Tschannen, M., Ritter, M., Zhai, X., Bachem, O., & Gelly, S. (2019). *High-Fidelity Image Generation With Fewer Labels*. Retrieved from https://arxiv.org/abs/1903.02271

Ma, S., Fu, J., Chen, C. W., & Mei, T. (2018). DA-GAN: Instance-Level Image Translation by Deep Attention Generative Adversarial Networks. In *Proceedings of the IEEE Computer Society Conference on Computer Vision and Pattern Recognition* (pp. 5657–5666). 10.1109/CVPR.2018.00593

Mariani, G., Scheidegger, F., Istrate, R., Bekas, C., & Malossi, C. (2018). *BAGAN: Data Augmentation with Balancing GAN*. Retrieved from https://arxiv.org/abs/1803.09655

McNitt-Gray, M., Armato, S. III, Meyer, C., Reeves, A., Mclennan, G., Pais, R., … Clarke, L. (2008). The Lung Image Database Consortium (LIDC) Data Collection Process for Nodule Detection and Annotation. *Academic Radiology, 14*(12), 1464–1474. doi:10.1016/j.acra.2007.07.021 PMID:18035276

Menze, B. H., Jakab, A., Bauer, S., Kalpathy-Cramer, J., Farahani, K., Kirby, J., … Van Leemput, K. (2015). The Multimodal Brain Tumor Image Segmentation Benchmark (BRATS). *IEEE Transactions on Medical Imaging, 34*(10), 1993–2024. doi:10.1109/TMI.2014.2377694 PMID:25494501

Mirza, M., & Osindero, S. (2014). *Conditional Generative Adversarial Nets*. Retrieved from https://arxiv.org/abs/1411.1784

Miyato, T., Kataoka, T., Koyama, M., & Yoshida, Y. (2018). *Spectral Normalization for Generative Adversarial Networks*. Retrieved from https://arxiv.org/abs/1802.05957

Moreira, I., Amaral, I., Domingues, I., Cardoso, A., Cardoso, M., & Cardoso, J. (2011). INbreast: Toward a Full-field Digital Mammographic Database. *Academic Radiology*, *19*(2), 236–248. doi:10.1016/j.acra.2011.09.014 PMID:22078258

Netzer, Y., Wang, T., Coates, A., Bissacco, A., Wu, B., & Ng, A. Y. (2011). Reading Digits in Natural Images with Unsupervised Feature Learning. *NIPS Workshop on Deep Learning and Unsupervised Feature Learning 2011*. Retrieved from http://ufldl.stanford.edu/housenumbers/nips2011_housenumbers.pdf

Odena, A., Buckman, J., Olsson, C., Brown, T. B., Olah, C., Raffel, C., & Goodfellow, I. (2018). *Is Generator Conditioning Causally Related to GAN Performance?* Retrieved from https://arxiv.org/abs/1802.08768

Odena, A., Olah, C., & Shlens, J. (2016). *Conditional Image Synthesis With Auxiliary Classifier GANs*. Retrieved from https://arxiv.org/abs/1610.09585

Onishi, Y., Teramoto, A., Tsujimoto, M., Tsukamoto, T., Saito, K., & Toyama, H. (2019). Automated Pulmonary Nodule Classification in Computed Tomography Images Using a Deep Convolutional Neural Network Trained by Generative Adversarial Networks. *BioMed Research International*, 1–9. doi:10.1155/2019/6051939 PMID:30719445

Ouyang, X., Cheng, Y., Jiang, Y., Li, C.-L., & Zhou, P. (2018). *Pedestrian-Synthesis-GAN: Generating Pedestrian Data in Real Scene and Beyond*. Retrieved from https://arxiv.org/abs/1804.02047

Pan, Z., Yu, W., Yi, X., Khan, A., Yuan, F., & Zheng, Y. (2019). Recent Progress on Generative Adversarial Networks (GANs): A Survey. *IEEE Access: Practical Innovations, Open Solutions*, *7*, 36322–36333. doi:10.1109/ACCESS.2019.2905015

Park, T., Liu, M.-Y., Wang, T.-C., & Zhu, J.-Y. (2019). *Semantic Image Synthesis with Spatially-Adaptive Normalization*. Retrieved from https://arxiv.org/abs/1903.07291

Parkhi, O. M., Vedaldi, A., & Zisserman, A. (2015). Deep Face Recognition. *British Machine Vision Conference*.

Radford, A., Metz, L., & Chintala, S. (2015). *Unsupervised Representation Learning with Deep Convolutional Generative Adversarial Networks*. Retrieved from https://arxiv.org/abs/1511.06434

Ravuri, S., & Vinyals, O. (2019). *Classification Accuracy Score for Conditional Generative Models*. Retrieved from https://arxiv.org/abs/1905.10887

Ren, J., Hacihaliloglu, I., Singer, E. A., Foran, D. J., & Qi, X. (2018). *Adversarial Domain Adaptation for Classification of Prostate Histopathology Whole-Slide Images*. Retrieved from https://arxiv.org/abs/1806.01357

Richter, S. R., Vineet, V., Roth, S., & Koltun, V. (2016). *Playing for Data: Ground Truth from Computer Games*. Retrieved from https://arxiv.org/abs/1608.02192

Ristani, E., Solera, F., Zou, R. S., Cucchiara, R., & Tomasi, C. (2016). *Performance Measures and a Data Set for Multi-Target, Multi-Camera Tracking*. Retrieved from https://arxiv.org/abs/1609.01775

Ronneberger, O., Fischer, P., & Brox, T. (2015). *U-Net: Convolutional Networks for Biomedical Image Segmentation*. Retrieved from https://arxiv.org/abs/1505.04597

Ros, G., Sellart, L., Materzynska, J., Vazquez, D., & Lopez, A. M. (2016). The SYNTHIA Dataset: A Large Collection of Synthetic Images for Semantic Segmentation of Urban Scenes. In *2016 IEEE Conference on Computer Vision and Pattern Recognition (CVPR)* (pp. 3234–3243). 10.1109/CVPR.2016.352

Salehinejad, H., Valaee, S., Dowdell, T., Colak, E., & Barfett, J. (2017). *Generalization of Deep Neural Networks for Chest Pathology Classification in X-Rays Using Generative Adversarial Networks*. Retrieved from https://arxiv.org/abs/1712.01636

Salimans, T., Goodfellow, I., Zaremba, W., Cheung, V., Radford, A., & Chen, X. (2016). *Improved Techniques for Training GANs*. Retrieved from https://arxiv.org/abs/1606.03498

Shaban, M. T., Baur, C., Navab, N., & Albarqouni, S. (2018). *StainGAN: Stain Style Transfer for Digital Histological Images*. Retrieved from https://arxiv.org/abs/1804.01601

Shijie, J., Ping, W., Peiyi, J., & Siping, H. (2017). Research on data augmentation for image classification based on convolution neural networks. *Proceedings - 2017 Chinese Automation Congress, CAC 2017*, 4165–4170. 10.1109/CAC.2017.8243510

Shin, H. C., Tenenholtz, N. A., Rogers, J. K., Schwarz, C. G., Senjem, M. L., Gunter, J. L., … Michalski, M. (2018). Medical image synthesis for data augmentation and anonymization using generative adversarial networks. Lecture Notes in Computer Science, 11037, 1–11. doi:10.1007/978-3-030-00536-8_1

Shmelkov, K., Schmid, C., & Alahari, K. (2018). How good is my GAN. In *Proceedings of the European Conference on Computer Vision* (pp. 1–20). ECCV. Retrieved from https://arxiv.org/abs/1807.09499

Silberman, N., Hoiem, D., Kohli, P., & Fergus, R. (2012). Indoor Segmentation and Support Inference from RGBD Images. In *Proceedings of the 12th European Conference on Computer Vision - Volume Part V* (pp. 746–760). Berlin: Springer-Verlag. 10.1007/978-3-642-33715-4_54

Simard, P. Y., Steinkraus, D., & Platt, J. C. (2003). Best practices for convolutional neural networks applied to visual document analysis. In *Proceedings of the International Conference on Document Analysis and Recognition, ICDAR* (pp. 958–963). 10.1109/ICDAR.2003.1227801

Simon, T., Joo, H., & Sheikh, Y. (2017). *Hand Keypoint Detection in Single Images using Multiview Bootstrapping*. CVPR. doi:10.1109/CVPR.2017.494

Sirinukunwattana, K., Pluim, J. P. W., Chen, H., Qi, X., Heng, P.-A., Guo, Y. B., … Rajpoot, N. M. (2016). *Gland Segmentation in Colon Histology Images: The GlaS Challenge Contest*. Retrieved from https://arxiv.org/abs/1603.00275

Sung, F., Yang, Y., Zhang, L., Xiang, T., Torr, P. H. S., & Hospedales, T. M. (2017). *Learning to Compare: Relation Network for Few-Shot Learning*. Retrieved from https://arxiv.org/abs/1711.06025

Sutskever, I., Hinton, G., Krizhevsky, A., & Salakhutdinov, R. R. (2014). Dropout : A Simple Way to Prevent Neural Networks from Overfitting. *Journal of Machine Learning Research.*

Tang, X., Wang, Z., Luo, W., & Gao, S. (2018). *Face Aging with Identity-Preserved Conditional Generative Adversarial Networks.* doi:10.1109/CVPR.2018.00828

Tang, Y., Cai, J., Lu, L., Harrison, A. P., Yan, K., Xiao, J., … Summers, R. M. (2018). *CT Image Enhancement Using Stacked Generative Adversarial Networks and Transfer Learning for Lesion Segmentation Improvement.* Retrieved from https://arxiv.org/abs/1807.07144

Taylor, L., & Nitschke, G. (2019). Improving Deep Learning with Generic Data Augmentation. In *Proceedings of the 2018 IEEE Symposium Series on Computational Intelligence, SSCI 2018* (pp. 1542–1547). 10.1109/SSCI.2018.8628742

Temel, D., Kwon, G., Prabhushankar, M., & AlRegib, G. (2017). *{CURE-TSR:} Challenging Unreal and Real Environments for Traffic Sign Recognition.* Retrieved from https://arxiv.org/abs/1712.02463

UCI. (2011). *UCI Machine Learning Repository: Breast Cancer Wisconsin (Diagnostic) Data Set.* Http:// Archive.Ics.Uci.Edu/Ml/Datasets/Breast+Cancer+Wisconsin+%2528Diagnostic%2529

Valstar, M., & Pantic, M. (2010). Induced disgust, happiness and surprise: An addition to the mmi facial expression database. *Proc. Int'l Conf. Language Resources and Evaluation, Workshop EMOTION*, 65–70.

Vandenhende, S., De Brabandere, B., Neven, D., & Van Gool, L. (2019). *A Three-Player GAN: Generating Hard Samples To Improve Classification Networks.* Retrieved from https://arxiv.org/abs/1903.03496

Vinyals, O., Blundell, C., Lillicrap, T. P., Kavukcuoglu, K., & Wierstra, D. (2016). *Matching Networks for One Shot Learning.* Retrieved from https://arxiv.org/abs/1606.04080

Volpi, R., Morerio, P., Savarese, S., & Murino, V. (2018). Adversarial Feature Augmentation for Unsupervised Domain Adaptation. *Proceedings of the IEEE Computer Society Conference on Computer Vision and Pattern Recognition*, 5495–5504. 10.1109/CVPR.2018.00576

Wah, C., Branson, S., Welinder, P., Perona, P., & Belongie, S. (2011). *The Caltech-UCSD Birds-200-2011 Dataset.* Academic Press.

Wang, G., Kang, W., Wu, Q., Wang, Z., & Gao, J. (2019). Generative Adversarial Network (GAN) Based Data Augmentation for Palmprint Recognition. *2018 International Conference on Digital Image Computing: Techniques and Applications, DICTA 2018*, 1–7. 10.1109/DICTA.2018.8615782

Wang, X., Wang, K., & Lian, S. (2019). *A Survey on Face Data Augmentation.* Retrieved from https://arxiv.org/abs/1904.11685

Wang, Z., She, Q., & Ward, T. E. (2019). *Generative Adversarial Networks: A Survey and Taxonomy.* Retrieved from https://arxiv.org/abs/1906.01529

Wei, X., Gong, B., Liu, Z., Lu, W., & Wang, L. (2018). *Improving the Improved Training of Wasserstein GANs: A Consistency Term and Its Dual Effect.* Retrieved from https://arxiv.org/abs/1803.01541

Wu, E., Wu, K., Cox, D., & Lotter, W. (2018). Conditional infilling GANs for data augmentation in mammogram classification. In Lecture Notes in Computer Science (including subseries Lecture Notes in Artificial Intelligence and Lecture Notes in Bioinformatics) (Vol. 11040 LNCS, pp. 98–106). Springer Verlag. doi:10.1007/978-3-030-00946-5_11

Wu, J., Zhang, C., Xue, T., Freeman, W. T., & Tenenbaum, J. B. (2016). *Learning a Probabilistic Latent Space of Object Shapes via 3D Generative-Adversarial Modeling*. Retrieved from https://arxiv.org/abs/1610.07584

Wu, Y., Yue, Y., Tan, X., Wang, W., & Lu, T. (2018). End-To-End Chromosome Karyotyping with Data Augmentation Using GAN. *Proceedings - International Conference on Image Processing, ICIP*, 2456–2460. 10.1109/ICIP.2018.8451041

Wu, Y., Lim, J., & Yang, M. (2013). Online Object Tracking: A Benchmark. In *2013 IEEE Conference on Computer Vision and Pattern Recognition* (pp. 2411–2418). 10.1109/CVPR.2013.312

Xiang, Y., Kim, W., Chen, W., Ji, J., Choy, C., Su, H., … Savarese, S. (2016). *ObjectNet3D: A Large Scale Database for 3D Object Recognition* (Vol. 9912). doi:10.1007/978-3-319-46484-8_10

Yan, K., Wang, X., Lu, L., Zhang, L., Harrison, A. P., Bagheri, M., & Summers, R. M. (2018). Deep Lesion Graphs in the Wild: Relationship Learning and Organization of Significant Radiology Image Findings in a Diverse Large-Scale Lesion Database. *Proceedings of the IEEE Computer Society Conference on Computer Vision and Pattern Recognition*. 10.1109/CVPR.2018.00965

Yan, M., Liu, K., Guan, Z., Xu, X., Qian, X., & Bao, H. (2018). Background Augmentation Generative Adversarial Networks (BAGANs): Effective Data Generation Based on GAN-Augmented 3D Synthesizing. *Symmetry*, *10*(12), 734. doi:10.3390ym10120734

Yang, J., Liu, S., Grbic, S., Setio, A. A. A., Xu, Z., Gibson, E., … Comaniciu, D. (2018). *Class-Aware Adversarial Lung Nodule Synthesis in {CT} Images*. Retrieved from https://arxiv.org/abs/1812.11204

Yang, J., Zhao, Z., Zhang, H., & Shi, Y. (2019). Data Augmentation for X-Ray Prohibited Item Images Using Generative Adversarial Networks. *IEEE Access: Practical Innovations, Open Solutions*, *7*, 28894–28902. doi:10.1109/ACCESS.2019.2902121

Yi, D., Lei, Z., Liao, S., & Li, S. Z. (2014). *Learning Face Representation from Scratch*. Retrieved from https://arxiv.org/abs/1411.7923

Yi, X., Walia, E., & Babyn, P. (2018). *Generative Adversarial Network in Medical Imaging: A Review*. Retrieved from https://arxiv.org/abs/1809.07294

Yu, S., Tan, D., & Tan, T. (2006). A Framework for Evaluating the Effect of View Angle, Clothing and Carrying Condition on Gait Recognition. In *18th International Conference on Pattern Recognition (ICPR'06)* (Vol. 4, pp. 441–444). 10.1109/ICPR.2006.67

Zhang, H., Goodfellow, I., Metaxas, D., & Odena, A. (2018). *Self-Attention Generative Adversarial Networks*. Retrieved from https://arxiv.org/abs/1805.08318

Zhang, J., Jiao, J., Chen, M., Qu, L., Xu, X., & Yang, Q. (2016). *3D Hand Pose Tracking and Estimation Using Stereo Matching*. Retrieved from https://arxiv.org/abs/1610.07214

Zhang, R., Che, T., Grahahramani, Z., Bengio, Y., & Song, Y. (2018). MetaGAN: An Adversarial Approach to Few-Shot Learning. *Advances in Neural Information Processing Systems, 31*. Retrieved from http://papers.nips.cc/paper/7504-metagan-an-adversarial-approach-to-few-shot-learning.pdf

Zhang, X., Wang, Z., Liu, D., & Ling, Q. (2018). *DADA: Deep Adversarial Data Augmentation for Extremely Low Data Regime Classification*. Retrieved from https://arxiv.org/abs/1809.00981

Zhang, Y., Jia, G., Chen, L., Zhang, M., & Yong, J. (2019). *Self-Paced Video Data Augmentation with Dynamic Images Generated by Generative Adversarial Networks*. Academic Press.

Zhang, Z., Yang, L., & Zheng, Y. (2018). *Translating and Segmenting Multimodal Medical Volumes with Cycle- and Shape-Consistency Generative Adversarial Network*. Retrieved from https://arxiv.org/abs/1802.09655

Zhao, G., Huang, X., Taini, M., Li, S. Z., & Pietikäinen, M. (2011). Facial expression recognition from near-infrared videos. *Image and Vision Computing*, *29*(9), 607–619. doi:10.1016/j.imavis.2011.07.002

Zheng, L., Shen, L., Tian, L., Wang, S., Wang, J., & Tian, Q. (2015). Scalable Person Re-identification: A Benchmark. In *2015 IEEE International Conference on Computer Vision (ICCV)* (pp. 1116–1124). 10.1109/ICCV.2015.133

Zheng, Z., Zheng, L., & Yang, Y. (2017). Unlabeled Samples Generated by GAN Improve the Person Re-identification Baseline in Vitro. *Proceedings of the IEEE International Conference on Computer Vision*, 3774–3782. 10.1109/ICCV.2017.405

Zhong, Z., Zheng, L., Zheng, Z., Li, S., & Yang, Y. (2017). *Camera Style Adaptation for Person Re-identification*. Retrieved from https://arxiv.org/abs/1711.10295

Zhou, S., Ke, M., & Luo, P. (2019). Multi-camera transfer GAN for person re-identification. *Journal of Visual Communication and Image Representation*. doi:10.1016/j.jvcir.2019.01.029

Zhu, J. Y., Park, T., Isola, P., & Efros, A. A. (2017). Unpaired Image-to-Image Translation Using Cycle-Consistent Adversarial Networks. *Proceedings of the IEEE International Conference on Computer Vision*, 2242–2251. 10.1109/ICCV.2017.244

Zhu, Y., Aoun, M., Science, C., Krijn, M., & Vanschoren, J. (2018). Data Augmentation using Conditional Generative Adversarial Networks for Leaf Counting in Arabidopsis Plants. *Computer Vision Problems in Plant Phenotyping (CVPPP2018)*, 1–11. Retrieved from https://www.semanticscholar.org/paper/Data-Augmentation-using-Conditional-Generative-for-Zhu-Aoun/0636eb841bf3480309a346587010f43f2a87633e

Zhuang, P., Schwing, A. G., & Koyejo, S. (2019). *{FMRI} data augmentation via synthesis*. Retrieved from https://arxiv.org/abs/1907.06134

Zimmermann, C., & Brox, T. (2017). *Learning to Estimate 3D Hand Pose from Single RGB Images*. Retrieved from https://lmb.informatik.uni-freiburg.de/projects/hand3d/

Zoumpourlis, G., Doumanoglou, A., Vretos, N., & Daras, P. (2017). Non-linear convolution filters for cnn-based learning. In *Proceedings of the IEEE International Conference on Computer Vision* (pp. 4761–4769). IEEE.

ENDNOTES

[1]   https://mitos-atypia-14.grand-challenge.org

[2]   http://adni.loni.usc.edu/

[3]   CASIA Palmprint Database, http://biometrics.idealtest.org/

[4]   IIT Delhi Palmprint Image Database version 1.0, http://www4.comp.polyu.edu.hk/csajaykr/ITD/

[5]   https://www.kaggle.com/alxmamaev/flowers-recognition

[6]   Dataset real driving images.

Chapter 12
Medical 3D Graphics With eXtensible 3D

Felix G. Hamza-Lup
ⓘ https://orcid.org/0000-0002-8532-4228
Georgia Southern University, USA

Nicholas Polys
Virginia Tech, USA

Athanasios G. Malamos
Hellenic Mediterranean University, Greece

Nigel W. John
ⓘ https://orcid.org/0000-0001-5153-182X
University of Chester, UK

ABSTRACT

As the healthcare enterprise is adopting novel imaging and health-assessment technologies, we are facing unprecedented requirements in information sharing, patient empowerment, and care coordination within the system. Medical experts not only within US, but around the world should be empowered through collaboration capabilities on 3D data to enable solutions for complex medical problems that will save lives. The fast-growing number of 3D medical 'images' and their derivative information must be shared across the healthcare enterprise among stakeholders with vastly different perspectives and different needs. The demand for 3D data visualization is driving the need for increased accessibility and sharing of 3D medical image presentations, including their annotations and their animations. As patients have to make decisions about their health, empowering them with the right tools to understand a medical procedure is essential both in the decision-making process and for knowledge sharing.

DOI: 10.4018/978-1-5225-5294-9.ch012

INTRODUCTION

The 3D medical visualization field, both research and commercial, is heavily fragmented due to the lack of information sharing. As a result there is a tremendous amount of incompatibilities and duplicated efforts in fundamental methods like: volumetric rendering, registration and segmentation. The lack of cooperation capabilities also results in limited access to interpreted studies, due to multiple proprietary file formats, which restrict data sharing and collaboration. While the DICOM and HL7 ([Health Level 7], n.d.) standards are complex and capable for medical data interchange and structured reports, they do not represent the presentation state information required for interactive 3D graphics and haptic simulation. Further, proprietary file formats and software and hardware platforms are not easily accessible due to intellectual property, cost, and technical constraints.

The Blue Button Initiative ([Blue button Implementation Guide], n.d.) in the United States is a standard that facilitates patients' electronic access to their medical information, wherever it may be stored. In Europe, the United Kingdom's NHS Constitution also guarantees this right to patients. Additionally, as a multinational effort coordinated by EuroRec (European Institute for Health Records), by 2020 all European Union (EU) citizens should be able to access their online medical records anywhere in Europe. Accountable care organizations are appearing in increasing numbers, and require partnerships between healthcare organizations and providers; high levels of communication are necessary among these constituents to minimize waste, provide timely care, improve quality and reduce costs over the patient lifetime.

Enterprise scale' systems are characterized by their high availability and speed. Maintenance is a key concern as in many ways these systems determine the inertia of an organization; thus premium is placed on both their durability and extensibility. 'Web scale' systems include these requirements, but in addition they must address the challenges of distributed information, heterogeneous users, and non-linear network behavior. As the Web becomes the primary and common interface for numerous information services, we must consider the requirements, emergent properties, and access patterns for health data from laboratory to clinic.

Historically, the medical communities' IT systems have been insular, focused on providing information for their specific function, without concern for data integration or aggregation across the enterprise. Now the changes are fast as the medical enterprises realized that sharing of information within the organization significantly reduces costs and increases efficiency. Finally, in the shift of reimbursement of care from volume to value, medical enterprises are being compelled to share data among and between themselves. This has proven to be especially challenging as Electronic Health Record (EHR) systems, the main clinical data input mechanism for healthcare providers, have been slow to adopt interoperability to deliver integrated services to patients and caregivers, especially where the interoperability and security of the web and mobile devices are concerned.

Meanwhile, the web and entertainment industry has been adding more and more realism to their graphical models and rendering pipelines, including representations and computation for bones, skin and musculature, as well as physics and inverse kinematics, for their virtual characters. However, these representations are often proprietary or physiological simplifications. There are efforts underway to bring together the graphics and physiological models to deliver high-fidelity patient-specific, interactive 3D models to surgeons and trainees. In this paper we demonstrate several examples that are enabled by the interoperability of the Web3D/ISO/IEC Standard, Extensible 3D (X3D). We present the case that, given the requirements of electronic health records and care coordination, the two worlds of Web3D graphics and electronic health records are converging to live as interactive, graphical hypermedia documents in the World Wide Web architecture and ecosystem.

In the real case of long-term care and the knowledge enterprise, it is 'mission-critical' that data becomes verifiable information and that views of this information are interoperable between systems and portable across platforms. We use the term 'enterprise' broadly to describe any organization (research, clinical, industrial) where the access of diversified workers to data must be scalable and efficient (through 'Enterprise' systems); however, the results and interpretations of a patient's pathology are only valid in so much as they are reproducible; that is, able to be independently read and evaluated by different parties and stakeholders across the 'enterprise'.

REAL ISSUES WITH MEDICAL IMAGING TODAY – A COMMON SCENARIO

The use of clinical imaging modalities, especially CT, MRI, PET and ultrasound, has been steadily increasing over the last decade. The CT and MRI modalities are creating increasingly more slices of images for a given patient/case. Despite the multitude of abstractions and interfaces for interactive volume rendering, we claim a premium on the requirement for a cross-platform representation of interactive rendering parameters and the accessibility of volume rendered views by a greatest common denominator - international standards and open source toolkits. This is especially important for enterprises that require interoperability among multiple applications and units, the portability across World Wide Web devices and the durability of their volumetric presentations and environments (Polys & Wood, 2012).

Consider the following scenario: a patient receives a CT exam at a Hospital A due to a malignancy. The image is reconstructed as a 3D volume, segmented and marked-up by the radiologist (and may even have a camera animation if the exam involved for example a virtual colonoscopy). The patient pursues a second opinion and brings a copy of the studies to a specialist who practices at Hospital B, which has a different vendor than Hospital A for viewing 3D medical images. The parameters generating the mark ups and camera animations must demonstrate interoperability and perceptual equivalence, or those from the initial radiologist will be lost. This could lead to a delay of care and/or a repeat (and redundant) imaging study, as the specialist at Hospital B tries to communicate with her counterpart at Hospital A leading to increased costs and possible increased radiation exposure.

In the case of durability, we ask: "How durable is this presentation; will it be accessible in 30 - plus years?" This is not an empty rhetorical challenge - human lifetimes mostly exceed that number. Not only is this interoperability and durability an imperative requirement for providing optimal and efficient clinical care, it is also the key to scientific progress, efficient realization of government, citizen's rights and the public interests. Such scenarios are occurring every day in uncounted numbers and are unfortunately ignored.

INTERNATIONAL 3D GRAPHICS STANDARDS AND APPLICATIONS FOR MEDICAL IMAGING

Interactive 3D renderings from CT, MRI, PET, X-Ray and other imaging modalities are increasingly used to better interpret the size, orientation and other spatial relationships of the patient's anatomy and pathology as necessary for diagnosis and therapy, and in the future, training and procedural preparation.

These images, their portrayals (presentations), their derived objects, and other metadata must be part of the patient's medical record and reproducible by stakeholders throughout the healthcare enterprise. International Standards provide the formalisms and recognition that can improve data richness, sharing, and access across the lifecycle and across stakeholders.

Consider the variety of health-related 3D graphical information in addition to image stacks and volumes. For example, segmentations and surfaces of anatomical structures, optical and laser-based body scans, exercise and ergonomic captures, are all native 3D information that could be ingested and shared in an electronic health record as illustrated in Figure 1.

Figure 1. Segmented MRI fused with dermatology scan as interactive, animated X3D environment

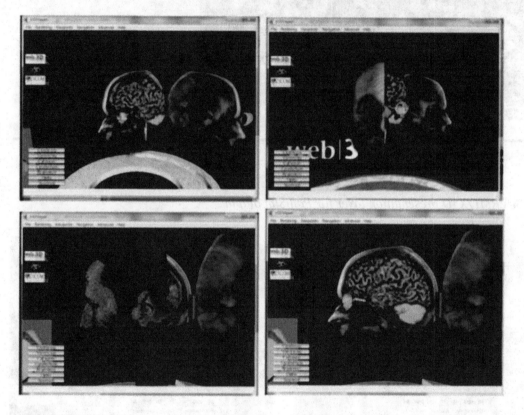

Thinking more broadly, the Standards for interactive 3D environments have seen a variety of healthcare and precision medical applications from microscopy (Figure 6) (Polys & Gurjarpadhye, 2016) and gene expressions (Marquart et al., 2017) (Figure 2) to BLAST alignment (Gardner et al., 2006) and agent-based immune system simulations (Polys et al., 2004) (Figure 3), to the physics of DNA stretching (Figure 4) (Savin et al., 2013). As our ecosystem of producers and consumers grows, a deliberate approach to common information models is required.

Figure 2. X3D HTML5 presentation for Zebrafish Genetic Neurophysiology (Interactive Volume Atlas)

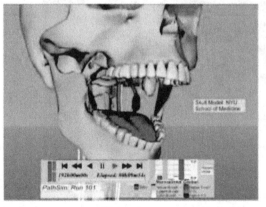

Figure 3. VRML/X3D presentation layer for PathSim output

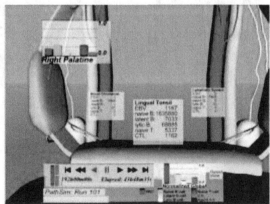

Figure 4. X3D presentation for Molecular Dynamics DNA physics Simulation in a CAVE

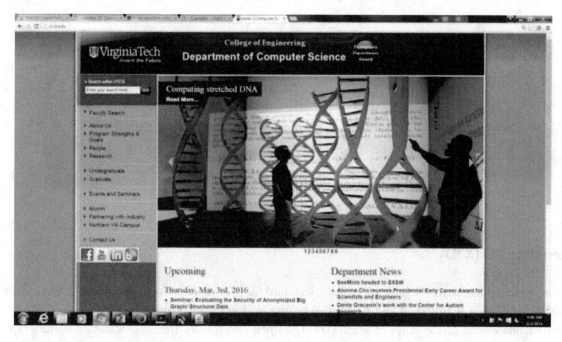

Figure 5. Spatial semantics estimated after model segmentation (Kontakis at al 2018)

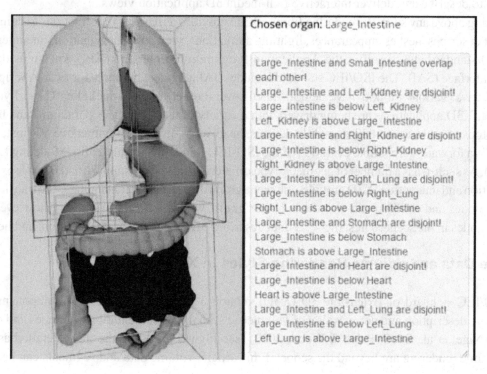

Figure 6. Example X3D volume rendering styles (Polys et al., 2013)

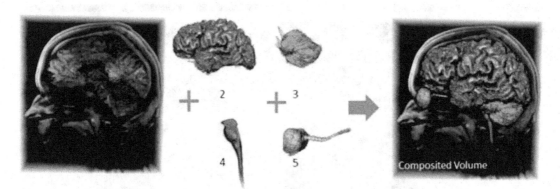

Extensible 3D (X3D)

The International Standards Organization (ISO) standard for 3D graphics over the Internet is Extensible 3D (X3D), which is maintained and developed by the Web3D Consortium (http://www.web3d.org), (Web3D Consortium, 2018; Polys et al., 2007). The open and royalty-free ISO standard scene graph has evolved through 18 years of hardware development and software boom-busts and still remains the greatest common denominator for communicating real-time interactive 3D scenes over the Web. With dozens of implementations across industries and operating systems, X3D specifies this scene graph in layers of functionality, known as 'Profiles' and several encodings, including binary, XML, UTF8, and JSON. The Extensible 3D scene graph, X3D (ISO/IEC 19775), provides an expressive and durable platform to describe and deliver interactive rich-media 3D application views.

Working above any specific rendering library, X3D provides a rich set of abstractions to compose 3D scenes; it describes meshes, appearances, lighting, animations, viewpoints, navigations and interactions. The X3D standard also specifies the Application Programming Interface (API), known as the Scene Access Interface (SAI). The ISO/IEC standard includes SAI language bindings for ECMAScript/JavaScript and Java; various toolkits have demonstrated several other bindings including C++, Python and VBScript. X3D applications are being driven with a variety of user interfaces paradigms and hardware from laptops to multi-touch tables, mobile devices, head-worn displays to immersive VR installations.

X3D is a forward-compatible evolution of the ISO-IEC standard Virtual Reality Modeling Language (VRML). As such, it has a number of geometry types, material and texture support, and flexible expression of animation and interaction. X3D provides the scene graph data structure that includes the transformation graph of nodes and children and also the behavior graph, which is the description of how events flow between nodes in the scene. Thus, the X3D data describes 3D objects, their presentation, and behaviors.

Volume Data and Volume Rendering Styles in X3D

The ISO/IEC standard of Extensible 3D (X3D) version 3.3 includes several key components which support the description and composition of volumetric scan data, segmentations, surfaces and other 3D models (Nigel et al., 2008; Polys & Wood, 2012) (see Figure 1). While the more detailed aspects of X3D volume rendering are beyond the scope of this article, volume data and segments can be 'styled', composed, and blended for interactive presentation. A lot of progress in recent years allow the adaptation of the X3D Volume rendering nodes to the Web platform and enhance their functionality based on feedback provided by the X3D and X3DOM open source communities For example the new description on the volume data node allows creation of 4D volume rendering real time visualizations as illustrated in Figure 7.

Figure 7. Proposed Scene for 4D volume visualization [OsiriX, 2018]

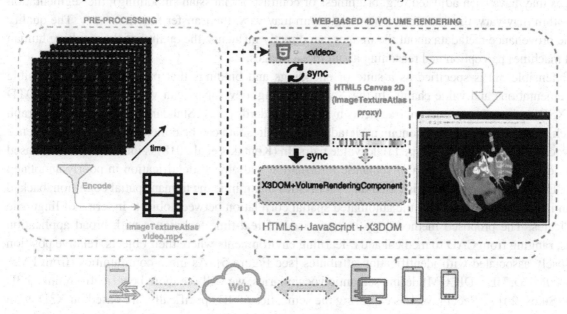

Future X3D functionalities will include: Transfer Functions, Multi Planar Reconstruction (MPR), intersection of the volume with 3D objects, clipping planes with volume data and control in the quality of the generated volume visualization (Arbelaiz et al., 2017).

Lossless Metadata in the Scene Graph

From the original design of X3D all nodes, including those used in Volume rendering, can transport metadata tags in the X3D scene graph. An X3D Metadata node can be used to store information about any node in an X3D scene graph (such as a segmentation), and is placed as a child of the node (Shape, Appearance, Geometry, etc.) that it describes. Metadata node values do not affect the visible rendering of a scene, however they are accessible to applications through the Scene Access Interface (SAI) (Web3D Consortium, 2018). Previously we have demonstrated the integration of SNOMED, FMA and the UMLS (Unified Medical Language System) with X3D objects and scenes (Nigel et al., 2008). Thus to support better search and decision making, each graphical or anatomical object can be referenced back to a knowledge base, catalog, or ontology.

The success of long-term digitally-enabled healthcare depends on the reproducibility of data and its graphical presentations and annotations across time, space and systems. However, better decision-making relies on knowledge of the quality and nature of the information that is available (its noisiness, variance, uncertainty, etc.). Metadata in the scene graph enables us to meet an additional requirement at web scale: to maintain record of the 2D and 3D image processing pipelines and presentation performed on imagery datasets (their transformation history, a.k.a. their provenance) *with the presentation.*

Let's consider a concrete example. In X3D, the source volume is not modified, but 'styled' for presentation (rendering); this might be a set of volumes or a set of segmentations within one volume. The source modality machine will have a response profile, but also at any point in the workflow the 2D images may have been adjusted (e.g. brightness or contrast or Gaussian smoothing); the segmentation algorithm may vary, the surface-meshing algorithm may vary, the transfer functions vary. The quality of the provenance metadata about the images can directly influence the quality of the resulting human (and machine) perception and reasoning about those images.

Extensible 3D is specified as a suite of encodings and bindings that provide a myriad possible implementations and value chains. In the XML encoding, developers can validate scenes with DTD and XSD tool, style, and encrypt fragments by W3C Standards (W3C Standards, n.d.). In a scene graph as rich as X3D, any node can contain a Metadata node. Metadata can be collected in sets that reference the vocabulary and specify a typed field-value pairs. In (Kontakis et al 2018) is introduced a web-based methodology for the extraction of semantic information and object identification in poorly annotated Web3D scenes. This approach is based on a set of rules that mimic the human spatial cognition, backed by an indexing mechanism for the automated spatial correlation between objects in terms of linguistic predicates. The proposed methodology is comprised of real-time techniques with broad application areas, ranging from CAD to medical and e-learning environments where their objects' relative position is closely associated with identification attributes [see Figure 5]. As more communities (from FMA to SNOMED, HL7, DICOM) define semantic vocabularies, we will see more benefits from linked 3D data (Sikos, 2017). Recent work is exploring the semantics of 3D specifically, are based on X3D, with published ontologies of 3D.

Scene Graph Interaction

For minimum conformance, sensor nodes that require interaction with the geometry (e.g. a TouchSensor in X3D) shall provide intersection information based on the volume's bounds. An implementation may optionally provide real intersection information based on performing ray casting into the volume space and reporting the first non-transparent voxel hit. Navigation and collision detection also require a minimal conformance requirement of using the bounds of the volume. In addition, implementations may allow greater precision with non-opaque voxels in a similar manner to the sensor interactions.

H3D ((Haptics 3D, n.d.) and Instant-Reality (Instant-Reality, n.d.) are two cross-platform software toolkits that support X3D 3.3 Volume rendering. The X3D scene graph provides the formal structure to unify several data types from resources and services across the Web and portray them as interactive scenes including lights, cameras, polygons, volumes animations and scripting. For application-specific user interfaces, metadata can be displayed and X3D Volume render styles (and their parameters) can be manipulated through the Scene Authoring Interface (SAI). For example, Figure 8 shows several X3D presentations of the public multi-channel microscopy slices in the online Cell Image Library (Cell Image Library, n.d.).

Figure 8. Cell Image Library data (multi-channel microscopy) presented with X3D VolumeRender styles; segmented by channel for volume rendering (left) and with isosurface style (right)

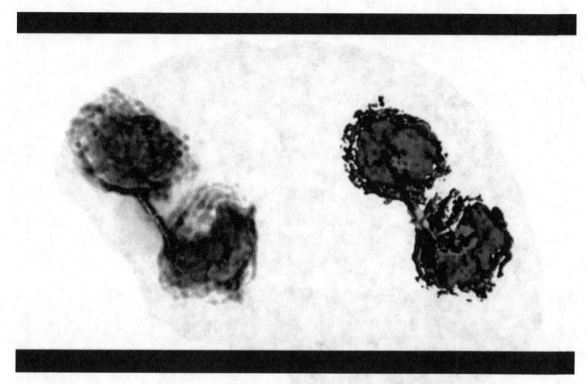

MED X3DOM

X3D provides the basis of interoperability for interactive 3D and 4D presentations, allowing them to break out of the hospital Picture and Archiving Communication System (PACS), be archived and shared across the enterprise and across the spectrum and lifespan of care. Most recently, this convergence has occurred between HTML5 applications and WebGL - enabled volume rendering. MED X3DOM is an open-source work-in-progress contributed by Vicomtech-IK4 to support Extensible 3D (X3D) volume rendering methods on the Web without the use of plug-ins or special installations. It is implemented as a component for the X3DOM (X3 Document Object Model, n.d.) framework, currently led by Fraunhofer IGD (Behr, et al., 2009). MED X3DOM is based on standardized web based technologies (X3D, JavaScript, WebGL and HTML5) enabling the visualization within any WebGL - powered browser on a wide range of devices: off-the-shelf computers, tablets and smart phones.

Figure 9. MRI volume in X3DOM/HTML5

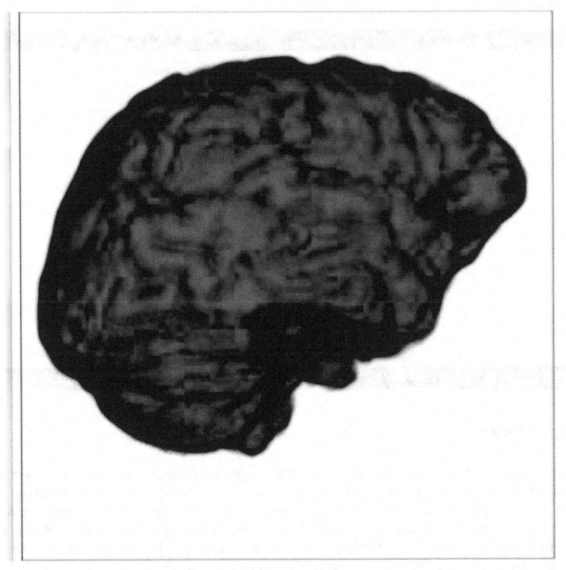

From the first developments shown at Web3D 2011 and SIGGRAPH 2012 (Congote, 2012; Congote et al., 2011) the implementation of MED X3DOM has been improved towards the compliance with the Extensible 3D (X3D) version 3.3. In the current implementation, any volume data provided as an ImageTextureAtlas (slices of the volume data tiled on a single image on a matrix configuration) can be loaded and visualized in the scene. Thus volume data can be rotated and inspected and styled interactively within any HTML5 client browser in real-time as illustrated in Figure 9. As the rendering is currently performed in the client browser, MED X3DOM is a scalable and cross-platform approach to share 3D medical imaging and 3D health information. By building for the Web as the platform, MED X3DOM enables greater access to imaging information for patients and caregivers at the World Wide "Web scale".

APPLICATIONS

X3D applications across the medical field range from visualization to procedural simulations and training tools for students and medical personnel. In the following section we present some of the latest research and innovation demonstrating the potential of X3D and associated APIs in developing clinical tools to provide higher quality and cost-efficient care.

NIH 3D Print Exchange

With an International Standard as the greatest common denominator for a multitude of data pipelines and types (Morse et al., 2011) there are clear advantages for governmental agencies are adopting the open format in their enterprise. When creating a community resource for Web users and makers, the NIH created the 3DPrint Exchange. Noting the deficiencies of industry formats (STL - no color; obj - no metadata or extensibility; fbx - changes every year by proprietary agendas), the developers chose a Coakley et al., 2014) prosthetics to molecules to heart and centrifuge parts, the NIH 3D Print Exchange creates a common platform for 3D data exchange and printing with ISO-IEC VRML and X3D (As 3D printing products such as CURA, NetFabb, and Shapeways have added X3D support, the sharing of 3D is even more seamless between bit, atom, and extensible reality.

Radiation (X-Ray/Proton) Therapy Simulation/Training

Radiation therapy is a proven, effective and widely accepted form of treatment for many types of cancer. External beam radiation therapy in the form of X-Ray and Proton therapy is an effective way for destroying the cancer cells reproductive capacity. Approximately 90% of patients treated with radiation in the United States receive external beam radiation either as X-Ray Therapy (XRT) or more recently as Proton Therapy (PT).

Unfortunately, both types of treatment planning systems (XRT, PT) have limited or no visual aid that combines a patient boundary representation (i.e. body shell) with the room view to provide a detailed understanding of potential collisions before the actual therapy begins. While partial patient-specific Computed Tomography (CT) is available, in general a full body CT scan is not possible due to the extra radiation dose to the patient. Therefore, treatment planners often find it difficult to determine precise treatment equipment setup parameters. In some cases, patient treatment is delayed or postponed due to unforeseen collisions between different parts of the treatment systems and the patient. In addition, the demand for better cancer targeting has created specific immobilization and on-board imaging devices, which can become additional collision sources.

An early prototype of an X3D Web-based simulator was developed in 2006 (Hamza-Lup et al., 2006) to pre-test for collision scenarios in XRT procedures (Figure 9 top). The simulator facilitates the development of an optimal, patient-specific treatment plan and also provides a safe training environment and the capability to educate patients about the procedure. Recent developments on the simulator involve simulation accuracy tests, the introduction of patient specific CT data, as well as novel boundary representations (Hamza-Lup et al., 2007a; Hamza-Lup et al., 2007b; Hamza-Lup et al., 2008) illustrated in Figure 10 bottom. A novel module for Proton Therapy simulation is under development (Hamza-Lup et al., 2015).

Figure 10. top: X3D simulation of X-Ray therapy; bottom: Patient CT data and real-time boundary representation for the 3DRTT simulator

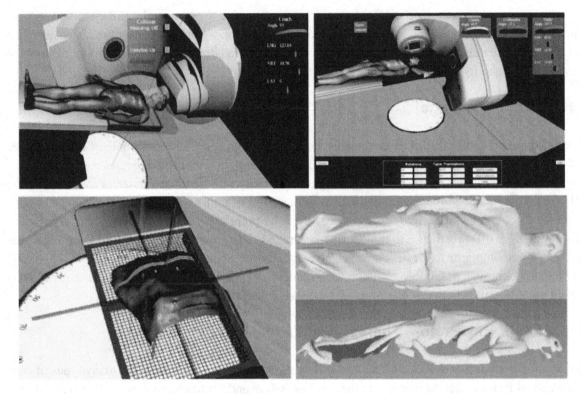

3D Medical Training with Tactile Feedback

Haptic technology applications are spreading rapidly in several fields due to the lower cost of haptic hardware devices. Specifically in medical training and education recent advancements have significantly reduced the cost of haptic hardware. H3D is an open source API for force-feedback (haptic) software development. The API uses the open standards OpenGL and X3D adding haptics capabilities in one unified scene. H3D (Haptics 3D, n.d.) is cross-platform and device-independent; it is released under the GNU GPL license, with options for commercial licensing. It includes audio integration as well as stereography for advanced and consumer displays. Most importantly in the context of this paper, H3D combines those features with X3D's volume rendering. For example, the Best Paper award at IEEE VR 2012 demonstrated successful application of haptics to medical training for realistic palpation procedures (Ullrich & Kuhlen, 2012).

Eye Surgery Training and Simulation

HelpMeSee is a global campaign to cure cataract blindness for the 22 million people currently suffering from this treatable disease. HelpMeSee's unique model combines best-in-class surgical partners, convergence and effective use of technology, and best practices to eliminate blindness caused by cataracts globally over the next 20 years. This H3D simulator is developed by Moog, SenseGraphics and InSimo (Bello et al., 2009) (Figure 11 left) for medical personnel training in eye surgery. It combines haptic devices, physical-based soft tissue simulation with Simulation Open Framework Architecture (SOFA) (Simulation Open Framework Architecture, n.d.) and realistic X3D models with GLSL shaders rendered in H3D. The models were created with the open source modeling software Blender (Blender n.d.). The official Blender X3D exporter has been extended to support X3D export including GLSL shaders, tessellation shaders and Humanoid-Animation (H-Anim) hierarchies and structures.

Figure 11. left: HelpMeSee – Eye Surgery simulator; right: X3D simulation with haptics for ultrasound-guided needle puncture

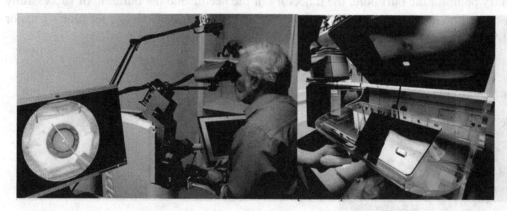

[PUB-1]

Needle Puncture Simulation

X3D and H3D were also successfully used in the ImaGiNe-S: Imaging Guided Needle Simulation – see Figure 11 right. This is a high fidelity simulation of ultrasound guided needle puncture that uses patient specific data to enable interventional radiology trainees to learn different visceral access procedures. The input data required is a computed tomography scan of the patient that is used to create 3D anatomy models. Force measurements have been made on real tissue and the resulting data is incorporated into the simulator. Respiration and soft tissue deformations are also carried out. The trainee interacts with the virtual patient using two force feedback joysticks - one for the ultrasound transducer and one for the needle. The ultrasound images are displayed on a second monitor.

Construct and content validation studies were carried out and indicated that this system is effective for training procedures such as nephrostomy (which involves needle puncture into a kidney). Some of the ideas used in ImaGiNe-S were later extended to create PalpSim, (Coles et al., 2011) the world's first augmented reality haptics surgical simulator, which integrates new technologies that we believe will be important for X3D to support in the future. PalpSim teaches palpation and needle puncture into blood vessels.

Mobile Learning

A great deal of medical education material is available for Web-based access or mobile devices such as tablet computers and smartphones. However, there is again a lack of standards in this broad area, particularly if interactive 3D computer graphics is being used within these educational materials. We have previously explored the impact of Web 3D technologies in this context (John, 2007) and have used classic VRML (the ISO forerunner of X3D) to produce web-based surgical training tools, for example ventricular catheterization for neurosurgeons - Figure 12 left. We have also implemented the same training tool for a tablet platform (Cenydd et al., 2012) - Figure 11 right.

These mobile learning tools may only offer a low fidelity user interface, for example the tablet relies on the iPad's finger gesture interface, but they are effective for certain skills. In a recent controlled study we found a statistically significant improvement in performance after using the tablet app in selecting the optimum entry point for the burr hole, the trajectory of the needle and the duration of successfully completing the procedure. Further, such tools are available at any time and from any location - a major benefit for both students and trainees.

Figure 12. Ventricular catheterization training tool. Left: VRML version. Right: Tablet version

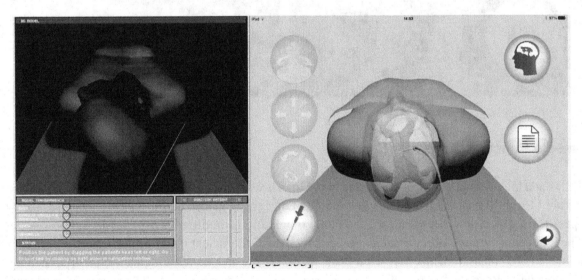

CONCLUSION AND FUTURE WORK

Extensible 3D (X3D) has proven to be a robust, extensible presentation and archival standard to improve the interactive visual access to volume and medical image data, clinical ontologies, simulations and training scenarios. Focusing on X3D Volume rendering tool support, conformance and extension can bring the full power of X3D to bear, improving healthcare efficiency and outcomes. The latest addition to the X3D standard enables volume rendering and X3D content to be displayed on any HTML5/WebGL enabled browser, making plugin-less 3D on the web a reality, and eliminating the highest barrier to its widespread adoption. For example, the creation of open workflows and delivery to mobile HTML5 clients for interactive presentation of medical imaging data will stimulate innovation and lower the barrier to entry for clinicians, students and the layperson alike.

As is evidenced by the variety of data sources and applications in this paper and the literature, the X3D ISO standard has more far reaching effects in that the imaging data is used not only for diagnosis and treatment, but also as content in physiological and surgical simulators supporting personalized medicine. The surgical simulation field has traditionally been a mosaic of parallel efforts that produce cutting edge simulations of specific organ systems, specific organs or general tissue dynamics that are isolated products that cannot communicate with each other. To align these efforts so that the 'best of breed' organ or system-specific models can be brought together and we can begin to realize a truly computational representation of a human being, standards such as X3D for 3D presentation of medical imaging data must be adopted. Additional extensions for standard haptics will enable simulators to conform to approved specifications and allow more valid comparisons between them when attempting to judge their fidelity, efficiency and utility.

The concept of sensors and event routing to fields in X3D allows for a very flexible implementation of interaction with a growing range of displays and input devices. The open source implementation H3D, with its API based on X3D, is also a prominent example with medical simulators, featuring complex interaction schemes quickly prototyped in Python and then implemented as C++ custom nodes. H3D can be run in stereo and integrated with a number of commercially available haptic devices. As consumer VR platforms (such as 3D TVs. game consoles, the Kinect and Leap controllers, Oculus and Sony head-mounted displays) become more widespread, we expect a continued explosion in the variety of web-connected hardware platforms sharing X3D assets and views.

The continuous improvement of 3D visualization hardware will make it increasingly feasible to store, transmit and present larger volume datasets, but it also brings out new scientific questions about data streaming and out-of-core volume rendering methods. Streaming 3D content to leverage server-side processing and mobile devices is also being explored. In future work, the X3D standard will be extended to further interaction concepts such as advanced haptic rendering and soft tissue response, for example (Ullrich et al, 2011). MEDX3DOM will focus on the compliance with the Extensible 3D (X3D) features (versions 3.4 and 4.0) for HTML5 delivery of volume presentations, possibly proposing the standardization of the ImageTextureAtlas node. The Web3D Consortium and its Working Groups welcome further research and development to address the challenges in interaction design and paths to support and standardize new interaction methods, means and metaphors for medical multimedia via Extensible 3D (X3D), HL7, and DICOM.

ACKNOWLEDGMENT

We would like to acknowledge Ander Arbelaiz, Abhijit Gurjarpadhye and Sebastian Ullrich for their ideas and collaboration on several projects related to X3D and H3D.

REFERENCES

W3C Standards. (n.d.). Retrieved from https://www.w3.org/standards

H3D. (n.d.). Retrieved from http://www.h3dapi.org

X3DOM. (n.d.). Retrieved from https://www.x3dom.org

Arbelaiz, A., Moreno, A., Kabongo, L., Polys, N., & García-Alonso, A. (2017). Community-driven extensions to the X3D volume rendering component. In *Proceedings of the 22nd International Conference on 3D Web Technology* (p. 1). ACM. 10.1145/3055624.3075945

Behr, J., Eschler, P., Jung, Y., & Zöllner, M. (2009). X3DOM: a DOM-based HTML5/X3D integration model. *Proceedings of the 14th International Conference on 3D Web Technology*, 127-135. 10.1145/1559764.1559784

Bello, F., Bulpitt, A., Gould, D. A., Holbrey, R., Hunt, C., How, T., . . . Zhang, Y. (2009). ImaGiNe-S: Imaging Guided Needle Simulation. *In Eurographics 2009, Medical Prize*, (pp. 5-8). Blender. Retrieved from https://www.blender.org

Blue Button. (n.d.). *Blue button Implementation Guide*. Retrieved from https://bluebutton.cms.gov/assets/ig/index.html

Cell Image Library. (n.d.). Retrieved from http://www.cellimagelibrary.org/home

Cenydd, L., John, N. W., Phillips N. I., & Gray, W. P. (2012). VCath: a tablet-based neurosurgery training tool. *Studies in Health Technology and Informatics, 184*, 20-23.

Coakley, M. F., Hurt, D. E., Weber, N., Mtingwa, M., Fincher, E. C., Alekseyev, V. & Yoo, T. S. (2014). The NIH 3D print exchange: a public resource for bioscientific and biomedical 3D prints. *3D Printing and Additive Manufacturing, 1*(3), 137-140.

Coles, T. R., John, N. W., Gould, D. A., & Caldwell, D. G. (2011). Integrating haptics with augmented reality in a femoral palpation and needle insertion training simulation. *Haptics. IEEE Transactions, 3*(4), 199–209. doi:10.1109/TOH.2011.32 PMID:26963487

Congote, J. (2012). MedX3DOM: MedX3D for X3DOM. *Proceedings of the 17th International Conference on 3D Web Technology*, 179.

Congote, J., Segura, A., Kabongo, L., Moreno, A., Posada, J., & Ruiz, O. (2011). Interactive visualization of volumetric data with webgl in real-time. *Proceedings of the 16th International Conference on 3D Web Technology*, 137-146. 10.1145/2010425.2010449

Gardner, M. K., Feng, W. C., Archuleta, J., Lin, H., & Ma, X. (2006). Parallel genomic sequence-searching on an ad-hoc grid: experiences, lessons learned, and implications. In *SC 2006 Conference, Proceedings of the ACM/IEEE* (pp. 22-22). ACM.

HL7. (n.d.). Retrieved from http://www.hl7.org/implement/standards

Hamza-Lup, F. G., Davis, L., & Zeidan, O. (2006). Web-based 3D planning tool for radiation therapy treatment. *Proceedings of the 11th international conference on 3D web technology, 1,* 59-162. 10.1145/1122591.1122613

Hamza-Lup, F. G., Farrar, S., & Leon, E. (2015) Patient specific 3D surfaces for interactive medical planning and training. In *Proceedings of the 20th International Conference on 3D Web Technology (Web3D '15).* ACM. 10.1145/2775292.2775294

Hamza-Lup, F. G., Sopin, I., & Zeidan, O. (2007a). Comprehensive 3D visual simulation for radiation therapy planning. *Studies in Health Technology and Informatics, 125,* 164–166.

Hamza-Lup, F. G., Sopin, I., & Zeidan O. (2007b). Towards 3D web-based simulation and training systems for radiation oncology. *ADVANCE for Imaging and Oncology Administrators,* 64-68.

Hamza-Lup, F. G., Sopin, I., & Zeidan, O. (2008). Online external beam radiation treatment simulator. *International Journal of Computer Assisted Radiology and Surgery, 3*(3-4), 275–281. doi:10.100711548-008-0232-7

Instant-Reality. (n.d.). Retrieved from http://www.instantreality.org

John, N. W. (2007). The impact of Web3D technologies on medical education and training. *Computers & Education, 1*(49), 19–31. doi:10.1016/j.compedu.2005.06.003

John, N. W., Aratow, M., Couch, J., Evestedt, D., Hudson, A. D., Polys, N. F., ... Wang, Q. (2008). MedX3D: standards enabled desktop medical 3D. *Studies in Health Technology and Informatics, 132,* 189–194.

Kontakis, K., Malamos, A. G., Steiakaki, M., Panagiotakis, S., & Ware, J. A. (2018). Object identification based on the automated extraction of spatial semantics from web3d scenes. *Annals of Emerging Technologies in Computing, 2*(4), 1–10. doi:10.33166/AETiC.2018.04.001

Marquart, G. D., Tabor, K. M., Horstick, E. J., Brown, M., Geoca, A. K., Polys, N. F., ... Burgess, H. A. (2017, August 1). High-precision registration between zebrafish brain atlases using symmetric diffeomorphic normalization. *GigaScience, 6*(8), gix056. doi:10.1093/gigascience/gix056 PMID:28873968

Morse, K. L., Brunton, R., & Schloman, J. (2011). *X3D - 3D manmade feature common data storage format. Fall Simulation Interoperability Workshop, Orlando,* FL.

Polys, N. F., Bowman, D. A., North, C., Laubenbacher, R., & Duca, K. (2004). PathSim visualizer: an Information-Rich Virtual Environment framework for systems biology. *Proceedings of the ninth international conference on 3D Web technology,* 7-14. 10.1145/985040.985042

Polys, N. F., Brutzman, D. P., Steed, A., & Behr, J. (2008). Future Standards for Immersive VR: Report on the IEEE Virtual Reality 2007 Workshop. *IEEE Computer Graphics and Applications, 28*(2), 94–99. doi:10.1109/MCG.2008.29 PMID:18350937

Polys, N. F., & Gurjarpadhye, A. A. (2016). Tradeoffs in multi-channel microscopy volume visualization: an initial evaluation. In *Proceedings of the 21st International Conference on Web3D Technology.* ACM. 10.1145/2945292.2945323

Polys, N. F., Ullrich, S., Evestedt, D., & Wood, A. D. (2013). A fresh look at immersive Volume Rendering: Challenges and capabilities. *IEEE VR Workshop on Volume Rendering*.

Polys, N. F., & Wood, A. (2012). New platforms for health hypermedia. *Issues in Information Systems*, *1*(13), 40–50.

Savin, A. V., Kikot, I. P., Mazo, M. A., & Onufriev, A. V. (2013). Two-phase stretching of molecular chains. *Proceedings of the National Academy of Sciences of the United States of America*, *110*(8), 2816–2821. doi:10.1073/pnas.1218677110 PMID:23378631

Sikos, L. (2017). F. A novel ontology for 3D semantics: Ontology-based 3D model indexing and content-based video retrieval applied to the medical domain. *International Journal of Metadata, Semantics and Ontologies*, *12*(1), 59. doi:10.1504/IJMSO.2017.087702

SOFA. (n.d.). Retrieved from https://www.sofa-framework.org/

Ullrich, S., & Kuhlen, T. (2012). Haptic palpation for medical simulation in virtual environments. *IEEE Transactions on Visualization and Computer Graphics*, *18*(4), 617–625. doi:10.1109/TVCG.2012.46 PMID:22402689

Ullrich, S., Kuhlen, T., Polys, N. F., Evestedt, D., Aratow, M., & John, N. W. (2011). Quantizing the Void: Extending Web3D for Space-Filling Haptic Meshes. *Medicine Meets Virtual Reality*, (163), 670-676.

Web3D Consortium. (2018). *Extensible 3D (X3D), ISO/IEC 19775-1:2008*. Retrieved from https://www.web3d.org/documents/specifications/19775-1/V3.2

Chapter 13
Visualization and Analysis of 3D Images Using Data Mining Approaches

Parimala Boobalan
Vellore Institute of Technology, India

ABSTRACT

With the recent advancements in supercomputer technologies, large-scale, high-precision, and realistic model 3D simulations have been dominant in the field of solar-terrestrial physics, virtual reality, and health. Since 3D numeric data generated through simulation contain more valuable information than available in the past, innovative techniques for efficiently extracting such useful information are being required. One such technique is visualization—the process of turning phenomena, events, or relations not directly visible to the human eye into a visible form. Visualizing numeric data generated by observation equipment, simulations, and other means is an effective way of gaining intuitive insight into an overall picture of the data of interest. Meanwhile, data mining is known as the art of extracting valuable information from a large amount of data relative to finance, marketing, the internet, and natural sciences, and enhancing that information to knowledge.

INTRODUCTION

The advent of innovative 3D technology and accruing sales of 3D consumer electronics, has accompanied an increase in demands of more and more 3D technology. This has led to wide interest in conversion of the already existing two-dimensional (2D) contents to three-dimensional (3D) contents in the field of image processing. This is a great issue in emerging 3D applications because the conventional 2D content do not provide the depth information which is required for the 3D displays. So 3D displays enhance visual quality more than two-dimensional (2D) displays.

The 2D to 3D conversion adds the binocular disparity depth indication or cue to the digital images perceived by the human brain. Therefore, if it is done appropriately, it significantly improves the immersive effect while one is viewing this stereo video in comparison to the original 2D video. However,

DOI: 10.4018/978-1-5225-5294-9.ch013

in order to be successful, this conversion needs to be done with sufficient accuracy and correctness, that is, the quality of the original 2D images should not deteriorate, and also the introduced disparity cue should not contradict to the other cues used for depth perception by the human brain. If this is done properly and thoroughly, the conversion produces stereo video of similar quality to "native" stereo video which is shot in stereo and accurately aligned and adjusted in post-production.

It has been found that the manual conversion of 2D - 3D image have been the most effective but then again are costly in terms of time. Many automatic conversion techniques have thus been proposed but each of these techniques consider assumptions that are not met in the real world.

The main difference between 2D and 3D images is clearly the presence of depth in 3D images which makes calculation of depth the most important factor during conversion of images from 2D to 3D. Several methods have been proposed for the same. Out of these we shall study mainly two methods. First, calculating the depth using the edge information of the existing 2D image and second, depth map evaluation by kNN based learning from training set of images. To compare these two methods, we use the generation of a depth map. A depth map is an image or image channel that contains information relating to the distance of the surfaces of scene objects from a viewpoint.

Data mining is defined as "extracting nonself-evident information from data". Included among the various analysis techniques available to suit specific data characteristics and objectives are pattern extraction, regression analyses, class separation and clustering. Another such technique is visual data mining intended to provide cutting-edge visualization to large volumes of data that are difficult to understand when visualized in a simple manner, thereby allowing heuristic analysis

Techniques aimed at analysis data in a 2D plane, such as wavelet analyses and pattern recognition, are commonly known means of applying visual data mining to numerical simulation data in the fields of natural sciences. Conversely, visualization and data mining techniques that target data in a 3D space have yet to be established regarding the extraction of information from 3D data. We have thus pursued visual data mining techniques capable of extracting information from 3D data and 3D time-varying data, and analyzing it heuristically. In this paper, we introduce various techniques for visual data mining for 3D time-varying data generated from 3D simulations for solar-terrestrial physics, and related applications.

Conversion of 2D to 3D Images

Calculating the depth using the edge information and second, depth map evaluation by kNN based learning. Using examples and with parameters, we compare these techniques to find out the optimum approach for conversion of 2D images to 3D images by introducing depth in the latter. Depth generation algorithms for 2D to 3D conversions face two major challenges. First is the depth uniformity inside the same object in the image. Because the image consists of 2D pixel arrays, information about the object grouping relation of pixels is lacking. A better grouping of pixels implies a better outcome for the depth uniformity inside the object. An effective grouping method should consider both color similarity and spatial distance. The other challenge involves figuring out an appropriate depth relationship among all the objects in an image.

To overcome these two challenges, algorithm can be designed that uses a simple depth hypothesis to assign the depth of each group rather than retrieving the depth value directly from the depth cue. Firstly, an effective grouping method is chosen which involves grouping pixels that have similar colours and spatial locality. Now the depth values are assigned according to the hypothesis depth value. To enhance the visual comfort, a cross bilateral filter can be applied.

Recently, mining techniques based on image parsing have been used for estimating the depth map from single monocular images. Such methods can generate depth maps for any 2D visual material, but currently work on only few types of images using carefully selected training data is done. The proposed approach is a simplified algorithm that "mines" the scene depth from a large repository of image and depth pairs and is computationally more efficient than the other algorithms.

Depth evaluation by learning from examples proposes a simplified data-driven 2D-to-3D conversion method and has objectively validated its performance against state-of-the-art Make3D algorithm. This algorithm compares favourably in terms of estimated depth quality as well as computational complexity. Admittedly, the validation was limited to a database of indoor scenes captured by Kinect camera. The generated anaglyph images produce a comfortable 3D perception but they are also not completely void of distortions. With the continuously accruing amount of 3D data online and rapidly growing computing power in the cloud, the proposed algorithm looks like a promising alternative to an operator assisted 2D to 3D conversion.

Depth evaluation using edge information has presented a novel 2D to 3D (Figure 1) conversion algorithm. The recent algorithms utilizes edge information to group the image into coherent regions. A simple depth hypothesis is adopted to assign the depth for each region and a cross bilateral filter is consequently applied to remove the blocky artifacts. Traditional algorithm is quality-scalable depending on the block size. Smaller block size results in better depth detail whereas larger block size has lower computational complexity. Capable of generating a comfortable 3D effect, the algorithm is highly promising for 2D-to-3D conversion in 3D applications. Depth evaluation by learning from examples proposes a simplified data-driven 2D-to-3D conversion method and has objectively validated its performance against state-of-the-art Make3D algorithm. This algorithm compares favourably in terms of estimated depth quality as well as computational complexity. Admittedly, the validation was limited to a database of indoor scenes captured by Kinect camera. The generated anaglyph images produce a comfortable 3D perception but they are also not completely void of distortions. With the continuously accruing amount of 3D data online and rapidly growing computing power in the cloud, the algorithm looks like a promising alternative to an operator assisted 2D to 3D conversion.

Depth evaluation using edge information has presented a novel 2D to 3D conversion algorithm. These algorithms utilizes edge information to group the image into coherent regions. A simple depth hypothesis is adopted to assign the depth for each region and a cross bilateral filter is consequently applied to remove the blocky artifacts. The algorithm is quality-scalable depending on the block size. Smaller block size results in better depth detail whereas larger block size has lower computational complexity. Capable of generating a comfortable 3D effect, the proposed algorithm is highly promising for 2D-to-3D conversion in 3D applications.

3D image in Virtual Reality

With the recent development of supercomputers, large scale 3D space plasma simulations to study electromagnetic environments have become practicable. We obtain a variety of 3D phenomena and configurations from 3D numerical simulations. To analyze 3D numerical simulation data has a great importance on the understanding of Earth's magnetospheric dynamics. However,it is difficult to analyze and understand 3D complex plasma phenomena or configurations. In particular, since magnetic field line's topology is strongly dependent on temporal and spatial change, it is not easy to understand time-dependent 3D configurations. Various types of 3D visualization and Visual Data Mining(VDM) techniques to analyze the time dependent change of magnetic field line's topology more effectively and efficiently are discussed.

Figure 1. Conversion of 2D to 3D Images

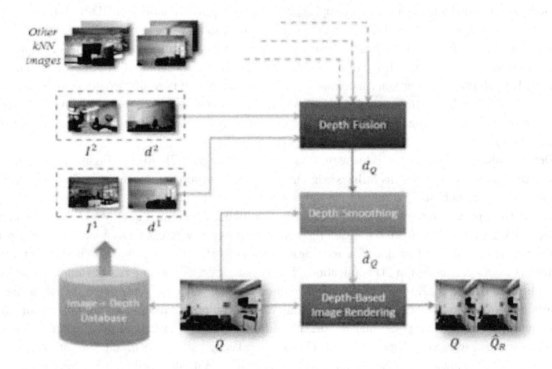

Visual data mining is a process dedicated to discovering scientific knowledge of interest from numeric data. Figure 2 shows the general flow of knowledge discovery, including data mining. The researcher selects the data to be analyzed, and then preprocesses, transforms or otherwise manipulates that data as needed. Then the researcher performs data mining on the data to evaluate the results. This sequence of processes is repeated based on the evaluation results to ultimately enhance the data to knowledge. In the knowledge discovery process, a key to discovering better knowledge is being able to feed back the results of evaluations conducted by humans and any known information to the knowledge discovery process with greater ease and in a more interactive manner.

The researcher selects time steps, physical components and other elements as the objects of analysis from numerical data, and then filters the data as needed, such as by reduction. Next, filtered discrete data in 3D space is transformed into geometric data, such as isosurfaces and stream lines. Since this geometric data is 3D data, it is rendered to generate image data with an eye direction and eye position being set. The analysis process may be pursued interactively with the eye position and visualization technique being modified, and data selection repeated as needed. Because the visualization dataflow model (Figure 3) is similar to an intellectual discovery process, the data mining process used in the intellectual discovery process is replaced by visualization.

Figure 2. Knowledge Discovery process

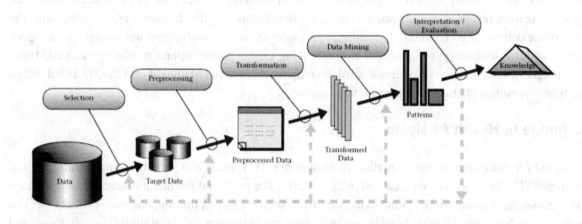

In the visual data mining process, human interactions occur between the understanding and feedback of results. More specifically, these interactions include a visual perception of the visualization results, the selection of physical components, parameters, regions, visualization techniques, eye position and more. Flat displays, mouse devices, keyboards and other equipment have traditionally been used as computer interfaces for these operations. It is difficult, however, to output stereo video or input 3D positions with such interfaces.

Figure 3. Visualizations Data Flow model

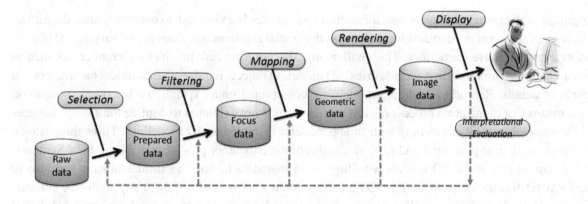

Typical applications of visual data mining aided by the use of various 3D visualization techniques with reference to magnetic flux rope - a complex magnetic structure observed in the magnetosphere is used. We gained insight into 3D structures, particularly with the aid of the 3D I/O interfaces of CAVE and PHANToM, and also achieved highly interactive visualization processing performance. Moreover, the visualization results were subjected to imaging operations to cut calculation costs, along with the batch processing of large volumes of visualization results to analyze spatiotemporal changes with higher precision. 3D visualization of separatrix surfaces using super spatiotemporal resolution data and time-trace magnetic field lines, with a view toward developing more detailed insight into the 3D distributions and time-dependent changes in magnetic field topology.

3D Image in Health Analysis

A method for automatic 3D segmentation of human brain CT scans using data mining techniques was developed. The brain scans are processed in 2D and 3D. The proposed method has several steps – image pre-processing, segmentation, feature extraction from segments, data mining, and post-processing. The method introduced implemented in 3D image processing extension for the RapidMiner platform, and both are provided as open source. With testing data the resultant performance selection of tissue slices from the brain image was 98.08% when compared to human expert results.

The selection of brain tissue is a challenging task because it is difficult to distinguish neural tissue from other neighbouring structures. Segmentation is often very important for the evaluation of medical treatment and its success for some diseases, e.g. for expressing the ratio between brain volume and the affected part of the brain. For an expert measuring brain volume is a relatively trivial but time consumption task. Recently in research, it introduces automatic human brain segmentation and selection from Computer Tomography (CT) scans. This method is based on data-mining principles. 438 CT slices were used for training and the trained model was tested on 262 slices. Extracted brain image represented by voxels can be used to measure and monitor the brain volume in time or for other medical purposes. The visualized 3D model can also help a surgeon to perform an operation more accurately.

4D and 5D Modelling

Digitizing and creating digital models for archaeological sites is a vital task to preserve cultural heritage. There is an emergent need to develop and assess the spatial and temporal diversity of varying 3D objects under a cost effective framework. This challenging 3D capturing task involves different actors such as researchers, curators and creative industries. 3D modeling objects requires digital model parameters and levels of details. Recently, 3D digital models are constructed under spatial and temporal framework. This means that digitization process of common surfaces is not exploited to digitize the similar surfaces of the same objects. 3D modelling with time parameter is treated as 4D modelling. Three dimensional geometry with time parameter and Line of details combine together provides the 5D models. Semantic enhancement allows the 5D models with high level metadata to link the similar objects and also to perform 3D digitization process. The 5D modelling framework is used widely in improving the automation and cost-effectiveness of 3D capturing of objects. There are five steps involved in the 5D digital model. First step deals with the visual representation such as color/texture of objects. The second step is to categorize the shape related object properties. The third step is the Line of Details that allows the scalable representation of 3D objects. Final step is the spatio-temporal analysis where temporal change in objects are created. So, this modelling is good in detecting object degradation through time due to environmental factors, structural problems and defects and potential failures.

CONCLUSION

Visualization and analysis methods are critical for understanding and using 3D microscopic images for various cell biology, structural biology, neurosciences, and systems biology applications. These tools become indispensable for the ever- increasing need to screen tens of gigabytes to many terabytes of microscopic images. Pipelining these tools and other data analysis/mining methods is a new trend for producing interesting biology.

REFERENCES

Doulamis, A., Doulamis, N., Ioannidis, C., Chrysouli, C., Grammalidis, N., Dimitropoulos, K., ... Ioannides, M. (2015). 5D Modelling: An Efficient Approach for creating spatiotemporal predictive 3D maps of Large scale cultural resources. *ISPRS Annals of Photogrammetry, Remote Sensing & Spatial Information Sciences*, 2.

Doulamis, A., Ioannides, M., Doulamis, N., Hadjiprocopis, A., Fritsch, D., Balet, O., ... Johnsons, P. S. (2013, August). 4D reconstruction of the past. In *First International Conference on Remote Sensing and Geoinformation of the Environment (RSCy2013)* (Vol. 8795, p. 87950J). International Society for Optics and Photonics. 10.1117/12.2029010

Doulamis, A., Soile, S., Doulamis, N., Chrisouli, C., Grammalidis, N., Dimitropoulos, K., ... Ioannidis, C. (2015, June). Selective 4D modelling framework for spatial-temporal land information management system. In *Third International Conference on Remote Sensing and Geoinformation of the Environment (RSCy2015)* (Vol. 9535, p. 953506). International Society for Optics and Photonics. 10.1117/12.2193464

Ganatra, Z., Chavda, R., & D'mello, L. (2014). *Conversion of 2D Images to 3D Using Data Mining Algorithm*. Academic Press.

Kyriakaki, G., Doulamis, A., Doulamis, N., Ioannides, M., Makantasis, K., Protopapadakis, E., ... Weinlinger, G. (2014). 4D reconstruction of tangible cultural heritage objects from web-retrieved images. *International Journal of Heritage in the Digital Era*, *3*(2), 431–451. doi:10.1260/2047-4970.3.2.431

Long, F., Zhou, J., & Peng, H. (2012). Visualization and analysis of 3D microscopic images. *PLoS Computational Biology*, *8*(6), e1002519. doi:10.1371/journal.pcbi.1002519 PMID:22719236

Matsuoka, D., Murata, K., Fujita, S., Tanaka, T., Yamamoto, K., & Ohno, N. (2009). 4-2-2 3D Visualization and Visual Data Mining. *Journal of the National Institute of Information and Communications Technology*, *56*(1-4).

Uher, V., & Burget, R. (2012, July). Automatic 3D segmentation of human brain images using data-mining techniques. In *Telecommunications and Signal Processing (TSP), 2012 35th International Conference on* (pp. 578-580). IEEE.

Chapter 14
Review on Various Machine Learning and Deep Learning Techniques for Prediction and Classification of Quotidian Datasets

Anisha M. Lal
Vellore Institute of Technology, India

B. Koushik Reddy
Vellore Institute of Technology, India

Aju D.
Vellore Institute of Technology, India

ABSTRACT

Machine learning can be defined as the ability of a computer to learn and solve a problem without being explicitly coded. The efficiency of the program increases with experience through the task specified. In traditional programming, the program and the input are specified to get the output, but in the case of machine learning, the targets and predictors are provided to the algorithm make the process trained. This chapter focuses on various machine learning techniques and their performance with commonly used datasets. A supervised learning algorithm consists of a target variable that is to be predicted from a given set of predictors. Using these established targets is a function that plots targets to a given set of predictors. The training process allows the system to train the unknown data and continues until the model achieves a desired level of accuracy on the training data. The supervised methods can be usually categorized as classification and regression. This chapter discourses some of the popular supervised machine learning algorithms and their performances using quotidian datasets. This chapter also discusses some of the non-linear regression techniques and some insights on deep learning with respect to object recognition.

DOI: 10.4018/978-1-5225-5294-9.ch014

INTRODUCTION

Machine learning can be defined as the ability of a computer to learn and solve a problem without being explicitly coded. The efficiency of the program increases with experience through the task specified. In traditional programming the program and the input are specified to get the output, but in the case of machine learning the targets and predictors are provided to the algorithm which makes the process trained. This chapter focuses on various machine learning techniques and its performance with quotidian datasets. A supervised learning algorithm consists of a target variable which is to be predicted from a given set of predictors. Using these established targets, a function that plots targets to the given set of predictors. The training process allows the system to train the unknown data and continues until the model achieves a desired level of accuracy on the training data. The supervised methods can be usually categorized as classification and regression. In classification, the data is classified into the groups based on the prior data that is used to train the machine learning model. In regression, the model is trained with the target data to make the predictions of the unknown predictors, when the parameters whose output is unknown is passed to the algorithm, it predicts based on the target that is used to train the data. This chapter discourses some of the popular supervised machine learning algorithms and their performances using quotidian datasets. This chapter also discusses some of the non-linear regression techniques and some insights on deep learning with respect to object recognition.

APPLICATIONS

Machine Learning concepts are used in various domains, such as in the field of medicine where these techniques can be used for the detection, diagnosis of the diseases in the patients with the minimal effort. In the field of sports, predictions are made for the combination of the players for which the probability of the team winning or losing is predicted, in stock market the predictions of the share value of being increased or decreased in the coming certain period of days if so what is the percentage of change and all sort of factors can be predicted. Earth is the largest reserve of natural mines such as gold, silver etc., these locations can be predicted accurately such that the mining can be performed without much effort in locating the resources. The websites are automatically customized based on the user taste. Artificial Limbs can be attached to the people. In the field of bio informatics, the gene classifications get way lot easier. The computer vision has played a great role in the field of security and Artificial Intelligence. So, the applications extend from spam filtering all the way to complex Artificial bots that are still being prototyped.

Important Terms

Cost Function

It is the function used to calculate the penalty based on the difference between the predicted output and the actual output. The more the cost the less is the accuracy of the algorithm and the less the cost the better the accuracy of the algorithm that is being applied.

Optimization Algorithm

Optimization Algorithm is used to minimize the cost from the cost function. It updates the parameters continuously so that the difference between the predicted value and the actual value gets to the minimum which in turn results in the cost from the cost function.

Some of the Optimization algorithms are Gradient Descent, Conjugate Decent, BFGS and L-BFGS. Here, the Gradient Descent algorithm model is used as it is less complicated and easy for the purpose of explanation. The Normal Equations method can also be used, in this method there is no need for iterating as the parameters are calculated with a formula. The method of normal equation is food for smaller data sets, as there is a need to invert the matrix and inverting above 10000 X 10000 increases the computational cost to the greater extent so hence, when a data set is taken with the data above 10000 elements it is better to use gradient descent or any other complex optimization algorithm.

Vectorization

Vectorization is a concept used to reduce the computational cost of the algorithm by writing it in a single line and let the high-level language compiler such as Octave, Matlab etc., take care of the rest instead of using a lot of loops.

Overfitting

The problem of overfititng occurs when there is less amount of data and lot of parameters that are taken into account. In such case it is better to drop the features that are unimportant and insignificant. In other case the hypothesis considered may be a higher order polynomial in this scenario it is better to apply the concept of regularization and to penalize the higher order polynomials.

Supervised Learning Algorithms

Linear Regression

Linear Regression is the most basic of all the machine learning algorithms where the output is dependent only on a single input parameter. The hypothesis or the fundamental equation that is taken for a linear regression is given in equation (1).

$$h_\theta(x) = \theta^T x = \theta_0 + \theta_1 x_1 \tag{1}$$

Here, $h_\theta(x)$ is the value that is predicted from the equation, θ is the set of values for which the cost function (explained later) is minimum and x is the set of all the dependent variable values (Neter et al. 1996).

The cost function is the equation which essentially calculates the difference between the predicted output and the actual output. Here, the mean of sum of squares is taken which was used by Hosmer et al. (2013) instead of sum of all the differences as given by Seber & Lee (2012) as it is easier for the smaller values for computational purposes. The entire equation is divided by 2 as further when the gradient descent(explained further) by differentiating the cost function and the 2 gets cancelled out.

$$J(\theta) = \frac{1}{2m} \sum_{i=1}^{m} \left(h_\theta \left(x^{(i)} \right) - y^{(i)} \right)^2 \tag{2}$$

To minimize the cost function is to equating the cost function to 0. So, hence the equation is differentiated and thus the equation obtained is the gradient descent which is shown in equation (2). The gradient descent is iterated for multiple times and the θ values are updated continuously until the cost function becomes reaches global minimum. In linear regression one need not worry about converging at local minimum as there is only one variable it is for sure converge at the global minima. There is a term α in the gradient descent called the learning rate which have to be selected with care.

The cost function is differentiated as given in equation (3),

$$\frac{\partial J(\theta)}{\partial \theta_j} = \frac{1}{m} \sum_{i=1}^{m} \left(h_\theta \left(x^{(i)} \right) - y^{(i)} \right) x_j^{(i)} \tag{3}$$

So, hence the gradient descent is evaluated as given in equation (4),

$$\theta_j := \theta_j - \alpha \frac{1}{m} \sum_{i=1}^{m} \left(h_\theta \left(x^{(i)} \right) - y^{(i)} \right) x_j^{(i)} \tag{4}$$

The concept of Linear Regression is applied on a data to predict the profits of a restaurant. Here, the profits are assumed to be depend only on the population of the city

Firstly, the data is loaded into the programming environment and then visualized as given in Figure (1).

The initial cost is calculated with theta = [0 ; 0] and the cost obtained is 32.072734. Now the gradient descent is made to run for 1500 times with the value of α being 0.01 and the value of theta obtained is [-3.630291, 1.166362].

The prediction line is drawn as shown in Figure (2)

Visualizing the value of $J(\theta)$ with respect to θ the graph obtained in surface form is shown in Figure (3).

Visualizing the value of $J(\theta)$ with respect to θ the graph obtained in contour form is shown in Figure (4).

From the above Visualization graphs, it shows Linear Regression method is acceptable for input data set for predicting cost function.

Multivariate Linear Regression

This algorithm is used when a single unknown entity is dependent upon multiple known parameters (Seber and Lee 2012). The data taken here is to estimate the cost of housing, here the cost is dependent on various parameters such as the size of the house and the number of rooms that the house contain. For the ease of calculation the entire data in the set is normalised. The gradient descent is used such that it can accommodate multiple features.

Figure 1. Visualization of data

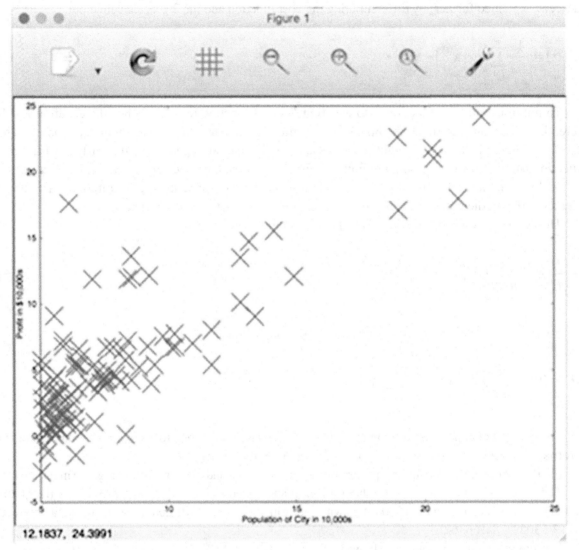

The hypothesis of the model is given as shown in equation (5).

$$h_\theta(x) = \theta^T x = \theta_0 + \theta_1 x_1 \tag{5}$$

Cost function is same as the previous algorithm and is given by equation (6).

$$J(\theta) = \frac{1}{2m} \sum_{i=1}^{m} \left(h_\theta \left(x^{(i)} \right) - y^{(i)} \right)^2 \tag{6}$$

Figure 2. Prediction line in the data visualized

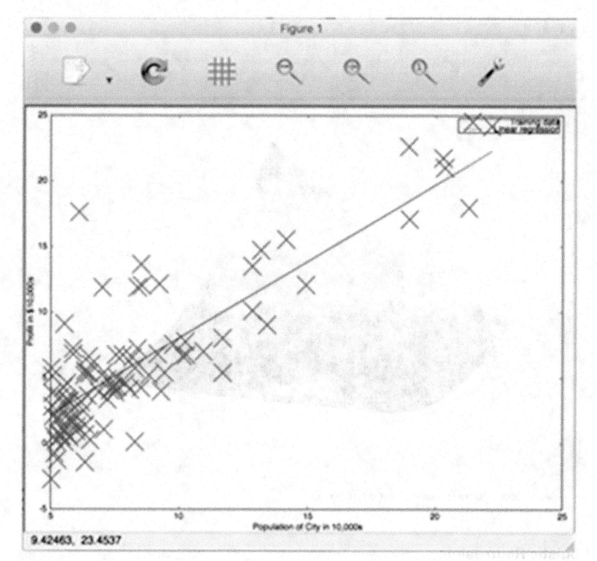

The gradient descent function is evaluated as given in equation (7).

$$\theta_j := \theta_j - \alpha \frac{1}{m} \sum_{i=1}^{m} \left(h_\theta \left(x^{(i)} \right) - y^{(i)} \right) x_j^{(i)} \tag{7}$$

(Simultaneously update θ_j for all j)

Predicting for other values [3] of population, for the population of 35,000 and 70,000, the predicted profits are 4519.767868 and 45342.450129 respectively.

The gradient descent that is computed can be visualised as shown in Figure (5).

Multivariate Linear Regression is not advisable for minor data sets.

Figure 3. Graph obtained using J(θ)

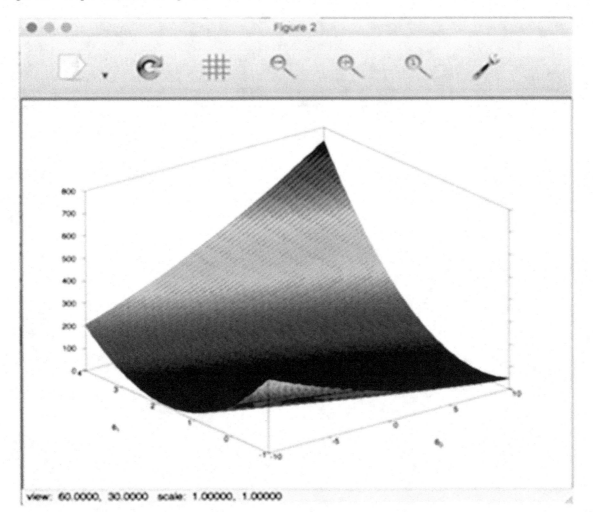

Logistic Regression

This is a classification algorithm, though the name suggests it is a regression algorithm, it is a classification algorithm that is applied for the discrete set of data (Menard 2002). This separates the unknown data into known number of classes, it has several applications in almost all the fields of study imaginable.

Here based on two exam scores a prediction is made whether the student can secure admission into a university or not. For any data set first it is better to visualize the data as shown in Figure (6).

The logistic regression [4] hypothesis is defined as shown in equation (8).

$$h_\theta\left(x\right) = g\left(\theta^T x\right) \qquad (8)$$

Figure 4. Graph obtained in contour form for J(θ)

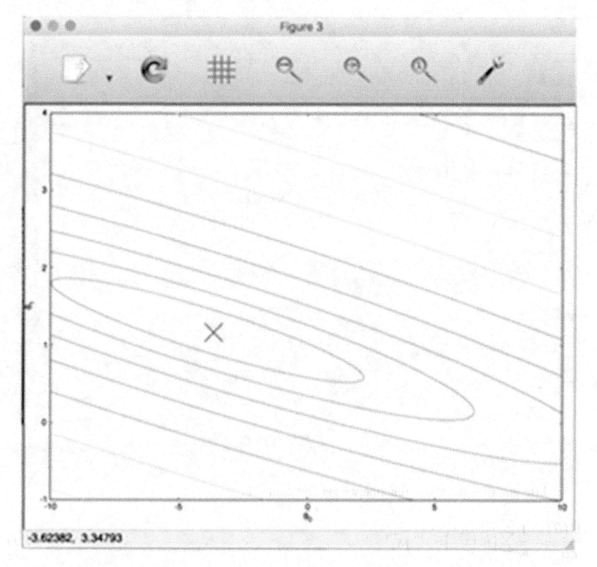

Here, g is the sigmoid function which converts the values in the range as shown in equation (9).

$$g(z) = \frac{1}{1 + e^{-x}} \qquad (9)$$

The cost function in logistic regression is described as given in equation (10).

$$J(\theta) = \frac{1}{m} \sum_{i=1}^{m} \left[-y^{(i)} \log\left(h_\theta\left(x^{(i)}\right)\right) - \left(1 - y^{(i)}\right) \log\left(1 - h_\theta\left(x^{(i)}\right)\right) \right] \qquad (10)$$

Figure 5. Visualization of gradient descent

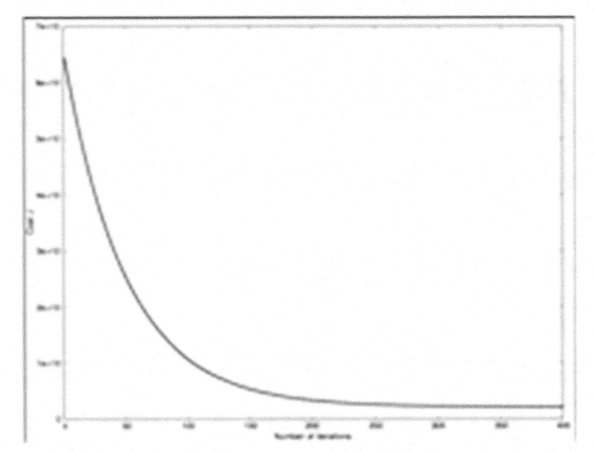

By differentiating the above function we get equation (11).

$$\frac{\partial J(\theta)}{\partial \theta_j} = \frac{1}{m} \sum_{i=1}^{m} \left(h_\theta \left(x^{(i)} \right) - y^{(i)} \right) x_j^{(i)} \tag{11}$$

The cost at initial values of theta is 0.693147 and the gradient at initial values of theta are -0.100000, -12.009217, and -11.262842. The minimum cost found is 0.203498 at the values of theta -25.161272, 0.206233, 0.201470. At the scores 45 and 85, the probability that the student will enter the college is 0.776289.

The training accuracy is 89.000000

The above Figure (7) is the visualization for the way the separation is made on the data set. This is for two dependent parameters, if there are more than two visualization may not be possible in the same manner but it works in the same way in multidimensional direction.

This algorithm can provide a classification model on the dependent variables and provide approximate results for two- class problem.

Figure 6. Visualization of data

Regularized Logistic Regression

This method is the same as the logistic regression with certain changes in the cost function. This is made to solve the problem of overfitting of the data for the model (Mernard 2002). Here the dataset taken is to verify if the microchips from a certain fabrication will pass the quality test or not (Kleinbaum & Klein 2010). Initially visualizing the data is performed as shown in Figure (8).

Calculating the cost at initial values of theta with the cost function the cost is evaluated as shown in equation (12).

$$J(\theta) = \frac{1}{m}\sum_{i=1}^{m}\left[-y^{(i)}\log\left(h_\theta\left(x^{(i)}\right)\right)-\left(1-y^{(i)}\right)\log\left(1-h_\theta\left(x^{(i)}\right)\right)\right]+\frac{\lambda}{2m}\sum_{j=1}^{n}\theta_j^2 \tag{12}$$

Figure 7. Visualization of separation in the dataset

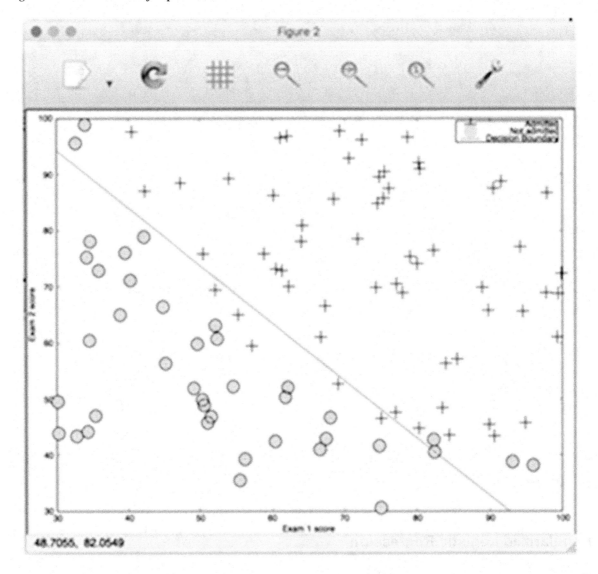

Here, λ is the regularization parameter.

The initial cost that is calculated is 0.693147. Finally when the gradient line is marked to visualize the data as shown in Figure (9).

The accuracy of the model is 86.440678 which is greater than the normal logistic regression.

This algorithm is more concentrated towards the cost function in order to focus and attain the precise value of the hypothesis.

Figure 8. Visualization of data

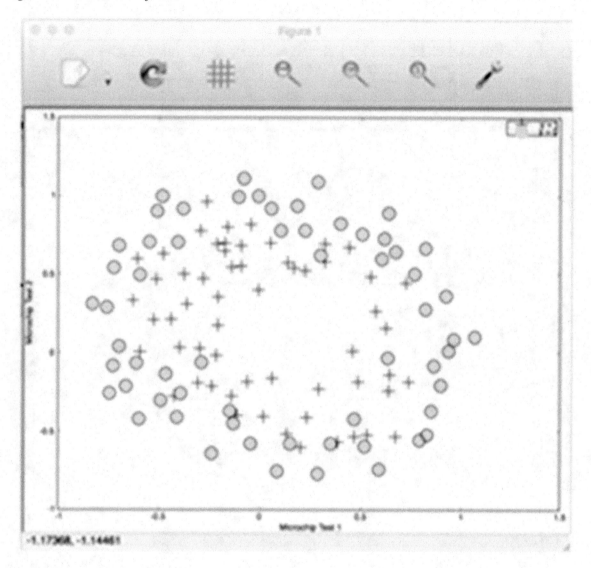

Multi-Class Logistic Regression

Here Logistic Regression algorithm is used to classify the data into various classes, for this purpose handwriting detection suggested by Rowley et al. (1998) is taken as input data, that too the digits ranging from 0 to 9.

Visualizing the input data is shown in Figure (10).

The vectorised cost function is given as shown in equation (13).

$$J(\theta) = \frac{1}{m} \sum_{i=1}^{m} \left[-y^{(i)} \log\left(h_\theta\left(x^{(i)}\right)\right) - \left(1 - y^{(i)}\right) \log\left(1 - h_\theta\left(x^{(i)}\right)\right) \right] \tag{13}$$

Figure 9. Visualizing the data with gradient line

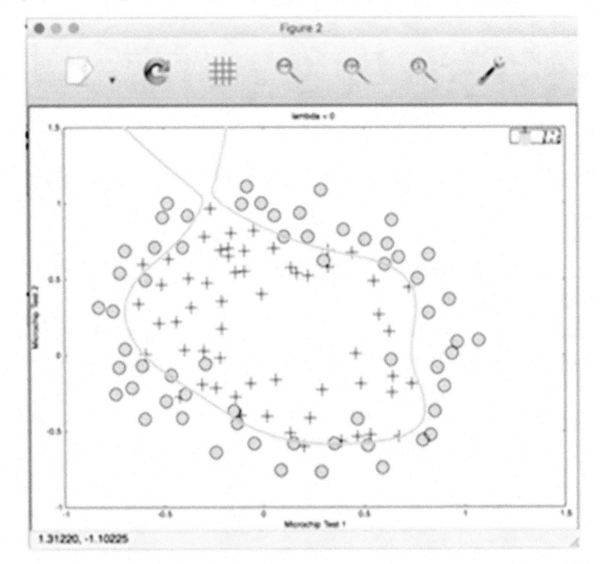

The vectorised gradient function is given in equation (14) as follows,

$$\frac{\partial J(\theta)}{\partial \theta_j} = \frac{1}{m} \sum_{i=1}^{m} \left(h_\theta \left(x^{(i)} \right) - y^{(i)} \right) x_j^{(i)} \tag{14}$$

The handwritings have been identified with an accuracy of 95.02%

This algorithm inferences with accurate values of predicting the raw data sets. It predicts the strength of the variables, changes impacts and future values (Lent et al. 1994).

Figure 10. Visualizing the data

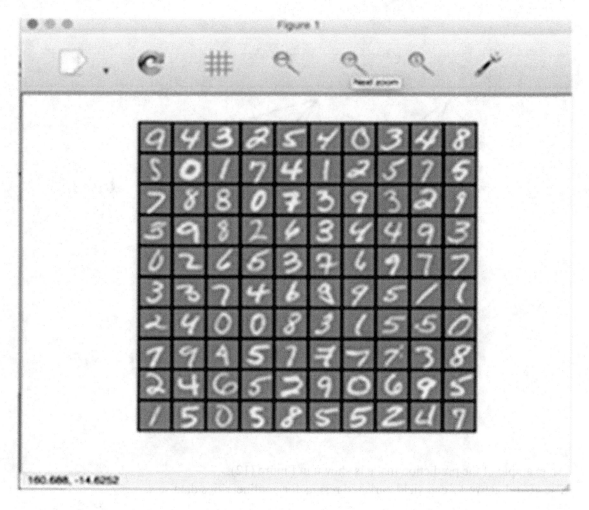

Neural Networks

A neural network works is the way in which our human brain functions (Demuth et al. 2014, Brooks 1991). Unlike the classical machine learning algorithms to detect an image it does not take parameters but takes sub parameters builds parameters upon them and finally recognises (Fury et al. 2000). To detect a face first the algorithm recognises pixels, then lines, shapes and finally face (Rowley et al. 1998). Hence, it works step by step analogous to the functioning of the brain. The same above task of identifying the handwriting is implemented using the neural networks algorithm the results with the accuracy of 97.52% has been attained.

From this it can be inferred that the neural networks though are complicated than the logistic regression have quite a few applications more than the logistic regression with the greater efficiency and accuracy (Russell &Norvig 2002, Bench & Dunne 2007, Horn & Schunck 1981).

In neural networks the input is passed through the series of functions before showing as the output. So, one can imagine the series of functions to be hidden layers in between the input and the output (Suykens et al. 1999, Ship et al. 2002). A neural network process is shown in Figure (11).

Figure 11. Neural Network Process

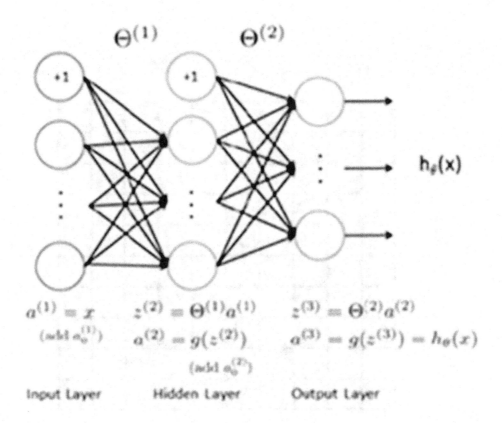

$a^{(1)} = x$ $z^{(2)} = \Theta^{(1)}a^{(1)}$ $z^{(3)} = \Theta^{(2)}a^{(2)}$

$(\text{add } a_0^{(1)})$ $a^{(2)} = g(z^{(2)})$ $a^{(3)} = g(z^{(3)}) = h_\theta(x)$

$(\text{add } a_0^{(2)})$

Input Layer   Hidden Layer   Output Layer

An example of the prediction made is shown in Figure (12).

The neural networks can yield enriched results for nonlinearities data sets.

Support Vector Machine

Support Vector Machine is a modern algorithm as discussed by Tong et al., (2001) it is similar to logistic regression algorithm, with changes in the cost function which led to the increase in the efficiency in the algorithm (Goldberg & Holland 1988, Perkowitz & Etzioni 2000). Here it is tested with two types of data as the algorithm can support various types of data. The cost function is the same as the regularized logistic regression except the fact that $C=1/\lambda$.

For example any general 2D data is considered for evaluation and the visualizing of the data is shown in Figure (13) (Bandhura 1989, Guyon et al. 2002).

With C = 1 we get the gradient line as shown in Figure (14).
With C = 100 we get the gradient line as shown in Figure (15).

This SMV algorithm concentrates on multi domain applications considering massive data for proving appropriate cost function results (Bandhura 2001, Melgani & Bruzzone 2004).

Figure 12. Prediction made from the input

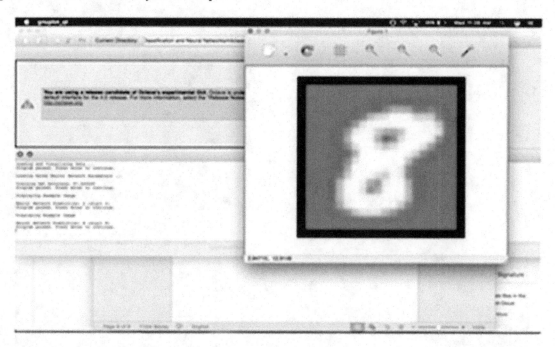

Figure 13. Visualizing the data

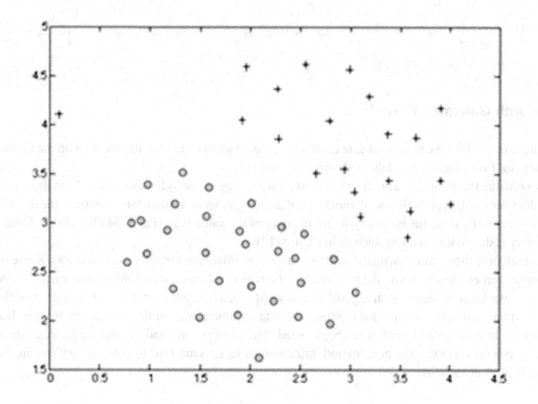

Figure 14. Gradient line with c = 1

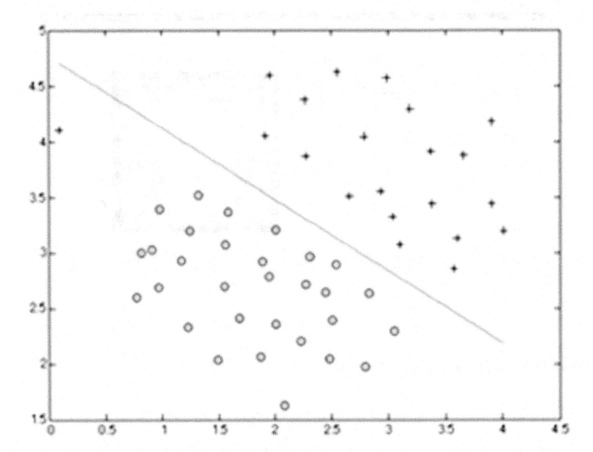

SVM with Gaussian Kernel

For the data in which the non linear data cannot be attained we need to train the model with the Gaussian Kernel. So, first visualize the data as shown in Figure (16).

Now, using the algorithm a boundary is marked separating the two classes of data. As in this case the data does not exists separately and all the data is existed together as a single bunch of data, the algorithm needs to carefully draw the boundary along the data of the same type (Pal & Mather 2005). Once the boundary is drawn it is in a way such as in Figure (17).

This algorithm assurances with the optimal with low estimation and approximation errors. Regression algorithm can efficiently frame the relationships between independent and dependent variables. Also the type like Logistic Regression algorithm can yield a better result on the two dependent variables. Based on the factors like application type, size of data set, linear and nonlinear data sets and number of classes the best suitable algorithm can be selected. The attempts are made to reduce the cost function and improve the accuracy. The benefits and limitations of various machine learning algorithms are listed in the Table 1 given below;

Figure 15. Gradient line with c=100

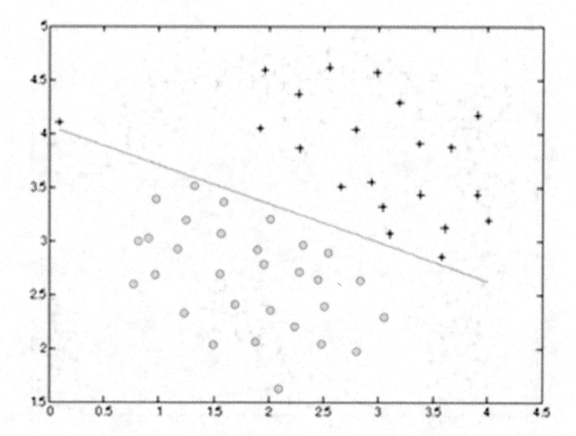

Non –Linear Regression Techniques

Nonlinear Regression techniques plays an important role in expressing whether that data is fit into a particular model or not. Nonlinear regression is a statistical analysis of nonlinear relationships in an experimental data.

Recursive Nonlinear Autoregressive Neural Network

The Nonlinear Auto-Regressive Neural Network (NARNN) is the method developed for multi-step ahead prediction which is based on Multilayer Feedforward Neural Network (MFNN) basically arranged in three or more layers (Al-allaf & AbdAlKader 2011). These consist of an input layer, a target layer and hidden layers in between. In generally only one hidden layer is adapted for most applications if there are enough number of neurons available. The sum of input patterns along with their respective weights produces an activation pattern resulting the number of neurons in the hidden layer. The type of neural network chosen is mainly based on its training algorithm. The most commonly used is Back Propagation Network (BP).

Figure 16. Visualizing the data

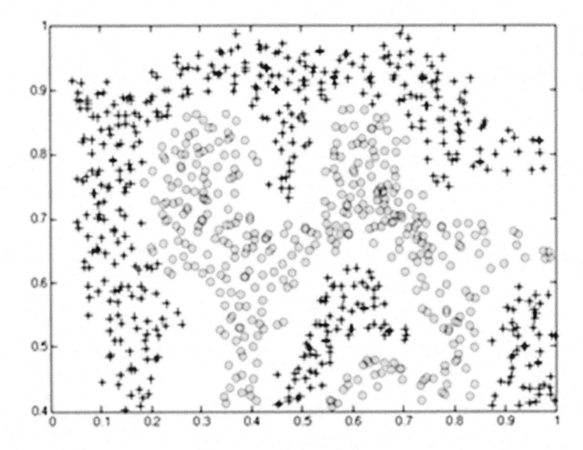

In this recursive NARNN method, first a single model g is trained to perform a one-step ahead estimation which is given in equation (15).

$$u_{x+1} = g\left(u_x,\ldots,u_{x-d+1}\right)+b$$

(15)

where, $x \in \{d,\ldots,M-1\}$, d is the number of previous inputs and b is the bias. For N steps ahead prediction, the first step is predicted by applying the model in (15) and the predicted value is included as the last entry in the input patterns to predict the next step using the same trained model. The process is repeated for the entire predictions. The recursive prediction is defined as a piecewise function with respect to window n and input length d as given in equation (16) (Ahmed & Khalid 2017).

$$\hat{u}_{M+n} = \begin{cases} g\left(u_M,\ldots,u_{M-d+1}\right) & if \; n=1 \\ g\left(\hat{u}_{M+n-1},\ldots,\hat{u}_{M+1},\ldots,u_M,\ldots,u_{M-d+n}\right) & if \; n \in \{2,\ldots,d\} \\ g\left(\hat{u}_{M+n-1},\ldots,\hat{u}_{M-d+n}\right) & if \; n \in \{d+1,\ldots,N\} \end{cases}$$

(16)

Figure 17. Boundary line after applying SVM

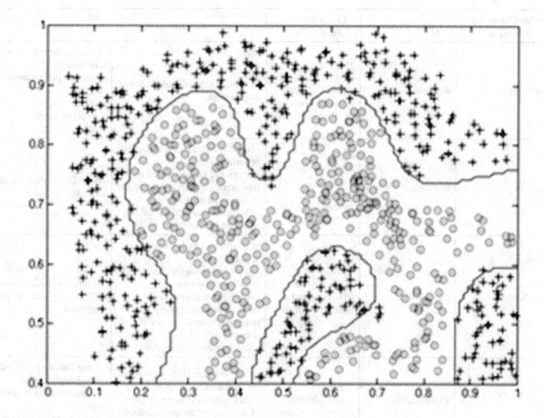

The BP network produces activation function based on the weighted sums of the input signal. The target j^{th} neuron of the hidden layer is given by the equation (17) as,

$$n_j = \sum_{i=0}^{d} w_{ij} u_i \ (i = 0, 1, \ldots, d, j = 1, \ldots, n) \tag{17}$$

where w_{ij} is the connection weight from input node i to hidden node j. u_i is the input node with u_0 as the bias W_{IH} with weight $w_{0j} = 1$.

The activation value of each neuron is passed through an activation function and is calculated using the sigmoid function. Thus the output of jth neuron is calculated as z_j. These outputs are fed to the single neuron of the target layer to produce the final target as given in equation (18).

$$\hat{u} = g_0 \left(\sum_{j=0}^{n} w_{jk} z_j \right) (j = 0, 1, 2, \ldots, n) \tag{18}$$

where, g_0 is a line function used for target layer activation, w_{jk} is the connection weight from hidden node j to target node k (here $k = 1$) and z0 $_i$s the bias WHO $_w$ith weight w0k $_=$ 1.

Table 1. Benefits and Limitation of various Machine Learning Techniques

Machine Learning Technique	Type of Problem	Efficiency with the data used	Benefits	Limitations
Linear Regression	Regression	This is a predictions based algorithm just the closeness provides its efficiency.	Very good at predicting the linear relationships.	· Cannot predict nonlinear relationships. · Can only predict numeric outputs. · Explanation about the content learnt is inappropriate.
Logistic Regression	Regression	89% without optimization techniques, the efficiency increases with the optimization.	· No need for normal distribution of variables · Dependent variables need not have equal variance in each group · Can handle nonlinear data · Can handle categorical variable and bounded variable	· Need large dataset for the purpose of training.
Neural Networks	Classification	Efficiency was 97%, can also be optimised further.	· Can detect complex non-linear relationships · There can be multiple training algorithms implemented · All different interactions between dependent and independent variables can be detected · Smaller data set is needed	· High computational cost. · This is very likely to get over fitted.
Support Vector Machines	Classification	Efficiency varied with the complexity of data.	· There is a flexibility in choice of the threshold. · Very robust algorithm. · Can compute complex nonlinear relationships.	· Large data set is needed. · The Regularization parameters are to be chosen with care. · Over fit and under fit is an major issue.

Training of the neural network is performed only once for the recursive method of forecasting using one-step ahead setting as suggested by Al-allaf & AbdAlKader (2011), i.e., target output being the next hour value ux_{+1} from the known training set. The Recursive Nonlinear Autoregressive Neural Network is shown in Figure 18.

Recurrent Dynamic Neural Network

As described, earlier Neural Networks can learn dynamic or time-series associations. In dynamic networks the target depends on the current data to the network, but also on the current or previous data and targets of the network. The nonlinear autoregressive network (NARX) is a recurrent dynamic network which has feedback connections enfolding several layers of the neural network (Doulamis et al. 2000).

The NARX model is generated from linear ARX model which is normally used in time-series modeling, where the next value of the reliant target signal g(x) is retreated on previous values of the target signal and previous values of an independent input signal (Chen & Billings 1989). The NARX model can be implemented using a feedforward ANN to approximate the function f (Lu 1998, Amari 2000) . The equation for NARX model can be defined as shown in equation (19),

Figure 18. Recursive Nonlinear Autoregressive Neural Network

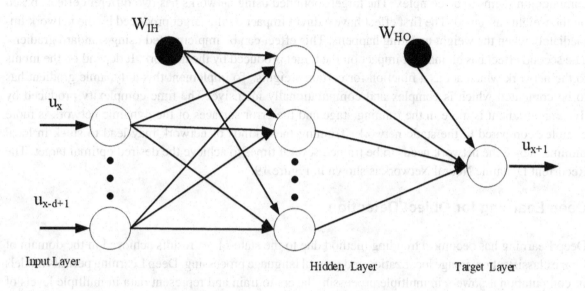

$$u_{x+1} = g(u_x, \ldots, u_{x-d+1}) + W_{HO}$$

Figure 19. Recurrent Dynamic Neural Network

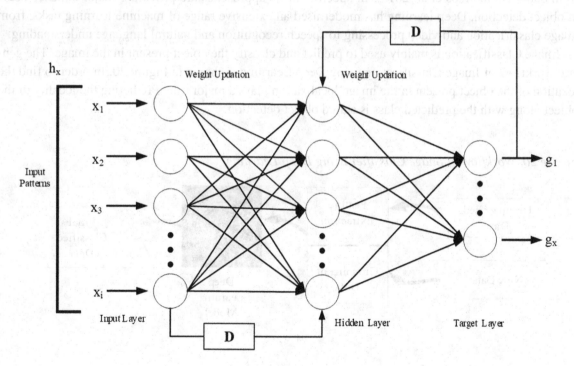

$$G(x) = F\Big(g(x-1), g(x-2), \ldots, g(x-n_g), h(x-1), h(x-2), \ldots, h(x-n_h)\Big) \qquad (19)$$

Even though the same gradient algorithms cab be used for both dynamic and static networks the performance of gradient based algorithms on dynamic networks can be quite different and the gradient computation seems to be complex. The targets obtained using networks has two different effects based on the weights assigned. The first effect have a direct impact on the target produced by the network immediately when the weight updating happens. This effect can be implemented using standard gradient. The second effect has an indirect impact on the target produced by the network. It depend on the inputs to the network which act as a function for certain weights. To implement this a dynamic gradient has to be computed which is complex and computationally intensive. The time complexity produced by dynamic gradient is more in the training stage and the error surfaces of the dynamic network is more complex compared to the static network. Training these kinds of network may lead to stuck in local minima, hence the network needs to be trained several times to achieve the desired optimal target. The Recurrent Dynamic Neural Network is shown in Figure 19.

Deep Learning for Object Detection

Deep Learning has become a trending method due to the state-of-art results achieved in the domain of image classification, image localization and natural language processing. Deep Learning permits models of computational powers in multiple processing layers to train and represent data in multiple levels of notion simulating, how the brain perceives and understands multimodal information. Nowadays, deep learning techniques have developed as dominant approaches for learning feature descriptors automatically from data (Voulodimos et al. 2018). In specific, these approaches are providing major enhancements in object detection. Deep learning has modernised an extensive range of machine learning tasks, from image classification and video processing to speech recognition and natural language understanding.

Image Classification is mainly used to predict and classify the object present in the image. The general workflow of Image Classification using Deep Learning is shown in Figure 20. In order to find the location of the object present in the image localization plays a major role. Predicting the locality of the object along with the predicted class is called object detection.

Figure 20. Workflow of Image Classifier using Deep Learning

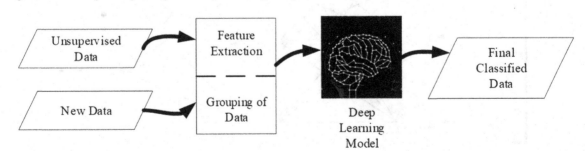

Object Detection is exhibited as a classification approach where windows of fixed sizes are taken from the input image at all the possible localities and these window patches are fed to an image classifier. Each window is fed to the classifier which predicts the class of the object in the window. Hence, both the class and location of the objects are identified in the image. The most commonly used object detection technique is extracting the HoG (Histogram of oriented gradients) features from the image and feeding it to the classifier. HoG features are computationally in expensive and good for many real world problems such as pedestrian detection, face detection, and so many other object detection use-cases. After the rise of deep learning, HoG based classifiers are replaced with CNN (Convolution Neural Network) based classifiers.

Convolutional Neural Networks

Convolutional Neural Networks (CNNs) is a Deep Learning model which is used to classify a image and detect the location of the object present in the image. It takes an input image, assign learnable weights and biases to various objects in the image and be able to discriminate one from the other.

A CNN comprises three main types of neural layers, namely, (i) convolutional layers, (ii) pooling layers, and (iii) fully connected layers. Figure 21 shows a CNN architecture for an object detection in image task. Every layer of a CNN transforms the input patches to an output patches of neuron activation, eventually leading to the final fully connected layers, resulting in a mapping of the input data to a 1D feature vector.

Figure 21. CNN architecture for object detection

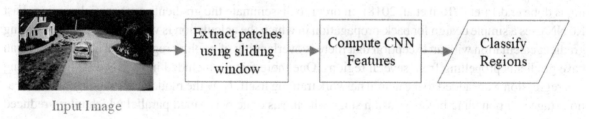

Typically, there are three stages in an object detection framework using CNN.

1. First, a model is used to generate patches of fixed windows from the input image. These patches are a large set of bounding boxes spanning the full image which is an object localisation stage.
2. In the second stage, visual features are extracted for each of the bounding boxes, they are evaluated and it is determined whether and which objects are present in the proposals based on visual features which is an object classification stage.
3. In the final post-processing stage, overlapping boxes are combined into a single bounding box which is an non maximum suppression stage.

However, CNNs are too slow and computationally very expensive which further makes impossible to run CNNs on so many patches generated by sliding window detector.

Region Based Convolutional Neural Networks

Region based Convolutional Neural Networks (RCNN) solves the above said problem raised by CNN using an object proposal approach called Selective Search which combines the bounding boxes to region proposals and fed to the classifier. Selective search uses texture, intensity, color, etc., to produce all the possible localities of the object (Girshick et al. 2015).

Hence, there are 3 important stages of RCNN:

1. Selective Search model is used to generate region proposal objects.
2. The patches generated using selective search are fed into CNN followed by SVM to predict the class of each patch.
3. Optimize the patches by training the bounding box regression separately.

Still, RCNN is too slow. Feeding patches generated by selective search to a classifier makes the process very slow. Spatial Pyramid Pooling Network SPP-Net solves the above said problem raised by RCNN by calculating CNN representations for the entire image only once and use that to calculate the CNN representations for each patch generated using selective search. The main limitation was it was not trivial to perform back propagation through spatial pooling layer which was introduced in the last convolution layer because of the fixed size of the fully connected layers.

Fast RCNN

Fast RCNN rectifies the limitations raised in SPP-Net. It combines both SPP-Net and RCNN and training is done end-to-end (Ren et al. 2018). In order to disseminate the gradients over spatial pooling, Fast RCNN uses a simple design for back-propagation in which the calculation is very similar to max-pooling gradient calculation with an exception that there is overlapping of pooling regions and hence a patch can have gradients propelling from several regions. One more feature included in RCNN was the bounding box regression were added to the neural network training itself. Now the model had two stages classification stage and bounding box regression stage which was done performed parallel which intern reduced the training time and increased the accuracy.

Faster RCNN

Even though, Fast RCNN is faster the stage which makes it slower is the selective search bounding box approach. Faster RCNN replaces this approach using a convolutional network called Region proposal network (RPN) which generate regions of interest in the image (Chen et al. 2018). The RPN model generates sliding windows for the last layer of initial CNN and creates regions from each sliding window based on k-fixed ratio anchor boxes. Each region proposal consists of patch score and the coordinated representing the bounding box. If the anchor box has a score above the threshold value then that coordinate value is passed as region proposal to the Fast RCNN model. Faster RCNN is the combination of RPN model and Fast RCNN. Faster RCNN is ten times faster than Fast RCNN as well its accuracy is better compared to all models related to CNN.

CONCLUSION

This chapter presents some supervised and non-linear classification models with respect to quotidian datasets. This chapter also discusses the deep learning models used for object detection. Supervised machine learning algorithms still provides better for lesser data sets and for applications such as material sciences, material informatics and data mining. Machine learning provides a basic prototype for the deep learning models. Faster RCNN, Fast RCNN and SSD are the best deep learning models used for object detection that is for identifying the location of the object present in the image. Compared to the above three Faster RCNN is faster in terms of speed and accuracy of detected object is perfect than the other two models.

REFERENCES

Ahmed, A., & Khalid, M. (2017). Multi-step ahead wind forecasting using nonlinear autoregressive neural networks. *Energy Procedia, 134*, 192–204. doi:10.1016/j.egypro.2017.09.609

Al-allaf, O. N., & AbdAlKader, S. A. (2011). Nonlinear Autoregressive neural network for estimation soil temperature: a comparison of different optimization neural network algorithms. *UBICC J*, 42-51.

Amari, S. (Ed.). (2000). *Neural Computing: New Challenges and Perspectives for the New Millennium* (Vol. 2). IEEE Computer Society.

Bandura, A. (1989). Human agency in social cognitive theory. *American Psychologist, 44*(9), 1175.

Bandura, A. (2001). Social cognitive theory: An agentic perspective. *Annual Review of Psychology, 52*(1), 1–26. doi:10.1146/annurev.psych.52.1.1 PMID:11148297

Bench-Capon, T. J., & Dunne, P. E. (2007). Argumentation in artificial intelligence. *Artificial Intelligence, 171*(10-15), 619–641. doi:10.1016/j.artint.2007.05.001

Brooks, R. A. (1991). Intelligence without representation. *Artificial Intelligence, 47*(1-3), 139–159. doi:10.1016/0004-3702(91)90053-M

Chen, S., & Billings, S. A. (1989). Representations of non-linear systems: The NARMAX model. *International Journal of Control, 49*(3), 1013–1032. doi:10.1080/00207178908559683

Chen, Y., Li, W., Sakaridis, C., Dai, D., & Van Gool, L. (2018). Domain adaptive faster r-cnn for object detection in the wild. In *Proceedings of the IEEE conference on computer vision and pattern recognition* (pp. 3339-3348). 10.1109/CVPR.2018.00352

Demuth, H. B., Beale, M. H., De Jess, O., & Hagan, M. T. (2014). *Neural network design*. Martin Hagan.

Doulamis, A. D., Doulamis, N. D., & Kollias, S. D. (2000, July). Recursive non linear models for on line traffic prediction of VBR MPEG coded video sources. In *Proceedings of the IEEE-INNS-ENNS International Joint Conference on Neural Networks. IJCNN 2000. Neural Computing: New Challenges and Perspectives for the New Millennium* (Vol. 6, pp. 114-119). IEEE. 10.1109/IJCNN.2000.859382

Furey, T. S., Cristianini, N., Duffy, N., Bednarski, D. W., Schummer, M., & Haussler, D. (2000). Support vector machine classification and validation of cancer tissue samples using microarray expression data. *Bioinformatics (Oxford, England)*, *16*(10), 906–914. doi:10.1093/bioinformatics/16.10.906 PMID:11120680

Girshick, R., Donahue, J., Darrell, T., & Malik, J. (2015). Region-based convolutional networks for accurate object detection and segmentation. *IEEE Transactions on Pattern Analysis and Machine Intelligence*, *38*(1), 142–158. doi:10.1109/TPAMI.2015.2437384 PMID:26656583

Goldberg, D. E., & Holland, J. H. (1988). *Genetic algorithms and machine learning*. Academic Press.

Guyon, I., Weston, J., Barnhill, S., & Vapnik, V. (2002). Gene selection for cancer classification using support vector machines. *Machine Learning*, *46*(1-3), 389–422. doi:10.1023/A:1012487302797

Horn, B. K. P., & Schunck, B. G. (1981). Determining Optical Flow. *Artificial Intelligence*, *17*(1-3), 185–203. doi:10.1016/0004-3702(81)90024-2

Hosmer, D. W. Jr, Lemeshow, S., & Sturdivant, R. X. (2013). *Applied logistic regression* (Vol. 398). John Wiley & Sons. doi:10.1002/9781118548387

Kleinbaum, D. G., & Klein, M. (2010). Maximum likelihood techniques: An overview. In *Logistic regression* (pp. 103–127). New York, NY: Springer. doi:10.1007/978-1-4419-1742-3_4

Lent, R. W., Brown, S. D., & Hackett, G. (1994). Toward a unifying social cognitive theory of career and academic interest, choice, and performance. *Journal of Vocational Behavior*, *45*(1), 79–122. doi:10.1006/jvbe.1994.1027

Lu, Z. (1998). On the geometric ergodicity of a non-linear autoregressive model with an autoregressive conditional heteroscedastic term. *Statistica Sinica*, *§§§*, 1205–1217.

Melgani, F., & Bruzzone, L. (2004). Classification of hyperspectral remote sensing images with support vector machines. *IEEE Transactions on Geoscience and Remote Sensing*, *42*(8), 1778–1790. doi:10.1109/TGRS.2004.831865

Menard, S. (2002). *Applied logistic regression analysis* (Vol. 106). Sage. doi:10.4135/9781412983433

Neter, J., Kutner, M. H., Nachtsheim, C. J., & Wasserman, W. (1996). *Applied linear statistical models*. Academic Press.

Pal, M., & Mather, P. M. (2005). Support vector machines for classification in remote sensing. *International Journal of Remote Sensing*, *26*(5), 1007–1011. doi:10.1080/01431160512331314083

Perkowitz, M., & Etzioni, O. (2000). Towards adaptive web sites: Conceptual framework and case study. *Artificial Intelligence*, *118*(1-2), 245–275. doi:10.1016/S0004-3702(99)00098-3

Ren, Y., Zhu, C., & Xiao, S. (2018). Object detection based on fast/faster RCNN employing fully convolutional architectures. *Mathematical Problems in Engineering*, *2018*, 2018. doi:10.1155/2018/3598316

Rowley, H. A., Baluja, S., & Kanade, T. (1998). Neural network-based face detection. *IEEE Transactions on Pattern Analysis and Machine Intelligence*, *20*(1), 23–38. doi:10.1109/34.655647

Russell, S., & Norvig, P. (2002). *Artificial intelligence: a modern approach*. Academic Press.

Seber, G. A., & Lee, A. J. (2012). *Linear regression analysis* (Vol. 329). John Wiley & Sons.

Shipp, M. A., Ross, K. N., Tamayo, P., Weng, A. P., Kutok, J. L., Aguiar, R. C., ... Ray, T. S. (2002). Diffuse large B-cell lymphoma outcome prediction by gene-expression profiling and supervised machine learning. *Nature Medicine*, *8*(1), 68–74. doi:10.1038/nm0102-68 PMID:11786909

Suykens & Vandewalle. (1999). Least squares support vector machine classifiers. *Neural Processing Letters*, *9*(3), 293-300.

Tong, S., & Koller, D. (2001). Support vector machine active learning with applications to text classification. *Journal of Machine Learning Research*, *2*(Nov), 45–66.

Voulodimos, A., Doulamis, N., Doulamis, A., & Protopapadakis, E. (2018). Deep learning for computer vision: A brief review. *Computational Intelligence and Neuroscience*, *2018*, 2018. doi:10.1155/2018/7068349 PMID:29487619

Chapter 15
Improved Automatic Anatomic Location Identification Approach and CBR–Based Treatment Management System for Pediatric Foreign Body Aspiration

Vasumathy M.
D.K.M College for Women, Vellore, India

Mythili Thirugnanam
Vellore Institute of Technology, Vellore, India

ABSTRACT

In general, the diagnosis and treatment planning of pediatric foreign body aspiration is done by medical experts with experience and uncertain clinical data of the patients, which makes the diagnosis a more approximate and time-consuming process. Foreign body diagnostic information requires the evidence such as size, shape, and location classification of the aspired foreign body. This evidence identification process requires the knowledge of human expertise to achieve accuracy in classification. The aim of the proposed work is to improve the performance of automatic anatomic location identification approach (AALIA) and to develop a reasoning-based systematic approach for pediatric foreign body aspiration treatment management. A CBR-based treatment management system is proposed for standardizing the pediatric foreign body aspiration treatment management process. The proposed approach considered a sample set of foreign body-aspired pediatric radiography images for experimental evaluation, and the performance is evaluated with respect to receiver operator characteristics (ROC) measure.

DOI: 10.4018/978-1-5225-5294-9.ch015

INTRODUCTION

Medical image analysis is a difficult task in which a medical expert makes extensive use of the knowledge of medical anatomy structure and imaging techniques such as X-ray, computer tomography (CT), and magnetic resonance imaging (MRI) and etc., In foreign body aspiration diagnosis process, the physicians and radiologists are ground their diagnosis based on their expertise for determining the anatomic location based on clinical cases. The manual diagnosis is often complex and involves many steps such as taking an appropriate history of symptoms and collecting relevant data, generating a provisional and differential diagnosis, physical examination, reviewing, referral to other experts to seek clarification if needed, reaching a final diagnosis, providing instructions and follow up, and documenting decisions made which are time consuming and cost effective steps in medical diagnosis process. vasumathy et al.,(2016) presented a framework for automatic intrude object identification in paediatric foreign body aspired radiography images. The developed framework of automatic intrude object identification approach adopted combination of image processing techniques such as median filtering, iterative thresholding, sobel edge detection and k-means clustering for segmenting the images and edge, shape and texture based features are extracted. The j48 decision tree is used for classification and achieves 80% of classification accuracy but the work has some limitations in mapping the anatomic region that is the pixel position and intensity value alone is used to distinguish similar region of interest and mapping is done by predefined template of anatomic location based on pixel coordinates. Hence a simple change in template pixel positions can largely affect the classification accuracy and which leads to misclassification. Motivated by this challenge, this work developed an improved automatic anatomic location identification approach to distinguish anatomic location by considering pixel, edge, shape and texture features on foreign body aspired pediatric radiography images and case based reasoning approach is used to improve classification accuracy. The CBR approach is usually used where the experts find it very difficult to expressive their thought processes while solving problems.

Related Work

In general, for foreign body aspiration diagnosis and treatment planning, assessing the radiological and clinical evidence such as size, type, shape and aspired location determines the accuracy of diagnosis process. Some of the existing work has been surveyed for assessing the significant usage of imaging features on identifying the anatomic location on radiography images are described in Table 1. Knowledge base systems and intelligent computing systems are used widely in areas that require heuristic and logic in reasoning where knowledge is predominant than data. A review is made to assess the benefits of knowledge based decision making in the field of medical diagnosis and treatment planning and the observation is presented in Table 2.

Table 1. Assessing the significant usage of imaging features on identifying the anatomic location

Author(s)	Used Imaging Features	Technique used for anatomic location classification	Considered Anatomic Location for the work	Observation of the proposed work
Oscar Jimenez-del-Toro et al., (2016)	Image segmentation and landmark detection techniques	Cloud-Based Evaluation, Intensity–based clustering, Shape and appearance segmentation models	large–scale 3D radiology image data set	The **visual concept extraction challenge in radiology** (VISCERAL) anatomy benchmarks are set to evaluate the processing techniques of anatomical structure detection.
Lalendra upreti et al. (2015)[14]	Pixel based feature extraction	Histogram approach	Airway, Trachea-bronchial	The histogram tool helps to identify foreign body lodgment and diagnosis on digital radiographs of pediatric chest.
Fabian Lecron et al. (2012)[15]	Region based feature extraction	Model-based vertebra detection, identification.	Vertebra detection	An automatic vertebra detection method based on the Generalized Hough Transform (GHT) and announces a detection rate of 92%.
Tatyana nuzhnaya et al. (2011)	Texture based feature extraction (skewness, coarseness, contrast, energy, and fractal dimension (FD))	Graph cut method	Ductal network in x-ray galactograms	The pixels are manually spotted to separate the foreground from background. The graph cut method randomly divides the image by grouping 8-neigborhood connection. To assess the accuracy, the receiver operating characteristic (ROC) curve is made and it achieves 0.76 accuracy rate.
Juhasz et al. (2010)[16]	Edge based features	KNN and curve fitting methods.	Chest Localization	Describe a method for segmenting anatomical structures on chest radiographs. The results are analyzed with an efficient GPU based real time evaluation.
Megalooikonomou et al., (2009)	Contrast, edge based labeling, branching properties, such as branch length, angle, and tortuosity	Symbolic graph representation with text mining techniques, support vector machines (SVM) for classification	Breast tree like structure in X-ray Galactograms	Constructing characterization strings helps to create location branching patterns to represent the tree structures in breast X-ray. The string encoding process is done manually and the performance is compared with ROC analysis.
Klinder, T (2009)[17]	Histogram features, edge based features	Multi-Class SVM	Vertebra Detection	A contrast limited adaptive histogram equalization, a Canny edge detection filter and an edge polygonal approximation are useful to automate the vertebra detection in X-Ray
Mohammed Benjelloun et al. (2009)[20]	Edge and region based features	Contour detection method for localization of vertebrae.	Vertebra detection	Manual seed selection is required. The contour detection method gives satisfactory results.
Scott C. Neu et al.(2008) [21]	shape, size, and location	Java GUI application (LONI ICE).	Brain Localization	Singular value decomposition method is used to identify the brain shape, size, and location. It is comparatively less computational time than other traditional methods.
Kerry A. Danelson (2008) [22]	Intensity, shape	threshold based shape and size prediction	Pediatric Brain	The shape and size is determined based on the intensity which is not sufficient for predicting brain structures.
Benjelloun, M.[18]	Intensity, contrast,	Interest Point Detection, support vector machine(SVM)	Spine Localization	Method to locate a vertebra by detecting its points of interest on X-ray images and support vector machine is used to classified regions.

The existing works focused on the issue of identifying anatomic location such as breast ductal network, lung region detection, brain tumor detection, spine localization, airway, Trachea-bronchial localization of the human organs with the help of radiography images. The researchers claim their proposed method performs better with experimental results. Most of them uses and a fixed template for labeling the anatomic regions based on pixel intensity. The use of texture features achieves 76% of classification accuracy in ductal network on x-ray galactograms. From the existing work it is observed that the use of texture features achieves good classification than the pixel based features. With this motivation the

Table 2. Assessing the benefits of knowledge based decision making in the field of medical diagnosis and treatment planning

Author(s)	Used Imaging Modality	Applied domain	Knowledge based approach	Observation of the proposed work
Souad Demigha et al.,(2016)	Mammograms	Breast cancer management	CBR	Breast Cancer Knowledge Management to improve breast cancer screening based on CBR, Combining CBR to Data Mining techniques will facilitate diagnosis and decision-making of medical experts.
Sharaf-El-Deen et al.,(2014)	Mammograms	breast cancer and thyroid diagnosis	Hybrid CBR(combination of case-based reasoning and rule-based reasoning)	Medical diagnosing contains complexities and diversities in predicting the rules for diagnosing. The proposed approach integrates the case-based reasoning and rule-based reasoning as a hybrid approach and achieves the diagnosing accuracy of 99.53% in breast cancer and thyroid diagnosis.
Shahina Begum et al.,(2012)	Imaging characteristics dataset	Review of CBR based medical diagnosis system	CBR	Presented a survey of recent medical CBR systems based on a literature review and concludes that CBR approach is capable of handling increasingly large, complex, and uncertain data in clinical environments.
Mariana Maceiras Cabrera et al.,(2010)	Image characteristics dataset	Diagnosis of Acute bacterial meningitis.	Hybrid CBR and RBR methods	Integration of the CBR and RBR methods in the development of a medical diagnosis take more computation time.
Rainer Schmidt et al.,(2010)			Case-based reasoning for medical knowledge-based Systems.	Discuss the appropriateness of CBR for medical knowledge based systems and concludes that CBR is capable of point out the problems, limitations and possibilities.
Mrs. S. S. Gulavani et al.,(2009)	Breast cancer dataset	Review of knowledge based systems in medical diagnosis	Experts systems with knowledge base	Expert systems can be enhanced with additions to the knowledge base or to the set of rules, knowledge based systems have been extensively used in the medical diagnosis
Mobyen Uddin Ahmed et al.,(2008)	Imaging dataset	Diagnosis of stress	CBR with enhanced cosine and fuzzy similarity	Hybrid case-based reasoning system for stress diagnosis. The proposed approach uses similarity estimates for improved case ranking and retrieval compared with traditional distance-based matching criteria. It achieves accuracy of 66% to 79%. Complexity of the algorithm is high. Takes more computation time.
Bichindaritz et al.,(2006)	Blood cell dataset	biology and medicine research	Artificial intelligence and knowledge acquisition, model based reasoning	Proposed a framework for semantic interoperability of case based reasoning systems in biology and medicine researches and achieves 70% of performance accuracy.
Montani M et al.,(2001)	Diabetes dataset	Diabetes monitoring system	Multi Modal Reasoning methodology	Integrated method of CBR and rule based reasoning, for supporting context detection, information retrieval and therapy revision in diabetes care.
C. Le Guillou et al.,(1999)	Imaging characteristics dataset	Endoscopic images diagnosis aid	Case based reasoning (CBR)	A knowledge base describing endoscopic pathologies is destined to take place of a control unit of coherence for similarities search.

proposed work aims to develop an improved automatic anatomic location identification approach for predicting the foreign body lodgment location on pediatric foreign body aspired radiography images.

From the literature the common advantage and disadvantages of case base reasoning are identified and presented in Table 3.

Table 3. Assessing the significant pros and cons of CBR approach

S.no	CBR Advantages	CBR Disadvantages
1	Knowledge acquisition process is simple with documented case library	If the similarity matching process is complex, computational cost is high.
2	Efficient knowledge maintenance process	Distance calculations between the desired and actual solution can be difficult
3	CBR is a cognitive problem solving model	Rules adaptation may be quite difficult
4	CBR performs better than rule-based systems	Building a case library may not be easy in some situations
5	The best experience of the previous case only can produce better knowledge base.	Learning, demands some considerations as to which cases are added to the case library

Based on the observation of existing work, it is concluded to make use of CBR approach for the treatment management process of pediatric foreign body aspiration. The CBR is mainly based on the reusability in which the case base is reused and matched against the problem with the help of similarity calculations. The main advantage of CBR approach is its closeness to the human thinking. The CBR method is implemented in a four step process-retrieval of the most similar cases compared to the case base by identifying relevant problems and matching the case, reuse the retrieved case to solve new problem, revise and adapt the proposed solution and retaining the useful information from final solution in the case base.

Proposed Work

The aim of the proposed work is to improve the performance of automatic anatomic location identification approach (AALIA) and to develop reasoning based systematic approach for pediatric foreign body aspiration treatment management with fastest learning capabilities, domain knowledge and better efficiency in retrieval algorithm. The proposed approach includes our previous research work of image segmentation, shape determination and automatic anatomic location identification, feature identification of the required region of interest based on pixel, edge, shape and texture and optimal feature selection on foreign body aspired pediatric radiographic images. Figure 1 shows the schematic view of systematic approach of automatic anatomic location identification and CBR based treatment management system for standardizing the pediatric foreign body aspiration treatment process.

Improved Automatic Anatomic Location Identification Algorithm (I-AALIA)

Identifying the anatomic location in pediatric radiography image is a challenging task in treatment management process. Complications arising from foreign body aspiration is usually depend on the anatomic location, type of the aspired foreign body and the duration of time the foreign body remained in the

Figure 1. Framework of CBR based for pediatric foreign body aspiration diagnosis and treatment management system

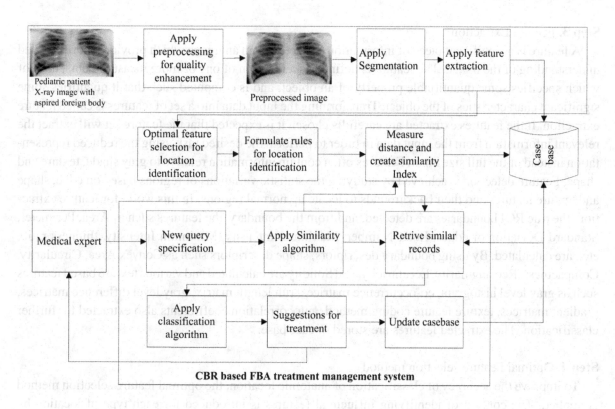

human body. The existing framework of automatic anatomic location identification approach (AALIA) involves corner identification method with a fixed template by considering the pixel position values of identified regions. The 8- connected block searching method, randomly takes seed point to begin the search, it increases the computation time. Hence the proposed work aims to improve the AALIA by introducing the feature based rules creation method to identify the common anatomic location such as esophageal, airway, bronchus, trachea, gastrointestinal in the pediatric FB aspired X-Ray image.

Steps Involved In Improved Automatic Anatomic Location Identification Algorithm (I-AALIA)

Step 1. Preprocessing

Image preprocessing is a low level process in which, the inputs and outputs both are images. It involves primitive operations such as reducing the noise, contrast enhancement and image sharpening.

Step 2. Segmentation

Image segmentation produces a binary representation of the object with features of interest such as shapes and edges. Foreign body anatomic localization is the significant task in treatment management process of foreign body aspiration. Isolating the foreign body region of interest is done by various image segmentation techniques such as median filtering, iterative thresholding, sobel edge detection and K-Means clustering technique for segmenting the meaningful regions from pediatric FB aspired radiography images.

Step 3. Feature Extraction

A feature is a significant piece of information extracted from an image which provides more detailed understanding of the image. The feature is defined as a function of one or more measurements, each of which specifies some quantifiable property of an object, and is computed such that it quantifies some significant characteristics of the object. Transforming the input data into a set of features is called feature extraction. If the features extracted are carefully chosen it is expected that the feature set will extract the relevant information from the input data in order to perform the desired task using the reduced representation instead of the full size input. Features often contain information relative to gray shade, texture and shape. Feature detection is achieved by studying the statistic variations of regions based on edge, shape and texture features and their backgrounds to locate up normal regions. In this work, for feature extraction, the true ROI boundaries are detected, and from the boundary, the features such as Area, Perimeter, Standard Deviation of edges, Eular Number, Maximum Intensity, Minimum Intensity, thinness ratio, etc., are calculated. By using boundary descriptors, shape descriptors such as Convex Area, Circularity, Compactness, Rectangularity, Eccentricity, and Solidity are calculated and various texture based features such as gray level histogram, co-occurrence matrices, run length matrix, gray level difference matrices, gradient matrices, texture feature coding method, autocorrelation coefficients also extracted for further classification. The extracted features are stored in case base.

Step 4. Optimal Feature selection method

To improve the accuracy of classification of anatomic location, the optimal feature selection method is applied. The concept of identifying influential features is introduced for each type of location by considering the receiver operator characteristic (ROC) measures. The influential features are identified by assessing the optimal features based on the features gain values which are calculated by Euclidean distance measure by WEKA tool. The ranking is applied from highest to lowest values of the features. The ranked features are considered for similarity measure in case base reasoning. The result of the same is discussed in Table 4, Table 5, Table 6, Table 7, and Table 8. The results obtained from the developed

Figure 2. Sample snapshot from WEKA tool showing selected location features

```
        13 ClusterShade
        12 ClusterProminence
        15 Energy1
        Merit of best subset found : 0.707

Attribute Subset Evaluator (supervised, Class (nominal): 30 Location):
        CFS Subset Evaluator
        Including locally predictive attributes

Selected attributes: 1,5,6,14,24,25,26 : 7
                     stddev
                     Dispersion
                     Size
                     Dissimilarity
                     Differenceentropy
                     Inmcorr1
                     Inmcorr2
```

Table 4. Assessing the optimal features for Bronchus location

Influenced optimal Feature for Bronchus	
Ranked Features	**Ranking Value**
Size	1.04
Cluster Shade	1.09
Sum entropy	0.89
Difference entropy	0.59
Inmcorr2	0.58

Table 5. Assessing the optimal features for Lung location

Influenced optimal Feature for lungs	
Ranked Features	**Ranking Value**
Entropy	0.98
Size	0.97
Sum entropy	0.94
maximum probability	0.92
energy1	0.81

Table 6. Assessing the optimal features for Airway and esophagus location

Influenced optimal Feature for Airway and esophagus	
Ranked Features	**Ranking Value**
Size	0.99
Cluster Shade	0.99
Sum entropy	0.99
Difference entropy	0.68
Inmcorr2	0.68

Table 7. Assessing the optimal features for GI region

Influenced optimal Feature for GI Region	
Ranked Features	**Ranking Value**
Standard deviation	0.95
Elongation	0.94
Correlation1	0.94
Difference entropy	0.93
IDHomom	0.81
Size	0.58

Table 8. Assessing the optimal features for Diaphragm

Influenced optimal Feature for Diaphragm	
Ranked Features	**Ranking Value**
Dispersion	0.99
Size	0.99
Solidity	0.98
Contrast	0.87
Cluster Shade	0.85
Dissimilarity	0.76
Difference variance	0.74
Inmcorr1	0.68

method are illustrated optimal features such Standard deviation, size, dissimilarity, difference entropy, information measure of correlation1, information measure of correlation2 with their corresponding ranking for location identification is presented in Figure 2.

Based on the experimental results, size, cluster shade, sum entropy and information correlation are identified as the influenced optimal features for classifying the bronchus anatomic location. Entropy, size, sum entropy maximum probability and energy are identified as the influenced optimal features for classifying the lung anatomic location. Size, cluster shade, sum entropy, difference entropy and information correlation are identified as the influenced optimal features for classifying the airway and esophagus anatomic location. Standard deviation, elongation, correlation, difference entropy, inverse difference homogenous measure and size are identified as the influenced optimal features for classifying the gastro intestinal anatomic location. Similarly size, dispersion, solidity, contrast, cluster shade, dissimilarity, difference variance, and information correlation are the influenced optimal features for diaphragm anatomic location.

Step 5. Formulate Decision Rules for Location Identification

The existing Automatic Anatomic Location Identification Approach AALIA make use of corner identification method and 8 connected block searching method to identify some of the common anatomic location such as esophageal, airway, bronchus, trachea, gastrointestinal in pediatric FB aspired X-ray image. The j48 decision tree is used for location and shape prediction and achieves 80% of performance accuracy but the work has some limitations in rules generation and mapping the anatomic region that is the pixel position and intensity value alone is used to distinguish similar region of interest and mapping is done by predefined template of anatomic location based on pixel coordinates. Hence a simple change in template pixel positions can largely affect the prediction accuracy and which leads to misclassification. To overcome the issue the proposed improved AALIA uses random forest decision tree algorithm for generating the rules. The rules are constructed with selected optimal features. As per the conclusion made by lakshmi Devasena et al., (2014), the random forest classifier performs best then by J48 Classifier, the random forest decision tree is used for generation the rules based on the optimal features selected for each anatomic location. The decision rules for predicting bronchus anatomic location based on the selected optimal features such as cluster shade, information measure correlation, standard deviation, entropy, autocorrelation and rectangularity are presented in figure 3. The decision rules for predicting diaphragm anatomic location based on the selected optimal features are presented in figure 4. The decision rules for predicting lung anatomic location based on the selected optimal features are presented in figure 5.

3.1 CBR based treatment management system

The proposed work adopts case base reasoning approach for its closeness to the human thinking. In general, case based reasoning is the process of providing the solutions to the unsolved problems based on the knowledge or information gathered from the solutions of the previous problems of similar nature. The proposed framework of the CBR based treatment management system consist the basic mechanisms for pediatric foreign body aspiration case representation with object localization and feature extraction, the similarity assessment, and the retrieval techniques of case based reasoning approach. For the development of treatment management system requires the following requirements.

Figure 3. The decision rules for predicting bronchus anatomic location

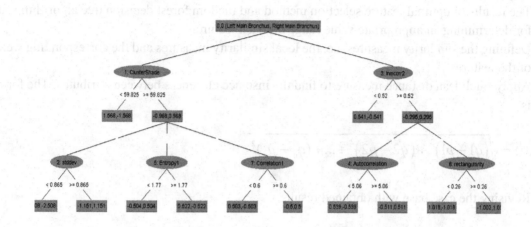

Figure 4. The decision rules for predicting diaphragm anatomic location

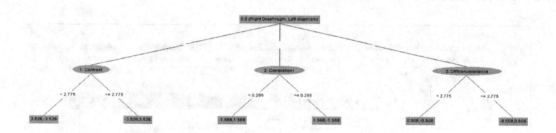

Figure 5. The decision rules for predicting lung anatomic location

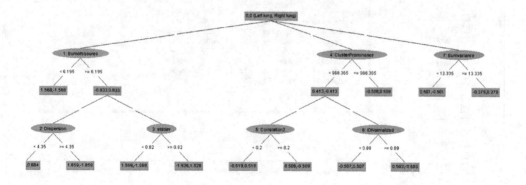

- Feature extraction methods are applied to segmented structure to extract the required data such as shape, size, texture and angle to describe a set of relevant information from the input image.
- The results of optimal feature selection method and random forest decision tree algorithm is used for determining an appropriate value range for each feature.
- Defining the similarity measures, i.e. the local similarity measures and the corresponding weights of the features.
- Apply Euclidean distance measure to find the instance closeness between attributes. The formula is

$$d(p,q) = \sqrt{\left(q1 - p1\right)^2 + \left(q2 - p2\right)^2 + ... + \left(q_n - p_n\right)^2} \tag{1}$$

- Revising the case base with obtained results.

The validation involves number of physicians, experienced radiologist and domain experts for further updates or improvements of the decision support system. In order to improve validation, a medical expert is required to decide whether a suggestion of the decision support system is appropriate. Sample result of the developed case based reasoning tool is shown is figure 6 and figure 7.

Figure 6. Sample result of developed case base reasoning tool

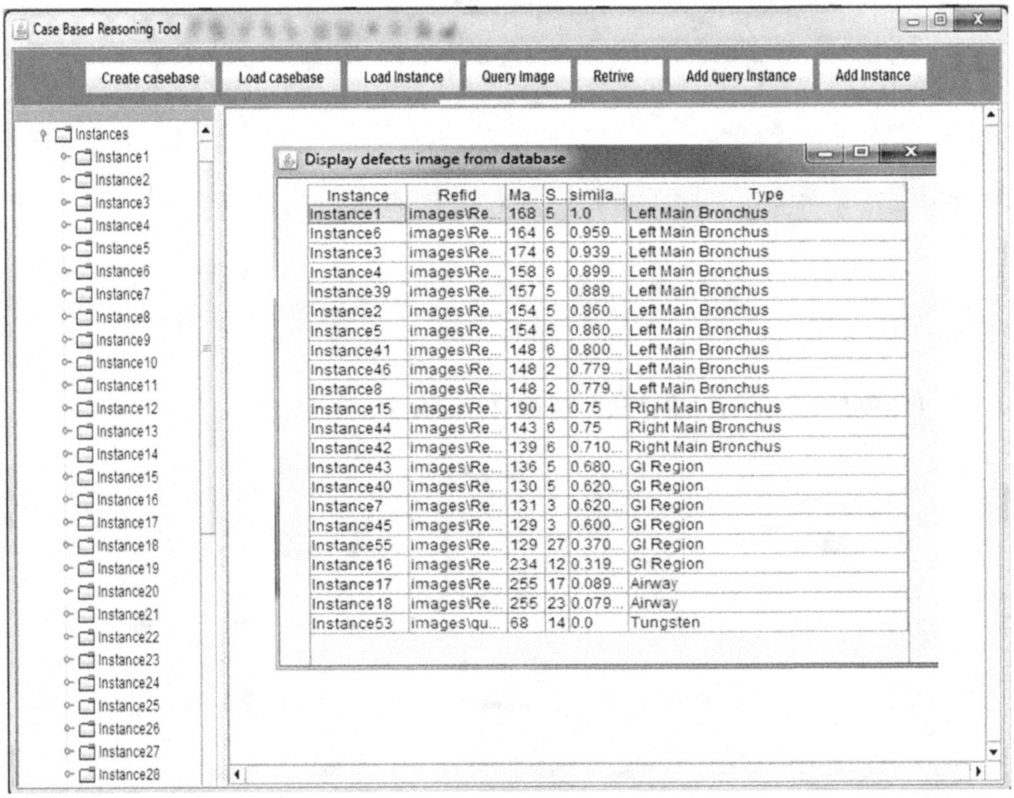

Figure 7. Sample similarity result from case base reasoning tool

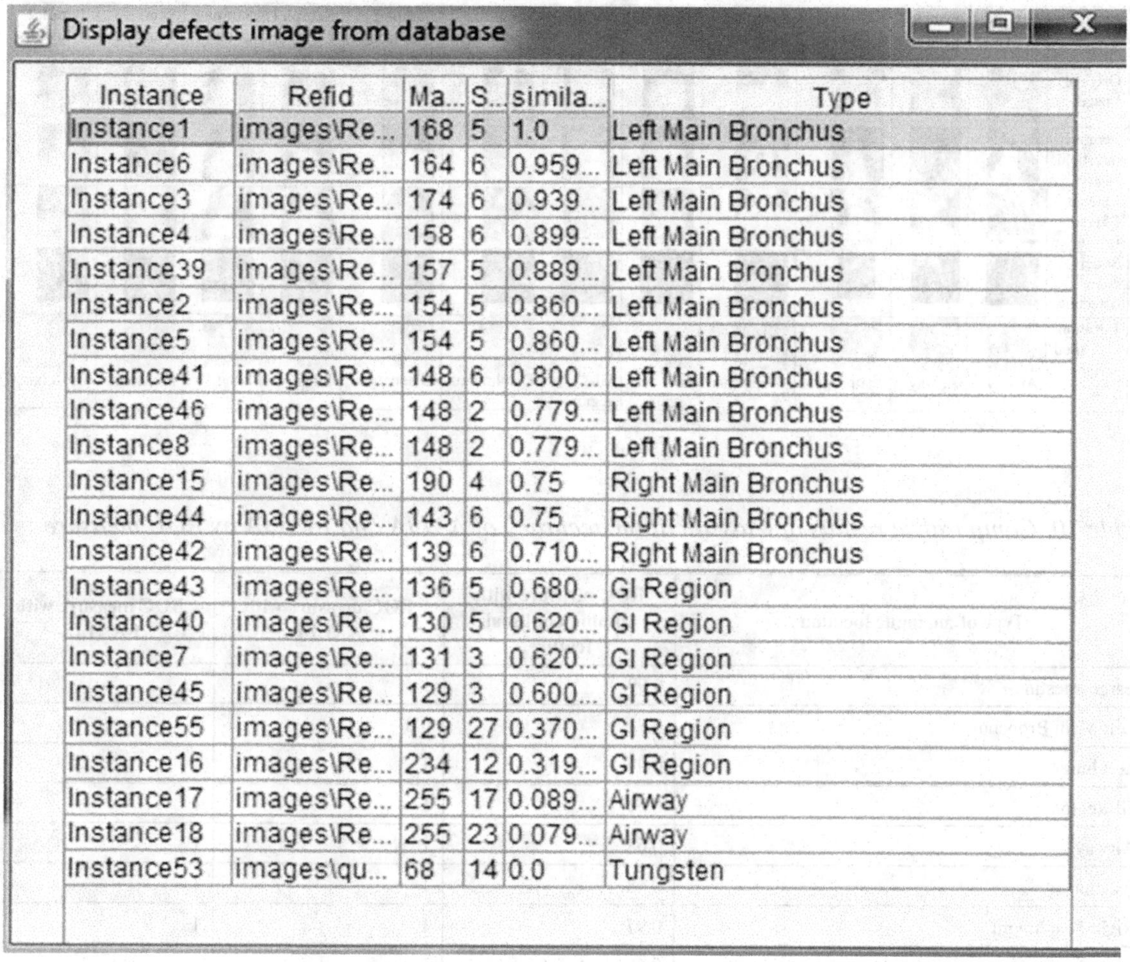
Display defects image from database

Instance	Refid	Ma...	S...	simila...	Type
Instance1	images\Re...	168	5	1.0	Left Main Bronchus
Instance6	images\Re...	164	6	0.959...	Left Main Bronchus
Instance3	images\Re...	174	6	0.939...	Left Main Bronchus
Instance4	images\Re...	158	6	0.899...	Left Main Bronchus
Instance39	images\Re...	157	5	0.889...	Left Main Bronchus
Instance2	images\Re...	154	5	0.860...	Left Main Bronchus
Instance5	images\Re...	154	5	0.860...	Left Main Bronchus
Instance41	images\Re...	148	6	0.800...	Left Main Bronchus
Instance46	images\Re...	148	2	0.779...	Left Main Bronchus
Instance8	images\Re...	148	2	0.779...	Left Main Bronchus
Instance15	images\Re...	190	4	0.75	Right Main Bronchus
Instance44	images\Re...	143	6	0.75	Right Main Bronchus
Instance42	images\Re...	139	6	0.710...	Right Main Bronchus
Instance43	images\Re...	136	5	0.680...	GI Region
Instance40	images\Re...	130	5	0.620...	GI Region
Instance7	images\Re...	131	3	0.620...	GI Region
Instance45	images\Re...	129	3	0.600...	GI Region
Instance55	images\Re...	129	27	0.370...	GI Region
Instance16	images\Re...	234	12	0.319...	GI Region
Instance17	images\Re...	255	17	0.089...	Airway
Instance18	images\Re...	255	23	0.079...	Airway
Instance53	images\qu...	68	14	0.0	Tungsten

EXPERIMENTAL RESULTS AND DISCUSSION

The 80 randomly taken pediatric foreign body aspired radiography images were used for the experimental test. Table 9 shows the identified features of sample input of anatomic locations such as Airway, Esophagus, Gastro Intestinal region (Small and Large intestine), Diaphragm, Lung and Bronchus in the pediatric foreign body identified image.

PERFORMANCE ANALYSIS

The ability of the developed improved anatomic location identification approach I-AALIA is measured with ROC classification accuracy. The performance comparison is made with AALIA for location identification. The comparative results of Classification accuracy of AALIA and IAALIA by ROC measure is presented in Table 10.

Table 9. Sample Experimental results of automatic anatomic location identification approach

Table 10. Comparative results of Classification accuracy of AALIA and IAALIA by ROC measure

Type of anatomic location	ROC measure with common optimal feature	ROC measure with AALIA	ROC measure with I-AALIA
Large intestine	0.99	1	1
Left Main Bronchus	0.72	0.8	1
Left lung	0.99	1	1
GI Region	0.51	1	1
Airway	0.68	1	1
Esophagus	0.98	1	1
Right Diaphragm	0.97	1	1
Right Lung	0.66	1	1
Right Main Bronchus	0.71	0.8	1
Left Diaphragm	0.71	1	1

CONCLUSION

In this work, a prototype of a CBR based treatment management system with improved automatic anatomic location identification approach. The underlying case base reasoning approach is based on the statistical and texture characteristics of anatomic location description and the similarity metric defined in the feature vector space. The developed I-AALIA approach is efficient for analyzing the pediatric foreign body aspired radiography images for doctors and medical practitioners. The optimal feature selection method gives optimal features for location determination. The experimental result proves that the ROC performance accuracy for all the location class, comparatively gives better results with the existing work of AALIA. This system can be further extended to large databases where the time consumption for data retrieval and analysis is more.

REFERENCES

Ahmed, M. U., Begum, S., Funk, P., & Xiong, N. (2008). Case-based reasoning for diagnosis of stress using enhanced cosine and fuzzy similarity. *Transactions on Case-Based Reasoning for Multimedia Data, 1*(1), 3–19.

Begum, S., Ahmed, M. U., Funk, P., Xiong, N., & Folke, M. (2012). Case-Based Reasoning Systems in the Health Sciences: A Survey of Recent Trends and Developments. *IEEE Transactions on Systems, Man and Cybernetics. Part C, Applications and Reviews, 41*(4), 421–434. doi:10.1109/TSMCC.2010.2071862

Benjelloun, M., & Mahmoudi, S. (2009). S Spine Localization in X-ray Images Using Interest Point Detection. *Journal of Digital Imaging, 22*(3), 309–318. doi:10.100710278-007-9099-3 PMID:18273669

Bichindaritz. (2006). A framework for semantic interoperability of case-based reasoning systems in biology and medicine. *Artificial Intelligence Medical Journal, 36*(2),177-92.

Cabrera, M. M. (2010). Integration of Rule Based Expert Systems and Case Based Reasoning in an Acute Bacterial Meningitis Clinical Decision Support System. *International Journal of Computer Science and Information Security, 7*(2), 20–29.

Danelson, K. A., Geer, C. P., Stitzel, J. D., Slice, D. E., & Takhounts, E. G. (2008). Age and Gender Based Biomechanical Shape and Size Analysis of the Pediatric Brain. *Stapp Car Crash Journal, 52*(2), 59–81. doi:10.4271/2008-22-0003 PMID:19085158

Demigha, S. (2016). A case-based reasoning tool for breast cancer knowledge management with data mining concepts and techniques. *SPIE Proceedings, 9789,* 1-10.

Gulavani & Kulkarni (2009). A review of knowledge based systems in medical diagnosis. *International Journal of Information Technology and Knowledge Management, 2*(2), 269-275.

Jimenez-del-Toro, O., Muller, H., Krenn, M., Gruenberg, K., Taha, A. A., Winterstein, M., ... Hanbury, A. (2016). Cloud-Based Evaluation of Anatomical Structure Segmentation and Landmark Detection Algorithms: VISCERAL Anatomy Benchmarks. *IEEE Transactions on Medical Imaging, 35*(11), 1–10. doi:10.1109/TMI.2016.2578680 PMID:27305669

Klinder, Ostermann, Ehm, Kneser, & Lorenz. (2009). C Automated model-based vertebra detection, identification, and segmentation in CT images. *Medical Image Analysis, 13*(3), 471–482.

Lakshmi Devasena, C. (2014). Comparative Analysis of Random Forest, REP Tree and J48 Classifiers for Credit Risk Prediction. *International Journal of Computers and Applications, 8*(7), 30–36.

Le Guillou, C. (1999). Case-based reasoning (CBR) in endoscopic images diagnosis aid, *Engineering in Medicine and Biology. IEEE Transactions on Systems, Man and Cybernetics. Part C, Applications and Reviews, 1*(4), 21–34.

Lecron, F., & Benjelloun, M. (2012). Fully Automatic Vertebra Detection in X-Ray Images Based on Multi-Class SVM. *Medical Imaging, SPIE proceedings, 8314*(2), 1-8.

Megalooikonomou, Barnathan, & Konto. (2009). A Representation and Classification Scheme for Tree-like Structures in Medical Images: Analyzing the Branching Pattern of Ductal Trees in X-ray Galacto-grams. *IEEE TMI*, *28*(4), 487-493.

Montani, M., & Bellazzi, R. (2001). Intelligent knowledge retrieval for decision support in medical applications. *Studies in Health Technology and Informatics*, *84*(1), 498–502. PMID:11604790

Neu, S. C., & Toga, A. W. (2008). Automatic Localization of Anatomical Point Landmarks for Brain Image Processing Algorithms. *Neuroinformatics*, *6*(2), 135–148. doi:10.100712021-008-9018-x PMID:18512163

Nuzhnaya. (2011). Segmentation of anatomical branching structures based on texture features and graph cut. *IEEE International Symposium on Biomedical Imaging*, *52*(20), 35-42.

Ochs, J. G., Goldin, J., Abtin, F., Kim, H., Brown, K., Batra, P., ... Brown, M. (2007). Automated classification of lung bronchovascular anatomy in CT using AdaBoost. *Medical Image Analysis*, *11*(3), 315–324. doi:10.1016/j.media.2007.03.004 PMID:17482500

Schmidt, R., & Gierl, L. (2010). Case-based Reasoning for Medical Knowledge-based Systems. *Medical Infobahn for Europe*, *7*(7), 720–725. PMID:11187647

Horvath, Nikhazy, Horvath, & Horvath. (2010). Segmentation of anatomical structures on chest radiographs. *International Journal of Medical Sciences*, *4*(3), 1–4.

Sharaf-El-Deen, D. A., Moawad, I. F., & Khalifa, M. E. (2014). A new hybrid case-based reasoning approach for medical diagnosis systems. *Journal of Medical Systems*, *38*(2), 1–11. doi:10.100710916-014-0009-1 PMID:24469683

Upreti & Gupta (2015). Imaging for Diagnosis of Foreign Body Aspiration in Children. *Indian Pediatrics*, *52*(1), 659-690.

Compilation of References

Advanced Realtime Tracking, A. R. T. (n.d.). Retrieved November 22, 2019, from https://ar-tracking.com/

Agarwal, S., Furukawa, Y., Snavely, N., Simon, I., Curless, B., Seitz, S. M., & Szeliski, R. (2011). Building Rome in a Day. *Communications of the ACM*, *54*(10), 105–112. doi:10.1145/2001269.2001293

Agisoft PhotoScan. (n.d.). Retrieved July 26, 2017, from https://www.agisoft.com/

Agisoft. (2010). *Metashape*. Retrieved from http://www.agisoft.com

Ahmed, M., Idrees, M., ul Abideen, Z., Mumtaz, R., & Khalique, S. (2016). Deaf talk using 3D animated sign language: A sign language interpreter using Microsoft's kinect v2. *2016 SAI Computing Conference (SAI)*, 330–335. 10.1109/SAI.2016.7556002

Ahmed, A., & Khalid, M. (2017). Multi-step ahead wind forecasting using nonlinear autoregressive neural networks. *Energy Procedia*, *134*, 192–204. doi:10.1016/j.egypro.2017.09.609

Ahmed, M. U., Begum, S., Funk, P., & Xiong, N. (2008). Case-based reasoning for diagnosis of stress using enhanced cosine and fuzzy similarity. *Transactions on Case-Based Reasoning for Multimedia Data*, *1*(1), 3–19.

AIM@SHAPE. (n.d.). http://visionair.ge.imati.cnr.it/ontologies/ shapes/

Al-allaf, O. N., & AbdAlKader, S. A. (2011). Nonlinear Autoregressive neural network for estimation soil temperature: a comparison of different optimization neural network algorithms. *UBICC J*, 42-51.

Albrecht, S., Wiemann, T., Gunther, M., & Hertzberg, J. (2011). Matching CAD object models in semantic mapping. In *Proceedings ICRA 2011 Workshop: Semantic Perception, Mapping and Exploration*. SPME.

Albuquerque, E. R., Sampaio, E. V., Pareyn, F. G., & Araújo, E. L. (2015). Root biomass under stem bases and at different distances from trees. *Journal of Arid Environments*, *116*, 82–88. doi:10.1016/j.jaridenv.2015.02.003

Alexanderson, S., & Beskow, J. (2015). Towards Fully Automated Motion Capture of Signs--Development and Evaluation of a Key Word Signing Avatar. *ACM Transactions on Accessible Computing*, *7*(2), 7. doi:10.1145/2764918

Alexiadis, D. S., Chatzitofis, A., Zioulis, N., Zoidi, O., Louizis, G., Zarpalas, D., & Daras, P. (2016). An integrated platform for live 3D human reconstruction and motion capturing. *IEEE Transactions on Circuits and Systems for Video Technology*, *27*(4), 798–813. doi:10.1109/TCSVT.2016.2576922

Al-khazraji, S., Berke, L., Kafle, S., Yeung, P., & Huenerfauth, M. (2018). Modeling the Speed and Timing of American Sign Language to Generate Realistic Animations. *Proceedings of the 20th International ACM SIGACCESS Conference on Computers and Accessibility*, 259–270. 10.1145/3234695.3236356

Almeida, S. G. M., Guimarães, F. G., & Ramírez, J. A. (2014). Feature extraction in Brazilian Sign Language Recognition based on phonological structure and using RGB-D sensors. *Expert Systems with Applications*, *41*(16), 7259–7271. doi:10.1016/j.eswa.2014.05.024

Almer, A., Schnabel, T., Stelzl, H., Stieg, J., & Luley, P. (2006). A tourism information system for rural areas based on a multi platform concept. In *International Symposium on Web and Wireless Geographical Information Systems* (pp. 31-41). Springer. 10.1007/11935148_4

Amari, S. (Ed.). (2000). *Neural Computing: New Challenges and Perspectives for the New Millennium* (Vol. 2). IEEE Computer Society.

Amberg, B., Romdhani, S., & Vetter, T. (2007, June). Optimal step nonrigid ICP algorithms for surface registration. In *2007 IEEE Conference on Computer Vision and Pattern Recognition* (pp. 1-8). IEEE. doi:10.1109/AVSS.2009.58

Anderson, E. F., McLoughlin, L., Liarokapis, F., Peters, C., Petridis, P., & De Freitas, S. (2010). Developing serious games for cultural heritage: A state-of-the-art review. *Virtual Reality (Waltham Cross)*, *14*(4), 255–275. doi:10.100710055-010-0177-3

Andreetto, M., Brusco, N., & Cortelazzo, G. M. (2004). Automatic 3-d modeling of textured cultural heritage objects. *IEEE Transactions on Image Processing*, *13*(3), 354–369. doi:10.1109/TIP.2003.821351 PMID:15376927

Ankerst, M., Breunig, M. M., Kriegel, H.-P., & Sander, J. (1999). OPTICS: Ordering Points to Identify the Clustering Structure. In *Proceedings of the 1999 ACM SIGMOD International Conference on Management of Data* (pp. 49–60). New York, NY: ACM. 10.1145/304182.304187

Antoniou, A., Storkey, A., & Edwards, H. (2017). *Data Augmentation Generative Adversarial Networks*. Retrieved from https://arxiv.org/abs/1711.04340

Antoniou, A., Lepouras, G., Bampatzia, S., & Almpanoudi, H. (2013). An approach for serious game development for cultural heritage: Case study for an archaeological site and museum. *Journal on Computing and Cultural Heritage*, *6*(4), 17. doi:10.1145/2532630.2532633

Apache. (2014). *Data Format Description Language (DFDL) v1.0 Specification*. https://daffodil.incubator.apache.org/docs/dfdl/

Arbelaiz, A., Moreno, A., Kabongo, L., Polys, N., & García-Alonso, A. (2017). Community-driven extensions to the X3D volume rendering component. In *Proceedings of the 22nd International Conference on 3D Web Technology* (p. 1). ACM. 10.1145/3055624.3075945

Argyriou, V., Zafeiriou, S., & Petrou, M. (2014). Optimal illumination directions for faces and rough surfaces for single and multiple light imaging using class-specific prior knowledge. *Computer Vision and Image Understanding*, *125*, 16–36. doi:10.1016/j.cviu.2014.01.012

Aristidou, A., Stavrakis, E., Charalambous, P., Chrysanthou, Y., & Himona, S. L. (2015). Folk Dance Evaluation Using Laban Movement Analysis. *Journal on Computing and Cultural Heritage*, *8*(4), 20:1–20:19. doi:10.1145/2755566

Aristidou, A., Stavrakis, E., Papaefthimiou, M., Papagiannakis, G., & Chrysanthou, Y. (2018). Style-based motion analysis for dance composition. *The Visual Computer*, *34*(12), 1725–1737. doi:10.100700371-017-1452-z

Arjovsky, M., & Bottou, L. (2017). *Towards Principled Methods for Training Generative Adversarial Networks*. Retrieved from https://arxiv.org/abs/1701.04862

Arjovsky, M., Chintala, S., & Bottou, L. (2017). *Wasserstein GAN*. Retrieved from https://arxiv.org/abs/1701.07875

Atazadeh, B., Kalantari, M., Rajabifard, A., Ho, S., & Ngo, T. (2016). Building Information Modelling for High Rise Land Administration. *Transaction in GIS*.

Attene, M., Robbiano, F., Spagnuolo, M., & Falcidieno, B. (2007). Semantic Annotation of 3D Surface Meshes Based on Feature Characterization, Semantic Multimedia. Springer Berlin/Heidelberg.

Attene, M., Robbiano, F., Spagnuolo, M., & Falcidieno, B. (2007). Semantic Annotation of 3D Surface Meshes Based on Feature Characterization. In Semantic Multimedia, (pp. 126–139). Springer Berlin Heidelberg.

Autodesk Inc. (2014a). *Basic concepts on solution in CAD*. Retrieved from https://www.autodesk.com/Solutions/Cad-software

Autodesk Inc. (2014b). *Building Information Modelling*. Retrieved from http://www.Architect-bim.com/what-is-bim-part2-building-information-modelling-and-bim-maturity-levels/

Azuma, R. T. (1997). A survey of augmented reality. *Presence: Teleoper. Virtual Environ.*, *6*(4), 355–385. doi:10.1162/pres.1997.6.4.355

Baillard, C., & Zisserman, A. (2000). A plane-sweep strategy for the 3D reconstruction of buildings from multiple images. *International Archives of Photogrammetry and Remote Sensing, 33*(B2), 56-62.

Bailo, O., Ham, D., & Shin, Y. M. (2019). *Red blood cell image generation for data augmentation using Conditional Generative Adversarial Networks*. Retrieved from https://arxiv.org/abs/1901.06219

Bakalos, N., Rallis, I., Doulamis, N., Doulamis, A., Protopapadakis, E., & Voulodimos, A. (2019). Choreographic Pose Identification using Convolutional Neural Networks. *2019 11th International Conference on Virtual Worlds and Games for Serious Applications (VS-Games)*, 1–7. 10.1109/VS-Games.2019.8864522

Ballas, A., Santad, T., Sookhanaphibarn, K., & Choensawat, W. (2017). Game-based system for learning labanotation using Microsoft Kinect. *2017 IEEE 6th Global Conference on Consumer Electronics (GCCE)*, 1–3. 10.1109/GCCE.2017.8229481

Banda-R, K., Delgado-Salinas, A., Dexter, K. G., Linares-Palomino, R., Oliveira-Filho, A., Prado, D., ... Rodríguez, M. (2016). Plant diversity patterns in neotropical dry forests and their conservation implications. *Science, 353*(6306), 1383–1387. doi:10.1126cience.aaf5080 PMID:27708031

Bandura, A. (1989). Human agency in social cognitive theory. *American Psychologist, 44*(9), 1175.

Bandura, A. (2001). Social cognitive theory: An agentic perspective. *Annual Review of Psychology, 52*(1), 1–26. doi:10.1146/annurev.psych.52.1.1 PMID:11148297

Bao, J., Chen, D., Wen, F., Li, H., & Hua, G. (2017). *CVAE-GAN: Fine-Grained Image Generation through Asymmetric Training*. Retrieved from https://arxiv.org/abs/1703.10155

Barmpoutis, P. (2017). *Design and Development of a System for the Processing of Wood Images of Greek Forest Species* (Doctoral dissertation). Aristotle University of Thessaloniki, Greece.

Barmpoutis, P., Dimitropoulos, K., Barboutis, I., Grammalidis, N., & Lefakis, P. (2018). Wood species recognition through multidimensional texture analysis. *Computers and Electronics in Agriculture, 144*, 241–248. doi:10.1016/j.compag.2017.12.011

Barone, S., Paoli, A., & Razionale, A. V. (2012). 3D virtual reconstructions of artworks by a multiview scanning process. In *2012 18th International Conference on Virtual Systems and Multimedia* (pp. 259–265). 10.1109/VSMM.2012.6365933

Basler AG – Industrial Camera Manufacturer. (n.d.). Retrieved November 22, 2019, from https://www.baslerweb.com/en/

Bastanlar, Y., Grammalidis, N., Zabulis, X., Yilmaz, E., Yardimci, Y., & Triantafyllidis, G. (2008). 3D Reconstruction for a Cultural Heritage virtual tour system. *Paper presented at the The International Archives of the Photogrammetry, Remote Sensing and Spatial Information Sciences, 37*(b5).

Bay, H. T. (2006). Surf: Speeded up robust features. *European conference on computer vision*, 404-417.

Bay, H., Tuytelaars, T., & Gool, L. V. (2006). SURF: Speeded Up Robust Features. In *Computer Vision – ECCV 2006* (pp. 404–417). Berlin: Springer. doi:10.1007/11744023_32

Becker, C., Häni, N., Rosinskaya, E., d'Angelo, E., & Strecha, C. (2017). Classification of Aerial Photogrammetric 3d Point Clouds. *ISPRS Annals of Photogrammetry, Remote Sensing and Spatial Information Sciences*, 3-10.

Begum, S., Ahmed, M. U., Funk, P., Xiong, N., & Folke, M. (2012). Case-Based Reasoning Systems in the Health Sciences: A Survey of Recent Trends and Developments. *IEEE Transactions on Systems, Man and Cybernetics. Part C, Applications and Reviews, 41*(4), 421–434. doi:10.1109/TSMCC.2010.2071862

Behr, J., Eschler, P., Jung, Y., & Zöllner, M. (2009). X3DOM: a DOM-based HTML5/X3D integration model. In *Proceedings of the 14th international conference on 3D web technology* (pp. 127-135). ACM.

Behr, J., Eschler, P., Jung, Y., & Zöllner, M. (2009). X3DOM: a DOM-based HTML5/X3D integration model. *Proceedings of the 14th International Conference on 3D Web Technology*, 127-135. 10.1145/1559764.1559784

Bell & Dee. (2016). *Aberystwyth leaf evaluation dataset*. Academic Press.

Bello, F., Bulpitt, A., Gould, D. A., Holbrey, R., Hunt, C., How, T., . . . Zhang, Y. (2009). ImaGiNe-S: Imaging Guided Needle Simulation. *In Eurographics 2009, Medical Prize*, (pp. 5-8). Blender. Retrieved from https://www.blender.org

Bellotti, F., Kapralos, B., Lee, K., Moreno-Ger, P., & Berta, R. (2013). Assessment in and of serious games: An overview. *Advances in Human-Computer Interaction, 2013*, 1. doi:10.1155/2013/120791

Bench-Capon, T. J., & Dunne, P. E. (2007). Argumentation in artificial intelligence. *Artificial Intelligence, 171*(10-15), 619–641. doi:10.1016/j.artint.2007.05.001

Benjelloun, M., & Mahmoudi, S. (2009). S Spine Localization in X-ray Images Using Interest Point Detection. *Journal of Digital Imaging, 22*(3), 309–318. doi:10.100710278-007-9099-3 PMID:18273669

Bentaieb, A., & Hamarneh, G. (2017). Adversarial Stain Transfer for Histopathology Image Analysis. *IEEE Transactions on Medical Imaging, PP, 1*. doi:10.1109/TMI.2017.2781228 PMID:29533895

Bentley. (2016). *ContextCapture*. Retrieved from https://www.bentley.com

Berndt, D. J., & Clifford, J. (1994). Using dynamic time warping to find patterns in time series. *KDD Workshop, 10*, 359–370.

Berners-Lee, T., Handler, J., & Lassila, O. (2001). *The Semantic Web. A new form of Web content that is meaningful to computers will unleash a revolution of new possibilities* (Vol. 284). Scientific American.

Berners-Lee, T., Hendler, J., & Lassila, O. (2001). The semantic web. *Scientific American, 284*(5), 34–43. doi:10.1038 cientificamerican0501-34 PMID:11681174

Beuchle, R., Grecchi, R. C., Shimabukuro, Y. E., Seliger, R., Eva, H. D., Sano, E., & Achard, F. (2015). Land cover changes in the Brazilian Cerrado and Caatinga biomes from 1990 to 2010 based on a systematic remote sensing sampling approach. *Applied Geography (Sevenoaks, England), 58*, 116–127. doi:10.1016/j.apgeog.2015.01.017

Bichindaritz. (2006). A framework for semantic interoperability of case-based reasoning systems in biology and medicine. *Artificial Intelligence Medical Journal, 36*(2),177-92.

Bigand, F., Prigent, E., & Braffort, A. (2019). Animating Virtual Signers: The Issue of Gestural Anonymization. *Proceedings of the 19th ACM International Conference on Intelligent Virtual Agents*, 252–255. 10.1145/3308532.3329410

Bilasco, M., Genzel, J., Villanova, M. O., & Martin, H. (2006). An MPEG-7 framework enhancing the reuse of 3D models. *Proceedings of Web3D Symposium '06*, 65-73.

Bilasco, I. M., Gensel, J., Villanova-Oliver, M., & Martin, H. (2005). 3DSEAM: a model for annotating 3D scenes using MPEG-7. *Seventh IEEE International Symposium on Multimedia (ISM'05)*. DOI 10.1109/ISM.2005.2

Bilasco, M., Genzel, J., Villanova, M. O., & Martin, H. (2005). On Indexing of 3D Scenes Using MPEG-7. *Proceedings of ACM Multimedia '05*, 471-474. 10.1145/1101149.1101254

Bilasco, M., Genzel, J., Villanova, M. O., & Martin, H. (2007). Semantic-based Rules for 3D Scene Adaptation. *Proceedings of IEEE International Symposium on Multimedia '07*, 97-100.

Bille, W., Pellens, B., Kleinermann, F., & De Troyer, O. (2004). Intelligent Modelling of Virtual Worlds Using Domain Ontologies. *IVEVA, 97*.

Bille, W., Pellens, B., Kleinermann, F., & De Troyer, O. (2004). Intelligent modelling of virtual worlds using domain ontologies. *Proceedings of the Workshop of Intelligent Computing (WIC), held in conjunction with the MICAI 2004 conference*, 272–279.

Bimber, O., & Raskar, R. (2005). *Spatial Augmented Reality: Merging Real and Virtual Worlds*. A. K. Peters, Ltd. doi:10.1201/b10624

Blais, F., & Beraldin, J. A. (2006). Recent Developments in 3D Multi-modal Laser Imaging Applied to Cultural Heritage. *Machine Vision and Applications, 17*(6), 395–409. doi:10.100700138-006-0025-3

Blanz, V., & Vetter, T. (1999, July). A morphable model for the synthesis of 3D faces. In Siggraph (Vol. 99, No. 1999, pp. 187-194). ACM.

BlenderA. P. I. (n.d.). https://www.blender.org/api/.JSON

Blue Button. (n.d.). *Blue button Implementation Guide*. Retrieved from https://bluebutton.cms.gov/assets/ig/index.html

Bobkov, D., Chen, S., Jian, R., Iqbal, Z., & Steinbach, E. (2018). Noise-resistant Deep Learning for Object Classification in 3D Point Clouds Using a Point Pair Descriptor. *IEEE Robotics and Automation Letters*.

Bodnar, J. L., Candoré, J. C., Nicolas, J. L., Szatanik, G., Detalle, V., & Vallet, J. M. (2012). Stimulated infrared thermography applied to help restoring mural paintings. *NDT & E International, 49*(0), 40–46. doi:10.1016/j.ndteint.2012.03.007

Booth, J., Antonakos, E., Ploumpis, S., Trigeorgis, G., Panagakis, Y., & Zafeiriou, S. (2017, July). 3D face morphable models "In-The-Wild". In *2017 IEEE Conference on Computer Vision and Pattern Recognition (CVPR)* (pp. 5464-5473). IEEE. 10.1109/CVPR.2017.580

Booth, J., Roussos, A., Zafeiriou, S., Ponniah, A., & Dunaway, D. (2016). A 3d morphable model learned from 10,000 faces. In *Proceedings of the IEEE Conference on Computer Vision and Pattern Recognition* (pp. 5543-5552). IEEE.

Bouritsas, G., Bokhnyak, S., Ploumpis, S., Bronstein, M., & Zafeiriou, S. (2019). Neural 3d morphable models: Spiral convolutional networks for 3d shape representation learning and generation. In *Proceedings of the IEEE International Conference on Computer Vision* (pp. 7213-7222). 10.1109/ICCV.2019.00731

Bournez, E., Landes, T., Saudreau, M., Kastendeuch, P., & Najjar, G. (2017). From TLS point clouds to 3D models of trees: A comparison of existing algorithms for 3D tree reconstruction. ISPRS-International Archives of the Photogrammetry. *Remote Sensing and Spatial Information Sciences, 42*, 2.

Bouzid, Y., & Jemni, M. (2014). A Virtual Signer to Interpret SignWriting. In K. Miesenberger, D. Fels, D. Archambault, P. Pevnáz, & W. Zagler (Eds.), *Computers Helping People with Special Needs* (pp. 458–465). Cham: Springer International Publishing. doi:10.1007/978-3-319-08599-9_69

Bowles, C., Gunn, R., Hammers, A., & Rueckert, D. (2018). *GANsfer Learning: Combining labelled and unlabelled data for GAN based data augmentation.* Retrieved from https://arxiv.org/abs/1811.10669

Braffort, A., Benchiheub, M.-F., & Berret, B. (2015). APLUS: a 3D Corpus of French Sign Language. *International ACM SIGACCESS Conference on Computers and Accessibility.* 10.1145/2700648.2811380

Brock, A., Donahue, J., & Simonyan, K. (2018). *Large Scale GAN Training for High Fidelity Natural Image Synthesis.* Retrieved from https://arxiv.org/abs/1809.11096

Broekstra, J., & Kampman, A. (2004). *SeRQL: An RDF query and transformation language. Semantic Web and Peer-to-Peer.* https://gate.ac.uk/sale/dd/related-work/SeRQL.pdf

Brooks, R. A. (1991). Intelligence without representation. *Artificial Intelligence, 47*(1-3), 139–159. doi:10.1016/0004-3702(91)90053-M

Broquetas, M. (2010). *List of BIM Software and Providers.* Retrieved from www.cad-addict.com

Bruno, F., Bruno, S., De Sensi, G., Luchi, M.-L., Mancuso, S., & Muzzupappa, M. (2010). From 3D reconstruction to virtual reality: A complete methodology for digital archaeological exhibition. *Journal of Cultural Heritage, 11*(1), 42–49. doi:10.1016/j.culher.2009.02.006

Brunton, A., Bolkart, T., & Wuhrer, S. (2014, September). Multilinear wavelets: A statistical shape space for human faces. In *European Conference on Computer Vision* (pp. 297-312). Springer. 10.1007/978-3-319-10590-1_20

Bujari, A., Ciman, M., Gaggi, O., & Palazzi, C. E. (2017). Using gamification to discover cultural heritage locations from geo-tagged photos. *Personal and Ubiquitous Computing, 21*(2), 235–252. doi:10.100700779-016-0989-6

Bunkhumpornpat, C., Sinapiromsaran, K., & Lursinsap, C. (2012). DBSMOTE: Density-based synthetic minority oversampling technique. *Applied Intelligence, 36*(3), 664–684. doi:10.100710489-011-0287-y

Burt, P. J., & Adelson, E. H. (1983). The Laplacian Pyramid as a Compact Image Code. *IEEE Transactions on Communications, 31*(4), 532–540. doi:10.1109/TCOM.1983.1095851

Cabrelles, M., Seguí, A. E., Navarro, S., Galcerá, S., Portalés, C., & Lerma, J. L. (2010). *3D Photorealistic modelling of stone monuments by dense image matching.* Paper presented at the International Archives of Photogrammetry, Remote Sensing and Spatial Information Sciences. Commission V Symposium, Newcastle upon Tyne, UK.

Cabrera, M. M. (2010). Integration of Rule Based Expert Systems and Case Based Reasoning in an Acute Bacterial Meningitis Clinical Decision Support System. *International Journal of Computer Science and Information Security, 7*(2), 20–29.

Callaham, J. (2015). *Kinect for Windows v2 sensor sales end, developers can use Xbox One version instead.* Retrieved November 22, 2019, from https://www.windowscentral.com/kinect-windows-v2-sensor-sales-end-developers-can-use-xbox-one-version

Camgoz, N. C., Hadfield, S., Koller, O., & Bowden, R. (2017, October). Subunets: End-to-end hand shape and continuous sign language recognition. In *2017 IEEE International Conference on Computer Vision (ICCV)* (pp. 3075-3084). IEEE. 10.1109/ICCV.2017.332

Cao, Z., Hidalgo, G., Simon, T., Wei, S. E., & Sheikh, Y. (2018). *OpenPose: realtime multi-person 2D pose estimation using Part Affinity Fields.* arXiv preprint arXiv:1812.08008

CapturingReality. (2016). *Reality Capture.* Retrieved from https://www.capturingreality.com

Cardoso, D., Särkinen, T., Alexander, S., Amorim, A. M., Bittrich, V., Celis, M., ... Giacomin, L. L. (2017). Amazon plant diversity revealed by a taxonomically verified species list. *Proceedings of the National Academy of Sciences of the United States of America, 114*(40), 10695–10700. doi:10.1073/pnas.1706756114 PMID:28923966

Casas, S., Portalés, C., García-Pereira, I., & Fernández, M. (2017). On a First Evaluation of ROMOT – a RObotic 3D MOvie Theatre – for Driving Safety. *Multimodal Technologies and Interaction.*

Caudell, T. P., & Mizell, D. W. (1992). Augmented reality: an application of heads-up display technology to manual manufacturing processes. *Proceedings of the Twenty-Fifth Hawaii International Conference on System Sciences.*

Celakovski, S., & Davcev, D. (2009). Multiplatform real-time rendering of mpeg-4 3D scenes with Microsoft XNA. In *International Conference on ICT Innovations.* Springer.

Cell Image Library. (n.d.). Retrieved from http://www.cellimagelibrary.org/home

Cenydd, L., John, N. W., Phillips N. I., & Gray, W. P. (2012). VCath: a tablet-based neurosurgery training tool. *Studies in Health Technology and Informatics, 184*, 20-23.

Cetto, A., Netter, M., Pernul, G., Richthammer, C., Riesner, M., Roth, C., & Sänger, J. (2014). *Friend inspector: a serious game to enhance privacy awareness in social networks.* arXiv preprint arXiv:1402.5878

Chang, A. X., Funkhouser, T. A., Guibas, L. J., Hanrahan, P., Huang, Q.-X., Li, Z., ... Yu, F. (2015). *ShapeNet: An Information-Rich 3D Model Repository.* Retrieved from https://arxiv.org/abs/1512.03012

Chang, K.-E., Chang, C.-T., Hou, H.-T., Sung, Y.-T., Chao, H.-L., & Lee, C.-M. (2014). Development and behavioral pattern analysis of a mobile guide system with augmented reality for painting appreciation instruction in an art museum. *Computers & Education, 71*(0), 185–197. doi:10.1016/j.compedu.2013.09.022

Chawla, N. V., Bowyer, K. W., Hall, L. O., & Kegelmeyer, W. P. (2002). SMOTE: Synthetic minority over-sampling technique. *Journal of Artificial Intelligence Research, 16*, 321–357. doi:10.1613/jair.953

Chen, K., Zhou, X., Zhou, Q., & Xu, H. (2019). Adversarial Learning-based Data Augmentation for Rotation-robust Human Tracking. In *ICASSP 2019 - 2019 IEEE International Conference on Acoustics, Speech and Signal Processing (ICASSP)* (pp. 1942–1946). IEEE. 10.1109/ICASSP.2019.8683451

Chen, L., Lin, S.-Y., Xie, Y., Tang, H., Xue, Y., Xie, X., ... Fan, W. (2018). *Generating Realistic Training Images Based on Tonality-Alignment Generative Adversarial Networks for Hand Pose Estimation.* Retrieved from https://arxiv.org/abs/1811.09916

Chen, B.-C., Chen, C.-S., & Hsu, W. H. (2014). Cross-Age Reference Coding for Age-Invariant Face Recognition and Retrieval. *Proceedings of the European Conference on Computer Vision ({ECCV}).* 10.1007/978-3-319-10599-4_49

Chen, C.-Y., Chang, B., & Huang, P.-S. (2014). Multimedia augmented reality information system for museum guidance. *Personal and Ubiquitous Computing, 18*(2), 315–322. doi:10.100700779-013-0647-1

Chen, F., & Vleeschouwer, C. D. (2011). Formulating Team-Sport Video Summarization as a Resource Allocation Problem. *IEEE Transactions on Circuits and Systems for Video Technology*, *21*(2), 193–205. doi:10.1109/TCSVT.2011.2106271

Cheng, S., Bronstein, M., Zhou, Y., Kotsia, I., Pantic, M., & Zafeiriou, S. (2019). *MeshGAN: Non-linear 3D Morphable Models of Faces*. arXiv preprint arXiv:1903.10384

Cheng, S., Kotsia, I., Pantic, M., & Zafeiriou, S. (2018). 4dfab: A large scale 4d database for facial expression analysis and biometric applications. In *Proceedings of the IEEE conference on computer vision and pattern recognition* (pp. 5117-5126). 10.1109/CVPR.2018.00537

Chen, S., & Billings, S. A. (1989). Representations of non-linear systems: The NARMAX model. *International Journal of Control*, *49*(3), 1013–1032. doi:10.1080/00207178908559683

Chen, Y., Li, W., Sakaridis, C., Dai, D., & Van Gool, L. (2018). Domain adaptive faster r-cnn for object detection in the wild. In *Proceedings of the IEEE conference on computer vision and pattern recognition* (pp. 3339-3348). 10.1109/CVPR.2018.00352

Cheok, M. J., Omar, Z., & Jaward, M. H. (2019). A review of hand gesture and sign language recognition techniques. *International Journal of Machine Learning and Cybernetics*, *10*(1), 131–153. doi:10.100713042-017-0705-5

Chittaro, L., & Ranon, R. (2007). Web3D technologies in learning, education and training: Motivations, issues, opportunities. *Computers & Education*, *49*(1), 3–18. doi:10.1016/j.compedu.2005.06.002

Chmielewski, J. (2008a). Interaction Descriptor for 3D Objects. *Proceedings of the International Conference on Human System Interaction*, 18-23.

Chmielewski, J. (2008b). Interaction Interfaces for Unrestricted Multimedia Interaction Descriptions. *Proceedings of the Mobile Computing and Multimedia Conference*, 397-400. 10.1145/1497185.1497270

Choi, Y., Choi, M., Kim, M., Ha, J. W., Kim, S., & Choo, J. (2018). StarGAN: Unified Generative Adversarial Networks for Multi-domain Image-to-Image Translation. *Proceedings of the IEEE Computer Society Conference on Computer Vision and Pattern Recognition*, 8789–8797. 10.1109/CVPR.2018.00916

Choudary, C., & Liu, T. (2007). Summarization of Visual Content in Instructional Videos. *IEEE Transactions on Multimedia*, *9*(7), 1443–1455. doi:10.1109/TMM.2007.906602

Chow, S.-K., & Chan, K.-L. (2009). Reconstruction of photorealistic 3D model of ceramic artefacts for interactive virtual exhibition. *Journal of Cultural Heritage*, *10*(2), 161–173. doi:10.1016/j.culher.2008.08.011

Christopoulos, D., Mavridis, P., Andreadis, A., & Karigiannis, J. N. (2011). *Using Virtual Environments to Tell the Story:" The Battle of Thermopylae"*. Paper presented at the Games and Virtual Worlds for Serious Applications (VS-GAMES), 2011 Third International Conference on.

Christou, C., Angus, C., Loscos, C., Dettori, A., & Roussou, M. (2006). A versatile large-scale multimodal VR system for cultural heritage visualization. *Proceedings of the ACM symposium on Virtual reality software and technology*. 10.1145/1180495.1180523

Chu, Y., & Li, T. (2012). Realizing semantic virtual environments with ontology and pluggable procedures. *Applications of Virtual Reality*.

Cignoni, P., Callieri, M., Corsini, M., Dellepiane, M., Ganovelli, F., & Ranzuglia, G. (2008). *MeshLab: an Open-Source Mesh Processing Tool*. The Eurographics Association.

Clapuyt, F. V., Vanacker, V., & Van Oost, K. (2016). Reproducibility of UAV-based earth topography reconstructions based on Structure-from-Motion algorithms. *Geomorphology*, *260*, 4–15. doi:10.1016/j.geomorph.2015.05.011

Coakley, M. F., Hurt, D. E., Weber, N., Mtingwa, M., Fincher, E. C., Alekseyev, V. & Yoo, T. S. (2014). The NIH 3D print exchange: a public resource for bioscientific and biomedical 3D prints. *3D Printing and Additive Manufacturing*, *1*(3), 137-140.

Cock, D. K., & Moor, D. B. (2002). Subspace angles between ARMA models. *Systems & Control Letters*, *46*(4), 265–270. doi:10.1016/S0167-6911(02)00135-4

Coenen, T., Mostmans, L., & Naessens, K. (2013). MuseUs: Case study of a pervasive cultural heritage serious game. *Journal on Computing and Cultural Heritage*, *6*(2), 8. doi:10.1145/2460376.2460379

Cohen, G., Afshar, S., Tapson, J., & van Schaik, A. (2017). *{EMNIST:} an extension of {MNIST} to handwritten letters*. Retrieved from https://arxiv.org/abs/1702.05373

Coles, T. R., John, N. W., Gould, D. A., & Caldwell, D. G. (2011). Integrating haptics with augmented reality in a femoral palpation and needle insertion training simulation. *Haptics. IEEE Transactions*, *3*(4), 199–209. doi:10.1109/TOH.2011.32 PMID:26963487

COLLADA Homepage. (n.d.). https://www.khronos.org/collada/

Congote, J. (2012). MedX3DOM: MedX3D for X3DOM. *Proceedings of the 17th International Conference on 3D Web Technology*, 179.

Congote, J., Segura, A., Kabongo, L., Moreno, A., Posada, J., & Ruiz, O. (2011). Interactive visualization of volumetric data with webgl in real-time. *Proceedings of the 16th International Conference on 3D Web Technology*, 137-146. 10.1145/2010425.2010449

Content4All Project website. (n.d.). Retrieved November 22, 2019, from http://content4all-project.eu/

Cooper, M. R., Raquet, J., & Patton, R. (2018). Range Information Characterization of the Hokuyo UST-20LX LIDAR Sensor. *Photonics*, *5*(2), 12. doi:10.3390/photonics5020012

Cordts, M., Omran, M., Ramos, S., Rehfeld, T., Enzweiler, M., & Benenson, R., … Schiele, B. (2016). The Cityscapes Dataset for Semantic Urban Scene Understanding. *Proceedings of the IEEE Computer Society Conference on Computer Vision and Pattern Recognition*, 3213–3223. 10.1109/CVPR.2016.350

Corti, A. G., Giancola, S., Mainetti, G., & Sala, R. (2016). A metrological characterization of the Kinect V2 time-of-flight camera. *Robotics and Autonomous Systems*, *75*, 584–594. doi:10.1016/j.robot.2015.09.024

Cosker, D., Krumhuber, E., & Hilton, A. (2011, November). A FACS valid 3D dynamic action unit database with applications to 3D dynamic morphable facial modeling. In *2011 International Conference on Computer Vision* (pp. 2296-2303). IEEE. 10.1109/ICCV.2011.6126510

Costineanu, D., Fosalau, C., Damian, C., & Plopa, O. (n.d.). *Triangulation-based 3D image processing method and system with compensating shadowing errors*. Academic Press.

Crowdsourcing definition. (n.d.). Retrieved November 22, 2019, from https://searchcio.techtarget.com/definition/crowdsourcing

Cruz-Neira, C., Sandin, D. J., DeFanti, T. A., Kenyon, R. V., & Hart, J. C. (1992). The CAVE: Audio visual experience automatic virtual environment. *Communications of the ACM*, *35*(6), 64–73. doi:10.1145/129888.129892

Cui, R., Liu, H., & Zhang, C. (2017). Recurrent convolutional neural networks for continuous sign language recognition by staged optimization. In *Proceedings of the IEEE Conference on Computer Vision and Pattern Recognition* (pp. 7361-7369). 10.1109/CVPR.2017.175

Cui, R., Liu, H., & Zhang, C. (2019). A Deep Neural Framework for Continuous Sign Language Recognition by Iterative Training. *IEEE Transactions on Multimedia*, *21*(7), 1880–1891. doi:10.1109/TMM.2018.2889563

CyberGlove Systems LLC. (n.d.). Retrieved November 22, 2019, from http://www.cyberglovesystems.com/

Da Silva, J. M. C., Leal, I. R., & Tabarelli, M. (Eds.). (2018). *Caatinga: The Largest Tropical Dry Forest Region in South America*. Springer.

Daakir, M. P.-D. (2016). Study of Lever-arm Effect Usign Embedded Photogrammetry and On-board GPS Receiver on UAV for Metrological Mapping Purpose and Proposal of a Free Ground Measurements Calibration Procedure. *ISPRS Annals of Photogrammetry, Remote Sensing & Spatial. Information Sciences*, *§§§*, 6.

Dachselt, R., Hinz, M., & Pietschmann, S. (2006). Using the AMACONT architecture for flexible adaptation of 3D web applications. In *Proceedings of the eleventh international conference on 3D web technology*. ACM.

Danelson, K. A., Geer, C. P., Stitzel, J. D., Slice, D. E., & Takhounts, E. G. (2008). Age and Gender Based Biomechanical Shape and Size Analysis of the Pediatric Brain. *Stapp Car Crash Journal*, *52*(2), 59–81. doi:10.4271/2008-22-0003 PMID:19085158

Dasiopoulou, S., Tzouvaras, V., Kompatsiaris, I., & Strintzis, M. G. (2010). Enquiring MPEG-7 based multimedia ontologies. *Multimedia Tools and Applications*, *46*(2-3), 331–370. doi:10.100711042-009-0387-4

Daszykowski, M., Walczak, B., & Massart, D. L. (2002). Looking for Natural Patterns in Analytical Data. 2. Tracing Local Density with OPTICS. *Journal of Chemical Information and Computer Sciences*, *42*(3), 500–507. doi:10.1021/ci010384s PMID:12086507

Daum, S., & Borrmann, A. (2013). Definition and implementation of temporal operators for a 4D query language. *Computing in Civil Engineering*, *2013*(2013), 468–475. doi:10.1061/9780784413029.059

Davidson, M. J. (2006). PAULA: A computer-based sign language tutor for hearing adults. *Intelligent Tutoring Systems 2006 Workshop on Teaching with Robots, Agents, and Natural Language Processing*.

Dawson-Haggerty. (2019). *trimesh*. Retrieved from https://trimsh.org

De Albuquerque, U. P., De Medeiros, P. M., De Almeida, A. L. S., Monteiro, J. M., Neto, E. M. D. F. L., de Melo, J. G., & Dos Santos, J. P. (2007). Medicinal plants of the caatinga (semi-arid) vegetation of NE Brazil: A quantitative approach. *Journal of Ethnopharmacology*, *114*(3), 325–354. doi:10.1016/j.jep.2007.08.017 PMID:17900836

De Amorim, C. C., Macêdo, D., & Zanchettin, C. (2019). *Spatial-Temporal Graph Convolutional Networks for Sign Language Recognition*. arXiv preprint arXiv:1901.11164

De Floriani, L., Hui, A., Papaleo, L., Huang, M., & Hendler, J. (2007). A semantic web environment for digital shapes understanding. In *Semantic Multimedia* (pp. 226–239). Springer. doi:10.1007/978-3-540-77051-0_25

De Troyer, O., Kleinermann, F., Pellens, B., & Bille, W. (2007). Conceptual modeling for virtual reality. In *Tutorials, posters, panels and industrial contributions at the 26th international conference on Conceptual modeling-Volume 83* (pp. 3-18). Australian Computer Society, Inc.

DeGroot, M. H. (2012). *Probability and statistics*. Pearson Education.

Demigha, S. (2016). A case-based reasoning tool for breast cancer knowledge management with data mining concepts and techniques. *SPIE Proceedings, 9789*, 1-10.

Demuth, H. B., Beale, M. H., De Jess, O., & Hagan, M. T. (2014). *Neural network design*. Martin Hagan.

Denker, J. S., Gardner, W. R., Graf, H. P., Henderson, D., Howard, R. E., & Hubbard, W. ... Guyon, I. (1989). Neural Network Recognizer for Hand-Written Zip Code Digits. In D. S. Touretzky (Ed.), *Advances in Neural Information Processing Systems 1* (pp. 323–331). Morgan-Kaufmann. Retrieved from http://papers.nips.cc/paper/107-neural-network-recognizer-for-hand-written-zip-code-digits.pdf

Denton, E., Chintala, S., Szlam, A., & Fergus, R. (2015). *Deep Generative Image Models using a Laplacian Pyramid of Adversarial Networks*. Retrieved from https://arxiv.org/abs/1506.05751

Dhall, A., Goecke, R., Lucey, S., & Gedeon, T. (2011). Static facial expression analysis in tough conditions: Data, evaluation protocol and benchmark. In *2011 IEEE International Conference on Computer Vision Workshops (ICCV Workshops)* (pp. 2106–2112). 10.1109/ICCVW.2011.6130508

Dimitropoulos, K., Manitsaris, S., Tsalakanidou, F., Nikolopoulos, S., Denby, B., Kork, S. A., ... Grammalidis, N. (2014). Capturing the intangible an introduction to the i-Treasures project. *2014 International Conference on Computer Vision Theory and Applications (VISAPP)*, *2*, 773–781.

Dimitropoulos, K., Barmpoutis, P., & Grammalidis, N. (2017). Higher order linear dynamical systems for smoke detection in video surveillance applications. *IEEE Transactions on Circuits and Systems for Video Technology*, *27*(5), 1143–1154. doi:10.1109/TCSVT.2016.2527340

Dimitropoulos, K., Barmpoutis, P., Kitsikidis, A., & Grammalidis, N. (2016). Classification of multidimensional time-evolving data using histograms of grassmannian points. *IEEE Transactions on Circuits and Systems for Video Technology*, *28*(4), 892–905. doi:10.1109/TCSVT.2016.2631719

Dimitropoulos, K., Barmpoutis, P., Kitsikidis, A., & Grammalidis, N. (2016). Classification of multidimensional time-evolving data using histograms of Grassmannian points. *IEEE Transactions on Circuits and Systems for Video Technology*.

Dimitropoulos, K., Barmpoutis, P., Zioga, C., Kamas, A., Patsiaoura, K., & Grammalidis, N. (2017). Grading of invasive breast carcinoma through Grassmannian VLAD encoding. *PLoS One*, *12*(9), e0185110. doi:10.1371/journal.pone.0185110 PMID:28934283

Dimitropoulos, K., Manitsaris, S., Tsalakanidou, F., Nikolopoulos, S., Denby, B., Kork, S. A., ... Grammalidis, N. (2014). Capturing the intangible an introduction to the i-Treasures project. *2014 International Conference on Computer Vision Theory and Applications (VISAPP)*, *2*, 773–781.

Dimitropoulos, K., Tsalakanidou, F., Nikolopoulos, S., Kompatsiaris, I., Grammalidis, N., Manitsaris, S., ... Hadjileontiadis, L. (2018). A multimodal approach for the safeguarding and transmission of intangible cultural heritage: The case of i-Treasures. *IEEE Intelligent Systems*, *33*(6), 3–16. doi:10.1109/MIS.2018.111144858

Ding, H., Sricharan, K., & Chellappa, R. (2017). *ExprGAN: Facial Expression Editing with Controllable Expression Intensity*. Retrieved from https://arxiv.org/abs/1709.03842

Ding, L. &. (2017). Fusing structure from motion and lidar for dense accurate depth map estimation. *IEEE International Conference on Acoustics, Speech and Signal Processing (ICASSP)*, 1283-1287. 10.1109/ICASSP.2017.7952363

Ding, W., Liu, K., Belyaev, E., & Cheng, F. (2018). Tensor-based linear dynamical systems for action recognition from 3D skeletons. *Pattern Recognition*, *77*, 75–86. doi:10.1016/j.patcog.2017.12.004

Djaouti, D., Alvarez, J., Rampnoux, O., Charvillat, V., & Jessel, J.-P. (2009). *Serious games & cultural heritage: a case study of prehistoric caves.* Paper presented at the Virtual Systems and Multimedia, 2009. VSMM'09. 15th International Conference on. 10.1109/VSMM.2009.40

Doller, M., & Kosch, H. (2008). The MPEG-7 Multimedia Database System (MPEG-7 MMDB). *Journal of Systems and Software, 81*(9), 1559–1580. doi:10.1016/j.jss.2006.03.051

Döller, M., Tous, R., Gruhne, M., Yoon, K., Sano, M., & Burnett, I. S. (2008). The MPEG Query Format: Unifying access to multimedia retrieval systems. *IEEE MultiMedia,* (4): 82–95.

Donahue, C., McAuley, J., & Puckette, M. (2018). *Adversarial audio synthesis.* ArXiv Preprint ArXiv:1802.04208

Doretto, G., Chiuso, A., Wu, Y. N., & Soatto, S. (2003). Dynamic textures. *International Journal of Computer Vision, 51*(2), 91–109. doi:10.1023/A:1021669406132

Doulamis, A. D., Voulodimos, A., Doulamis, N. D., Soile, S., & Lampropoulos, A. (2017). Transforming Intangible Folkloric Performing Arts into Tangible Choreographic Digital Objects: The Terpsichore Approach. *VISIGRAPP, 5,* 451–460.

Doulamis, A., Soile, S., Doulamis, N., Chrisouli, C., Grammalidis, N., Dimitropoulos, K., . . . Ioannidis, C. (2015). Selective 4D modelling framework for spatial-temporal land information management system. *Third International Conference on Remote Sensing and Geoinformation of the Environment (RSCy2015), 9535,* 953506.

Doulamis, N., Ceacero, C., Collantes, L., & Tektonidis, D. (2006). DESYME: Development System for Mobile Services. 15th IST Mobile & Wireless Communications Summit, Mykonos, Greece.

Doulamis, N., Doulamis, A., Ioannidis, C., Klein, M., & Ioannides, M. (2017). Modelling of Static and Moving Objects: Digitizing Tangible and Intangible Cultural Heritage. In Mixed Reality and Gamification for Cultural Heritage (pp. 567–589). Springer. doi:10.1007/978-3-319-49607-8_23

Doulamis, A. D., & Doulamis, N. D. (2004). Optimal content-based video decomposition for interactive video navigation. *IEEE Transactions on Circuits and Systems for Video Technology, 14*(6), 757–775. doi:10.1109/TCSVT.2004.828348

Doulamis, A. D., Doulamis, N. D., & Kollias, S. D. (2000). A fuzzy video content representation for video summarization and content-based retrieval. *Signal Processing, 80*(6), 1049–1067. doi:10.1016/S0165-1684(00)00019-0

Doulamis, A. D., Doulamis, N. D., & Kollias, S. D. (2000, July). Recursive non linear models for on line traffic prediction of VBR MPEG coded video sources. In *Proceedings of the IEEE-INNS-ENNS International Joint Conference on Neural Networks. IJCNN 2000. Neural Computing: New Challenges and Perspectives for the New Millennium* (Vol. 6, pp. 114-119). IEEE. 10.1109/IJCNN.2000.859382

Doulamis, A. D., Doulamis, N., & Kollas, S. (2000). Non-sequential video content representation using temporal variation of feature vectors. *IEEE Transactions on Consumer Electronics, 46*(3), 758–768. doi:10.1109/30.883444

Doulamis, A., Doulamis, N., Ioannidis, C., Chrysouli, C., Grammalidis, N., Dimitropoulos, K., ... Ioannides, M. (2015). 5D Modelling: An Efficient Approach for creating spatiotemporal predictive 3D maps of Large scale cultural resources. *ISPRS Annals of Photogrammetry, Remote Sensing & Spatial Information Sciences, 2.*

Doulamis, A., Doulamis, N., Ioannidis, C., Chrysouli, C., Grammalidis, N., Dimitropoulos, K., ... Ioannides, M. (2015). 5D modelling: An efficient approach for creating spatiotemporal predictive 3D maps of large-scale cultural resources. *ISPRS Annals of the Photogrammetry. Remote Sensing and Spatial Information Sciences, 2*(5), 61.

Doulamis, A., Ioannides, M., Doulamis, N., Hadjiprocopis, A., Fritsch, D., Balet, O., ... Johnsons, P. S. (2013, August). 4D reconstruction of the past. In *First International Conference on Remote Sensing and Geoinformation of the Environment (RSCy2013)* (Vol. 8795, p. 87950J). International Society for Optics and Photonics. 10.1117/12.2029010

Doulamis, A., Soile, S., Doulamis, N., Chrisouli, C., Grammalidis, N., Dimitropoulos, K., ... Ioannidis, C. (2015, June). Selective 4D modelling framework for spatial-temporal land information management system. In *Third International Conference on Remote Sensing and Geoinformation of the Environment (RSCy2015)* (Vol. 9535, p. 953506). International Society for Optics and Photonics. 10.1117/12.2193464

Doulamis, N. D., Voulodimos, A. S., Kosmopoulos, D. I., & Varvarigou, T. A. (2010). Enhanced Human Behavior Recognition Using HMM and Evaluative Rectification. *Proceedings of the First ACM International Workshop on Analysis and Retrieval of Tracked Events and Motion in Imagery Streams*, 39–44. 10.1145/1877868.1877880

Doulamis, N., & Doulamis, A. (2005). Non-sequential multiscale content-based video decomposition. *Signal Processing*, *85*(2), 325–356. doi:10.1016/j.sigpro.2004.10.004

Doulamis, N., & Voulodimos, A. (2016). FAST-MDL: Fast Adaptive Supervised Training of multi-layered deep learning models for consistent object tracking and classification. *2016 IEEE International Conference on Imaging Systems and Techniques (IST)*, 318–323. 10.1109/IST.2016.7738244

Doumanoglou, A., Vretos, N., & Daras, P. (2019). Frequency--based slow feature analysis. *Neurocomputing*, *368*, 34–50. doi:10.1016/j.neucom.2019.08.067

Dou, P., Shah, S. K., & Kakadiaris, I. A. (2017). End-to-end 3D face reconstruction with deep neural networks. In *Proceedings of the IEEE Conference on Computer Vision and Pattern Recognition* (pp. 5908-5917). 10.1109/CVPR.2017.164

Drap, P., Papini, O., Sourisseau, J. C., & Gambin, T. (2017). Ontology-based photogrammetric survey in underwater archaeology. In *European Semantic Web Conference*, (pp. 3–6). Springer.

Dzitsiuk, M., Sturm, J., Maier, R., Ma, L., & Cremers, D. (2017, May). De-noising, stabilizing and completing 3d reconstructions on-the-go using plane priors. In *Robotics and Automation (ICRA), 2017 IEEE International Conference on* (pp. 3976-3983). IEEE.

Eastman, C. T., Sacks, R., & Liston, K. (2008). BIM Handbook: A guide to building information modelling for owners, Managers, designers, engineers and contractors. Hoboken, NJ: John Wiley.

Eastman, C., Fisher, D., Lafue, G., Lividini, J., Stocker, D., & Yessios, C. (1974). *An outline of the building description system*. Institute of Physical Planning, Carnegie – Mellon University.

Eastman, C., Tiecholz, P., Sacks, R., & Liston, K. (2011). *BIM Handbook: A guide to building information modelling for owners, Managers, designers, engineers and contractors* (2nd ed.). Hoboken, NJ: John wiley.

EasyTV Project website. (n.d.). Retrieved November 22, 2019, from https://easytvproject.eu/

Elliott, R., Glauert, J. R. W., Kennaway, J. R., & Marshall, I. (2000). The development of language processing support for the ViSiCAST project. *Annual ACM Conference on Assistive Technologies, Proceedings*, 101–108. 10.1145/354324.354349

Elliott, R., Glauert, J. R. W., Kennaway, J. R., Marshall, I., & Safar, E. (2008). Linguistic modelling and language-processing technologies for Avatar-based sign language presentation. *Universal Access in the Information Society*, *6*(4), 375–391. doi:10.100710209-007-0102-z

Elsken, T., Metzen, J. H., & Hutter, F. (2019). Neural Architecture Search: A Survey. *Journal of Machine Learning Research*, *20*(55), 1–21. Retrieved from http://jmlr.org/papers/v20/18-598.html

Emem, O. (2002). *Three dimensional Modelling: Design and applications*. Istanbul: Yildiz Technological University.

EncoderA. P. I. (n.d.). https://docs.python.org/2/library/json.html.urllib, https://docs.python.org/2/library/urllib.html.Restlet

EngineU. (2019). https://www.unrealengine.com/what-is-unreal-engine-4

Epikoinwnw Project. (n.d.). Retrieved November 22, 2019, from http://iti.gr/iti/projects/Επικοινωνώ.html

Ercek, R., Viviers, D., & Warzée, N. (2010). 3D reconstruction and digitalization of an archeological site, Itanos, Crete. *Virtual Archaeology Review, 1*(1). doi:10.4995/var.2010.4794

Ester, M., Kriegel, H.-P., Sander, J., Xu, X., & Associates. (1996). A density-based algorithm for discovering clusters in large spatial databases with noise. In *Kdd* (Vol. 96, pp. 226–231). Retrieved from https://www.aaai.org/Papers/KDD/1996/KDD96-037

Evans, A., Romeo, M., Bahrehmand, A., Agenjo, J., & Blat, J. (2014). 3D graphics on the web: A survey. *Computers & Graphics, 41*, 43–61. doi:10.1016/j.cag.2014.02.002

Fang, G., Gao, W., & Zhao, D. (2004). Large vocabulary sign language recognition based on fuzzy decision trees. *IEEE Transactions on Systems, Man, and Cybernetics. Part A, Systems and Humans, 34*(3), 305–314. doi:10.1109/TSMCA.2004.824852

Fang, H. S., Xie, S., Tai, Y. W., & Lu, C. (2017). Rmpe: Regional multi-person pose estimation. In *Proceedings of the IEEE International Conference on Computer Vision* (pp. 2334-2343). IEEE.

Favorskaya, M. N., & Jain, L. C. (2017). Overview of LiDAR Technologies and Equipment for Land Cover Scanning. In *Handbook on Advances in Remote Sensing and Geographic Information Systems* (pp. 19–68). Cham: Springer. doi:10.1007/978-3-319-52308-8_2

Ferrari, C., Lisanti, G., Berretti, S., & Del Bimbo, A. (2017). A dictionary learning-based 3D morphable shape model. *IEEE Transactions on Multimedia, 19*(12), 2666–2679. doi:10.1109/TMM.2017.2707341

Ferreira, A. (2017). *Character Animation Using Sign Language Character Animation Using Sign Language*. Academic Press.

Finn, C., Abbeel, P., & Levine, S. (2017). *Model-Agnostic Meta-Learning for Fast Adaptation of Deep Networks*. Retrieved from https://arxiv.org/abs/1703.03400

Fitbit Official Site for Activity Trackers and More. (n.d.). Retrieved November 22, 2019, from https://www.fitbit.com/eu/home

Flotyński, J., & Walczak, K. (2017). Knowledge-based Representation of 3D Content Behavior in a Service-oriented Virtual Environment. In *Proceedings of the 22Nd International Conference on 3D Web Technology, Web3D '17*, (pp. 14:1–14:10). New York, NY: ACM.

Flotyński, J. (2014). Semantic modelling of interactive 3D content with domain-specific ontologies. *Procedia Computer Science, 35*, 531–540. doi:10.1016/j.procs.2014.08.134

Flotynski, J., Krzyszkowski, M., & Walczak, K. (2017). Semantic Composition of 3D Content Behavior for Explorable Virtual Reality Applications. In *Proceedings of EuroVR 2017* (pp. 3–23). Springer. doi:10.1007/978-3-319-72323-5_1

Flotyński, J., & Walczak, K. (2013). Semantic Multi-layered Design of Interactive 3D Presentations. In *Proceedings of the Federated Conference on Computer Science and Information Systems*, (pp. 541–548). Krakow, Poland: IEEE.

Flotyński, J., & Walczak, K. (2013a). Microformat and microdata schemas for interactive 3d web content. In *2013 Federated Conference on Computer Science and Information Systems*. IEEE.

Flotyński, J., & Walczak, K. (2013b). Semantic multi-layered design of interactive 3d presentations. In *2013 Federated Conference on Computer Science and Information Systems*. IEEE.

Flotyński, J., & Walczak, K. (2014). Semantic representation of multi-platform 3D content. *Computer Science and Information Systems*, *11*(4), 1555–1580. doi:10.2298/CSIS131218073F

Flotyński, J., & Walczak, K. (2015). Conceptual knowledge-based modeling of interactive 3D content. *The Visual Computer*, *31*(10), 1287–1306. doi:10.100700371-014-1011-9

Flotyński, J., & Walczak, K. (2015). Ontology-based creation of 3D content in a service-oriented environment. In *International Conference on Business Information Systems*. Springer. 10.1007/978-3-319-19027-3_7

Flotyński, J., & Walczak, K. (2016). Customization of 3D content with semantic meta-scenes. *Graphical Models*, *88*, 23–39. doi:10.1016/j.gmod.2016.07.001

Flotyński, J., & Walczak, K. (2017). Ontology-Based Representation and Modelling of Synthetic 3D Content: A State-of-the-Art Review. *Computer Graphics Forum*, *36*(8), 2017. doi:10.1111/cgf.13083

FOCUS K3D Homepage. (n.d.). http://www.focusk3d.eu/

Francis, R. (2006). Revolution: Learning about history through situated role play in a virtual environment. *Proceedings of the American educational research association conference.*

Frid-Adar, M., Diamant, I., Klang, E., Amitai, M., Goldberger, J., & Greenspan, H. (2018). GAN-based synthetic medical image augmentation for increased CNN performance in liver lesion classification. *Neurocomputing*, *321*, 321–331. doi:10.1016/j.neucom.2018.09.013

Funkhouser, T., Min, P., Kazhdan, M., Chen, J., Halderman, A., Dobkin, D., & Jacobs, D. (2003). A search engine for 3D models. *ACM Transactions on Graphics*, *22*(1), 83–105. doi:10.1145/588272.588279

Furey, T. S., Cristianini, N., Duffy, N., Bednarski, D. W., Schummer, M., & Haussler, D. (2000). Support vector machine classification and validation of cancer tissue samples using microarray expression data. *Bioinformatics (Oxford, England)*, *16*(10), 906–914. doi:10.1093/bioinformatics/16.10.906 PMID:11120680

Gaitatzes, A., Christopoulos, D., & Papaioannou, G. (2004). The ancient olympic games: being part of the experience. *Proceedings of the 5th International conference on Virtual Reality, Archaeology and Intelligent Cultural Heritage.*

Gaitatzes, A., Christopoulos, D., & Roussou, M. (2001a). Reviving the past: cultural heritage meets virtual reality. *Proceedings of the 2001 conference on Virtual reality, archeology, and cultural heritage.* 10.1145/584993.585011

Galteri, L., Ferrari, C., Lisanti, G., Berretti, S., & Del Bimbo, A. (2019, August). Deep 3D Morphable Model Refinement via Progressive Growing of Conditional Generative Adversarial Networks. *Computer Vision and Image Understanding*, *185*, 31–42. doi:10.1016/j.cviu.2019.05.002

Ganah, A.A., Bouchalaghem, N.M., & Anumba, C.J. (2005). VISCON: Computer Visualization Support for Constructability. *Journal of Information Technology in Construction.*

Ganatra, Z., Chavda, R., & D'mello, L. (2014). *Conversion of 2D Images to 3D Using Data Mining Algorithm.* Academic Press.

Ganin, Y., & Lempitsky, V. (2015). Unsupervised Domain Adaptation by Backpropagation. In *Proceedings of the 32Nd International Conference on International Conference on Machine Learning - Volume 37* (pp. 1180–1189). JMLR.org. Retrieved from https://dl.acm.org/citation.cfm?id=3045118.3045244

Gao, H., Shou, Z., Zareian, A., Zhang, H., & Chang, S.-F. (2018). *Low-shot Learning via Covariance-Preserving Adversarial Augmentation Networks.* Retrieved from https://arxiv.org/abs/1810.11730

Gardner, M. K., Feng, W. C., Archuleta, J., Lin, H., & Ma, X. (2006). Parallel genomic sequence-searching on an ad-hoc grid: experiences, lessons learned, and implications. In *SC 2006 Conference, Proceedings of the ACM/IEEE* (pp. 22-22). ACM.

Gaus, Y. F. A., & Wong, F. (2012, February). Hidden Markov Model-based gesture recognition with overlapping hand-head/hand-hand estimated using kalman filter. In *2012 Third International Conference on Intelligent Systems Modelling and Simulation* (pp. 262-267). IEEE. 10.1109/ISMS.2012.67

Gecer, B., Bhattarai, B., Kittler, J., & Kim, T.-K. (2018). *Semi-supervised Adversarial Learning to Generate Photorealistic Face Images of New Identities from 3D Morphable Model*. doi:10.1007/978-3-030-01252-6_14

Geiger, A., Lenz, P., & Urtasun, R. (2012). Are we ready for autonomous driving? The KITTI vision benchmark suite. In *2012 IEEE Conference on Computer Vision and Pattern Recognition* (pp. 3354–3361). 10.1109/CVPR.2012.6248074

Georgopoulos, A., Kontogianni, G., Koutsaftis, C., & Skamantzari, M. (2017). *Serious Games at the Service of Cultural Heritage and Tourism. In Tourism, Culture and Heritage in a Smart Economy* (pp. 3–17). Springer. doi:10.1007/978-3-319-47732-9_1

Gibson, I., Kvan, T., & Ming, L.W. (2002). *Rapid prototyping for Architectural Models*. doi:10.1108 / 13552540210420961

Gimeno, J., & Morillo, P. (n.d.). *A Mobile Augmented Reality System to Enjoy the Sagrada Familia*. Academic Press.

Gimeno, J., Olanda, R., Martinez, B., & Sanchez, F. M. (2011). Multiuser augmented reality system for indoor exhibitions. *Proceedings of the 13th IFIP TC 13 international conference on Human-computer interaction*. 10.1007/978-3-642-23768-3_86

Gimeno, J., Portalés, C., Coma, I., Fernández, M., & Martínez, B. (2017). Combining Traditional and Indirect Augmented Reality for Indoor Crowded Environments. A Case Study on the Casa Batlló Museum. *Computers & Graphics*, *69*, 92–103. doi:10.1016/j.cag.2017.09.001

Giner Martínez, F., & Portalés Ricart, C. (2005). *The Augmented User: A Wearable Augmented Reality Interface*. Paper presented at the International Conference on Virtual Systems and Multimedia (VSMM'05), Ghent, Belgium.

Girardeau-MontautD. (2003). *CloudCompare*. Retrieved from http://www.cloudcompare.org

Girshick, R., Donahue, J., Darrell, T., & Malik, J. (2015). Region-based convolutional networks for accurate object detection and segmentation. *IEEE Transactions on Pattern Analysis and Machine Intelligence*, *38*(1), 142–158. doi:10.1109/TPAMI.2015.2437384 PMID:26656583

Giubilato, R. C. (2018). Scale correct monocular visual odometry using a lidar altimeter. *IEEE/RSJ International Conference on Intelligent Robots and Systems (IROS)*, 3694-3700. 10.1109/IROS.2018.8594096

Glantz, A., Krutz, A., Sikora, T., Nunes, P., & Pereira, F. (2010). Automatic MPEG-4 sprite coding Comparison of integrated object segmentation algorithms. *Journal of Multimedia Tools and Applications*, *49*(3), 483–512. doi:10.100711042-010-0469-3

Goesele, M., Snavely, N., Curless, B., Hoppe, H., & Seitz, S. M. (2007). Multi-View Stereo for Community Photo Collections. In *2007 IEEE 11th International Conference on Computer Vision* (pp. 1–8). 10.1109/ICCV.2007.4408933

Goldberg, D. E., & Holland, J. H. (1988). *Genetic algorithms and machine learning*. Academic Press.

Golovinskiy, A., Kim, V. G., & Funkhouser, T. (2009). Shape-based recognition of 3D point clouds in urban environments. In *Computer Vision, 2009 IEEE 12th International Conference on* (pp. 2154-2161). IEEE.

Golshani, F., Vissicaro, P., & Park, Y. (2004). A Multimedia Information Repository for Cross Cultural Dance Studies. *Multimedia Tools and Applications, 24*(2), 89–103. doi:10.1023/B:MTAP.0000036838.87602.71

Gong, X., Chang, S., Jiang, Y., & Wang, Z. (2019). *AutoGAN: Neural Architecture Search for Generative Adversarial Networks*. Retrieved from https://arxiv.org/abs/1908.03835

Goodfellow, I. J., Erhan, D., Carrier, P. L., Courville, A., Mirza, M., Hamner, B., ... Bengio, Y. (2015). Challenges in representation learning: A report on three machine learning contests. *Neural Networks, 64*, 59–63.

Goodfellow, I. J., Pouget-Abadie, J., Mirza, M., Xu, B., Warde-Farley, D., Ozair, S., ... Bengio, Y. (2014). *Generative Adversarial Networks*. Retrieved from https://arxiv.org/abs/1406.2661

Goodfellow, I., Pouget-Abadie, J., Mirza, M., Xu, B., Warde-Farley, D., Ozair, S., . . . Bengio, Y. (2014). Generative adversarial nets. In Advances in neural information processing systems (pp. 2672-2680). Academic Press.

Grana, C., & Cucchiara, R. (2006). Performance of the MPEG-7 Shape Spectrum Descriptor for 3D objects retrieval. In *Second Italian Research Conference on Digital Library Management Systems*. IRCDL.

Granero-Montagud, L., Portalés, C., Pastor-Carbonell, B., Ribes-Gómez, E., Gutiérrez-Lucas, A., Tornari, V., . . . Dietz, C. (2013). *Deterioration estimation of paintings by means of combined 3D and hyperspectral data analysis*. Paper presented at the SPIE - Optics for Arts, Architecture, and Archaeology IV. 10.1117/12.2020336

Groves, R. M., Portalés, C., & Ribes-Gómez, E. (2014). *Assessment of Mechanical and Chemical Deterioration of Artworks*. Paper presented at the International Conference on Ageing of Materials & Structures (AMS), Delft, The Netherlands.

Gruber, T. (2009). *Encyclopedia of database systems*. http://tomgruber.org/writing/ontology-definition- 2007.htm

Grussenmeyer, P., Landes, T., Voegtle, T., & Ringle, K. (2008). Comparison methods of terrestrial laser scanning, photogrammetry and tacheometry data for recording of cultural heritage buildings. *The International Archives of the Photogrammetry, Remote Sensing and Spatial Information Sciences, 37*(B5), 213–218.

Gu, G., Kim, S. T., Kim, K., Baddar, W. J., & Ro, Y. M. (2017). *Differential Generative Adversarial Networks: Synthesizing Non-linear Facial Variations with Limited Number of Training Data*. Retrieved from https://arxiv.org/abs/1711.10267

Guan, H., Yu, Y., Ji, Z., Li, J., & Zhang, Q. (2015). Deep learning-based tree classification using mobile LiDAR data. *Remote Sensing Letters, 6*(11), 864–873. doi:10.1080/2150704X.2015.1088668

Guarnieri, A., Remondino, F., & Vettore, A. (2006). Digital photogrammetry and TLS data fusion applied to Cultural Heritage 3D modeling. *International Archives of Photogrammetry, Remote Sensing and Spatial Information Sciences. ISPRS Commission V Symposium, Dresden, Germany, 36*(part 5).

Guevara Lopez, M. A., González Posada, N., Moura, D., Pollán, R., Franco-Valiente, J., Ortega, C., ... Ferreira M Araújo, B. (2012). BCDR: A breast cancer digital repository. Academic Press.

Guidi, G., Russo, M., & Angheleddu, D. (2014). 3D Survey and virtual reconstruction of archeological sites. *Digital Applications in Archaeology and Cultural Heritage, 1*(2), 55–69. doi:10.1016/j.daach.2014.01.001

Gulavani & Kulkarni (2009). A review of knowledge based systems in medical diagnosis. *International Journal of Information Technology and Knowledge Management, 2*(2), 269-275.

Gulrajani, I., Ahmed, F., Arjovsky, M., Dumoulin, V., & Courville, A. (2017). *Improved Training of Wasserstein GANs*. Retrieved from https://arxiv.org/abs/1704.00028

Gutierrez, M., Vexo, F., & Thalmann, D. (2005). Semantics-based representation of virtual environments. *International Journal of Computer Applications in Technology, 23*(2-4), 229-238.

Gutierrez, D., Seron, F. J., Magallon, J. A., Sobreviela, E. J., & Latorre, P. (2004). Archaeological and cultural heritage: Bringing life to an unearthed Muslim suburb in an immersive environment. *Journal of Cultural Heritage, 5*(1), 63–74. doi:10.1016/j.culher.2003.10.001

Gutierrez, M., Garcıa-Rojas, A., Thalmann, D., Vexo, F., Moccozet, L., Magnenat-Thalmann, N., ... Spagnuolo, M. (2007). An ontology of virtual humans: Incorporating semantics into human shapes. *The Visual Computer, 23*(3), 207–218.

Guyon, I., Weston, J., Barnhill, S., & Vapnik, V. (2002). Gene selection for cancer classification using support vector machines. *Machine Learning, 46*(1-3), 389–422. doi:10.1023/A:1012487302797

H3D. (n.d.). Retrieved from http://www.h3dapi.org

Haala, N., & Rothermel, M. (2012). Dense multiple stereo matching of highly overlapping UAV imagery. *ISPRS-International Archives of the Photogrammetry. Remote Sensing and Spatial Information Sciences, 39*(B1), 387–392.

Hachimura, K., & Nakamura, M. (2001). Method of generating coded description of human body motion from motion-captured data. *Proceedings 10th IEEE International Workshop on Robot and Human Interactive Communication. ROMAN 2001 (Cat. No.01TH8591)*, 122–127. 10.1109/ROMAN.2001.981889

Hackbusch, W., & Uschmajew, A. (2017). On the interconnection between the higher-order singular values of real tensors. *Numerische Mathematik, 135*(3), 875–894. doi:10.100700211-016-0819-9 PMID:28615745

Halabala, P. (2003). Semantic metadata creation. *Proceedings of CESCG 2003: 7th Central European Seminar on Computer Graphics.*

Halko, N., Martinsson, P. G., & Tropp, J. A. (2011). Finding structure with randomness: Probabilistic algorithms for constructing approximate matrix decompositions. *SIAM Review, 53*(2), 217–288. doi:10.1137/090771806

Halkos, D., Doulamis, N., & Doulamis, A. (2009). A Secure Framework Exploiting Content Guided and Automated Algorithms for Real Time Video Searching. *Multimedia Tools and Applications, 42*(3), 343–375. doi:10.100711042-008-0234-z

Hamza-Lup, F. G., Sopin, I., & Zeidan O. (2007b). Towards 3D web-based simulation and training systems for radiation oncology. *ADVANCE for Imaging and Oncology Administrators,* 64-68.

Hamza-Lup, F. G., Davis, L., & Zeidan, O. (2006). Web-based 3D planning tool for radiation therapy treatment. *Proceedings of the 11th international conference on 3D web technology, 1,* 59-162. 10.1145/1122591.1122613

Hamza-Lup, F. G., Farrar, S., & Leon, E. (2015) Patient specific 3D surfaces for interactive medical planning and training. In *Proceedings of the 20th International Conference on 3D Web Technology (Web3D '15).* ACM. 10.1145/2775292.2775294

Hamza-Lup, F. G., Sopin, I., & Zeidan, O. (2007a). Comprehensive 3D visual simulation for radiation therapy planning. *Studies in Health Technology and Informatics, 125,* 164–166.

Hamza-Lup, F. G., Sopin, I., & Zeidan, O. (2008). Online external beam radiation treatment simulator. *International Journal of Computer Assisted Radiology and Surgery, 3*(3-4), 275–281. doi:10.100711548-008-0232-7

Han, C., Kitamura, Y., Kudo, A., Ichinose, A., Rundo, L., Furukawa, Y., ... Li, Y. (2019). *Synthesizing Diverse Lung Nodules Wherever Massively: 3D Multi-Conditional GAN-based {CT} Image Augmentation for Object Detection.* Retrieved from https://arxiv.org/abs/1906.04962

Han, C., Murao, K., Noguchi, T., Kawata, Y., Uchiyama, F., Rundo, L., ... Satoh, S. (2019). *Learning More with Less: Conditional PGGAN-based Data Augmentation for Brain Metastases Detection Using Highly-Rough Annotation on MR Images.* Retrieved from https://arxiv.org/abs/1902.09856

Han, C., Rundo, L., Araki, R., Furukawa, Y., Mauri, G., Nakayama, H., & Hayashi, H. (2019). *Infinite Brain MR Images: PGGAN-based Data Augmentation for Tumor Detection.* Retrieved from https://arxiv.org/abs/1903.12564

Hanke, T. (2004). HamNoSys-representing sign language data in language resources and language processing contexts. *LREC, 4,* 1–6.

Haralick, R. M. (2000). *Propagating covariance in computer vision.* Performance Characterization in Computer Vision.

Harris, C., & Stephens, M. (1988). A combined corner and edge detector. In *Alvey vision conference* (Vol. 15, pp. 10–5244). Retrieved from http://courses.daiict.ac.in/pluginfile.php/13002/mod_resource/content/0/References/harris1988.pdf

Harris, H., & Sagnis, G. (1999). *Structural Modelling and Experimental Techniques.* CRC Press LLC. doi:10.1201/9781420049589

Hassner, T. (2013). Viewing real-world faces in 3D. In *Proceedings of the IEEE International Conference on Computer Vision* (pp. 3607-3614). IEEE.

Hassner, T., & Basri, R. (2006, June). Example based 3D reconstruction from single 2D images. In *2006 Conference on Computer Vision and Pattern Recognition Workshop (CVPRW'06)* (pp. 15-15). IEEE. 10.1109/CVPRW.2006.76

Hassouna, M. S., & Farag, A. A. (2007). Multistencils fast marching methods: A highly accurate solution to the eikonal equation on cartesian domains. *IEEE Transactions on Pattern Analysis and Machine Intelligence, 29*(9), 1563–1574. doi:10.1109/TPAMI.2007.1154 PMID:17627044

Haugstvedt, A.-C., & Krogstie, J. (2012). *Mobile augmented reality for cultural heritage: A technology acceptance study.* Paper presented at the Mixed and Augmented Reality (ISMAR), 2012 IEEE International Symposium on. 10.1109/ISMAR.2012.6402563

Haymaker, J., & Fischer, M. (2001). *Challenges and Benefits of 4D Modelling on the Walt Disney Concert Hall Project.* Working paper No.64. Stanford University.

Heath, M., Bowyer, K., Kopans, D., Moore, R., & Kegelmeyer, P. (2001). The digital database for screening mammography. *Proceedings of the Fifth International Workshop on Digital Mammography.* 10.1007/978-94-011-5318-8_75

Hejazi, M. R., & Ho, Y.-S. (2007). An efficient approach to texture-based image retrieval. *International Journal of Imaging Systems and Technology, 17*(5), 295–302. doi:10.1002/ima.20120

Hejazi, M. R., & Ho, Y.-S. (2007). Efficient approach to extraction of texture browsing descriptor in MPEG-7. *Electronics Letters, 43*(13), 709–711. doi:10.1049/el:20070208

Heloir, A., & Nunnari, F. (2013). Towards an intuitive sign language animation authoring environment for the deaf. *Proceedings of the 2nd Workshop in Sign Language Translation and Avatar Technology.*

Hertzmann, A. (1999). *Interactive 3D Scene Reconstruction from Images.* Academic Press.

Heusel, M., Ramsauer, H., Unterthiner, T., Nessler, B., & Hochreiter, S. (2017). *GANs Trained by a Two Time-Scale Update Rule Converge to a Local Nash Equilibrium.* Retrieved from https://arxiv.org/abs/1706.08500

Hisatomi, K., Katayama, M., Tomiyama, K., & Iwadate, Y. (2011). 3D Archive System for Traditional Performing Arts. *International Journal of Computer Vision, 94*(1), 78–88. doi:10.100711263-011-0434-2

HL7. (n.d.). Retrieved from http://www.hl7.org/implement/standards

Hokuyo. (2010). *UTM-30LX.* Retrieved from https://www.hokuyo-aut.jp

Horn, B. K. P., & Schunck, B. G. (1981). Determining Optical Flow. *Artificial Intelligence, 17*(1-3), 185–203. doi:10.1016/0004-3702(81)90024-2

Horn, B. K., & Brooks, M. J. (1989). *Shape from shading*. MIT Press.

Horn, H. S. (1971). *The adaptive geometry of trees*. Princeton, NJ: Princeton University Press.

Horvath, Nikhazy, Horvath, & Horvath. (2010). Segmentation of anatomical structures on chest radiographs. *International Journal of Medical Sciences, 4*(3), 1–4.

Hosmer, D. W. Jr, Lemeshow, S., & Sturdivant, R. X. (2013). *Applied logistic regression* (Vol. 398). John Wiley & Sons. doi:10.1002/9781118548387

Huang, G. B., Ramesh, M., Berg, T., & Learned-Miller, E. (2007). *Labeled Faces in the Wild: A Database for Studying Face Recognition in Unconstrained Environments*. Academic Press.

Huang, J., Zhou, W., Li, H., & Li, W. (2015, June). Sign language recognition using 3d convolutional neural networks. In 2015 IEEE international conference on multimedia and expo (ICME) (pp. 1-6). IEEE.

Huang, S. W., Lin, C. T., Chen, S. P., Wu, Y. Y., Hsu, P. H., & Lai, S. H. (2018). AugGAN: Cross domain adaptation with GAN-based data augmentation. Lecture Notes in Computer Science, 11213, 731–744. doi:10.1007/978-3-030-01240-3_44

Huang, C.-H., & Huang, Y.-T. (2013). An annales school-based serious game creation framework for taiwanese indigenous cultural heritage. *Journal on Computing and Cultural Heritage, 6*(2), 9. doi:10.1145/2460376.2460380

Huang, H., Brenner, C., & Sester, M. (2013). A generative statistical approach to automatic 3D building roof reconstruction from laser scanning data. *ISPRS Journal of Photogrammetry and Remote Sensing, 79*, 29–43. doi:10.1016/j.isprsjprs.2013.02.004

Huenerfauth, M. (2014). Learning to generate understandable animations of American Sign Language. *Proceedings of the 2nd Annual Effective Access Technologies Conference*.

Hughes, S., Brusilovsky, P., & Lewis, M. (2002). Adaptive navigation support in 3D e-commerce activities. *Proc. of Workshop on Recommendation and Personalization in eCommerce at AH*, 132-139.

Hullo, J. F., Grussenmeyer, P., & Fares, S. (2009). Photogrammetry and dense stereo matching approach applied to the documentation of the cultural heritage site of Kilwa (Saudi Arabia). *Proceedings of CIPA*.

Imposa, S. (2010). Infrared thermography and Georadar techniques applied to the "Sala delle Nicchie" (Niches Hall) of Palazzo Pitti, Florence (Italy). *Journal of Cultural Heritage, 11*(3), 259–264. doi:10.1016/j.culher.2009.04.005

Instant-Reality. (n.d.). Retrieved from http://www.instantreality.org

Intel RealSense Depth and Tracking Cameras. (n.d.). Retrieved November 22, 2019, from https://realsense.intel.com/stereo/

Ioannides, M., Hadjiprocopi, A., Doulamis, N., Doulamis, A., Protopapadakis, E., Makantasis, K., ... Julien, M. (2013). Online 4D reconstruction using multi-images available under Open Access. *ISPRS Photogr. Rem. Sens. Spat. Inf. Sc., 2*(W1), 169–174. doi:10.5194/isprsannals-II-5-W1-169-2013

ISO 15938:3. (2002). Multimedia Content Description Interface – Part 3: Visual.

ISO 15938:5. (2003). Multimedia Content Description Interface – Part 5: Multimedia Description Schemes. May.

Isola, P., Zhu, J. Y., Zhou, T., & Efros, A. A. (2017). Image-to-image translation with conditional adversarial networks. In *Proceedings - 30th IEEE Conference on Computer Vision and Pattern Recognition, CVPR 2017* (pp. 5967–5976). Institute of Electrical and Electronics Engineers Inc. 10.1109/CVPR.2017.632

Izadi, S., Kim, D., Hilliges, O., Molyneaux, D., Newcombe, R., Kohli, P., ... Fitzgibbon, A. (2011). KinectFusion: Real-time 3D Reconstruction and Interaction Using a Moving Depth Camera. In *Proceedings of the 24th Annual ACM Symposium on User Interface Software and Technology* (pp. 559–568). New York, NY: ACM. 10.1145/2047196.2047270

Jackson, A. S., Bulat, A., Argyriou, V., & Tzimiropoulos, G. (2017). Large pose 3D face reconstruction from a single image via direct volumetric CNN regression. In *Proceedings of the IEEE International Conference on Computer Vision* (pp. 1031-1039). 10.1109/ICCV.2017.117

JenaA. (n.d.). http://jena.apache.org/

Jendele, L., Skopek, O., Becker, A. S., & Konukoglu, E. (2019). *Adversarial Augmentation for Enhancing Classification of Mammography Images*. Retrieved from https://arxiv.org/abs/1902.07762

Jiménez Fernández-Palacios, B., Morabito, D., & Remondino, F. (2016). Access to complex reality-based 3D models using virtual reality solutions. *Journal of Cultural Heritage*.

Jimenez-del-Toro, O., Muller, H., Krenn, M., Gruenberg, K., Taha, A. A., Winterstein, M., ... Hanbury, A. (2016). Cloud-Based Evaluation of Anatomical Structure Segmentation and Landmark Detection Algorithms: VISCERAL Anatomy Benchmarks. *IEEE Transactions on Medical Imaging, 35*(11), 1–10. doi:10.1109/TMI.2016.2578680 PMID:27305669

Jin, D., Xu, Z., Tang, Y., Harrison, A. P., & Mollura, D. J. (2018). *CT-Realistic Lung Nodule Simulation from 3D Conditional Generative Adversarial Networks for Robust Lung Segmentation*. Retrieved from https://arxiv.org/abs/1806.04051

Jobst, M., & Dollner, J. (2008). 3D City Model Visualization with cartography-oriented design. REAL CORP 2008 Proceedings.

John, N. W., Aratow, M., Couch, J., Evestedt, D., Hudson, A. D., Polys, N. F., ... Wang, Q. (2008). MedX3D: standards enabled desktop medical 3D. *Studies in Health Technology and Informatics, 132*, 189–194.

John, N. W. (2007). The impact of Web3D technologies on medical education and training. *Computers & Education, 1*(49), 19–31. doi:10.1016/j.compedu.2005.06.003

Jourabloo, A., & Liu, X. (2016). Large-pose face alignment via CNN-based dense 3D model fitting. In *Proceedings of the IEEE conference on computer vision and pattern recognition* (pp. 4188-4196). 10.1109/CVPR.2016.454

Kalogerakis, E., Christodoulakis, S., & Moumoutzis, N. (2006). Coupling ontologies with graphics content for knowledge driven visualization. In *IEEE Virtual Reality Conference (VR 2006)*. IEEE. 10.1109/VR.2006.41

Kamachi, M., Lyons, M., & Gyoba, J. (1997). *The Japanese female facial expression (jaffe) database*. Http://Www. Kasrl. Org/Jaffe. Html

Kamberov, G., Kamberova, G., Chum, O., Obdržálek, Š., Martinec, D., & Kostková, J. ... Šára, R. (2006). 3D Geometry from Uncalibrated Images. In Advances in Visual Computing (pp. 802–813). Springer. doi:10.1007/11919629_80

Kandoth, C., McLellan, M. D., Vandin, F., Ye, K., Niu, B., & Lu, C. ... Ding, L. (2013). Mutational landscape and significance across 12 major cancer types. *Nature*. doi:10.1038/nature12634 PMID:24132290

Kankare, V., Holopainen, M., Vastaranta, M., Puttonen, E., Yu, X., Hyyppä, J., ... Alho, P. (2013). Individual tree biomass estimation using terrestrial laser scanning. *ISPRS Journal of Photogrammetry and Remote Sensing, 75*, 64–75. doi:10.1016/j.isprsjprs.2012.10.003

Kapahnke, P., Liedtke, P., Nesbigall, S., Warwas, S., & Klusch, M. (2010). ISReal: An Open Platform for Semantic-Based 3D Simulations in the 3D Internet. *International Semantic Web Conference, 2*, 161–176. 10.1007/978-3-642-17749-1_11

Karpathy, A., Miller, S., & Fei-Fei, L. (2013). Object discovery in 3d scenes via shape analysis. In *Robotics and Automation (ICRA), 2013 IEEE International Conference on* (pp. 2088-2095). IEEE.

Karras, T., Aila, T., Laine, S., & Lehtinen, J. (2017). *Progressive Growing of GANs for Improved Quality, Stability, and Variation*. Retrieved from https://arxiv.org/abs/1710.10196

Kaur, K., & Kumar, P. (2016). HamNoSys to SiGML conversion system for sign language automation. *Procedia Computer Science*, *89*, 794–803. doi:10.1016/j.procs.2016.06.063

Kazeminia, S., Baur, C., Kuijper, A., van Ginneken, B., Navab, N., Albarqouni, S., & Mukhopadhyay, A. (2018). *GANs for Medical Image Analysis*. Retrieved from https://arxiv.org/abs/1809.06222

Kendon, A. (2004). *Gesture: Visible action as utterance*. Cambridge University Press. doi:10.1017/CBO9780511807572

Keselman, L., Woodfill, J. I., Grunnet-Jepsen, A., & Bhowmik, A. (2017). Intel(R) RealSense(TM) Stereoscopic Depth Cameras. *2017 IEEE Conference on Computer Vision and Pattern Recognition Workshops (CVPRW)*, 1267–1276. 10.1109/CVPRW.2017.167

Kim, D., Kim, D.-H., & Kwak, K.-C. (2017). Classification of K-Pop Dance Movements Based on Skeleton Information Obtained by a Kinect Sensor. *Sensors (Basel)*, *17*(6), 1261. doi:10.339017061261 PMID:28587177

Kim, J. S., Jang, W., & Bien, Z. (1996). A dynamic gesture recognition system for the Korean sign language (KSL). *IEEE Transactions on Systems, Man, and Cybernetics. Part B, Cybernetics*, *26*(2), 354–359. doi:10.1109/3477.485888 PMID:18263039

Kim, O. &. (2015). A sensor fusion method to solve the scale ambiguity of single image by combining IMU. *15th International Conference on Control, Automation and Systems (ICCAS)*, 923-925. 10.1109/ICCAS.2015.7364754

Kinect—Windows app development. (2017). https://developer.microsoft.com/en-us/windows/kinect

Kingma, D. P., & Welling, M. (2013). *Auto-Encoding Variational Bayes*. Retrieved from https://arxiv.org/abs/1312.6114

Kiourt, C., Koutsoudis, A., & Pavlidis, G. (2016). DynaMus: A fully dynamic 3D virtual Museum framework. *Journal of Cultural Heritage*, *22*, 984–991. doi:10.1016/j.culher.2016.06.007

Kipp, M., Nguyen, Q., Heloir, A., & Matthes, S. (2011). Assessing the Deaf User Perspective on Sign Language Avatars. *The Proceedings of the 13th International ACM SIGACCESS Conference on Computers and Accessibility*, 107–114. 10.1145/2049536.2049557

Kipp, M., Heloir, A., & Nguyen, Q. (2011). Sign Language Avatars: Animation and Comprehensibility. In H. H. Vilhjálmsson, S. Kopp, S. Marsella, & K. R. Thórisson (Eds.), *Intelligent Virtual Agents* (pp. 113–126). Berlin: Springer Berlin Heidelberg. doi:10.1007/978-3-642-23974-8_13

Kitsikidis, A., Dimitropoulos, K., Uğurca, D., Bayçay, C., Yilmaz, E., Tsalakanidou, F., ... Grammalidis, N. (2015, August). A game-like application for dance learning using a natural human computer interface. In *International Conference on Universal Access in Human-Computer Interaction* (pp. 472-482). Springer. 10.1007/978-3-319-20684-4_46

Klare, B. F., Klein, B., Taborsky, E., Blanton, A., Cheney, J., & Allen, K., ... Jain, A. K. (2015). Pushing the frontiers of unconstrained face detection and recognition: IARPA Janus Benchmark A. In *2015 IEEE Conference on Computer Vision and Pattern Recognition (CVPR)* (pp. 1931–1939). 10.1109/CVPR.2015.7298803

Kleinbaum, D. G., & Klein, M. (2010). Maximum likelihood techniques: An overview. In *Logistic regression* (pp. 103–127). New York, NY: Springer. doi:10.1007/978-1-4419-1742-3_4

Klinder, Ostermann, Ehm, Kneser, & Lorenz. (2009). C Automated model-based vertebra detection, identification, and segmentation in CT images. *Medical Image Analysis, 13*(3), 471–482.

Knapitsch, A. P., Park, J., Zhou, Q.-Y., & Koltun, V. (2017). Tanks and temples: Benchmarking large-scale scene reconstruction. *ACM Transactions on Graphics, 36*(4), 78. doi:10.1145/3072959.3073599

Koller, D., Frischer, B., & Humphreys, G. (2009). Research challenges for digital archives of 3D cultural heritage models. *ACM J. Comput. Cult. Herit., 2*(3).

Koller, O., Forster, J., & Ney, H. (2015). Continuous sign language recognition: Towards large vocabulary statistical recognition systems handling multiple signers. *Computer Vision and Image Understanding, 141*, 108–125. doi:10.1016/j.cviu.2015.09.013

Koller, O., Zargaran, O., Ney, H., & Bowden, R. (2016). Deep sign: Hybrid CNN-HMM for continuous sign language recognition. *Proceedings of the British Machine Vision Conference 2016*. 10.5244/C.30.136

Koller, O., Zargaran, S., & Ney, H. (2017). Re-sign: Re-aligned end-to-end sequence modelling with deep recurrent CNN-HMMs. In *Proceedings of the IEEE Conference on Computer Vision and Pattern Recognition* (pp. 4297-4305). 10.1109/CVPR.2017.364

Kong, W. W., & Ranganath, S. (2008). Signing exact english (SEE): Modeling and recognition. *Pattern Recognition, 41*(5), 1638–1652. doi:10.1016/j.patcog.2007.10.016

Konstantinidis, D., Dimitropoulos, K., & Daras, P. (2018, June). Sign language recognition based on hand and body skeletal data. In *2018-3DTV-Conference: The True Vision-Capture, Transmission and Display of 3D Video (3DTV-CON)* (pp. 1-4). IEEE. 10.1109/3DTV.2018.8478467

Konstantinidis, D., Dimitropoulos, K., & Daras, P. (2018, September). Skeleton-based action recognition based on deep learning and Grassmannian pyramids. In *2018 26th European Signal Processing Conference (EUSIPCO)* (pp. 2045-2049). IEEE. 10.23919/EUSIPCO.2018.8553163

Konstantinidis, D., Dimitropoulos, K., & Daras, P. (2018, October). A deep learning approach for analyzing video and skeletal features in sign language recognition. In *2018 IEEE International Conference on Imaging Systems and Techniques (IST)* (pp. 1-6). IEEE. 10.1109/IST.2018.8577085

Kontakis, K., Steiakaki, M., Kapetanakis, K., & Malamos, A. G. (2014). DEC-O: An Ontology Framework and Interactive 3D Interface for Interior Decoration Applications in the Web. In *Proceedings of the 19th International ACM Conference on 3D Web Technologies, Web3D '14*, (pp. 63–70). New York, NY: ACM.

Kontakis, K., Steiakaki, M., Kapetanakis, K., & Malamos, A. G. (2014). DEC-O: an ontology framework and interactive 3D interface for interior. In *Proceedings of the 19th International ACM Conference on 3D Web Technologies* (pp. 63-70). Vancouver, British Columbia, Canada: ACM.

Kontakis, K., Malamos, A. G., Steiakaki, M., & Panagiotakis, S. (2017). Spatial Indexing of Complex Virtual Reality Scenes in the Web. *International Journal of Image and Graphics, 17*(2), 00523. doi:10.1142/S0219467817500097

Kontakis, K., Malamos, A. G., Steiakaki, M., Panagiotakis, S., & Ware, J. A. (2018). Object Identification Based on the Automated Extraction of Spatial Semantics from Web3D Scenes. *Annals of Emerging Technologies in Computing, 2*(4), 1–10. doi:10.33166/AETiC.2018.04.001

Kontakis, K., Steiakaki, M., Kalochristianakis, M., & Malamos, A. G. (2015). Applying Aesthetic Rules in Virtual Environments by means of Semantic Web Technologies. In *Augmented and Virtual Reality* (Vol. 9254, pp. 344–354). Springer International Publishing; doi:10.1007/978-3-319-22888-4_25

Kosmidou, V. E., & Hadjileontiadis, L. J. (2009). Sign language recognition using intrinsic-mode sample entropy on sEMG and accelerometer data. *IEEE Transactions on Biomedical Engineering*, *56*(12), 2879–2890. doi:10.1109/TBME.2009.2013200 PMID:19174329

Kosmopoulos, D. I., Doulamis, A., & Doulamis, N. (2005, September). Gesture-based video summarization. In *IEEE International Conference on Image Processing 2005* (Vol. 3, pp. III-1220). IEEE. 10.1109/ICIP.2005.1530618

Kosmopoulos, D. I., Voulodimos, A. S., & Varvarigou, T. A. (2010). Robust Human Behavior Modeling from Multiple Cameras. *2010 20th International Conference on Pattern Recognition*, 3575–3578. 10.1109/ICPR.2010.872

Kosmopoulos, D. I., Voulodimos, A. S., & Doulamis, A. D. (2013). A System for Multicamera Task Recognition and Summarization for Structured Environments. *IEEE Transactions on Industrial Informatics*, *9*(1), 161–171. doi:10.1109/TII.2012.2212712

Kriegel, H.-P., Kröger, P., Sander, J., & Zimek, A. (2011). Density-based clustering. *Wiley Interdisciplinary Reviews. Data Mining and Knowledge Discovery*, *1*(3), 231–240. doi:10.1002/widm.30

Kristan, M., Matas, J., Leonardis, A., Felsberg, M., Cehovin, L., Fernandez, G., ... Solis Montero, A. (2015). The Visual Object Tracking VOT2015 Challenge Results. In *2015 IEEE International Conference on Computer Vision Workshop (ICCVW)* (pp. 564–586). 10.1109/ICCVW.2015.79

Krizhevsky, A., Sutskever, I., & Hinton, G. E. (2012). Imagenet classification with deep convolutional neural networks. In Advances in neural information processing systems (pp. 1097-1105). Academic Press.

Krizhevsky, A. (2012). *Learning Multiple Layers of Features from Tiny Images*. University of Toronto.

Kumar, P., Gauba, H., Roy, P. P., & Dogra, D. P. (2017). Coupled HMM-based multi-sensor data fusion for sign language recognition. *Pattern Recognition Letters*, *86*, 1–8. doi:10.1016/j.patrec.2016.12.004

Kurach, K., Lucic, M., Zhai, X., Michalski, M., & Gelly, S. (2018). *A Large-Scale Study on Regularization and Normalization in GANs*. Retrieved from https://arxiv.org/abs/1807.04720

Kyriakaki, G., Doulamis, A., Doulamis, N., Ioannides, M., Makantasis, K., Protopapadakis, E., ... Weinlinger, G. (2014). 4D Reconstruction of Tangible Cultural Heritage Objects from Web-Retrieved Images. *International Journal of Heritage in the Digital Era*, *3*(2), 431–452. doi:10.1260/2047-4970.3.2.431

Laggis, A., Doulamis, N., Protopapadakis, E., & Georgopoulos, A. (2017). A low-cost markerless tracking system for trajectory interpretation. *ISPRS International Workshop of 3D Virtual Reconstruction and Visualization of Complex Arhitectures, Nafplio*, 1–3. 10.5194/isprs-archives-XLII-2-W3-413-2017

Laiserin, J. (2003). *The BIM Page*. Laiserin Letter.

Lake, M., Salakhutdinov, R., & Tenenbaum, J. B. (2015). Human-level concept learning through probabilistic program induction. *Science*, *350*(6266), 1332–1338. doi:10.1126cience.aab3050 PMID:26659050

Lakshmi Devasena, C. (2014). Comparative Analysis of Random Forest, REP Tree and J48 Classifiers for Credit Risk Prediction. *International Journal of Computers and Applications*, *8*(7), 30–36.

Lalos, C., Voulodimos, A., Doulamis, A., & Varvarigou, T. (2014). Efficient tracking using a robust motion estimation technique. *Multimedia Tools and Applications*, *69*(2), 277–292. doi:10.100711042-012-0994-3

Larsen, R. M. (1998). Lanczos bidiagonalization with partial reorthogonalization. *DAIMI Report Series*, *27*(537).

Latoschik, M. E., Blach, R., & Iao, F. (2008). *Semantic modelling for virtual worlds a novel paradigm for realtime interactive systems?* VRST. doi:10.1145/1450579.1450583

Le Guillou, C. (1999). Case-based reasoning (CBR) in endoscopic images diagnosis aid, *Engineering in Medicine and Biology. IEEE Transactions on Systems, Man and Cybernetics. Part C, Applications and Reviews, 1*(4), 21–34.

Leal, I. R., da Silva, J. O. S. E., Cardoso, M., Tabarelli, M., & Lacher, T. E. (2005). Changing the course of biodiversity conservation in the Caatinga of northeastern Brazil. *Conservation Biology, 19*(3), 701–706. doi:10.1111/j.1523-1739.2005.00703.x

Leap Motion. (n.d.). Retrieved November 22, 2019, from https://www.leapmotion.com/

Lecron, F., & Benjelloun, M. (2012). Fully Automatic Vertebra Detection in X-Ray Images Based on Multi-Class SVM. *Medical Imaging, SPIE proceedings, 8314*(2), 1-8.

Lecun, Y., Bottou, L., Bengio, Y., & Haffner, P. (1998). Gradient-based learning applied to document recognition. *Proceedings of the IEEE, 86*(11), 2278–2324. doi:10.1109/5.726791

Ledig, C., Theis, L., Huszar, F., Caballero, J., Aitken, A. P., Tejani, A., … Shi, W. (2016). *Photo-Realistic Single Image Super-Resolution Using a Generative Adversarial Network.* Retrieved from https://arxiv.org/abs/1609.04802

Lee, K., Choi, M.-K., & Jung, H. (2019). DavinciGAN: Unpaired Surgical Instrument Translation for Data Augmentation. In M. J. Cardoso, A. Feragen, B. Glocker, E. Konukoglu, I. Oguz, G. Unal, & T. Vercauteren (Eds.), *Proceedings of The 2nd International Conference on Medical Imaging with Deep Learning* (Vol. 102, pp. 326–336). London, UK: PMLR. Retrieved from http://proceedings.mlr.press/v102/lee19a.html

Lee, K.-L., & Chen, L.-H. (2005). An efficient computation method for the texture browsing descriptor of MPEG-7. *Image and Vision Computing, 23*(5), 479–489. doi:10.1016/j.imavis.2004.12.002

Lee, R. S., Gimenez, F., Hoogi, A., Miyake, K. K., Gorovoy, M., & Rubin, D. L. (2017). Data Descriptor: A curated mammography data set for use in computer-aided detection and diagnosis research. *Scientific Data, 4*(1), 170177. doi:10.1038data.2017.177 PMID:29257132

Lent, R. W., Brown, S. D., & Hackett, G. (1994). Toward a unifying social cognitive theory of career and academic interest, choice, and performance. *Journal of Vocational Behavior, 45*(1), 79–122. doi:10.1006/jvbe.1994.1027

Lercari, N., Mortara, M., & Forte, M. (2013). *Unveiling California history through serious games: Fort Ross virtual warehouse.* Paper presented at the International Conference on Games and Learning Alliance.

Lerma, J. L., Cabrelles, M., & Portalés, C. (2011). Multitemporal thermal analysis to detect moisture on a building façade. *Construction & Building Materials, 25*(5), 2190–2197. doi:10.1016/j.conbuildmat.2010.10.007

Lerones, P. M., Fernández, J. L., Gil, Á. M., Gómez-García-Bermejo, J., & Casanova, E. Z. (2010). A practical approach to making accurate 3D layouts of interesting cultural heritage sites through digital models. *Journal of Cultural Heritage, 11*(1), 1–9. doi:10.1016/j.culher.2009.02.007

Lewis, R. (1996). Generating 3D Building Models from 2D Architectural Plans (Master's Project). University of California, Berkeley, CA.

Li, C., & Wand, M. (2016). *Precomputed Real-Time Texture Synthesis with Markovian Generative Adversarial Networks.* Retrieved from https://arxiv.org/abs/1604.04382

Li, X., Flohr, F., Yang, Y., Xiong, H., Braun, M., Pan, S., … Gavrila, D. (2016). *A new benchmark for vision-based cyclist detection.* doi:10.1109/IVS.2016.7535515

Liang, R. H., & Ouhyoung, M. (1998, April). A real-time continuous gesture recognition system for sign language. In *Proceedings third IEEE international conference on automatic face and gesture recognition* (pp. 558-567). IEEE. 10.1109/AFGR.1998.671007

Liarokapis, F., Petridis, P., Andrews, D., & de Freitas, S. (2017). *Multimodal Serious Games Technologies for Cultural Heritage. In Mixed Reality and Gamification for Cultural Heritage* (pp. 371–392). Springer. doi:10.1007/978-3-319-49607-8_15

Li, L., & Lan, H. (2019). Recovering absolute scale for Structure from Motion using the law of free fall. *Optics & Laser Technology, 112*, 514–523. doi:10.1016/j.optlastec.2018.11.045

Lim, K. M., Tan, A. W., & Tan, S. C. (2016a). Block-based histogram of optical flow for isolated sign language recognition. *Journal of Visual Communication and Image Representation, 40*, 538–545. doi:10.1016/j.jvcir.2016.07.020

Lim, K. M., Tan, A. W., & Tan, S. C. (2016b). A feature covariance matrix with serial particle filter for isolated sign language recognition. *Expert Systems with Applications, 54*, 208–218. doi:10.1016/j.eswa.2016.01.047

Liu, D., Hua, G., & Chen, T. (2010). A Hierarchical Visual Model for Video Object Summarization. *IEEE Transactions on Pattern Analysis and Machine Intelligence, 32*(12), 2178–2190. doi:10.1109/TPAMI.2010.31 PMID:20975116

Liu, T., Zhou, W., & Li, H. (2016, September). Sign language recognition with long short-term memory. In *2016 IEEE International Conference on Image Processing (ICIP)* (pp. 2871-2875). IEEE. 10.1109/ICIP.2016.7532884

Li, W., Zhao, R., Xiao, T., & Wang, X. (2014). DeepReID: Deep Filter Pairing Neural Network for Person Re-identification. In *2014 IEEE Conference on Computer Vision and Pattern Recognition* (pp. 152–159). 10.1109/CVPR.2014.27

Li, Z., Schuster, G. M., & Katsaggelos, A. K. (2005). MINMAX optimal video summarization. *IEEE Transactions on Circuits and Systems for Video Technology, 15*(10), 1245–1256. doi:10.1109/TCSVT.2005.854230

Loewenstein, Y., Raimondo, D., Redfern, O. C., Watson, J., Frishman, D., Linial, M., ... Tramontano, A. (2009). Protein function annotation by homology-based inference. *Genome Biology, 10*(2), 207. doi:10.1186/gb-2009-10-2-207 PMID:19226439

Logitech - Webcams for Video Conferencing and Video Calling. (n.d.). Retrieved November 22, 2019, from https://www.logitech.com/en-us/video/webcams?filters=consumer

Long, F., Zhou, J., & Peng, H. (2012). Visualization and analysis of 3D microscopic images. *PLoS Computational Biology, 8*(6), e1002519. doi:10.1371/journal.pcbi.1002519 PMID:22719236

Lorenzi, H. (2002). Brazilian Trees. A Guide to the Identification and Cultivation of Brazilian Native Trees, Vol. 2 (2nd ed.). Instituto Plantarum de Estados da Flora LTDA, Nova.

Lowe, D. G. (2004). Distinctive image features from scale-invariant keypoints. *International Journal of Computer Vision, 60*(2), 91–110. doi:10.1023/B:VISI.0000029664.99615.94

Lucic, M., Kurach, K., Michalski, M., Gelly, S., & Bousquet, O. (2017). *Are GANs Created Equal? A Large-Scale Study.* Retrieved from https://arxiv.org/abs/1711.10337

Lucic, M., Tschannen, M., Ritter, M., Zhai, X., Bachem, O., & Gelly, S. (2019). *High-Fidelity Image Generation With Fewer Labels.* Retrieved from https://arxiv.org/abs/1903.02271

Lüthi, M., Jud, C., Gerig, T., & Vetter, T. (2016). *Gaussian Process Morphable Models.* Academic Press.

Lu, Y. L. (2020). *Sharing heterogeneous spatial knowledge: Map fusion between asynchronous monocular vision and lidar or other prior inputs.* Robotics Research.

Lu, Z. (1998). On the geometric ergodicity of a non-linear autoregressive model with an autoregressive conditional heteroscedastic term. *Statistica Sinica, §§§,* 1205–1217.

Maarif, H., Akmeliawati, R., & Gunawan, T. S. (2018). Survey on Language Processing Algorithm for Sign Language Synthesizer. *International Journal of Robotics and Mechatronics, 4*(2), 39–48. doi:10.21535/ijrm.v4i2.1001

Madeira, R. N., Silva, A., Santos, C., Teixeira, B., Romão, T., Dias, E., & Correia, N. (2011). LEY! Persuasive pervasive gaming on domestic energy consumption-awareness. *Proceedings of the 8th International Conference on Advances in Computer Entertainment Technology.* 10.1145/2071423.2071512

Madsen, C. B. (1997). A comparative study of the robustness of two pose estimation techniques. *Machine Vision and Applications, 9*(5-6), 291–303. doi:10.1007001380050049

Maglo, A., Lee, H., Lavoué, G., Mouton, C., Hudelot, C., & Dupont, F. (2010). Remote scientific visualization of progressive 3D meshes with X3D. In *Proceedings of the 15th International Conference on Web 3D Technology* (pp. 109-116). ACM.

Maicas, J. M., & Viñals, M. J. (2016). Edeta 360° Virtual Tour for visiting the heritage of Lliria (Spain). *Proceedings of the Archaeologica 2.0. 8th International Congres on Archaeology, Computer Graphics, Cultural Heritage and Innovation.*

Makantasis, K. D., Doulamis, A., Doulamis, N., & Ioannides, M. (2016). In the wild image retrieval and clustering for 3D cultural heritage landmarks reconstruction. *Multimedia Tools and Applications, 75*(7), 3593–3629. doi:10.100711042-014-2191-z

Malala, V. D., Prigent, E., Braffort, A., & Berret, B. (2018). Which Picture? A Methodology for the Evaluation of Sign Language Animation Understandability. In Multimodal Signals: Cognitive and Algorithmic Issues (pp. 83–93). Berlin: Springer Berlin Heidelberg.

Malamos, A. G., & Mamakis, G. (2006). VCLASS-3D: A Multimedia Educational Collaboration Platform With 3D Virtual Workspace Support. WBE '06, Puerto Vallarta.

Malamos, A. G., & Mamakis, G. (2009). Extending X3D-based Educational Platform for Mathematics with Multicast Networking Capabilities. WBE ' 09, 644-038, Phuket, Thailand.

Manus, V. R. | World's leading VR gloves for training. (n.d.). Retrieved November 22, 2019, from https://manus-vr.com/

Marčiš, M. (2013). Quality of 3D models generated by SFM technology. *Slovak Journal of Civil Engineering,* 13-24.

Mariani, G., Scheidegger, F., Istrate, R., Bekas, C., & Malossi, C. (2018). *BAGAN: Data Augmentation with Balancing GAN.* Retrieved from https://arxiv.org/abs/1803.09655

Marolt, M., Vratanar, J. F., & Strle, G. (2009). Ethnomuse: Archiving folk music and dance culture. *IEEE EUROCON, 322–326,* 322–326. doi:10.1109/EURCON.2009.5167650

Marquart, G. D., Tabor, K. M., Horstick, E. J., Brown, M., Geoca, A. K., Polys, N. F., ... Burgess, H. A. (2017, August 1). High-precision registration between zebrafish brain atlases using symmetric diffeomorphic normalization. *GigaScience, 6*(8), gix056. doi:10.1093/gigascience/gix056 PMID:28873968

Martell, A. L. (2018). Benchmarking structure from motion algorithms of urban environments with applications to reconnaissance in search and rescue scenarios. *IEEE International Symposium on Safety, Security, and Rescue Robotics,* 1-7. 10.1109/SSRR.2018.8468612

Martinelli, G., & Moraes, M. A. (2013). *Livro vermelho da flora do Brasil.* Academic Press.

Ma, S., Fu, J., Chen, C. W., & Mei, T. (2018). DA-GAN: Instance-Level Image Translation by Deep Attention Generative Adversarial Networks. In *Proceedings of the IEEE Computer Society Conference on Computer Vision and Pattern Recognition* (pp. 5657–5666). 10.1109/CVPR.2018.00593

Masood, S., Srivastava, A., Thuwal, H. C., & Ahmad, M. (2018). Real-time sign language gesture (word) recognition from video sequences using CNN and RNN. In *Intelligent Engineering Informatics* (pp. 623–632). Singapore: Springer. doi:10.1007/978-981-10-7566-7_63

Masurelle, A., Essid, S., & Richard, G. (2013). Multimodal classification of dance movements using body joint trajectories and step sounds. *2013 14th International Workshop on Image Analysis for Multimedia Interactive Services (WIAMIS)*, 1–4. 10.1109/WIAMIS.2013.6616151

Matsuoka, D., Murata, K., Fujita, S., Tanaka, T., Yamamoto, K., & Ohno, N. (2009). 4-2-2 3D Visualization and Visual Data Mining. *Journal of the National Institute of Information and Communications Technology, 56*(1-4).

McCann, S. (2015). *3D Reconstruction from Multiple Images*. Academic Press.

McDonald, J., Wolfe, R., Schnepp, J., Hochgesang, J., Jamrozik, D. G., Stumbo, M., ... Thomas, F. (2016). An automated technique for real-time production of lifelike animations of American Sign Language. *Universal Access in the Information Society, 15*(4), 551–566. doi:10.100710209-015-0407-2

McNitt-Gray, M., Armato, S. III, Meyer, C., Reeves, A., Mclennan, G., Pais, R., ... Clarke, L. (2008). The Lung Image Database Consortium (LIDC) Data Collection Process for Nodule Detection and Annotation. *Academic Radiology, 14*(12), 1464–1474. doi:10.1016/j.acra.2007.07.021 PMID:18035276

Megalooikonomou, Barnathan, & Konto. (2009). A Representation and Classification Scheme for Tree-like Structures in Medical Images: Analyzing the Branching Pattern of Ductal Trees in X-ray Galactograms. *IEEE TMI, 28*(4), 487-493.

Melgani, F., & Bruzzone, L. (2004). Classification of hyperspectral remote sensing images with support vector machines. *IEEE Transactions on Geoscience and Remote Sensing, 42*(8), 1778–1790. doi:10.1109/TGRS.2004.831865

Menard, S. (2002). *Applied logistic regression analysis* (Vol. 106). Sage. doi:10.4135/9781412983433

Menze, B. H., Jakab, A., Bauer, S., Kalpathy-Cramer, J., Farahani, K., Kirby, J., ... Van Leemput, K. (2015). The Multimodal Brain Tumor Image Segmentation Benchmark (BRATS). *IEEE Transactions on Medical Imaging, 34*(10), 1993–2024. doi:10.1109/TMI.2014.2377694 PMID:25494501

Michele, G., Michele, D. D., & Fabio, S. (2013). *VisitAR: a mobile application for tourism using AR*. Paper presented at the SIGGRAPH Asia 2013 Symposium on Mobile Graphics and Interactive Applications, Hong Kong, Hong Kong. 10.1145/2543651.2543665

Micmac - LOGICIELS. (n.d.). Retrieved July 26, 2017, from http://logiciels.ign.fr/?Micmac

Miguélez Fernández, L. (2013). *Tour virtual por la red de museos de Gijón* (Master). Univeridad de Oviedo.

Mikolajczyk, K., Zisserman, A., & Schmid, C. (2003). Shape recognition with edge-based features. *BMVC'03*, 779–788.

Min, P., Kazhdan, M., & Funkhouser, T. (2004). A comparison of text and shape matching for retrieval of online 3D models. *Proc. European conference on digital libraries*, 209. 10.1007/978-3-540-30230-8_20

Min, R., & Cheng, H. D. (2009). Effective image retrieval using dominant color descriptor and fuzzy support vector machine. *Pattern Recognition, 42*(1), 147–157. doi:10.1016/j.patcog.2008.07.001

Mirza, M., & Osindero, S. (2014). *Conditional Generative Adversarial Nets*. Retrieved from https://arxiv.org/abs/1411.1784

Miyato, T., Kataoka, T., Koyama, M., & Yoshida, Y. (2018). *Spectral Normalization for Generative Adversarial Networks.* Retrieved from https://arxiv.org/abs/1802.05957

Montani, M., & Bellazzi, R. (2001). Intelligent knowledge retrieval for decision support in medical applications. *Studies in Health Technology and Informatics, 84*(1), 498–502. PMID:11604790

Moons, T., Van Gool, L., & Vergauwen, M. (2010). 3D reconstruction from multiple images part 1: principles. *Foundations and Trends® in Computer Graphics and Vision, 4*(4), 287-404.

Moreira, I., Amaral, I., Domingues, I., Cardoso, A., Cardoso, M., & Cardoso, J. (2011). INbreast: Toward a Full-field Digital Mammographic Database. *Academic Radiology, 19*(2), 236–248. doi:10.1016/j.acra.2011.09.014 PMID:22078258

Morse, K. L., Brunton, R., & Schloman, J. (2011). *X3D - 3D manmade feature common data storage format. Fall Simulation Interoperability Workshop, Orlando,* FL.

Mortara, M., Catalano, C. E., Fiucci, G., & Derntl, M. (2013). *Evaluating the effectiveness of serious games for cultural awareness: the Icura user study.* Paper presented at the International Conference on Games and Learning Alliance.

Mortara, M., Catalano, C. E., Bellotti, F., Fiucci, G., Houry-Panchetti, M., & Petridis, P. (2014). Learning cultural heritage by serious games. *Journal of Cultural Heritage, 15*(3), 318–325. doi:10.1016/j.culher.2013.04.004

MPEG-4 Homepage. (n.d.). https://mpeg.chiariglione.org/standards/mpeg-4/mpeg-4.htm

MPEG-7 Homepage. (n.d.). https://mpeg.chiariglione.org/standards/mpeg-7/mpeg-7.htm

Muja, M., & Lowe, D. G. (2009). Fast approximate nearest neighbors with automatic algorithm configuration. *VISAPP, 1*(2)331–340.

Mulayim, A. Y., Yilmaz, U., & Atalay, V. (2003). Silhouette-based 3-D model reconstruction from multiple images. *IEEE Transactions on Systems, Man, and Cybernetics. Part B, Cybernetics, 33*(4), 582–591. doi:10.1109/TSMCB.2003.814303 PMID:18238208

Murtagh, I. E. (2019). *A Linguistically Motivated Computational Framework for Irish Sign Language.* Trinity College.

Nassar, N. M., Hashimoto, D., & Fernandes, S. (2008). Wild Manihot species: Botanical aspects, geographic distribution and economic value. *Genetics and Molecular Research, 7*(1), 16–28. doi:10.4238/vol7-1gmr389 PMID:18273815

Navarro, S., Seguí, A. E., Portalés, C., Lerma, J. L., Akasheh, T., & Haddad, N. (2009). *Integration of tls data and non-metric imagery to improve photo models and recording-a case study on djin block no. 9, petra (jordan).* Paper presented at the Virtual Systems and Multimedia.

Nelson, D. (2009). Using a Signing Avatar as a Sign Language Research Tool. Academic Press.

Neter, J., Kutner, M. H., Nachtsheim, C. J., & Wasserman, W. (1996). *Applied linear statistical models.* Academic Press.

Netzer, Y., Wang, T., Coates, A., Bissacco, A., Wu, B., & Ng, A. Y. (2011). Reading Digits in Natural Images with Unsupervised Feature Learning. *NIPS Workshop on Deep Learning and Unsupervised Feature Learning 2011.* Retrieved from http://ufldl.stanford.edu/housenumbers/nips2011_housenumbers.pdf

Neu, S. C., & Toga, A. W. (2008). Automatic Localization of Anatomical Point Landmarks for Brain Image Processing Algorithms. *Neuroinformatics, 6*(2), 135–148. doi:10.100712021-008-9018-x PMID:18512163

Nguyen, M., Tran, H., & Le, H. (2017). Exploration of the 3D World on the Internet Using Commodity Virtual Reality Devices. *Multimodal Technologies and Interaction, 1*(3), 15. doi:10.3390/mti1030015

Nikolov, I. A. (2016). Benchmarking close-range structure from motion 3D reconstruction software under varying capturing conditions. *Euro-Mediterranean Conference*, 15-26. 10.1007/978-3-319-48496-9_2

Nikolov, I., & Madsen, C. (2019). Performance Characterization of Absolute Scale Computation for 3D Structure from Motion Reconstruction. *International Conference on Computer Vision Theory and Applications.* 10.5220/0007444208840891

Ni, X., Ding, G., Ni, X., Ni, X., Jing, Q., Ma, J., ... Huang, T. (2013, August). Signer-independent sign language recognition based on manifold and discriminative training. In *International Conference on Information Computing and Applications* (pp. 263-272). Springer. 10.1007/978-3-642-53932-9_26

Nuzhnaya. (2011). Segmentation of anatomical branching structures based on texture features and graph cut. *IEEE International Symposium on Biomedical Imaging, 52*(20), 35-42.

O'Connor, M. J., & Das, A. (2009). *SQWRL: A Query Language for OWL* (Vol. 529). OWLED.

Ochs, J. G., Goldin, J., Abtin, F., Kim, H., Brown, K., Batra, P., ... Brown, M. (2007). Automated classification of lung bronchovascular anatomy in CT using AdaBoost. *Medical Image Analysis, 11*(3), 315–324. doi:10.1016/j.media.2007.03.004 PMID:17482500

Odena, A., Buckman, J., Olsson, C., Brown, T. B., Olah, C., Raffel, C., & Goodfellow, I. (2018). *Is Generator Conditioning Causally Related to GAN Performance?* Retrieved from https://arxiv.org/abs/1802.08768

Odena, A., Olah, C., & Shlens, J. (2016). *Conditional Image Synthesis With Auxiliary Classifier GANs.* Retrieved from https://arxiv.org/abs/1610.09585

Onishi, Y., Teramoto, A., Tsujimoto, M., Tsukamoto, T., Saito, K., & Toyama, H. (2019). Automated Pulmonary Nodule Classification in Computed Tomography Images Using a Deep Convolutional Neural Network Trained by Generative Adversarial Networks. *BioMed Research International*, 1–9. doi:10.1155/2019/6051939 PMID:30719445

Orange. (2017). *Fundación Orange. Hablando con el arte.* Retrieved from http://www.fundacionorange.es/aplicaciones/hablando-con-el-arte-apps/

Orbbec – Intelligent computing for everyone everywhere. (n.d.). Retrieved November 22, 2019, from https://orbbec3d.com

Orghidan, R., Salvi, J., Gordan, M., Florea, C., & Batlle, J. (2014). Structured light self-calibration with vanishing points. *Machine Vision and Applications, 25*(2), 489–500. doi:10.100700138-013-0517-x

Ouyang, X., Cheng, Y., Jiang, Y., Li, C.-L., & Zhou, P. (2018). *Pedestrian-Synthesis-GAN: Generating Pedestrian Data in Real Scene and Beyond.* Retrieved from https://arxiv.org/abs/1804.02047

Özyeşil, O. V., Voroninski, V., Basri, R., & Singer, A. (2017). A survey of structure from motion*. *Acta Numerica, 26*, 305–364. doi:10.1017/S096249291700006X

Pal, M., & Mather, P. M. (2005). Support vector machines for classification in remote sensing. *International Journal of Remote Sensing, 26*(5), 1007–1011. doi:10.1080/01431160512331314083

Panagiotakis, C., Doulamis, A., & Tziritas, G. (2009). Equivalent Key Frames Selection Based on Iso-Content Principle. *IEEE Transactions on Circuits and Systems for Video Technology, 19*(3), 447–451. doi:10.1109/TCSVT.2009.2013517

Pan, Z., Yu, W., Yi, X., Khan, A., Yuan, F., & Zheng, Y. (2019). Recent Progress on Generative Adversarial Networks (GANs): A Survey. *IEEE Access: Practical Innovations, Open Solutions, 7*, 36322–36333. doi:10.1109/ACCESS.2019.2905015

Papadogiorgaki, M., Grammalidis, N., Tzovaras, D., & Strintzis, M. G. (2005). Text-to-sign language synthesis tool. *2005 13th European Signal Processing Conference*, 1–4.

Papadopoulos, S., Zigkolis, C., Kompatsiaris, Y., & Vakali, A. (2010). Cluster-based Landmark and Event Detection on Tagged Photo Collections. *IEEE MultiMedia.* doi:10.1109/mmul.2010.68

Papaleo, L., & De Floriani, L. (2009). Semantic-Based Segmentation and Annotation of 3D Models. In Image Analysis and Processing – ICIAP 2009, (pp. 103-112). Springer Berlin/Heidelberg.

Park, T., Liu, M.-Y., Wang, T.-C., & Zhu, J.-Y. (2019). *Semantic Image Synthesis with Spatially-Adaptive Normalization.* Retrieved from https://arxiv.org/abs/1903.07291

Parkhi, O. M., Vedaldi, A., & Zisserman, A. (2015). Deep Face Recognition. *British Machine Vision Conference.*

Patel, A., & Smith, W. A. (2009). Shape-from-shading Driven 3D Morphable Models for Illumination Insensitive Face Recognition. In BMVC (pp. 1-10). Academic Press.

Pavlopoulos, G. A., Wegener, A.-L., & Schneider, R. (2008). A survey of visualization tools for biological network analysis. *BioData Mining, 1*(1), 12. doi:10.1186/1756-0381-1-12 PMID:19040716

Paysan, P., Knothe, R., Amberg, B., Romdhani, S., & Vetter, T. (2009, September). A 3D face model for pose and illumination invariant face recognition. In *2009 Sixth IEEE International Conference on Advanced Video and Signal Based Surveillance* (pp. 296-301). IEEE.

Pein, R. P., Amador, M., Lu, J., & Renz, W. (2008). Using CBIR and semantics in 3D-model retrieval. In *8th IEEE International Conference on Computer and Information Technology.* IEEE. 10.1109/CIT.2008.4594669

Pennington, R. T., & Ratter, J. A. (Eds.). (2006). *Neotropical savannas and seasonally dry forests: plant diversity, biogeography, and conservation.* CRC Press. doi:10.1201/9781420004496

Perez-Gallardo, L. C., Crespo, G., & de Jesus, G. (2017). GEODIM: A Semantic Model-Based System for 3D Recognition of Industrial Scenes. In Current Trends on Knowledge-Based Systems (pp. 137–159). Springer.

Perkowitz, M., & Etzioni, O. (2000). Towards adaptive web sites: Conceptual framework and case study. *Artificial Intelligence, 118*(1-2), 245–275. doi:10.1016/S0004-3702(99)00098-3

Pfister, A., West, A. M., Bronner, S., & Noah, J. A. (2014). Comparative abilities of Microsoft Kinect and Vicon 3D motion capture for gait analysis. *Journal of Medical Engineering & Technology, 38*(5), 274–280. doi:10.3109/03091902.2014.909540 PMID:24878252

Pitarello, F., & Faveri, A. (2006). Semantic Description of 3D Environments: a Proposal Based on Web Standards. *Proceedings of Web3D Symposium '06*, 85-95.

Pittarello, F., & Faveri, A. (2006). Semantic Description of 3D Environments: A Proposal Based on Web Standards. In *Proceedings of the Eleventh International Conference on 3D Web Technology, Web3D '06*, (pp. 85–95). New York, NY: ACM.

PlatformA. P. I. (n.d.). http://restlet.com/.Apache

Ploumpis, S., Ververas, E., Sullivan, E. O., Moschoglou, S., Wang, H., Pears, N., . . . Zafeiriou, S. (2019). *Towards a complete 3D morphable model of the human head.* arXiv preprint arXiv:1911.08008

Polys, N. F., Bowman, D. A., North, C., Laubenbacher, R., & Duca, K. (2004). PathSim visualizer: an Information-Rich Virtual Environment framework for systems biology. *Proceedings of the ninth international conference on 3D Web technology*, 7-14. 10.1145/985040.985042

Polys, N. F., Brutzman, D. P., Steed, A., & Behr, J. (2008). Future Standards for Immersive VR: Report on the IEEE Virtual Reality 2007 Workshop. *IEEE Computer Graphics and Applications*, 28(2), 94–99. doi:10.1109/MCG.2008.29 PMID:18350937

Polys, N. F., & Gurjarpadhye, A. A. (2016). Tradeoffs in multi-channel microscopy volume visualization: an initial evaluation. In *Proceedings of the 21st International Conference on Web3D Technology*. ACM. 10.1145/2945292.2945323

Polys, N. F., Ullrich, S., Evestedt, D., & Wood, A. D. (2013). A fresh look at immersive Volume Rendering: Challenges and capabilities. *IEEE VR Workshop on Volume Rendering*.

Polys, N. F., & Wood, A. (2012). New platforms for health hypermedia. *Issues in Information Systems*, 1(13), 40–50.

Portalés Ricart, C. (2009). *Entornos multimedia de realidad aumentada en el campo del arte* (Doctoral Thesis). Universidad Politécnica de Valencia, Valencia.

Portalés Ricart, C., Giner Martínez, F., & Sanmartín Piquer, F. (2005). Back to the 70's. *Proceedings of the ACM SIGCHI International Conference on Advances in Computer Entertainment Technology*.

Portalés, C., & Perales, C. D. (2009). *Sound and Movement Visualization in the AR-Jazz Scenario.* Paper presented at the International Conference on Entertainment Computing (ICEC). 10.1007/978-3-642-04052-8_15

Portalés, C., Alonso-Monasterio, P., & Viñals, M. J. (2017). 3D virtual reconstruction and visualisation of the archaeological site Castellet de Bernabé (Llíria, Spain). *Virtual Archaeology Review*, 8(16), 75–82. doi:10.4995/var.2017.5890

Portalés, C., Casas, S., Alonso-Monasterio, P., & Viñals, M. J. (2017). Multi-Dimensional Acquisition, Representation and Interaction of Cultural Heritage Tangible Assets. An Insight on Tourism Applications. In J. M. F. Rodrigues, C. M. Q. Ramos, P. J. S. Cardoso, & C. Henriques (Eds.), *Handbook of Research on Technological Developments for Cultural Heritage and eTourism Applications*. IGI-Global.

Portalés, C., Casas, S., Coma, I., & Fernández, M. (2017). A Multi-Projector Calibration Method for Virtual Reality Simulators with Analytically Defined Screens. *Journal of Imaging*, 3(2), 19. doi:10.3390/jimaging3020019

Portalés, C., Gimeno, J., Casas, S., Olanda, R., & Giner, F. (2016). Interacting with augmented reality mirrors. In J. Rodrigues, P. Cardoso, J. Monteiro, & M. Figueiredo (Eds.), *Handbook of Research on Human-Computer Interfaces, Developments, and Applications* (pp. 216–244). IGI-Global. doi:10.4018/978-1-5225-0435-1.ch009

Portalés, C., Lerma, J. L., & Pérez, C. (2009). Photogrammetry and augmented reality for cultural heritage applications. *The Photogrammetric Record*, 24(128), 316–331. doi:10.1111/j.1477-9730.2009.00549.x

Portalés, C., Viñals, M. J., Alonso-Monasterio, P., & Morant, M. (2010). AR-Immersive Cinema at the Aula Natura Visitors Center. *IEEE MultiMedia*, 17(4), 8–15. doi:10.1109/MMUL.2010.72

Prado, D. E. (2000). Seasonally dry forests of tropical South America: From forgotten ecosystems to a new phytogeographic unit. *Edinburgh Journal of Botany*, 57(3), 437–461. doi:10.1017/S096042860000041X

Protégé. (2019). https://protege.stanford.edu/

Protopapadakis, E., Grammatikopoulou, A., Doulamis, A., & Grammalidis, N. (2017). Folk Dance Pattern Recognition Over Depth Images Acquired via Kinect Sensor. *3D ARCH-3D Virtual Reconstruction and Visualization of Complex Architectures*.

Protopapadakis, E., Voulodimos, A., Doulamis, A., Doulamis, N., Dres, D., & Bimpas, M. (2017b). *Stacked Autoencoders for Outlier Detection in Over-The-Horizon Radar Signals*. Academic Press.

Protopapadakis, E., & Doulamis, A. (2014). Semi-Supervised Image Meta-Filtering Using Relevance Feedback in Cultural Heritage Applications. *International Journal of Heritage in the Digital Era, 3*(4), 613–627. doi:10.1260/2047-4970.3.4.613

Protopapadakis, E., Niklis, D., Doumpos, M., Doulamis, A., & Zopounidis, C. (2019). Sample selection algorithms for credit risk modelling through data mining techniques. *Int. J. Data Mining, Modelling and Management, 11*(2), 103–128. doi:10.1504/IJDMMM.2019.10019369

Protopapadakis, E., Voulodimos, A., & Doulamis, A. (2018a). On the Impact of Labeled Sample Selection in Semisupervised Learning for Complex Visual Recognition Tasks. *Complexity, 2018*, 1–11. doi:10.1155/2018/6531203

Protopapadakis, E., Voulodimos, A., Doulamis, A., Camarinopoulos, S., Doulamis, N., & Miaoulis, G. (2018). Dance Pose Identification from Motion Capture Data: A Comparison of Classifiers. *Technologies, 6*(1), 31. doi:10.3390/technologies6010031

Protopapadakis, E., Voulodimos, A., Doulamis, A., Doulamis, N., Dres, D., & Bimpas, M. (2017a). Stacked autoencoders for outlier detection in over-the-horizon radar signals. *Computational Intelligence and Neuroscience, 2017*, 2017. doi:10.1155/2017/5891417 PMID:29312449

Protopapadakis, E., Voulodimos, A., & Doulamis, N. (2018b). Multidimensional Trajectory Similarity Estimation via Spatial-Temporal Keyframe Selection and Signal Correlation Analysis. *Proceedings of the 11th PErvasive Technologies Related to Assistive Environments Conference*, 91–97. 10.1145/3197768.3201533

Psaltis, A., Apostolakis, K. C., Dimitropoulos, K., & Daras, P. (2017). Multimodal student engagement recognition in prosocial games. *IEEE Transactions on Games, 10*(3), 292–303. doi:10.1109/TCIAIG.2017.2743341

Psaltis, A., Kaza, K., Stefanidis, K., Thermos, S., Apostolakis, K. C., Dimitropoulos, K., & Daras, P. (2016, October). Multimodal affective state recognition in serious games applications. In *2016 IEEE International Conference on Imaging Systems and Techniques (IST)* (pp. 435-439). IEEE. 10.1109/IST.2016.7738265

Puliti, S., Gobakken, T., Ørka, H. O., & Næsset, E. (2017). Assessing 3D point clouds from aerial photographs for species-specific forest inventories. *Scandinavian Journal of Forest Research, 32*(1), 68–79. doi:10.1080/02827581.2016.1186727

Punchimudiyanse, M. (2015). *3D Animation framework for sign language*. Academic Press.

Punchimudiyanse, M., & Meegama, R. G. N. (2015). 3D signing avatar for Sinhala Sign language. *2015 IEEE 10th International Conference on Industrial and Information Systems (ICIIS)*, 290–295.

Rabah, M. B. (2018). *Using RTK and VRS in direct geo-referencing of the UAV imagery*. NRIAG Journal of Astronomy and Geophysics.

Rabattu, P. Y., Massé, B., Ulliana, F., Rousset, M. C., Rohmer, D., Léon, J. C., & Palombi, O. (2015). My Corporis Fabrica Embryo: An ontology-based 3D spatio-temporal modeling of human embryo development. *Journal of Biomedical Semantics, 6*(1), 36. doi:10.118613326-015-0034-0 PMID:26413258

Radford, A., Metz, L., & Chintala, S. (2015). *Unsupervised Representation Learning with Deep Convolutional Generative Adversarial Networks*. Retrieved from https://arxiv.org/abs/1511.06434

Radics, P. J., Polys, N. F., Neuman, S. P., & Lund, W. H. (2015). OSNAP! Introducing the open semantic network analysis platform. In Visualization and Data Analysis 2015 (vol. 9397, pp. 38–52). International Society for Optics and Photonics, SPIE.

Rallis, I., Georgoulas, I., Doulamis, N., Voulodimos, A., & Terzopoulos, P. (2017). Extraction of key postures from 3D human motion data for choreography summarization. *2017 9th International Conference on Virtual Worlds and Games for Serious Applications*, 94–101. 10.1109/VS-GAMES.2017.8056576

Rallis, I., Langis, A., Georgoulas, I., Voulodimos, A., Doulamis, N., & Doulamis, A. (2018). An Embodied Learning Game Using Kinect and Labanotation for Analysis and Visualization of Dance Kinesiology. *2018 10th International Conference on Virtual Worlds and Games for Serious Applications (VS-Games)*, 1–8. 10.1109/VS-Games.2018.8493410

Rallis, I., Doulamis, N., Doulamis, A., Voulodimos, A., & Vescoukis, V. (2018). Spatio-temporal summarization of dance choreographies. *Computers & Graphics*, *73*, 88–101. doi:10.1016/j.cag.2018.04.003

Rallis, I., Protopapadakis, E., Voulodimos, A., Doulamis, N., Doulamis, A., & Bardis, G. (2019). Choreographic Pattern Analysis from Heterogeneous Motion Capture Systems Using Dynamic Time Warping. *Technologies*, *7*(3), 56. doi:10.3390/technologies7030056

Raptis, M., Kirovski, D., & Hoppe, H. (2011). Real-time classification of dance gestures from skeleton animation. *Proceedings of the 2011 ACM SIGGRAPH/Eurographics Symposium on Computer Animation*, 147–156. 10.1145/2019406.2019426

Raumonen, P., Casella, E., Calders, K., Murphy, S., Åkerblom, M., & Kaasalainen, M. (2015). Massive-scale tree modelling from TLS data. ISPRS Annals of the Photogrammetry. *Remote Sensing and Spatial Information Sciences*, *2*(3), 189.

Raumonen, P., Kaasalainen, M., Åkerblom, M., Kaasalainen, S., Kaartinen, H., Vastaranta, M., ... Lewis, P. (2013). Fast automatic precision tree models from terrestrial laser scanner data. *Remote Sensing*, *5*(2), 491–520. doi:10.3390/rs5020491

Rautaray, S. S., & Agrawal, A. (2011). A real time hand tracking system for interactive applications. *International Journal of Computers and Applications*, *18*(6), 28–33. doi:10.5120/2287-2969

Ravichandran, A., Chaudhry, R., & Vidal, R. (2013). Categorizing dynamic textures using a bag of dynamical systems. *IEEE Transactions on Pattern Analysis and Machine Intelligence*, *35*(2), 342–353. doi:10.1109/TPAMI.2012.83 PMID:23257470

Ravuri, S., & Vinyals, O. (2019). *Classification Accuracy Score for Conditional Generative Models*. Retrieved from https://arxiv.org/abs/1905.10887

Rebolledo-Mendez, G., Avramides, K., de Freitas, S., & Memarzia, K. (2009). Societal impact of a serious game on raising public awareness: the case of FloodSim. *Proceedings of the 2009 ACM SIGGRAPH Symposium on Video Games*. 10.1145/1581073.1581076

Reffat, R. M., & Nofal, E. M. (2013). Effective Communication with Cultural heritage using Virtual Technologies. *The International Archives of the Photogrammetry, Remote Sensing and Spatial Information Sciences*, *XL-5*(W2), 519–524. doi:10.5194/isprsarchives-XL-5-W2-519-2013

Rekimoto, J., & Nagao, K. (1995). The world through the computer: computer augmented interaction with real world environments. *Proceedings of the 8th annual ACM symposium on User interface and software technology*. 10.1145/215585.215639

Ren, J., Hacihaliloglu, I., Singer, E. A., Foran, D. J., & Qi, X. (2018). *Adversarial Domain Adaptation for Classification of Prostate Histopathology Whole-Slide Images*. Retrieved from https://arxiv.org/abs/1806.01357

Ren, Y., Zhu, C., & Xiao, S. (2018). Object detection based on fast/faster RCNN employing fully convolutional architectures. *Mathematical Problems in Engineering*, *2018*, 2018. doi:10.1155/2018/3598316

Richardson, E., Sela, M., & Kimmel, R. (2016, October). 3D face reconstruction by learning from synthetic data. In *2016 Fourth International Conference on 3D Vision (3DV)* (pp. 460-469). IEEE. 10.1109/3DV.2016.56

Richardson, E., Sela, M., Or-El, R., & Kimmel, R. (2017). Learning detailed face reconstruction from a single image. In *Proceedings of the IEEE Conference on Computer Vision and Pattern Recognition* (pp. 1259-1268). 10.1109/CVPR.2017.589

Richter, S. R., Vineet, V., Roth, S., & Koltun, V. (2016). *Playing for Data: Ground Truth from Computer Games*. Retrieved from https://arxiv.org/abs/1608.02192

Ridel, B., Reuter, P., Laviole, J., Mellado, N., Couture, N., & Granier, X. (2014). The Revealing Flashlight: Interactive spatial augmented reality for detail exploration of cultural heritage artifacts. *Journal on Computing and Cultural Heritage, 7*(2), 6. doi:10.1145/2611376

Ristani, E., Solera, F., Zou, R. S., Cucchiara, R., & Tomasi, C. (2016). *Performance Measures and a Data Set for Multi-Target, Multi-Camera Tracking*. Retrieved from https://arxiv.org/abs/1609.01775

Rodrigues, N., Magalhaes, L. G., Moura, J. P., & Chalmers, A. (2008). Automatic Reconstruction of Virtual Heritage Sites. *Proceedings International Symposium on Virtual Reality, Archaeology and Intelligent Cultural Heritage.*

Rolland, J. P., Holloway, R. L., & Fuchs, H. (1994). *A comparison of optical and video see-through head-mounted displays.* Paper presented at the SPIE - Telemanipulator and Telepresence Technologies.

Ronchetti, F., Quiroga, F., Estrebou, C., Lanzarini, L., & Rosete, A. (2016). LSA64: A dataset of Argentinian sign language. *XX II Congreso Argentino de Ciencias de la Computación (CACIC).*

Ronneberger, O., Fischer, P., & Brox, T. (2015). *U-Net: Convolutional Networks for Biomedical Image Segmentation.* Retrieved from https://arxiv.org/abs/1505.04597

Ros, G., Sellart, L., Materzynska, J., Vazquez, D., & Lopez, A. M. (2016). The SYNTHIA Dataset: A Large Collection of Synthetic Images for Semantic Segmentation of Urban Scenes. In *2016 IEEE Conference on Computer Vision and Pattern Recognition (CVPR)* (pp. 3234–3243). 10.1109/CVPR.2016.352

Rosten, E. &. (2006). Machine learning for high-speed corner detection. *European conference on computer vision,* 430-443.

Rosten, E., & Drummond, T. (2005). Fusing points and lines for high performance tracking. In *Tenth IEEE International Conference on Computer Vision (ICCV'05)* (Vol. 2, pp. 1508–1515). 10.1109/ICCV.2005.104

Rowley, H. A., Baluja, S., & Kanade, T. (1998). Neural network-based face detection. *IEEE Transactions on Pattern Analysis and Machine Intelligence, 20*(1), 23–38. doi:10.1109/34.655647

Ro, Y. M., Kim, M., Kang, H. K., Manjunath, B. S., & Kim, J. (2001). MPEG-7 Homogeneous Texture Descriptor. *ETRI Journal, 23*(2), 41–51. doi:10.4218/etrij.01.0101.0201

Rublee, E. R. (2011). ORB: An efficient alternative to SIFT or SURF. *International Conference for Computer Vision,* 2. 10.1109/ICCV.2011.6126544

Russell, S., & Norvig, P. (2002). *Artificial intelligence: a modern approach.* Academic Press.

Saito, S., Li, T., & Li, H. (2016, October). Real-time facial segmentation and performance capture from rgb input. In *European Conference on Computer Vision* (pp. 244-261). Springer. 10.1007/978-3-319-46484-8_15

Salehinejad, H., Valaee, S., Dowdell, T., Colak, E., & Barfett, J. (2017). *Generalization of Deep Neural Networks for Chest Pathology Classification in X-Rays Using Generative Adversarial Networks.* Retrieved from https://arxiv.org/abs/1712.01636

Salimans, T., Goodfellow, I., Zaremba, W., Cheung, V., Radford, A., & Chen, X. (2016). *Improved Techniques for Training GANs.* Retrieved from https://arxiv.org/abs/1606.03498

Salvi, J., Fernandez, S., Pribanic, T., & Llado, X. (2010). A state of the art in structured light patterns for surface profilometry. *Pattern Recognition, 43*(8), 2666–2680. doi:10.1016/j.patcog.2010.03.004

Santos, J. C., Leal, I. R., Almeida-Cortez, J. S., Fernandes, G. W., & Tabarelli, M. (2011). Caatinga: The scientific negligence experienced by a dry tropical forest. *Tropical Conservation Science*, 4(3), 276–286. doi:10.1177/194008291100400306

Sarbolandi, H. L., Lefloch, D., & Kolb, A. (2015). Kinect range sensing: Structured-light versus Time-of-Flight Kinect. *Computer Vision and Image Understanding*, 139, 1–20. doi:10.1016/j.cviu.2015.05.006

Sarker, M. M., Ali, T. A., Abdelfatah, A., Yehia, S., & Elaksher, A. (2017). A cost-effective method for crack detection and measurement on concrete surface. *The International Archives of the Photogrammetry, Remote Sensing and Spatial Information Sciences*, 42(W8), 237–241. doi:10.5194/isprs-archives-XLII-2-W8-237-2017

Särkinen, T., Iganci, J. R., Linares-Palomino, R., Simon, M. F., & Prado, D. E. (2011). Forgotten forests-issues and prospects in biome mapping using Seasonally Dry Tropical Forests as a case study. *BMC Ecology*, 11(1), 27. doi:10.1186/1472-6785-11-27 PMID:22115315

Savin, A. V., Kikot, I. P., Mazo, M. A., & Onufriev, A. V. (2013). Two-phase stretching of molecular chains. *Proceedings of the National Academy of Sciences of the United States of America*, 110(8), 2816–2821. doi:10.1073/pnas.1218677110 PMID:23378631

Schmidt, R., & Gierl, L. (2010). Case-based Reasoning for Medical Knowledge-based Systems. *Medical Infobahn for Europe*, 7(7), 720–725. PMID:11187647

Schonberger, J. L. (2016). Structure-from-motion revisited. *Proceedings of the IEEE Conference on Computer Vision and Pattern Recognition*, 4104-4113.

Schöning, J. (2016). Taxonomy of 3D sensors. *Argos*, 9–10.

Schöps, T. S. (2015). 3D modeling on the go: Interactive 3D reconstruction of large-scale scenes on mobile devices. *International Conference on 3D Vision*, 291-299. 10.1109/3DV.2015.40

Seber, G. A., & Lee, A. J. (2012). *Linear regression analysis* (Vol. 329). John Wiley & Sons.

Sela, M., Richardson, E., & Kimmel, R. (2017). Unrestricted facial geometry reconstruction using image-to-image translation. In *Proceedings of the IEEE International Conference on Computer Vision* (pp. 1576-1585). 10.1109/ICCV.2017.175

Sengupta, S., Kanazawa, A., Castillo, C. D., & Jacobs, D. W. (2018). SfSNet: Learning Shape, Reflectance and Illuminance of Faces in the Wild'. In *Proceedings of the IEEE Conference on Computer Vision and Pattern Recognition* (pp. 6296-6305). 10.1109/CVPR.2018.00659

Sevilla, J., Martin, G., Casillas, J., Martinez, B., Blasco, J., & Pérez, M. (2000). *Utilización de entornos de visualización inmersiva en la transmisión del conocimiento. Un museo virtual de Santiago Ramón y Cajal.* Paper presented at the CEIG 2000:X Congreso Español de Informática Gráfica.

Shaban, M. T., Baur, C., Navab, N., & Albarqouni, S. (2018). *StainGAN: Stain Style Transfer for Digital Histological Images.* Retrieved from https://arxiv.org/abs/1804.01601

Sharaf-El-Deen, D. A., Moawad, I. F., & Khalifa, M. E. (2014). A new hybrid case-based reasoning approach for medical diagnosis systems. *Journal of Medical Systems*, 38(2), 1–11. doi:10.100710916-014-0009-1 PMID:24469683

Shay, A., & Sellers-Young, B. (2016). *Dance and Ethnicity.* doi:10.1093/oxfordhb/9780199754281.013.38

Shen, Y., Ong, S. K., & Nee, A. Y. C. (2008). Product information visualization and augmentation in collaborative design. *Computer Aided Design*, 40(9), 963–974. doi:10.1016/j.cad.2008.07.003

Shi, J., & Tomasi, C. (1994). Good features to track. In *1994 Proceedings of IEEE Conference on Computer Vision and Pattern Recognition* (pp. 593–600). 10.1109/CVPR.1994.323794

Shijie, J., Ping, W., Peiyi, J., & Siping, H. (2017). Research on data augmentation for image classification based on convolution neural networks. *Proceedings - 2017 Chinese Automation Congress, CAC 2017*, 4165–4170. 10.1109/CAC.2017.8243510

Shin, H. C., Tenenholtz, N. A., Rogers, J. K., Schwarz, C. G., Senjem, M. L., Gunter, J. L., … Michalski, M. (2018). Medical image synthesis for data augmentation and anonymization using generative adversarial networks. Lecture Notes in Computer Science, 11037, 1–11. doi:10.1007/978-3-030-00536-8_1

Shipp, M. A., Ross, K. N., Tamayo, P., Weng, A. P., Kutok, J. L., Aguiar, R. C., … Ray, T. S. (2002). Diffuse large B-cell lymphoma outcome prediction by gene-expression profiling and supervised machine learning. *Nature Medicine*, 8(1), 68–74. doi:10.1038/nm0102-68 PMID:11786909

Shmelkov, K., Schmid, C., & Alahari, K. (2018). How good is my GAN. In *Proceedings of the European Conference on Computer Vision* (pp. 1–20). ECCV. Retrieved from https://arxiv.org/abs/1807.09499

Shreyl, S., & Atub, K. (2007). 3D and 4D Modelling for Design and Construction Coordination: Issues and lessons learned. Academic Press.

Sikora, T. (2001). The MPEG-7 Visual standard for content description an overview. *IEEE Trans. on Circuits and Systems for Video Technology*, 11(6), 696–702.

Sikos, L. F. (2020). 3D Modeling Ontology (3DMO). http://purl.org/ontology/x3d/

Sikos, L. F. (2017a). A novel ontology for 3D semantics: Ontology-based 3D model indexing and content-based video retrieval applied to the medical domain. *International Journal of Metadata, Semantics and Ontologies*, 12(1), 59–70. doi:10.1504/IJMSO.2017.087702

Sikos, L. F. (2017b). *Description Logics in Multimedia Reasoning* (1st ed.). Springer Publishing Company, Incorporated. doi:10.1007/978-3-319-54066-5

Silberman, N., Hoiem, D., Kohli, P., & Fergus, R. (2012). Indoor Segmentation and Support Inference from RGBD Images. In *Proceedings of the 12th European Conference on Computer Vision - Volume Part V* (pp. 746–760). Berlin: Springer-Verlag. 10.1007/978-3-642-33715-4_54

Simard, P. Y., Steinkraus, D., & Platt, J. C. (2003). Best practices for convolutional neural networks applied to visual document analysis. In *Proceedings of the International Conference on Document Analysis and Recognition, ICDAR* (pp. 958–963). 10.1109/ICDAR.2003.1227801

Simon, T., Joo, H., Matthews, I., & Sheikh, Y. (2017). Hand keypoint detection in single images using multiview bootstrapping. In *Proceedings of the IEEE conference on Computer Vision and Pattern Recognition* (pp. 1145-1153). IEEE. 10.1109/CVPR.2017.494

Sirinukunwattana, K., Pluim, J. P. W., Chen, H., Qi, X., Heng, P.-A., Guo, Y. B., … Rajpoot, N. M. (2016). *Gland Segmentation in Colon Histology Images: The GlaS Challenge Contest*. Retrieved from https://arxiv.org/abs/1603.00275

Sirmacek, B., & Lindenbergh, R. (2015). Automatic classification of trees from laser scanning point clouds. ISPRS Annals of Photogrammetry, Remote Sensing & Spatial. *Information Sciences*, 2.

Sitnik, R., & Karaszewski, M. (2010). Automated Processing of Data from 3D Scanning of Cultural Heritage Objects. In *Digital Heritage* (pp. 28–41). Berlin: Springer. doi:10.1007/978-3-642-16873-4_3

Slamtec. (2013). *rpLidar A1*. Retrieved from http://www.slamtec.com/en/lidar/a1

Smith, D. (2007). An Introduction to Building Information Modelling. *Journal of Building Information Modelling*.

Smith, R., Morrissey, S., & Somers, H. (2010). *HCI for the Deaf community: Developing human-like avatars for sign language synthesis*. Academic Press.

Smith, R. G., & Nolan, B. (2016). Emotional facial expressions in synthesised sign language avatars: A manual evaluation. *Universal Access in the Information Society*, *15*(4), 567–576. doi:10.100710209-015-0410-7

Snavely, N., Seitz, S. M., & Szeliski, R. (2006). Photo Tourism: Exploring Photo Collections in 3D. In *ACM SIGGRAPH 2006 Papers* (pp. 835–846). New York, NY: ACM; doi:10.1145/1179352.1141964

SOFA. (n.d.). Retrieved from https://www.sofa-framework.org/

Soile, S., Adam, K., Ioannidis, C., & Georgopoulos, A. (2013). Accurate 3D textured models of vessels for the improvement of the educational tools of a museum. *Proceedings of 3D-ARCH*, 219–226.

Songer, A. D., Dickmann, J., & Al Rasheed, K. (1998). The Impact of 3D Visualization on construction planning. In *Proceedings of the international congress on computing in civil engineering*. ASCE.

Spagnuolo, M., & Falcidieno, B. (2008). *The Role of Ontologies for 3D Media Applications* (pp. 185–205). Springer London. doi:10.1007/978-1-84800-076-6_7

Spagnuolo, M., & Falcidieno, B. (2009). 3D media and the semantic web. *IEEE Intelligent Systems*, *24*(2), 90–96. doi:10.1109/MIS.2009.20

Spala, P., Malamos, A. G., Doulamis, A. D., & Mamakis, G. (2012). Extending MPEG-7 for efficient annotation of complex web 3D scenes. *Multimedia Tools and Applications*, *59*(2), 463–504. doi:10.100711042-011-0790-5

Starner, T., Weaver, J., & Pentland, A. (1998). Real-time american sign language recognition using desk and wearable computer based video. *IEEE Transactions on Pattern Analysis and Machine Intelligence*, *20*(12), 1371–1375. doi:10.1109/34.735811

Stavrakis, E., Aristidou, A., Savva, M., Himona, S. L., & Chrysanthou, Y. (2012). Digitization of Cypriot Folk Dances. In M. Ioannides, D. Fritsch, J. Leissner, R. Davies, F. Remondino, & R. Caffo (Eds.), *Progress in Cultural Heritage Preservation* (pp. 404–413). Springer. doi:10.1007/978-3-642-34234-9_41

Stuetzle, W. (2003). Estimating the Cluster Tree of a Density by Analyzing the Minimal Spanning Tree of a Sample. *Journal of Classification, 20*(1), 25–47. doi:10.100700357-003-0004-6

Su, H., Maji, S., Kalogerakis, E., & Learned-Miller, E. (2015). Multi-view convolutional neural networks for 3d shape recognition. In *Proceedings of the IEEE international conference on computer vision* (pp. 945-953). 10.1109/ICCV.2015.114

Sun, C., Zhang, T., & Xu, C. (2015). Latent support vector machine modeling for sign language recognition with Kinect. *ACM Transactions on Intelligent Systems and Technology*, *6*(2), 20. doi:10.1145/2629481

Sung, F., Yang, Y., Zhang, L., Xiang, T., Torr, P. H. S., & Hospedales, T. M. (2017). *Learning to Compare: Relation Network for Few-Shot Learning*. Retrieved from https://arxiv.org/abs/1711.06025

Sutskever, I., Hinton, G., Krizhevsky, A., & Salakhutdinov, R. R. (2014). Dropout : A Simple Way to Prevent Neural Networks from Overfitting. *Journal of Machine Learning Research*.

Suykens & Vandewalle. (1999). Least squares support vector machine classifiers. *Neural Processing Letters, 9*(3), 293-300.

Sweeney, C. H. (2015). Theia: A fast and scalable structure-from-motion library. *Proceedings of the 23rd ACM international conference on Multimedia*, 693-696. 10.1145/2733373.2807405

Sylaiou, Liarokapis, Kotsakis, & Patias. (2009). Virtual museums, a survey and some issues for consideration. *Journal of Cultural Heritage*, *10*(4), 520–528.

Szejner, M., & Emanuelli, P. (2016). Tree Species Identification in the Tropics. *Tropical Forestry Handbook*, 451-470.

Tack, K., Lafruit, G., Catthoor, F., & Lauwereins, R. (2006). Platform independent optimisation of multi-resolution 3D content to enable universal media access. *The Visual Computer*, *22*(8), 577–590. doi:10.100700371-006-0036-0

Tang, X., Wang, Z., Luo, W., & Gao, S. (2018). *Face Aging with Identity-Preserved Conditional Generative Adversarial Networks*. doi:10.1109/CVPR.2018.00828

Tang, Y., Cai, J., Lu, L., Harrison, A. P., Yan, K., Xiao, J., ... Summers, R. M. (2018). *CT Image Enhancement Using Stacked Generative Adversarial Networks and Transfer Learning for Lesion Segmentation Improvement*. Retrieved from https://arxiv.org/abs/1807.07144

Tangelder, J. W. H., & Veltkamp, R. C. (2008). A survey of content based 3D shape retrieval methods. *Multimedia Tools and Applications*, *39*(3), 441–471. doi:10.100711042-007-0181-0

Tanibata, N., Shimada, N., & Shirai, Y. (2002, May). Extraction of hand features for recognition of sign language words. In *International conference on vision interface* (pp. 391-398). Academic Press.

Taylor, L., & Nitschke, G. (2019). Improving Deep Learning with Generic Data Augmentation. In *Proceedings of the 2018 IEEE Symposium Series on Computational Intelligence, SSCI 2018* (pp. 1542–1547). 10.1109/SSCI.2018.8628742

TechnologiesU. (2019). *Unity*. http://unity3d.com

Tejada, S., Knoblock, C. A., & Minton, S. (2001). Learning object identification rules for information integration. *Information Systems*, *26*(8), 607–633. doi:10.1016/S0306-4379(01)00042-4

Temel, D., Kwon, G., Prabhushankar, M., & AlRegib, G. (2017). *{CURE-TSR:} Challenging Unreal and Real Environments for Traffic Sign Recognition*. Retrieved from https://arxiv.org/abs/1712.02463

Thomas, S., & Baltzer, J. (2002). Tropical forests. Encyclopedia of life sciences.

Tilden, F. (1957). Interpreting our heritage (R. B. Graig, Ed.; 4th ed.). The University of North Carolina Press.

Toldo, R., Gherardi, R., Farenzena, M., & Fusiello, A. (2015). Hierarchical structure-and-motion recovery from uncalibrated images. *Computer Vision and Image Understanding*, *140*, 127–143. doi:10.1016/j.cviu.2015.05.011

Tong, S., & Koller, D. (2001). Support vector machine active learning with applications to text classification. *Journal of Machine Learning Research*, *2*(Nov), 45–66.

Torello-Raventos, M., Feldpausch, T. R., Veenendaal, E., Schrodt, F., Saiz, G., Domingues, T. F., ... Lloyd, J. (2013). On the delineation of tropical vegetation types with an emphasis on forest/savanna transitions. *Plant Ecology & Diversity*, *6*, 101–137. doi:10.1080/17550874.2012.762812

Tran, A. T., Hassner, T., Masi, I., Paz, E., Nirkin, Y., & Medioni, G. G. (2018, June). Extreme 3D Face Reconstruction: Seeing Through Occlusions. In CVPR (pp. 3935-3944). Academic Press.

Trellet, N., Férey, N., Flotyński, J., Baaden, M., & Bourdot, P. (2018). Semantics for an integrative and immersive pipeline combining visualization and analysis of molecular data. *Journal of Integrative Bioinformatics*, *15*(2), 1–19. doi:10.1515/jib-2018-0004 PMID:29982236

Triggs, B. M. (1999). Bundle adjustment—a modern synthesis. *International workshop on vision algorithms*, 298-372.

Trinchão Andrade, B., Mazetto Mendes, C., de Oliveira Santos Jr, J., Pereira Bellon, O. R., & Silva, L. (2012). 3D preserving xviii century barroque masterpiece: Challenges and results on the digital preservation of Aleijadinho's sculpture of the Prophet Joel. *Journal of Cultural Heritage, 13*(2), 210–214. doi:10.1016/j.culher.2011.05.003

Tuan Tran, A., Hassner, T., Masi, I., & Medioni, G. (2017). Regressing robust and discriminative 3D morphable models with a very deep neural network. In *Proceedings of the IEEE Conference on Computer Vision and Pattern Recognition* (pp. 5163-5172). 10.1109/CVPR.2017.163

Turner, D. L., Lucieer, A., & Watson, C. (2012). An automated technique for generating georectified mosaics from ultra-high resolution unmanned aerial vehicle (UAV) imagery, based on structure from motion (SfM). *Remote Sensing, 4*(5), 1392–1410. doi:10.3390/rs4051392

Tuytelaars, T., Mikolajczyk, K., & others. (2008). Local invariant feature detectors: a survey. *Foundations and Trends® in Computer Graphics and Vision, 3*(3), 177–280.

Tzompanaki, K., & Doerr, M. (2012). A new framework for querying semantic networks. *Proceedings of Museums and the Web 2012: the international conference for culture and heritage on-line.*

Uchida, T., Sumiyoshi, H., Miyazaki, T., Azuma, M., Umeda, S., Kato, N., ... Yamanouchi, Y. (2019). Systems for Supporting Deaf People in Viewing Sports Programs by Using Sign Language Animation Synthesis. *ITE Transactions on Media Technology and Applications, 7*(3), 126–133. doi:10.3169/mta.7.126

UCI. (2011). *UCI Machine Learning Repository: Breast Cancer Wisconsin (Diagnostic) Data Set.* Http://Archive.Ics.Uci.Edu/Ml/Datasets/Breast+Cancer+Wisconsin+%2528Diagnostic%2529

Uher, V., & Burget, R. (2012, July). Automatic 3D segmentation of human brain images using data-mining techniques. In *Telecommunications and Signal Processing (TSP), 2012 35th International Conference on* (pp. 578-580). IEEE.

Ullrich, S., Kuhlen, T., Polys, N. F., Evestedt, D., Aratow, M., & John, N. W. (2011). Quantizing the Void: Extending Web3D for Space-Filling Haptic Meshes. *Medicine Meets Virtual Reality,* (163), 670-676.

Ullrich, S., & Kuhlen, T. (2012). Haptic palpation for medical simulation in virtual environments. *IEEE Transactions on Visualization and Computer Graphics, 18*(4), 617–625. doi:10.1109/TVCG.2012.46 PMID:22402689

Upreti & Gupta (2015). Imaging for Diagnosis of Foreign Body Aspiration in Children. *Indian Pediatrics, 52*(1), 659-690.

Valanis, A., Tapinaki, S., Georgopoulos, A., & Ioannidis, C. (2009). *High resolution textured models for engineering applications.* Retrieved from https://dspace.lib.ntua.gr/handle/123456789/28564

Valstar, M., & Pantic, M. (2010). Induced disgust, happiness and surprise: An addition to the mmi facial expression database. *Proc. Int'l Conf. Language Resources and Evaluation, Workshop EMOTION,* 65–70.

Van Uitert, R., & Bitter, I. (2007). Subvoxel precise skeletons of volumetric data based on fast marching methods. *Medical Physics, 34*(2), 627–638. doi:10.1118/1.2409238 PMID:17388180

Vandenhende, S., De Brabandere, B., Neven, D., & Van Gool, L. (2019). *A Three-Player GAN: Generating Hard Samples To Improve Classification Networks.* Retrieved from https://arxiv.org/abs/1903.03496

Vasilakis, G., García-Rojas, A., Papaleo, L., Catalano, C. E., Robbiano, F., Spagnuolo, M., ... Pitikakis, M. (2010). Knowledge-Based Representation of 3D Media. *International Journal of Software Engineering and Knowledge Engineering, 20*(5), 739–760.

Verykokou, S., Doulamis, A., Athanasiou, G., Ioannidis, C., & Amditis, A. (2016). UAV-based 3D modelling of disaster scenes for Urban Search and Rescue. In *2016 IEEE International Conference on Imaging Systems and Techniques (IST)* (pp. 106–111). 10.1109/IST.2016.7738206

VICON I Award Winning Motion Capture Systems. (n.d.). Retrieved November 22, 2019, from https://www.vicon.com/

Vidal, C., & Muñoz, G. (2015). Métodos avanzados para el análisis y documentación de la arqueología y la arquitectura maya: los "mascarones" de Chiloé y La Blanca. In C. Vidal & G. Muñoz (Eds.), *Artistic Expressions in Maya Architecture: Analysis and Documentation Techniques* (pp. 75–90). Oxford, UK: Archaeopress.

Vidal, R., Sapiro, G., & Elhamifar, E. (2012). See all by looking at a few: Sparse modeling for finding representative objects. *2012 IEEE Conference on Computer Vision and Pattern Recognition*, 1600–1607.

Vinyals, O., Blundell, C., Lillicrap, T. P., Kavukcuoglu, K., & Wierstra, D. (2016). *Matching Networks for One Shot Learning*. Retrieved from https://arxiv.org/abs/1606.04080

Visual, S. F. M. (n.d.). *A Visual Structure from Motion System - Documentation*. Retrieved July 26, 2017, from http://ccwu.me/vsfm/doc.html

Vive I Discover Virtual Reality Beyond Imagination. (n.d.). Retrieved November 22, 2019, from https://www.vive.com/eu/

Vlahakis, V., Ioannidis, N., Karigiannis, J., Tsotros, M., Gounaris, M., Stricker, D., ... Almeida, L. (2002). Archeoguide: An Augmented Reality Guide for Archaeological Sites. *IEEE Computer Graphics and Applications*, 22(5), 52–60. doi:10.1109/MCG.2002.1028726

Vögele, A., Krüger, B., & Klein, R. (2015). Efficient unsupervised temporal segmentation of human motion. *Proceedings of the ACM SIGGRAPH/Eurographics Symposium on Computer Animation*, 167–176.

Volpi, R., Morerio, P., Savarese, S., & Murino, V. (2018). Adversarial Feature Augmentation for Unsupervised Domain Adaptation. *Proceedings of the IEEE Computer Society Conference on Computer Vision and Pattern Recognition*, 5495–5504. 10.1109/CVPR.2018.00576

Voulodimos, A., Doulamis, N., Doulamis, A., & Rallis, I. (2018). Kinematics-based Extraction of Salient 3D Human Motion Data for Summarization of Choreographic Sequences. *2018 24th International Conference on Pattern Recognition (ICPR)*, 3013–3018. 10.1109/ICPR.2018.8545078

Voulodimos, A. D., Doulamis, N., Fritsch, D., Makantasis, K., Doulamis, A., & Klein, M. (2016). Four-dimensional reconstruction of cultural heritage sites based on photogrammetry and clustering. *Journal of Electronic Imaging*, 26(1), 011013. doi:10.1117/1.JEI.26.1.011013

Voulodimos, A. S., Doulamis, N. D., Kosmopoulos, D. I., & Varvarigou, T. A. (2012). Improving Multi-Camera Activity Recognition by Employing Neural Network Based Readjustment. *Applied Artificial Intelligence*, 26(1–2), 97–118. doi:10.1080/08839514.2012.629540

Voulodimos, A. S., Kosmopoulos, D. I., Doulamis, N. D., & Varvarigou, T. A. (2014). A top-down event-driven approach for concurrent activity recognition. *Multimedia Tools and Applications*, 69(2), 293–311. doi:10.100711042-012-0993-4

Voulodimos, A., Doulamis, N., Doulamis, A., & Protopapadakis, E. (2018). Deep learning for computer vision: A brief review. *Computational Intelligence and Neuroscience*, 2018, 2018. doi:10.1155/2018/7068349 PMID:29487619

Voulodimos, A., Kosmopoulos, D., Veres, G., Grabner, H., Van Gool, L., & Varvarigou, T. (2011). Online classification of visual tasks for industrial workflow monitoring. *Neural Networks*, 24(8), 852–860. doi:10.1016/j.neunet.2011.06.001 PMID:21757322

Voulodimos, A., Rallis, I., & Doulamis, N. (2018). Physics-based keyframe selection for human motion summarization. *Multimedia Tools and Applications*. doi:10.100711042-018-6935-z

VRgluv | Force Feedback Haptic Gloves for VR Training. (n.d.). Retrieved November 22, 2019, from https://vrgluv.com/

Vuori, V., Aksela, M., Laaksonen, J., Oja, E., & Kangas, J. (2000). Adaptive character recognizer for a hand-held device: Implementation and evaluation setup. *Proc. of the 7th IWFHR*, 13–22.

W3C Consortium. (2012). *OWL*. https://www.w3.org/TR/owl2- syntax/

W3C Consortium. (2013). *SPARQL*. https://www.w3.org/TR/ sparql11-query/

W3C Consortium. (2014a). *RDF*. https://www.w3.org/TR/rdf11- concepts/

W3C Consortium. (2014b). *RDFS*. https://www.w3.org/TR/rdfschema/

W3C Consortium. (2019). *WebXR*. https://www.w3.org/TR/ webxr/

W3C Standards. (n.d.). Retrieved from https://www.w3.org/standards

W3C. (2004). *RDQL a query language for RDF (member submission)*. http://www.w3.org/Submission/2004/SUBM-RDQL-20040109/

W3C. (2008). *SPARQL query language for RDF*. http://www.w3.org/TR/2008/REC-rdf-sparql-query-20080115/

W3C. (2013). *SPARQL 1.1 update*. http://www.w3.org/tr/sparql11-update/

Wah, C., Branson, S., Welinder, P., Perona, P., & Belongie, S. (2011). *The Caltech-UCSD Birds-200-2011 Dataset*. Academic Press.

Walczak, K., & Flotyński, J. (2016). Semantic query-based generation of customized 3D scenes. In *Proceedings of the 20th International Conference on 3D Web Technology*. ACM.

Walczak, K. (2008). Flex-VR: Configurable 3D Web Applications. *Proceedings of the International Conference on Human System Interaction, HSI'08*, 135-140.

Walczak, K., & Flotyński, J. (2014). On-demand generation of 3D content based on semantic meta-scenes. In *International Conference on Augmented and Virtual Reality*. Springer. 10.1007/978-3-319-13969-2_24

Walczak, K., & Flotynski, J. (2019). Inference-based creation of synthetic 3D content with ontologies. *Multimedia Tools and Applications*, 78(9), 12607–12638. doi:10.100711042-018-6788-5

Wan Idris, W. M. R., Rafi, A., Bidin, A., Jamal, A. A., & Fadzli, S. A. (2019). A systematic survey of martial art using motion capture technologies: The importance of extrinsic feedback. *Multimedia Tools and Applications*, 78(8), 10113–10140. doi:10.100711042-018-6624-y

Wang, X., Wang, K., & Lian, S. (2019). *A Survey on Face Data Augmentation*. Retrieved from https://arxiv.org/abs/1904.11685

Wang, Z., She, Q., & Ward, T. E. (2019). *Generative Adversarial Networks: A Survey and Taxonomy*. Retrieved from https://arxiv.org/abs/1906.01529

Wang, G., Kang, W., Wu, Q., Wang, Z., & Gao, J. (2019). Generative Adversarial Network (GAN) Based Data Augmentation for Palmprint Recognition. *2018 International Conference on Digital Image Computing: Techniques and Applications, DICTA 2018*, 1–7. 10.1109/DICTA.2018.8615782

Wang, H., Chai, X., Hong, X., Zhao, G., & Chen, X. (2016). Isolated sign language recognition with grassmann covariance matrices. *ACM Transactions on Accessible Computing*, *8*(4), 14. doi:10.1145/2897735

Wang, H., Zhihong, D., Bo, F., Hongbin, M., & Yuanqing, X. (2017). An adaptive Kalman filter estimating process noise covariance. *Neurocomputing*, *223*, 12–17. doi:10.1016/j.neucom.2016.10.026

Wang, L., & Zhang, Z. (2017). Automatic detection of wind turbine blade surface cracks based on UAV-taken images. *IEEE Transactions on Industrial Electronics*, *64*(9), 7293–7303. doi:10.1109/TIE.2017.2682037

Wang, R., Peethambaran, J., & Chen, D. (2018). LiDAR Point Clouds to 3-D Urban Models: A Review. *IEEE Journal of Selected Topics in Applied Earth Observations and Remote Sensing*, *11*(2), 606–627. doi:10.1109/JSTARS.2017.2781132

Wang, Y., Weinacker, H., & Koch, B. (2008). A lidar point cloud based procedure for vertical canopy structure analysis and 3D single tree modelling in forest. *Sensors (Basel)*, *8*(6), 3938–3951. doi:10.33908063938 PMID:27879916

Web3D Consortium. (1995). *VRML*. https://www.w3.org/ MarkUp/VRML/.Web3D

Web3D Consortium. (2004). *Extensible 3D (X3D) ISO/IEC 19775:2004*. http://www.web3d.org/x3d/specifications/ ISOIEC-19775-X3DAbstractSpecification/2004S

Web3D Consortium. (2013). *X3D*. https://www.web3d.org/ documents/specifications/19775-1/V3.3/Part01/ X3D.html

Web3D Consortium. (2018). *Extensible 3D (X3D), ISO/IEC 19775-1:2008*. Retrieved from https://www.web3d.org/ documents/specifications/19775-1/V3.2

Web3D Consortium. (2018). *X3D Semantic Web Working Group*. https://www.web3d.org/working-groups/x3d- semantic- web/.Web3D

Web3D Consortium. (2019a). *X3D Ontology for Semantic Web*. https://www.web3d.org/x3d/content/semantics/ semantics.html

Web3D Consortium. (2019b). *X3D Unified Object Model (X3DUOM)*. https://www.web3d.org/specifications/ X3DUOM. html

Web3D Consortium. (2019c). *Export stylesheet to convert X3D XML models into Turtle RDF/OWL triples*. https://www. web3d.org/x3d/stylesheets/X3dToTurtle.xslt

Webb, J., & Ashley, J. (2012). *Beginning Kinect Programming with the Microsoft Kinect SDK*. Apress. doi:10.1007/978-1-4302-4105-8

Webel, S., Olbrich, M., Franke, T., & Keil, J. (2013). *Immersive experience of current and ancient reconstructed cultural attractions*. Paper presented at the Digital Heritage International Congress (DigitalHeritage). 10.1109/DigitalHeritage.2013.6743766

WebG. L. (2020). https://get.webgl.org/

Wei, X., Gong, B., Liu, Z., Lu, W., & Wang, L. (2018). *Improving the Improved Training of Wasserstein GANs: A Consistency Term and Its Dual Effect*. Retrieved from https://arxiv.org/abs/1803.01541

Wei, S.-E., Ramakrishna, V., Kanade, T., & Sheikh, Y. (2016). Convolutional Pose Machines. *The IEEE Conference on Computer Vision and Pattern Recognition (CVPR)*.

Wessels, S., Ruther, H., Bhurtha, R., & Schröeder, R. (2014). *Design and creation of a 3D Virtual Tour of the world heritage site of Petra, Jordan*. Paper presented at the AfricaGeo.

Wiebusch, D., & Latoschik, M. E. (2012). Enhanced Decoupling of Components in Intelligent Realtime Interactive Systems using Ontologies. In *Software Engineering and Architectures for Realtime Interactive Systems (SEARIS), Proceedings of the IEEE Virtual Reality 2012 Workshop*. IEEE.

Wojciechowski, R., Walczak, K., White, M., & Cellary, W. (2004). Building virtual and augmented reality museum exhibitions. *Proceedings of the ninth international conference on 3D Web technology*. 10.1145/985040.985060

Woodham, R. J. (1980). Photometric method for determining surface orientation from multiple images. *Optical Engineering (Redondo Beach, Calif.)*, *19*(1), 191139. doi:10.1117/12.7972479

Wu, C. (2011). *VisualSFM: A visual structure from motion system*. Retrieved from http://ccwu.me/vsfm/doc.html

Wu, C. (2017). *VisualSFM: A Visual Structure from Motion System*. Retrieved from http://ccwu.me/vsfm/

Wu, C., Agarwal, S., Curless, B., & Seitz, S. M. (2011). Multicore bundle adjustment. In CVPR 2011 (pp. 3057–3064). doi:10.1109/CVPR.2011.5995552

Wu, E., Wu, K., Cox, D., & Lotter, W. (2018). Conditional infilling GANs for data augmentation in mammogram classification. In Lecture Notes in Computer Science (including subseries Lecture Notes in Artificial Intelligence and Lecture Notes in Bioinformatics) (Vol. 11040 LNCS, pp. 98–106). Springer Verlag. doi:10.1007/978-3-030-00946-5_11

Wu, J., Zhang, C., Xue, T., Freeman, W. T., & Tenenbaum, J. B. (2016). *Learning a Probabilistic Latent Space of Object Shapes via 3D Generative-Adversarial Modeling*. Retrieved from https://arxiv.org/abs/1610.07584

Wu, Y., Yue, Y., Tan, X., Wang, W., & Lu, T. (2018). End-To-End Chromosome Karyotyping with Data Augmentation Using GAN. *Proceedings - International Conference on Image Processing, ICIP*, 2456–2460. 10.1109/ICIP.2018.8451041

Wu, Y., Lim, J., & Yang, M. (2013). Online Object Tracking: A Benchmark. In *2013 IEEE Conference on Computer Vision and Pattern Recognition* (pp. 2411–2418). 10.1109/CVPR.2013.312

Wu, Z., Xu, G., Zhang, Y., Cao, Z., Li, G., & Hu, Z. (2012). GMQL: A graphical multimedia query language. *Knowledge-Based Systems*, *26*, 135–143. doi:10.1016/j.knosys.2011.07.013

X3DOM. (n.d.). Retrieved from https://www.x3dom.org

Xiang, Y., Kim, W., Chen, W., Ji, J., Choy, C., Su, H., … Savarese, S. (2016). *ObjectNet3D: A Large Scale Database for 3D Object Recognition* (Vol. 9912). doi:10.1007/978-3-319-46484-8_10

Xiao, F., & Fan, C. (2014). Data mining in building automation system for improving building operational performance. *Energy and Building*, *75*, 109–118. doi:10.1016/j.enbuild.2014.02.005

Xiu, Y., Li, J., Wang, H., Fang, Y., & Lu, C. (2018). *Pose flow: Efficient online pose tracking*. arXiv preprint arXiv:1802.00977

Xu, F., Buhalis, D., & Weber, J. (2017). Serious games and the gamification of tourism. *Tourism Management*, *60*, 244–256. doi:10.1016/j.tourman.2016.11.020

Yang, J., Liu, S., Grbic, S., Setio, A. A. A., Xu, Z., Gibson, E., … Comaniciu, D. (2018). *Class-Aware Adversarial Lung Nodule Synthesis in {CT} Images*. Retrieved from https://arxiv.org/abs/1812.11204

Yang, J., Zhao, Z., Zhang, H., & Shi, Y. (2019). Data Augmentation for X-Ray Prohibited Item Images Using Generative Adversarial Networks. *IEEE Access: Practical Innovations, Open Solutions*, *7*, 28894–28902. doi:10.1109/ACCESS.2019.2902121

Yan, K., Wang, X., Lu, L., Zhang, L., Harrison, A. P., Bagheri, M., & Summers, R. M. (2018). Deep Lesion Graphs in the Wild: Relationship Learning and Organization of Significant Radiology Image Findings in a Diverse Large-Scale Lesion Database. *Proceedings of the IEEE Computer Society Conference on Computer Vision and Pattern Recognition.* 10.1109/CVPR.2018.00965

Yan, M., Liu, K., Guan, Z., Xu, X., Qian, X., & Bao, H. (2018). Background Augmentation Generative Adversarial Networks (BAGANs): Effective Data Generation Based on GAN-Augmented 3D Synthesizing. *Symmetry, 10*(12), 734. doi:10.3390ym10120734

Yastikli, N. (2007). Documentation of cultural heritage using digital photogrammetry and laser scanning. *Journal of Cultural Heritage, 8*(4), 423–427. doi:10.1016/j.culher.2007.06.003

Yi, D., Lei, Z., Liao, S., & Li, S. Z. (2014). *Learning Face Representation from Scratch.* Retrieved from https://arxiv.org/abs/1411.7923

Yi, X., Walia, E., & Babyn, P. (2018). *Generative Adversarial Network in Medical Imaging: A Review.* Retrieved from https://arxiv.org/abs/1809.07294

Ying, S., Xu, G., Li, C., & Mao, Z. (2015). Point Cluster Analysis Using a 3D Voronoi Diagram with Applications in Point Cloud Segmentation. *ISPRS International Journal of Geo-Information, 4*(3), 1480–1499. doi:10.3390/ijgi4031480

Yorganci, R., Kindiroglu, A. A., & Kose, H. (2016). Avatar-based Sign Language Training Interface for Primary School Education. *Workshop: Graphical and Robotic Embodied Agents for Therapeutic Systems.*

Yu, S., Tan, D., & Tan, T. (2006). A Framework for Evaluating the Effect of View Angle, Clothing and Carrying Condition on Gait Recognition. In *18th International Conference on Pattern Recognition (ICPR'06)* (Vol. 4, pp. 441–444). 10.1109/ICPR.2006.67

Zaharia, T., & Preteux, F. (2001). 3D Shape-based retrieval within the MPEG-7 framework. *Proceedings of the SPIE/EI Conference on Nonlinear Image Processing, SPIE/EI 2001.*

Zampoglou, P., Spala, K., Kontakis, A. G., Malamos, & Ware, J. A. (2013). Direct mapping of x3d scenes to mpeg-7 descriptions. *Proceeding of the 18th International Conference on 3D Web Technology.*

Zbigniew, K., & Tomasz, K. (2014). Building Information Modelling- 4D Modelling Technology on the example of the reconstruction of stairwell. Academic Press.

Zhang, H., Goodfellow, I., Metaxas, D., & Odena, A. (2018). *Self-Attention Generative Adversarial Networks.* Retrieved from https://arxiv.org/abs/1805.08318

Zhang, J. M., Xu, X., & Yuan, B. (2007). Rotation Invariant Image Classification Based on MPEG-7 Homogeneous Texture Descriptor. *Eighth ACIS International Conference on Software Engineering, Artificial Intelligence, Networking, and Parallel/Distributed Computing (SNPD 2007), 3,* 798-803.

Zhang, J., Jiao, J., Chen, M., Qu, L., Xu, X., & Yang, Q. (2016). *3D Hand Pose Tracking and Estimation Using Stereo Matching.* Retrieved from https://arxiv.org/abs/1610.07214

Zhang, R., Che, T., Grahahramani, Z., Bengio, Y., & Song, Y. (2018). MetaGAN: An Adversarial Approach to Few-Shot Learning. *Advances in Neural Information Processing Systems, 31.* Retrieved from http://papers.nips.cc/paper/7504-metagan-an-adversarial-approach-to-few-shot-learning.pdf

Zhang, X., Wang, Z., Liu, D., & Ling, Q. (2018). *DADA: Deep Adversarial Data Augmentation for Extremely Low Data Regime Classification.* Retrieved from https://arxiv.org/abs/1809.00981

Zhang, Y., Jia, G., Chen, L., Zhang, M., & Yong, J. (2019). *Self-Paced Video Data Augmentation with Dynamic Images Generated by Generative Adversarial Networks*. Academic Press.

Zhang, Z., Yang, L., & Zheng, Y. (2018). *Translating and Segmenting Multimodal Medical Volumes with Cycle- and Shape-Consistency Generative Adversarial Network*. Retrieved from https://arxiv.org/abs/1802.09655

Zhang, D. B. (2017). Remote inspection of wind turbine blades using UAV with photogrammetry payload. *56th Annual British Conference of Non-Destructive Testing-NDT*.

Zhang, X., Chen, X., Li, Y., Lantz, V., Wang, K., & Yang, J. (2011). A framework for hand gesture recognition based on accelerometer and EMG sensors. *IEEE Transactions on Systems, Man, and Cybernetics. Part A, Systems and Humans*, *41*(6), 1064–1076. doi:10.1109/TSMCA.2011.2116004

Zhang, Z. (2012). Microsoft Kinect Sensor and Its Effect. *IEEE MultiMedia*, *19*(2), 4–10. doi:10.1109/MMUL.2012.24

Zhang, Z., & Huang, F. (2013, December). Hand tracking algorithm based on superpixels feature. In *2013 International Conference on Information Science and Cloud Computing Companion* (pp. 629-634). IEEE. 10.1109/ISCC-C.2013.77

Zhao, G., Huang, X., Taini, M., Li, S. Z., & Pietikäinen, M. (2011). Facial expression recognition from near-infrared videos. *Image and Vision Computing*, *29*(9), 607–619. doi:10.1016/j.imavis.2011.07.002

Zheng, L., Shen, L., Tian, L., Wang, S., Wang, J., & Tian, Q. (2015). Scalable Person Re-identification: A Benchmark. In *2015 IEEE International Conference on Computer Vision (ICCV)* (pp. 1116–1124). 10.1109/ICCV.2015.133

Zheng, Y.-T., Zhao, M., Song, Y., Adam, H., Buddemeier, U., & Bissacco, A., … Neven, H. (2009). Tour the world: Building a web-scale landmark recognition engine. In *IEEE Conference on Computer Vision and Pattern Recognition, 2009. CVPR 2009* (pp. 1085–1092). 10.1109/CVPR.2009.5206749

Zheng, Z., Zheng, L., & Yang, Y. (2017). Unlabeled Samples Generated by GAN Improve the Person Re-identification Baseline in Vitro. *Proceedings of the IEEE International Conference on Computer Vision*, 3774–3782. 10.1109/ICCV.2017.405

Zhong, Z., Zheng, L., Zheng, Z., Li, S., & Yang, Y. (2017). *Camera Style Adaptation for Person Re-identification*. Retrieved from https://arxiv.org/abs/1711.10295

Zhou1, N., & Deng, Y. (2009). Virtual reality: A state-of-the-art survey. *International Journal of Automation and Computing*, *6*(4), 319-325.

Zhou, D. D. (2016). Reliable scale estimation and correction for monocular visual odometry. *IEEE Intelligent Vehicles Symposium*, 490-495.

Zhou, F., la Torre, F. D., & Hodgins, J. K. (2013). Hierarchical Aligned Cluster Analysis for Temporal Clustering of Human Motion. *IEEE Transactions on Pattern Analysis and Machine Intelligence*, *35*(3), 582–596. doi:10.1109/TPAMI.2012.137 PMID:22732658

Zhou, S., Ke, M., & Luo, P. (2019). Multi-camera transfer GAN for person re-identification. *Journal of Visual Communication and Image Representation*. doi:10.1016/j.jvcir.2019.01.029

Zhou, Y., & Toga, A. W. (1999). Efficient skeletonization of volumetric objects. *IEEE Transactions on Visualization and Computer Graphics*, *5*(3), 196–209. doi:10.1109/2945.795212 PMID:20835302

Zhu, Y., Aoun, M., Science, C., Krijn, M., & Vanschoren, J. (2018). Data Augmentation using Conditional Generative Adversarial Networks for Leaf Counting in Arabidopsis Plants. *Computer Vision Problems in Plant Phenotyping (CVPPP2018)*, 1–11. Retrieved from https://www.semanticscholar.org/paper/Data-Augmentation-using-Conditional-Generative-for-Zhu-Aoun/0636eb841bf3480309a346587010f43f2a87633e

Zhuang, P., Schwing, A. G., & Koyejo, S. (2019). *{FMRI} data augmentation via synthesis*. Retrieved from https://arxiv.org/abs/1907.06134

Zhu, J. Y., Park, T., Isola, P., & Efros, A. A. (2017). Unpaired Image-to-Image Translation Using Cycle-Consistent Adversarial Networks. *Proceedings of the IEEE International Conference on Computer Vision*, 2242–2251. 10.1109/ICCV.2017.244

Zimmermann, C., & Brox, T. (2017). *Learning to Estimate 3D Hand Pose from Single RGB Images*. Retrieved from https://lmb.informatik.uni-freiburg.de/projects/hand3d/

Zoumpourlis, G., Doumanoglou, A., Vretos, N., & Daras, P. (2017). Non-linear convolution filters for cnn-based learning. In *Proceedings of the IEEE International Conference on Computer Vision* (pp. 4761–4769). IEEE.

Zou, X., Cheng, M., Wang, C., Xia, Y., & Li, J. (2017). Tree Classification in Complex Forest Point Clouds Based on Deep Learning. *IEEE Geoscience and Remote Sensing Letters*, *14*(12), 2360–2364. doi:10.1109/LGRS.2017.2764938

About the Contributors

Athanasios Voulodimos is Assistant Professor with the Department of Informatics and Computer Engineering at the University of West Attica. He received his Dipl.-Ing., MSc and PhD degrees from the School of Electrical and Computer Engineering of the National Technical University of Athens (NTUA) with the highest honor. He has received awards for his academic performance and scientific achievements by the Greek State Scholarships Foundation (IKY), the National Technical University of Athens (NTUA), the Hellenic Mathematical Society (HMS) and the European Neural Network Society (ENNS). From 2007 to 2017 he was a research associate of the Institute of Communication and Computer Systems (ICCS) of NTUA. He has been involved in several European and national research & development projects, as researcher, senior researcher, and/or technical manager. Dr. Voulodimos is the author of more than 100 papers in international journals, conference proceedings and books. His research interests lie in the areas of machine learning, computer vision, artificial intelligence, multimedia analysis and pervasive computing. He has served as Organizing and Program Committee member in several conferences and workshops, and has guest edited collective book volumes and special issues in international journals. He is a member of IEEE, IEEE Signal Processing and Computational Intelligence Societies, ACM and INNS.

Anastasios Doulamis received the Diploma degree in Electrical and Computer Engineering from the National Technical University of Athens (NTUA) with the highest honour (second ranked among all classmates) and the PhD degree in Electrical and Computer Engineering from NTUA. He is currently Associate Professor in National Technical University of Athens. Prof. Anastasios Doulamis has received several awards and prizes during his studies, including the Best Greek Student in all fields of engineering at the national level, the Best Graduate Thesis Award in the area of Electrical Engineering and several prizes from the National Technical University of Athens. He is author of more than 350 papers in the area of signal processing, image analysis, decision making and artificial intelligence among them more than 35 in IEEE/ACM journals papers of high impact factors and more than 80 journal papers. He has also more than 4600 citations in the respective field. He has served as organizer in many major workshops, like the ones sponsored by ACM, and IEEE.

* * *

Panagiotis Barmpoutis is a Research Fellow at the Computer Science department of University College London and Visiting Researcher at the Electrical and Electronic Engineering department of Imperial College London. He received his B.Eng./M.Eng. in Electrical and Computer Engineering from the Aristotle University of Thessaloniki in 2009. He also received his MSc in Forestry Informatics and his MSc in Medical Informatics from the Aristotle University of Thessaloniki in 2012 and 2013 respectively. In 2017 he received his PhD in Forestry Informatics from the Aristotle University of Thessaloniki. He has worked as Research Assistant, Research Associate and Research Fellow in Centre for Research &Technology Hellas, Aristotle University of Thessaloniki, Imperial College London and University College London. His current development and research interests lie in the areas of computer vision and applications, image and video processing, analysis and visualization, pattern recognition and machine learning. He has co-authored numerous highly cited journal and conference publications and has participated in national and European funded research projects.

Stefano Berretti (PhD, Univ. of Florence, 2001) is an Associate Professor at the Department of Information Engineering, University of Florence, since 2011. His research interests are in computer vision, pattern recognition and computer graphics, with applications to face biometrics, human emotion and behavior understanding from body and face, 3D face reconstruction, 3D modeling and retrieval. On these themes, he has published more than 170 papers, receiving three best paper awards. He has been Visiting Professor at the University of Lille, France, and at the University of Alberta, Canada. He is the Information Director and an Associate Editor of the ACM Transactions on Multimedia Computing, Communications, and Applications, and an Associate Editor of the IET Computer Vision Journal.

Sergio Casas-Yrurzum has a master's degree in Computer Engineering and also a bachelor's degree in Telecommunications Engineering - Telematics Specialty. He received the Spanish National Award on University Studies in 2008. He received his PhD in Computational Mathematics at the University of Valencia in 2014. He works as a senior researcher in the Robotics Institute (IRTIC) of the University of Valencia, where he is also a part-time professor at the School of Engineering (ETSE). His expertise is in the simulation field with special focus on Virtual Reality, Augmented Reality and motion cueing.

Aju D. received his PhD. in Computer Science and Engineering from VIT University, Vellore, India. He received his M.Tech. degree in Computer Science and IT from Manonmaniam Sundaranar University, Tirunelveli. He received his M.C.A degree from Madras University. Presently, he is working as Associate Professor at VIT University in the department of Computer Science and Engineering. He has published more than 30 research articles in different reputed international peer-reviewed journals. And, he is also serving as reviewer for few international journals. He is having more than 15 years of teaching experience. His area of interest includes Digital Image Processing, Medical Imaging, Computer Graphics and Digital Forensics.

Petros Daras is a Research Director at the Information Technologies Institute of the Centre for Research and Technology Hellas. He received the Diploma in Electrical and Computer Engineering, the MSc degree in Medical Informatics and the Ph.D. degree in Electrical and Computer Engineering all from the Aristotle University of Thessaloniki, Greece in 1999, 2002 and 2005, respectively. He is the head researcher of the Visual Computing Lab coordinating the research efforts of more than 50 scientists. His research interests include 3D media processing and compression, multimedia indexing, classification and retrieval, annotation propagation and relevance feedback, bioinformatics and medical image processing. He has co-authored more than 200 papers in refereed journals and international conferences, and has been involved in more than 50 national and international research projects.

Kosmas Dimitropoulos is a research fellow at Visual Computing Lab of Information Technologies Institute - Centre for Research and Technology Hellas (ITI-CERTH) and an academic faculty member of AIMove (Artificial Intelligence and Movement in Industries and Creation) Post-Master Programme at MINES ParisTech University. He holds a diploma in Electrical and Computer Engineering and a Ph.D. degree in Applied Informatics. His main research interests lie in the fields of multi-dimensional data modelling and analysis, human computer interaction, virtual reality and serious games. His involvement with these research areas has led to the co-authoring of more than 100 publications in refereed journals and international conference proceedings. He has participated in several European and national research projects and has served as a regular reviewer for a number of international journals and conferences. He is a member of IEEE and the Technical Chamber of Greece.

Nikolaos Doulamis received the Dipl.-Ing. degree in Electrical and Computer Engineering from the National Technical University of Athens (NTUA) in 1995 with the highest honor and the PhD degree in electrical and computer engineering from NTUA in 2000. His PhD thesis was supported by the Bodosakis Foundation Scholarship. He is currently Assistant Professor at the National Technical University of Athens. Dr. Doulamis was awarded the Best Greek Student Award in the field of engineering at a national level by the Technical Chamber of Greece in 1995. In 1996, he was received the Best Graduate Thesis Award in the area of electrical engineering. During his studies, he has also received several prizes and awards from the National Technical University of Athens, the National Scholarship Foundation and the Technical Chamber of Greece. In 1997, he was given the NTUA Medal as Best Young Engineer. He has also served as program committee in several international conferences and workshops. He is reviewer of several IEEE journals and conferences as well as other leading international journals, and has served as guest editor in many special issues. His research interests include machine learning, computer vision, and signal processing for remote sensing as well as biomedical applications. Prof. Nikolaos Doulamis is the author of 53 journal papers, 21 book chapters and 200 conference papers. In total, the cumulative sum of journals' impact factors is 78.345. In addition, among the 200 conferences, more than 100 papers are within IEEE archives. He has received 2788 citations in his work with h-index=24 and g-index=45 (according to Google Scholar). One of his works has been cited as the "Doulamis Model" in the literature.

Claudio Ferrari received a master's degree cum laude in computer engineering and the Ph.D. in Information Engineering from the University of Florence in 2014 and 2018 respectively. He has been a visiting research scholar at the IRIS lab, University of Southern California, Los Angeles under the supervision of Prof. Gérard Medioni (march – September 2014). Currently, he is a PostDoc researcher at MICC. His research interests are computer vision, 3D vision and Deep Learning mostly focused on "in-the-wild" face recognition, statistical 3D face modeling and single-view 3D face reconstruction.

Jakub Flotyński is an Assistant Professor in the Department of Information Technology at the Poznań University of Economics and Business, Poland. He holds a Ph.D. degree in computer science (multimedia systems). His research interests include VR/AR, semantic web, and service-oriented architectures. He is a Co-Chair of the X3D Semantic Web Working Group and was a Program Co-Chair of the International ACM Conference on 3D Web Technology, in 2017 and 2018.

Athanasios Kalvourtzis received his diploma from the Department of Electrical and Computer Engineering of Aristotle University of Thessaloniki in November 2017. Since May 2018, he has been working as a research assistant at Information Technologies Institute (ITI) of the Centre for Research and Technology Hellas (CERTH). His main interest is in the development of web applications, involving technologies of computer vision and graphics.

Maria Kaselimi studied surveying engineering at NTUA. Her education background includes a M. Sc. degree in geoinformatics. She is a PhD candidate at NTUA. Her research interests focus on geodata analysis and modeling, machine learning and signal processing for geodetic and energy applications.

Dimitrios Konstantinidis is a postdoctoral researcher in the Visual Computing Lab (VCL) of CERTH-ITI. He received his B.Sc degree in Electrical and Computer Engineering from the Aristotle University of Thessaloniki (AUTH) in 2009. He then received an Advanced Master degree in Artificial Intelligence from KU Leuven in 2012 and a PhD from Imperial College of London with the topic of monitoring urban changes from satellite images in 2017. His main research interests lie in the fields of computer vision, image processing, machine/deep learning and artificial intelligence.

Anisha M. Lal is an Associate Professor in the School of Computer Science and Engineering at VIT University, Vellore, India. She received her B.E degree in Computer Science from Manonmanium Sundaranar University and M.E degree in Computer Science from Anna University. She has been awarded Doctorate in Computer Science and Engineering at VIT University. She has teaching and research experience of about 14 years. She has published more than 22 papers in international journals and presented around 5 papers in national and international conferences. Her research interests include image processing, remote sensing, biomedical and soft computing. She has served as a reviewer in many academic conferences and journals in the related areas.

Jonathan Lloyd is a Professor of Global Ecosystem Function at Imperial College London and a Royal Society Wolfson Research Merit Award holder. He holds a Ph.D in Agricultural Science from the University of Adelaide (Australia) and has after positions at the New South Wales Department of Agriculture and the Australian National University he headed the Biosphere-Atmosphere Interactions Group at the Max Planck Institute for Biogeochemistry in Jena, Germany (1997-2004) after which he was Centenary Chair in Earth System Science in the School of Geography at Leeds (2004-2009). He has extensive experience in the modelling and measurement of terrestrial fluxes at the leaf, canopy and global level with much of his recent research focusing on vegetation-soil interactions.

Vasumathy M. is a PhD Research Scholar in the School of Computing Science and Engineering at VIT University, Vellore, India. She received her Master's in Software Engineering from VIT University. She has industry experience of three years. Her area of specialization includes image processing and knowledge engineering. She has a research experience of two years as a junior research fellow for the sponsored projects funded by government of India.

Claus B. Madsen received his M.Sc. and Ph.D. from Aalborg University in 1990 and 1994 respectively. He held post doc positions at University of Coimbra in Portugal (1994 to 1995) and at the Royal Institute of Technology in Sweden (1995) before assuming a position as assistant professor at Aalborg

University, Denmark. He is now an associate professor at the Department of Media Technology, Aalborg University (CREATE/AAU), where he heads the Computer Graphics Group. Claus B. Madsen has authored or co-authored more than 90 papers in the areas of computer vision, computer graphics, robotics, augmented and virtual reality. He serves on the programme committee of the Graphics Theory and Applications conference (GRAPP), he regularly acts as reviewer for international journals and conferences, and he organized the 2007 edition of the Scandinavian Conference on Image Analysis (www.scia2007. dk). He has co-proposed and been technical manager of two large EU funded projects (PUPPET, The Educational Puppet Theatre of Virtual Worlds, 1998 to 2000, and BENOGO, Being There Without Going, 2002 to 2005). He has held a grant from the Danish Research Council for project CoSPE, Computer Vision-Based Estimation of Scene Parameters, 2004 to 2012, and is currently PI for the EUDP project Leading Edge Roughness, and the Innovation Foundation Denmark project DARWIN. Claus B. Madsen current research interest lie in the field between computer graphics and computer vision, especially on estimating and modelling the illumination conditions in real scenes so as to make it possible to render virtual objects into the scenes with consistent illumination. He primarily teaches subjects relating to computer graphics rendering.

Athanasios G. Malamos is professor in the Hellenic Mediterranean University and an active member of the WEB3D community. He is leading the Spatial Sound group of interest. His team contributed the spatial sound, the Humanoid and the Physics libraries in X3DOM platform. He has served as Guest Editor in Graphical Models Journal (Springer), Special Issues Advances in Web3D and in The Journal of Virtual Worlds Research. He was also General Chair of the 20th International Conference on 3D Web Technology. Dr. Malamos has served as program and organizational committee in several IEEE and ACM international conferences and workshops. He is regular reviewer of IEEE, Springer as well as other international journals. Dr. Malamos is honored with the ACM Recognition of Service Award and by the WEB3D consortium with recognition of his efforts as a member. Dr. Malamos is a member of ACM SIGGRAPH, IEEE computer society and of the WEB3D consortium. His research interests include multimedia services, multimedia semantics, WEB3D.

Ioannis Maniadis studied Electrical and Computer Engineering at Aristotle University of Thessaloniki, Greece. His main area of interest is deep learning and its applications. Upon graduation he worked in CERTH as an associate researcher focusing on the subject of data augmentation with GANs. Currently, he is doing an Artificial Intelligence MSc at Queen Mary University, London.

Magna S B Moura is researcher at the Brazilian Agricultural Research Corporation (EMBRAPA), working at the Embrapa Tropical Semi-Arid Unit since 2003. She received her B. degree in Agronomic Engineering from the Federal Rural Semi-Arid University in 1999. She also received her MSc in Meteorology from the Federal University of Paraíba in 2001 and her PhD in Natural Resources from the Federal University of Campina Grande in 2005. She is responsible for the Agrometeorology Lab of the Embrapa Tropical Semi-Arid, where she coordinates a network of 16 Agrometeorological Stations. She is a professor of the Master Program in Agricultural Engineering of the Federal University of the São Francisco Valley; and of the Development and Environment Program of the Federal University of Pernambuco, at MSc and PhD level. She is Advisor of Master and PhD students. She participates in research projects as PI and as researcher in partnership. Her current development and research interests lie in the areas of evapotranspiration, environmental instrumentation, energy and radiation balance, energy-carbon fluxes, remote sensing, atmosphere-biosphere interaction in natural and agricultural systems. She has co-authored numerous journal and conference publications and has participated in national and international funded research projects. She is a council member of the Brazilian Society of Agrometeorology (2017-2021).

Ivan A. Nikolov received his B.Sc. from the Technical University Sofia in 2012 and later his M.Sc. from Aalborg University in 2014. He is currently pursuing a Ph.D. in the topic of 3D reconstruction and computer graphics, with a focus on mesh analysis for industrial inspection. Ivan Nikolov has taken part and was one of the main contributors in the EUDP project Leading Edge Roughness. He regularly reviews paper for conferences and journals, and has started to publish a number of papers in both computer graphics and computer vision. His main interests are in the field of 3D reconstruction, virtual and augmented reality, as well as robotics and drones.

Cristina Portalés (PhD in Geodesy and Cartography, 2008) is senior researcher at the Institute of Robotics and Information and Communication Technologies at Universitat de València (Spain), where she previouslyhad been a Juan de la Cierva post-doc fellow. She formerly graduated with a double degree: Engineer in Geodesy and Cartography from the Universidad Politécnica de Valencia (Spain) and MSc in Surveying and Geoinformation from Technische Universität Wien (Austria). Afterwards she was a PhD research fellow at the Mixed Reality Laboratory of the University of Nottingham (UK, 2005) and at the Interaction and Entertainment Research Centre of the Nanyang University of Singapore (Singapore, 2006). She was the first woman to receive the best paper EH Thompson Award, given by the Remote Sensing and Photogrammetry Society (2010). From 2011-2012 she worked at AIDO (technological institute of Optics, Colour and Imaging), being primarily involved in the technical management of the FP7 project SYDDARTA. She is the author of more than 50 scientific publications including international conferences, high impact journals, books and book chapters. Her current research interests are focused on geometric calibration, image processing, 3D reconstruction, multispectral imaging, HCI and augmented reality.

Eftychios Protopapadakis studied production engineering and management at technical university of Crete. His educational background includes a M.S. degree in management and business administrator and a Ph.D. in decision systems design, both at the same university. He is working as engineer in European and Interegg projects since 2010. Currently, he is working on intangible cultural assets digitization. His research interests focus on machine learning applications in real life problems. He has explored the applicability of semi-supervised techniques in maritime surveillance, elder people support, industrial workflow monitoring, and cultural heritage applications. Other investigated areas involve stock market share trends' forecasting and credit risk assessment. Additionally, he has worked on structural assessment in transportation tunnel infrastructures, via deep-learning techniques and robotic platforms, intelligent parking management policies, and radar signal processing for target identification. Eftychios co-authored more than thirty publications. His paper on industrial workflow recognition received the best paper award in INFOCOMP 2012. Other awards include university scholarships for excellence, Technical Chamber of Greece award for excellence in studies, state scholarship foundation – SIEMENS doctorate scholarship 2012 and post PhD scholarship of the National Strategic Reference Framework 2014-2020.

Javier Sevilla is graduated in Computer Science from the Valencia Polytechnic University (Spain) in 1995. He worked at iSOCO, S.A where he researched the semantic web visualisation area, and participated in many international projects. He has managed many national and international IT projects related to disability. He is co-founder of the ADAPTA Foundation and researcher in the Autism & IT Group at the IRTIC Technological Institute of the University of Valencia (Spain). In these organizations, he is leading IT projects that apply the technology to improve the quality of life of people with autism.

Leslie F. Sikos, Ph.D., is a computer scientist specializing in data science and artificial intelligence applications, in particular formal knowledge representation and automated reasoning. He developed knowledge organization systems for 3D modeling, and is a founding member and co-chair of the X3D Semantic Web Working Group at the Web3D Consortium.

Vassilios Solachidis, PhD, received the Diploma in Mathematics in 1996 and the PhD degree in Informatics in 2004, both from the Aristotle University of Thessaloniki, Greece. He has worked as researcher in twenty one (21) European and national research projects in the Informatics Department of Aristotle University of Thessaloniki, Information Technologies Institute and the Applied Electronics Department of Università degli Studi Roma TRE. He has also served as an adjunct lecturer at the Aristotle University of Thessaloniki, the University of Western Macedonia and at the Technological Institutes of Thessaloniki, Kavala, Serres and Western Macedonia. His research interests focus in technologies of image and video analysis, and multimedia watermarking. He has eleven (11) papers in international scientific peer review journals and forty seven (47) papers in international and national conferences. Currently he is working in the Centre for Research and Technology Hellas as Postdoctoral Research Fellow.

Tania Stathaki was born in Athens, Hellas. In September 1991 she received the Masters degree in Electronics and Computer Engineering from the Department of Electrical and Computer Engineering of the National Technical University of Athens (NTUA) and the Advanced Diploma in Classical Piano Performance from the Orfeion Athens College of Music. She received the Ph.D. degree in Signal Processing from Imperial College in September 1994. She is currently a Reader (Associate Professor) in the Communications and Signal Processing Research Group of the Department of Electrical and Electronic Engineering of Imperial College. Previously, she was Lecturer in the Department of Information Systems and Computing of Brunel University in UK, Visiting Lecturer in the Electrical Engineering Department of Mahanakorn University in Thailand and Assistant Professor in the Department of Technology Education and Digital Systems of the University of Pireus in Greece. Her current research interests lie in the areas of Signal and Image Processing and Computer Vision.

Kiriakos Stefanidis graduated with honors from the Department of Informatics of the Aristotle University of Thessaloniki (AUTh) in 2011. He has participated in several EU research projects for information technology and since January 2015 he works as a research assistant at the Information Technologies Institute (ITI) of the Centre for Research and Technology Hellas (CERTH). His research interests include machine learning, computational intelligence, and information retrieval.

Mythili Thirugnanam is an Associate Professor Senior in the School of Computer Science and Engineering at Vellore Institute of Technology, Vellore, India. She received a Master's in Software Engineering from VIT University. She has been awarded a Doctorate in Computer Science and Engineering at VIT University in 2014. She has teaching experience of around 12 years. She has research experience of 3 years in handling sponsored projects funded by Govt. Of India. Her area of specialization includes Image Processing, Software Engineering, and Machine Learning. She has published more than 40 papers in international and national journals and presented around 12 papers in various national and international conferences.

Lucia Vera is graduated in Computer Science from the University of Valencia (Spain) in 1999. She received an extraordinary prize by the University of Valencia for the best academic record of the Computer Engineering promotion in 1999. Also she has an Executive Master in Project Management by the University of Valencia. She works as a senior researcher in the Robotics Institute (IRTIC) of the University of Valencia. Her expertise is in virtual characters and in the development of applications for simulation, training or learning mainly in the areas of Virtual and Augmented Reality.

Nicholas Vretos, PhD, is a research fellow at CERTH-ITI. He obtained the degree of BSc in Computer Science from the University Pierre et Marie Currie (Paris VI) in 2002 and his Ph.D. from the Aristotle University of Thessaloniki in 2012. During elaboration of his thesis, he taught as assistant and worked as a research assistant in Artificial Intelligence and Information Analysis Laboratory. He has worked in 15 European projects as a researcher. He has published more than 60 articles in scientific journals and conference proceedings and 2 book chapters. He has committed as a reviewer for several journals and conferences in the field of image, video and 3D processing. His main interests are in image and video processing, semantic analysis, neural networks and 3-D data processing.

Krzysztof Walczak is an Associate Professor in the Department of Information Technology at the Poznań University of Economics and Business. He holds a habilitation degree (higher Ph.D. degree) in computer science (multimedia systems). His research interests focus on virtual and augmented reality, distance teaching and learning, semantic web and databases. He is the author or co-author of over 140 scientific publications and several patents in these domains.

Index

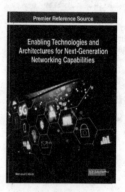

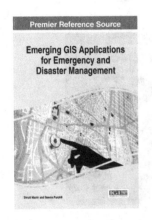

Printed in the United States
By Bookmasters